Official Publisher Partnership

7

Graham Thompson
sta Wiggins-James
Rob James

DYNAMIC LEARNING

HODDER
EDUCATION
AN HACHETTE UK COMPANY

Graham Thompson would like to thank his family for their support during the writing of this book.

Rob James and Nesta Wiggins-James would like to thank Ffion, Ellie, Rees and Cai for putting up with them, their support and patience during the writing of this book.

Orders: please contact Bookpoint Ltd, 130 Milton Park, Abingdon, Oxon OX14 4SB.
Telephone: (44) 01235 827720. Fax: (44) 01235 400454. Lines are open from 9.00 – 5.00,
Monday to Saturday, with a 24-hour message answering service. You can also order
through our website www.hoddereducation.co.uk.

British Library Cataloguing in Publication Data
A catalogue record for this title is available from the British Library

ISBN: 978 0 340 95 899 5

First Published 2009
Impression number   10 9 8 7 6 5 4 3 2 1
Year   2014 2013 2012 2011 2010 2009

Hachette UK's policy is to use papers that are natural, renewable and recyclable
products and made from wood grown in sustainable forests. The logging and
manufacturing processes are expected to conform to the enviromental regulations of
the country of origin.

Cover photo © Aflo Photo Agency/Alamy
Typeset by Pantek Arts Ltd
Artwork by Simon Tegg
Printed in Italy for Hodder Education, an Hachette UK Company, 338 Euston Road,
London NW1 3BH

Contents

Acknowledgements

3.5	Hulton Archive/Getty Images
3.6	Hulton Archive/Getty Images
3.8	Hulton Archive/Getty Images
4.3	Tennis Players, 1885, Cauty, Horace Henry (1846-1909)/Private Collection/© Christopher Wood Gallery, London, UK/The Bridgeman Art Library
4.6	The Women's Match, c.1811 (ink & w/c on paper), Rowlandson, Thomas (1756-1827)/© Marylebone Cricket Club, London, UK, The Bridgeman Art Library
6.6	© Icon/Action Plus
7.4	© Nick Wilson/Allsport/Getty Images
8.1	© David Rogers/Getty Images
9.1 (a)	© Shaun Botterill/Getty Images
9.1 (b)	© Leo Mason/Action Plus
9.7 (a)	© EMPICS Sport/PA Photos
9.7 (b)	© Laurence Griffiths/Getty Images
9.10	© Ryan Pierse/Getty Images
9.13	© Ryan Pierse/Getty Images
10.1	© Action Plus
10.2	© AP/Press Association Images
10.3	© Neil Tingle/Action Plus
11.1 (a)	© Bob Thomas/Getty Images
11.1 (b)	© Photocome/PA Photos
11.10	© Barry Bland/Action Plus
12.1	© Neil Tingle/Action Plus
12.2	© Neil Tingle/Action Plus
12.3	© Deborah Davis/Photonica/Getty Images
12.5	© Glyn Kirk/Action Plus

13.1	© Phil Walter/Getty Images
13.3 (a)	© Neil Tingle/Action Plus
13.3 (b)	© Leo Mason/Action Plus
13.3 (c)	© Mark Dadswell/Getty Images
13.3 (d)	© Bob Martin/Sports Illustrated/Getty Images
13.4	© Kent Horner/Getty Images
13.9	© Neil Tingle/Action Plus
14.1	© Getty Images/Getty Images for Speedo
14.10	© Glyn Kirk/Action Plus
15.1	© Glyn Kirk/Action Plus
15.2	© Glyn Kirk/Action Plus
15.3	© Robert Michael/Corbis
15.12	© Atsushi Tomura/AFLO/Action Plus
15.13	© Glyn Kirk/Action Plus
17.3	© Sipa Press/Rex Features
17.14	© Gary I Rothstein/Action Plus
18.8	© Neil Tingle/Action Plus
19.2	© Sean Aidan/Eye Ubiquitous/Corbis
19.13	© Shelly Gazin/The Image Works/TopFoto
21.1	© Helene Rogers/Alamy
22.1	© Glyn Kirk/Action Plus

Introduction

Welcome to the new edition of *OCR PE for A2*!

This book has been specifically written to support those students following the OCR AS specification in Physical Education (H554). It has been designed to follow the exact requirements of the specification and, in doing so, will help to prepare you for both the written and coursework units of the qualification.

The book is divided into two sections – one for each area of study:

- **Section 1:** Principles and concepts across different areas of Physical Education (G453)
- **Section 2:** The improvement of effective performance and the critical evaluation of practical activities in Physical Education (G454).

How will each section be assessed?

What do I need to do to satisfy the synoptic requirement of the examination?

The word **synoptic** comes to us from the Greek 'sunoprikos', which means 'seeing the whole together' or 'taking a comprehensive view'. Students must show that they have an overall understanding of the subjects they are studying. Synoptic assessment tests a candidate's grasp of the connections between the different elements of a subject and should also:

- require candidates to exercise higher order skills (as identified in the specification) in constructing answers
- be based upon knowledge, understanding and skills specified in the identified unit, but also draw upon those in previously studied units

Unit G453: Principles and concepts across different areas of Physical Education	Unit G454: The improvement of effective performance and the critical evaluation of practical activities in Physical Education
Externally assessed written paper 105 marks available 2 ½ hours duration	Internally assessed, but externally moderated 60 marks available
This is an options paper that is divided into two sections:	
1. Section A Socio-cultural focus A1 Historical studies, A2 Comparative studies **2. Section B Scientific focus** B1 Sports Psychology, B2 Biomechanics, B3 Exercise and Sport Physiology	You will be assessed in one activity out of 40 marks (assessed as a performer or coach or official) + Oral assessment on the evaluation, appreciation and the improvement of performance out of 20 marks
You will be required to answer 3 × 35 mark questions, with at least one of these that *must* come from Section A	
The final part of each question answered is synoptic	
70% of overall A2 mark 35% of the total Advanced GCE marks	30% of overall A2 mark 15% of the total Advanced GCE marks

- sometimes ask candidates to make proposals/predictions/hypotheses/explanations/responses to problems that go beyond the strict limits of the knowledge, skills and understanding studied within the unit and which may frequently present candidates with questions in an unfamiliar setting.

For this specification, synoptic assessment is defined as:

'...the requirement of candidates to draw together 4the three aims of GCE Physical Education.'

Where the three aims of this Physical Education specification are:

1   These specifications will encourage candidates to become increasingly physically competent by:
    (a) developing the skills and techniques they require to perform effectively in physical activities
    (b) applying and adapting a wide range of skills and techniques effectively in different types of physical activity
    (c) developing and applying their skills in different roles, such as performer, leader/coach and official within physical activities
    (d) applying their skills in different contexts within a physical activity.
2   These specifications will enable candidates to maintain and develop their involvement and effectiveness in physical activity through:
    (a) developing their knowledge and understanding of factors that enable them and others to be physically active
    (b) as part of a balanced lifestyle
    (c) as part of a lifelong involvement in an active and healthy lifestyle
    (d) developing their knowledge and understanding of the relationship between skill, strategy/composition and body and mind readiness so as to ensure that both their own and other's performance is both effective and efficient in roles such as performer, leader/coach and official.
3   These specifications will enable candidates to be informed and discerning decision-makers who understand how to be involved in physical activity through helping them to understand:
    (a) how they and others make the most of the opportunities and pathways available to be involved in physical activity
    (b) and critically evaluate how contemporary products and consumer-focused influences related to physical activity affect and inform young people's decisions about being involved in a range of physical activities;
    (c) and critically evaluate current key influences that might limit or encourage young people's involvement in physical activity.

In unit G453, the part (d) questions require 'critical evaluation' of the topics being examined. Candidates are asked to make judgements, attach a value or level of importance to certain developments or initiatives, and to discuss issues related to physical education and participation. The part (d) questions seek to draw together Aims 2 and 3 from the specification. In order to achieve the higher grades A – B candidates must demonstrate the ability to 'accurately apply diverse knowledge taken from the wider context of the A2 specification' and 'skills of critical analysis and evaluation'.

In unit G454, the Evaluation and Appreciation oral response is aimed at offering synoptic assessment related to Aim 1, which is becoming increasingly physically competent. Candidates will have to demonstrate evaluative judgements about the quality of performance, and propose a viable and detailed action plan to address the issues observed. Candidates also draw upon their theoretical knowledge in the physiological, psychological and socio-cultural aspects that relate to the activity being evaluated, bringing in Aims 2 and 3.

Throughout the course you must relate and apply knowledge **to lifelong involvement in an active and healthy lifestyle**. You will be aware that physical education is a multi-faceted discipline that encompasses a number of theoretical areas. Therefore, it is imperative that you reflect on the impact of each area upon **lifelong participation and the contribution of each to the promotion of healthy lifestyle.**

You will be required to engage in 'higher order thinking' and this text will help you develop those necessary skills of **critical evaluation** and **analysis**

What is 'higher order thinking'?

Higher order thinking skills require you to do more than simply show your knowledge and understanding. To be successful on this course you must show your abilities of **application, analysis, synthesis and evaluation** (see table).

Feature boxes

Look out for the feature boxes and symbols that appear throughout the text. There are a number of different features that are designed to give you all the information you need to be successful and to help you reinforce your learning. A brief overview of each feature is given below:

- **Key terms** – definitions of significant words or phrases that are required knowledge
- **In context** – real-life case studies that demonstrate the application of theoretical knowledge to sporting situations
- **Activities** – opportunities to apply and reinforce your knowledge through a range of student-centred tasks

Skill	What's involved?	What could I do?	Question cues
Application	Making use of your knowledge in a particular situation	Use your knowledge in a sporting context such as problem solving. For example, illustrate the pattern of heart rate during a game of netball	apply demonstrate illustrate examine
Analysis	Taking something apart or breaking it down	Look at the effect that individual components have on the 'whole'. For example, break a skill down into its component parts and identify strengths and weaknesses of each part	explain classify compare
Synthesis	Pulling ideas together, rebuilding and solving problems	Formulate an 'action plan' or 'development plan' for improvement For example, suggest how a coach can improve the skills of a performer	create design compose formulate
Evaluation	Judging the value of material or methods as they might be applied in a particular situation	Reflect on the impact of methods or action plan. Give recommendations. For example, judge the relative benefits of exercise compared to any negative aspects	assess measure recommend convince judge

- **Examiner's tips** – helpful hints on examination technique and revision tips from real examiners
- **What you need to know** – a summary of key points found at the end of each chapter that can be used as a quick progress check; can also be used as a handy revision tool
- **Exam-style questions** – apply your knowledge to the sorts of questions you can expect in your written examination

- **Review questions** – check your progress with these questions at the end of each chapter; these questions address the key aspects of each chapter.

There are several main themes that underpin this course and it is really important that you reflect upon these when completing your assessment activities

UNIT 1

Historical Studies

This section focuses on the historical factors that had an impact on and continue to affect participation and improved competence in physical activity as part of a balanced, active and healthy lifestyle. We will learn to apply historical concepts in order fully to understand the factors that led to young people and other societal groups being physically active.

The application of historical concepts will enable you to evaluate critically consumer-focused and other key societal influences that in both the past and the present have limited or encouraged involvement in physical activity.

Sport influences, and is in turn influenced by, the social system operating at the time – economic, geographical, educational, social and political. Therefore, whatever we discover about sport must not be seen in isolation.

Over the next few chapters we shall:

- chart some social changes that have been influential and analyse how recreational activities and the education system have been affected
- apply knowledge gained to provide an analysis of the development of a variety of recreational and sporting activities from their origins to the present day, as specific case studies.

Popular recreation in pre-industrial Britain and its impact on contemporary participation and performance

Learning outcomes

By the end of this chapter you should be able to:

- understand the term 'popular recreation'
- describe the characteristics of popular recreation such as simple/natural; occasional; local; wagering; violence/cruelty; simple unwritten rules; courtly/popular; rural; occupational
- explain the social and cultural factors that influenced the nature and development of popular recreations;
- explain how popular recreation affected the physical competence and health of participants
- describe the varying opportunities for participation
- explain the impact of popular recreation on contemporary participation and performance.

CHAPTER INTRODUCTION

In this chapter you will look at the origins of popular recreation in Britain, and the impact of popular recreation on contemporary participation and performance.

The origins of sports and pastimes were initially functional, e.g., for military and hunting purposes. When societies depended less on survival, many activities took on a recreational dimension, such as children's play and the feasts and festivals which often had religious associations, either pagan or Christian.

Specific reference will be made to the development of football within the 'In context' feature.

Characteristics and societal determinants

You will need to have a basic grasp of British history. It is not useful to refer to Regency or Victorian times if you have no idea where they fall in the overall scheme. Use the chart giving the different eras in chronological order (see Figure 1.1).

Medieval England (1066–1485)

The years between 1066 and 1485 are generally known as the Middle Ages. The bulk of the population were peasants in rural areas, but there was an increase in the townsmen, who were mainly merchants, lawyers and doctors. The townsmen formed the beginnings of the middle class, which was later to grow even more powerful. Festivals and feasts played an important part of life in the Middle Ages. Many recreational pastimes took place at this time. The horse was a significant feature for the nobility, who used them for hunting and the

Roman Britain	43–450AD
Anglo Saxon invasion	450–613
Division into Kingdoms	613–1017
Danish Rule	1017–1066
William I	1066
William II	1087
Henry I	1100
Stephen	1135
Henry II	1154
Richard I	1189
John	1199
Henry III	1216
Edward I	1272
Edward II	1307
Edward III	1327
Richard II	1377
Henry IV	1399
Henry V	1413
Henry VI	1422
Edward IV	1461
Edward V	1483
Richard III	1483
Henry VII	1485
Henry VIII	1509
Edward VI	1547
Mary I	1553
Elizabeth I	1558
James I	1603
Charles I	1625
Commonwealth	1649
Charles II	1660
James II	1685
William III & Mary	1689
Anne	1702
George I	1714
George II	1727
George III	1760
George IV	1820
William IV	1830
Victoria	1837
Edward VII	1901
George V	1910
Edward VIII	1936
George VI	1936
Elizabeth II	1952

Fig 1.1 Dates of the coronations of the monarchs of England and (from 1603) Great Britain

tournaments. Military activities were favoured over purely recreational ones, and archery became a compulsory aspect of young men's lives, for defence of the realm.

Festivals were held in honour of events that were important to people's daily lives – for example, the change of seasons, the harvest and the summer and winter solstices. As the pagan customs were taken over by the Church they were given new religious meanings. 'Holy days' were put aside for feasting. Many towns and villages had their own special festivals and saints' days, which often celebrated the death of a saint.

Easter is the most important feast of the Christian Church, and its date fixed the dates of the holy days connected to it – Lent, Shrove Tuesday, Ash Wednesday. Shrove Tuesday is the last day before the fasting of Lent, and was a time for feasting and fun. Popular recreations took place within a wide social pattern, and activities included mob football, wrestling, animal baiting, skittles and bowls.

Fig 1.3 Frontispiece to the *Book of Falconrie*, 1498

Fig 1.2 Functional and recreational origins of sport

IN CONTEXT

Lakeland Sports was a traditional sporting festival based in the Lake District.

1787 'Upon Stone Carr there have been held, time out of mind, races and other sports, such as wrestling, leaping (high jump) tracing with dogs (hound trailing).'

The English Lake District can draw a parallel between the sheep-based economy and many of the sporting occasions. During the early nineteenth century these tended to have a social significance. Shepherds travel to buy and sell sheep. A show would be born – families would treat the occasion as a 'day out'. Following the showing and selling of sheep, there would be sports and dance. They were based on a seasonal economy.

Table 1.1 Seasonal activities in the countryside

Season	Activity	Social/sporting activity
Spring	Lambing	No time for sport
Whitsuntide	Lambing over	Hiring fairs (hiring of labour, but also a social occasion)
Autumn	Sheep fairs	'Wrestling or hurdle race for a fleece'

Fig 1.4 Stag hunting was a popular pastime during the sixteenth and seventeenth centuries

Activity 1

Consider how many local villages and churches still retain annual or seasonal festivities.

EXAMINER'S TIP

It is necessary to understand that in pre-industrial Britain there was a two-tier social-class system. The two social classes had their distinctive activities, such as real tennis for the upper classes and mob football for the lower classes, but would also enjoy sporting social occasions together, such as the Lakeland Games and the Cotswold Olimpick Games.

The Tudor and Stuart era (1485–1714)

The Tudors

England changed rapidly under the Tudors.

Under Henry VIII's rule, there was even greater prosperity and more time for cultural pursuits. Henry was a great sports lover. He participated in all-day hunts and wrestling, and ordered his own real tennis court to be built at Hampton Court (it is still well worth a visit). Access to education, equipment and facilities enabled the upper classes the privilege of exclusive recreational activities.

Under Elizabeth, games and sports flourished. This was the age of the Renaissance gentleman, who was knowledgeable, partook in the appropriate physical activities and was appreciative of all art forms.

The mass of the population also enjoyed traditional pastimes such as mob football, and the baiting and killing of animals were also a great treat. People lived in harsh conditions, and held different attitudes about the treatment of animals compared with modern values. Activities such as cock fighting, bull baiting and bull running were all popular. They originated in rural areas but were also enjoyed in the towns until social forces led to their decline; there is an account of bull running in London as late as 1816. There were, however, once again, distinct social class divisions in the enjoyment and participation in physical activities.

The Stuarts

After the death of Elizabeth I, James VI of Scotland (the son of Mary Queen of Scots) became James I of England. He had been brought up a Protestant, and in 1617 issued a declaration known as the 'Book of Sports', which encouraged the notion of traditional pastimes, so long as they did not interfere with Church attendance.

IN CONTEXT

The Cotswold Olimpick [sic] Games were an annual public celebration of games and sports held in the Cotswolds in the West Country of England. The games began somewhere between 1604 and 1612 and have continued on and off to the present day.

The games were organised during the reign of James I of England on Dover's Hill above the town of Chipping Campden, Gloucestershire. The games were originally organised by a local attorney, Robert Dover, as a protest against the growing Puritanism of the day. These sports were referred to by contemporary writers as 'Mr. Robert Dovers Olimpick Games upon the Cotswold Hills'. The games were held on Thursday and Friday of Whit-Week, or the week of Whitsuntide, which would normally fall between the middle of May and the middle of June. They continued for many years as a spectacle until about the time of Dover's death. He presided over the games on horseback. Horses and men were abundantly decorated with yellow ribbons (Dover's colour), and he was duly honoured by all as king of their sports for a series of years. Tents were erected for the gentry, and refreshments were supplied in abundance. Tables stood in the open air, or cloths were spread on the ground, for the common folk.

EXAMINER'S TIP

The focus of this specification is not 'dates and dust', but an understanding of how changes in society affected sport and recreation activities.

Following the Civil War and execution of Charles I (James I's son) in 1646, Oliver Cromwell was made Protector of Britain. He was intent on establishing parliamentary rule allied with a Puritan lifestyle. Puritanism particularly objected to:

- practising sport on a Sunday
- inflicting cruelty on animals
- the idleness, drinking and profanity generally associated with sport and the public houses.

The effect of the Puritans on the development of sport was to be significant. They believed that people should concentrate on working hard and praying for salvation, and were opposed to recreational activities, which they considered as sinful and a waste of time. As many of the traditional activities took place after church services on a Sunday, they came under fierce attack from the Puritans.

Cromwell failed to unite all the different factions, and Charles II returned as monarch in 1660. This period was known as the Restoration. Charles II was in favour of many sports. His court enjoyed a lifestyle of ease, affluence and leisure; they occupied themselves lavishly on sporting pursuits. The Restoration helped to restore many of the previously banned popular activities, but never again to their past glories.

Popular recreation's effect on physical competence, health and opportunities for participation

Popular recreation tended to be:

- played occasionally
- simple in nature
- local in nature
- mainly male-dominated.

As popular games were played occasionally, this meant that physical **competency skills** were not developed and refined. Instead, rather more crude methods were utilised. For example, in mob football, where hundreds of bodies would forcibly move a ball to its intended target, *force* rather than *skill* was used. Participants were not developing specific skills such as dribbling, passing and heading. These skills were only to emerge during the transition of mob football to its rational form.

As popular games were not participated in regularly (i.e. on a daily, weekly or even monthly basis), the benefits to health would have been questionable. Also, owing to the lack of official rules, health was often threatened by the number of serious injuries that would occur during the course of a match. Injured workers could lose days, perhaps weeks, of production because of the time taken to play these mob games and then recover from their injuries. This was one of the reasons given by the ruling classes for banning such recreations.

The games played by the working classes did not use sophisticated equipment and facilities, which meant that the working classes tended not to develop wider skills as a result of their play. In contrast, the middle and upper classes could develop skills such as hand-to-eye coordination by using equipment, e.g. rackets, when playing games such as lacrosse and real or lawn tennis.

The many variations of the same sport that existed between the different localities meant that regional competitions could not be held until the rules were codified. Therefore, general standards of play remained limited.

Working-class games tended to be mainly male dominated, but some activities such as smock races were popular with women.

Contemporary participation

The legacy of popular recreation on contemporary participation has been significant. Forms of mob football are still played today. Notable examples are Ashbourne's Royal Shrovetide football and the Haxey Hood Game (see *OCR PE for AS*, pages 232–233). These are local events, which are popular with participants and spectators alike and which foster a community spirit at a local level.

Rural areas still have festivals and fetes that are linked to seasonal events. Many churches, both those in the town and those in the countryside, still hold annual fetes where many traditional activities take place. Some areas have surviving ethnic sports, such as the Highland Games in Scotland and Cheese Rolling in Gloucestershire.

Many blood sports were banned, especially those enjoyed by the lower classes such as cock-fighting. Sports such as fox hunting survived much longer due to the favour shown to it by the upper classes. However, the legacy of activities such as cock fighting have survived as coconut shies at fairs.

Pedestrianism as a form of road racing still exists for the masses as road races.

EXAMINER'S TIPS

Let's pose a possible exam question and consider how you might approach it.

Evaluate the social and cultural factors that affected the emergence of physical activity during the nineteenth century and which may still affect contemporary participation. **[20 marks]**

First, you must realise that there will be an allocation of marks to deal with both sides of the question: historical *and* present day.

When a question indicates the nineteenth century, ideally you should understand the pre-industrial and industrialisation of society, and show appreciation of how both these changes would affect recreation activities.

You could begin by stating how society changed with regard to:

- the loss of space, time and money
- poor working and living conditions
- increasing control being exerted by the ruling classes, especially the newly emerging middle classes.

Then later, you could look at how improvements to transport, increases in free time, the development of public provision, and the rationalisation of sport via the public schools, all had an affect on participation. Organisations such as the Church and national governing bodies were to be influential — who you were in society and which social class (and gender) would also influence the type of activity you would become involved with.

Contemporary participation
Try to view this from a personal perspective as it can help you truly understand the significance of how societal factors can influence you – rather than seeing these factors as external and, therefore, meaningless.

Do consider social class; race and religion; ability/disability; social attitudes such as stereotypes and prejudices; gender (not only the constraints, but also the growing opportunities for women); location in the country; and political factors that can influence funding.

The following feature will begin tracing the development of football as a case study throughout this section of the book. In Chapter 4 other sporting activities will be studied in similar detail.

Key term

Puritanism The extreme form of Protestants in the sixteenth and seventeenth centuries with a strict moral outlook to life shunning the more pleasurable activities

Case Study: Mob football

Shrovetide football, as it was called, belonged in the 'mob football' category, where the number of players was unlimited and the rules were fairly vague (for example, according to an ancient handbook from Workington in England, any means could be employed to get the ball to its target with the exception of murder and manslaughter). Football flourished for over a thousand years in diverse forms. The repeated unsuccessful intervention of the authorities shows how powerless they were to restrict it, in spite of their condemnation and threats of severe punishment.

Disapproval of authorities

During the 100 Years War between England and France from 1338 to 1453 the court was unfavourably disposed towards football. This well-loved recreation prevented its subjects from practising more useful military disciplines, particularly archery, which played an important and valuable role in the English army at that time.

Despite several interventions by kings and parliaments to discourage people from playing football, none of these efforts had much effect.

The popularity of the game and people's obvious delight in the rough and tumble for the ball went far too deep to be uprooted.

Resentment of football up to this time had been mainly for practical reasons. The game had been regarded as a public disturbance that resulted in damage to property, – for example, in Manchester in 1608 football was banned because so many windows had been smashed.

With the spread of Puritanism, the cry went up against 'frivolous' amusements, and sport was classified as such, football in particular. The main objection was that it supposedly constituted a violation of peace on the Sabbath.

All told there was scarcely any progress at all in the development of football for hundreds of years. But, although the game was persistently forbidden for 500 years, it was never completely suppressed. As a consequence, it remained essentially rough, violent and disorganised. A change did not come about until the beginning of the nineteenth century, when school football became the custom, particularly in the famous English public schools. This was the turning point in the rationalisation of the game.

Activity 2

- List the social factors that made mob football popular with the working classes.
- List the social factors that were to threaten the existence of mob football.

Exam-style Questions

How did mob football reflect the lifestyle of a peasant in pre industrial Britain?

[4 marks]

EXAMINER'S TIPS

When the instruction is to 'list', remember that the first points in your list will be considered until the mark allocation is reached. Thus, if the question says 'list', and '5 marks' are available, the first five answers will be taken.

CHALLENGE YOURSELF

Describe the structural changes that have occurred in association football from its popular origins to its rational form and explain the social determinants that have been influential. [20 marks]

What you need to know

Popular recreations were:

* occasional, because of limited free time and energy; they would often occur on 'holy days' and be a reflection of the changing seasons
* simple in nature, as few facilities and equipment were available; many activities therefore used natural facilities such as rivers and fields
* orally passed down through the generations, as the mass of the population were uneducated and therefore could not write down rules
* violent and cruel, as there were few rules in activities such as boxing, mob football and blood sports; this merely reflected a violent society where hangings were part of the social entertainment
* affected by prohibitions if they were considered unnecessary by the ruling class and by religious groups such as the Puritans
* functional first – that is, they served a specific purpose for that society, such as hunting and defence

* occupational – such as the watermen transporting people across rivers before the development of rowing competitions began
* recreational, as they were participated in during feasts and festivals as outlets for leisure pursuits
* linked with wagering as part of the entertainment and to provide people with other ways of making money; both social classes enjoyed this aspect of their recreations
* courtly as well as for the peasantry; the nobility and upper classes enjoyed recreational activities equally
* mainly local in nature because of lack of mobility and frequent wars; thus many geographical areas in the United Kingdom developed their own unique recreations, such as the Lakeland Games, the Highland Games in Scotland, Gloucestershire's cheese rolling and Ashbourne's Royal Shrovetide football.

Review Questions

1 What do the terms **functional**, **recreational** and **religious** mean in relation to the influence physical activities have within a particular culture? Give specific examples.
2 Write down in table form summaries of the Medieval and the Tudor and Stuart eras.
3 What was the significance of Shrove Tuesday in the recreational lives of people?

4 Compare the characteristics of the games of real tennis and mob football.
5 What were the characteristics of the Cotswold Olimpick Games?
6 What was Puritanism and what effect did it have on the recreational pursuits of the working classes?

CHAPTER 2

Rational recreation in post-industrial Britain and its impact on contemporary participation and performance

Learning outcomes

By the end of this chapter you should be able to:

- describe the characteristics of rational recreation (including respectability, regularity, regionalisation, codification, more controlled wagering)
- understand how these characteristics differed from the characteristics of popular recreation
- explain how social and cultural factors influenced the nature and development of rationalised sports and pastimes, with reference to:
  - the Industrial Revolution and the associated urban and agrarian revolutions
  - the emergence of the urban middle class
  - changes in work conditions that improved health and affected participation
  - the increase in free time for the industrial working class
  - the transport revolution and the impact of the railways
  - the changing views of the Church towards sport and recreation
  - amateurism and professionalism
  - the place and status of women in Victorian Britain, and the increased participation by middle-class women by the end of the nineteenth century.
- explain how rational recreation impacted on physical competence and health of participants
- describe the varying opportunities for participation
- explain how rational recreation impacted on physical competence and health of participants and the varying opportunities for participation
- relate these features to the activity of football as a case study activity.

Activity 1

Remind yourselves of the characteristics of popular recreation and how these activities reflected the society of which they formed an integral part.

The Hanoverian era (1714–1790)

The Industrial Revolution began in England in the middle of the 1700s and developed over a hundred years. It signified a dramatic movement of people from rural areas to the towns. Farming had become less important, as small farms had been taken over by large landowners as a result of the enclosure system. The efficiency of the urban factories also put many people who had been employed in the cottage industry out of work. Factory work required unskilled workers, who worked long hours in cramped, dirty conditions six days a week; young children were often employed in difficult and dangerous conditions.

Key terms

Industrial Revolution The period running from the middle of the 1700s to the end of the nineteenth century during which towns were developed from rural areas and manufacturing industries replaced agriculturally based employment.

Agrarian revolution A change in farming practice, after small farms had been taken over by large landowners as a result of the enclosure system and the development of machinery had reduced the need for labour.

Urban revolution The process whereby the mass of the population changes its lifestyle from living in villages and rural areas to living in towns and cities, usually as a result of the need to find alternative employment.

Impact on popular recreation

Moving from rural areas to the new towns and cities had an enormous impact on people's lifestyles, not least on their recreational pursuits.

- Their previous games were increasingly difficult to accommodate – for example, mob football.
- Space was at a premium and so were facilities, so there was to be a shift in emphasis from a participation base to a more spectator-based type of leisure pursuits.
- The economic conditions of people had changed, and their long working hours also curbed their opportunities for recreation.

Some activities such as cricket, racing, rowing and pugilism (a forerunner to boxing) had already begun their first phases of organisation.

Rules developed in activities:

- that began to occur more frequently
- in which the upper classes had control
- when the moral climate within society began to change.

Sports clubs and governing bodies developed to meet the recreation needs of 'Old Boys' who had left their public school and university and wanted to continue participating in sport. Evidence for this can be found in:

- the publication of the Racing Calendar from 1727
- the formation of the Jockey Club in 1752
- the rules for cricket, which were first drawn up in 1727.

In the eighteenth century, the Methodists continued the Puritan work ethic; they strengthened the attack on popular sports, believing that sport and drinking on a Sunday would lead to an afterlife in hell. The violence associated with many of the pastimes, such as wrestling, football and animal sports, was believed to be the cause of social unrest; employees would use them as an excuse to miss work, at a time when eighteenth-century employers required a more disciplined workforce in the mills.

Victorian Britain (1837–1901)

Victoria became queen in 1837. Her reign was a period of dramatic social change, which is reflected in the development of games and sports during the nineteenth century.

The working class

Under Queen Victoria's reign, social reformers campaigned for improvements in the physical and mental health of workers in society.

Parliament passed many laws and reforms to address the problems of women and children being employed in factories under terrible conditions and for long working hours – for example, the Reform and Factory Act 1832, the Ten Hours Act 1847 and the Factory Act 1878. The custom of a half-day Saturday began early in her reign, followed by the movement for early closing for shop-workers on Wednesdays.

Factory-owners created factory sports facilities and sponsored work teams. The development of the railways enabled them to send their workers on recreational trips, such as to the seaside. Employers hoped to gain the goodwill of their workers, increase morale and encourage the moral benefits of participating in team games.

From the 1870s onwards, there was a move to encourage a healthy, moral and orderly workforce, as can be seen in the provision of parks, museums, libraries and public baths. Sport developed into an important part of working life. The Municipal Reform Act 1835 led to the building of parks in the towns and cities; the general public were encouraged to use these parks for recreational use after 1870. The reasons for providing parks were:

- to improve the health of the population
- to discourage crime on the streets
- to wean people away from the evils of alcohol and gambling, as part of the Temperance movement
- to instil morality in workers by following the rules of rational, organised sport
- to demonstrate a sense of social justice.

Popular	Rational
· Occasional	· Regular
· Few, simple rules	· Complex, written rules
· Limited structure and organisation	· Highly structured
· Participation sport	· Spectator sport
· Physical force	· Refined skills
· Lower-class development	· Upper class development
· Local	· Regional/national
· Limited equipment and facilities	· Sophisticated equipment and facilities
↓	↓
e.g. MOB FOOTBAL	e.g. REAL TENNIS

Fig 2.1 Definition of popular and rational sports

The skilled workforce gradually shifted its attentions and interests away from the traditional popular sports, taking up pastimes such as reading and quieter exercise in the park:

> The decline of traditional sports, especially those which involved fighting, was not simply a question of pressure from well-organised groups of evangelicals and businessmen; in addition to the agitation from abolitionists there was evidence of a gradual shift in public taste, especially amongst the literate and more highly skilled elite of working people themselves. (R. Holt)

Fig 2.2 Prize fighting, c. 1840

By 1900, working people were heavily involved in sporting activity. There was continuity between the traditional and modern sports: bowls, darts, billiards, fishing, pigeon racing and dog racing provided sporting entertainment.

The upper classes

The upper classes were wealthy and powerful, possessed vast tracts of property and dominated Parliament well into the nineteenth century. They enjoyed a life of leisure, and were waited on by an army of servants. The aristocracy took part in local sports and affairs, usually in the form of patronage of prize fights (a forerunner to boxing) and pedestrianism (road walking).

Wealthy aristocrats who wanted to be associated with new styles and trends would sometimes spend large amounts of money on sporting events and particular athletes. A group of patrons would join together and form an association – for example, the Pugilistic Club – which would then organise the sport. When patrons withdrew their funds, preferring to sponsor different, perhaps more elite, sports, the effect was similar to modern-day commercial sponsors pulling out of sports events; it usually led to a decline in the activity.

Key term

Patron a person who sponsors any kind of artist or athlete from his or her own private funds; patronage tends to occur amongst a privileged class within a hierarchical society.

With regard to animal sports, on the one hand the upper classes supported the ban on cock fighting, while, on the other hand, maintaining their own passion for fox hunting – an example of the powerful safeguarding their own interests?

The French Revolution had shown the possible results of a breakdown in relations between the aristocracy and the ordinary people. The English gentry was, therefore, now not so confident of the respect that had previously been shown to them by the lower classes.

The middle classes

The new rich (or nouveau riche) who emerged from the Industrial Revolution became a strong 'middle-class' section of society. They wished to emulate the upper classes by buying old estates, educating their children in the established public schools and establishing their own recreations, which would separate them from the working classes. They also brought Christian morality to their recreations.

EXAMINER'S TIP

When giving an answer about social class, ensure that you clearly stipulate which group you are referring to.

Rational recreation

Table 2.1 shows the generally accepted characteristics of popular and rational recreation. However, as with any other generalisation, there are occasions when the general does not hold true.

Recreational activities did not just change overnight. In some cases the changes were very gradual, whilst in others they were more dramatic. Table 2.1 shows the transition phase that became evident, sometimes stretching over a number of years.

Concern over the amusements of the lower classes became a more pressing concern in the nineteenth century.

Sports, museums, libraries and baths were to play a large part in the way in which the ruling classes and new middle-class reformers saw the development of the lower classes into a more orderly, disciplined and moral workforce.

The urban developments had left the Established Church with little influence – a religious census in 1851 revealed very little attendance at any sort of church by a large section of the population.

Large groups of youth were regarded as potential social problems.

The Boys' Brigade (founded in 1883), the Church Lads' Brigade and the Young Men's Christian Association were all used to improve the appeal of organised religion and also as a form of social discipline.

Aston Villa, Everton, Fulham and Bolton were all church-based football clubs.

Street football was banned under the Highways Act, so adult workers usually had poor experiences of physical activity.

Table 2.1 The changing characteristics of popular and rational recreation

Popular recreation	Transition phase	Rational recreation
Played locally	Some athletes would have travelled to some festivals, games and race meetings.	Played regionally, nationally and later internationally.
Rural in nature/participant rather than spectator based	Larger towns retained the rural pursuits such as mob games and bull baiting.	The lack of space in towns would lead to provision for more spectators than participants.
Few/simple rules	Rules did not occur in all activities at the same time. Games such as cricket had early forms of rules, and even mob games played to similar but limited rules year after year.	Complex, written and later codified rules.
Played occasionally	There were approximately 46 holy days in the year, allowing for animal sports, archery etc.	More regular time off work meant more regularity of play.
Violent	Not all activities were violent – e.g. archery, bathing.	Activities relied on skill rather than force.
Festivals and feasts involved the whole village	Festival occasions could also be smaller occasions.	Festivals retained their popularity.
Working class	Many activities were lower class in their association, but the gentry often had some control, in the form of either land ownership or patronage.	All social classes would participate in the rational recreations.
Mostly male	Many activities were male based, but women ran the smock race, and played cricket early on.	Female sport was to increase greatly with independence, but there would still be less than for men.
Association with pagan rites	The church did allow some traditions to be maintained.	Muscular Christianity was the acceptance by the church of rational recreation.

Industrial influences

Industrial recreation programmes were not very widespread, although several individual projects were almost revolutionary in their social thinking.

> **Key term**
>
> **Rational recreation** Activities that developed a higher level of organisation and structure, especially as a result of the Industrial Revolution.

West Ham Football Club developed from the philanthropic industrial policy of A. F. Hills, an old Harrovian. A range of activities was introduced as well as profit-sharing schemes. A sports stadium was built to cater for a variety of sports clubs.

The Cadbury family were Quakers who founded the model industrial community at Bournville, Birmingham. George Cadbury required women workers to learn to swim (for cleanliness) and men with heavy jobs to do weight lifting to protect themselves from industrial injury. Good sports facilities were provided as part of a company policy, which 'rested on the importance of quick, well-executed work. Athletics and swimming, medical and dental care, proper breaks for meals and rest – all that helps to develop manual dexterity and visual awareness which are the commercial object.' The company was the first in England to implement the half-day Saturday.

> **Key term**
>
> **Philanthropy** The practice of performing charitable or benevolent actions.

Religion

The Victorian era was a climate of suppressing vice and encouraging religion and virtue. Non-conformism and the Protestant ethic became more firmly entrenched. Sports became less brutal, gambling was driven underground and there was a decline in blood sports.

IN CONTEXT

OPE

The inn had always been a social rural meeting place, and was used as a stopping place for the gentry on long journeys.

A tradition of games developed, which was encouraged by the inn-keepers to increase their business; examples are fives, rackets, boxing, coursing and quoits.

Many of the new sports clubs met in pubs, and they formed mutually beneficial partnerships:

- The village cricket teams would often use the field next to the pub.
- The hunt would have its stirrup cup at the pub followed by dinner.
- Liquor tents would be provided by publicans at sporting events.
- Bowling greens and boxing rings were built onto pubs, and pubs often organised a football team.

Those associated with sports were often regulars at the inns, so it was in the interests of the publican to encourage sport.

The English alehouse had to adapt to the new urban recreational needs. The pub became a focal point for workers trying to maintain a sense of identity, which was being eradicated in the new urban culture. As early as 1879 there were strings of football clubs in Blackburn, which were the culmination of the formalising of street corner teams. Boxing took over from the previous animal baiting sports of cock fighting and ratting.

Some religious sects had a restraining influence on working-class leisure – not only the Puritans, but also the Protestants, Evangelists, Methodists and Sabbatarians.

Protestants. The work ethic of the Protestant religion is associated with the Calvinists and Lutherans of the seventeenth century. The emphasis is on worldly work, which should be treated as a duty and as a means of earning salvation from God. Worldly success was seen as a sign that you were one of the 'chosen' to be saved, though reckless spending and enjoyment were not encouraged, but rather a thrifty outlook towards life. Leisure time and recreational activities were, therefore, given very low status. This was to be a particular constraint for the working class, whose members had no private means for recreation and who were subjected to the values of the moral middle classes.

Evangelists. Evangelism is the practice of spreading the Christian gospel. Evangelists emphasise personal conversion and faith for salvation. In the nineteenth century the Evangelists restricted the recreations of the working classes, believing their popular recreations to be sinful and associated with gambling and alcohol.

Methodists. Methodism was a system of faith developed by John Wesley and a nonconformist denomination. In the nineteenth century Methodists believed that popular recreations were sinful, being associated with drinking and gambling. The Methodists were among the strongest opponents of animal sport in the eighteenth and nineteenth centuries and were to have a detrimental effect on recreation pastimes for the lower classes. They tried to provide alternative religious activities combining the vigour of the wake with a spiritual cause.

Sabbatarians. Sabbatarianism was a religious sect that followed a strict observance of Sunday as the Sabbath. This had the effect of restricting the leisure activities of the working classes in the nineteenth century.

However, during the nineteenth century there was a distinct change in attitude of the Church towards recreational activities. This was due to a variety of reasons. In particular, rational recreation had begun to take shape, and this acceptance of recreation was useful in promoting the Church as a more attractive place to be, as church attendance was declining.

The Muscular Christians, the YMCA and the youth movements like the Boys Brigade and Scouts were examples of the new approach.

Activity 2

What constituted the basis of Protestantism, Evangelism and Sabbatarianism, and what influence did they have on working-class leisure?

IN CONTEXT

OPE

'No sport on Sunday': the proclamationists and muscular Christians were united by their desire to observe Sunday as a day of complete rest, without physical activity. This signified a slow development of working-class sports, as workers were prevented from joining the elite sports, and parks were closed on Sundays. Wealthy people, who usually had private facilities, seemed to escape from the Sunday ban on sport; golf, tennis and croquet were regularly played on Sundays.

Alternative Sunday pastimes were encouraged by the muscular Christians, such as cycling, rambling and boating. The bicycle had revolutionised the English Sunday, and the clergy might with advantage arrange short services for cyclists passing through their parishes.

Since the nineteenth century, **how** and **why** did the **Church** develop leisure opportunities for the British public?

[4 marks]

Key term

Temperance Restraint or moderation, especially abstinence from alcoholic drink

The transport revolution

The roads and canal systems in Britain were vastly improved during the eighteenth and nineteenth centuries. People, ideas, services and goods were mobile and could be transported around the country. Areas that had hardly been influenced by the outside world were now open to change. In terms of sport, inter-town fixtures could be held and spectators could travel to watch the spectacles. This tendency was to be transformed in the nineteenth century with the advent of the **railways**:

- Increased wealth and mobility enabled the sports of hare, stag and fox hunting to be more easily accessible to the middle classes. Animals could be transported with relative ease and comfort, and competitions changed from being on a local club level to national competitions between England, Ireland and Scotland.
- Ramblers, cyclists and mountaineers could access the countryside and more isolated areas.
- Fishing was revolutionised. In 1867 a book titled *The Rail and the Rod* was published – a guide to angling spots that could be reached within a 30-mile radius of London.

The major spectator sports of racing, cricket and football became national sports. Special excursion trains would carry spectators. William Clarke of Nottingham formed the first All-England Cricket XI and transported the team about the country, playing games against a variety of sides. The railways enabled them to play thirty or more matches a season, and allowed a high level of cricket to be enjoyed by those who would otherwise have been unable to experience such an event.

National sporting events then developed into international events, and foreign competition improved standards further. The rebirth of the Olympic Games in 1896 was made possible only by rail travel.

The present day

We have already established that sport is an integral part of the society in which it exists. It is, therefore, important to understand also that society is still changing and that this will inevitably impact on recreational and sporting activities.

Activity 3

Using a variety of sports, explain how the communications by water, road and rail influenced the development of different sports.

- Consider the importance of rivers for sports and development of towns.
- Consider the development of roads to the present day.
- Consider the railway for transport of animals, and for bridging the link between rural and urban areas.

Cheap flights have enabled ordinary people to access other parts of the world. Dubai is now in the top six destinations! This has also meant that other sports and recreations have become accessible. Consider water sports such as white water rafting on the Zambezi; skiing has become even more accessible; golf is a major recreational activity that is closely tied with leisure and tourism. The most recent initiatives to develop golf in the Himalayas reflect how people wish to integrate leisure activities with experiencing vastly different cultures.

Why were the majority of sports rationalised in the nineteenth century?

5 marks

Professionalism and amateurism

The concept of amateurism was thought to reflect the Ancient Olympian spirit, placing the ideals of fair play and team spirit high above any material objectives. In the 1850s Dr Penny Brookes founded the Much Wenlock Olympic Games and formed a National Olympic Association. He had a pure sense of amateurism, and encouraged the citizens of Much Wenlock to delight in the challenge of sport with no thought for a reward. The first Games were held in 1850, and included events such as football, cricket, quoits, a blindfold wheelbarrow race and chasing a pig through the town. The Games had all the trappings of a rustic festival and perhaps reinvented the Cotswold Games first started in 1612 in Chipping Camden. By 1870 the events included track and field athletics, such as the pentathlon and tilting at the ring (a version of the jousting tournament).

Key terms

Amateur One who participates in sport for the love of it without monetary gain.
Professional One who participates in a sport in order to earn an income.

The public-school influence established its own definition of amateurism, which superseded the Much Wenlock version. Much of the public-school version of athleticism was Olympian in outlook: combining physical endeavour with moral integrity, where the struggle was fought for the honour of the house or school. Baron Pierre de Coubertin visited both Much Wenlock and Rugby School in 1890, in the years preceding the foundation of the modern Olympic Games. He looked forward to a time when anyone would be able to participate, regardless of social standing or race.

In England there were two distinct phases of amateurism:

1 Originally, amateurs were gentlemen of the middle and upper classes who played sports in the spirit of fair competition.
2 There was a shift in definition of an amateur, from a straightforward social distinction to a monetary one. Originally there had been no problems perceived by earning money from amateur sport.

Fair play was the bedrock upon which amateurism was based. It was important to adhere to the rules of the game, but it was expected that a player would discipline himself rather than wait for a referee's decision. A situation was recorded that the Corinthian Casuals, founded in 1882, would withdraw their goalkeeper on the awarding of a penalty to the opposing side, on the principle that they should accept the consequences of a foul.

There were advantages and disadvantages to the amateur code. It promoted restraint in victory and graciousness in defeat; the acceptance of rules and consequent respect for decisions. However, it excluded the working classes, and this was a moral argument for its abolition. In 1894 the Rugby Football Union and the Northern Union split because of the refusal of the authorities to allow northern players to have enough leisure time to compete on the same basis as players in the south. Employers could not accept 'broken time payments' (compensation for loss of wages), and by so doing excluded manual workers who needed time to train and travel for sport. Similar conflicts were felt in rowing and cricket.

Table 2.2 is an attempt to organise the developments of these two concepts with the effect they have had on certain sports.

Table 2.2 A comparison between the changing concepts and sporting activities of the codes of Amateurism and Professionalism

Amateurism	Professionalism
Evolved in nineteenth-century England.	Earning money from sport is a very old concept – it goes back to ancient civilisations such as Rome.
Code brought in by upper class.	
An ideal based upon participation for the love of sport rather than for monetary gain; participation deemed more important than the winning.	Professional sport is an avenue of upward and downward social mobility.
	The Gladiator was an early form of a professional sportsman.
The gentleman amateur was a social class distinction of the amateur code.	The similarities between a gladiator and a professional footballer are that both athletes:
The gentleman amateur was drawn only from the upper classes and was regarded as having qualities of refinement associated with a good family; a man who is courteous, cultured and well-educated. Although gentlemen amateurs may have participated in some activities with their lower-class professional counterparts, there was no shame should they lose, as they were not being paid, neither were they involved in serious training.	• are involved in a physical contact sport relying on physical strength and speed • have a strong likelihood of injury resulting in an early end to a career • are treated as expendable; the 'hire and fire' policy; • are bought and sold through transfer deals and treated as a commodity • are paid by results • have little control as they are 'owned' by a coach/manager • have high media status and are treated as heroes.
Amateurism encompassed the belief in fair play and abiding by the spirit as well as the rules of the game.	Certain social factors are necessary for professional sport to flourish. It has been suggested that ancient Rome and industrial England in the nineteenth century shared similarities:
Amateurism originally had a monetary as well as a social-class distinction in its efforts to exclude the lower class.	• mass of a population living in close proximity • large section of population with disposable income and leisure time • need for excitement • commercialism.
The Corinthians were the epitome of amateurism.	
The Corinthians were consistent with St Paul's letter to the Corinthians that 'not everyone can win but those that do, should do so according to the rules and spirit of the time.' The Corinthians were drawn from the elite of Victorian society and followed this code during games.	

Amateurism

These meanings are arbitrary and socially determined hence they change over a period of time.

Sports have undergone major changes in their amateur/professional status.

For example, rowing was originally open to amateurs and professionals but the gentleman amateurs disliked being beaten by their social inferiors. This resulted in a strict amateur definition instigated by the 'Amateur Rowing Association' called the 'manual labour clause', instigated in 1882 to lead to the formal exclusion of manual workers. It was abolished in 1890.

Also, Rugby football developed in the nineteenth-century English public schools based upon amateurism. The working class in the northern industrial towns adopted the game, but needed to be paid to play or at least to receive compensation for loss of earnings while playing.

In 1896 these payments led to the North–South split into southern amateurs/northern professional. A hundred years later, even the Union game had moved over to professionalism as a result of player pressure.

In cricket amateurs and professionals could play together under the auspices 'gentlemen vs players'. The gentlemen were the amateurs and the players were the professionals.

The revival of the modern Olympic Games in 1896 was based on the amateur code as founder Pierre de Coubertin had been impressed with the values associated with athleticism in the English public schools of the time.

During the twentieth century other terms emerged to describe performers who receive some form of payment, including:

- 'shamateurism' – describes amateurs who receive 'under the table' payments. Trust funds were set up to try to combat this problem.
- 'stamateur' – describes state-sponsored amateurs and was common in Eastern bloc countries.

In the twenty-first century, amateurs can now officially receive financial aid from sponsorship, trust funds and organisations such as Sport Aid and the National Lottery.

CHALLENGE YOURSELF

Explain, using examples, how the concepts of amateurism and professionalism have changed since the nineteenth century.   **[20 marks]**

Professionalism

Bread and circuses theory: suggests that the mass of a population can be kept relatively content; a cynical viewpoint may suggest that sporting activities can be used by governments to alleviate social problems by channelling people's energies in a socially acceptable form.

Professionalism was evident in a variety of sports in the nineteenth century:

- **pedestrianism:** an early form of race-walking. In the eighteenth and nineteenth centuries, with only horse racing and boxing as rivals, pedestrianism was very popular, with much gambling involving men against time, distance and other walkers. On famous walker was Captain Barclay who, in 1809, walked 1,000 miles in 1,000 consecutive hours. A pedestrian was also a group of lower-class individuals who earned part of their money by competing in sporting activities for money, particularly rowing, footraces and cricket. It was the forerunner to the term 'professional'.
- **prizefighting:** individuals were taught to defend themselves in gladiatorial schools in 'sword and buckle' contests. Prizefighting was patronised by the wealthy and powerful, who wagered huge sums on the outcome of contests even though they themselves would never have been combatants. The activity employed virtually a professional core of men fighting in regular circuits, mostly centred on London. Rules were fairly loosely enforced and death was not uncommon. When the sport was outlawed contests were organised on private land away from magistrates. Notable figures were Broughton, Mendoza and Tom Cribb.
- **athletics:** developed under amateur rules in the public schools, but in society a professional circuit was very popular. As with many professional sports in the nineteenth century, there were problems with bribery, corruption and fixing of events.
- **rowing:** public schools employed professional watermen to coach the school rowing teams when the prestige of winning became ever more important.

In professional sport in the nineteenth century in England the role of the different social classes would tend to be:

- **lower class** – performer
- **middle class** – agents, promoters, managers
- **upper class** – patrons.

The inclusion of sports such as tennis and basketball in the Olympic Games in the twentieth-first century highlights the problems encountered by the modern-day sports world in trying to adhere to the pure ideal of amateurism.

Broken time payments Payments made to compensate working-class players for loss of earnings while playing sports such as soccer and rugby football. This tended to lead to professionalism in some sports and was looked down upon by the gentleman amateurs.

Gladiator Trained to fight in arenas to provide entertainment. This began as a concept in Ancient Greece/Rome but is now used to denote professional sport.

Professionalism Engaging in a sporting activity for financial gain or as a means of livelihood means training is synonymous with improving standards and specialising in an activity.

Activity 4

1 How has the concept of amateurism changed for the top performer over the last few years?

2 The role and status of amateurs and professionals within sport have changed a great deal during the nineteenth and twentieth centuries.

   (i) In the late nineteenth century the 'gentleman amateur' was highly regarded. Describe the characteristics of the gentleman amateur.

   (ii) From 1850 to 1900 the status of amateurs and professionals varied between sports. Comment upon this statement in relation to

● cricket
● rowing
● rugby football.

Exam-style Questions

Describe the factors that played their part in initially decreasing the leisure opportunities for the industrial working classes as they moved to the towns and the later improvements.

The changing role of women

The role of women in society has undergone some radical changes. However, it is important to distinguish between women in the upper, middle and working classes.

The involvement of women in football since the late nineteenth century highlights quite clearly that public interest in their competitive participation was high, until the Football Association banned them from playing on Football League grounds in 1921. Since then, the female game has made a slow recovery and is now beginning to attract media coverage at the higher levels. The members of the US female

soccer team are household names, and the Football Association and FIFA are taking positive steps to encourage the game.

Victorian female stereotypes in health, medicine, exercise, and social limitations resulted in the following:

● More social sports – croquet; tennis; golf – and school sports – lacrosse; hockey; netball.
● Headmistresses had autonomy; games were played in peace and privacy; there was balance between emancipation and social respectability.
● Distinctions were made between the characteristics and capabilities of men and women; ladies did not have to compromise status as ladies' fashion signalled changes; this was used to maintain the status quo.

IN CONTEXT

1895	First women's football game played between a northern and a southern team.
1902	The Football Association Council forbade its teams to play 'lady teams'.
1917–19	A boom in women's football – often to raise money for charity. Especially popular was Dick Kerr's Ladies Teams, which attracted up to 25,000 spectators.
1921	Football Association banned women from Football League grounds, deeming the game 'quite unsuitable for ladies'.
1960s	Interest in the game revived for women.
1969	The Women's Football Association formed.
1983	The FA invited the WFA to affiliate on the same basis as a county Football Association.
1989	Channel 4 increased interest, with 3 million viewers.
1994/5	The Football Association Women's Premier League established.

Rational recreation's impact on physical competence, health and opportunities for participation

Rational recreation tended to:

● take place regularly
● be codified by the public schools
● have clearly defined roles for working and other classes
● be played at a regional and national level
● increase participation by females.

With activities being played on a regular basis, the physical competence (i.e. skill) and health of people participating in these activities would improve, with most benefit being felt by those participating in rational recreation. Initially, it was the upper and middle classes who had this privilege. There was a delay in opportunities for the working classes owing to the lack of free time, disposable income and available facilities. But when the many social reforms of the nineteenth

Table 2.3 Women through the centuries

Upper class	Middle class	Lower class
Eighteenth Century		**Pre-nineteenth Century**
• Cricket; croquet; riding	• Aspire to upper-class lifestyle	• Popular recreations/occasional/ festivals/rural
Nineteenth Century	• Proprietary colleges	**Post-nineteenth Century**
• Pretentious education/social/ leisure/time/money/femininity/ fashion	• Own activities – lawn tennis/cycling	• Working/urban/industrial
• Rational sport	• Time and money not social breeding = restrictions	• Little time or money
• Copy boys' education	• Professions e.g. teaching	• Few sport opportunities
• Athleticism modelled for women	• Garden suburbs – golf/tennis	• Education from 1870/drill/femininity/sport male domain
• Victoria – sport and refinement	• Sports clubs administrators	• Improved work conditions/ gradual work outings/half-day Saturday/Bank holidays
• Limited on medical grounds	• Cheltenham Ladies' College/Roedean 1885 Miss Lawrence 1884 first ladies' singles Wimbledon	
• Social mixing		
• Development of ladies' universities (Girton Hockey team 1890)		

CHALLENGE YOURSELF

Women's participation in recreation and sporting activities has varied over time.

How did the role of working-class women change between the late nineteenth century (1890) and the middle of the twentieth century (1950) and how did this affect their participation in recreational and sporting activities?

[20 marks]

Exam-style Questions

Why was lawn tennis suitable for middle-class ladies in the nineteenth century?

[4 marks]

century began to be influential and factors such as the public provision of parks and baths and increasing rights within the education system became more widespread, opportunities for working-class participation increased.

The public schools were predominantly responsible for the rationalisation of traditionally working-class sports such as mob football. Therefore, public schools negatively impacted on the continuity of the 'old' ways of playing by changing,

and even banning, some activities. However, because the public schools then encouraged the workforce to participate in rational recreation, the working classes ended up with more opportunities than they had previously enjoyed.

Rational recreation made clear the division of labour. One of the earliest sports to be rationalised was cricket. Here, there were clear role-positions in the game and also clearly defined roles for the different social classes. Similarly in football there emerged the roles of attack and defence. Social class was more clearly defined by the amateur and professional divide in games such as rugby and football.

Amateurism tended to be the favoured code for the middle and upper classes, while professionalism was favoured by the working classes.

Owing to the massive growth in participants during the nineteenth century, clubs and governing bodies emerged, providing an administrative and competitive structure that could be enjoyed by people across the country, who all then played using one set of nationally accepted rules.

Rational recreation was especially helpful in allowing females to participate with social acceptance. They could now participate in rule-bound, civilised activities, which required skill development rather than brute force.

Contemporary participation

The legacy of rational recreation on contemporary participation has been significant. Many of the sports institutionalised in the nineteenth century can still be recognised today. There have been some rule developments and skills have evolved as a result of training and the technology now available, but by and large we would still recognise the **technical** aspects of activities such as, for example, lawn tennis, cricket, football and rugby.

The activities are still using many of the **moral** codes developed in the nineteenth century such as sportsmanship and etiquette.

Sports clubs and governing bodies still retain many of their original characteristics. There are, however, fewer amateur sports than there used to be. This means that there is now **less exclusivity** in sport and so **more sports are more accessible to greater numbers of people** than before.

Table 2.4 Sport in the nineteenth century and today

Sport	Contemporary participation as a reflection of the past
Rowing	University Boat Race/Henley Regatta
Lawn Tennis	Wimbledon ('The Championships') still a major competition in world tennis
Athletics	The Olympics, re-established in 1896, are still the pinnacle of every athlete's career
Football	Has become the most popular sport in the world at amateur and professional level
Cricket	'The Ashes' is still the most hotly contested event in cricket

Case Study: Mob football to rational football

Over approximately 100 years the British Isles had undergone a dramatic transformation from a rural and agricultural-based economy to the first industrialised country in the world. It was no coincidence that the birth of modern sport also began here. The old popular recreations were giving way to rational sport, which was seen as reflecting the civilising of society.

A change did not come about to the variety of mob games until the beginning of the nineteenth century, when school football became the custom, particularly in the famous public schools. This was the turning point in the rationalisation of the game.

Innovations and refinements were made to the game. This can be referred to as *the technical development of games*, where the skills, tactics, facilities and general organisation of the game developed.

Each school in fact developed its own adaptations. Where there was simply not enough space for the old hurly-burly mob football, schools such as Charterhouse, Westminster, Eton and Harrow gave birth to the type of game in which more depended on the players' dribbling virtuosity than the robust energy required in a scrum. On the other hand, schools such as Cheltenham and Rugby were more inclined towards the more rugged game, in which the ball could be touched with the hands or even carried.

The Clarendon Commission, a government report on public schools, formally recognised the educational value of team games. This time also witnessed the change in attitude of the Church towards sporting activities. The use of sport in developing Sunday school teams and church youth groups indicated that rational sport had won the approval of the Church.

In 1863 at Cambridge University an initiative began to establish some uniform standards and rules that would be accepted by everyone. This was codification.

Only eight years after its foundation, the Football Association already had fifty member clubs. The first football competition in the world was started in the same year - the FA Cup, which preceded the League Championship by seventeen years.

The game of soccer flourished, particularly in the newly industrial counties of Lancashire and Yorkshire. The teams and supporters travelled by rail. A team started by the Lancashire and Yorkshire Railway became Manchester United Football Club.

International matches were being staged in Great Britain before football had hardly been heard of in Europe. The first match was played in 1872 and was contested by England and Scotland.

This sudden boom of organised football, accompanied by staggering crowds of spectators, brought with it certain problems. Professionalism was one of them. Broken-time payments saw the beginnings of professional football. The first moves in this direction came in 1879, when Darwin, a small Lancashire club, twice managed to draw against the supposedly invincible Old Etonians in the FA Cup, before the famous team of London amateurs finally scraped through to win at the third attempt. This practice of compensating players for time lost at work grew rapidly, and the Football Association found itself obliged to legalise professionalism as early as 1885.

The foundation of the Football League in 1888 increased the popularity of the game. The following twelve clubs were to become the League's founder members: Accrington, Aston

Villa, Blackburn Rovers, Bolton Wanderers, Burnley, Derby County, Everton, Notts County, Preston North End, Stoke, West Bromwich Albion and Wolverhampton Wanderers.

The spread of football outside Great Britain, mainly because of British influence abroad, started slowly, but it soon gathered momentum and spread rapidly to all parts of the world.

This international football community grew steadily, although it sometimes met obstacles and setbacks. In 1912 twenty-one national associations were already affiliated to the Fédération Internationale de Football Association (FIFA).

By 1925 the number had increased to 36, in 1930 – the year of the first World Cup – it was 41, in 1938 it was 51 and in 1950, after the interval caused by the Second World War, the number had reached 73. At present FIFA has over 200 members in every part of the world.

Origins of football clubs

Many of our well-known football clubs developed as a result of encouragement from the Church and factory owners.

Table 2.4 Origins of football clubs

Church	Industry
Aston Villa	Arsenal
Queens Park Rangers	Manchester United
Wolves	Millwall
Fulham	West Ham

Activity 5

Discover the actual origins of the clubs shown in Table 2.4.

EXAMINER'S TIP

Be prepared to draw comparisons between the past and the present. For example, how does lawn tennis today reflect the era from which its emerged?

What you need to know

* The gentry detached themselves from the people as a result of social change and pressures.
* New wealth and ambitions from the urban areas were beginning to be felt in the country lifestyle.
* Despite legislation some activities persisted – traditional activities do not simply die out overnight.
* Reformers and abolitionists tried to discipline the industrialised workforce.
* The upper classes tried to remove themselves from the middle classes, who in turn tried to disassociate themselves from the working classes.

The Empire was at its height, famous for the phrase 'the sun shall never set on the British Empire'. However, Queen Victoria died and dramatic social changes that would change the face of the world began.

The industrial urban working classes emerged as a significant numerical body and were starting to understand the power they could yield as a united force. The Labour Party with its trade union connections was to put this power into effect.

Transport was increasingly affordable, particularly the railways.

Sport became part of the fabric of working-class culture and was budgeted for. International sport competitions were to become more organised, evident by the London Games 1908; World Series baseball was conceived in America; the first Grand Prix was held at Le Mans in 1906; the Tour de France was staged in 1903.

Spectator problems occurred – for example, a wooden stand collapsed at Ibrox in 1902 and in 1909 people were injured at a riot at Hampden.

Traditions that had started early in the century took hold so fast they can still be recognised today, particularly in football, cricket and rugby.

Rational sport was characterised by:

* respectability with codified rules, enabling competitions between regions many miles apart; this was a reflection of the civilising of society
* regularity of play, with increasing leisure time; public school and club developments
* the curbing of the bribery and corruption of the old professionalism, with more restrictions made upon it.

Review Questions

1 How did the constraints on free time and wages influence working-class sport and how were conditions improved towards the end of the nineteenth century?

2 The Municipal Reform Act of 1835 led to the provision of public parks. What were the motives behind this provision?

3 Explain the influence of a shorter working week on working-class sport for men and women.

4 Why did some industrialists encourage young working-class men to participate in sport and exercise?

5 What effect did the emergence of the middle classes have on recreational pursuits in Britain in the nineteenth century?

6 How did the inns and public houses cater for recreation?

7 Give some specific examples of how the railways affected recreation in the nineteenth century.

8 Contrast popular and rational recreation.

CHAPTER 3

Public and state schools: their impact on the development of physical activities and the participation and promotion of healthy lifestyles

Learning outcomes

By the end of this chapter you should be able to:

- describe the characteristics of the nineteenth century public schools, in particular appreciating that these schools were for the middle and upper classes and were therefore elitist educational institutions
- explain the impact that public schools had on the development of activities such as rugby and football and upon opportunities provided for participation, then and now
- describe and explain the legacy of the public schools on our present day sporting and education systems, including the state school system
- demonstrate knowledge of the Clarendon Report, especially its acknowledgement of the educational value of team games
- outline the three stages of athleticism (bullying & brutality; Dr Arnold, muscular Christianity & social control; cult of athleticism)
- describe the characteristics of the state schools, in particular appreciating that they provided a basic education for the working classes
- describe the objectives, content and methodology of the:
  — 1902 Model course with its emphasis on military drill
  — the 1933 syllabus, which was the last of the government-directed Syllabuses of Physical Training
  — *Moving & Growing* and *Planning the Programme*, which were designed specifically to help primary schools provide an educational approach to the teaching of physical activities such as gymnastics and dance.
- explain the societal influences on the opportunity and provision for young people to participate in physical activity in state schools today
- describe the aims of the National Curriculum.

CHAPTER INTRODUCTION

This chapter explores the origins of physical education, looking closely at the key role played by the English public schools in the development and popularity of sport in the nineteenth century, how culture and history have shaped the way physical education has been taught, and how physical education is now taught today in state schools.

It is important that, by the end of this chapter, you are able to understand the link to the present day education system. Although for ease of study we will deal with the state and private sector separately, it is important to remember that after 1870 both state and private sectors were running parallel to each other, each providing an education for the different social classes in the United Kingdom.

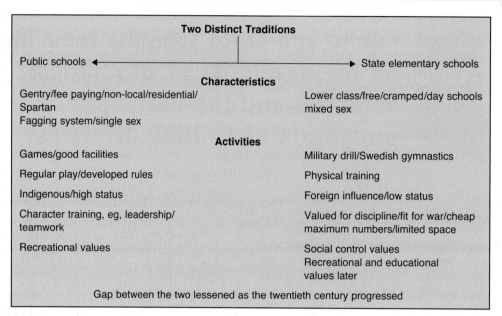

Fig 3.1 School traditions

Nineteenth–century public schools

The sons of the gentry were educated at large, prestigious, fee-paying boarding schools. Separate schools for daughters were founded much later, and catered for very different needs; boys' schools were academic while girls' schools concentrated on social accomplishments like sewing and managing a household.

There were originally nine elite institutions, which were called 'Barbarian' schools as they maintained the gentry tradition: Eton, Harrow, Rugby, Shrewsbury, Charterhouse, Westminster, Winchester, St Paul's and Merchant Taylors'.

The emergence of the middle classes has already been mentioned as a major change in the social structure of nineteenth-century Britain. When they acquired the necessary funds for their sons to attend these prestigious schools, the middle classes were unfairly rejected, as the schools wished to remain exclusive, and so they began to build their own proprietary colleges, which were based on the elite schools. Examples of these 'Philistine' schools are Cheltenham College, Marlborough and Clifton.

The development of games in the public schools occurred in three distinct stages.

> ### Key term
>
> **Public school** An elitist, independent, **fee-paying** school.

Stage 1 Bullying and brutality

The development of sport in the public schools radically changed previous concepts of sport. The boys brought to their schools their experiences of games like cricket and mob football and country pursuits such as fishing and coursing. Before the formalisation of team games, the boys would leave the school grounds, and participate in rowdy behaviour; this often involved poaching, fighting and trespassing, drinking alcohol and generally bringing the school's reputation into disrepute, causing conflict with local landowners and gamekeepers.

However, during this stage, they had begun the process of organising their own activities and devising new ways of playing; these were often associated with individual architectural features of the different schools, such as cloisters for fives, and the Eton wall game. This is an old form of football, and survives to this day. It developed from the unique architectural feature of a long red brick wall that separates the school playing fields from the Slough road. Ten players per side work the small ball along a narrow strip, 4–5 yards wide and 118 yards long. The players are assigned their playing position and specialised role according to their physique. The wall was built in 1717, but the game became popular in the nineteenth century.

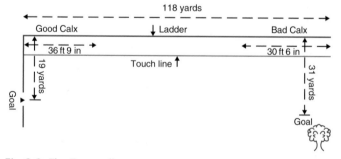

Fig 3.2 The Eton wall game

> ## Activity 1
>
> Can you think of reasons why a game peculiar to this school should continue to be played today?

Stage 2 Dr Arnold and social control

Doctor Thomas Arnold became headmaster of Rugby School in 1828, where he directed a crusade against personal sin – bullying, lying, swearing, cheating, running wild. Pupils were to remain on the school grounds, he forbade shooting and beagling as these activities encouraged poaching, and fights should occur only within his presence and be supervised by the prefects, who enforced his authority.

Arnold is known for his contribution to Muscular Christianity, but he valued games only for what they could contribute towards the social control of the boys. The development of athleticism followed the cooperation of the boys in maintaining discipline and achieving Arnold's reforms.

Thomas Arnold encouraged the boys to develop activities that could be played on the school grounds and that would also highlight the more moral features of teamwork, such as self-discipline, loyalty and courage; character-building qualities suitable for the prospective leaders of society.

Tom Brown's Schooldays by Thomas Hughes was published in 1860 and highlighted the Victorian ideal towards the physical side of the Christian gentleman. Hughes expanded the manliness ideals of Charles Kingsley – moral manliness became extrovert masculinity.

The government was forced to intervene in public-school education in 1861, when the Clarendon Commission was set up to 'inquire into the revenues and management of certain colleges and schools and the studies pursued and the instruction given there'. When the **Clarendon Report** was published in 1864, it strengthened the position of the headmasters by stressing the positive, educational features of team games as agents of training character. It did not place too much emphasis on skilled performance, but stressed moral qualities such as group loyalty. It also highlighted sports that were less useful, including hare and hounds, and gymnastics – both activities that focused on individual qualities. However, the report also revealed the extent to which games were becoming central to the school lives of the boys.

> ### Key term
>
> **Clarendon Report** A government report in 1864 that resulted in the acceptance of the educational importance and value of organised games as agents of character building.

The Taunton Commission Report, published in 1868, examined other schools. This also regarded gymnastics as inferior and less lively than the indigenous English games, which they recognised as having educational value. The headmasters rallied together at a conference in 1869 under the leadership of Edward Thring, and agreed that sport should encourage conformity in boys' lives.

Cricket was already a fairly well-established game in society and as such was considered suitable for the boys; mob football, on the other hand, was played by the lower classes in society and was not so acceptable, until the boys devised a more organised format. The game of rugby supposedly began at Rugby School, when William Webb Ellis picked up the ball during a game of football and ran with it.

The boys were in charge of organising the games, and senior bands of boys (normally called prefects) would be in control, which reflected the fagging system. Games committees were formed – for example, the Harrow Philathletic Club. The masters actively discouraged some activities (poaching and gambling), while others were allowed to exist on an informal recreational basis among the boys (fives and fighting). The boys were actively encouraged to organise team games.

Initially, inter-school fixtures were not feasible, as no two schools had the same rules. However, by the mid-nineteenth century, the headmaster and staff started to organise sports. Games were seen as a medium for achieving educational aims with a moral social sense; they could also help combat idleness and as such were a form of social control. Boys who excelled in games were admired by the other pupils.

Games developed technically because:

- boys brought local variations to the schools from their villages
- boys played regularly in their free time
- boys developed individual school rules/skills/boundaries, etc
- boys played competitively, i.e., house matches
- self-government meant boys organised activities initially
- later codified rules allowed inter-school fixtures
- development of games elite.

Muscular Christianity

Muscular Christianity was an evangelical movement, of which Charles Kingsley was one of its most influential exponents. Kingsley helped to combine the Christian and the chivalric ideal of manliness. It was the return of the Platonic concept,

Table 3.1 The origins of cricket and football

Cricket	Football
• Earliest established game in English society accepted by boys' families	• Still a 'mob' game in the nineteenth century
• Differing positional roles made it acceptable for both social classes to play	• Played by lower classes in society
• Reflected the ideals of athleticism: teamwork/ honour/etiquette; team before individual	• Not popular with gentry until boys devised rules within the schools
	• 'Contact' nature of the game meant that the social classes would play separately for a long time

the 'whole man'. It improved man's ability to be gentle and courteous, brave and enterprising, reverent and truthful, selfless and devoted.

Kingsley believed healthy bodies were needed alongside healthy minds: to neglect health was to be as lazy as to neglect the mind. He also led the hygienic movement, which was to have a deep effect on the working conditions of the poor.

There was little or no support for sport for its own sake at this time; sport should increase physical health and military valour, and create Christian soldiers. It was a fusion of physical with moral training.

Evangelical developments were directly linked with two philosophies – the muscular Christians were promoting things of which the nonconformists were sceptical.

- Muscular Christians regarded cricket, boating and football as positive recreation.
- The Church was attempting to attract workers from the pubs by forming alternative social clubs, such as Hand in Hand clubs.

Eventually there was a strong link between the churches and the club development of working-class sport, particularly football – for example:

- Barnsley: 1887, Revd Preedy appointed
- QPR: 1881, Revd Young appointed
- Aston Villa: 1874, a Wesleyan Chapel.

In Birmingham approximately a quarter of football clubs were explicitly connected to religious organisations between 1870 and 1885.

> ### Key term
> **Muscular Christianity** Embodied the belief that healthy bodies were needed alongside healthy minds in order to serve God. Moreover it believed that moral understanding could be developed through rational, athletic activity.

Stage 3 The cult of athleticism

> ### Key term
> **Athleticism** Physical endeavour with moral integrity.

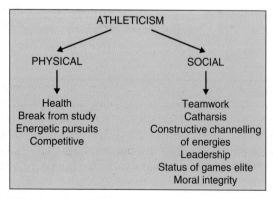

Fig 3.3 The benefits of athleticism

The cult of athleticism stressed the physical and social benefits of sports:

- The physical benefits were seen to counteract the effects of sedentary lifestyles, and sport was viewed as therapeutic, invigorating and cathartic. It was also seen as a break from work.
- Sport would take place within a competitive situation, which would help the boys to learn how to cope with winning and losing, all in a dignified manner. It helped to develop leadership qualities, and being captain was a high-status office to hold.

The house system was instrumental to the competitive sport events, in which the manner of the performance was considered more important than the result.

Games developed morally. Athleticism also met middle-class values of respectability and order – values such as:

- sportsmanship
- leadership
- abiding by rules.

The middle classes were to become the organisers and administrators of society – as was highlighted particularly in their role within governing bodies of sports clubs.

There were also opponents of this emphasis on athleticism, with many people believing it was becoming more important than the boys' studies, and could lead to a regimentation of boys' thoughts and behaviour with a destruction of individuality. Old boys who returned as teachers after university were often employed for their games prowess as much as for their intellectual teaching contribution. They brought to the schools the new sports they had learnt at university, the fully codified versions of the games and also the philosophy to excel at their sport.

The public schools instituted the idea of the Sports Day, which operated as a public-relations exercise to the old boys, parents and governors of the school. The funds of the school could benefit from generous donations and valuable publicity could be gained.

Exam-style Questions

The nineteenth-century English public schools were the first centres of sporting excellence. Discuss.

Exam-style Questions

Compare the two movements of Athleticism and Muscular Christianity.

Activity 2

Read the extract from *Tom Brown's Schooldays*, and consider the following questions:

1 Comment on the level of technical development of the physical activity described.

2 Explain the different social relationships being identified.

3 Discuss the values being reinforced as part of a character-building process.

'Huzza, there's going to be a fight between Slogger Williams and Tom Brown!'

The news ran like wildfire about, and many boys who were on their way to tea at their several houses turned back, and sought the back of the chapel, where the fights come off.

'Just run and tell East to come and back me,' said Tom to a small School-house boy, who was off like a rocket to Harrowell's, just stopping for a moment to poke his head into the School-house hall, where the lower boys were already at tea, and sing out, 'Fight! Tom Brown and Slogger Williams.'

In another minute East and Martin tear through the quadrangle, carrying a sponge, and arrive at the scene of action just as the combatants are beginning to strip.

Tom felt he had got his work cut out for him, as he stripped off his jacket, waistcoat, and braces. East tied his handkerchief round his waist, and rolled up his shirt-sleeves for him: 'Now, old boy, don't you open your mouth to say a word, or try to help yourself a bit,—we'll do all that; you keep all your breath and strength for the Slogger.' Martin meanwhile folded the clothes, and put them under the chapel rails; and now Tom, with East to handle him, and Martin to give him a knee, steps out on the turf, and is ready for all that may come: and here is the Slogger too, all stripped, and thirsting for the fray.

It doesn't look a fair match at first glance: Williams is nearly two inches taller, and probably a long year older than his opponent, and he is very strongly made about the arms and shoulders,—'peels well,' as the little knot of big fifth-form boys, the amateurs, say; who stand outside the ring of little boys, looking complacently on, but taking no active part in the proceedings. But down below he is not so good by any means; no spring from the loins, and feeblish, not to say shipwrecky about the knees. Tom, on the contrary, though not half so strong in the arms, is good all over, straight, hard, and springy, from neck to ankle, better perhaps in his legs than anywhere. Besides, you can see by the clear white of his eye, and fresh bright look of his skin, that he is in tip-top training, able to do all he knows; while the Slogger looks rather sodden, as if he didn't take much exercise and ate too much tuck. The time-keeper is chosen, a large ring made, and the two stand up opposite one another for a moment, giving us time just to make our little observations. The combatants, however, sit there quietly, tended by their seconds, while their adherents wrangle in the middle. East can't help shouting challenges to two or three of the other side, though he never leaves Tom for a moment, and plies the sponges as fast as ever.

The spread of athleticism nationally and worldwide

So far we have studied the development of games and sport in the public schools. However, the boys left the schools and mostly went on to the universities of Oxford and Cambridge. The universities acted as a melting pot for the nine schools where the variety of games and rules had arrived.

It was at the universities that:

- many rules became standardised;
- new sports emerged;
- further technical developments were made;
- standards of performance increased.

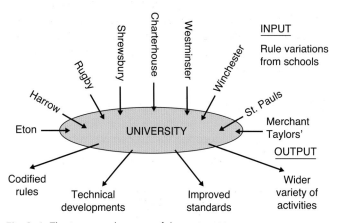

Fig 3.4 The input and output of the universities

The question remains: how could the sporting developments within nine public schools in the United Kingdom have such an impact on the sporting systems across the world? The answer lies in the status of the British Empire at the time. Britain had colonised much of the world, and this resulted in an economic and cultural legacy. The old boys occupied high-status positions that enabled them to influence the working classes within the United Kingdom and abroad.

- The Old Boys'/Girls' network provided contacts.
- The universities codified rules, developed activities technically, and improved and devised new ways of playing.
- Sports clubs and governing bodies became significant administrative features.
- Officers in the army and navy were influential on troops.
- The clergy influenced parishioners.
- Teachers went back into schools.
- Employers encouraged games in their workforce.
- The Empire enabled these developments to be spread worldwide.

Female education

In the late 1800s the education of girls was very patchy. Where provision was made for schooling the children of the poor, this was almost always focused upon boys. Among the upper classes, education for girls was pretentious and costly, with an emphasis on the accomplishments that a girl would require to function in 'good society' rather than for her intellectual development. Music and dancing counted much higher than with writing and arithmetic. 'Medical' reasons to limit women's sports participation were legitimised; it was believed that women who participated in strenuous physical activity would become muscle bound, which would be detrimental to child-bearing. As physical activity and educational examinations incorporated a degree of competitiveness, this was not conducive to the social image of how women should behave.

Attitudes towards educating women were not that much more enlightened at the beginning of the Victorian era, when constructive education for women was regarded as a threat to the norms for behaviour for society. As the struggle for women's rights developed, the pioneers of female education had to overcome much prejudice. Two such pioneers were Frances Mary Buss and Dorothea Beale. Buss founded the North London Collegiate School and Camden School for Girls, while Beale transformed the derelict Cheltenham Ladies College, turning this into a serious educational establishment for girls of the upper and middle classes. The efforts of both women were influential in changing the Victorian ideals of womanhood. However, it was not easy. Dorothea Beale wanted to teach the rudiments of science, but had to call this 'physical geography' to escape widespread condemnation. The introduction of physical education caused the most controversy. At this time, girls were not supposed to

exercise at all. In the nineteenth century the idea of allowing girls to run and jump and to remove their restricting corsets, was as culturally radical in Britain as the unbinding of women's feet in Japan.

Thus, physical activities for girls developed much later than those for boys, and this gradual development was linked to sociological factors and the development of female education in general. When prejudicial attitudes began to change, girls began to participate in activities such as tennis, hockey, gymnastics and cricket. Girls then developed their activities along similar lines to the boys; they established clubs and entered competitions. There was a concentration on female sports developing separately to boys, partly due to the single sex developments in schools, but social games like tennis did allow a mixing of the sexes.

IN CONTEXT

Each school developed its own adaptation of football and, at times, these varied considerably. Examples include the Eton Wall Game and Field Game; the Cloister game and Association games at Charterhouse; Harrow football and Rugby football. These variations would eventually lead to a split in the dribbling and handling versions of the game. At this time the public schools could play only inter-house competitions, as all schools did not recognise the same rules. Innovations depended for the most part on the playing ground available. If use had to be made of a paved school playground, surrounded by a brick wall, then there was simply not enough space for the old hurly-burly mob football.

All these early styles were given a great boost when it was given official recognition by the Clarendon Report that football was not merely an excuse to indulge in a childish romp, but could actually be beneficial educationally.

A new attitude began to permeate the game, eventually leading to a 'games cult' in public schools. This materialised when it was observed how well the team game served to encourage such fine character-building qualities as loyalty, selflessness, cooperation, subordination and deference to the team spirit. Games became an integral part of the school curriculum and participation in football became compulsory. A more organised form of football matched the concept of athleticism, a movement developed in public schools, and Muscular Christianity, a movement developed in society.

Dr Thomas Arnold, the head of Rugby school, made further advances in this direction, when in 1846 in Rugby the first truly standardised rules for an organised game were laid down. These were in any event quite rough enough – for example, they permitted kicking an opponent's legs below the knees, with the reserve that he should not be held still whilst his shins were being worked on. Handling the ball was also allowed and, ever since the memorable occasion in 1823 when William Webb Ellis, to the amazement of his own team and his opponents, made a run with the ball tucked under his arm, carrying the ball has been permitted. Many schools followed suit and adopted the rules laid down in Rugby; others, such as Eton, Harrow and Winchester, rejected this form of football, and gave preference to kicking the ball, and carrying it was forbidden. Charterhouse and Westminster were also against handling the ball.

Finally, in 1863, developments reached a climax. At Cambridge University, where in 1848 attempts had already been made by former pupils from the various schools to find a common denominator for all the different adaptations of the game, a fresh initiative began to establish some uniform standards and rules that would be accepted by everyone. This was codification.

Exam-style Questions

1 What has been the legacy of the nineteenth-century public schools on our present-day physical education system?

2 How does football match the concept of athleticism?

EXAMINER'S TIP

It is important to understand who the schools were catering for, their characteristics and overall purpose.

State education

Prior to 1870, the education of the masses had been the responsibility of the parish, and was very inconsistent. The Forster Education Act of 1870 was a great milestone in social welfare, as it created a state system of education. There was a developing initiative to build more schools, and the Act was the result of some radical changes in social thinking by philanthropists and social reformers.

Ever since the first Board Schools had been built in 1870, teachers in the poorest districts had been faced with the extreme poverty of many of their pupils. As many as three to four million children were living below the poverty line.

There were two main principles of state education:

1 There should be efficient schools everywhere throughout Great Britain.
2 There would be compulsory provision of such schools if and where needed, but only if such need could be proved.

The existing British schools, foreign schools, under the Foreign Schools Society 1808, and national schools, under the National Schools Society 1811, would continue to provide the bulk of the nation's education, provided they were good enough. The main points of the Education Act were as follows:

● England and Wales were divided into 2,500 school districts.
● The Churches were to decide if they needed to build new schools.
● Failing this, a School Board had to be elected by local people, to finance schools from the rates.
● The children would pay a small fee, with an increase in government grants. The very poor could receive free education.
● The school age was not less than 5 years but no more than 13 years. In London children were exempt at the age of 10 if they had passed grade V and were needed to work for the family income.

Mundella's Education Act of 1880 made education compulsory for all children between the ages of 5 and 10, without exception. In 1893 the compulsory school leaving age was raised to 11 and in 1899 to 12 years.

Overview of the development of state school physical education

Table 3.2 outlines the key dates and developments from drill to physical training to physical education within state schools.

Experiences of children at state schools were very different from those of their counterparts in the gentry schools. Small buildings with little space and no recreational facilities, allied with a philosophy that denied any recreational rights to the working class, placed constraints on the physical activities available to the state school system. Moreover, these schools were also day schools and catered for both sexes.

Early activities

Gymnastics formed the bedrock of early state-school physical exercise. Foreign influences, in the form of Swedish and German gymnastics, combined with the English style under Archibald MacLaren. The Schools Boards tended to favour the Swedish system for its free-flowing, free-standing exercises, possibly because of the employment of Swedish inspectors, while the strength-based German gymnastics that utilised apparatus developed within the club structure.

The lack of fitness and discipline and the poor general health of the working classes had been noted in the Boer War (1899–1902) and blamed for the heavy loss of life suffered. Swedish gymnastics also came under threat as not being effective enough in improving the fitness of the working classes sufficiently for the hardships of war.

Swedish gymnastics were deemed suitable for state schools as they aimed to:

- suit the diverse objectives of physical exercise for the working classes
- promote health and fitness based on scientific principles, so gaining approval with the School Board
- encourage military preparedness
- improve industrial efficiency/work productivity
- foster social order/social control/discipline of large numbers of children
- promote the harmonious development of the whole body
- be safe and cheap
- be easy to learn and instruct.

Fig 3.5 Massed drill in yard of an Elementary school

Fig 3.6 Drill in a classroom of Townsend Road School 1905

The Model Course: military drill

A policy of military drill and physical training was initiated but had little recreational value. In 1902 the Model Course was instituted by Colonel Fox of the War Office, but was to last only two years.

The main objectives of the course were to:

- improve the fitness of the working classes for military preparation
- increase their familiarity with combat and weapons
- improve discipline and obedience amongst the working classes
- prepare the working classes for their lives in employment and the armed forces.

Content

- Children stood in uniform military-style rows.
- Children obeyed the commands given by non-commissioned officers (NCOs).
- Actions were carried out in unison, requiring a class response rather than an individual response.
- Large numbers could be catered for in a small space.
- The movements were free standing and required no apparatus; they were cheap.
- Actions such as marching and handling dummy weapons occurred.

Methodology

- Commands were issued by the teacher or NCOs.
- There was little interaction between the teachers and pupils.
- The centralised system made it a requirement within state schools nationwide.

The problems with this approach were that they were essentially adult exercises for children. They did not take children's needs and physical and mental development into account. There was no educative content, and individualism was submerged within a group response. The use of NCOs also reduced the status of the subject, as it did not use qualified teachers.

In addition, it was recognised that these static and boring activities did not improve the health and fitness of the urban working classes and therefore were not being successful in producing productive workers and healthy soldiers.

Activity 3

- As a class prepare a practical session where the group is led in a drill-style activity.
- What qualities were required by the teacher and the pupils in military drill?
- How do the pupil requirements compare with those being generated through team games within the public-school system?

Table 3.2

Date	Type of activity	Characteristics	Reasons	Problems
1870 Forster Education Act State schools/ Elementary schools	Military Drill	• War office exercises • Regimented/straight lines • NCO and teachers command – obey • Dummy weapons • Static/free standing • Boys first – girls later • No age distinctions • Compulsory/centralised • Working class children not required to think/class response no interaction	To train working classes for: • military preparation • work preparation • discipline/obedience • fitness Useful for: • accept place in society • cheap/little space needed	• No education content • Adult exercises for children • Low status NCO
1890	Swedish drill included gymnastics	• Led by teachers • Free standing • Still instruction-based • Based on scientific principles of the day (knowledge of body) P.H. Ling 'father of gymnastics	Suitable for state schools: • Free standing/cheap/little space needed • Promote health and fitness • Military preparation • Discipline/social control	• Blamed for lack of fitness of troops in Boer War (1899–1902) • Replaced by Model Course
1902–1904	Model Course devised by Colonel Fox of War Office	As for military drill	Due to poor showing in Boer War	• No educational focus • Adult exercises for children • Did not cater for children's needs • Replaced by gymnastics focus and syllabuses of PT
1904–1919	Reinstatement of Swedish gymnastics	• Therapeutic approach • Recognised different • Improve health	• Non-trained teachers • Rehabilitation of soldiers ages/sexes • Value of recreation for morale increase, fun/enjoyment • Allow scope for teachers to use some initiative • Still mainly instruction	• Centralised • Rehabilitation of soldiers in content and style of teaching
1914–1918 World War I	First Syllabus of P.T. Board of Education	• Physical development • Medical basis • Development of games (playground) • Compulsory/centralised based Great War: • Static trench warfare • War glorified • Millions died/followed by flu epidemic 1926 General Strike 1930s Economic depression/social unrest/unemployment/need for some government recreation provision/social control		

Table 3.2 Continued

Date	Type of activity	Characteristics	Reasons	Problems
1933	Last of the syllabuses of P.T.	● More free movement ● More creativity ● Group work ● More interaction between pupils/teachers ● Beginning of decentralisation	● Influence of Laban training of specialist teachers being felt ● Women's training influential	Teachers were specialists and could plan their own lessons
1939–1945 World War II		● Mobile fighting – different training of troops led to obstacle/problem solving/assault courses led to apparatus in primary schools ● Bombing 5 destruction of facilities/re-building programme ● Men enlisted/women took over men's jobs ● 1944 LEA to provide sport/recreation facilities in schools		

1952–1953	Moving and Growing, Planning the Programme	● For primary schools
		● Obstacle training from army/apparatus
		● Movement training from Centres of Dance
		  ● exploratory
		  ● creative
		  ● individual
		  ● fun
		● Major games
		● Skills/dance/movement/swimming/ national dances
			● Result in changes in educational thinking
			● Child-centred approach
			● Teacher autonomy/initiative
			● Decentralised approach
			● Properly trained teachers	

1950s–1988		● Decentralised ● Total teacher autonomy/choice of activities ● Rise in use of educational gymnastics ● Heuristic/guidance style of teaching ● Children given a stimulus, children respond through movement ● Within their capabilities ● Imagination/creativity ● School recreation facilities improved since 1944 Education Act	● Society less formal ● Fully trained teachers ● Educational rather than physical training ● Term 'Physical Education' now in use	● Government wanting more control ● Need for more teacher accountability ● Replaced by National Curriculum
1988	National Curriculum	(see Chapter 10)		

Military Drill Strict and repetitive training in procedures or movements, as for ceremonial parades or the use of weapons.
Physical training Training of the physical body as distinguished from the mind and spirit.
Physical education The instilling of skills, knowledge and values through the medium of physical activity.

Syllabuses of physical training

Owing to the problems and concerns over the Model Course, the Board of Education established a syllabus of physical training in 1904, 1909, 1919, 1927 and 1933. They stressed the physical and educative effect of sport. Initially there would have been many similarities between the early syllabuses and the Model Course, except for the absence of military content.

IN DEPTH

The First World War, also known as the Great War, was fought from 1914 to 1918, mainly in Europe and the Middle East. The allies (France, Russia, Britain, Italy and the United States after 1917) defeated the central powers (Germany, Austria, Hungary and Turkey). Millions were to die in static trench warfare.

Nationalism revealed itself in war. Public schoolmen with their ideals of service were enthusiastic about the coming conflict. It was glorified like a football match, and the football match between British and German soldiers at Christmas 1914 set the tone for how sport was to be used during war time. Football grounds were used extensively for recruiting, and eventually the Football League bowed to moral pressure to stop fixtures for the duration of the war. Following the war there were hopes of a more equal society because of the massive loss of life sustained from all echelons of society.

1933 Syllabus of Physical Training

The 1933 syllabus was the last syllabus of physical training. The physical content would have been very much influenced by the government's primary concern for the medical and physiological base from which it approached the subject.

The syllabus reflected a more holistics approach to the teaching of the subject. As such its aims included:

- therapeutic effect;
- correction of posture faults and defects;

- improvement to the circulatory systems would have been foremost in their aims.

The educational aims would try to develop alertness and decision-making and reflected a more holistic approach to the teaching of this subject.

Content

There was more variety of activities, such as skill-based work from sports such as athletics, gymnastics and games.

- There was a reduction in the number of tables.
- More variety of equipment was being used, including the building of gymnasiums.
- The ages of the children were taken into account, especially whether they were under or over the age of 11.

Methodology

- The lessons were becoming more decentralised, which meant children were no longer standing in ranks, but the teacher would work with individuals and the whole class.
- There was more interaction between teachers and pupils.

This was to be the last centralised programme for the teaching of physical activity in state schools until 1988 with the introduction of the National Curriculum. There were now fully trained physical education specialists who required less strict guidance from the government. They were able to plan their own work and this reflected the decentralised nature of the political situation in the United Kingdom, whereby local authorities were encouraged to develop initiatives and programmes to suit their local needs.

Activity 4

Consider the similarities and differences between the 1904 and the 1933 syllabuses in Figures 3.7 (a) and (b).

The Second World War

Key effects on the development of physical education:

- destruction of schools/deterioration of equipment
- evacuation of children to rural areas
- male physical education teachers enlisted
- work taken over by older men and women
- more mobile style of fighting
- apparatus for schools from commando training
- movement away from therapeutic and medical value of physical education
- more emphasis on heuristic/guidance style of teaching.

I	PLAY RUNNING OR MARCHING	Play or running about. The children should, for a minute or two, be allowed to move about as they please.
II	PRELIMINARY POSITIONS AND MOVEMENTS	Attention. Standing at ease. Hips firm. Feet close. Neck rest. Feet astride. Foot outward place. Foot forward place. Stepping sideways. Heels raising. Right turn and right half turn. Left turn and left half turn.
III	ARM FLEXIONS AND EXTENSIONS	Arms downward stretching. Arms forward stretching. Arms sideways stretching. Arms upward stretching.
IV	BALANCE EXERCISES	Heels raising. Knees bending and stretching. Preparation for jumping. Heels raising (neck rest). Heels raising (astride, hips firm). Heels raising (astride, neck rest). Head turning in knees bend position. Knees bending and stretching (astride). Leg sideways raising with arms sideways raising. Knee raising.
V	SHOULDER EXERCISES AND LUNGES	Arms forward raising. Arms sideways raising. Hands turning. Arms flinging. Arms forward and upward raising. Arms sideways and upward raising.
VI	TRUNK FORWARD AND BACKWARD BENDING	Head backward bending. Trunk forward bending. Trunk backward bending. Trunk forward bending (astride). Trunk backward bending (astride).
VII	TRUNK TURNING AND SIDEWAYS BENDING	Head turning. Trunk turning. Trunk turning (astride, neck rest). Trunk turning (feet close, neck rest). Trunk sideways bending. Trunk sideways bending (feet close, hips firm). Trunk sideways bending (feet close, neck rest).
VIII	MARCHING	Marking time (from the halt). Turnings while marking time. Quick march. Marking time (from the march). Changing direction.
IX	JUMPING	Preparation for jumping. *Note:* Work from this Column should be omitted until above exercise has been taught under IV.
X	BREATHING EXERCISES	Breathing exercises without arm movements. With deep breathing, arms sideways raising.

Note: Exercises bracketed should be taken in succession.

Fig 3.7 (a) The 1904 syllabus for physical education

PART ONE

1

Introductory Activity
1. Free running, at signal, children run to 'homes' in teams. (Four or more marked homes in corners of playground.) All race round, passing outside all the homes, back to places and skip in team rings.
2. Free running, at signal all jump as high as possible and continue running. Brisk walking, finishing in open files, marking time with high knee raising.
3. Aeroplanes. (Following the leaders in teams.)

Rhythmic Jump
1. Skip jump on the spot, three low, three high (continuously) (*Low, 2, 3, high, 2, 3, etc.*)
2. Astride jump. *Astride jumping – begin! 1., 2., 1., 2., etc. stop!*
3. Skip jump, four on the spot, four turning round about (8 counts) and repeat turning the opposite way (8 counts).

2

1. (Astride [Long sitting]) Trunk bending downward to grasp ankles. Unroll. (*With a jump, feet astride – place! [with straight legs – sit.!] Grasp the ankles – down! With unrolling, trunk upward – stretch! With a jump, feet together – place!*)
2. (Astride [Astride long sitting]) Trunk bending downward to touch one foot with opposite hand.
3. (Feet close [Cross-legged sitting].) Head dropping forward and stretching upward. (*Feet – close!) Head forward – drop! Head upward – stretch! (Crouch) Knee stretching and bending. ('Angry Cats') (Crouch position – down!) Knees – stretch! bend! up! down! etc. stand – up!*

3

1. As small as possible, as tall as possible. [(Crook sitting, Back to wall) Single arm swinging forward-upward to touch wall.] [(Crook sitting) Drumming with the feet, loud and soft.]
2. Single arm circling at a wall. (Run and stand with side to wall, nearest hand supported against wall about shoulder height. Circling with free arm. Turn about and repeat.)

4

1. Free running like a wooden man. Finish in open files in chain grasp. (One foot forward, heel level with the other toe). Knee full bending and stretching with knees forward. (Several times. Move the back foot forward and repeat.) (Lean standing) Hug the knee. [(Crook lying) Hug the knees. (Lower the feet quietly.)]
2. Running in twos, change to skipping, finish in a double ring facing partner holding hands. Knees full bend. Knee springing. Hands on ground and jump up. *Knees full bend! Knee springing – begin! 1, 2, 1, 2, etc. Stop! Placing the bands on the ground, with a jump stand – up!*
3. Form a ring. Gallop step left and right, at signal, run and stand with side to wall, nearest hand supported against wall (the other arm sideways). Kick the hand. (Turn about, or run to opposite wall and repeat several times with each leg.)

5

1. Brisk walking anywhere, change to walking on heels or toes, at signal run to open files facing partners. (Feet-close, Arms forward, Fists touching.) Trunk turning with single elbow bending. (Elbow raised and pulled back. 'Drawing the bow.') (Feet – close! With fists touching, arms forward – raise!) With the right arm, draw the bow – pull! Let go! With the left arm – pull! Let go! etc. Arms – lower!
2. Race to a wall and back to centre line and join right hand across with partner. Tug of war with one hand.
3. (Informal lunge with hand support.) Head and trunk turning with arm raising to point upward. (Left (right) *foot forward with knee bent and left (right) hand on knee (informal lunge) – ready!) With arm raising to point upward, head and trunk to the right, (left) – turn! With arm lowering, forward – turn. (Repeat several times.) With a jump, feet change!*

6

Class Activity
1. Running, jumping over a series of low ropes. (In ranks of six or eight in stream.)
2. Frog jump anywhere.
3. Free running or skipping, tossing up a ball and catching it. (A ball each. Who can make the greatest number of catches without missing.)

Group Practices
1. Running or galloping with a skipping rope. (A rope each.)
2. Running Circle Catch, with a player in the centre, throwing, or bouncing and catching a ball.
3. Sideways jumping over a low rope, partner helping. (Partner astride rope, performer holding partner's hands does several preparatory skip jumps on the spot and then a high jump over the rope landing with knees bent and standing up again.)
4. In two's, crawling or crouch jump through a hoop, held by partner.

Game
Odd Man.
Free Touch with 6 or 7 'He's.' ('He's' carry a coloured braid or bean bag as distinguishing mark.).
Tom Tiddler.

7

Free walking, practising good position, lead into school.

Fig 3.7 (b) The 1933 syllabus for physical education – excerpt

Developments in education since 1945

IN DEPTH

The Butler Education Act of 1944 was a major social reform, which had a wide-ranging impact on education in Britain. It aimed to remove special privileges and ensure equality of opportunity for all. Its main provisions were as follows:

- There were to be 146 local education authorities to replace the previous 300. They were required to provide recreational facilities to specific sizes.
- The school leaving age was to be raised to 15 from 1947.
- All education in state-maintained grammar schools was to be free. To attend grammar schools children now needed to pass the eleven plus exam, rather than pay.
- All children would leave the elementary school at 11 and move to a secondary school – either grammar or secondary modern. This was a complete separation of the primary from secondary education, and meant that new schools had to be built.
- More mature forms of physical education were required to suit the higher ages of the children. His Majesty's Inspectorate (HMI) for PE now reported to the Chief Inspector, not to the Chief Medical Officer.
- The 1944 McNair Report gave PE teachers the same status as other teachers.

After the war there was an extensive rebuilding programme, and facilities were more sophisticated than before. The therapeutic effect of recreational activities was again valued. The commando training during the war had developed the use of obstacle training, and this was how the first apparatus began to appear in schools – scramble nets, rope ladders, mats and frames, hoops, wooden tables and benches.

The 'movement' approach began in physical-education lessons; children were required to use their initiative and learn by discovery. This also demanded new teaching methods, and there was the development of a more heuristic style, which placed the teacher in the role of guiding the children rather than being purely instructional.

The influence of Isadora Duncan and Laban, with their form of dance using the body as an expressive medium, was taken up by women teachers. Modern Educational Dance 1948 gave sixteen basic movement themes and rudiments of free dance technique and space orientation. The word 'movement' came to reflect the 1940s and 1950s, as 'posture' had reflected the 1930s.

Summary

- Destruction of schools/deterioration of equipment during the Second World War led to new facilities
- Male physical education teachers were enlisted so the work was taken over by older men and women, which led to an emphasis on the movement approach
- The more mobile style of fighting (i.e. commando training) led to the development of new apparatus for schools such as rope ladders and, combined with a more heuristic/guidance style of teaching, developed a problem-solving approach to learning
- There was a movement away from the therapeutic and medical approach to the value of a 'physical education'.

CHALLENGE YOURSELF 1

Explain the development of gymnastics in the UK school system and discuss its effectiveness as a lifelong activity. [20 marks]

Moving and Growing and Planning the Programme

These two publications were issued by the Ministry of Education in 1952 and 1953 respectively. These publications developed as a result of changes in educational thinking that were to make learning stem from a more child-centred approach. They replaced the old syllabuses and were to be implemented in primary schools. They combined the two influences of:

- obstacle training from the army
- movement training from centres of dance.

Running parallel to these changes were:

- circuit training (devised by G. T. Adamson and R. E. Morgan at the University of Leeds)
- weight training – progressive resistance exercises
- Outward Bound schools promoting adventurous activities to develop the personality within the natural environment in challenging conditions.

The physical-education teacher was now more autonomous, with personal control over the physical-education syllabus.

Aims

The term physical education had truly arrived, with the emphasis on combining the physical, intellectual, social and emotional aspects of a child's development.

Enjoyment was now considered an important feature of a physical-education lesson, enhancing the learning process.

Content

The activities included:

- agility, playground and more major game skills
- educational gymnastics
- dance and movement to music
- national dances
- swimming.

The key words that separate these activities from earlier forms of physical activity in state schools are:

- exploratory
- creative
- individual
- fun.

Methodology

- Teaching styles had become more heuristic or guidance oriented, where children were encouraged to find solutions through movement.
- It was a problem-solving approach, which stimulated the cognitive and intellectual abilities of the child.
- The content and style of teaching were determined by the child's needs – that is, they were child centred.
- There was more variety of equipment and apparatus such as ropes, boxes, mats and so on.

IN CONTEXT

Children were encouraged to respond with movement to a stimulus, or movement problem. For example, a teacher might set a task of finding as many different ways to travel across, along or over a bench. The child would be required to use a certain amount of imagination and creativity to answer the task.

However, there would be no right or wrong solution. Children were not forced to perform cartwheels, but they could answer the task by responding with movements within their capabilities and therefore would develop confidence as they achieved a level of success.

This was very much a heuristic or guidance style of teaching as opposed to the more didactic and prescribed approach of the early twentieth century.

Key term

Heuristic A teaching style that encourages children to learn by discovery. The sense of failure is eliminated, as tasks set have open-ended possibilities rather than predetermined goals set by adults.

Fig 3.8 Physical Education in the 1950s

1870	Drill	centralised
1904–1933	Syllabuses of Physical Training	centralised
1933–1988	Physical Education teachers devise syllabus	decentralised
1988+	National Curriculum	more centralised

Fig 3.9 Syllabus development of physical education in the UK

The Decentralised Years (1945–1988)

This was a period when physical education teachers were fully trained. Therefore, teachers required less strict guidance from the government. They were able to plan their own work and Local Education Authorities (LEAs) were encouraged to develop initiatives and programmes to suit local needs. The benefits of decentralised systems are that good teachers are able to display initiative and flair and are able to cater for their local areas. However, one negative aspect can be an abuse of the system whereby teachers are not fully accountable for what they teach and may teach activities of their own choice, not providing children with a wide range of activities.

The situation regarding school sport or extra-curricular activities was the same. Children could receive very different experiences depending upon where they lived and which schools they attended.

In the early 1980s industrial action by teachers – the contractual hours and lack of monetary incentives tended to diminish teachers' goodwill, with the result that physical education lessons and extra-curricular clubs were negatively affected.

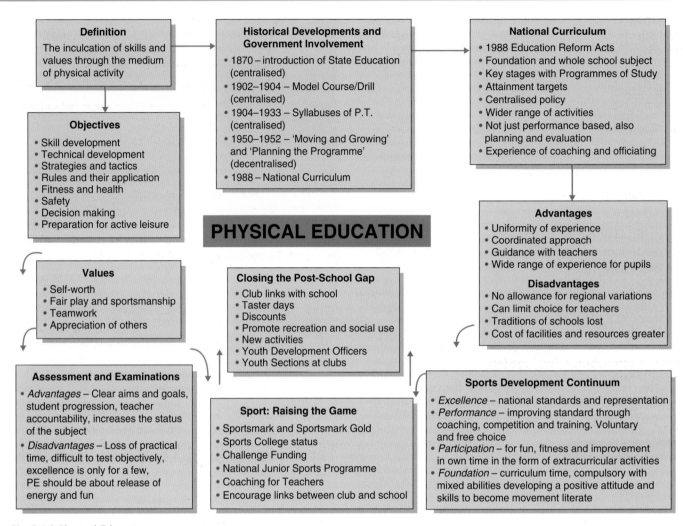

Definition
The inculcation of skills and values through the medium of physical activity

Objectives
- Skill development
- Technical development
- Strategies and tactics
- Rules and their application
- Fitness and health
- Safety
- Decision making
- Preparation for active leisure

Historical Developments and Government Involvement
- 1870 – introduction of State Education (centralised)
- 1902–1904 – Model Course/Drill (centralised)
- 1904–1933 – Syllabuses of P.T. (centralised)
- 1950–1952 – 'Moving and Growing' and 'Planning the Programme' (decentralised)
- 1988 – National Curriculum

National Curriculum
- 1988 Education Reform Acts
- Foundation and whole school subject
- Key stages with Programmes of Study
- Attainment targets
- Centralised policy
- Wider range of activities
- Not just performance based, also planning and evaluation
- Experience of coaching and officiating

PHYSICAL EDUCATION

Advantages
- Uniformity of experience
- Coordinated approach
- Guidance with teachers
- Wide range of experience for pupils

Disadvantages
- No allowance for regional variations
- Can limit choice for teachers
- Traditions of schools lost
- Cost of facilities and resources greater

Values
- Self-worth
- Fair play and sportsmanship
- Teamwork
- Appreciation of others

Closing the Post-School Gap
- Club links with school
- Taster days
- Discounts
- Promote recreation and social use
- New activities
- Youth Development Officers
- Youth Sections at clubs

Assessment and Examinations
- *Advantages* – Clear aims and goals, student progression, teacher accountability, increases the status of the subject
- *Disadvantages* – Loss of practical time, difficult to test objectively, excellence is only for a few, PE should be about release of energy and fun

Sport: Raising the Game
- Sportsmark and Sportsmark Gold
- Sports College status
- Challenge Funding
- National Junior Sports Programme
- Coaching for Teachers
- Encourage links between club and school

Sports Development Continuum
- *Excellence* – national standards and representation
- *Performance* – improving standard through coaching, competition and training. Voluntary and free choice
- *Participation* – for fun, fitness and improvement in own time in the form of extracurricular activities
- *Foundation* – curriculum time, compulsory with mixed abilities developing a positive attitude and skills to become movement literate

Fig 3.10 Physical Education

This all led to the government wishing to take more control of education, setting national standards of attainment and making schools and teachers accountable for their results. Hence, the introduction of the National Curriculum in 1988.

Physical Education Today

Administration of physical education in the UK

The UK has a system of private and state school education. The nature of schools can be as diversified as the people they house. Local authorities used to have a large influence on how education operated in their areas; they would be the middle man between the schools and the government. During the 1980s the government implemented increasingly **centralised** policies, such as the **National Curriculum**, the Local Management of Schools (LMS) and the growing number of grant maintained schools (GMS), which resulted in them leaving local authority control. The government sought more direct control of education, and through the Education Reform Acts of 1986 and 1988, it has restricted the freedom of teachers, schools and local authorities to construct their own syllabus.

Key terms

Centralised To draw under central control. The central government directs policy across a country. State legislation coordinates and supports policies such as an education curriculum.

Decentralised Dispersal away from the centre towards outlying areas. It is a system of government that is organised into smaller, more autonomous units. Examples are local authorities in the United Kingdom and the individual states in the United States of America. The government in power often gives guidelines, which can be interpreted at a local level.

Who chooses the physical-education programme?

In the United Kingdom the National Curriculum for Physical Education now sets out which subjects are to be taught at each Key Stage [1–4] of a pupil's schooling. Physical education is one of the statutory subjects to be delivered.

At this point it will be useful to remind yourself about the meaning of the terms 'centralised' and 'decentralised'. The advantages of a centralised system are that it:

- provides uniformity of experience;
- is a coordinated system;
- is funded by the government.

The disadvantages of a centralised system are that it:

- can be rigid and inflexible;
- may not cater for different local needs.

As for a decentralised system, it:

- can be difficult to monitor the system effectively, particularly in large countries;
- can reduce the initiatives of individuals such as good teachers.

The National Curriculum

The National Curriculum sets out the stages and core subjects that children will be taught during their time at school in the UK. The National Curriculum applies to all pupils of compulsory school age (ages 5–16) in community and foundation schools, including community special schools and foundation and voluntary-controlled schools.

The National Curriculum is a framework used by all maintained (i.e. state) schools to ensure that teaching and learning are balanced and consistent. The National Curriculum sets out:

- the subjects to be taught;
- the knowledge, skills and understanding required in each subject;
- the standards or attainment targets for each subject;
- how each child's progress is to be assessed and reported.

Within the framework of the National Curriculum, all schools are free to plan and organise teaching and learning in the way that best meets the needs of their pupils.

Key stages

The National Curriculum is organised into blocks of years called 'key stages'.

There are four key stages as well as a 'Foundation Stage'. The 'Foundation Stage' covers education for children before they reach 5 (compulsory school age in the UK).

Measuring progress

For each subject, there is a programme of study. The programmes of study describe the subject knowledge, skills and understanding that pupils are expected to develop during each key stage.

National Curriculum levels

The programmes of study also map out a scale of attainment within the subject. In most Key Stage 1, 2, and 3 subjects, these 'attainment targets' are split into eight levels, plus a description of 'exceptional performance'.

Table 3.3 Key stages of the National Curriculum

Age	Stage	Year	Assessment
3–4	Foundation		
4–5		Reception	
5–6	**Key Stage 1**	Year 1	
6–7		Year 2	Teacher assessments in English, maths and science
7–8	**Key Stage 2**	Year 3	
8–9		Year 4	
9–10		Year 5	
10–11		Year 6	National tests and teacher assessments in English, maths and science
11–12	**Key Stage 3**	Year 7	
12–13		Year 8	
13–14		Year 9	National tests in English, maths and science; and teacher assessments in other foundation subjects
14–15	**Key Stage 4**	Year 10	Some children take GCSEs
15–16		Year 11	Most children take GCSEs or other national qualifications

Children develop at different rates, but National Curriculum levels can give an idea of how a child's progress compares to what is typical for his or her age. For example, by the end of Key Stage 1, most children will have reached level 2, and by the end of Key Stage 2 most will be at level 4.

National Curriculum aims

Aim 1: The school curriculum should aim to provide opportunities for all pupils to learn and to achieve.

The school curriculum should develop enjoyment of, and commitment to, learning as a means of encouraging and stimulating the best possible progress and the highest attainment for all pupils. It should build on pupils' strengths, interests and experiences and develop their confidence in their capacity to learn and work independently and collaboratively. It should equip them with the essential learning skills of literacy, numeracy, and information and communication technology, and promote an enquiring mind and capacity to think rationally.

The school curriculum should contribute to the development of pupils' sense of identity through knowledge and understanding of the spiritual, moral, social and cultural heritages of Britain's diverse society and of the local, national, European, Commonwealth and global dimensions of their lives. It should encourage pupils to appreciate human aspirations and achievements in aesthetic, scientific, technological and social fields, and prompt a personal response to a range of experiences and ideas.

By providing rich and varied contexts for pupils to acquire, develop and apply a broad range of knowledge, understanding and skills, the curriculum should enable pupils to think creatively and critically, to solve problems and to make a difference for the better. It should give them the opportunity to become creative, innovative, enterprising and capable of leadership to equip them for their future lives as workers and citizens. It should also develop their physical skills and encourage them to recognise the importance of pursuing a healthy lifestyle and keeping themselves and others safe.

Aim 2: The school curriculum should aim to promote pupils' spiritual, moral, social and cultural development and prepare all pupils for the opportunities, responsibilities and experiences of life.

The school curriculum should promote pupils' spiritual, moral, social and cultural development and, in particular, develop principles for distinguishing between right and wrong. It should develop their knowledge, understanding and appreciation of their own and different beliefs and cultures, and how these influence individuals and societies. The school curriculum should pass on enduring values, develop pupils' integrity and autonomy and help them to be responsible and caring citizens capable of contributing to the development of a just society.

It should promote equal opportunities and enable pupils to challenge discrimination and stereotyping. It should develop their awareness and understanding of, and respect for, the environments in which they live, and secure their commitment to sustainable development at a personal, local, national and global level. It should also equip pupils as consumers to make informed judgements and independent decisions and to understand their responsibilities and rights.

The school curriculum should promote pupils' self-esteem and emotional wellbeing and help them to form and maintain worthwhile and satisfying relationships, based on respect for themselves and for others, at home, school, work and in the community. It should develop their ability to relate to others and work for the common good.

It should enable pupils to respond positively to opportunities, challenges and responsibilities, to manage risk and to cope with change and adversity.

It should prepare pupils for the next steps in their education, training and employment and equip them to make informed choices at school and throughout their lives, enabling them to appreciate the relevance of their achievements to life and society outside school, including leisure, community engagement and employment.

National Curriculum for physical education

Physical education (PE) has a distinctive contribution to make to the aims of the National Curriculum. The PE programme of study provides opportunities to plan sequences of work, learning outcomes and teaching approaches that develop success, confidence and responsibility.

Successful learners. PE helps pupils acquire the knowledge, skills and understanding they need to participate successfully in, and enjoy, physical activities both now and in the future. Pupils develop analytical and evaluation skills by deciding how to improve the quality of their own and others' work. This is essential in developing learners who are creative, resourceful and able to solve problems. It also helps them to understand how they learn and how to set themselves targets based on their mistakes and successes.

Pupils also have the opportunity to evaluate their own and others' success. They can use ICTs to develop their skills in a range of real contexts, recording, analysing and evaluating data to create short reviews and films.

By working in a variety of contexts on their own, in groups and in teams, pupils learn to work both independently and collaboratively. By participating as performers, leaders and officials, pupils develop the ability to communicate effectively in a range of ways both verbally and non-verbally. They also learn to listen and act on what they hear, to understand and appreciate alternative viewpoints and to learn to compromise, particularly when working in pairs or groups to create final products.

Confident individuals. Competence in physical activity and the sense of enjoyment brought about by being active and successful engender a sense of confidence and self-esteem in pupils and enable them to become increasingly independent. This confidence encourages them to get involved in physical activity for its own sake and as part of a healthy lifestyle choice.

Experiencing a range of activities, roles and contexts helps pupils gain the confidence to try new things, take managed risks and stay safe, make the most of opportunities, recognise their talents and develop ambitions.

Taking on responsible roles like leading, coaching, choreographing, officiating, managing a team or mentoring and being responsible for their own and others' safety also gives pupils confidence. Working in groups and teams in different activities provides opportunities for pupils to learn to work with others and form good relationships.

In PE pupils engage in competitive, creative, artistic, aesthetic and challenging activities that require them to become self-aware and to deal with their emotions – for example, when winning or losing or when being supportive of others.

Responsible citizens. PE encourages learners to be enterprising and work cooperatively and effectively with others. Taking on the roles of leader or official helps develop a sense of respect for others and the ability to apply rules fairly and to act with integrity.

PE encourages pupils to make regular physical activity part of their lives and to get involved in healthy physical activity, sport and dance regularly both in school and in the community. PE helps pupils consider the impact of their lifestyle choices on the community, environment and sustainability.

Learning how to perform, lead, coach and officiate provides pupils with a broad range of skills and attributes that they can use within their local communities, allowing them to contribute positively to make them better places in which to live and work.

> **EXAMINER'S TIP**
>
> It is important to read carefully what the question is asking for, such as specific reference to comparing objectives, content and teaching methods and the different physical activity programmes in state schools.

What you need to know

Physical education aims to:

* develop a range of psycho-motor skills;
* maintain and increase physical mobility and flexibility, stamina and strength;
* develop understanding and appreciation for a range of physical activities;

* develop positive values and attitudes like sportsmanship, competition and abiding by the rules;
* help children acquire self-esteem and confidence through the acquisition of skills, knowledge and values;
* develop an understanding of the importance of exercise in maintaining a healthy lifestyle.

Requirements at Key Stage 1 and Key Stage 2

	Key Stage 1	Key Stage 2
Acquiring and developing skills	1) Pupils should be taught to: a. explore basic skills, actions and ideas with increasing understanding b. remember and repeat simple skills and actions with increasing control and coordination.	1) Pupils should be taught to: a. refine and adapt existing skills b. develop them into specific techniques that suit different activities and perform these with consistent control.
Selecting and applying skills, tactics and compositional ideas	2) Pupils should be taught to: a. explore how to choose and apply skills and actions in sequence and in combination b. vary the way they perform skills by using simple tactics and movement phrases c. apply rules and conventions for different activities.	2) Pupils should be taught to: a. use principles to plan and implement strategies, compositional and organisational ideas in individual, pair, group and team activities b. modify and develop their plans c. apply rules and conventions for different activities.

	Key Stage 1	Key Stage 3
Evaluating and improving performance	3) Pupils should be taught to: a. describe what they have done b. observe, describe and copy what others have done c. use what they have learnt to improve the quality and control of their work	3) Pupils should be taught to: a. be clear about what they want to achieve in their own work, and what they have actually achieved b. take the initiative to analyse their own and others' work, using this information to improve its quality.
Knowledge and understanding of fitness and health	4) Pupils should be taught: a. how important it is to be active b. to recognise and describe how their bodies feel during different activities	4) Pupils should be taught:: a. how to prepare for and recover from specific activities b. how different types of activity affect specific aspects of their fitness c. the benefits of regular exercise and good hygiene d. how to go about getting involved in activities that are good for their personal and social health and well-being
Breadth of study	5) During the key stage, pupils should be taught the knowledge, skills and understanding through dance activities, games activities and gymnastic activities.	5) During the key stage, pupils should be taught the knowledge, skills and understanding through four areas of activity. These should include: a. games activities and three of the following, at least one of which must be dance or gymnastic activities: b. dance activities c. gymnastic activities d. swimming activities and water safety e. athletic activities f. outdoor and adventurous activities

State education: opportunities in primary schools

As mentioned above, in the state system physical education is compulsory and is a statutory subject of the National Curriculum: students must spend at least two hours a week on this subject. The class teacher is usually in charge, though is not usually a specialist. Some schools may hire specialist help for certain activities, such as swimming.

The content of the lessons is usually based on movement and ball skills. Learning by 'moving and doing' is considered essential to the physical, emotional, intellectual and social education of young children. Children's own play is generally very physical and enjoys a lot of repetition, as this enables them to master skills that increase their sense of worth. The physical-education programme can use this as a foundation. Variety is also important, as children's concentration span can be limited and they need to be stimulated by interesting situations.

In addition to the curriculum, many schools also offer club activities, such as gymnastics, netball, soccer, country dancing, and so on. These tend to be at the discretion and goodwill of the teachers.

The policy of PESSCLS and the 'family of schools' policy within the specialist schools programmes have provided funds, staffing and specialist expertise for teachers to draw upon.

Many primary schools adopted a non-competitive approach towards physical activity, but this is now in decline, with the government beginning to stress the value of competitive sport once again.

State education: opportunities in secondary schools

As children approach the end of the compulsory years of schooling, it is necessary to foster in them an awareness of the opportunities available in the community.

As a result of the philosophy of educating children for their leisure time, schools began to offer options programmes in the later years, where a wider variety of activities, sometimes using community facilities, could be experienced. Smaller groups, guided by additional non-specialist staff, made this possible. Students should be informed about and put into contact with local clubs and sports centres. This is an area of weakness in the United Kingdom; there are traditionally poor links between schools and community sport, as a result of trying to keep a distance between sport and physical education, though recent policies are trying to reverse this situation.

Physical education as an examination subject has flourished. A rapidly growing number of students opt to take GCSE and A level examinations as well as a variety of vocational courses.

The importance of physical education

A recent survey showed that a third of secondary schools were failing to meet the earlier two-hour requirement. This does not bode well for the new 4- or 5-hour offer that is now being publicised by the Government.

The Department for Children, Schools and Families (DCSF) is to help increase the take-up of sporting opportunities by 5–16-year-olds.

By 2008 the plan was to engage 75 per cent of children in each School Partnership in two hours of high-quality PE and school sport per week, within and beyond the curriculum.

By 2010 the ambition is to offer all children at least four hours of sport made up of at least two hours of high-quality PE within the curriculum and at least an additional two–three hours out of school, delivered by a range of school, community and club providers.

Developments in school sport and extra-curricular activities

The term 'school sport' refers to the 'physical activities with established rules engaged in by individuals attempting to outperform their competitors' (Wuest, Bucher, 1991). Its main focus is on improving performance standards rather than the educational process and mainly takes place outside the formal curriculum. It is usually viewed as an opportunity for children to extend their interest or ability in physical activities.

The changes in society and education in the last twenty years have affected school sport (that is, the extra-curricular opportunities), with a reduction in emphasis on the sporting elite, which sometimes required a disproportionate amount of resources for a few children. Extra-curricular clubs, open to all, became more acceptable. The situation did not change overnight, however; many teachers continued to focus on competitive sports, and extra-curricular activities were affected by the following factors:

1   The teachers' strikes in the early 1980s – the contractual hours and lack of monetary incentives tended to diminish teachers' goodwill, and clubs were disbanded.
2   Financial cuts were felt in terms of transport.
3   The local management of schools allowed schools to supplement their funds by selling off school fields.
4   The increasing amount of leisure and employment opportunities for children meant they were less attracted to competing for their school team.
5   The anti-competitive lobby became more vocal: they espoused the theory that competition in sport was not good for children's development.

IN CONTEXT

Sport England's Chairman welcomed the Prime Minister's children and young people's sports announcement.

'The injection of another £100m is good news for school sport and good news for community sport. It means more coaches working across schools and community sports clubs and extends the offer to 16–19-year-olds. Sport England will do its part in getting 5–16-year-olds to do 5 hours of sport each week and 16–19-year-olds to do 3 hours.

'Extending the offer to 16–19-year-olds will help address the dramatic drop in sports participation which happens at 16. At the moment 33,000 young people stop doing sport after the age of 16 every year. The Prime Minister's announcement will help bring the worlds of school and community sport together to create a seamless sporting pathway for youngsters of all levels of ability.

'We know there is a sport that can reach out to every child and every young person. Sport England's job is to make participating in sport fun, easy to do and life enhancing.'

Working in partnership with the Youth Sport Trust, Sport England's role in the National School Sport Strategy has been to invest in creating new and stronger links between schools and sports clubs. Through the Step into Sport programme it has provided leadership and volunteering opportunities for older children and young people in schools and the wider community. This has increased the percentage of youngsters participating in club sport to 27 per cent last year, up from 19 per cent in 2003. The percentage of young people actively engaged in sports leadership and volunteering has risen from 9 per cent in 2003 to 13 per cent last year.

The funding also builds on our £20 million investment into a network of 3,000 community sports coaches working with schools and clubs. The coaches have been deployed through our network of forty-nine County Sports Partnerships across England.

Together this provides a firm foundation on which to take participation to the next level.

Activity 5

What threats have schools' extracurricular programmes faced in the twentieth and twenty-first centuries?

CHALLENGE YOURSELF 2

Explain how and why the teaching of games has developed in public and state schools within the UK since the nineteenth century.   **[20 marks]**

Post-school gap

Key term

Post-school gap The drop in sport participation when people leave full-time education.

As early as 1960 the Wolfenden Report was concerned that the provision of sport in the UK was poorer than in other European countries, leading to the post-school gap, which results in a drop in participation on leaving school. The UK still has one of the largest post-school gaps in Europe.

There are various reasons for this drop in participation.

- Children had poor experiences of physical education whilst at school.
- There are traditionally poor links between schools and local sport clubs.
- Young adults have less leisure time and experience changing domestic circumstances.
- There are competing leisure interests with age.
- Facilities are less accessible than at schools.

Impact of National Curriculum on Physical Education

As with any system there will be advantages and disadvantages.

Advantages	Disadvantages
Increasing the range of activities taught	Too much time spent on testing
Making teachers accountable	Possibly reducing the flair of better teachers
Setting national standards of attainment	Enjoyment factor may be lost if children feel they are being evaluated all the time
Focusing on other roles in sport, such as officials and coaches	

Exam-style Questions

What factors determine the amount and type of physical activity children in the UK state school system receive today?

CHALLENGE YOURSELF 3

Discuss how the current National Curriculum for Physical Education compares with the Syllabuses of Physical Training in the early twentieth century in preparing children to develop their health and fitness. Comment on the people they cater for.

[20 marks]

What you need to know

Nineteenth-century public schools:
* provided an education for the social elite
* developed many traditional activities and games
* gave rise to the cult of athleticism parallel with the muscular Christian movement
* allowed games associated with character-building qualities – for example, courage and loyalty
* influenced the development of sport nationally and worldwide through their positions of leadership in society.

Female education:
* developed later but was to be based on the boys' system
* helped in the growing liberation of women at the end and beginning of the twentieth century.

State schools at the end of the nineteenth century:
* concentrated on physical activity based on Swedish gymnastics and Military Drill
* emphasised activities suitable for the poor conditions in state schools and the discipline of the working classes.

There was disenchantment with these systems:
* The Board of Education produced syllabuses in the first three decades of the twentieth century that schools were required to follow.
* The syllabuses laid out the content and style of teaching as a guideline for teachers to follow.
* Strong emphasis was placed on teacher authority.
* There was still very limited teaching of major games.

Syllabuses became defunct with the improvements in teacher training:

* The publications of Planning the Programme and Moving and Growing reflected the change in emphasis from purely physical and organic developments to a focus on the development of the 'whole' child through the Movement approach.

* The use of different terms over the years (drill, physical training and then physical education) reflects the gradual development of certain ideas. Changes occurred in content as well as in the relationship between the teacher and the class.

State schools:

* The National Curriculum was introduced in 1988.
* It was a move towards a centralised policy for education.
* There are four key stages.
* A broad range of activities is offered.
* As well as the role of performer, other roles such as choreographer, coach, official, manager and so on are also taught in order to develop 'critical performers'.

Review Questions

1 What were the characteristics of the nineteenth-century public and state schools?
2 Describe the process in the technical development of team games in the public schools.
3 Define the term 'athleticism' and discuss its influence on society.
4 What influence did the universities bring to bear in the development of sports?
5 Why were team games encouraged in the public schools?
6 What is meant by the term 'self-government' in relation to the organisation of games in the nineteenth-century public schools? Give examples of how this system operated.
7 In what way was gymnastics used in state schools?
8 How did the role of a child change from 1904 to 1988?
9 What are the aims of the National Curriculum for Physical Education?
10 What impact did the National Curriculum have on physical education?

CHAPTER 4

Physical Activity Case Studies: Popular Origins to Rational Developments

Learning outcomes

By the end of this chapter you should be able to:
- discuss increases in participation and increased physical competence in the specified activities
- analyse the activity as popular recreation
- assess the influence of nineteenth-century schools on the development of the activity
- demonstrate knowledge and understanding of the activity as rational recreation
- demonstrate knowledge and understanding of both participation and barriers to participation in the activities today.

CHAPTER INTRODUCTION

In previous chapters we analysed the game of football as it developed from its popular origins to its rational form. Similarly, in this chapter we will study the following activities:

- swimming
- tennis
- football
- cricket
- athletics.

The development of the various physical activities within their overall social context should now make more sense. Always try to see the historical, political, economic, geographical, educational and social and cultural aspects – as they will affect the sports and pastimes under study.

As well as learning about the history of specific sports, it is also important that you can apply that knowledge and link it to present day developments.

Historical development of physical activities

The development of various physical activities should always be considered within their overall social context. Always try

to see the historical, political, economic, geographical, educational and socio-cultural aspects, as these will affect the pastimes and sports that we will be studying.

In this chapter each activity will be considered specifically under the following four headings:

- as a popular recreation
- within the public schools
- as rational recreation
- impact on contemporary participation.

Activity 1

Remind yourselves of the key characteristics of popular and rational recreation and then answer the following question.

Rationalised sport had a new set of characteristics that were shaped by the changing cultural and social conditions of the time.

(a) Identify **four** characteristics of rationalised sport.
(b) What were the underlying cultural factors that influenced **each** of the characteristics you have identified?

[4 marks]

Swimming

Swimming is a method of propulsion through water and has been valued as a recreational activity for thousands of years.

Swimming as a popular recreation

Swimming is older than the ancient civilisations of Greece and Rome and has been a human activity since people have had to learn to negotiate the waters around them. Many communities were built around features such as rivers, lakes and seas, for reasons of defence, hygiene, safety, as well as trade and transport. Military skills often involved learning to swim, as many battles were fought out on the seas. Swimming was also considered an important aspect of the chivalric code of medieval England.

Class distinction in medieval England resulted in many middle and upper classes being unwilling to use the same facilities as the lower classes. Therefore, as the nineteenth century progressed, working-class children were pushed further away and discouraged from using bathing facilities at the same time as their upper- and middle-class contemporaries so as not to offend the eyes of the gentry.

The social class divide was also highlighted by the fact that many upper-class people would act as patrons to the lower class, resulting in many working-class men performing in the name of their upper-class patron. Money would exchange hands in the numerous races such as those on the river Thames, given royal encouragement by King Charles II (1660–85).

The fashion for sea bathing began in the eighteenth century when it was initially regarded as serving medical purposes. The seaside resort took over in popularity from the spa towns.

Bathing became popular in the 1720s, with the first bathing machines making their appearance in Scarborough in 1753. Bathing nude was not uncommon at this time and the bathing machine afforded some privacy when costumes were heavy and difficult to remove without help. These bathing machines would be pulled by men or horses into the sea, and the occupants would descend down wooden steps into the water. Later, at the turn of the twentieth century, these machines would be replaced by bathing tents. Men and women would have separate bathing areas. Mixed bathing and the wearing of costumes came later in the nineteenth century.

During the Victorian era (1837–1901), the railways and steamers with their cheap excursion fares made the seaside resorts accessible to larger numbers of people, including the working class. In 1841 Thomas Cook established his travel company and lay on excursion trains. This resulted in an exodus of the upper classes to more isolated areas like the West Country resorts. The creation of Bank Holidays in 1871 resulted in even more people visiting the seaside, sometimes as day trippers.

Swimming within the public schools

In the public schools swimming was used as a recreational activity for the boys, who used natural facilities such as ponds on the school grounds. At Harrow school the boys would leave school grounds to find suitable facilities. Swimming was not officially encouraged in the same way that team games were, as swimming was not thought to possess the character-building qualities ascribed to games such as cricket. However, swimming was considered positively for its **therapeutic** and **hygienic** effects. As swimming developed rationally in society, so it was mirrored in the public schools, with purpose-built facilities appearing at Charterhouse in 1863.

In *Tom Brown's School-days'* reference is made to the river Avon at Rugby:

a slow and not very clear stream in which chub, dace, roach and other coarse fish are plentiful enough, together with a sprinkling of small jack . . . It is, however, a capital river for bathing, as it has many nice small pools and several good reaches for swimming, all within about a mile of one another, and at an easy ten minute mile walk from the school. This mile of water is rented, or used to be rented, for bathing purposes, by the Trustees of the School, for the boys . . . Sleath's, the first bathing place where all new boys had to begin, until they had proved to the bathing men [three steady individuals who were paid to attend daily through the summer to prevent accidents] that they could swim pretty decently . . . Swift's was reserved for the sixth and fifth forms, and had a springboard and two sets of steps, the others had one set of steps each, and were used indifferently by the lower boys, though each house addicted itself more to one hole than another . . . Tom and East, who had learnt to swim like fishes, were to be found there as regular as the clock through the summer, always twice, and often three times a day . . . they spent a large portion of their day in nature's garb by the river side, and so, when tired of swimming, would get out on the other side and fish, or set night lines till the keeper hove in sight.

Activity 2

Read the extract about swimming in *Tom Brown's School-days* above. Comment on the **technical** developments and the **social relationships** evident in this excerpt.

Swimming as rational recreation

In the UK, swimming for recreation developed in the eighteenth century. The following factors were influential in the rationalisation of swimming:

1734   First open-air swimming pool built in London

1840   An increase in public baths following the Public Baths and Wash-Houses Act. (Note that there were separate baths for the different social classes!)

1873   Developments in technique came from overseas, e.g. the front crawl developed from the stroke that John Trudgeon had learned in South America, where natives would bring both arms over the water when swimming (it was Trudgeon who is credited with introducing this stroke to the UK).

1875   Captain Webb swam the English Channel, providing a role model and creating national interest in the sport

1886   Amateur Swimming Association (ASA) formed

1896   The first modern Olympics at Athens included the 100m, 500m and 1200m freestyle

1908 Fédération Internationale de Natation Amateur (FINA) formed

1912 Women's swimming introduced at the Stockholm Olympic Games

The success in swimming races in Britain from the mid-nineteenth century led to a proportional increase in prizes, which were usually won by 'professional swimmers', who were swimming teachers involved in giving lessons in return for money.

The nature of the sport places it in the category of an athletic activity. The keeping of records by 'racing against the clock' is an important element. Other factors have also played a part – social acceptability and regulation governed both the style and materials worn by male and female swimmers.

Activity 3

Pre-industrial popular recreation had certain characteristics that, to a greater or lesser extent, were evident in most early sports and pastimes.

To what extent did early swimming show the characteristics of popular recreation? **[3 marks]**

Swimming and contemporary participation
Regional Offices

The plan is for the ASA's eight new Regions to lead the ASA into a challenging new phase. Each Region will have its own full-time professional staff to build the necessary

IN CONTEXT

From the 135 clubs affiliated in 1890, there are now over 1,500 clubs, representing some 300,000 swimmers in the UK.
   The educational work of the ASA has an extensive programme of teacher and coach qualifications, which come under the auspice of the ASA's education department.

1869 London Swimming Clubs form an association to promote and encourage the art of swimming; shortly after the association adopts the title 'Metropolitan Swimming Association'

1883 Laws of Amateur Swimming distributed throughout Europe and the USA

1884 The Metropolitan Swimming Association divides because of a dispute over amateurism

1886 Both sides of the dispute are brought together under new title 'The Amateur Swimming Association' (ASA), and its objects are revised to include:
   ● the control of race meetings
   ● the uniformity of rules
   ● the enforcement of the observance of the laws
   Other changes include:
   ● a new definition of 'amateur'
   ● a new constitution
   ● work now carried out through an executive committee, not the whole body, as before

1890 First Annual General Meeting of ASA

1901 ASA divides into five Districts
   First Women's Championship – the 100 yards Freestyle – instituted.

1908 ASA takes leading part in Olympic Games in London

1934 British Empire and Commonwealth Games held at Wembley

1935 Diving comes under control of ASA

1938 European Championships held at Wembley

1947 Junior Championships instituted

1948 ASA takes leading part in Olympic Games in London

1952 Alice M. Austin becomes the ASA's first female President

1962 Survival Awards introduced

1972 First National Age Group Championships held

1973 Junior European Championships held at Leeds

1974 Introduction of National Development Officers to cover disciplines of the court

1980 Duncan Goodhew wins Gold for 100m Breaststroke at the Moscow Olympics

1981 Introduction of Masters swimming at national level

1984 Introduction of drug testing

1988 Adrian Moorhouse wins Gold for 100m Breaststroke at the Seoul Olympics

1993 European Championships return to England (held at Sheffield)

2005 ASA changes from 5 to 8 districts

2008 Increase of medals won at the Beijing Olympics greatly helped by Team GB's swimmers, including twice-Gold medallist Rebecca Adlington

infrastructures and partnerships that will enable the ASA to deliver its vision.

Each Region will be underpinned by good corporate governance, but will focus on:

- improving talent pathways;
- getting more people involved in all swimming disciplines;
- providing more and better coaches, volunteers and officials.

At the forefront of these initiatives is **Swim 21**, the club development and accreditation programme. Currently, one-third of all ASA-affiliated clubs are now signed up to **Swim 21**.

CHALLENGE YOURSELF 1

Describe the development of recreational and competitive swimming in the UK and explain how its development reflected the changing social conditions.

[20 marks]

IN CONTEXT

More people are taking part in swimming and diving than any other sport or physical activity, according to a government report.

The Taking Part survey commissioned by the Department of Culture, Media and Sport (in partnership with a number of public bodies, including Sport England) asked people what sports they had participated in during the past four weeks.

Swimming or diving (indoors) was the most popular activity, with 14.5 per cent having participated. This was higher than those who had taken part in gym activities, cycling, football or golf. And a further 3.4 per cent had taken part in swimming/diving outdoors.

More than 24,000 adults took part in the second Taking Part survey which details all public participation in cultural, leisure and sporting activities between 2006 and 2007.

Other figures showed that 40 per cent of adults said they had participated in moderate intensity sport for at least half an hour within the past week.

The survey also revealed that 47 per cent of those who had not participated in active sport for at least a year cited poor health as the reason, while 18 per cent said a lack of time stopped them from participating.
http://www.culture.gov.uk/reference_library/publications/5396.aspx

Tennis

Real tennis – popular or rational recreation?

The game of real tennis originated in France, as suggested by much of the terminology – for example, 'dedans', 'tambour' and 'grille'. It was an activity of the French Royal court, and was made popular in England by the Tudors. A famous scene in Shakespeare's *Henry V* is one of the earliest literary references to the game. At Hampton Court, one of the most famous courts, constructed in 1529, is still in use.

Real tennis was the sport of the noblemen and royalty and in 1536 there were restrictive acts that forbade servants and labourers to play and helped to retain the privileged status of the elite. The game was originally played with the hand, 'le jeu de paume', until the sixteenth century when rackets were used, and as such it did have its roots with the peasantry. There is a reference to peasants playing a version of 'field tennis', which was a form of handball.

That the game was established prior to the Industrial Revolution, and had some evidence of peasantry participation, albeit not in the more exclusive closed facilities, could give it some credence as a popular recreation. However, this was a very sophisticated, exclusive game, requiring expensive facilities, equipment and an understanding of the complex rules and social etiquette of the game. The emphasis was on the individual's skill and tactical and strategic awareness; as ever, wagering was evident. It was the epitome of rational sport.

Table 4.1 Swimming and participation

Opportunities for participation	Barriers to participation
Public provision since nineteenth century	Limited on the National Curriculum
Swimming on National Curriculum	Lack of 50m pools for elite development
Not associated with any gender stereotypes	Lack of access to elite training facilities means unsociable training times
Highly valued for safety and therapeutic benefits	
Social encouragement and provision from toddlers upwards	
Early recognition of rehabilitative effects led to early development for people with disabilities	
Natural facilities can be used for recreational and sporting aspects – e.g. swimming the Channel	

THE COURT

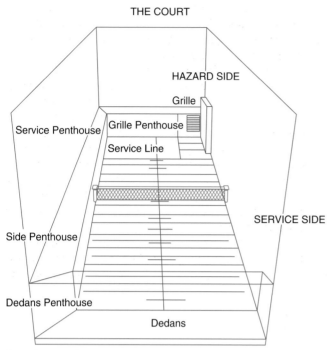

Fig 4.1 A Real Tennis court

Fig 4.2 An early version of tennis, taken from *Orbis Sensualium Pictus* by John Comenius, 1659

Racket sports with the public schools

Rackets at public schools

In its earliest form during the eighteenth century, rackets was played in the open on the walls of the yards of the two main debtors' prisons; the King's Bench and the Fleet. Gentlemen, imprisoned until they could repay their creditors, amused themselves with many different activities around the prison yard. These included skittles and fives, which was played both with the hand and a bat (as at Westminster School), and some brought tennis rackets with them and improvised against any convenient wall, sometimes with no side walls and always without a back wall.

Fig 4.3 Lawn tennis was one of the few recreational activities that men and women could enjoy together in Victorian England

The game of rackets began in fairly humble circumstances in England. Open courts existed in the back yards of taverns and inns, and in many towns. They were social meeting places and there was always a wall to be used. Equipment could also be hired from publicans wishing to make the most of their business opportunities. They had all the requirements – willing opponents, alcohol and wagering.

The game was a test of strength and accuracy. In a four-handed match the players took alternate 'out' and 'in' games, which would lead to exciting rallies.

Rackets was taken up by the public schools for its simple qualities and the possibilities of using architectural features within the school grounds. It was a game that suited the cult of athleticism, containing rules, etiquette and sportsmanship.

Squash at public schools

Squash is derived from the older game of rackets and originated at Harrow school. The use of a softer spongier ball gave it its name. However, its simplicity also made it suitable for wealthy people to develop on their country estates and also in the West End social clubs. A lack of development in the rules detracted from the growth of the game. Rules were not laid down until 1922. It generally tended to be an addition to other sports clubs, especially tennis and cricket, and therefore developed along elitist lines.

Fives at public schools

Fives is a hand-ball game played between two teams of players in a three-walled court.

It originated from a knockabout game played by schoolboys at Eton College. The original court is the area between two buttresses of the Eton College Chapel. The architectural features of the court, with a step across the middle, a buttress protruding from the left-hand wall and several ledges, made the game unique.

The first purpose-built Fives courts, built at Eton in the 1840s, were based on the original court with certain modifications to improve the game. Some of the copies showed little respect for accurate dimensions, and non-standard examples still exist, but modern courts are built to exact specifications, replicas of the Eton courts.

Fives is played with the palm of the hand, wearing a glove, and the ball is hit against the wall. It was played in inns and other public places, and was a much more individual game than rackets. In the public schools it tended to be played more in the boys' recreation time, using unique architectural features, and consequently did not establish well-known formal rules. As the game was not taken up at the universities, individual schools' variations continued. These qualities tended to make it a less favourable game than rackets as far as the staff were concerned.

The game is played in 45 centres (35 active and 10 non-active), mostly in independent schools. Eton Fives is an amateur game, played primarily by men and boys, but in recent years several schools and clubs have introduced the game to female players. A total of forty-two schools play the game (twenty-nine independent schools, three grammar schools, one comprehensive and nine preparatory schools). There are currently thirty Fives clubs, comprised of twenty-four active Old Boys' clubs, The Jesters, two teams each from Oxford and Cambridge universities (a team is usually 3 pairs) and one team from London University. A number of local clubs are developing, playing in school courts.

Activity 4

How did rackets match the concept of athleticism whilst Fives did not?

Lawn tennis as rational recreation

Real or Royal tennis was an aristocratic pastime and was not conducive to the lives of the middle and lower classes. However, in the nineteenth century the middle classes, with their increasing wealth and leisure time, wanted to establish their own form of recreation, which would set them apart from the lower classes, and the subsequent game became enormously popular midway through Queen Victoria's reign.

Major Wingfield took most of the credit for the game's popularity. His invention, which he called Sphairistike, had an hour-glass shaped court. He provided a commercial product that could be bought in kit form, making it

attractive to the middle classes, whose wealth was often determined by trade. The Marylebone Cricket Club (MCC) then took it one stage further, calling it lawn tennis and adopting an oblong-shaped court.

It ousted croquet from the lawns of the middle classes, and proved to be an ideal game for large suburban gardens to be played by both social classes, in their increasingly leisured society. There were few recreational activities at this time that both sexes could enjoy together. The ladies were able to play privately away from the public gaze, and it was a game that helped to remove some of the stereotypes. They could run around becoming increasingly energetic and clothing began to be slightly less restrictive. Their schools also accepted the game, as it was non-contact, had rules and was acceptable to the parents.

The middle classes also ensured its club development and the administrative structures. The lower classes had to wait until there was public provision, so their participation was delayed.

IN CONTEXT

The most famous tennis tournament is held each summer at The All England Lawn Tennis & Croquet Club, a private club based in Wimbledon, London. The first competition for the Gentlemen's Singles was held in 1877 as an attempt to raise funds for the repair of the club's roller. There were 22 entrants, with the eventual winner, W. Spencer Gore, being awarded the prize of 12 guineas before a crowd of some 200 spectators, each of whom had paid one shilling to attend.

The success of the tournament ensured that it returned a year later, and has become a constant on the sporting calendar ever since.

Since 1877 the Championships (as they are formally known) have only ever been disrupted by the two world wars – four years being lost during the First World War and six during the Second.

In 1884 competitions for the Ladies' Singles and Men's Doubles were introduced.

For the first thirty years British tennis players dominated proceedings, with the likes of Ernest and William Renshaw and Laurie and Reggie Doherty. The Renshaw brothers created such an interest in the game that the 1880s were dubbed the 'Renshaw Rush', as people took to the sport.

In 1905 American May Sutton became the first overseas champion, winning the Ladies' Singles title. Two years later, the first male champion from overseas, Norman Brookes, won the Gentlemen's Singles.

Tennis and contemporary participation

Table 4.2 Tennis and participation

Opportunities for participation	Barriers to participation
Public provision started in the twentieth century	White, middle-class origins are still influential
Game developed for people with disabilities – e.g. wheelchair tennis	Club development can make it exclusive and less accessible
Acceptable for both genders to play	
Can be taught in schools	
Mini game for children	
NGB made efforts to democratise the sport – e.g. inner-city tennis schemes	
Included as an Olympic sport	

Activity 5

(a) Why was lawn tennis suitable for middle-class ladies to play?

(b) Why was working-class participation in tennis delayed?

CHALLENGE YOURSELF 2

Describe the factors influencing the development of lawn tennis. Explain its suitability for middle class ladies in the nineteenth century and the delay in the participation of the working classes.

[20 marks]

Football

Football as popular recreation

Football has been discussed in some detail in earlier chapters, but a summary will be useful here.

Football began as a mob game. It lacked the organisational features of the modern game and was characterised by large numbers of players, exclusively male and from the lower classes, involved in a territorial struggle. The game tended to be played occasionally on annual holidays like the Wakes as the people had limited free time, and would cover distances between villages. Because it was played only a few times a year, there were limited rules, and hence violence, injury and sometimes death were common, as the game was determined by force rather than skill. There was no division of labour; players had no particular roles, and there was a loose distinction between participating and spectating. This was originally a rural activity and reflected the harsh way of life lived by uneducated, rural people.

Football and the public schools

What changed the game out of all proportion to its original character? The gentry sons in the public schools began to play the game regularly on the school grounds. Though they started with variations in rules from school to school, they gradually began to develop them in the form of shape of goals, boundaries, limits on the size of the team and so on. A competitive structure emerged, with inter-house and inter-school matches. Some variations remained and some unique facilities gave rise to features that were distinctive to individual schools – for example, the soft turf of the Close at Rugby, and the Quad at Charterhouse, where the dribbling game emerged. There is also the Eton Wall game, which still exists today.

Football as rational recreation

The game was further codified by university graduates, who also established associations; the Football Association was established in 1863. When university graduates became employers, they encouraged the game among workers, partly to boost morale and loyalty, but also to instil middle-class values and discipline. They also established their middle-class sports clubs based on amateurism.

The roads and pavements were the playgrounds of working-class children and they devised numerous types of street games. Football was one of them and most streets had a football team associated with a strong community feeling. The cramped living conditions and shortage of facilities led to a more spectator-based interest in the game. Developments in transport opened up the rest of the country for fixtures further afield.

There was therefore a curious development across the different social classes. The game began as a mob game by and for the lower classes. The public schools made it popular with the gentry in the south of England, who also incorporated middle class values within the game as it developed along strictly amateur lines – the southern amateurs. However, in the north of England it developed in the industrial towns, and professionalism soon crept in with clubs like Sheffield Wednesday being established, when Wednesday became early closing day. The Football League was established in 1885. When the two sides met there was a culture shock!

Fig 4.4 England vs Scotland at the Oval, 6 March 1875

Football and contemporary participation

See Table 4.3.

Activity 6

Why was the development of cricket different from that of football?

Cricket

Cricket as popular recreation

Cricket is one of the oldest established games and was played from the outset by both social classes – the aristocrats and the commoners played together. There were

not many activities that both social classes played together, though they had particular roles within the game to signify their status. The game reflected the feudal structure of the village. The early clubs emerged from the rural village sides, with the gentry acting as patrons. There were a variety of reasons for this: the game took place in the summer season when light was at its best, allowing the workers time to participate, and, because of its non-violent nature, there were no threats to the gentry in playing with the peasants. The early rules and gentlemanly behaviour ensured a level of respectful behaviour.

At this level of organisation cricket appeared to be a development in the southern counties and London, and was not yet national in its appeal. Thus it can still be recognised as a popular recreation, even though rules had been in existence for some time. It was still organised along rural and feudal lines. Patrons would sponsor teams to come up to London for big money matches.

Key term

Feudal A medieval and socioeconomic system; vassals were protected by the lords, but were required to serve under them in war.

In terms of its **technical development**, players tended to wear everyday clothes; lines were intended to keep spectators at bay rather than to delineate a boundary and overarm bowling was not yet established.

Women from both social classes were also involved in playing cricket at this stage (remember this was before the constraints imposed by Victorian society). There is an early reference to a game being played near Guildford between 'the eleven maids of Bramley and the eleven maids of Hambledon dressed all in white'. Matches were great spectacles, with refreshment tents and a festival atmosphere.

Cricket in the public schools

Cricket was immediately acceptable in the public schools, as it matched all the criteria for social control for the masters and athleticism for the boys. The game was already well developed by the eighteenth century. The rules meant a

Table 4.3 Football and participation

Opportunities for participation	Barriers to participation
Fastest growing sport for women	Still a major male sport
One of the most accessible sports	Hooligan element can put people off
Disabled adaptation	Ticket prices have continued to rise resulting in the working classes being marginalised with the corporate tickets having greater prominence.
Core game on National Curriculum	
Opportunities to earn an income – semi professional or professional	
Included as an Olympic sport	

code of behaviour for the boys, who would be expected to behave within the spirit of the game. The fags, or younger boys, would help the older boys in practice, and the assistant masters would also play. When fixtures became prestigious and important to win, professionals were employed to raise the standards of play amongst the team.

Cricket reflected the technical and moral developments in public-school sport:

> play was regular; serious training and coaching were undertaken; fags were used to assist the older boys; the equipment and facilities were refined; inter-house and later inter-school matches became important fixtures and were used as PR exercises to impress parents and governors. As a team game it was believed to develop the all-important character-building qualities.

Cricket as rational recreation

Games would attract spectators in their thousands. The first written rules were drawn up by the Duke of Richmond in 1727 to help control country-house games, where sometimes large sums of money would hinge on the outcome. The MCC emerged as an organisational feature comparatively early in the game's development. The terms 'gentlemen' and 'players' emerged to distinguish the amateurs from the professionals. Though they played together, they had very different roles to play. The captain would always be an amateur; the professionals would be consigned to different changing facilities. Gentlemen versus players began in 1806 and would exist until 1963, when performers would be referred to as 'cricketers'.

Activity 7

Read the following extract from *Tom Brown's School-days* and comment on the *technical* developments and *moral values* attributed to the game of cricket.

> The clock strikes eight and the whole field becomes fevered with excitement. Arthur, after two narrow escapes, scores one; and Johnson gets the ball. The bowling and fielding are superb, and Johnson's batting worthy of the occasion. He makes here a two and there a one, managing to keep the ball to himself, and Arthur backs up and runs perfectly; only eleven runs to make now, and the crowd scarcely

breathe. At last Arthur gets the ball again, and actually drives it forward for two, and feels prouder than when he got the three best prizes, at hearing Tom's shout of joy, 'Well played, well played, young 'un!' . . . Before Winter can get in, the omnibus which is to take the Lord's men to the train pulls up at the side of the close, and Mr Aislabie and Tom consult, and give out that the stumps will be drawn after the next over. And so ends the great match. Winter and Johnson carry out their bats and it being a one day's match, the Lord's men are declared the winners, they having scored the most in the first innings. But such a defeat is a victory: so think Tom and all the School eleven, as they accompany their conquerors to the omnibus, and send them off with three ringing cheers, after Mr Aislabie has shaken hands all round, saying to Tom, 'I must compliment you, sir, on your eleven, and I hope we shall have you for a member if you come up to town'.

Key term

Gentlemen v Players game A first-class cricket match, generally played on an annual basis, between teams consisting of amateurs (the Gentlemen) and professionals (the Players).

Though it was a game to appeal to all social classes, county cricket remained quite exclusive, with matches held mid-week. The suburban middle classes began to take out county membership, and the large grounds began to take over from the smaller, more portable fixtures. This would detach it even more from the working classes. The Lancashire League was established in a very similar way to the Football League, to cater for the needs of the working classes.

William Clarke, a professional player, was the first person to organise a national professional touring side in 1847, realising the possibility of making money and running parallel to the gentry teams like MCC. County gentlemen's clubs raised sides to play the England XI, and huge crowds turned out to see cricket of the highest standard for the day. This was one of the major influencing factors in making cricket popular across the country. In due course national sides would supersede the county sides, as epitomised by the Test series such as The Ashes.

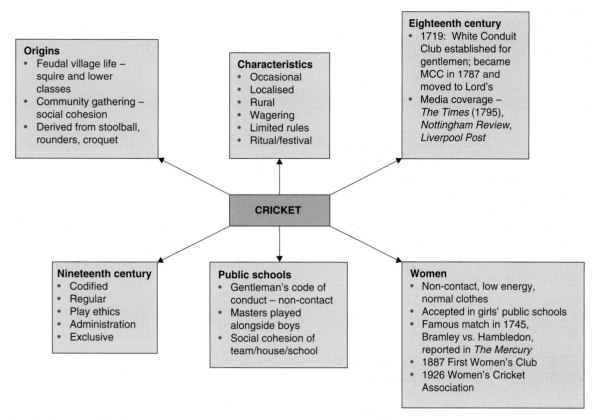

Origins
- Feudal village life – squire and lower classes
- Community gathering – social cohesion
- Derived from stoolball, rounders, croquet

Characteristics
- Occasional
- Localised
- Rural
- Wagering
- Limited rules
- Ritual/festival

Eighteenth century
- 1719: White Conduit Club established for gentlemen; became MCC in 1787 and moved to Lord's
- Media coverage – *The Times* (1795), *Nottingham Review*, *Liverpool Post*

CRICKET

Nineteenth century
- Codified
- Regular
- Play ethics
- Administration
- Exclusive

Public schools
- Gentleman's code of conduct – non-contact
- Masters played alongside boys
- Social cohesion of team/house/school

Women
- Non-contact, low energy, normal clothes
- Accepted in girls' public schools
- Famous match in 1745, Bramley vs. Hambledon, reported in *The Mercury*
- 1887 First Women's Club
- 1926 Women's Cricket Association

Fig 4.5 The development of cricket

Fig 4.6 'Rural Sports' by Rowlandsen, c. 1811

The Ashes is a Test cricket series played between England and Australia. Dating back to 1882, it is currently played every two years, alternating between venues in England and Australia.

A series of The Ashes now comprises five Test matches, two innings per match, under the regular rules for international Test-match cricket. If a series is drawn, then the country holding the Ashes retains them.

The series is named after a satirical obituary published in an English newspaper, the *Sporting Times*, in 1882, after the match at The Oval in which Australia beat England on an English ground for the first time. The obituary stated that English cricket had died, and 'the body will be cremated and the ashes taken to Australia'. The English media then dubbed the next English tour to Australia (1882–3) as 'the quest to regain The Ashes'.

Cricket and contemporary participation

Kerry Packer, an Australian media magnate, changed cricket. He replaced revered white cricket flannels with coloured clothing and took the game to floodlit grounds with his World Series cricket series in the late 1970s. Seeing cricket as a business that could bring in money and profit the game, Packer turned cricket into a huge television spectacle and adorned it with the biggest names in the sport.

The commercialisation of cricket since the 1970s

After the series, the players returned as highly paid professionals (some may say they got their rightful remuneration), while Packer got the television rights he wanted, and millions of people who had never been interested in cricket were suddenly interested by the game.

A new game called Tape Ball Cricket was launched in 2008 at Stoke Newington School, in Hackney, East London, with £66,360 from Sport England. This fast, exciting and fresh new style of cricket leaves the days of whites, long barriers and playing for a draw with the old school.

Tape Ball Cricket has been developed by 'Opportunity through Cricket's' Director of Programmes.

Inner London has only four clubs and eleven cricket pitches to cater for over two million people. Tape Ball Cricket will offer a new alternative.

The first summer's pilot programme involved over thirty estates and was funded by Sport England. It could be the game that ensures that England remains on top of the world for years to come.

Tape Ball Cricket will offer young people from recreationally deprived inner-city areas the chance to share in the success of the England team whilst also offering them the chance to try a game that might one day make them one of England's great heroes.

The project was particularly suited to receive Community Investment Funding, because of its commitment to creating and supporting sustainable innovative multi-activity environments in areas of social, sport and health deprivation. It introduces a new and creative solution that will engage people in sport and physical activity by addressing some of the perceived barriers to participation.

Table 4.4 Cricket and participation

Opportunities for participation	Barriers to participation
Village activity and club development	Selectors can still be discriminatory towards public schools and certain clubs
Can be taught at school	
	Still associated with males
Options to make it more acceptable: limited overs; 1-day cricket; 20–20; indoor; kwik cricket; beach cricket; etc.	Discriminatory practices by MCC
Lifelong activity	
Development of female cricket	
Growth of commercialisation – advertising on pitch and clothing	
More sponsored competitions, such as Nat West Pro 40; Friends Provident Trophy	
Indian Cricket League	

Packer invented day–night cricket, played under lights and with coloured clothing and different coloured balls. Cricket's ruling body called it 'pyjama' cricket at the time, but it is one-day cricket that is selling the game in the early twenty-first century. Another advantage of the World Series Cricket was the decision to transfer the pitch from one place to another so that a good pitch was always available to play on. The World Series meant that the best players got to compete against the greatest players of the era.

Activity 8

The acceptability of cricket as a respectable game was such that nineteenth-century public schools adopted it as a vehicle for the development of Christian gentlemen.

The engraving by Rowlandsen called *Rural Sports* captures the mood of a three-day county match between Hampshire and Surrey (see Figure 4.6).

(a) What technical features point to this being an eighteenth-century match?

(b) What do you understand by the term 'gentlemen' and 'players' in relation to cricket?

(c) What aspects of nineteenth-century cricket made it such an attractive activity in boys' public schools?

(d) Why was cricket an acceptable game for women to play by the end of the nineteenth century?

(e) The emergence of the West Indies in world standard cricket was no coincidence. What may have motivated an emerging country to specialise in such an activity?

(f) Cricket is still as popular in modern times, but some elements of the game have changed. Suggest what some of these changes have been and account for them.

CHALLENGE YOURSELF 3

Cricket has undergone many changes from its popular to its present day form. Comment on the changes and possible societal causes. **[20 marks]**

Athletics

Athletics as popular recreation

Many athletic activities developed from functional activities, like the throwing events, while others came from agricultural pursuits like hunting and clearing obstacles.

The traditional commercial fairs and festivals were the backdrop to many athletic pursuits. Men, in particular, would use activities such as stick fighting, shin kicking and running to prove their masculinity and to impress a future employer who might be planning to hire people at the hiring fairs. These were the earliest forms of multi-sport festivals.

Earlier mention has been made of the Highland Games and the Dover or Cotswold Festivals as well as the Much Wenlock Olympic Games. Ancient festivals were not exclusive to the United Kingdom. The ancient civilisations of Greece and Rome also enjoyed these events. They were one of the ways in which human beings could celebrate the joy of life and serve their gods (especially in pagan festivals), as well as providing an opportunity for people to test their strength and power – skills that were highly valued in the earlier agricultural societies. Unfortunately many of these events were lost with the advent of industrialisation and the mobilisation of the population to new areas of the country.

Church holy days provided a direct link with the earlier pagan days. The principal days were at Christmastide, Eastertide and Whitsuntide; at a later date, after the Reformation, other days were added, such as Boxing Day, Easter Monday and Whit Monday. Wakes or parish feasts had pagan origins, and each village had a church and its own day of dedication, where the whole community enjoyed the recreational and sporting festivals. Activities involved bull baiting, smock races and prize fighting. The nineteenth century was to bring a rationalisation of many of the more vulgar activities.

Pedestrianism, a term embraced by race walkers, was developed in Stuart and Georgian society, where young men were sent ahead of a coach to warn an innkeeper of the coach's imminent arrival. Wagers were placed, and the gentry acted as patrons. This developed into an endurance event covering long distances against the opponent or the clock. It involved a working-class performer and a gentry patron, and came to include other activities, such as running and boating. Pedestrianism was a commercial attraction, with notable characters like Deerfoot, the American, earning large sums of money, but it was rife with corruption.

Table 4.5 Working class professional vs Gentleman amateur

Pedestrian	Gentleman amateur
Working class	Middle/upper class
Aim to earn a living	Personal challenge rather than challenge against the lower-class professional
Serious training towards a serious outcome	Test of temperament
Enjoyable form of occupation	

The 'gentleman amateur' would also walk competitively, usually to test himself and as a wager, but would not usually compete against the lower-class pedestrian. Matches could take place over as short a distance as 100 yards up to twenty-four hours. Spectators came in their thousands, making the events into festival occasions. The sporting spectacles of the Much Wenlock Olympian Games and the Cotswold and Lakeland Games were the forerunners to the modern Olympic Games.

Athletics and the public schools

Athletics became more refined at the public schools, with the addition of rules, techniques and purpose-built equipment and facilities. The school sports day was born, when headmasters would use physical prowess to impress parents and governors, and the media would report on the notable victories.

Most public schoolboys would make the transition to university, mostly Oxford and Cambridge, where once again there was plenty of time to participate in sporting activities. The Boat Race between the two universities is still a national event. The universities acted as a melting pot for the rules of many activities.

Athletics at Oxford in the 1850s was organised on the same basis as horse racing, but was to undergo awkward times as people tried to adapt from the old concept of pedestrianism to this new era of amateur and moral values being attributed to healthy exercise. A former member of Oxford helped to found the Amateur Athletic Association in 1880. At the time, the idea of being beaten by a lower-class person and the problems that ensued from not being able to socialise properly after the event led to restrictions. So lower-class performers were excluded from sports such as athletics and rowing.

In 1880 the clause was removed, and 'no financial gain' became the main value attached to this association and its members. The new association was reorganised on a relatively non-discriminatory basis by three Oxford men –

Jackson, Sherman and Wise. This was to lead the way to the doors of athletics being opened to the working classes. It was a reflection of the Gladstonian 'widening of opportunity for the professional and industrial elites' and the concept of 'let the best man win'. Between the two world wars the best British athletes were generally of modest origins – athletics was relatively cheap – but these individuals showed the capacity for hard training and were beginning to carry the national expectation of proving British superiority at a time when invasion was imminent.

Hurdling is said to have evolved from the boys at public schools improvising in their leisure time and re-enacting events they saw at home – like the association between hunting, hare and hounds, and hurdling with horse racing. Today the **steeplechase** features in the programme of events for men and women in all major championships. It is a test of middle-distance running, endurance and hurdling skill. The first steeplechase took place in Oxford in 1850 over a two-mile cross-country course. Today it is on a running track with a variety of obstacles, including the water jump.

Other events were included, like high and standing broad jumps, athletics meetings began, and athletics clubs – such as the London Athletic Club – were developed.

Athletics as rational recreation

In 1896 the revival of the modern Olympic Games heralded an international appeal for athletics. Specialisation was taking over from the traditional all-round English amateur sportsman. By the end of the nineteenth century many of the big towns had purpose-built facilities and the equipment to record and measure athletic feats was becoming more refined. The Amateur Athletics Association was formed in 1880 by ex-university gentlemen who wished to continue to be able to challenge themselves but disassociate themselves from the 'old' corrupted version of the professional contests. To this end they adopted an exclusion clause to prevent lower-class professionals from joining their clubs and competitions.

Table 4.6 Technical aspects vs Values during Hare and hounds

Technical aspects	Values
9 miles across country	Hunt undertaken as a pack, but essentially an individual activity
40–50 boys	
Good runners for the hares (use bag filled with scent, usually paper)	Need to look after yourself
	Develops ability to stick to a task
Six-minute advantage for hares	
'Running & fencing' = jumping over fences	
Tactics – casting to find the scent	
Forerunner of cross country	

EXAMINER'S TIP

Make sure that you remember the difference between technical and moral values.

Key term

Exclusion clause Mechanics, artisans and labourers were excluded from participating alongside the middle-class amateurs.

Athletics and contemporary participation

Table 4.7 Athletics and participation

Opportunities for participation	Barriers to participation
The Olympic and Paralympic Games biggest worldwide athletic events	Age an issue – not considered a lifelong activity
Core activity on the National Curriculum	Facilities not readily accessible or available
At the heart of all school sports days	Lack of media coverage for certain activities – e.g. running has a positive image, but throwing events a less positive one
Adaptations to most events for people with disabilities	
Popularity of running increased by fun runs and half-marathons	
Steady increase of women's events	

IN CONTEXT

In 1896 the modern Olympic Games were established by a French aristocrat, Baron Pierre de Coubertin. Deeply interested in education, and concerned by the poor physical health of his countrymen and by their apparent lack of national pride, the Baron thought that sport could help. He was also aware of the Much Wenlock Olympian Games in Shropshire that had been organised by Dr William Penny Brookes since the first such games in 1850. Following several visits to England, the Baron had been impressed by the amateur code of team games prevalent in English public schools and by the code for athleticism that had developed. Upon returning to France, Baron de Coubertin revived the ancient Olympic Games of Greece based upon these ideals, hoping to regenerate a sense of French nationalism as well as a romantic view of furthering international understanding.

In 1894 de Courbertin convened a conference in Paris to determine the nature of the competition he envisaged.

- Eligibility standards of participation were introduced.
- An administrative body (the International Olympic Committee) was established to oversee the running of the event.
- The first Games were awarded to Athens for 1896.

Exam-style Questions

1 Modern track and field athletics have their roots in popular recreation. Describe 'pedestrianism' and outline its attraction as a popular recreation.

[4 marks]

2 By the mid- to late-nineteenth century, urban track and field athletics meetings were extremely popular, with athletics having a strict class divide. Identify reasons why there was a class divide in late-nineteenth-century athletics.

[2 marks]

What you need to know

From this selection of activities, you can see how sport within society is a dynamic experience, constantly changing to adapt to new pressures and sometimes exerting its own influence on society.

* Sporting activities changed to adapt to a system where legislation curtailed activities – for example, mob football – or caused modifications.
* The change in emphasis from rural to urban sport with a philosophy of participation was hindered by lack of facilities and space.
* The emphasis of watching in small local groups changed to mass spectator sport, accompanied by business enterprise, improved communications and a national interest in sport.

* There was a change from local rules to fully codified rules formulated by governing bodies.
* Control passed from the aristocracy to the middle classes.
* Bribery, corruption and vice were largely eliminated, and with them the old concept of professionalism.
* Recreation was no longer the privilege of the nobility. By the end of the nineteenth century the working class had won the same right to recreation.

Review Questions

1 List four characteristics of popular and rational recreation.
2 What were the first professional race walkers called?
3 What was the 'manual labour' clause and which sport did it affect in particular?
4 Explain why Real Tennis was for the upper classes while Lawn Tennis developed for the middle classes.
5 Explain the influence of the various social classes on the development of football.
6 What is the link between the hunt, hare and hounds and cross country as athletic activities?
7 Who invented the game that he called Sphairistike and what is the game called today?
8 How did the structure of Real Tennis differ from mob football and how did this reflect the class of people who played them?
9 The democratisation of tennis has become an important issue in the late twentieth century.
   (a) How has this been reflected in the approach of the Lawn Tennis Association (LTA) towards the game?
   (b) Discuss the view that tennis has changed from a Victorian garden party game to a highly commercial enterprise.

UNIT 2

Comparative Studies

Within this unit we will look at the way physical education has developed in three different countries:

- the United Kingdom (UK)
- the United States of America (USA)
- Australia.

We will look at how the history and culture of each of these countries has influenced the way in which different sports have developed and are played today.

Physical activities or games are cultural institutions that are determined by the culture operating in a particular country, but physical activities or games also influence how that culture operates. Discovering the significance and meanings of games in various cultures, along with their function in relation to cultural values and related social structures, is an interesting project of study.

Using a comparative approach

A comparative approach is widely used in many other academic disciplines. It attempts to describe, analyse and explain factors occurring within society. A reformative approach occurs when different cultures borrow and adopt ideas that may be beneficial to their own society.

Problems with initial attempts at comparative research lay in isolating a topic of study and in not viewing it within the context of the whole system. By 1900 it was recognised that each individual aspect being studied had to be seen as an integral part of the society that produced it. Only then can the value orientations that surround particular parts of a culture be fully understood. Thus, a multi-disciplinary approach has emerged involving economics, history, philosophy, sociology, psychology, anthropology, social science and science. Pioneered by George Bereday, this has four main stages:

- **description**: the systematic collection of data
- **interpretation**: analysis in terms of social sciences
- **juxtaposition**: a review of similar systems to determine the framework to be used to compare
- **comparison**: first of select problems and then the relevance to the various cultures.

Comparative physical education and sport is still a fairly recent field of study. The International Society on Comparative Physical Education and Sport (ISCPES) was formed in 1980. ISCPES publications can be useful sources of information.

Central to the themes in the Comparative section are the key terms – **Opportunity, Provision** and **Esteem.**

[O] **Opportunity** – individuals experience different opportunities/constraints, such as family background, socio-economic status, leisure time and disposable income

[P] **Provision** – participation by different community groups is influenced by increasing accessibility of facilities, transport, equipment, space and a variety of activities

[E] **Esteem** – to have great respect or high regard for someone or something. Talented athletes who reach the pinnacle of their sport are awarded honour and prestige that raises their social status. Such athletes may become role models to the wider community. An individual's own self-esteem is also raised by a sense of achievement through participating in physical and sporting activities.

Throughout this Comparative Studies unit, look for the symbol [OPE]. Any text with this symbol will be relevant to these themes.

CHAPTER 5

The United Kingdom

Learning outcomes

By the end of this chapter you should be able to:
- appreciate the cultural context of the United Kingdom (UK), including the historical and social, geographical and political, social and equality values embedded in the UK sport system
- understand the physical education and school sports systems in the UK
- understand the issues surrounding mass participation, especially amongst young people, in the UK
- appreciate the pursuit of excellence in the UK, from young children's leagues to the professional sport scene, and the barriers and opportunities that certain sections of society can experience
- describe the role of the major sports within the UK.

CHAPTER INTRODUCTION

This chapter explores the important role played by Britain in the development of sport since the nineteenth century, and the key factors – historical and cultural – that impact upon sport in the UK today.

In this chapter you will examine the organisation and administration and policy-making process of sport, helping you to reflect on major sporting and social issues.

You will explore many of the issues that people discuss in their everyday life: those that are reported in the media; those that arouse our passions, and those that force us to develop personal opinions. The information in this chapter should help you to participate in discussions about sport in an informed manner. Also, you will need the information here to make a comparison of the sporting and educational systems of the USA and Australia.

Historical and social determinants
English public schools

The sons and daughters of the gentry were educated at large, prestigious, fee-paying boarding schools such as Eton, Harrow and Rugby. When the newly emerging middle classes acquired the necessary funds, but not the social standing, they began to build their own proprietary colleges such as Cheltenham College, Marlborough and Clifton.

The development of sport in the public schools radically changed previous concepts of sport. The boys brought their experiences of games like cricket and mob football to the schools, where they began the process of organising their own activities and devising new ways of playing.

Thomas Arnold, the headmaster of Rugby School, encouraged the boys to develop activities that could be played on the school grounds and that would also highlight the more moral features of teamwork, such as self-discipline, loyalty, courage – character-building qualities suitable for the prospective leaders of society.

The senior boys or prefects were in charge of organising the games, and games committees, such as the Harrow Philathletic Club, were formed.

When the Clarendon Report was published in 1864, it stressed the positive, educational features of team games as agents of training character. From this time team games have been accepted as an essential part of education.

Cricket was already a fairly well-established game in society and as such was already fairly well developed.

Professionalism and amateurism [OPE]

The concept of amateurism was thought to reflect the Ancient Olympian spirit, placing the ideals of fair play and team spirit high above any material objectives.

The public-school influence established its own definition of amateurism. Much of the public-school version of athleticism was Olympian in outlook: it combined physical endeavour with moral integrity, with the struggle being fought for the honour of the house or school.

Table 5.1 The development of sport

Technical development of sport	Moral development of sport
Local variations brought to the schools from the boys' villages	Character training, such as courage, bravery, loyalty and teamwork
Games played regularly in free time	Abiding by rules, both written and unwritten
Individual school rules, skills, boundaries, etc.	The individual less important than the team
Games played competitively – e.g. house matches	Honour in victory and defeat
Self-government meant that initially the boys organised activities	
Later codified rules allowed inter-school fixtures	
Development of games elite	

In England there were two distinct phases of amateurism:

1 Originally, amateurs were gentlemen of the middle and upper classes who played sports in the spirit of fair competition.
2 There was then a shift in definition of an amateur, from a straightforward social distinction, to a monetary one.

Originally there had been no problems perceived by earning money from amateur sport. Fair play was the bedrock upon which amateurism was based.

There were advantages and disadvantages to the amateur code. It promoted restraint in victory and graciousness in defeat, the acceptance of rules and a consequent respect for decisions. However, it excluded the working classes, and this was a moral argument for its abolition.

Social class

Before the Industrial Revolution the United Kingdom had a two-tier class system, the working or lower classes, and the upper classes, mainly the gentry or aristocracy. The middle classes emerged with the advent of new ways of making money.

The working classes initially found their recreational pursuits limited by industrialisation, but gradually improvements were made. Middle-class factory-owners created factory sports facilities and sponsored work teams. The development of the railways enabled them to send their workers on recreational trips, such as to the seaside. Employers hoped to gain the goodwill of their workers, increase morale and encourage the moral benefits of participating in team games.

900 working people were heavily involved in sporting activity. There was continuity between the traditional and modern sports – bowls, darts, billiards, fishing, pigeon racing and dog racing provided sporting entertainment.

The upper classes were wealthy and powerful, possessed vast tracts of property and dominated Parliament well into the nineteenth century. They enjoyed a life of leisure, and were waited on by an army of servants. The aristocracy took part in local affairs and local sports, usually in the form of patronage of prize fights (the forerunner to boxing) and pedestrianism (road walking). Wealthy aristocrats who wanted to be associated with new styles and trends spent large amounts of money on sporting events and particular athletes.

The middle classes aspired to the lifestyle of the upper classes. They became the moral force in society, disapproving of the traditional popular activities enjoyed by both the working and upper classes. They encouraged rational sport, concepts such as amateurism, banned cruel blood sports and also became the agents and promoters of sport in order to accrue a commercial return.

Geographical and political determinants

Government policy

Policy suggests that decision making is based on the ideology (set of ideas) or philosophy of those in power. This is relevant from local to international situations. Sport and physical activities have sometimes been used by various governments, individuals and administrators for political reasons.

A decentralised political system is one where the administration of government is reorganised into smaller, more autonomous units. Local authorities in the United Kingdom are examples, as are the individual states in the USA, which control their own affairs while the federal government becomes involved in matters of national importance. The government in power can give guidelines, but would not normally enforce them. The local authority can then use the guidelines to suit their particular needs.

In recent years the UK governments, both Conservative and Labour, have sought increasingly to assume more control over physical education and sport. This represents a change in the policy and funding of the Department of Culture, Media and Sport (DCMS) to promote social inclusion in the context of the National Strategy for Neighbourhood Renewal.

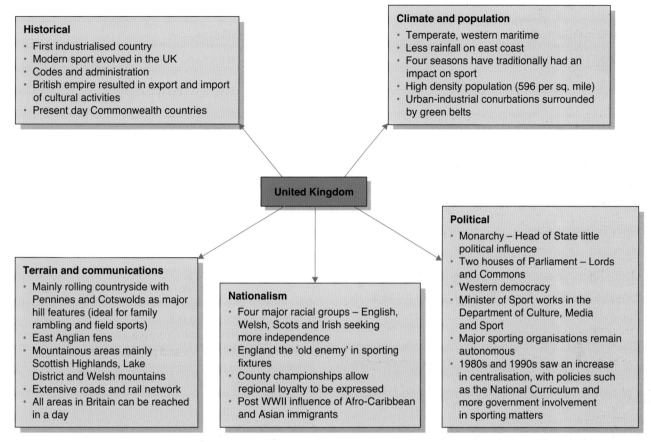

Historical
- First industrialised country
- Modern sport evolved in the UK
- Codes and administration
- British empire resulted in export and import of cultural activities
- Present day Commonwealth countries

Climate and population
- Temperate, western maritime
- Less rainfall on east coast
- Four seasons have traditionally had an impact on sport
- High density population (596 per sq. mile)
- Urban-industrial conurbations surrounded by green belts

United Kingdom

Political
- Monarchy – Head of State little political influence
- Two houses of Parliament – Lords and Commons
- Western democracy
- Minister of Sport works in the Department of Culture, Media and Sport
- Major sporting organisations remain autonomous
- 1980s and 1990s saw an increase in centralisation, with policies such as the National Curriculum and more government involvement in sporting matters

Terrain and communications
- Mainly rolling countryside with Pennines and Cotswolds as major hill features (ideal for family rambling and field sports)
- East Anglian fens
- Mountainous areas mainly Scottish Highlands, Lake District and Welsh mountains
- Extensive roads and rail network
- All areas in Britain can be reached in a day

Nationalism
- Four major racial groups – English, Welsh, Scots and Irish seeking more independence
- England the 'old enemy' in sporting fixtures
- County championships allow regional loyalty to be expressed
- Post WWII influence of Afro-Caribbean and Asian immigrants

Fig 5.1 The United Kingdom

Why should the government wish to spend money on sport and leisure?

The stance taken is that sport can make a valuable contribution to delivering the four key national outcomes of:

- lower long-term unemployment
- less crime
- better health
- better qualifications.

Sport can also develop individual pride and community spirit, which will enable communities to run regeneration programmes themselves.

The Department of Culture, Media and Sport (DCMS) (see **www.culture.gov.uk**) assumed control of sport in the 1990s. As a result, a 'Sports Cabinet' was set up under the chairmanship of the Secretary of State for Culture, Media and Sport to work alongside UK Sport and to bring together ministers with responsibility for sport in the four Home Countries.

The department promotes its policies for:

- Sport for All, aiming to widen access to sport and recreation to the masses
- Achieving Excellence in national and international competition.

Fig 5.2 A map of the UK

Table 5.2 Policies for sport in the UK

Policies for participation	Policies for excellence
A Sporting Future for All (2000)	A Sporting Future for All
Game Plan (2002)	Game Plan
Best Value through Sport	Best Value through Sport
Step into Sport: Leadership and Volunteering	Step into Sport: Leadership and Volunteering
5 hour offer	PE School Sport and Club Links Strategy (PESSCL)

The Youth Sports Unit promotes the importance of physical education and sport for young people, in conjunction with the Department for Children, Schools and Families (DfCSF), and also has responsibility for children's play, via education and training.

Attracting major international events such as the World Cup or the Olympic Games is a high priority. The DCMS supports the relevant organisations in bidding for and staging such events.

Local authorities [OPE]

There is a huge pressure on local authorities, from the district and county councils, to provide leisure facilities in their area. Since the year 2000 leisure has been mainly the responsibility of one specialist department. As legislation is mainly permissive, it is not surprising that wide variations in provision and expenditure can be found between local authorities.

Positive features emerge, nonetheless:

- Financial expenditure has remained reasonably steady.
- Leisure is a popular demand by local residents.
- Leisure is increasingly valued for its own benefits and not just as a means of meeting other policy objectives such as reducing vandalism or improving the nation's health.
- Leisure in the 1990s was also perceived to be of economic benefit to a local area, particularly in its ability to attract tourism.

Many local authorities place sport as a central feature in their work on:

- healthy living
- regeneration
- social inclusion and other key objectives.

The document 'The Value of Sport' responds to the challenge 'Why invest in sport?' and demonstrates that sport can make a difference to people's lives and to the communities in which they live. It emphasises that, for every pound spent on sport, there are multiple returns in improved health, reduced crime, economic regeneration and improved employment opportunities.

These policies have been a result of the public sector being forced to account more for the use of local taxes in order to improve the efficiency of provision and use of resources.

Social and equality determinants [OPE]

Many of the qualities assigned to sport are well recognised – development of self-esteem via the opportunity for self-knowledge, personal achievement, good health, enjoyment, skill acquisition, social interaction, responsibility, development of confidence and so on. We should, therefore, be concerned that certain sections of the population are missing the chance to benefit from such an enriching experience.

The need for a more coordinated and fair approach to the provision of sporting activities addresses two main areas:

1. sports development: enabling people to learn basic sports skills with the possibility of reaching a standard of sporting excellence.
2. sports equity: redressing the balance of inequalities in sport– that is, equality of access/opportunity for everyone, regardless of race, age, gender or level of ability.

Stratification of society

Society can be divided into layers, in much the same way as rocks can be divided into strata. The divisions are based on biological, economic and social criteria – for example, age, gender, race and social class. The dominant group in society, which controls the major social institutions like the media, law, education and politics, can exercise control over the more subordinate groups. This need not be the majority – take the case of the previous minority white rule in South Africa. Using this classification, the dominant group in the UK could be described as white, male and middle class; the subordinate groups would be women, ethnic minorities, people with disabilities and members of the working class. Discrimination can occur when opportunities available to the dominant group are not available to all social groups.

Although 'sport for all' campaigns are no longer a direct function of Sport England, the target groups (i.e. those groups against which there may be discrimination) are still under-represented in sport participation. More recently they are being dealt with at governmental level, under the DCMS, using the term 'Social Exclusion Groups'.

Social exclusion

Aspects of exclusion include:

- ethnicity
- gender
- disability
- youth
- age.

Constraints and exclusion in sport can be broken down into three main categories:

- environmental/structural factors (economic, physical and social)
- personal constraints (internal and psychological)
- attitudes of society and provider systems (policies and managers' practices can act as barriers or enablers).

The evidence suggests that:

- large numbers of people are affected
- policies such as discount schemes/adaptations for disability sport will have little impact if managers do not actively promote their facilities and services – the target population (e.g. women, ethnic, poor, aged and disabled) must be made to feel secure in attending these venues.

The main factors of constraint are poverty, time and unemployment.

- Poverty is constantly being highlighted as the factor that contributes to 'locking people in', accentuating their feelings of isolation and powerlessness.
- Time is quoted by many groups – e.g. the rich, the poor and the retired.
- Chronic unemployment is a constraint, in particular because of the problem of structuring time.

Combinations of aspects of exclusion can be said to lead to double deprivation – for example, being elderly and from an ethnic minority. If exclusion is prolonged in youth, it can have lasting effects in terms of opportunities to play sport recreationally, to socialise and to compete to achieve.

Values

The following values are inseparable from any study of sport within its society.

Democracy. This is relevant both in a political sense and also in the growing democratisation of many sports. Sports are opening their doors when once they would have barred particular social groups. Examples are rugby for women and tennis initiatives in inner cities.

Teamwork. The social benefits from people understanding teamwork are enormous. Any functional society requires its citizens to work together and to conform to the wider social norms and values. Team games were encouraged for this very value; the idea was that, if you could learn to be loyal to a sports team, a school house and a school, then you would also serve your country well.

Individuality. The Industrial Revolution required individuals to show flair and entrepreneurial skills in order to capitalise on the competitive economic environment. Within the sports context, skills such as dribbling in football were highly valued. However, this individualism was also supposed to be for the greater good. In sports such as cricket the individual was valued less than the team as a whole.

Fair play. Sportsmanship or fair play is a code of etiquette that has been highly regarded since the nineteenth century. The ability to abide by the written and unwritten rules of the sports was expected. It was the bedrock upon which amateurism was based.

Competitiveness. A competitive economic system emerged and with it new horizons for those people who recognised the opportunities available through trade and commerce. Team games were valued for the competitive spirit that they encouraged and needed for successful performance. Competitiveness tested a person's character and temperament when under pressure.

Participation. Traditional pastimes, such as mob football, encouraged active participation by large numbers of people. However, urbanisation and the loss of space, as well as the mass of the population needing entertainment to keep them occupied, meant that spectator sports, such as association football, became the national pastime. Today, there is widespread concern that participation levels of young children in particular have fallen dramatically and the obesity problem in the UK involves all social agencies in their attempt to combat the problem.

Overcoming discrimination. Since the nineteenth century the following groups have experienced fewer opportunities than the dominant group in society (namely white, male and middle class): the working classes; women; the disabled; ethnic minority groups. Overcoming discrimination can be achieved through:

- recognising your own prejudice
- understanding the difficulties
- talking to people
- getting support from others
- thinking of alternatives
- going on a training course
- using a policy or guidelines
- sharing common values
- promoting equality through sport
- working in partnership
- endorsing the law
- challenging discrimination.

The commercialism of sport

The commercial world plays an extremely important role in sports decision making, at local, national and international level. The cost of staging sports events, particularly at international level, is extraordinarily high:

- The construction of stadiums requires capital that often only governments can raise.
- The running of events increasingly involves those who pay international television fees.
- Revenue for major events requires huge commitment from governments.

Equally, sport is now a major market for governments, and the trend in the United Kingdom has been for the government to receive more money from sport than it contributes.

Historically, sport has been used as a way of entertaining the public. As it developed the qualities to attract large crowds, the term 'spectator sports' emerged. Initially, sports would generate money on a more personal level. The participants could receive some monetary reward and the spectators would wager on the event, partly to increase the excitement of the event but also to have the opportunity of winning more money than they could from their everyday occupation. When these entertainments became more regular, certain individuals recognised the opportunity to make more money using an organised approach. Promoters and patrons started to accrue more profit than the participants, and even the wagering became more structured.

Today this has evolved into a situation where sport is heavily commercialised, packaged and presented to worldwide audiences. Countries with a market economy have been most open to this kind of development; capitalism encourages its population to work in competitive conditions to create profitable enterprises. The availability of widespread television coverage has attracted large-scale businesses that can use sport to promote their products, and the development of technology has meant that sports that were once national pastimes – for example, basketball in the USA – are now able to look further afield and to seek global audiences.

The potential for profit in the television age was realised in the 1980s, with the emergence of entrepreneurs such as Robert Maxwell, Bernard Tapie, Kerry Packer and Rupert Murdoch. They recognised the loyal fans as captive customers and clubs as unexploited assets. More importantly, they realised that gate receipts were no longer the key to profits. Media rights, sponsorship deals and merchandising were to become the future potential.

The large audiences needed to support sport, either as live spectators providing gate receipts and because they own television sets and can view the sports at home, tend to be found predominantly in advanced technological societies, where people tend to possess enough free time, disposable income and the means to travel easily to different sporting venues. It is no coincidence, therefore, that commercial sports originally began in the nineteenth century in Britain – the first country to develop industrialisation and communication networks. Professional sport grew steadily and included activities such as cricket, ball games, prize fighting and pedestrianism. Competitors could be paid for their efforts, and coaching and training methods developed alongside.

It is interesting to see this development in Britain, which had, as its ruling class, the elite upper class, which had developed the 'amateur' concept that was aimed at keeping monetary values out of sport. The business side of sport was delayed in Britain in comparison to the USA, which had no compunction about linking sport and money. By the 1990s, even in Britain, sport had become big business.

The organisations in charge of individual sports have found that their remit has changed over the years. This can again be highlighted in Britain, where the governing bodies originally subscribed to the principle of amateurism. They have had to adapt to commercial pressures to ensure that their sport maintains its status. Amateur sport receives its main funding from sponsorship and individual donations. Some sports are wealthier than others, but they all need to pay for athletes' training, operating expenses and the staging of events. Staff with expertise in financial management and publicity are hired rather than those with an interest purely in the sport itself, and decisions related to revenue are not necessarily made with the good of the athletes at heart. This has led to some athletes seeking more control, 'taking on' the organisations concerned, and setting up their own players' association in order to project a collective voice – for example, the Professional Golf Association (PGA) and the Association of Tennis Professionals (ATP). Athletes' protests include such matters as rule changes, an extension of the competitive season and the need to create more revenue for themselves.

- Commercial sports have developed under certain social and economic conditions – urbanisation, industrialisation, effective communications, surplus disposable income and a large population with high living standards and sufficient leisure time.
- The basic structures of many sports have remained the same, but commercialisation has been influential.
- Mass audiences may demand drama and excitement rather than aesthetic appreciation.
- Control of sport needs to be balanced between the owners and the athletes.
- Amateur sports are becoming pressurised by the need to generate more money.

Key term

Sponsorship The provision of funds or other form of support to an individual or event in return for a commercial return. It is of mutual benefit to both parties.

Sponsorship

Sponsorship is now an intrinsic aspect of sports funding. Through the medium of television, business sponsors of sport can create the images they want, allow identification with the sports stars and introduce the 'new' populations into the game to their product.

School sport and physical education

What is meant by 'physical activity'?

- 'Physical activity' is an umbrella term encompassing any activity that requires an individual to exert a certain amount of energy, resulting in an increase in heart rate.
- Physical activity may include many different activities, from walking, skipping and playing games, to athletic, outdoor and adventurous activities such as skiing or canoeing.
- Physical activity involves participating on a recreational basis and/or performing in a competitive and organised sporting structure, including adhering to externally enforced rules.
- When individuals raise their heart rate sufficiently, a certain number of times a week, they can be said to be improving their health and potentially reducing their risk of cardiovascular disease.

Key terms

Healthy, balanced lifestyle Where an individual achieves a healthy state or equilibrium, especially in the ratio of time shared between the active and non-active aspects of their life.

Obesity A condition that accompanies a sedentary or inactive lifestyle, caused by an imbalance between energy intake and expenditure that results in an excessive increase in the body's total quantity of fat.

What are the aims of physical education within the UK context?

Physical education aims to:

- develop a range of psycho-motor skills
- maintain and increase physical mobility and flexibility, stamina and strength
- develop understanding and appreciation for a range of physical activities
- develop positive values and attitudes such as sportsmanship, competition and an ability to abide by the rules
- help children acquire self-esteem and confidence through the acquisition of skills, knowledge and values
- develop an understanding of the importance of exercise in maintaining a healthy lifestyle.

Who chooses the physical education programme?

In the United Kingdom there is a decentralised system where the teacher and the individual school have the power to produce their own programme, though they are increasingly bound by government guidelines. The National Curriculum now sets out which subjects are to be taught at each Key Stage of a pupil's schooling. Physical education is compulsory from Key Stage 1 (ages 5–7) through to Key Stage 4 (up to age 16).

National Curriculum

The National Curriculum attempts to raise standards in education and make schools more accountable for what they teach. Physical education continues to be one of only five subjects that pupils of all abilities must pursue, from their entry to school at age 5 until the end of compulsory schooling at age 16. For more details about the National Curriculum, see Chapter 4.

Physical education as preparation for leisure

As children approach the end of the compulsory years of schooling, it is necessary to foster in them an awareness of the opportunities available in the community. Schools offer:

- options programmes in the later years
- use of community facilities where necessary or appropriate
- information about local clubs and sports centres.

However, one of the big problems in the United Kingdom is the traditionally poor link between schools and community sport, as a result of trying to keep a distance between sport and physical education. Various policies and initiatives have been set up during the last decade to try to improve activity levels amongst school children, as part of both the curriculum and extra-curricular programmes.

Developments in school sport

The term 'sport' refers to the 'physical activities with established rules engaged in by individuals attempting to outperform their competitors' (Wuest, Bucher, 1991). It provides different opportunities for physical activity whilst at school. Its main focus is on improving performance standards rather than the educational process and mainly takes place outside the formal curriculum. It is usually viewed as an opportunity for children to extend their interest or ability in physical activities.

Key points to note:

- Extracurricular activities are optional in the UK
- Teachers are not paid extra for this provision
- Opportunity and provision are therefore very different across the country
- The traditional stance of keeping school sport and physical education separate is a challenge to the new initiatives and philosophy to try to improve these links.
- There was a reduction in emphasis on the sporting elite, with a more recreational focus being adopted in many schools.

The government, through its Department for Children, Schools and Families (DfCSF) has an increasing number of initiatives to increase the range and amount of school sport available to young people aged 5–16.

The aim is that by 2008 75 per cent of children in each School Partnership will have engaged in two hours of high-quality PE and school sport per week, within and beyond the curriculum.

By 2010 the ambition is to offer all children at least four hours of sport made up of at least two hours of high-quality PE within the curriculum and at least an additional two–three hours out of school, delivered by a range of school, community and club providers.

The following are some of the initiatives in operation.

- Club Links is a programme that links schools with local sports clubs and is being delivered through the National Governing Bodies of twenty-two sports.
- Competition Managers are being appointed by the DCMS to develop a programme of inter-school competitions in a number of pilot areas. The Department aims to have a Competition Manager in all School Sport Partnerships by 2010.
- Step into Sport provides sports leadership and volunteering opportunities for young people aged 14–19 years. It is a joint initiative with the Department for Children, Schools and Families – one of the eight strands in the national School Sports Strategy.
- Sport Kitemarks for Schools will in future reward delivery of the national PE, School Sports and Club Links strategy. They will, therefore, be open only to schools that are in a Schools Sport Partnership.
- School Sport Matters was conceived in 2005 as a pioneering campaign to highlight exemplary practice in physical education and sport in schools, and to generate debate on the delivery of sport in schools.

Key term

School sport The term 'sport' refers to the 'physical activities with established rules engaged in by individuals attempting to outperform their competitors' (Wuest, Bucher, 1991).

A **high-quality physical education** for all children is central to the Government's new PE School Sport and Club Links Strategy (PESSCL).

The achievements of England's School Sport Partnership schools in the past eight years has certainly helped stabilise a clear decline. Government figures now put at 80 per cent the number of pupils in partnership schools who participate in at least two hours of high-quality PE and school sport a week, while 97 per cent of partnership schools held at least one school sports day or equivalent during the academic year.

Across School Years 5–11, some 189,000 pupils in partnership schools are now registered as gifted and talented because of their ability in PE or sport – up from 106,100 in 2004/5. The figures are from the latest 2005/6 School Sport Survey, which reports on what over 5 million schoolchildren at 16,882 schools are doing.

For a third year, the *Daily Telegraph*, with Norwich Union as commercial sponsors, will continue the 'School Sport Matters' campaign to highlight exemplary practice in

physical education and sport in schools. The aim is also to rally the government to give the necessary infrastructure and facilities for schools to be able to deliver what we believe will strengthen the lives of all our children. The 'School Sport Matters' campaign will culminate with a national awards ceremony. To enter in any of the ten categories, go to **http://juniorsport. telegraph.co.uk/school-sports-matters**.

IN CONTEXT

The **UK School Games** is a multi-sport event for the UK's elite young athletes of school age.

The sports programme was increased for 2008 to include a second team sport – hockey – which, combined with the existing programme of Athletics, Badminton, Fencing, Gymnastics, Judo, Swimming, Table Tennis and Volleyball, brought the total to nine sports. The integrated programme of disability events in Athletics, Swimming and Table Tennis increased the athletes competing in 2008 to over 1,500.

Each of the nine sports was combined into a four-day Games environment designed to replicate the feel of major events such as the Olympic Games and Paralympic Games.

The UK School Games seek to create an inspirational and motivational setting, which encourages more young people to take part and succeed in sport.

Responsibility for the development and organisation of the UK School Games lies with the Youth Sport Trust.

Mass participation

Participation trends can be summarised as follows:

- Only 46 per cent of the population participate in sport more than 12 times a year.
- Only 32 per cent of adults in England take 30 minutes of moderate physical activity five times a week, compared to 57 per cent of Australians.
- Young white males are most likely to take part in sport and physical activity. The least likely to take part in sport and physical activity are the most disadvantaged groups.
- Participation falls dramatically after people leave school, and continues to drop with age.

According to research highlighted by Sport England, the most popular recreation activities during a one-month period were:

- walking (20 per cent)
- swimming (14 per cent)
- fitness-related activities (10.5 per cent).

Activity 1

Read the article opposite and comment in table format on the advantages and disadvantages of midnight leagues.

IN CONTEXT

A keen young footballer who almost gave up on sport but for a unique social experiment has defied the odds to be picked to play for Great Britain at the Paralympic Games in Beijing. Mark Robertson, 17, who suffers from cerebral palsy, is the first Midnight League player from Scotland to make it to an Olympic or Paralympic Games. The selection of Mark, from Penicuik, Midlothian, for the cerebral palsy (CP) team at Beijing is testimony to the way the Midnight Leagues, which started life as a bid to keep youngsters off the streets on Friday and Saturday nights, have taken off. Mark was young player of the tournament when he was part of the Scotland team which took part in the CP 7-a-side world championships in Brazil last year, when they finished in sixth place and helped the UK qualify for Beijing.

Nicky Wilson, a trustee of the Coalfields Regeneration Trust (CRT), which sponsors the Dalkeith Midnight League where Mark plays, said: 'It is a tremendous achievement for him and a real boost for the thousands of young people who play Midnight League football over the dark and dismal winter evenings. Mark's success proves that Midnight League football does more than keep young boys and girls off the streets and out of trouble on Friday and Saturday nights. It also helps them develop their talents.'

Wilson, an ex-miner, and president of the NUM in Scotland, witnessed at first hand the devastation pit closures brought to mining towns and villages. He now devotes much of his time to the work of the CRT to rebuild these communities. Since its formation in 1999, the CRT has invested £10m in supporting local organisations to revitalise their former colliery areas, and seen these organisations go onto raise a further £30m from other sources.

Wilson explained the CRT's commitment to the Midnight Leagues: 'We believe sporting initiatives like the Midnight Leagues have a huge role to play in the regeneration of mining areas which are still struggling to catch up with other communities. Not only do they make local areas safer by diverting youngsters who were often driven by sheer boredom into anti-social behaviour, they provide social cohesion by helping young people build relationships with each other. They also strengthen teenagers' links with former mining communities such as Penicuik and Dalkieth, and that's what regeneration is all about.'

The CRT sponsors Midnight Leagues involving around 1000 youngsters in association with the Bank of Scotland and the SFA. It also organises Scottish Coalfields Finals of Midnight Leagues and a highly successful Home International series. Apart from on-the-field success, the Midnight Leagues are already proving a winner at home.

Inspector Derek Fairlie, a liaison officer with Lothian and Borders Police, said: 'Around 36 per cent of all the calls we receive are complaints of anti-social behaviour involving young people. The Midnight Leagues have had a significant effect in reducing these calls at their peak period on Friday and Saturday nights by giving youngsters something positive to do rather than hang around street corners.'

But the Broxburn Midnight League has thrown up some interesting figures. Inspector Fairlie added: 'Our analysis suggests that in 2006–2007 when the Midnight Leagues were being played, the number of youth calls dropped by 50 per cent compared with the previous year. From April to September, when there is no Midnight League football, these calls increased by 24 per cent.'

Almost 200 youngsters taking part in Midnight Leagues across West Lothian responded to a survey. Over half of them said they would either be 'out drinking on the streets' or 'just hanging around' (20 per cent) if they were not playing Midnight League Football.

The Leagues have grown from just three in 2003 to being established in all of Scotland's 32 Local Authorities, covering 74 venues with over 10,000 young people taking part. The Bank of Scotland, which has invested £1.5 million in supporting grassroots football — most of it Midnight Leagues — predicts that with an additional £1 million from the Scottish Government's Cashback for Communities fund, the number of youngsters involved will rise to around 140,000 by the year 2010.

(*Source*: *The Herald*, 30 November 2008. 'Midnight league star set to shine at Beijing Paralympics' reported by John Scott)

Sport and the Pursuit of Excellence [OPE]

Remind yourselves of the key terms – opportunity, provision and esteem.

Organisations with a specific remit to develop sporting excellence in the UK are:

1   UK Sport
2   UK Sport Institute (UKSI).

UK Sport

UK Sport is funded by, and responsible to, the Department for Culture, Media and Sport. It has a remit to develop world-class standards, and coordinates overall policy in the support of elite sport at the UK level, as well as UK-wide programmes such as anti-doping and major events. In addition, it manages the international relationships of the UK and coordinates a UK-wide approach to any international issues.

Olympic and Paralympic sport can no longer be the preserve of all-round, talented amateurs. Medals are won by as little as thousandths of a second or fractions of a centimetre by dedicated, often full-time athletes.

Once talent has been identified and nurtured, an army of support providers is required – from coaches to physiotherapists and doctors to bio-mechanists.

UK Sport's mission is to support the delivery of medal success at the world's most significant sporting events – principally the Olympic and Paralympic Games. Investment over £100m annually is made to the most talented athletes.

- World Class Performance Pathway: World-class performance can be delivered only by world-class personnel, and the challenge for Olympic Games is to develop home-grown expertise to support our athletes.
- Worldwide Impact: Our international programme will enable us to bring best practice in other sporting nations to the UK. We will also provide clear strategic support to enable sports to bid for and stage major events in this country.
- World Class Standards: UK Sport will promote the highest standards of sporting conduct whilst continuing to lead a world-class anti-doping programme for the UK and being responsible for improving the education and promotion of ethically fair and drug-free sport.

UK Sport Institute (UKSI)

The UK Sport Institute is the name given to a network of centres and a central team of experts that support the UK's top sportsmen and women.

It is made up of four Home Country Sports Institutes in England, Scotland, Wales and Northern Ireland, along with a central services team, which is part of UK Sport, based in London. The four Sports Institutes of England, Scotland, Wales and Northern Ireland provide world-class facilities to elite athletes. They provide state-of-the-art facilities and services for sports science and medicine.

Case studies of cricket, rugby league, rugby union and association football will be studied later in this unit (see Chapter 8).

CHALLENGE YOURSELF

Comment on the cultural factors that have led to the more widespread promotion of sporting excellence in the USA in comparison to the UK.

[20 marks]

What you need to know

- ✱ Sport and physical education have developed gradually over time and reflect the society of which they form an integral part.
- ✱ The traditions of amateurism and middle-class values had a significant impact on the development of different sports.
- ✱ The compulsory nature of physical education and the option of participating in school sport have caused controversy, and the government is trying to redress the balance by encouraging school sport and a more competitive approach within schools. Unlike in the USA, physical education is compulsory.
- ✱ The problem of obesity and sedentary lifestyles is leading to the development of participation initiatives.
- ✱ Sports policy is characterised by a high degree of fragmentation between central government departments. There is heavy reliance on local government to provide facilities and opportunities for sport and recreation.

- ✱ In local authorities, there is a decentralised approach towards the organisation of sport and recreation, reflecting the political system in the UK. As with much of the administration of sport in the UK it is a mixture of tradition and compromise.
- ✱ There has been a steady expansion in the commercialisation of sport. This has brought challenges for the National Governing Bodies to adjust their rules and take note of the international sporting calendar.
- ✱ Funding for UK sport is dominated by sponsorship. This is supplemented by government grants (both local and central) and funds from governing bodies and private individuals. British sports bodies, such as the RFU, have had to cast off their traditional amateur, elitist approach to join the modern, professional sports world.

Review Questions

1. What is meant by the terms opportunity, provision and esteem?
2. How did the nineteenth-century public schools exemplify amateurism?
3. How has local government tried to improve opportunities for the more disadvantaged groups in the UK?
4. Outline contemporary initiatives to promote school sport in the UK. Why should the UK government be concerned at the lack of fitness amongst the general population?
5. What is the role of UK Sport in the pursuit of excellence in the UK?

CHAPTER 6

The United States of America

Learning outcomes

By the end of this chapter you should be able to:

- appreciate the cultural context of the USA, including historical, geographical, political, economic, equality and values such as 'the American dream' embedded in the US sport system
- define the terms 'WASP', 'isolationism', 'frontierism', 'stacking', 'centrality' and 'tokenism'
- describe the physical education and school sport systems in the USA, with reference to intra-mural and inter-scholastic sport
- understand the issues surrounding mass participation, especially amongst young people, in the USA
- appreciate the pursuit of excellence in the USA, from Little League to the professional sport scene, and the barriers and opportunities that certain sections of society can experience
- understand the Lombardian, radical and counter-culture sport ethics
- understand the role of the major sports within the USA.

CHAPTER INTRODUCTION

This chapter explores the role played by the USA in the development of sports in the twentieth century, and the key factors – historical and cultural – that impact upon sport in the USA today.

The links between the USA and the United Kingdom cannot be ignored, especially in the cultural legacy left by the colonial power. However, the USA was to go on and carve for itself a new and unique future.

EXAMINER'S TIP

Throughout this chapter, try to compare the information here to that which you have already learned about the United Kingdom.

Cultural context

Activity 1

Consider the impact of the factors in Figure 6.1 on the system of sport in the USA.

Activity 2

Imagine the trek west to settle in uninhabited wilderness areas, with a hostile indigenous population to overcome.

- What personal qualities would be most likely to prove successful?
- Can you relate any of these qualities to success in sport?

Activity 3

How does professional sport reflect a capitalist system?

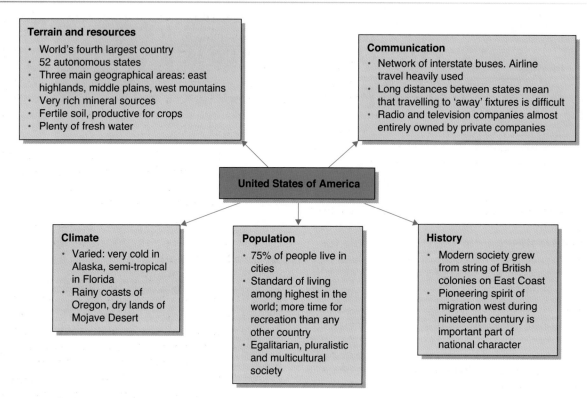

Terrain and resources
- World's fourth largest country
- 52 autonomous states
- Three main geographical areas: east highlands, middle plains, west mountains
- Very rich mineral sources
- Fertile soil, productive for crops
- Plenty of fresh water

Communication
- Network of interstate buses. Airline travel heavily used
- Long distances between states mean that travelling to 'away' fixtures is difficult
- Radio and television companies almost entirely owned by private companies

United States of America

Climate
- Varied: very cold in Alaska, semi-tropical in Florida
- Rainy coasts of Oregon, dry lands of Mojave Desert

Population
- 75% of people live in cities
- Standard of living among highest in the world; more time for recreation than any other country
- Egalitarian, pluralistic and multicultural society

History
- Modern society grew from string of British colonies on East Coast
- Pioneering spirit of migration west during nineteenth century is important part of national character

Fig 6.1 An overview of the USA

Fig 6.2 The United States of America

Development and structure of the US government

Following the American War of Independence (1775–83), the American colonies achieved their objective of complete political independence from Britain. The causes of the war were complex, but one key factor was the desire of the colonists to break free from controls imposed by a pro-British elite. Also, the colonists were growing in a self-confidence born of their experiences and from the opportunities for self-improvement, now they were no longer limited by the tightly closed class system of the British – a system that excluded the majority of people from self-improvement on the grounds that they did not possess the preferred social status.

A new government with a federal constitution was founded, effectively creating a republic. A federal constitution is where the powers of government are divided between the national and the state or provincial governments. This was an important concept: the people had just broken away from a distant system of power over which they had little control, and did not want to replace it with another, so they sought to restrict the powers of the new national government via the Constitution of the United States, which serves as the Supreme Law of the Land. This **isolation** of the USA was to extend itself to sport as well as to politics. The Bill of Rights guaranteed the basic rights of American citizens. The constitution establishes **federalism** with three separate branches:

- legislative (responsible for creating laws)
- executive (power to enforce laws)
- judicial (power to operate laws).

The government operates on three different levels – national, state and local:

- national government – with delegated powers
- state government – with residual powers (where they work together, it is called concurrent power).

The country of the United States of America (USA) is a:

- **democracy** with a representative government, which means the people elect leaders who will represent them
- **republic**, which is where the chief of state is also elected by the people, unlike a monarch, who inherits the title
- **constitutional** government operating under a set of laws and principles outlined in the constitution
- **federal** system, with a sharing of power between the national, state and municipal governments.

Fig 6.3 The American government

The powers of the federal government have expanded since the constitution was first designed. By 1983 the American government had involved itself in matters concerning sport in eleven areas: antitrust, criminal activities, restructuring sport, discrimination, capital funding, tax/duty exemption, social work projects, sponsored publicity, health/ fitness promotion, boycott and international athletic tours. Some of these areas are outlined below.

Antitrust. This is where the US government regulates or opposes trusts, monopolies, cartels or similar organisations in an attempt to prevent unfair competition. Some incidences have involved the NCAA.

Criminal activities. This involves organised crime in horse racing and betting. The 'fixing' of events was made a criminal offence in 1963.

Restructuring sport. Numerous attempts have been made to curb the violence in boxing, but efforts have failed, as Congress is unwilling to impose sanctions on what is effectively a privately owned sport business. However, in 1978 the Amateur Sports Act was passed as an attempt to solve problems between the NCAA and the Amateur Athletic Union (AAU). They had been unable to agree, and this led to the establishing of the United States Olympic Committee. It effectively streamlined the amateur sports scene and allowed federal intervention.

Discrimination. Title IX, or the Education Amendment of 1972, made equal treatment of men and women in education compulsory. In 1975 the Education for All Handicapped Children Act was passed, which ensured the inclusion of children with special educational needs to regular physical education programmes.

Capital funding. Generally, Congress does not directly support sporting events, though this has become more prevalent, particularly for the Olympic Games and other prestigious events.

Tax exemptions. These have also been granted in the area of sport. About three-quarters of the stadia and arenas have been funded from federal sources. Few managers own the facilities, because, if they are owned by the federal government, they are exempt from taxes, maintenance and insurance costs – these are picked up by the tax-payer.

Health/fitness promotion. With health costs escalating, the government has turned its attention to preventative medicine and established the Office of Health Information, Health Promotion and Physical Fitness, and Sports Medicine. Its role is to coordinate all matters relating to education for health.

Boycott. The most famous boycott was the one ordered by President Carter in 1980, to pressurise the National Olympic Committee to boycott the Moscow Games. It was successful in its campaign.

Overall, the government will act in sports matters but generally prefers to maintain a low profile; it intervenes only when it is deemed necessary.

The spread of white American culture was not without a price. The indigenous population of native Americans, made up of many different Indian tribes (each with its own customs and language), was defeated and resettled, with the result that native Americans lost many of their ancient pastimes.

In the mid-1800s, plantations in the South produced huge cotton crops, and black slaves were relied upon to do the manual labour. The different values held in the North finally led to the Civil War in 1861; Abraham Lincoln issued the Emancipation Proclamation in 1863, pronouncing all slaves in the confederacy to be free. However, the Southern states continued to limit the rights of black people. Within living memory black Americans were treated as second-class citizens in their own country; in some states, not allowed to marry or attend school with white Americans, or even sit in the same part of a bus. The election of Barack Obama as President of the USA has gone some way to giving hope that, although the experiences of black people in America are still not equal to those of white people in many respects, self-improvement and opportunities to participate are truly open to all.

The new competitive capitalist economy in America aimed to provide people with determination, talent and the opportunity to be successful. Thus, in theory at least, people can experience upward social mobility regardless of social class. This is popularly called 'rags to riches' in the 'land of opportunity'. In sport this can be achieved from Little League to Professional and Olympic sport. Sporting terms such as 'win at all costs', 'nice guys finish last' and 'Lombardian ethic' reflect this need to achieve within American culture.

> **Key term**
>
> **American Dream** The idea that in America anyone with talent, drive and ambition can achieve success, regardless of social class.

Sport in America developed as a result of the fact that:

- American society was trying to produce a new identity/escape from its older European culture
- America had a growing variety of emigrants in a pluralist culture no longer dominated by Britain
- sport in America tended to be professional rather than follow the nineteenth-century class-based ideal of amateurism prevalent in Britain
- the 'win at all costs' ideology became more important than the ethos of 'how you play the game'
- this was a reflection of the technological changes of the new era.

> **Key term**
>
> **Isolationism** A national policy of abstaining from political or economic relations with other countries; was an official US government policy in the late nineteenth and early twentieth centuries.

In the United States, the frontier was the term applied to the impact of the zone of unsettled land outside the region of existing settlements of Europeans. Unlimited free land was available and thus offered the psychological sense of unlimited opportunity. This, in turn, had many consequences, such as increasing optimism about opportunities to progress, influencing the future orientation of settlements, and the increasing wastefulness of natural resources. Throughout American history, the expansion of settlement was largely from the east to the west, and thus the frontier is often identified with 'the west'. Sport has often been called the last frontier, as we have yet to discover the boundaries of human sporting achievement.

> **Key term**
>
> **Pluralism** A theory of society as several autonomous but interdependent groups having equal power.

Pluralism is a theory that refuses to accept that only an elite can make decisions on national policy. Rather, pluralism proposes that the state should consider the opinions of many different interest groups and then act in the best interests of everyone.

> ## Exam-style Questions
>
> How realistic is the premise that the New World was created on pluralistic lines?

> **Key term**
>
> **WASP (acronym)** White Anglo-Saxon Protestant – a descendant of the early European settlers in America.

The term WASP originated in the United States in reference to White Americans of Anglo-Saxon descent, whose early colonial ancestors were from North-Western Europe and were Protestant in religious affiliation. In the present day, the term is generally used to describe those who form a powerful elite based on a particular ethnic origin and social class and, consequently, has largely negative connotations. For our purposes here, the term WASP reflects that segment of the US population that founded the American nation. Technically, this segment is now less than 25 per cent of the US population, but continues to have a disproportionate influence over American institutions.

A WASP is a member of the group with the greatest access to opportunities, provision and esteem. Minority groups did not thrive so well. The first minority group comprising the Native Americans was decimated by disease and violence at the hands of the early European settlers. Today, the general premise is that the last immigrant group in has the least power.

Social determinants [OPE]

Among the flood of immigrants to North America, one group – 500,000 Africans – were brought over as slaves between 1619 and 1808. Great Britain had made moves to abolish the Slave Trade in 1807, with slavery made illegal in 1834. In the USA slavery continued until after the American Civil War. Slavery was finally abolished throughout the United States in 1865.

However, even after the end of slavery, American blacks were hampered by segregation and inferior education. In search of opportunity, African-Americans formed an internal wave of immigration, moving from the rural South to the urban North. But many urban blacks were unable to find work; by law and custom they had to live apart from whites, in run-down neighbourhoods called ghettos.

In the late 1950s and early 1960s, African-Americans, led by Dr Martin Luther King, Jr, used boycotts, marches and other forms of non-violent protest to demand equal treatment under the law and an end to racial prejudice.

Today, African-Americans comprise about 13.5 per cent of the total US population. In recent decades blacks have made great strides, and a black middle class has grown substantially. In 2002 50.8 per cent of employed blacks held white-collar jobs – managerial, professional and administrative positions rather than service jobs or those requiring manual labour. In 2003 58.3 per cent of all black high-school graduates enrolled in college within one year (compared to 35.8 per cent in 1982). For whites, the college participation rate in 2003 was 66.1 per cent. Thus, the racial gap was less than 8 percentage points. The average income of blacks is still lower than that of whites, however, and unemployment of blacks – particularly of young men – remains higher than that of whites.

The term 'Hispanic' is a generic term used to describe people whose origins can be traced to Spanish-speaking countries (approximately twenty-two million) and whose cultures are related by language, colonial history or Catholicism. Examples would be Chicanos and Puerto Ricans.

There are approximately 6.7 million Asian-Americans in the United States. Very little sociological research has been done on any of these groups in relation to sport participation. Generally, they are discriminated against in terms of racial stereotypes, which make belonging to sports groups difficult. Also, their traditions may not always coincide with the true American sports.

African-Americans have tended to be the group that has suffered the most discrimination, owing to the way they arrived in the country as slaves. Economically and socially, African-Americans began life in the United States suffering extreme discrimination. In terms of participation in sports, this tended to place them in the more working-class sports and, within mixed-race teams, they were often placed in outfield positions with less decision-making roles (note: centrality and stacking). We will discuss this further in the chapter.

Exam-style Questions

Explain why achievement in sport is increasing among ethnic minorities in the USA.

[4 marks]

Development of rational sport in the United States

As with Britain, in the nineteenth century there was an increasing rationalisation of sport in the USA.

- Club membership was exclusive.
- Spectator sports were developing.
- Social class distinctions became more defined and were reinforced through the amateur/professional divide.
- Organised sport carried the burden of achieving social and economic objectives and became serious in its orientation.
- Positive male character traits were closely allied to those needed to be successful in sport, as well as being useful in serving God and country.

By the 1920s these cultural links had become clearly defined, with the growth of spectator sports cleverly marketed in order to raise money and create profits. This occurred at both professional and intercollegiate level, and national organisations were being established to control the rapid growth – for example, the National Collegiate Athletic Association (NCAA).

> **Key term**
>
> **Rational sport** Rational sport became prevalent after the Industrial Revolution when sports became more organised and highly structured.

Commercialisation of sport

The United States was set up as a **capitalist** or **market economy** – an economic system based on free trade and the private ownership of the means of production, property and capital. Some would argue that the focus on maximising profits has led to the development of the 'good life'. Others would claim that the single scale of success – namely, monetary values – can alienate many people within a population. The USA is a typical example of a capitalist society.

Professional sport in particular shares some of the characteristics of capitalism, with its heavy emphasis on competition and on winning as the only important outcome, and the offer of rewards that are mostly materialistic. Very often the terms commercialisation and

Americanisation are synonymous. The terms are associated with the manner in which the sports are played and perceived as well as how they are marketed.

The USA did not get tied down with the limiting amateur ethos in the UK during the late nineteenth and twentieth centuries. Nor did it become involved with the state-funded Eastern-bloc approach to sport.

The scholarships and spectator appeal, which began in American universities, are said to have been the beginnings of modern professional sport. The development of the media, especially television, was the ideal environment for professional sport to flourish. Combined with the Lombardian ethic of winning and the potential material rewards for success, this became the dominating influence of American sport.

The four main popular sports in the USA are:

- American football
- ice hockey
- baseball
- basketball.

Each sport is run as a business and its athletes marketed as assets.

Professionalism at a price

In the twentieth and twenty-first centuries, many sports have become professional. Many professional performers have a high status in their sport and, if the sport receives a high level of media coverage, these performers become household names. As professional performers they are paid by results, and therefore success in their sport is crucial. This places heavy expectations on performers – from themselves, coaches, spectators, sponsors and the media. The pressure to perform consistently and at a high level can cause the 'win at all costs' ethic to be adhered to. Sponsorship and endorsements can be lucrative for performers, and a charismatic, high-profile performer such as Tiger Woods or Serena Williams is more likely to attract sponsorship deals. However, sponsors bring with them their own pressures, particularly expecting the performer to make regular appearances at specific tournaments and among the public. This may lead to players being encouraged to be active when they should be resting from injury.

Commercialisation and the media

Commercialisation has brought about profound changes in the structure of many sports, with media companies often able to call the shots.

Initial commercial developments occurred in the nineteenth century, as spectator sports emerged. It is no coincidence that commercial sports first appeared in England – the first country to develop industrialisation and communication networks. Allied with this was the emergence of a mass of the population with increasing free time and disposable income in need of excitement and entertainment. People's entertainment value was exploited by individuals who saw the opportunity to organise regular sporting events. Promoters and agents emerged, and **commercialism** became an integral part of sport. Since then:

- Sport has become a global product, advertised and marketed across the world.
- The vast profit potential of sport in the television age, first recognised in the 1980s, has attracted entrepreneurs.
- Media rights, sponsorship deals and merchandising have become important issues.
- The huge sums paid for TV and other media rights have turned sport into a global business.
- Sports clothing and equipment industries, such as Nike and Adidas, have formed another important part of the global sport complex.
- Building brand awareness through sport has become an important part of modern marketing.
- The richest clubs buy the best players they can afford – a system that has opened a wide gap between the top ranking clubs and those without financial backing.
- The old **turnstile** system of **cash receipts** – attractive to money launderers but a nightmare for club auditors as the system could be abused by the people manning the turnstile – has given way to sophisticated electronic systems, which enable supporters to buy merchandise as well as tickets.
- Organising bodies such as the National Basketball Association, National Football League and National Hockey League have started to behave like multinational companies, spreading their influence and products around the globe through aggressive marketing and well-directed media campaigns.

Table 6.1 Sports and athletes as businesses

Sports as businesses	Athletes as assets
Primary aim is to make a profit.	Are expendable (hire and fire).
Salaries, contracts and overheads are features.	Act as role models and ambassadors of the company.
Products are advertised.	Are salaried.
Merchandise is sold.	Can be transferred and sold.
Have owners and employees.	Must endorse products/company.
Make investments with shareholders.	Must generate funds.

- The success of US-style business practices has jolted even traditional sports such as rugby and cricket in the United Kingdom.
- The betting industry has long been bound up with sports such as horse racing, boxing and football. In the UK horse racing accounts for 70 per cent of revenue for the top three bookmakers, yet less then a tenth of the UK population are regular race followers.
- New technology could transform the gambling industry in the future, broadening the range of sports betting (e.g. online betting) and making it a more regular part of daily life.
- The increasing concentration of money and power in a limited number of giant sporting **conglomerates**, especially those that combine media clout with club ownership or merchandising interests, has caused increased unease.
- Many athletes do not have much control over their own careers.

Golf and tennis are amongst the few major sports that have a relatively democratic form of government. The players decide very much how things should be run and make their own decisions about when and where they will play and which sponsorship deals to take.

The characteristics of commercial sport

Commercial sport has close links with:

- professional sport
- sponsorship/business
- entertainment (sport becomes a spectacle or display for spectators)
- gate receipts/an affluent population
- contracts (athletes/clubs/businesses/stock market/merchandise/TV rights)
- athletes as commodities/endorsements/an asset to the company
- the media
- winning and success.

Concepts of American sport

There are three main sporting concepts operating in the United States.

1   The dominant concept is the **Lombardian** ethic, which is based on the Protestant work ethic of self-discipline, clean living and mental alertness. The popular image of this ethic is taken from the saying of the coach, Vince Lombardi: 'Winning isn't the most important thing, it's the only thing.' This emphasises the competitive, achievement-oriented, reward-based type of sport behaviour.

2   The **counter-culture** is an attempt by some sections of American society to change the emphasis in sport to one where the process is the important thing and the outcome is unimportant. It comes from Grantland Rice's slogan: 'It's not whether you won or lost but how you played the game.' This tends to take an anti-competitive viewpoint, and Eco Sport has evolved from it – cooperative rather than competitive games. The New Games Foundation aims to change the way people play by reducing the amount of equipment and skill and replacing them with informal situations, emphasising group effort rather than group reward.

3   The middle line is the **radical** ethic and this is perhaps the nearest to the British stance, where the outcome is important but so too is the process. The quest for excellence can be strived for and achieved, but not at the expense of other values.

Exam-style Questions

Identify the cultural factors which have prevented cricket from becoming a popular game in the USA.

[2 marks]

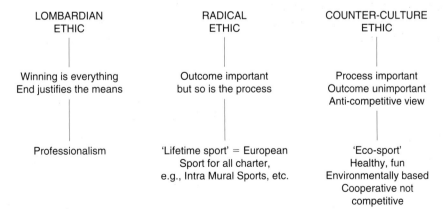

LOMBARDIAN ETHIC	RADICAL ETHIC	COUNTER-CULTURE ETHIC
Winning is everything End justifies the means	Outcome important but so is the process	Process important Outcome unimportant Anti-competitive view
Professionalism	'Lifetime sport' = European Sport for all charter, e.g., Intra Mural Sports, etc.	'Eco-sport' Healthy, fun Environmentally based Cooperative not competitive

Fig 6.4 Concepts of American sport

School sport and physical education

The American system houses a private and a public sector, with the former being self-financing and often associated with church groups. A decentralised system operates, which means each state is in charge of its own education, administration and jurisdiction. This has the advantage of being more likely to meet the needs of each state, as considerations of wealth and climate can be catered for. The state is responsible for providing a free education, teaching programmes, certification of teachers, building standards and financial support.

At 4–5 years children begin nursery (kindergarten), which aims to prepare them for their elementary education at the ages of 6–12 years. Advancement to each grade is based on achieving specialised skills in a number of subjects. The secondary schools allow considerable choice in the upper grades, as subjects are career-based. The final aim is to pass the high school diploma.

In one sense, the system is similar to the UK, where local authorities have some input. However, the teacher in the USA does not have the same amount of freedom as the British teacher in choosing a teaching programme, as the superintendent of the local school board draws up a programme that the teachers implement. Thus at local level the system is more centralised. To summarise:

- state level – decentralised;
- local level – more centralised by local school board.

Activity 4

What are the advantages and disadvantages of a local school board, with some teacher representatives creating the physical education programme?

Physical education is an essential and basic part of the total educational programme from kindergarten to age 12. Physical activities are valued for their ability to enhance the unique characteristics of students on a physical, mental, emotional and social level. Children are encouraged to develop motor skills, knowledge and attitudes necessary to help them function within their society. You may well

Table 6.2 The American education system

Ages	4–5	6–12	12–17	17–19	17–22
	Kindergarten	Elementary	High School	College	University
		Grades 1–6	*Junior Senior*	*Junior*	
		Grades 7–12	*Technical*		

Table 6.3 The English, Scottish and US systems of education

Age	England & Wales	Scotland	USA
4–5	Reception	Reception	Kindergarten
5–6	Year 1	1	1st Grade
6–7	Year 2 (KS1)	2	2nd Grade
7–8	Year 3	3	3rd Grade
8–9	Year 4	4	4th Grade
9–10	Year 5	5	5th Grade
10–11	Year 6 (KS2)	6	6th Grade
11–12	Year 7	7	7 (Junior High)
12–13	Year 8	8	8th Grade
13–14	Year 9 (KS3)	9	9 (High School)
14–15	Year 10	10	10 (Sophomore)
15–16	Year 11 (KS4, GCSE)	Standard Grade	11 (Junior)
16–17	Lower 6th	Highers	12 (Senior)
17–18	Upper 6th (A-level)	(6th Year Studies)	(Junior College)

As many sites are US-based, there is frequent reference to school years as 'K to 12'. This translation is given in the table. Source: http://www.pearson.co.uk/education.

recognise some similarities to the British philosophy. Physical education is an integral part of most of the curriculum's content, and is seen as part of the whole sporting continuum.

In the secondary sector in the USA a fitness-testing approach takes over; teachers in the UK tend to take the child-centred approach for a greater length of time. Fitness testing tends to suit a culture that is based on objectivity, accountability, quantification and the determination to produce the best they can. The Physical Fitness Movement was influential in introducing fitness tests.

The physical education teacher in the USA is separate from the sports coach and generally has a lower status.

There are various organisations that have responsibility for sport in schools. The State Athletic Association coordinates and regulates inter-scholastic athletic competition; the National Federation of State High School Associations (NFSHSA) establishes uniform rules for competition and gives guidelines and advice.

Health, fitness and obesity levels

IN CONTEXT

In 2003 58 per cent of boys and 51 per cent of girls in high school played on a sports team. The most popular sports for boys are American football, basketball, track and field, baseball and soccer (international football). For girls, the most popular are basketball, track and field, volleyball, softball and soccer. As a result of a US law that encourages women to take part in athletics, girls' participation in high-school athletics has increased by 800 per cent over the past 30 years. Other organised high-school sports often include gymnastics, wrestling, swimming, tennis and golf. Away from school, teenagers participate year-round in community-sponsored sports leagues. In addition, particularly in the summer, they engage in informal 'pick-up' games of one sport or another in the streets and parks of their neighbourhoods.

Physical education is a planned instructional programme with specific objectives. An essential part of the total curriculum, physical education programmes increase the physical competence, health-related fitness, self-responsibility and enjoyment of physical activity for all students, so that they can establish physical activity as a natural part of everyday life.

This is the traditional philosophy. What is the reality of the situation as reported in the latest 'Shape of the Nation Report' – a report that is conducted every five years?

SHAPE OF THE NATION REPORT

Most States Receive a Failing Grade on Physical Education Requirements

May 2006 – Despite skyrocketing childhood obesity rates and calls from Congress, the Surgeon General and Centers for Disease Control and Prevention for high quality daily physical education programmes, most states receive a **failing grade** on their physical education requirements. Those are the findings of the latest *Shape of the Nation Report: Status of Physical Education in the USA*, released by the National Association for Sport and Physical Education (NASPE) and the American Heart Association (AHA). 'This report shows that state physical education requirements are extremely weak. Furthermore, a vast array of "loopholes" such as exemptions, waivers and on-line physical education classes too often eradicate those minimal standards at the local level at a time when more and more children are obese or at risk of obesity.'

'Unbeknownst to many policymakers, the federal No Child Left Behind Act (NCLB) of 2001 is threatening the amount of time available for physical education,' said NASPE Executive Director. 'NCLB focuses on student achievement in defined core academic subjects. As states develop or select standardised tests to hold schools and students accountable, **content that is not tested, such as physical education, has become a lower priority**.'

According to the American Heart Association, 'Children are more overweight than ever before and they're at great risk of developing cardiovascular disease as they reach adulthood. Now is not the time for schools to cut physical education, and deprive children of the chance to adopt healthy lifestyles. We must **mandate** that quality physical education be required at all grade levels and that it be taught by qualified teachers.'

Since the last *Shape of the Nation Report* in 2001, there has been a continued increase in childhood and adult overweight and obesity. Currently 17 per cent (over nine million) of children and teens age 6 to 19 years are overweight and an additional 31 per cent are at risk for overweight. Even though a majority of states mandates physical education, most do not require a specific amount of instructional time and about half allow exemptions, waivers, and/or substitutions. These 'loopholes' significantly reduce the effectiveness of the mandate.

Another general pattern with differential impact on physical education is **local control** of education. Some states establish standards or very broad guidelines for curriculum content and defer specific decisions regarding time, class size and student assessment to local school districts or even schools. This results in very diverse patterns of delivery for physical education within states.

Highlights

- Forty-seven states and the District of Columbia have their own state standards for physical education.
- Approximately 30 per cent of states do not mandate physical education for elementary and middle school students.
- Almost one-quarter of states (24 per cent or 12) allow required physical education credits to be earned through online physical education courses.

- 43 per cent of states (22) require physical education grades to be included in a student's grade point average (GPA).
- 16 states have a required comprehensive assessment test for graduation, but none includes physical education.
- 36 states have an educational report card that rates specific subject areas individually, but only three of those states (California, Hawaii, Kentucky) include physical education on their state report card.
- Currently only three states – Arkansas, California and Illinois – require schools to measure body mass index (BMI) for each student.

Recommendations for action

NASPE and AHA want to remind America that 'Physically active, healthy kids learn better!' School age youth need at least 60 minutes of moderate to vigorous physical activity every day. To achieve that level of activity, NASPE and AHA recommend that schools across the country make physical education instruction the cornerstone of a comprehensive school physical activity programme that also includes health education, elementary school recess, after-school physical activity clubs and intramurals, high school interscholastic athletics, walk/bike to school programmes, and staff wellness programmes. It is particularly important that voluntary programmes (i.e., after-school physical activity clubs, intramurals) are designed to attract all students, especially those not interested in traditional athletic programmes.

Activity 5

What are the similarities and differences between the United Kingdom and the United States of America in their approach towards physical education and school sport?

Equality

Title IX

Women in the USA have historically experienced similar gender inequality as their British counterparts. Sport evolved along the male and masculinity concepts of competition, achievement, aggression and dominance, which led to poorer opportunities for women and resulted in lower participation rates. Their positive female sporting images have tended to be similar to other Western cultures: activities that require grace and have little physical contact and so a lower level of aggression, and activities in the supporting or cheerleading role, which has its own high status, based on a glamorous, entertainment approach to women in the sporting arena.

The female participation rate did not change radically until the 1970s, when a sudden rise in female participation in sports occurred and was visible at all levels from the youth sports to intercollegiate to amateur and professional. This can be attributed to several factors:

- the women's movement
- federal legislation
- the fitness movement
- an increased public awareness of women athletes helped by increased media coverage of female sport.

Federal legislation in the guise of Title IX, the Education Amendment of 1972, was one of the most influential factors, as it made compulsory the equal treatment of men and women in education programmes that were in receipt of federal funding. It was enacted in 1972 by the Department of Health Education and Welfare and released in 1975. Women could take a case as far as the Supreme Court, and, since then, numerous cases and judgments have been made. It stated that no discrimination should occur in the programmes offered, the quality of teaching and the availability of facilities, medical services, travel allowances and so on. All efforts should be made to teach co-educationally, though for heavy contact sports separation could occur. The equality should be proportional to the number of men and women participating.

Colleges and universities are required to disclose funding and participation rates broken down by gender.

Title IX has had a marked impact on overall academic educational achievement in the United States. It has also levelled the playing fields of America's schools. Title IX bans unfair treatment based on sex in any programme of a school receiving money from the federal government. Schools and universities lose government aid if their sports programmes do not treat men and women equally.

Title IX has helped girls and women participate in interscholastic and intercollegiate athletics in far greater numbers than they had in the past. Just one year before the enactment of Title IX, in 1971, a Connecticut judge was allowed by law to disallow girls from competing on a boys' high-school cross country team, even though there was no girls' team at the school. And that same year fewer than 300,000 high-school girls played interscholastic sports. Today, that number is 2.4 million. Today in the USA over one-third of all female students in high school play sports, and the number of women participating in university sports has tripled. Women now compete in almost every sport, whether the competition is team, individual or mixed gender.

Activity 6

- If there is a scholarship fund of $200,000 with 70 men and 30 women athletes, how much would the male and female athletes be entitled to?
- What problems do you think Title IX has caused within the educational institutions? Refer to teaching staff, students and administrative details.
- What are the arguments for and against the UK adopting a similar policy to Title IX?

Girls and women also are increasingly participants in sports that have traditionally been seen as out of bounds for women, including soccer, ice hockey, lacrosse, wrestling and rugby. In one sport that is more and more a favourite for young girls – soccer – the results led to a World Cup championship in 1999 and Olympic medals. Players like Mia Hamm and Brandi Chastain have helped make the sport more popular.

Since 1990 hundreds of lawsuits and Civil Rights complaints have been filed under Title IX and State Equal Rights Amendments charging gender discrimination in sports in high school and college. Most of these have been resolved in favour of women, resulting in women's teams being reinstated when they were due to be cut, women's club sports being upgraded to varsity status and women coaches receiving equal pay.

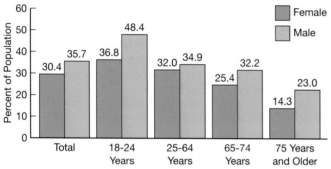

* Recommended physical activity is defined as moderate activity 5 times a week for 30 minutes or vigorous activity 3 times a week for 20 minutes

Fig 6.5 Adults aged 18 and older who engaged in recommended amounts of physical activity by age and sex, 2000

IN CONTEXT

Among many other things, the 2006 data show the highest ever participation by women in the US intercollegiate athletics programmes. On the other hand, the data also continue to show a depressed representation of women as head coaches and as head administrators of their programmes. Indeed, 2006 represents the lowest ever ratio of female coaches for women's teams.

Title IX and the growth of youth and college soccer

The growth of women's soccer was dramatic at both the youth, high school and college levels. By 1980, the growth in youth soccer was already dramatic, with almost 900,000 youth participating. By the year 2000 nearly 2.7 million participated with female participation growing steadily; by now over half of youth participation was female.

At the high school level, participant growth was no less dramatic. In 1976, barely 10,000 girls played in high school, less than 10 per cent of the total. By 2000, nearly 270,000 girls played high school soccer, almost 42 per cent of total high school participants.

The change was no less dramatic at the college level. Although participation numbers are not readily available, a good estimate can be gleaned from the number of NCAA institutions sponsoring soccer. In 1981, men's soccer was already well established, with 521 varsity teams, compared to 77 for women. By 1999, there were MORE women's varsity programmes in the NCAA than men's, 790 to 719. Women, who could only count on 1 per cent of the NCAA institutions to provide them a soccer opportunity, now had a choice from 77 per cent of the colleges, while men remained steady at 70 per cent. This growth was equally dramatic at all divisions, not just at the smaller colleges, and this was an important factor in the attempts to grow the women's game beyond the professional level.

A number of factors made this possible in addition to the growth in women's participation. The number of NCAA colleges had grown dramatically from 750 to over 1,000 during this time. Also, the impact of Title IX, which required not only equal expenditures among all men's and women's sports, also required equal participation. This had a negative impact on men's varsity programmes because so much of men's sport participation and expenditure was gobbled up by varsity football that often men's teams had to be dropped to keep things in balance. Even at that, many NCAA programmes were not in full compliance with Title IX even by 2000, although they were making enormous effort and progress.

Disability sport
Adaptive sporting programmes

According to the 2000 US Census, there are 49.7 million Americans over the age of 4 with a disability. That represents 19 per cent of the population. Among that 19 per cent, 14.3 million Americans have a mental disability and 2.2 million say they use a wheelchair. Depending on community offerings and the ability of each athlete, sports as diverse as hockey, horseback riding, rock climbing, scuba diving, cycling, water skiing, rugby, soccer, basketball and many, many others are available to disabled athletes.

Three pieces of federal legislation have opened doors in all aspects of life for people with disabilities in the United States.

1   The Rehabilitation Act, adopted in 1973, was the first major initiative in this regard. The main purpose of the Act was to prevent discrimination in employment, transportation and education programmes that received federal funding. Sports programmes were not the focus of the Act, but the law says that colleges and universities that receive federal funding for their physical education programmes, including intramural and interscholastic sports, must make them accessible to disabled persons.

2   The Individuals with Disabilities Education Act (IDEA) governs the education of students with disabilities in the public schools. The most recent pieces of federal

legislation aimed at ending discrimination against persons with disabilities were enacted in 1990. IDEA states that physical education is a required educational service; thus the law facilitates participation of students with disabilities in public school and interscholastic sports programmes.

3 The Americans with Disabilities Act (ADA) is a comprehensive law that bans discrimination against persons with disabilities, specifically in 'places of exercise'. The ADA goes further than the previous laws and says that school, university and community sports programmes must all comply with ADA provisions.

Adapted physical education is an umbrella term used to encompass areas such as dance, sport, fitness and rehabilitation for individuals with impairment across the lifespan. It has evolved from two major areas – the medical and educational perspectives – and was integrated in the 1950s. It recognised that teaching styles, facilities and equipment should be adapted to meet the individual needs of both regular and special students. The USA has again led the way in terms of legislation – federal legislation in 1975 required that there should be more inclusion in regular classes; in other words the mainstreaming of children with special educational needs – a movement from a medical to educational emphasis, with specialist training for teachers to help them deal more effectively with these children, and consultant monitoring. The Joseph F. Kennedy Jr Foundation has been active in this area. The Sport for All and the Paralympics movements continue to exert pressure for change, in the way that people view disability and the possibilities for physical education and sport programmes.

Outdoor education and recreation

Key terms

The main key terms for outdoor education are:
1 education/learning
2 outdoor
3 environment/nature/wilderness
4 adventure.

The importance attached to the 'great outdoors' in American society is evident in its literature and films. The links go back to the days of the pioneers and their efforts to overcome numerous obstacles in their attempts to push back the geographical frontiers. The scale and size of the country, with its varied land relief and climates, make for rich and exciting experiences. The character-building qualities that emerge from such experiences are still considered as important to America's future.

The National Parks are administered by the Bureau of Outdoor Education, which has developed a coherent structured approach. The land is classified according to its level of isolation; Class I would be close to towns and would be widely used, while Class V would be classed as wilderness

areas where it is possible to wander undisturbed for days. There is nothing comparable to this latter section in Britain.

There has been an increase in the participation of high-risk sports in the USA since the 1970s. These sports can be classed as a counter-culture, because they oppose the social values of competition and chance, favouring stimulation and vertigo. The rise in popularity of such sports can be attributed to several factors.

- Wide variety of topography/climate
- Moderate density of population
- Large country (comparable to Europe)
- Part of school curriculum
- Outward-bound traditions of pioneer/frontier spirit
- National Parks classification areas: 'Wilderness areas'
- Federal control/safety measures
- Variety of camp schools

Concerns over safety have led to action to regulate these sports in the form of the Federal Aviation Administration, and the National Park Service of the Department of the Interior, which controls rock climbing and mountaineering. However, is not this sort of regulation exactly what people may be trying to get away from?

Wilderness areas

Class I Areas intensively developed near towns and designed for intensive use

Class II Areas with substantial development for a variety of recreational use

Class III Areas that are suitable for recreational use in the natural environment but within easy reach of habitation

Class IV Areas of outstanding scenic beauty some distance from civilisation

Class V Undisturbed roadless areas/natural wild conditions – 'wilderness'

Class VI Historic and cultural sites

Key term

Frontier The limit of knowledge of a particular field. Sport is often called 'the last frontier', as we still do not know the limitations of human achievement in sport. It is an emotive term for Americans, as it also links to the history of the settlement of their country as each frontier was moved from east to west. Qualities required to push back any frontier, be it geographical or of a sporting nature, are bravery, courage, strength and determination.

Outdoor education camps

The camping movement did not gain acceptance until 1900. The first 100 camps were initiated by teachers and were supplemented by the YMCA, the Boy and Girl Scouts,

Campfire Girls and so on. The American Camping Association was formed, and camping programmes gradually gained educational acceptance and helped to raise the status of welfare and general camps.

There are several thousand summer camps for children throughout the USA and Canada, mostly permanent camps where children can reside for 1–8 weeks. The camps take children from between the ages of 6 and 16 years, and are responsible for their welfare twenty-four hours a day. 'Going to camp' for an extended period of time is a well-established tradition in the USA. There has been a tradition of sending urban children to the natural environment, and, in a country where the summer holidays last three months, it is accepted that children spend time away from their parents.

There are different types of camps:

- **Private residential**. These are privately owned and cater for the high/middle-income families. They run on a profit-making basis, providing permanent residential facilities, and operate all over the country. They have a range of facilities for various sports and crafts.
- **Day camps**. These can also be privately owned or run by organisations such as the YMCA or local towns.
- **Organisational camps**. These are run by Christian-based organisations like the Girl and Boy Scouts and the YMCA, though the emphasis on religion can vary.
- **Camps for underprivileged children**. These are operated by various social, philanthropic or religious agencies like the Salvation Army, and aim to give inner-city children a break from the urban environment. They are very heavily subsidised, with families paying little or nothing at all towards the cost. The facilities are more basic, and the emphasis is on the recreational experience and appreciating the environment.
- **Special-needs camps**. These are for people with physical or mental disabilities (adults as well as children), diabetics, people who are overweight (often termed Fat Camps), or who have special learning or behavioural problems.

A typical day at camp

07.15	Reveille. Short optional dip or jog.
07.45	Flag raising and personal inspection.
08.00	Breakfast, followed by clean-up of the cabin or tent.
09.30	1st activity period.
10.30	2nd activity period.
11.45	Optional general swim.
12.30	Lunch.
13.30	Rest hour supervision.
14.30	1st afternoon activity period.
15.30	2nd afternoon activity period.
16.30	Free time supervision.
18.00	Dinner.
19.00	Flag lowering – followed by special evening events.
21.00	First bell – lights out for younger children.
22.00	Lights out for the seniors.

'While some routine is essential there is always something different planned to bring new experience into a busy, happy, healthy existence.'

Exam-style Questions

Identify two different types of summer camps in the USA. Describe the benefits that a child would gain as a result of attending a summer camp.

[4 marks]

Extra-curricular activities
Extra-mural activities

These generally refer to inter-school competitions, which again can be informal or highly organised and serious. The students go through a more selective process, the activities are widely reported by the press and considerable interest is taken by the local community.

Inter-scholastic sports as a pathway to professional sport

Schools belong to the State High School Athletic Associations, which in turn belong to the National Federation of State High School Associations. This organisation coordinates and regulates contests in sport, as well as other activities.

Inter-scholastic competition achieves its greatest emphasis in grades 10–2. Those who are carefully selected practise a few hours each day. Rivalry in the local school leagues is intense, and competitions from local, district and regional levels occur that culminate in the championship of the state. State tournaments exist, but the size of the country inhibits national school tournaments. (It is worth noting here that the size of each state is comparable to a European country.) Schools can be classified into divisions, depending on the size of enrolment. The coach is a member of the high-school faculty, and money comes from donations from local booster clubs and local taxes.

These programmes are an accepted and high-status part of the school and college system, and are thought to deliver positive educational goals. There are, however, critics who believe that their effects are more negative than positive. Table 6.4 offers both arguments.

Activity 7

How does extra-curricular sport differ in the USA and the UK?

Table 6.4 Comparison between physical education in the UK and USA

UK	USA
Traditionally decentralised	Decentralised at state level
National Curriculum = more centralised Key Stages 1–4	Centralised at local level (school board)
Primary heuristic/movement approach/non-specialist teacher	Primary/heuristic/movement approach/non-specialist and specialist teachers
Secondary/skills focus/qualified teacher	Secondary/skills/fitness testing/measuring qualified teacher
PE programme guided by National Curriculum but teacher choice included	Programme drawn up by local school board/less flexibility
PE compulsory Exams voluntary GCSE/A level	PE compulsory/low status compared to sport programme
Extra-curricular = voluntary/low status/poor school and club links/teacher responsibility based on goodwill	Extra-curricular = high profile/sports coaches/funding
Government initiatives 'Raising the Game' Sportsmark 'A Sporting Future for All 2000' Active Schools	Government involvement Title IX Adaptive PE

Mass participation

- Participation rates
- National fitness levels
- Amateur sports clubs (lack of tradition)
- Community participation (midnight leagues; other contemporary community initiatives).

Participation rates

According to the US Bureau of Labour Statistics in May 2008:

- Approximately 16 per cent of 15 year olds and older participated in sports and exercise in an average day. The rate for watching television was 5 times higher.
- People with higher levels of education – e.g. Bachelor's degree and higher – were more than twice as likely to participate than those with high-school diplomas.
- Of the relatively small group of people who participated in exercise on a daily basis, walking was the most popular activity with basketball the most popular team game.
- Football, basketball, golf and soccer were dominated by men; women participated more in yoga and aerobics; gender neutral activities tended to be bowling, swimming, surfing and water skiing.
- Team sports had a lower age bracket, walking the highest and activities such as racket sports had the most equal distribution.

National fitness levels

In 2003 President Bush highlighted his **HealthierUS** initiative designed to help Americans, especially children, live longer, better and healthier lives. The President's HealthierUS initiative helps Americans to take steps to improve personal health and fitness and encourages all Americans to follow some basic advice.

Be physically active every day. Many chronic diseases can be prevented with modest exercise, in some cases as simple as walking for half an hour. For example, if just 10 per cent of adults began walking regularly, America could save $5.6 billion in costs related to heart disease.

Eat a nutritious diet. Americans should make simple adjustments to their diet and avoid excessive portions. Increasing fruit and vegetable consumption is a central part of a healthier diet, and good overall nutrition lowers the risk of getting heart disease, stroke, cancer and osteoporosis.

Get preventive screenings. Americans may be surprised to learn how a simple test like a cholesterol screen or a blood-pressure check can reveal current health status and identify a need to adjust diet or behaviour.

Make healthy choices. Avoid tobacco and drugs as well as the abuse and underage use of alcohol and make smart and safe choices in your everyday life.

The President's 2004 budget requested $125 million for Steps to a HealthierUS. The President's Council on Physical Fitness and Sports has set the goal of attracting an additional twenty million Americans to physical fitness and exercise. Physical activity has been identified as one of the USA's leading health indicators in Healthy People 2010, the national health objectives for the decade.

Amateur sport clubs

We have already mentioned that the United States embraced the idea of professional sport and that the education system has provided for physical fitness and extra-curricular activities for young people. The system of grass-roots amateur sports clubs did not become the norm as it did in the UK. Those interested and skilful in sport were provided with the route of staying on in education via a sport scholarship and the high-quality facilities within the education system provided non-sport-related students with the opportunities to maintain their participation levels whilst at college/university. The problem for many Americans arises when they leave full-time education. Expensive and exclusive country clubs do not provide for the majority.

Senior programmes

At the other end of the age spectrum is the US National Senior Sports Classic VI, the Senior Olympics. The US National Senior Sports Organisation promotes the image of healthy old age, aiming to establish positive role models for health and physical fitness. The opening ceremonies usually attract 10,000 athletes.

Community participation

While serving as Town Manager of Glen Arden, Maryland, Mr G. Van Standifer studied police reports that showed decisively that most crime occurred during the hours of 10 p.m. and 2 a.m. and was committed by individuals from a narrow age group (17–25 years old). In response to the escalating crime rate in his town, he established **Midnight Basketball League** Inc. (MBL) in June 1986. He used basketball as the tool to attract the target audience, but participants then had to take part in the other MBL programme components to be able to play in league games. Thus the programme Mr Standifer founded provided an alternative late-night activity in addition to workshops and educational opportunities. From the beginning, the MBL programme was a success, embraced and supported by local businesses, law enforcement and political/community leaders.

MBL's success in Glen Arden generated national attention. Programmes sprang up throughout the United States and eventually spread to fifty cities nationwide throughout the 1990s and early 2000s.

The Pursuit of Excellence [OPE]
Children's organised sports programmes

If sporting activities carry socially desirable values, it is not surprising that a culture will try to develop such qualities in its young. An example of a well-organised sports programme for children is Little League Baseball, which was established in 1939 and is now a business organisation employing full-time professional employees and volunteers. It was initially set up by parents who wanted a well-structured sporting programme. The league caters for 8–18-year-olds and is the largest of its kind in the world attracting media coverage. A senior division for youngsters aged 13–15 and a big league for the 16–18-year-olds are also part of the programme.

Children are selected by competitive trials for their specified age range, and the winning of leagues and tournaments is highly valued. Following local and regional playoffs, an annual world series is held where foreign teams can also enter.

The league is based on adult leagues, with some modifications: the diamond is two-thirds the size and the games are limited to six innings. The season lasts fifteen games, with no more than two games a week being permitted.

A provision of the official national Little League rules holds that 'at no time should payment of any fee be a prerequisite for participation in any level of the Little League program'. This stipulation stems from the founder's own personal experience of poverty in the Great Depression.

Divisions

Little League affiliated programmes are divided into six divisions based on the ages of the children playing: Tee Ball (ages 5–8), Minors (7–12), Little (or Majors) (9–12), Junior (13–14), Senior (14–16 baseball, 13–16 softball) and Big (16–18 baseball, 14–18 softball). Little League welcomes both boys and girls between the ages of 5 and 18.

Another division of Little League is the 'Challenger Division', which is designed for children with disabilities. One of the aims of Little League, other than simply to have fun, is to teach children about teamwork, sportsmanship and fair play. Their watchwords are Character, Courage, Loyalty. Little League has developed many equipment changes over the years to protect young ball players, including the introduction of the full batting helmet and the use of the throat guard for catchers. In recent years, Little League has developed rules to assist young ball players. Little League baseball has instituted a pitch count to protect young pitchers' arms.

Fig 6.6 Little League Baseball

Activity 8

What are the characteristics of adult-organised children's sports programmes, and what problems can be associated with them?

Inter-collegiate sport

Sports also play an important role in the everyday social scene at American colleges and universities. University sports programmes are offered at the inter-collegiate (organised competition) and the intra-mural (club-like, less competitive) levels. Many universities offer sports scholarships at the inter-collegiate level to students who are both academically qualified and skilled in a particular sport. Athletic scholarships are awarded for everything from archery to wrestling, with an eye on gender equality to achieve a balance between men's and women's scholarships.

Playing for a college team on a scholarship is one way students help pay for the cost of earning an undergraduate degree. About $1 billion in athletic scholarships are awarded through the National Collegiate Athletic Association (NCAA) each year. Over 126,000 student-athletes receive either a partial or a full athletic scholarship. These scholarships are awarded and administered directly by each academic institution, not the NCAA. Award amounts vary from a few thousand dollars to nearly $30,000 for one academic year and do not necessarily cover the full cost of tuition and living expenses. Scholarships are offered on a percentage basis, and universities have strict limits on the total amount they can award each year.

America based its colleges and sporting activities on the nineteenth-century English universities and public schools. Harvard and Yale reflected the developing traditions of their British counterparts, Oxford and Cambridge. Professionalism hit inter-collegiate sport very soon and possessed the following characteristics:

- competition was for non-cash prizes or for money prizes
- competition was against professionals
- money was charged at the gates
- the costs of a training table (food costs) were not borne by the athlete
- athletes were recruited and paid, and professional coaches employed.

American students soon abandoned the British ideal of amateurism. There was a feeling that the college students were being distracted from the primary aims of a college education, and the management of college athletics was becoming too large for the students to handle. By 1900 nearly every college had an athletic committee, with control of athletics shared between the students and alumni, or the sole prerogative of the institution. Then, with further development and expansion, inter-college regulation was needed. The National Collegiate Association was established in 1906 to control and create order in collegiate athletics; the NAIA in 1952; and the Association of Intercollegiate Athletics for Women in 1972.

Table 6.5 Principle of play, adult sporting programmes and Little League

Pure characteristics of play	Adult-organised sports programmes	Description of Little League
Spontaneous	Organised	Established in 1930s
Creative	Serious	Business oganisation
Developmental	Institutionalised	Full-time professionals and volunteers involved
Experimental	Rationalised	World's largest sports league for children
Enjoyable	Socialisation	Television coverage
Use initiative	Bureaucracy	Specified age groups
Rule-making and enforcing	Competitive	Highly competitive
Develop moral judgements	Success valued highly	High degree of commitment required

Inter-collegiate athletics is based on two foundations:

1 the NCAA Division III for small institutions, where sport and physical education are an integral part of students' lives.
2 Division I, where sport is run as an entertainment business and a training ground for professional and high-level amateur sport, namely the Olympic Games.

Division II is a transition ground between the two. The lack of an effective club structure in the USA has made this an inevitable route for athletes wishing to pursue a career in sport.

Activity 9

What is the benefit of a system which develops such interest in college sport? Consider the value placed on the British colleges sport scene.

Amateurs?

All North American university sports are conducted by amateurs. Even the most commercialised college sports, such as NCAA football and basketball, do not compensate competitors financially, although coaches and trainers are often the highest-paid state employees, drawing salaries of over $1 million annually. Athletic scholarship programmes, unlike academic scholarship programmes, cannot cover more than the cost of food, housing, tuition and other university-related expenses. A school can pay an athlete to attend classes. However, a school cannot pay an athlete to play.

In order to ensure that the rules are not circumvented, stringent rules restrict gift giving during the recruitment process as well as during and even after a collegiate athlete's career; moreover, college athletes cannot endorse products. Some have criticised this system as exploitative; prominent university athletics programmes are major commercial endeavours, and can easily rake in millions of dollars in profit during a successful season. College athletes spend a great deal of time 'working' for the university, and earn nothing from it at the time; basketball and football coaches, meanwhile, earn salaries that can compare with those of professional teams' coaches.

Supporters of the system say that college athletes can always make use of the education they earn as students if their athletic career does not pan out, and that allowing universities to pay college athletes would rapidly lead to deterioration of the already marginal academic focus of college athletics programmes. They also point out that athletic scholarships allow many young men and women who would otherwise be unable to afford to go to college, or would not be accepted, to get a quality education.

IN CONTEXT

A breeding ground for some of the most prolific sportsmen and women, American Collegiate Sport is renowned for its standard and quality throughout the world.

Participating athletes enjoy an amateur status. However, with scholarship budgets exceeding $1 billion, television companies playing over $5 billion for rights to broadcast events and some sports attracting more than 80,000 regular supporters, it is as close to professional as you can get.

In an era where multimedia and public relations have a prominent role in the marketing process, the success of a institution's sports programmes provides the ideal platform and an integral role in the recruitment of new students to the respective universities or colleges.

The US scholarship system allows individuals to combine their educational needs with the opportunity to pursue their sporting ambitions on a full-time basis. Upon the completion of their four years of study they will leave with an excellent degree and an experience that will offer them the ideal platform to realise career goals.

There are over 2,500 universities and colleges throughout the United States, with over 1,000 of these institutions offering funded sporting scholarships. Three athletics associations govern these sports.

Table 6.6 The advantages and disadvantages of inter-scholastic sport

Advantages	Disadvantages
Encourages pride and loyalty to school	Too much emphasis on competition and winning
Improves fitness levels	Most students are spectators, while players are often seriously injured during play
Develops teamwork skills, valuable for later life	
Strengthens links between school and community	Takes too many resources away from other educational programmes
Encourages students to become involved in school activities	Can assume too much importance; academic studies can suffer
	Encourages outdated 'macho' ideals

Olympic reserve

The Olympic reserve in the United States is drawn from the education sector via scholarships and collegiate sport programmes. The college tradition acts as a nursery for professional and Olympic performers.

'Big time' programmes

Generally it would be the responsibility of the principal to ensure that educational objectives are adhered to and that winning does not become overstated. The problems become more obvious at the inter-collegiate 'big-time' programmes, where incentives can distract athletes from academic work and are characterised by commercialism, poor rights of athletes and distorted views of gender and race; in such instances these are more negatives in their outcomes. Criticisms have been made about the lip service paid by some athletes and college administrators to the academic courses being undertaken by the high-level college athlete. A difference needs to be made between the 'big-time' collegiate sports and the lower-profile levels, which do not have scholarships and do not have the entertainment label tagged on; research has shown that academic studies do not suffer at this level.

Coaching

Sports coaching emerged as a specialised profession in the 1870s and coincided with the growth of competitive sport. Similarly to Britain at the same time, the elite institutions had a vested interest in achieving team records and individual achievements. A split occurred between sports coaching and physical education. The former concentrated on competitive success and rewards, an approach that culminated in an intense pressure to win, particularly at inter-collegiate and professional levels. The latter, on the other hand, stressed health, enjoyment and personal development as its major goals.

The role of the coach will often determine the type of behaviour that will most successfully achieve the desired outcome. Coaches are generally assertive, tough and focused on high achievement. As athletes progress up the sporting ladder, from high school to the youth leagues, to inter-collegiate and professional ranks, these aspects of a coach's behaviour would be expected to increase. As coaches are held accountable for the results and the results are scrutinised and publicly reported, they have a lot of pressure to succeed. This can lead to 'role strain' and ultimately to role conflict (Coakley, 1993). The coach has to interact with many different people, each with different expectations, and can find it difficult to meet everyone's needs. In America, young coaches need a mentor, and they usually rely on the sponsorship of established coaches. This has tended to reinforce the perpetuation of values and can exclude women and ethnic groups.

> ### Key term
>
> **The National Collegiate Athletic Association (NCAA)**
> The National Collegiate Athletic Association is a voluntary association of about 1,200 colleges and universities, athletic conferences and sports organisations which administers inter-collegiate athletics.

Equality and discrimination

How have equality and discrimination affected sport participation? A 'race logic' was developed by the early colonialists in America, the WASPs, that black people were physically superior but mentally inferior to white people. Historically, the sports associated with black people during the slavery era were boxing and horse racing.

- In boxing, the white owners would train up a black boxer, and use the fight as a way of entertainment and opportunity for wagering. The boxer would have gained considerably less from the situation, and parallels can be drawn to the gladiatorial concept.
- In horse racing, white owners were involved in the training and planning but the jockeys were usually black, fulfilling a role that required a more mechanical and physical input.

These racial prejudices have been difficult to overthrow, and are still common within the social institution of sport. The tennis player Arthur Ashe was not allowed to play in certain parts of America, as tennis was at that time still a white, middle-class sport. A similar situation was highlighted in 1997 with the emergence in the golfing arena of Tiger Woods, who has also experienced prejudice and discrimination.

Stacking

Racial stacking in sports teams is a well-reported issue, where players from a certain racial group are either over- or under-represented in certain positions in a sports team. Traditionally black players have not occupied positions that require decision making but have been placed in positions that rely on the physical attributes of speed, reflexes and strength. In football there have been few black quarterbacks, though in recent times, when the role of quarterback has become more physical, there has been a corresponding increase in black quarterbacks. It does not necessarily mean that there has been an improvement in equal opportunities within the sport.

In baseball, black people have tended to occupy the outfield positions, despite the fact that there used to be a highly successful black baseball league, in which black players would have fulfilled all the roles themselves! It was only when the white owners moved in that their status within the game began to change. There is a parallel with cricket in the nineteenth century, when the lower classes would occupy more physical positions, leaving the central positions that required thinking, strategy and closer social interaction to the upper classes. This is also closely tied to Grusky's theory of **centrality**. A vicious circle is created and these beliefs perpetuated, as few black people become coaches or sports administrators.

The lower sport participation rates and ethnic sport preferences have also been determined by these ideological factors. The dominant group determines the access and opportunities available, and it is not easy for minority groups to challenge those social determinants, despite the exception who manages to create the American dream. They can become role models for their ethnic groups, but this can reinforce the stereotypes that only a particular type of sport is suitable for black people, and that sport rather than education is the most suitable avenue for social mobility.

Affirmative action generally means that specific steps are taken to help redress the inequalities that have arisen over the centuries. It is always controversial and often used in relation to employment practices, but 'tokenism' can prevail whereby nondiscrimination can be claimed but may not necessarily be genuine. In the case of sport, places in the professional leagues would be available on a limited basis to African-Americans (see the case of baseball).

Key term

Tokenism Actions that are the result of pretending to give advantage to those groups in society who are often treated unfairly, in order to give the appearance of fairness.

Activity 10

- How has 'stacking' influenced the opportunities of ethnic baseball players in the United States of America?
- Explain why black Americans have achieved such success in the game of basketball.

Sport and entertainment

There are four major popular sports in the USA – American football, baseball, basketball and ice hockey. Sport in this instance has become a business, and athletes are marketed as assets who are well known and who can help generate funds and advertise products with their skill, showmanship and positive health images. The sports are packaged and presented to the public, and sports tend to be loud, brash and energetic and involve huge productions – a show rather than a game, display rather than play?

The concept of '**sport space**' has emerged whereby opportunities for other sports may have been limited by the domination of the 'big four' in American culture. As the dominant sports, the big four share the following characteristics:

- all team sports
- high scoring/excitement/no draws
- high media/spectator interest
- professional sport
- family entertainment
- heavily marketed as businesses
- excellent social and sporting facilities
- racial identities (e.g. basketball = African-American, ice hockey = white)
- social class identities (e.g. American football = middle class, baseball = working class)
- well-developed children's leagues
- professional players coming through the collegiate system
- they reflect capitalism/the American Dream
- the win ethic.

Exam-style Questions

1 Why is compulsory Physical Education being withdrawn from many USA High Schools?

[2 marks]

2 Explain why opportunities for mass participation in sport in the USA are limited.

[2 marks]

Exam-style Questions

The culture of the USA influences professional sport, and this influence extends to young children who engage in community sport.

1 Identify one community recreation sports initiative involving children in the USA and describe the benefits that can be gained by the child who participates in community sports initiatives.

[4 marks]

CHALLENGE YOURSELF

Explain how the nature of professional sports in the USA might deter people from taking part in sport.

[4 marks]

Explain how cultural factors have influenced the development of professional sport in America.

[5 marks]

Explain how professional sport was conducive to the culture of the USA and explain how this concept of sport might deter people from taking part.

[20 marks]

What you need to know

* There is a decentralised system – each state operates its own administration.
* There are exclusive, private clubs, which are different from British sports clubs.
* Careers in sport tend to take the route of collegiate sport as a feeder for the professional leagues as well as maintaining amateur eligibility.
* Inter-scholastic and collegiate sport is run on business and commercial lines, with control exerted by cartels.
* There is still discrimination in sport for female and black athletes, though legislation has laid the foundations for change.
* The dominant sports reflect the capitalist culture from which they evolved.
* The government tries not to become too involved in sport, but has produced much legislation in particular areas. Where business interests occur, the government tends to favour the sports bodies that will bring revenue and civic prestige.
* Children's sports programmes stress the dominant sporting values of adults, and there is a tendency for an over-emphasis on winning.

Review Questions

1 What does the term federal mean?
2 What was the fate of the Native American Indians following the spread of white culture?
3 What are the three concepts of American sport? Briefly outline what is meant by each.
4 Why does the physical education teacher in the USA not have the same amount of freedom in designing a curriculum as his or her British counterpart?
5 Why does fitness testing suit the American culture?
6 What is Title IX and what have been its effects in the American sport system?
7 What is meant by the term adaptive physical education?
8 What are the advantages and disadvantages of inter-scholastic sport in the American education system?
9 What are the common characteristics of the dominant American sports of football, basketball, ice hockey and baseball?
10 What is the difference between the roles of the sports coach and of a physical education teacher in America?
11 What does 'stacking' mean and how can this be reflected in a sporting situation?
12 How does Little League reflect the culture of the United States?
13 What are wilderness areas and what type of recreational pursuits can be undertaken there?
14 What are the different types of summer camps in the United States of America?
15 How do capitalism and professional sport complement each other?

CHAPTER 7

Australia

Learning outcomes

By the end of this chapter you should be able to:

- understand the cultural context of Australia, including geographical, political and economic values
- understand how Australia's colonial past has affected Aboriginal culture and sports
- define terms such as 'the Land of Fair-Go' and 'bush culture'
- describe the growth of multiculturalism
- understand the relationship between state and federal government
- describe initiatives such as exemplary schools, fundamental skills programme, state award schemes, cluster schools and teacher games
- understand ACPHER and the Australian Sports Commission (ASC)
- define PASE and SEPEP
- describe More Active Australia
- understand the Institutes of Sport, especially the Australian Institute of Sport (AIS) and the Victorian Institute of Sport (VIS).

CHAPTER INTRODUCTION

This chapter explores the role of sport in Australia and Oceania. The term 'Oceania' usually refers to the Pacific Basin, Melanesia, Polynesia and Australia. The peoples within this region and their cultures are as varied as the land they inhabit.

In Australia the Aboriginal societies were to suffer a deliberate attempt to decimate their traditions, but today Australian government apologies and policies are statements of intent to try to right the wrongs of the past.

After gaining independence in 1901, Australia has become a confident, modern nation with its own unique outlook, while maintaining its relationship with its colonial past. This past is evident in the education, legal and sporting traditions, being very similar to the United Kingdom.

EXAMINER'S TIPS

Remember to compare the information in this chapter with that provided in earlier chapters on the UK and the USA.

Activity 1

Consider the impact of the factors in Figure 7.1 on the system of sport in Australia.

Historical determinants

Australian culture is as broad and varied as the country's landscape. Australia is multicultural and multiracial, and this is reflected in the country's lifestyle and cultural practices, including recreational and sporting experiences.

Australia has an important heritage from its indigenous (Aboriginal) peoples, which plays a defining role in the cultural landscape.

Cultural heritage is seen as 'the total ways of living built up by a group of human beings, which is passed from one generation to the next', given to them by reason of their birth.

In Australia, indigenous communities keep their cultural heritage alive by passing their knowledge, arts, rituals and performances from one generation to another, speaking and teaching languages and protecting cultural materials, sacred and significant sites and objects.

Since the late 1700s, the settling of Australia by colonists, initially from England, has inevitably left its cultural legacy, none more so than in sport. This has led to the term

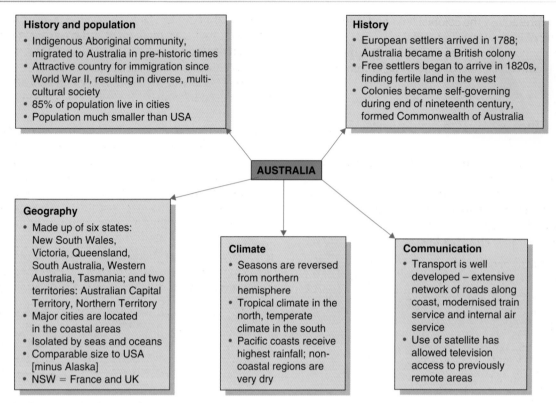

History and population
- Indigenous Aboriginal community, migrated to Australia in pre-historic times
- Attractive country for immigration since World War II, resulting in diverse, multi-cultural society
- 85% of population live in cities
- Population much smaller than USA

History
- European settlers arrived in 1788; Australia became a British colony
- Free settlers began to arrive in 1820s, finding fertile land in the west
- Colonies became self-governing during end of nineteenth century, formed Commonwealth of Australia

AUSTRALIA

Geography
- Made up of six states: New South Wales, Victoria, Queensland, South Australia, Western Australia, Tasmania; and two territories: Australian Capital Territory, Northern Territory
- Major cities are located in the coastal areas
- Isolated by seas and oceans
- Comparable size to USA [minus Alaska]
- NSW = France and UK

Climate
- Seasons are reversed from northern hemisphere
- Tropical climate in the north, temperate climate in the south
- Pacific coasts receive highest rainfall; non-coastal regions are very dry

Communication
- Transport is well developed – extensive network of roads along coast, modernised train service and internal air service
- Use of satellite has allowed television access to previously remote areas

Fig 7.1 An overview of Australia

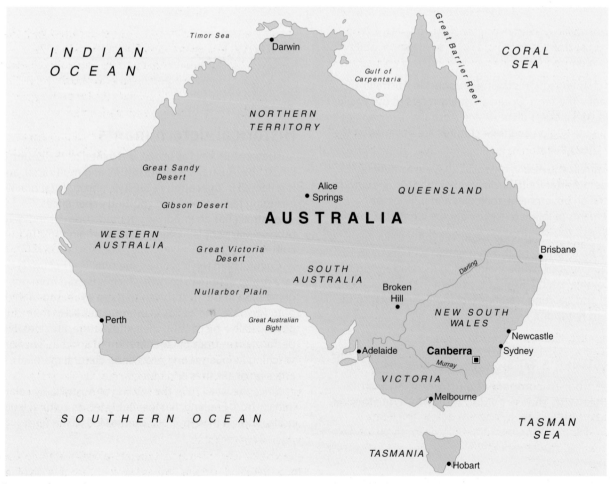

Fig 7.2 Map of Australia

'motherland' representing the colonial links and inevitable cultural sharing of ideas and values, politically and educationally. Independence was gained in 1901, but Australia still maintains its links as part of the Commonwealth.

The English influence is evident in the sporting traditions of the Australians, both in the type of games played – such as cricket and rugby – and in the attitudes of how to play the games, dress codes, etc. There is a strong middle-class influence on, and participation in, sport. The working-class element is not as traditional as in the UK.

- One of the first recorded cricket games was between two teams of HMS Calcutta in 1803, and today Australian cricket attracts thousands of spectators. Competition against England (the Ashes) incites nationalist fervour.
- Australian tennis players (e.g. Lleyton Hewitt, Rod Laver and Margaret Court) are renowned, and the Australian Davis Cup team has been successful on many occasions.
- Horse racing is an Australian passion (e.g. the Melbourne Cup).
- Swimming is popular, perhaps as a result of the favourable climate and extensive coastline.

Recent Australian government pronouncements for sport indicate an awareness of the improvements being made by the UK in high-performance sport and a determination to be successful against the 'old' country.

Geographical determinants

Australia is an island continent and the world's sixth largest country (7,682,300 square km). Lying between the Indian and Pacific oceans, Australia is approximately 4,000 km from east to west and 3,200 km from north to south, with a coastline 36,735 km long.

Canberra is Australia's capital city. With a population of approximately 320,000 and situated in the Australian Capital Territory, Canberra is roughly halfway between the two largest cities of Melbourne and Sydney.

As of July 2007, Australia's population was roughly twenty-one million people. The most populous states were New South Wales and Victoria, with their respective capitals, Sydney and Melbourne, the largest cities in Australia. The centre of Australia is sparsely populated.

The majority of Australia experiences temperate weather for most of the year. The northern states of Australia are typically warm all the time, with the southern states experiencing cool winters but rarely sub-zero temperatures. Snow falls on the higher mountains during the winter months, enabling skiing in southern New South Wales and Victorian ski resorts, as well as the smaller resorts in Australia's island state, Tasmania.

Australia is a member of the Commonwealth of Nations. The federal government is located in Canberra and conducts the national affairs. Similar to the United States, the Australian states have their own parliament and governor. It is a society based on democracy, with all citizens entitled to vote once they reach the age of 18.

Legislative authority is held by the Federal Parliament, and political power rests with the Prime Minister, who heads the government.

Australia has a multi-tiered system of government: a Commonwealth government, eight state and territory governments and a large number of local or municipal governments. Following a national vote in 1999, the Queen, through her representative, the Governor-General, is head of state. The political system follows the British Westminster system of bicameral parliamentary democracy.

Organisation of Australian sport

The Australian system evolved from a community-based club structure catering mainly for mass participation in sport:

- *advantage*: participation to individual's level of ability
- *disadvantage*: concentration on amateurism and volunteers (Australia even slower to accept professionalism in participation and sport management than the UK, from where it had inherited the amateur ethos)
- *result*: increased government involvement and funding in the 1980s recognised the need for a more professional approach.

A controversial but successful catalyst occurred with the attempts of media giant Kerry Packer, who in 1977 pioneered the commercialisation and professionalisation of cricket by establishing a professional World Series of Cricket.

Up to the 1980s the Australian focus for youth sport tended to be on developing elite performance:

- *disadvantage*: high drop-out rate of adolescents
- *result*: more programmes in the 1980s and 1990s to stimulate 'sport for all' policies.

Also up to the 1980s clubs and associations were uncoordinated and fragmented:

- *disadvantage*: catered for individual needs rather than promoting an integrated approach for federal funding.

Current organisation

Figure 7.3 represents the current state of the organisation of sport. From the top to the bottom one can see that the government gives elite and funding support in general. The Australian Institute of Sport (AIS) and the Australian Sports Commission (ASC) supply the national sporting organisations with funds and services. Similar state organisations fulfil a similar role at state level. Local government is mostly involved in supporting the regional and local sport organisations with services and facilities in which to participate.

Government involvement therefore occurs at three levels: local, state and national. We will look at the state involvement in sport in greater detail.

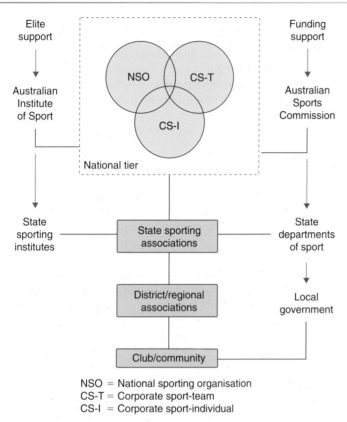

NSO = National sporting organisation
CS-T = Corporate sport-team
CS-I = Corporate sport-individual

Fig 7.3 The Australian sport system (*Source:* Westerbeck, 1995)

State departments of sport

- Government involvement in sport at state level began in the early 1970s.
- Each state or territory has its own government department with responsibility for sport and recreation (e.g. Sport and Recreation Victoria).
- Mass participation promoted, as well as State Academies housed.
- State Academies are centralised to some extent through the meeting of executive officers at the National Elite Sports Council (NESC).

IN CONTEXT

Since 2007 the Department of Health and Ageing has responsibility for information on the development of a stronger and internationally competitive Australian sports sector and encouragement of greater participation in sport by all Australians.

The Australian Government is committed to supporting sport, particularly at the community level, and increasing Australians' participation in physical and recreational activities to promote physical and mental health.

This commitment contributes to a competitive and clean Australian sports sector, based on excellence, integrity and leadership, and encourages greater participation in sport by all Australians.

The Australian Government aims to meet this commitment by establishing a best practice anti-doping framework and by developing the Australian sports system to support excellence in high performance and enhance grass-roots participation.

The major activities and key directions in 2008–9 are:

- work to improve rates of participation in sport and physical activity, including efforts to improve water and snow safety
- support of sport and recreation infrastructure and facilities
- support of national anti-doping efforts to ensure they continue to reflect the World Anti-Doping Program, the internationally accepted framework for anti-doping
- increase in the active participation of Indigenous Australians in sport and physical recreation activities
- support of sport agencies, the Australian Sports Commission and the Australian Sport Anti-Doping Authority, in improving Australia's sporting competitiveness and integrity.

Key term

Department of Health and Ageing Government department with responsibility for developing a stronger and internationally competitive Australian sports sector and encouragement of greater participation in sport by all Australians.

Key organisations

The Australian Sports Commission (ASC) is responsible for implementing the Australian Government's national sports policy, which is based on a sports philosophy of excellence and participation. It is the primary national sports administration and advisory agency, and the cornerstone of a wide-ranging sports system (Australian Sports Commission, 2004b).

The National Sporting Organisations (NSOs) are the pre-eminent organisations that take responsibility for the development of the sport in Australia and they are accountable at the national level for providing their members with technically and ethically sound sport programmes, policies and services (Australian Sports Commission, 2004a).

Sport and commercialisation

Sport and recreation are major components of the national economy, be it through employment in the sport and recreation industry (75,155 people in 2006), sales of goods and services both domestically and internationally or small business development.

Key term

Capitalism An economic system based on free trade with the focus on individual profit.

In 2004–5, the total income generated by the sport and recreation industry in Australia was estimated at $8.82 billion. The income reported by sports and physical recreation clubs, teams and sports professionals was $1.88 billion and by sports and physical recreation administrative organisations was $1.53 billion. Sport is also a powerful tool for international engagement.

Australia has developed an international reputation for sporting excellence, through national team performances, the staging of major international events including the 2004 Olympic and Paralympic Games, and the 2003 Rugby World Cup; the Federal Government is supportive of the Football Federation's bid to bring the World Cup to Australia in 2018.

Major international sporting events yield opportunities in tourism. Such activities attract people to Australia's rural and regional areas as well as major cities, generating income and employment for local economies. Further, it can be said that major events attract sizeable global television audiences, providing significant opportunities to promote Australia as a tourism destination.

Moral responsibilities and the problems resulting from the commercialisation of sport are lively issues that are now being debated in all Western countries.

Ruben Hernandez (2002) points out that 'idealistic principles are in a state of crisis; materialism and financial profit have gained the upper hand'. As new sporting structures emerge globally, National Sporting Organisations (NSOs) are forced to rethink their role in relation to business and profit-making interests in sport.

Corporate governance is now a major issue at government level. Inappropriate behaviour among leading business organisations has contributed to this. Conduct such as a lack of disclosure of information to shareholders and the transparency of financial reports has resulted in corporate law reform, particularly in the United Kingdom, America and Australia.

One of the ASC's goals within the 2002–5 Strategic Plan is to assist NSOs to adopt sound business and management practices. *A paper on National Sporting Organisations Governance: Principles of Best Practice* (Australian Sports Commission, 2002) identifies some important governance principles for boards such as transparency, accountability and responsibility to members.

Corporate sport

As more and more sports turned professional or semi-professional, new organisations were needed to cater for this section. They could only exist with corporate interest and support. There are five professional leagues:

- Australian Football League (AFL)
- New South Wales Rugby League (NSWRL)
- National Basketball League (NBL)
- National Soccer League (NSL)
- Australian Baseball League (NBL).

The NSOs still administer responsibility in relation to rules and international competition – as, for example, in basketball.

Private sport management companies (such as the IMG International Management Group) emerged to:

- secure sponsorships
- advise in marketing strategies
- manage sport teams/personalities
- negotiate television rights and endorsement contracts.

Their influence has grown, as is very evident in golf with the Australian Open, the Australian Masters and the Greg Norman Classic.

- *Advantage*: ensured ongoing professionalism.
- *Disadvantage*: blamed for focusing on commercial rather than sporting interests.

Sponsorship

The Australian Sports Commission has an elite corporate partnership programme that provides for category-exclusive corporate partners. These partners have opportunities to be involved with both the Australian Institute of Sport and the wider Australian Sports Commission.

The Australian Sports Commission helps its corporate partners maximise their partnership benefits by providing measurable outcomes and excellent leveraging opportunities. Australian Sports Commission corporate partnerships can take the form of financial contributions, value-in-kind goods or services, or a combination of both.

In 2007-08 the ASC's current major sponsors were Nestlé, Berlei and Gatorade.

The ASC's Official Suppliers have included:

- *sports programmes*: 2XU; Hart Sport; GKA Sports Distribution; Shimano Australia; Signature Mouthguards; Speedo; Sykes Racing
- *athlete career and education*: Energy Australia; Victoria University of Technology
- *science, medicine, education and training*: a range of companies.

Through visible and successful programming with national reach in both elite and community-based sports programmes, Australian Sports Commission initiatives can deliver the corporate sector significant commercial benefits.

Social determinants

Australia strives to be a pluralistic and inclusive society, though clearly this has not always been the case, especially with the indigenous peoples, but also because of the gender discrimination that has been the result of a very masculine-based culture.

Women

The role of women in Australia has often been subservient to that of men. As in the settlement of the United States of America, the qualities required for survival were synonymous with masculinity, and it was the male section of society that established itself in relation to power and decision making. Again, similarly to the USA and the UK, the female stereotype was born out of medical arguments used to restrict serious female participation in sport. It is still low in proportion to that of men.

The government is attempting to redress the balance by some schemes.

- A commitment has been made to help televise a new national soccer league for women and has also invested in the new Trans-Tasman netball competition.
- More training opportunities for women will be put in place to recognise achievement appropriately and to take real and practical steps to tackle the under-representation of women in sport.
- In conjunction with the Office for Women, the Australian Sports Commission also provides funding through the Sports Leadership Grants for Women Program in five key areas:
  - high performance coaching and officiating
  - indigenous women
  - women in disability sport
  - women from culturally and linguistically diverse backgrounds
  - women in general sports leadership.

Cathy Freeman has raised the profile of female and indigenous people's profile in society and in sport.

Maximising the effectiveness of the indigenous sport programme

The Aborigines of Australia

Aborigines were the first original inhabitants of Australia. For over 40,000 years they lived in nomadic tribes and spread out across the continent, creating and maintaining their own territory in which they had freedom to hunt and fish, though they established only temporary accommodation. They lived in clans, and several clans made up an extended family. The spiritual world was an integral part of the philosophy of the Aborigines. Boomerangs were used for

Fig 7.4 Cathy Freeman, Olympic Gold Medallist

hunting (non-returning) and sport (the returning boomerang). The Aborigine population has been decimated by military action, disease and exile into remote areas. Colonisation led to disease and death through military action and the loss of land rights has only recently being recognised and compensated for in the 'Native Title Act' (1994). This is an example of an ethnic people who were affected by the White Policy and whose fate was similar to that of the American Indians. They now form less than 2 per cent of the population. Traditional physical activities would have a functional base – for example, hunting and games as preparation for battles; they would also have had a strong religious and ritual meaning. The National Aboriginal Sport Foundation is part of the ASC and has founded the 'Aboriginal Sport and Recreation Programme'. Aboriginal culture has seen a revival within a more liberal society, though Aborigines still suffer severe discrimination.

National competitions exclusive to Aborigines have been organised – for example:

- National Aboriginal Australian Rules Carnival
- Interstate Aborigine Rugby League Carnivals
- Special Aborigine Sports Days.

Colonisation has resulted in the Anglicisation of Aboriginal culture. In the schools, reserves and missions, the main games are now cricket, rugby and netball.

Many sports were linked to the Aboriginal subsistence lifestyle. With the exception of inter-tribal tournaments, rules were few, easy to understand and often temporary; officials were not needed; winners were rarely honoured, as this was not the main purpose of participation.

- Males maintained fitness and military prowess through play and friendly contests.
- Tournaments were inter-tribal, called 'pruns' in Central Queensland. They followed rules of fair play and were used to settle personal scores or tribal disagreements.
- Sport was used to strengthen internal relationships, promote goodwill and encourage social intercourse.

Key term

White Australia Policy An Anglo-centric policy to keep Australia free of immigration from the East. It was not until the 1950s that large numbers from Europe and Asia were accepted. This policy also limited the amount of friction between different religious sects and was mainly restrained to the Protestant and Catholic divide.

Some Aboriginal sports included:

- Pit throwing, where a heavy stick or bone attached to a piece of twine was thrown over an emu net into a hole dug specifically for the game
- Kangaroo Rat, or *Weet Weet*: in this group game, the kangaroo 'rat', which was made out of a single piece of wood, was thrown so that it slid or bounced along the

ground; the main aim was to achieve the furthest distance and/or the greatest number of hops.

- *Mungan-Mungan*: in the centre of the designated playing areas a wormar (a white painted stick representing a young girl) was placed, and the object of the game was for the young boys to keep the *wormar* away from the older men. Passing and tackling were essential features of the game, which continued until one team was too exhausted to play.

Aboriginal and Torres Strait Islander participation

The Sydney Organising Committee for the Olympic Games (SOCOG) tried to reflect the rich culture of these indigenous peoples. It appointed a National Indigenous Advisory Committee, which made recommendations to SOCOG on issues and projects that should include indigenous involvement, such as:

- the logo reflecting elements of the old cultures
- Aborigines and Torres Strait Islanders playing a role in the Olympic Arts Festival
- Aboriginal and Torres Strait Islander protocol observed in Olympic ceremonies
- the torch relay visiting sites of ancient interest
- Australia's Aboriginal Cathy Freeman was the Olympic torchbearer
- the Australian Olympic Committee (AOC) in conjunction with SOCOG and the ASC established an Olympic Training Centre for Aboriginal and Torres Strait Islander (OTCATS) athletes in Canberra. There were approximately twenty-four indigenous athletes on such scholarships in the lead-up to the Sydney Games.

Emerging challenges

Research indicates that between 2001 and 2005 there was a shift towards lower levels of physical activity by Aboriginal and Torres Strait Islander people. There was also an increase in the proportion of sedentary behaviour amongst Aboriginal and Torres Strait Islander peoples aged 15 years and over during this period from 37 per cent to 47 per cent.

Sport and physical activity can help close the gap between indigenous and non-indigenous Australians' life expectancy by providing a practical tool for indigenous communities to achieve positive outcomes in areas such as physical wellbeing and mental health, education and social dysfunction.

New directions

For too long the funding of indigenous sport has been heavily fragmented between the Federal Government, the State Governments, non-governmental organisations and sporting bodies. This needs greater coordination.

The Federal Government must work closely with National Sporting Organisations on their existing indigenous sport initiatives and ensure that the government itself has the most effective funding structure in place. Major sports, such as Australian Rules Football, have already made great strides in building links with indigenous communities.

The government must build on existing programmes such as its commitment to help fund a team from the Northern Territory to play in either the South Australian National Football League or the West Australian Football League. Such a programme is aimed at maximising the career potential of young indigenous players without forcing them away from their homes and also at offering a clearer pathway to the Australian Football League for the elite players.

The government will enhance the capacity and coordination of sport participation and development programmes for indigenous Australians in partnership with state and territory government sport and recreation agencies, through the engagement of Indigenous Sport Development Officers, and National Sporting Organisations.

Traditional Indigenous Games and Cross Cultural Awareness programmes, as well as support for talented indigenous Australians to progress along mainstream sporting pathways, are planned.

IN CONTEXT

The Australian Sports Commission (ASC) has been involved in a number of programmes to encourage Aboriginal peoples to take part in sport. One such national scheme, ISP, is aimed at giving Aborigines opportunities to play, organise and manage community-based sport.

In 2008 through ISP the ASC supported a 6-week scheme to attract more indigenous women in the Illawara region to play netball. 'Come and try' sessions were set up, with modified rules, and older women were encouraged to attend.

Ray Smith, Indigenous Sport Development Officer with NSW Sport and Recreation, said the programme ensured that players, through undertaking coaching and officiating courses, were equipped with the skills and knowledge to help run the competition.

The competition's success was due to a number of factors, including accessibility to local courts, a playing time convenient for busy mothers, providing activities for their children, and training and support for coaching, umpiring and administration.

Disability and sport

The first opportunities for athletes with disabilities in Australia occurred in 1954 under the Australian Deaf Sports Federation; wheelchair sports began in 1972. The Australian Confederation of Sports for the Disabled speaks on behalf of all handicapped sport groups to the government. Associations represented include paraplegic and quadriplegic people, deaf people, those suffering with cerebral palsy, amputees and so on. They generally have national governing bodies, with state associations.

Emerging challenges

There are clear impediments to participation in organised sport and physical activity for people with disabilities. In line with the government's commitment that everyone will have the opportunity to participate in sport, recreation and physical activity, it is necessary to ensure that, at the community level, there are no barriers for people with disabilities to participate.

It is essential to ensure effective links between sports and disability groups. Sports CONNECT is a national programme coordinated by the Disability Sport Unit, with the aim to ensure that all Australians with disabilities have opportunities to participate in sporting activities at the level of their choice. It aims to improve sporting options for people with disabilities, such as increasing participation, coaching, officiating, involvement in administration or volunteering – that is, creating an inclusive environment.

To achieve this, the Disability Sport Unit (DSU) has committed to a national framework (see Figure 7.5).

Fig 7.5 Disability Sport Unit's national framework

The objectives of the DSU are:

- to provide direct practical assistance to national sports organisations (NSOs) and to assist them with the inclusion of people with disabilities in both disability and non-disability specific sport (supply);
- to provide direct links between people with disabilities and sport (demand);
- to coordinate the disability sport network, who work with NSOs, SSOs and other stakeholders to achieve the objectives of the supply/demand framework.

New directions

Elite athletes with disabilities are still elite athletes and should be recognised as such. Having opportunities and access to sporting pathways is paramount to the success of these athletes.

The Federal Government will consult with State and Territory Governments, various sporting groups for the disabled, including the Australian Paralympic Committee, and national sports organisations to ensure that there are appropriate opportunities and access to sporting pathways to support athletes with a disability (see section on 'Sport and the pursuit of Excellence').

Values

Bush culture

What is it about 'the bush' that is so special to Australians? The bush has an iconic status in Australian life and features

strongly in any debate about national identity, especially as expressed in Australian literature, painting, popular music, films and foods and, of course, sport.

The bush was something that was uniquely Australian. The bush was revered as a source of national ideals, and romanticising the bush in this way was a big step forward for Australians in their steps towards self-identity.

The skills of indigenous people in 'the bush', especially their tracking abilities, was seen as miraculous and became legendary in the minds of European Australians. Indigenous people's knowledge of the land, at the core of their spiritual beliefs, is expressed in stories, arts and performance – music, songs, dance and ceremony.

The bush was a symbol for a national life and yet, by 1910, most Australians were urban.

The idea of the bush as integral to Australian identity was reinforced in 1958 when Russel Ward published *The Australian Legend*. He argued that traits such as 'mateship', anti-authoritarianism, swearing and hard drinking came from the frontier experiences of real bush workers.

Australia as a social 'melting pot'

We have already established that Australia was settled by many different cultures, very similar to the settlement of the USA. Whilst the dominant values were those of white, male middle class, there is a desire now to show that the Australian spirit is one of multiculturalism and opportunity for everyone.

'Land of Fair Go'

As the USA became the land of opportunity epitomising the slogan 'rags to riches', so Australia is seen as the 'land of fair go'. This means everyone has a chance to succeed in an egalitarian society.

> **Key term**
>
> **Egalitarianism** Philosophy of the equality of mankind and the desirability of political, social and economic equality. In sport this has led to opening up access to all sections of society, such as women and indigenous peoples.

Physical education and school sport

Education is compulsory for all Australian children between the ages of 6 and 15. Infant classes, however, are available from age 5. A free education is provided by the government in schools in all populated areas of the country. Similar to most other countries, fee-paying schools also operate and are often associated with religious denominations. Similar to the USA, the individual states have overriding responsibility for education. Therefore generalisations are dangerous, although a centralised system does operate. Some funds are allocated by federal government from levied taxes, but the government does not have control over the states' spending. New policies show some similarities to the British

Table 7.1 Comparison between Physical Education in the UK and Australia

UK	Australia
Traditionally decentralised National Curriculum = more centralised	Decentralised – States State Department of Education/lays down educational content and trains teachers/similar to USA
Key Stages 1-4	
Primary/heuristic/movement approach	Primary/movement-based/should have non-specialist teacher access to trained staff (ACHPER)
Secondary/skills focus/qualified teacher	Secondary/skills/qualified teacher PHASE upgrade teacher qualifications
PE compulsory	PE compulsory
Voluntary PE exams GCSE/A level	VCE – similar to A level PE Testing similar to France
Extra curricular = voluntary/low status/poor school and club links/teacher responsibility based on goodwill	Sports afternoons supplement PE lessons 1975 National School Sports Council = formalising of school sport
Outdoor Education not compulsory Government initiatives 'Raising the Game' Sportsmark 'A Sporting Future for All 2000' Active Schools	Not on level found in France & USA 1980 Australian curriculum Dev. Centre (dev. aims for O.Ed) Wide interest in Duke of Edinburgh Award and Outward Bound Physical and Sport Education in Schools Policy 1995

model of Local Management of Schools, where responsibility for salaries and maintenance, among other issues, has passed from the central administration to the individual schools. The State Department of Education lays down the educational content of syllabuses, trains the teachers and acts as a final authority.

Children who live in the outback are too far away from official schools, so they receive instruction over the air waves and send work to be graded. This operates under a programme called School of the Air. They can also attend a school that travels to them by railroad.

There are approximately twenty universities and a number of colleges that offer courses leading to undergraduate and advanced degrees.

Australian school system

Schooling in Australia starts with a kindergarten or preparatory year followed by twelve years of primary and secondary school. In the final year of secondary school, Year 12, you can study for a government-endorsed certificate that is recognised by a range of further education institutions.

Subjects

Australia has a national curriculum framework to ensure high academic standards across the country. All schools provide subjects in the **eight key learning areas:** English, mathematics, studies of the society and the environment,

science, arts, languages other than English, technology, and personal development, health and **physical education**.

Many students use senior secondary study to gain university-entry qualifications. Around nine out of every ten Australian secondary schools also offer vocational education programmes in addition to the standard school curriculum.

Academic year

The school year is divided into four terms and runs from late January/early February until December. There is a short holiday between terms and a long summer holiday in December and January.

Students attend school from Monday to Friday each week. School hours vary slightly across Australia but are generally from 9.00 a.m. to 3.30 p.m. each school day.

Teachers are trained at colleges in two- or three-year diploma courses. Degree programmes have taken longer to establish. The teacher training programmes require the students to enter into a contract to complete the course and to serve as teachers for a certain period of time.

Each state develops its own physical education. In some states, a considerable integration of school and council personnel and facilities has been realised. Local committees with subcommittees made up of voluntary youth organisations and junior sport organisations have developed a number of play centres, recreation leadership programmes and coaching clinics.

Outdoor activities are the norm in this favourable climate. Schools generally have good playing-field facilities, swimming pools and outdoor gymnasia. In elementary schools, the emphasis tends to be on posture, gymnastics games and movement activities. At secondary level, conditioning or fitness activities, gymnastics, track and field games and swimming are integral parts of the programme. Girls participate more positively than their American counterparts.

There are sports afternoons, morning coaching session or sports day supplement physical education lessons. All pupils and teachers are expected to participate, with the more specialised teachers taking inter-scholastic teams. In reality, however, there is a high absentee rate from students who are not interested.

Competitive sports are controlled by amateur athletic associations and annual state championships are held in separate sports.

Activity 2

Describe the programmes of physical and sport education in Australian secondary schools and compare it to the system in the UK.

Important bodies such as the Australian Council for Health, Physical Education and Recreation (ACHPER) have agreed that all government schools should have weekly timetabled physical-education lessons. However, constraints limited the schools' implementation of the recommended compulsory 60 minutes of physical education every day.

ACHPER has also proposed that all primary schools should have access to trained physical-education specialists, whether from a permanent or peripatetic resource.

Physical education in Victoria

It is useful to study a particular state as this can give more specific information about physical education as well as allowing a more general understanding of sport in Australia to take place. There has generally, across Australia, been a lack of political will to put in place coordinated and well-funded sports policies. However, there are exceptions and the state of Victoria is one of them.

The Sport Education and Physical Education Project (SEPEP) provided a framework that schools can follow in their teaching of physical activities, but they are also able to adapt them to their local needs and according to their pupil profiles.

Key term

SEPEP A framework that schools can use, according to their needs, in order to deliver an effective physical-education programme.

Hugging the tip of the Australian east coast, Victoria is Australia's second-smallest state, covering 227,600 square kilometres – roughly the size of the British Isles. Victoria's

capital, Melbourne, is located around the shores of Port Phillip Bay. The city itself sits beside the Yarra River, about 5 kilometres from the bay.

Victoria occupies the south-east corner of the continent between latitudes 34 and 39 south and longitudes 141 and 150 east. It covers 227,600 square kilometres – about the same area as England, Wales and Scotland; three-fifths of Japan and slightly larger than the US State of Utah.

About 36 per cent of Victoria is covered by forest with the major forest belt in the east. The highest peaks are Mount Bogong (1,986 metres) and Mount Feathertop (1,922 metres).

Victoria's 1,800-kilometre coastline borders on Bass Strait, which separates the mainland from Tasmania, and in the west on the Southern Ocean. It is a generally rugged coastline but includes many wide sandy beaches and three large, almost fully enclosed harbours. Melbourne and Geelong are on the shores of the most important of these harbours, Port Phillip Bay.

Victoria's state parliament consists of an eighty-eight-member Legislative Assembly and a forty-four-member Legislative Council. The State Governor, as representative of the Queen, is Head of State and gives formal assent to legislation. The judiciary comprises Magistrates' Courts, Country Courts and the Supreme Court and is the final arbiter of legal disputes.

Education

Schooling is compulsory for all children between the ages of six and 15. Thirty-nine per cent of graduating final-year secondary students go on to tertiary studies. The State has eight universities in Melbourne and in country areas. There is a comprehensive technical education system catering for trades and sub-professional training needs.

The Review of Physical and Sport Education in Victorian Schools was begun in 1993 by the Minister for Education in an attempt to develop a coordinated approach towards improving children's experiences and participation in physical and sport education. This resulted in the implementation of the Physical and Sport Education in Schools Policy in 1995, which proved to be a watershed for Australian policy.

The main recommendations were as follows:

- PE and sport to be a high priority in the school charter and to receive accreditation for courses
- the training of non-specialist teachers to be upgraded.

As a result:

- The Victorian Primary and Secondary School Sports Associations organise inter-school sports throughout the state, benefiting from federal government grants.
- The Directorate of School Education supports staff development, and helps with the promotion of sport through these associations.
- School Sports Awards recognise excellence in major school sports and can be given to individuals, teams and coaches, and those who help the school in its attempts to improve the standards of school sport. You may recognise a similarity here with the Sportsmark Awards.

- Similarly to the USA, the national television networks are becoming involved to show features on school sport, from school initiatives to information on individual students and sports events. This can encourage a community interest in school sport.

Victorian Curriculum and Assessment Authority

The Victorian Curriculum and Assessment Authority (VCAA) is an independent statutory body directly responsible to the Victorian Minister for Education, serving both government and non-government schools.

> **Key term**
>
> **Victorian Curriculum and Assessment Authority** The VCAA is an independent statutory body directly responsible to the Victorian Minister for Education, serving both government and non-government schools.

Its mission is to provide high-quality curriculum, assessment and reporting that promotes individual lifelong learning in Victoria.

Physical education and sport education programmes were made compulsory for pupils up to year 10.

Years Prep to 4: laying the foundations

In these years the curriculum focuses on developing the fundamental knowledge, skills and behaviours in literacy and numeracy and other areas including physical and social capacities that underpin all future learning.

About the Victorian Certificate of Education (VCE)

The VCE is a certificate that recognises the successful completion of secondary education in Victoria. It provides pathways to further study at university, to Technical and Further Education (TAFE) and to the world of work. It is even possible to undertake a school-based apprenticeship or traineeship within the VCE.

> **Key term**
>
> **Victorian Certificate of Education (VCE)** A certificate that recognises the successful completion of secondary education in Victoria.

The VCAA develops courses that enable VCE students to acquire skills and knowledge in a wide range of studies. It also has responsibility for ensuring the quality of the school-assessed component of the VCE, the external examinations and the delivery of all VCE results to students across the state every year.

Physical education is an elective subject – the following table (from 2008 statistics) is a useful indication of choice by students.

Table 7.3 Top 10 subjects (i.e. biggest enrolment) in Victoria schools

1.	English (including English as a Second Language)	47,411
2.	Further Mathematics	27,668
3.	Mathematical Methods (including CAS)	16,532
4.	Psychology	16,024
5.	Health and Human Development	13,099
6.	Business Management	12,470
7.	Biology	10,968
8.	Physical Education	9,658
9.	Chemistry	9,089
10.	Legal Studies	8,332

At VCE level physical education is assessed on theoretical knowledge.

> **Key term**
>
> **Elective** Activity options that aim to prepare young people for lifelong participation in physical activity.

Table 7.2 Fundamental Skills Programme

About Early Childhood	
Mission statement is:	**Values include:**
Early Childhood Australia will advocate to ensure quality, social justice and equity in all issues relating to the education and care of children from birth to eight years.	• The rights of children • Leadership, excellence and respect • Courage, honesty and openness • Collaboration and diversity • Justice • Social inclusion of children

The **Victorian Essential Learning Standards (VELS)** describe what is essential for Victorian students to achieve from Prep to Year 10. VELS provide a whole school curriculum planning framework that sets out learning standards for schools to use to plan their teaching and learning programmes, including assessment and reporting of student achievement and progress.

Structure

The Health and Physical Education domain is organised into six sections, one for each level of achievement from Level 1 to Level 6. Each level includes a learning focus statement and a set of standards organised by dimension.

IN CONTEXT

Table 7.4 Standards by Domain

Strand	Domain	Dimension
Physical, Personal and Social Learning	Health and Physical Education	Movement and physical activity Health knowledge and promotion

The Victorian Essential Learning Standards recognise the differing learning needs of students at three stages of learning. Curriculum expectations for student achievement are set at six levels over the eleven years of compulsory schooling. The six levels are broadly associated with Years Prep to 10 and are consistent with the levels for student achievement introduced in the Curriculum and Standards Framework (CSF) in 1995. General expectations of when students will achieve the various standards are:
- Level 1 – Preparatory Year
- Level 2 – Years 1 and 2
- Level 3 – Years 3 and 4
- Level 4 – Years 5 and 6
- Level 5 – Years 7 and 8
- Level 6 – Years 9 and 10.

At Level 1, standards are written for English, Mathematics, Health and Physical Education, The Arts and Interpersonal Development. At Level 2, standards are introduced for ICT.

In Health and Physical Education, standards for the *Health knowledge and promotion* dimension are introduced at Level 3.

Learning focus

Learning focus statements are written for each level. These outline the learning that students need to focus on if they are to progress in the domain and achieve the standards at the levels where they apply. They suggest appropriate learning experiences from which teachers can draw to develop relevant teaching and learning activities.

Standards

Standards define what students should know and be able to do at different levels and are written for each dimension. In Health and Physical Education, standards for assessing and reporting on student achievement apply from Level 1.

Dimensions

Standards in the Health and Physical Education domain are organised into two dimensions.

- Movement and physical activity – from Level 1
- Health knowledge and promotion – from Level 3.

The *Movement and physical activity* dimension from Level 1:

- focuses on the important role that physical activity, sport and recreation need to play in the lives of all Australians
- provides opportunities for challenge, personal growth, enjoyment and fitness
- promotes involvement in a manner that reflects awareness that everyone has the right to participate in a healthy and active lifestyle
- develops students' confidence in using movement skills and strategies to increase their motivation to become active
- increases students' motivation to improve their performance
- motivates students to maintain a level of fitness that allows them to participate in physical activity without undue fatigue
- builds understanding of how training and exercise in areas such as strength, flexibility and endurance relate to physical performance.

The *Health knowledge and promotion* dimension from Level 3:

- examines physical, social, emotional and mental health and personal development across various stages of the lifespan
- focuses on safety and the identification of strategies to minimise harms associated with particular situations or behaviours
- encourages students to examine the promotion of health of individuals and the community through the use of specific strategies and the provision of health resources, services and products
- encourages students to examine the factors that influence food selection and the role of nutrition on health growth and development.

The fundamental skills programme believes that promotion of high level skills can be more easily transferred into a wide variety of activities later on. That is when a 'game sense' can be developed through the sport education programme, promoting enjoyment and a sense of fair play.

Activity 3

Compare the physical education curriculum in Australia with that of the National Curriculum in the UK

Government exemplary schools

Schools compete to achieve the exemplary schools status. Once achieved these schools act as role models to a cluster of schools providing and sharing good practice, This could be seen as similar to the system of specialist schools in the UK, where the term 'family of schools' is used.

> **Key term**
>
> **Cluster schools** Schools that come under the aegis of an exemplary school in order to raise the overall standards of education in that area.

Teachers in Australia have more autonomy than the UK teachers, but with this comes the idea of professional development and of maintaining their own identity as sport specialists. They engage in 'Teacher Games', which are residential and promote the idea of lifelong participation in sport as well as providing a communication network and opportunities for sharing good practice.

Teachers in all schools in Victoria are provided with guidelines that link the rational and structure of VELS to individual programme development and assessment for students who have disabilities.

The guidelines reflect current educational reform at a state, national and international level, and are informed by inclusive education principles and practices.

Inclusive education, a term that has been used to articulate the rights of every student to participate in, or have access to, the full range of programmes and services offered by the education system, supports and celebrates the diversity found among all learners.

Teacher professional development

Professional development occurs at many levels and in many different forms.

The activities can range from informal school-based programmes and on-line, self-paced programmes to structured professional development activities that may lead to a formal qualification.

Primary teachers tend to take a Physical Education course whilst secondary school teachers undertake sport education. They all come under the umbrella term of PASE (Physical and Sport Education).

> **Key term**
>
> **PASE** A professional development programme for teachers delivering physical activity as part of the education system.

The range of professional development activities can be categorised as follows:

School-based/initiated activities: Activities in this category can include teachers participating in seminars or workshops that are initiated and conducted by and for teachers at that school.

School-based curriculum project programmes: This category includes activities that involve teachers in a project that originates from outside a school but is conducted at the school level.

Professional development at schools and resource centres of excellence: Included in this category are activities that are initiated and conducted by schools that have been developed/chosen as sites of excellence.

Programmes initiated by an employing authority: Typical of this category are courses that are developed and implemented by education systems. These are often run on a large scale and may lead to a formal qualification.

Teacher professional association programmes: The Australian education community is supported by a large number of teacher professional associations, which are typically curriculum-based.

Professional development resources: This category includes resources that have been developed for use by teachers, teacher educators and trainers as the basis of a professional development programme.

Award schemes

> **What are the Pierre de Coubertin Awards?**
>
> The Pierre de Coubertin Awards, an initiative of the Victorian Olympic Council and the Department of Education and Early Childhood Development, are named after the founder of the modern Olympic Games and take place on an annual basis to recognise senior secondary students who demonstrate attributes consistent with Olympism through participation and commendable behaviour in sporting activities.
>
> All secondary government and non-government schools are invited to nominate one recipient from year 10, 11 or 12 for the Pierre de Coubertin Award each year. Each nominee must participate actively in the school's physical education programme with a consistently positive attitude and must have represented the school in a sport.

Every two years, a student from Victoria is awarded the opportunity to represent Australia at the International Pierre de Coubertin Youth Forum.

IN CONTEXT

Table 7.5 Level 6 Movement and physical activity

Excerpts from the standard	Terms and definitions/examples
Demonstrate proficiency in manipulative and movement skills during the execution of complex activities	**Proficiency** means that the skill is almost automatic. For example, students: ● focus on opponents while still performing the skill ● perform movements that seem effortless and can be reproduced in a variety of situations ● apply biomechanical principles to improve task performance. **Manipulative skills** are developed when a student controls an object such as a bat or ball. For example students: ● consistently perform skills required in sports such as golf, tennis, basketball, cricket, volleyball, hockey, netball, lacrosse and football ● use a variety of clubs during a round of golf ● maintain a rally for a series of consecutive shots during a volleyball match ● perform a backhand overhead shot in squash or badminton ● deliberately strike or place a ball through a gap in the field of play from a variety of deliveries (cricket, softball or volleyball). **Movement skills** are the skills we require to participate in a range of movement, including walking, running swimming, fleeing, pursuing, leaping, turning, dodging. For example, students: ● adapt, transfer and improvise movement in increasingly demanding contexts ● perform and refine swimming strokes for speed endurance and survival ● use dance or gymnastics to perform technically complex movement sequences ● complete a medley relay in the pool.
Demonstrate advanced skills in selected activities	**For example, students:** ● perform a range of advanced skills such as: basketball – a lay-up rebounding or crossover dribble volleyball – spike or dig soccer – goal keeping racing dive, chest trap, heading or dribble with either foot softball – bunting, pitching or base stealing ● use a digital camera and computer software to evaluate their own or a partner's skill technique ● develop a plan for improving a specific skill including improving the smoothness, accuracy of and the ability to reproduce specific skills.
Use training methods to improve their fitness level	For example, students: ● identify different components of fitness and how their importance varies between activities ● become aware of the principles of training such as specificity, overload, frequency, intensity and duration ● experience a variety of training methods such as weight training, flexibility training, plyometric training, interval training, fartlek, circuit training, Pilates, Nautilus, resistance bands and Swiss balls ● set personal fitness goals, undertake a fitness programme and evaluate its success ● devise a movement and skill analysis of a partner/player in a team game and then develop a fitness plan which aims to improve specific fitness components.
Participate in sports, games, recreational and leisure activities that maintain regular participation in moderate to vigorous physical activity	For example, students: ● evaluate their participation in relation to Australia's Physical Activity Recommendations for Children and Young People ● participate in a range of physical activities that are new to them such as tai-chi, kayaking or water polo and evaluate their potential as a physical activity for different age groups ● analyse strategies to enhance enjoyment and to improve their participation in physical activity ● collaboratively design and conduct an action plan for their school to increase participation and enjoyment in physical activity ● reflect on their current levels of physical activity and propose short-term and long-term goals that will assist them to maintain regular participation in the future ● analyse barriers to regular participation in physical activity and suggest strategies to overcome them ● locate information about opportunities for physical activity in their local area.

Excerpts from the standard	Terms and definitions/examples
Employ and devise skills and strategies to counter tactical challenges in game situations	For example, students: ● are able to use tactical skills such as zone, one-on-one and the offside trap ● use game strategies for scoring, stopping scoring and restarting play after scoring ● devise a set play to counter their opposition or particularly skilful opponent ● develop, interpret and apply team and individual strategies and rules to meet the demands of a new situation ● view a video of a challenge by an opposing team in a game and identify their team strengths, areas for team improvement and develop a team strategy to counter this challenge
Assume responsibility for the conduct of aspects of a sporting competition in which roles are shared	For example, students: ● select and perform a variety of roles as they organise, manage and participate in a sporting competition such as player, umpire, coach, scorer, administrator ● organise a mini sports competition for junior or primary school students.
Appropriate sporting behaviour	For example, students: ● develop and implement a code of conduct for sporting behaviour, which could include the following features: perform to the best of their ability at all times accept the decisions of umpires and officials shake hands at the completion of all matches be gracious in victory and defeat play within the competition rules and regulations respect all participants in the game and treat them courteously ● analyse their team's adherence to a sporting code of conduct ● analyse and evaluate the sporting behaviour of elite athletes.

School Sport Australia

Since its establishment in 1981, School Sport Australia has been responsible for the development and promotion of **school sport** in Australia.

The focal point of School Sport Australia activities has been the **interstate** competitions offered at both **Primary and Secondary** levels. These are the culmination of state-based programmes and offer the gifted and talented students the opportunity to participate in higher levels of sporting competition. These events are an integral part of the School Sport Australia programme, not only for their sporting benefits, but also for the immense educational, cultural and social benefits they provide for the participants.

The essential focus of School Sport Australia relates to the organisation and conduct of a broad range of school sporting programmes for all students appropriate to their age and ability. In order to undertake this role effectively in an educational environment, School Sport Australia:

● operates within a framework of accepted state and national policies, frameworks and guidelines for the development and conduct of sport in schools
● ensures that educational outcomes form the basis for all school-based sporting programmes/activities
● liaises with and promote cooperation between school sport and community sport agencies
● provides leadership in the area of sport development and programming and other key educational and sporting issues related to the delivery of sport in schools

● identifies and address equity standards in the participation of students and officials in school sport, particularly in relation to gender
● acts as a forum for the sharing of effective practice in the development and conduct of sporting programmes for students
● identifies and further develops the links between sport and relevant learning areas (in particular Health and Physical Education)
● provides opportunities for students in sport within and beyond state or territory boundaries
● involves students in the leadership of their own sporting programmes
● maintains and enhances the quality of those teachers and other volunteers who deliver sporting programmes to students
● ensures that the Australian Education Systems Officials Committee is kept informed of developments in school sport and make recommendations to the Committee regarding policy and new initiatives
● promotes and publicises the range of sporting activities conducted in schools to the wider community.

Secondary School Sport Associations

The Victorian Secondary Schools' Association (VSSA) in Victoria is one of the six school sport associations that organise intra-state competitions. Participation is maximised at the lower levels between local schools with the most successful schools progressing on to the state finals.

Research the mission statement and purpose of the VSSA.

Excellence in School Sport Awards 2008

This particular award:

- is presented in recognition of sporting excellence to ACT school students who have competed at a local, national or international level over the past 12 months
- is the highest schools sporting honour presented to ACT school students.

Nomination guidelines

- Principals, sports coordinators, School Sport ACT, PSSA, SSSA or team officials may make nominations.
- Sporting achievements are to be restricted to achievements in school sport teams and/or events. Community-based teams/events will not be taken into consideration.
- Students sporting conduct needs to meet the principles outlined in the School Sport Australia Fair Play in School Sport Policy, specifically in relation to displaying appropriate qualities of sportsmanship.
- Sporting achievements in most instances would need to be at national, state or regional levels.
- Students must be enrolled at an ACT school. All nominations must carry the endorsement of the principal of the school attended.
- In an effort to ensure prompt contact is made with Award winners, it is appreciated if home addresses and contact numbers are included on nomination forms.
- A maximum number of two females and two males in the primary, and two females and two males in the secondary sector, will be awarded in any one year.
- A maximum of two awards may be presented to acknowledge the achievements of athletes with a disability in any one year.

Exam-style Questions

Describe the Australian High Schools' initiatives entitled SEPEP and PASE.

[4 marks]

Victorian Institute of Sport (VIS)

VIS was set up in 1990 to assist the development of Victoria's best athletes. VIS is located at Olympic Park, Melbourne. Formerly known as the Glasshouse, the facility was the site of the swimming pool for the 1956 Olympic Games.

VIS is funded by the State Government through Sport and Recreation Victoria, the Commonwealth Government through the Australian Sports Commission and numerous corporate sector sponsors. VIS programmes are conducted in partnership with State Sporting Organisations.

VIS is a non-residential institute, which utilises Melbourne's outstanding sporting facilities, to allow high-performance athletes to live and train in Melbourne, the sporting capital of Australia.

Over 400 athletes from a wide range of sports participate in VIS programmes. Both able-bodied athletes and athletes with a disability have scholarships.

Advanced and specialised coaching, sport science and sports medicine services, career and education advice, and training and competition support are provided to all VIS athletes.

Several sports have established National Training Centre programmes at the VIS to enable many of Australia's best athletes to prepare for international competition.

Thirty athletes from Victoria have become Olympic Champions since the inception of the VIS, before which only 12 such athletes had ever succeeded at this level. The VIS contribution to the Australian national Olympic and Paralympic medal tally is always a significant one.

VIS paralympic athletes have won 113 medals at Paralympic Games level, including 17 in Barcelona (1992), 10 in Atlanta (1996), 39 in Sydney (2000), 29 in Athens (2004) and 18 in Beijing (2008).

Other VIS athletes have achieved international success in non-Olympic sports such as netball, cricket, squash and golf. This success has raised Interest in the VIS model of elite athlete development and has attracted athletes, coaches and administrators from all over the world to Melbourne, to ascertain and study the VIS methods for success.

Key term

Victoria Institute of Sport VIS is an Australian state-sponsored organisation established to aid in the growth of Victoria's best athletes.

In an article 'British lead the way' (*Daily Telegraph* by Gareth A Davies, 2007) reference was made to the manner in which school sport and participation figures in the UK have led to the Australians looking to our strategies to help them combat similar problems.

Australian sports administrators have enlisted the support of the Youth Sport Trust, the charity involved in the delivery of school sports policy for the British Government, for their advice and guidance.

Steve Grainger, chief executive of the Youth Sport Trust (YST), explained: 'Many of the issues facing PE and sport in Australia are those that we were facing in the UK 10 years ago. Although we still have lots to learn and more work to do in this country, it was immensely encouraging to realise how far we have come and to receive such positive feedback from a nation that many people look up to in the sporting world.'

While the systems in Australian elite sport appear to be in place, the Australian nation has genuine concerns about the state of grassroots sport, and the delivery of Physical Education and sport in schools. Grainger, with Sue Campbell, the YST Chair, returned from a week-long round of discussions and idea-sharing with Australian government officials and representatives of Austrade (the Australian Trade Commission).

Outdoor education

There is strong interest in the international Outward Bound Movement and the Duke of Edinburgh Award Scheme.

However, the level of Outdoor Education is not comparable to that found in France or the USA. It is lacking in organisation and funding and similar to the UK it relies on local government support and staff initiative. It was only in 1980 that the Australian Curriculum Development Centre developed aims for Outdoor Education and began a campaign for taking people to the natural environment.

Australia has four levels of Residential Centres:

- Outdoor Schools – extension of classrooms but they get first hand experience of natural environment
- Environmental Centres – focus on environmental studies
- Outdoor Pursuit Centres – largest group of field centres
- Outdoor Leisure & Environmental Centres – combined outdoor pursuits & environmental focus.

Outdoor recreation

Though it has topography and climate similar to the USA the population is much smaller and therefore there are large areas that are unpopulated. They do not grade areas as in the USA but they do have National Parks, which are run by individual States rather than by the Federal Government. Australians are becoming more aware of the natural environment but traditionally they have led more affluent/urban lifestyles.

- National Parks
- State Parks
- Regional Parks (5 mile radius of cities)

Mountain areas which have the benefit of snow are popular venues for weekenders and holiday enthusiasts. Swimming is the most popular sport – heavy emphasis is placed on this within the school curriculum, and it is the most popular participant sport.

In the Darwin region:

City limits	Open picnic sites
30 miles	Nature parks (rambling/mountain biking etc.)
50 miles	Katherine Gorge National Park
	Kakadu National Park

Exam-style Questions

Identify the cultural factors that make outdoor education an important subject in Australian schools.

[4 marks]

Mass participation

Mass participation in sporting activities serves a dual function:

- To widen the base of the sporting pyramid, which will enhance the quality of life for the mass of the population, especially as it impacts on health.
- It serves to increase the potential pool of talent from which the sports organisations, with a remit for high-performance sport, can draw upon.

More Active Australia: a national programme run by the ASC where the focus is on participation and 'sport for all'. This programme integrated other programmes such as 'Aussie Sport' (est. 1986) and 'Aussie Able' into getting Australians 'up and active' at the foundation level of sport. This requires the adoption of a cohesive framework and corporate plan by Local State Sport Recreation Departments. A pack (provider model) is supplied to help clubs and organisations.

More Active Australia identifies three main aims:

- to increase and enhance lifelong participation
- to realise the social, health and economic benefits of participation
- to develop a quality infrastructure with opportunities and services to support participation.

Its focus is entirely on sport for all rather than excellence. The principles of More Active Australia are:

- ensure access and equity
- lifelong involvement
- enjoyment in activity
- diversity and choice
- encourage improvement and quality of experience.

Its strategic directions are:

- policy and planning
- monitoring and evaluation
- training
- education advocacy
- industry
- organisation and facility development
- promotion
- consultation and coordination.

The fundamental building blocks of Australian sports are the 26,000 local sporting clubs that have played a key role in communities for more than 100 years. Grassroots sporting clubs provide better health outcomes for Australians of all ages.

They also help teach important Australian values – volunteerism, cooperation, leadership, teamwork, meeting challenges, defeating adversity and pursuing excellence. Sport plays a fundamental role in building healthy communities.

In many schools sport is now given a critically low level of priority and young people have more choices for their leisure time.

The Australian Government is committed to enhancing and promoting community sport and, through it, to building healthy and active Australian communities.

The Australian Sports Commission (ASC) delivers the Government's sports participation policy through a range of programmes including the:

- Active After-schools Communities Programme
- Junior Sport Framework
- Club Development Network
- Disability Education Program
- National Coaching Accreditation Scheme
- National Officiating Accreditation Scheme.

The Australian Sports Foundation (ASF) is the Australian Government organisation that generates funds from the community and business sectors to assist schools and community groups develop sport.

The Australian Government is committed to promoting healthy lifestyles, addressing obesity, and taking preventative measures to improve the health of all Australians. The Government is helping all Australians achieve healthier lives through initiatives such as:

- Get Set 4 Life – Habits for Healthy Kids – Guide is provided to parents/carers as part of the **Healthy Kids Check** for all four-year old children who are permanently resident in Australia or who are covered by a Reciprocal Health Care Arrangement.
- Healthy Spaces and Places – The *Healthy Spaces and Places* project aims to promote the on-going development and improvement of built environments where Australian people live, work and play, which will facilitate lifelong active living and promote good health outcomes for all. The project has a national approach to raising awareness of the relationship between health and the built environment, and to contributing to the development of a national policy setting.
- Community and Schools Grants Program – In 2007 the then Minister for Health and Ageing announced grants totalling over $37 million for 320 community organisations under the Grants Program, as part of the Australian Better Health Initiative (ABHI).
- Healthy Active Ambassadors – The Healthy Active Ambassadors Program is an initiative of the Australian Government, funded under the Australian Better Health Initiative: A joint Australian, State and Territory government initiative. The programme was announced in July 2006 and ran for two years.

  The programme aims to raise awareness among Australians of the importance of healthy living and particularly maintaining healthy body weight. It will target all Australians, with a particular focus on youth.
- Healthy Weight information and resources

Increasing participation rates and making sport part of the preventative health agenda

The Federal Government believes rather than debating the merits of elite sports versus community sport, it should recognise the vital interconnections between the two. The reality is that the elite sport system only prospers when there is a strong talent base on which to draw. Equally, having successful and high-performing role models in sport is integral to encouraging children to take up sport and aspire to reach their own dreams.

In recent times, junior and community sport has been approached with a focus, almost exclusively, on increasing the pool from which our elite athletes can be drawn. It must now recognise that everyone's involvement in sport and physical activity brings its own rewards.

Whereas early federal sports policy had a clear focus on community physical activity and 'Life. Be In It' style programmes, this has declined over time to become virtually non-existent.

Community participation in sport spans a number of central objectives: developing basic skills and healthy disciplines in young children; contributing directly and significantly to better health and prevention of chronic disease across all segments of the community; and promoting a more inclusive and engaged community.

Yet at a community level, participation in sport and local activities is declining. Federal sports policy must fill this void and play a central role in a preventative health agenda. It is why the first decision of the Rudd Government in this area was to shift Sport into the Health portfolio.

Emerging challenges

There are obvious challenges. In 2004-05, 70 per cent of Australians aged 15 years and over were classified as sedentary or having low exercise levels. No improvements have been seen since exercise levels were measured in 1995. These low exercise levels have been a major contributor to Australia's current status as one of the world's most overweight developed nations.

Over a 15-year period, from 1989-90 to 2004-05, the proportion of obese adults in Australia has doubled (from 9 per cent to 18 per cent). These dramatic increases in body weight have already seen the number of Australians with diabetes triple over the past two decades. This will dramatically escalate if the historical growth rate in obesity is not abated. That growth rate, when combined with demographic ageing, could see obesity rise to some 29 per cent of the population by 2025.

Sport and physical activity offer powerful defences against obesity and associated chronic diseases such as Type 2 Diabetes and the Federal Government is determined to get Australia active again.

At the community level, participation in sport and local activities is declining. In the past decade, time spent by Australians on sport and outdoor activity decreased on average by nearly an hour a week, while time spent on activities such as watching television and using the Internet increased by an hour.

In a recent survey, approximately 11.8 million Australians (73 per cent) reported no involvement in organised sport. In 2005–06, approximately 5.5 million people reported that they did not participate in any sports or physical recreation activities of any kind over the preceding year.

Junior Sport

The vision for the Australian Sports Commission's (ASC) Junior Sport Unit is to provide safe, enjoyable environments to encourage the long-term participation of young people. Junior sport refers to the organisation and management of sport and pre-sport activities for young people aged 5 to 17 years. It is the most important time to nurture, educate and have fun with sport and is important because it provides the entry to a lifelong involvement in sport which is increasingly important with our changing lifestyles.

The Active After-school Communities programme is a national initiative that provides primary school-aged children with access to free, structured physical activity programmes in the after-school timeslot of 3.00pm to 5.30pm.

IN CONTEXT

The Exercise, Recreation and Sport Survey (ERASS) collected information on the frequency, duration, nature and type of activities of persons aged 15 years and over for exercise, recreation and sport during the 12 months prior to interview. The survey was conducted quarterly in 2006 with total of 13,710 respondents. A summary of key findings is provided below.

Overall, 66 per cent of people aged 15 years and over (10.9 million) participated in exercise at least once a week, down from 69.2 per cent in 2005. The proportion of people participating in sport three or more times a week remained relatively steady (42.8 per cent compared with 44.2 per cent in 2005).

Females continued to be more likely to participate more often than males (with half of all females undertaking 2.5 sessions or more per week for all females (that is, median), compared with 2.0 sessions for all males). However, male participants were more likely to participate for five hours or more in the two weeks prior to their interview (35.7 per cent compared with 26.7 per cent of female participants).

The activities with the highest participation (at least once in the year) in 2006, in participation rate order, were: walking (36.2 per cent); aerobics/fitness activities (19.1 per cent); swimming (13.6 per cent); cycling (10.1 per cent); and running (7.4 per cent, replacing tennis which now has the eighth highest participation rate with 6.8 per cent).

An estimated 1.6 million persons aged 15 years and over participated three or more times per week in a physical activity for exercise, recreation and sport that was organised by a club, association, fitness centre or other type of organisation. This represented a participation rate of 9.7 per cent, compared with 11.3 per cent in 2006. A further 2.6 million persons participated once or twice a week, resulting in one quarter all of participants (25.3 per cent) participating in organised activity at least once per week.

Males were more likely to participate in organised sport compared to females (40.8 per cent and 37.4 per cent respectively). Females were more likely to participate in sports organised by fitness, leisure or indoor sports centres (14.6 per cent compared with 12.7 per cent of males), while males were more likely to participate at a sports and recreation club or association (30.8 per cent compared with 23.5 per cent for females).

In 2006, the non-organised activity with the highest participation rate (at least once in the year) was:

- walking (other than bushwalking) (35.6 per cent), followed by aerobics/fitness activities (12.1 per cent),
- swimming (12.1 per cent), cycling (9.7 per cent) and running (6.9 per cent). Activities most likely to be non-organised
- included walking (98.5 per cent of all walking is non-organised), cycling (95.7 per cent), running (94.2 per cent),
- bushwalking (91.9 per cent) and swimming (88.9 per cent).

The programme aims to engage traditionally non-active children in structured physical activities and to build pathways with local community organisations, including sporting clubs.

The Australian Sports Commission (ASC)

The Australian Sports Commission (ASC) is responsible for implementing the Government's national sports policy. Working together with other sporting organisations at all levels, the two delivery arms of the ASC – the AIS and Sport Performance and Development Group – promote the basic sports philosophy of the Australian Government: Excellence and Participation.

The ASC has developed an organisational and evaluation design based on a hierarchy of interdependent outcomes. The overarching goal (articulated as the mission statement) is dependent on achieving the three major objectives drawn from the Australian Sports Commission Act, which in turn rely on successful implementation of the seven major strategies described in the Strategic Plan.

The Commission is divided into seven primary groups:

Australian Institute of Sport (AIS)

The AIS is the Australian Government's national institute of sport. It is recognised as a world centre of excellence for the training and development of elite athletes and coaches, providing innovative and integrated support services to enhance athlete and programme performance. The AIS manages 35 scholarship sports programmes. It provides expert coaching, state of the art facilities and equipment, world-class integrated sports science and medical services, athlete welfare services and implementation of the technical requirements for sporting success.

Sport Performance and Development

The Sport Performance and Development Division comprises the Sport Services and Innovation and Best Practice sections. This division supports the development of the Australian sport system from the grassroots community level to high performance sport, by giving national sporting organisations access to advice and resources, including funding, policy development advice and management models, education, emerging information technologies and evaluation frameworks.

Corporate Services

The Corporate Services Division is responsible for the integration of the Commission's corporate operations as well as the provision of general services to sports and enhancement of the national sports information network. It is also responsible for the ASC's Legal Services and Research and Corporate Planning branches.

Commercial and Facilities

The Commercial and Facilities Division provides services to the other Divisions of the ASC in a client service environment. It administers the Australian Sports Foundation, manages and operates sporting/conference/accommodation facilities, generates off-budget revenue through commercial activities, and creates and maintains the buildings and infrastructure for the ASC.

National Sports Programs

The National Sports Programs Division comprises the National Programs section (which administers initiatives in the areas of Indigenous sport, women in sport, sport for people with a disability, coaching and officiating, and sport ethics), the International Relations section, the National Talent Identification and Development section and National Coach and Athlete Career and Education section.

Community Sport

The Community Sport Division includes the Active After-school Communities programme along with the National Junior Sport Unit. Recognising the importance of an active grass roots participation base in Australia, this division supports sport at the national level by assisting national sporting organisations to develop appropriate junior sport frameworks as well as building the base of Australian sport through actively delivering opportunities at the community level through the Active After-school Communities programme.

Financial Services

The Financial Services Division is responsible for the ASC's financial management, business support, accounts processing and financial reporting. The Financial Services area focuses on the provision of responsive and proactive

support within the ASC while continuing to ensure that the ASC satisfies the Government's financial management and accountability requirements.

Sport and the pursuit of excellence

The elite talent pool is estimated at 200,000. Compare this with the United States' 2 million. Programmes such as the National Talent Identification and Development Program, which assist sports in identifying talented athletes and preparing them for participation in domestic, national and eventually, international competition are crucial in finding the next generation of athlete.

Likewise, the development of the European Training Centre is evidence of a creative approach to equipping athletes to meet global competition. The Centre will provide and facilitate high-level support for Australian athletes whilst training and competing overseas in key international sporting events, in particular in the lead-up to the 2012 London Olympic and Paralympic Games.

The achievements of Australian athletes over recent years have been outstanding and a source of great national pride, helping to unite Australian communities. The number of Olympic, Paralympic and Commonwealth Games medal-winners combined with world champions and place-getters far exceeds the achievements of other nations of comparable population.

Australia can justifiably claim a model high performance sports system. Increasingly, other nations are looking at the Australian experience. However, to maintain its international reputation as a leading sporting nation, Australia will need to work even harder to maintain its current level of success.

The Australian Sports Commission (ASC) has responsibility for delivering high-performance programmes to meet the Government's objectives of supporting Australian athletes, their coaches and support staff as they compete in a large number of high-performance sports. These events include sports represented at the Olympics, the Paralympics, the Commonwealth Games and various World Championships.

The ASC achieves this through a range of programmes including Australian Institute of Sport (AIS) scholarship programmes (involving 26 sports), the AIS Athlete Career and Education programme, The High Performance, Innovation, Management and Systems programme and the High Performance Success Programme.

Activity 5

Research the ASC via its website (http://www.ausport.gov.au). What information about the AIS scholarships can you find?

CHALLENGE YOURSELF

Comment on the advantages and disadvantages of countries funding high-level sport and compare the approach of the Australian and the UK Institutes of Sport.

[20 marks]

Key term

Academies of Sport or Sports Institutes Training centres for the development of elite athletes usually with the aim of raising the profile of sport within a country, forming part of a national strategy in sport policy.

Australian Institute of Sport (AIS)

The AIS was established in 1981 as a result of a decline in world standing, lack of medals at world sporting events and lack of a formal structure to develop elite athletes. Its aim was 'to contribute to the development of elite sport in Australia through residential training programmes, camps and scholarship assistance'.

- Initially centralised in Canberra
- In 1985 it began to decentralise due to social problems encountered by young athletes (hockey to Perth; diving to Brisbane; volleyball to Sydney)
- States established their own Institutes (South Australia 1982; Western Australia 1984; Tasmania 1986; Victoria 1990)
- Funded 95 per cent by federal government; 5 per cent from commercial sponsorship, e.g., Kellogg's
- 1989 merged with ASC
- Provides training in 36 programmes in 26 sports across Australia
- Organises training camps for national teams
- Provides grants to elite athletes and coaches
- Delivers athlete advisory and employment services.

The AIS achieves its objectives through a variety of programmes as shown in Table 7. 6 below.

National talent search

The Australian Sports Commission (ASC) through the National Talent Identification and Development Program (NTID) aims to identify and fast-track Australia's next

generation of talented elite athletes with potential to win medals at the Olympics and World Championships. NTID is part of the ASC's Division of National Sports Programs.

The Australian Government has committed almost $20 million over four years to fund and support the delivery of National Talent Identification and Development Initiatives including:

- $4.8 million to strengthen the national talent identification network, regional and sport-specific talent identification initiatives.
- $8.8 million for the delivery of a national talent identification scheme focusing on the unique potential and needs within the Indigenous community.
- $7.2 million to promote regionally significant sports and other sports which have high potential to improve their results in international competition.

The ASC is delivering a number of national talent identification projects through a nationally integrated approach (across State Institutes of Sport and State Academies of State) in 18 specific sports which have the potential to achieve success at particularly the 2010 Commonwealth Games in India and the 2012 London Olympics. NTID projects will focus on the following Olympic sports including:

- Asian-centric – badminton, judo, tae-kwon-do, shooting, beach volleyball, triathlon, diving and short-track skating
- Indigenous communities – boxing, athletics, hockey, basketball and softball
- Other national sports – cycling, rowing, sprint and slalom canoeing and skeleton sled racing (Winter Olympics).

Australia is well equipped to fast-track athletes to success through its State Institutes of Sport and State Academies of Sport. The NTID programme will draw on the AIS cutting-edge sports science and technology, some of the world's best coaches and newly improved sport facilities.

The AIS has a long history of identifying talent, using the skills of its sports scientists to fast-track people with athletic ability. Back in 1988 Allan Hahn and colleagues from the Australian Institute of Sport (AIS) Physiology Department introduced a historic talent identification programme for rowing which discovered and fast-tracked exceptional talent like Atlanta gold medallist Megan Still.

The aim of talent identification projects is to help broaden Australia's sporting base and to maximise its relatively small talent pool of about 280,000 athletes (including all football codes, cricket, basketball and Olympic sports). China's talent pool is estimated at more than 16 million potential elite athletes and the United Kingdom has about 1.2 million.

In order for Australian sport to punch above its weight, National Talent Identification Initiatives must work smarter and harder to stay internationally competitive.

AIS facilities include:

- synthetic athletics track
- indoor swimming centre
- AIS Arena – catering for all indoor court sports
- Ansett Sports visitor centre
- gymnastic hall

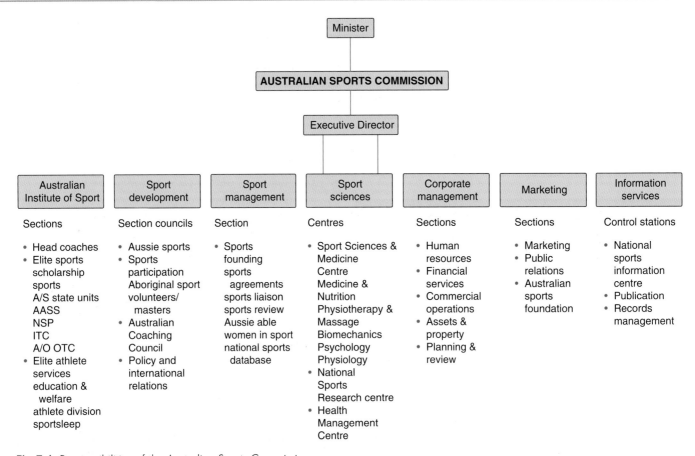

Fig 7.6 Responsibilities of the Australian Sports Commission

Table 7.6 The AIS

Programme	Explanation
Sport Talent Encouragement Plan (STEP)	Provide direct financial assistance to high-performance athletes
Elite Coaching Scheme	Raise standard of coaching for high-performance athletes
National Sports Plan/Sports Assistance Scheme (SAS)	Assistance to NSOs for training camps and technical seminars for athletes, coaches and officials
Intensive Training Centres (ITC)	Full-time Commonwealth funded coaches appointed to work with national and state-based coaches
Lifeskills for Elite Athletes Programme (SportsLEAP)	Reduce burden on athletes; short-term financial management of daily existence and career planning following retirement from performance
Scholarship Sports Programme	Main programme of AIS. Scholarship provides access to coaching, training facilities, sports science and medicine services; assistance with education and welfare; athletes receive full room and board (approx. $11 million per annum on around 500 scholarships)
Australian Athlete Scholarship Scheme	Similar to SportAid in the United Kingdom, but it receives federal money and has a larger budget. The primary aim is to give direct financial aid to elite athletes who will have been nominated by their National Sporting Bodies
Olympic Athlete Programme (OAP)	Six-year $135 million programme following successful Olympic bid

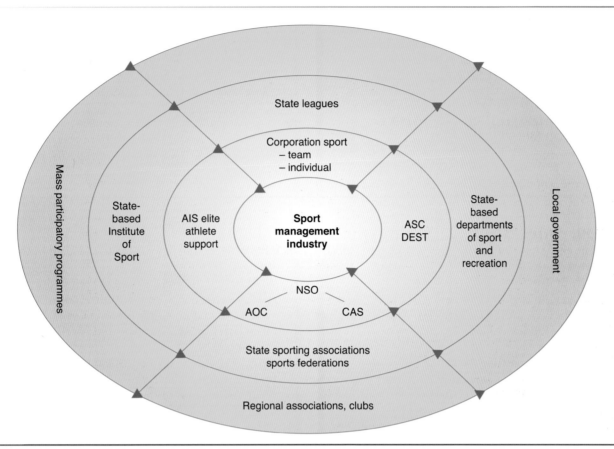

Fig 7.7 The four pyramids of Australian Sport

Pyramid A	Government involvement	Four pyramids show the peak agency/organisation at the apex of each
Pyramid B	Traditional sport system	Vertical channel of communication
Pyramid C	Sports development	Increasing width at lower level represents larger number of organisations and increased number of participants
Pyramid D	Corporate sport	Concentric circles show pattern and level of communication between organisations in each sector (only recently becoming more successful)

- soccer and hockey synthetic pitches
- outdoor tennis courts
- sports training facility
- National Sports Information Centre
- AIS residences.

Alternative pathways into professional sport

Throughout the country a wide variety of sports are played. According to official government statistics, in 2005–6 the most popular sports in terms of crowd attendance were Australian rules football, horse racing, motor sport, rugby league, cricket, rugby union and soccer (Association football).

Professional sport leagues in Australia use a model based on franchises and closed league membership, as is standard in North America. The 'European' system of professional sports league organisation, characterised by promotion and relegation, is foreign to Australia, at least at the professional level.

What you need to know

* Geographically, Australia is similar to the USA, and a variety of scenery and climate allows for wide variations in sports, though with fewer opportunities for winter sports.
* Australia has felt the influence of the British sports scene and has maintained links with the 'motherland' for a longer period of time.

* Australia has similar government administrations to the USA.
* Mass participation and the pursuit of excellence are important objectives, though the latter has attracted more world attention.

* The original characteristics of sports have been adapted within the more isolated continent and now have their own unique character such as Australian Rules football.
* International sport is high on the agenda for the Australians though professional sport is organised in a different format.
* Sport and physical education are given time on the timetable, and outside sports coaches are used within the school setting.

* The national sport institutes such as the VIS and the AIS share similar characteristics to the EIS in the UK and the American colleges and universities – these are high-level facilities and provide expert coaching.
* Traditional discrimination, especially against women, indigenous peoples and people with disabilities, is being reversed with specific policies.

Review Questions

1 Explain the impact of colonialism on Australian sport.
2 How has 'bush culture' influenced the national identity of Australia?
3 What does ACPHER stand for and what is its role?
4 Explain the PASE professional development programme.
5 Explain the fundamental skills programme.
6 Name three elements of the 'More Active Australia' programme and describe the aim of such a programme.
7 Talent identification is an important part of the Australian sport system. Describe how the Australians have implemented such an approach.
8 Each state has its own Sport Institute. What are the characteristics of these organisations?

9 What are the European influences evident in the game of Aussie Rules football?
10 What do the Australians have in their education system that is similar to the British Sportsmark Award?
11 What have been the similarities between the experiences of the Aborigine and American Indian populations?
12 What are the aims of the AIS and how does it attempt to achieve these aims?
13 What are the aims of the ASC and how does it attempt to achieve these aims?
14 Why has the Australian government placed so much emphasis on achieving excellence in sport?

Comparative examination techniques

The preparation of physical-education teachers

Having studied each country within its own context, you will need to find a method of directly comparing aspects of sport and physical education across all three countries. A useful method would be to take a topic such as 'the preparation of physical-education teachers'. You need to pull aspects of the topic together and then draw up a table and place key words under each country. This can be an effective way of revising.

Having considered how the subject of physical education is taught, we can assess how the teachers are prepared for their future role.

It is important that when you are asked to compare or contrast between different countries, you clearly state each, rather than assuming that, by mentioning one, the examiner will know that you understand the other. The examiner must be able to see a direct comparison in order to link the two together.

Example 1

Question

What are the different values inherent in school sport in the UK and the USA?

Answer

UK	USA
Value from playing intrinsic	Success in victory
Equality between girls and boys	Male games playing elite/female cheerleader
Less status for games elite	Elite sportspersons separate from mainstream
No cheerleaders in UK	Heavily financed
No financial privileges	Professional/deviance orientation
Amateur/PE value system	

Example 2

A response to a question about teaching and extracurriculum responsibilities in the UK and the USA could be shown as:

UK	USA
Teacher responsible	Coach responsible
Goodwill/no extra pay	Coach highly paid
Job security	Hire and fire
Low community profile	High media/community profile
Range of activities	Specialist

A descriptive account will usually gain minimum marks. You will need to show a deeper understanding by applying knowledge gained from each country and showing what effects this will have had on physical education and sport. Thus, political and sociological analysis is required. Terms that you should incorporate in your responses are:

- decentralised/centralised
- democracy/egalitarian
- pluralist/assimilation/ethnic groups
- dominant culture/subculture
- legislative
- nationalism
- functional/utilitarian/recreational
- autonomous/state-controlled
- capitalist/socialist
- republic/federal.

Conclusion

Globalisation

It is important to recognise the globalisation of sport that is due to the technological developments of transport and the media. Countries learn from each other, and the issues of human rights are slowly being addressed. Sports like baseball and American football are gaining acceptance outside the USA.

A 'core' programme

Despite the many differences existing across the countries we have looked at, there are also many similarities, such as mass participation, elite sport programmes, compulsory physical education and the development of sports for people with disabilities. A wider variety of sports has taken over from the traditional sports of gymnastics, football and track and field.

Commercial sport

Sport is big business and forms a significant income for governments. The development of the consumer market for sports goods, as well as extensive coverage by the media of sports events, contribute to this.

National government involvement in sport

This was summarised by Semoutiak as being for:

- political indoctrination
- labour and military efficiency
- national prestige
- international goodwill
- individualising and socialising function
- economic and legislative functions.

The reasons for different governments becoming involved in sport can reveal a lot about the values of that government and its opinion of physical education and sport.

Values

- The old concept of amateurism has undergone many changes, and abuse is prevalent in many systems, where eligibility for the prestigious Olympic Games is at stake. Situations like trust funds have changed the nature of amateur athletics and the full-time training of student athletes for the inter-collegiate competitions are examples of double standards operating. This begs the question – is there a place for amateurism in the twenty-first century?
- Physical education or sport? This is a question of educational philosophy – if the achievement of sporting excellence is the primary aim, the sport ethic can become too dominant and consequently damaging to children's personal development.
- The preparation of the sports professionals is consequently highlighted. Can the physical-education teacher, with his or her primary concern being the individual development of each child through a variety of physical activities, really take on board the win ethic associated with sport and the increasing specialisation required for each individual sport? Consider the priority given to sport in the 1995 publication 'Sport: Raising the Game'. Do they need to separate and remain with different aims? Does a system where there is a strong link developed between the school and community sport associations, such as in France, show an effective balance?
- Activity versus study? In an era when the industrialised countries of the world are concerned about the increasingly sedentary lifestyles of their citizens, physical education is showing a greater tendency to be examined on a theoretical level, possibly reducing the amount of physical energy expended.
- Nationalist tendencies can be reinforced through sport and can move from a unifying constructive factor to one that incites hatred, exploitation of athletes and unequal distribution of resources.
- The Olympic Games have moved from the original de Coubertin aims of reviving French nationalism based on the English tradition of athleticism, to one of providing a world stage for governments to raise their prestige and for political power groups to vent their tensions.
- Is the sports business world beginning to edge out the ordinary supporter, with the increased admission prices? The characteristics of these sports may well continue to change.
- The deviant acts of aggression, drug abuse and lack of respect for sports officials are becoming all too prevalent, as the win ethic assumes greater prominence.

Let us hope that in the future we can learn the best practices from each other and keep the positive nature of physical education and sport high on the agenda, for the development of future generations.

CHAPTER 8

Comparative studies of major sports in Australia, UK and USA

Learning outcomes

By the end of this chapter you should be able to:

- understand the major influencing factors on:
  - **cricket** (tradition, mythology of 'The Ashes', growth of commercialism, and development of the game)
  - **Association Football** (history as a working-class game, amateurism and professionalism, spectator and media interest, marginalisation in Australia but contemporary popularity)
  - **Rugby League football** (high-level competitions, history of professionalism, north–south divide, inclusive game in Australia, State of Origin, tri-nations)
  - **Rugby Union** (middle-class game, professionalism, commercialism, influence of rugby World Cup, and colonial game in Australia)
  - the 'big four' of American sports (i.e. **American Football, baseball, ice hockey,** and **basketball**) looking at their origins, the nature of the game, the impact of universities, the sport as an industry, and sport, sponsorship and media)
  - **Aussie Rules football** (cultural and ethnic diversity, appeal for both players and spectators)
- understand how the above sports developed within their own culture
- appreciate the impact of different cultures upon these sports.

CHAPTER INTRODUCTION

This chapter explores the effect of different cultures on the development of sport and physical activities. The UK has been a significant influence on how American and Australian sports evolved. Colonialism left its legacy of introducing British forms of sport and with it values such as amateurism. However, the more exclusive status of sport in the UK was never entirely adopted by these younger cultures, as it went against their social philosophy. Nevertheless, common to all three countries was the belief that sport should be encouraged for its individual character-building qualities and consequent benefits for society.

Cricket in Australia

For the history of 'the Ashes' and the growth of commercialism in cricket, see Chapter 6.

Cricket has a long history in Australia and is the most popular sport, played on local, national and international levels. Cricket is Australia's national summer sport and, unlike the various football codes, enjoys consistent support from a wide range of people throughout Australia.

EXAMINER'S TIP

The colonial influence is evident in a variety of sports. Some sports are unique to that culture; be prepared to explain this phenomenon.

The Australian national cricket team was the winner of the very first Test match, and is today regarded as one of the leading international teams in world cricket, having been the unquestionably dominant cricketing team since 2000.

In the summer of 1868 a team of Aboriginal cricketers toured England. This was the very first Australian cricket team to play overseas, and attracted wide interest at the time.

Australia has dominated world cricket since the mid-1990s. Australia has won the Cricket World Cup four out of the nine times it has been held, including the last three. Since 1996 its team has appeared in every World Cup final.

Domestic competitions among the Australian states include:

- the Sheffield Shield first-class competition
- the Ford Ranger One Day Cup List-A cricket competition
- the KFC Twenty20 Big Bash Twenty20 competition.

The Sheffield Shield and Ford Ranger One Day Cup tournaments involve each team playing against its opponents both at home and away, with the two highest-placed teams playing in the final match. The KFC Twenty20 Big Bash is similar, but with only one match against each other team before the final.

Established in 1999, the Commonwealth Bank Cricket Pathway offers a series of dedicated programmes and competitions for talented cricketers starting at the Under-13 level and moving through to senior cricket. The Pathway allows players, parents, coaches and administrators to understand the road from junior cricket to representing Australia at an international level. The Commonwealth Bank has been the official sponsor of the Pathway since 2003.

The eight metropolitan and eight country regions within the state of Victoria are all represented in every Pathway programme, with the result that players can participate in a programme suitable for their level irrespective of where in Victoria they live.

Within the eight metropolitan regions of West, North West, North, North East, Inner East, Outer East, South East and South, a player's alignment to a region is via where they live (i.e. their home address).

Within the eight country regions (Mallee-Murray, West Country, Central Highlands, Barwon, Northern Rivers, North East, Gippsland and South East) a player's alignment to a region is via the cricket association they participate in at a community cricket club level.

The Commonwealth Bank Cricket Pathway has three competition phases:

1   Under-14 Commonwealth Bank State Championships (played in January on Premier 3rd & 4th XI grounds).
2   Under-16 Commonwealth Bank Dowling Shield (played in January on Premier 1st & 2nd XI grounds).
3   Under-18 Commonwealth Bank Cup (played in January on Premier grounds and in a Victorian Country Cricket League (VCCL) region).

There are five state representative components of the Commonwealth Bank Cricket Pathway:

● Under-13 (controlled by the VPSSA with assistance from Cricket Victoria)
● Under-15 (controlled by the VSSSA with assistance from Cricket Victoria)
● Under-17 (National Championships in January)
● Under-19 (National Championships in December)
● Bushrangers (Pura Cup, ING Cup and Cricket Australia Cup).

Competitions such as VMCU Carnivals, VCCL Junior Country Weeks, VSDCA Under-15 Hatch Shield and inter-association cricket are not direct components of the Commonwealth Bank Cricket Pathway, but are valuable feeder competitions that assist with future pathway selection.

The significant contribution local clubs and associations in Victoria make in the development of cricketers is recognised in Pathway programmes. Players are not taken away from clubs for Pathway squad participation. Regional cricket managers are in regular discussion with association and club representatives over the selection of squads and use club/association performances as major factors in selection.

Fig 8.1 The Wallabies

The cricket Pathway programmes is one way how a cricketer from the state of Victoria in Australia could be sponsored by the VIS while playing for the cricket academy. However, this route is not essential to high-performance sport.

Association Football

For the development of Association Football (also known as 'football' or 'soccer') in the UK, see Chapter 2.

Association Football is a popular recreational and professional sport in Australia. The sport has the highest level of participation in Australia for all football codes. The fully professional A-League domestic competition has been operating since 2005 and the national team competes in the Asian Football Confederation. The national governing body is Football Federation Australia (formerly Soccer Australia).

The development of football in Australia

The early governing bodies of the sport in Australia had to distinguish themselves from Australian Rules football and Rugby Football—rival sports that had become very popular in the various Australian colonies during the 1860s and 1870s. The first inter-state match was played in 1883 between New South Wales (NSW) and its neighbouring colony of Victoria.

The first football (soccer) association was founded in 1882 in New South Wales by John Walter Fletcher, as the South British Football Association (some sources refer to it as the New South Wales English Football Association). In 1898 this became the NSW British Football Association.

While native-born Australians overwhelmingly played and watched Australian Rules football (or either code of Rugby Football), Association Football was highly popular among the various British and Southern European immigrant communities, all of which expanded rapidly during the 1950s and 1960s. Of these, the Croatian, Greek, Italian and Serbian communities gave rise to many of the largest clubs. At the time, the game served as a bonding force within these ethnic minority communities, and as a point of identity amongst them and the wider Australian community. A similarly increasing number of British migrants also retained an interest in the sport.

League system

Since 1977 the league system in Australia has involved a one-divisional league controlled by the national body, and many leagues run within each state below that with no promotion or relegation between the two. The A-League and Football Federation Australia are currently at the top of the sport. The first season of the new league began in August 2005. The average attendance (including finals) for the inaugural season was 11,627 attendees, which was significantly higher than the average of 4,119 for the NSL's final season the year before.

The A-League is the premier Australasian domestic association football competition. Run by the Australian governing body, Football Federation Australia, it was founded in 2004 and staged its inaugural season in 2005–2006. At the time of writing, it is sponsored by Hyundai Motor Company Australia, and is therefore officially known as the Hyundai A-League.

Football Federation Australia (FFA) is the governing body for the sport of football (soccer) in Australia. Before 2005, it was known as the Australian Soccer Association (ASA), which succeeded Soccer Australia in this role in 2003.

Among other duties, the FFA oversees:

- Australia's national football teams (including the Socceroos (men), the Matildas (women), and various youth teams)
- national coaching programmes
- coordination with the various state and territory governing bodies
- the national club competition.

Until 2004 the national competition was the National Soccer League (NSL). In 2005, FFA launched a new national league, the A-League. This league is contested by eight teams: seven covering Australia's major cities and regional centres and one from New Zealand. From the 2009–2010 season this is expanded to ten teams. Related leagues include a National Youth League for youth development, and the W-League also known as the women's league, which is the top level women's Association Football league in Australia. Established in 2008, it will be composed of

eight teams comprising the seven Australian A-League clubs and one based in Canberra.

The following state and territory federations are responsible for administering local league systems, which sit beneath the A-League:

- Football NSW
- Football Queensland
- Northern New South Wales Football
- Football Federation Victoria
- Football Federation Tasmania
- Football Federation of South Australia
- Football West
- Capital Football (ACT)
- Football Federation Northern Territory.

There is currently no national FA Cup-style knock-out competition as found in the UK. However, each state, except for Victoria and Queensland (which have regional cups), has its own cup competitions run by the state and territory federations. Some restrict participants to only the top flight or semi-pro clubs, while others have more open entries via invitation or qualifying rounds.

National teams

Australia enters national teams into women's and men's competitions, including all under-age competitions, as recognised by FIFA. The men's national football team is nicknamed the Socceroos and the women's national football team is nicknamed the Matildas.

Men's national team

In 2006 the Socceroos secured a place in the FIFA World Cup, when the then Prime Minister, John Howard, asked employers to turn a blind eye to workers turning up late for work the following day. Such was the widespread interest in the match!

During the 2006 World Cup the Japan and Italy games were the top-rating television programmes in Australia in their respective weeks, and the game against Croatia was the second highest in its week, despite the matches being broadcast during the work-day, between 11 pm and 5 am. However, the games were still out-rated by other sport-related programmes broadcast during 2006. The second round game against Italy was tenth on OzTam's survey of the most watched Australian TV events for 2006.

Women's national football team

The Australian national women's football team regularly qualifies for the FIFA Women's World Cup and Olympic Games. The Matildas are widely acknowledged as one of the most improved teams currently in the women's competition, following their quarter-final showing at the 2007 FIFA Women's World Cup. Currently, the Matildas are ranked inside the top 20 nations in the world at number 12 (England's national women's team is ranked 17 points ahead at position 11).

Association Football in the media

Pay television is the predominant outlet for both domestic and international football in Australia. Some games can also be heard on local radio stations. The anti-siphoning list that controls what must be kept on free-to-air television in Australia includes only the FA Cup games.

Following a A$120 million, seven-year deal between the FFA and Fox Sports, from 2007 Fox Sports have exclusive rights to all Socceroos' home internationals, all *A-League* and AFC Asian Cup fixtures, FIFA World Cup qualifiers through the AFC, and all AFC Champions League matches. Representing the most significant TV rights agreement for football in Australia, this is still relatively small beer compared to European football leagues, such as the English Premier League.

SBS shows live UEFA Champions League games and retains the Australian broadcast rights to the 2010 FIFA World Cup and 2014 FIFA World Cup finals. Pay Television stations (Fox Sports, ESPN and Setanta) also show English, Scottish, German, Dutch and Spanish leagues.

Exam-style Questions

Explain why the popularity of Association Football (soccer) has now begun to increase in Australia.

Rugby League

Rugby League is one of the two major codes of Rugby Football, the other being Rugby Union. The league code is prominent in Great Britain and Australia, where the sport is played professionally.

Rugby League takes its name from what was initially a breakaway faction of the English Rugby Football Union (RFU), known as the Northern Rugby Football Union when established in 1895. Since then, Rugby League and Rugby Union have been very different sports.

Although many factors, including the success of working-class northern teams, played a part in the split, the main division was caused by the RFU decision to enforce the amateur principle of the sport, thus preventing 'broken time payments' to players who had taken time off work to play. Northern teams typically had more working-class players who could not afford to play without this compensation, in contrast to southern teams which often had other sources of income to sustain the amateur principle.

Worldwide, Rugby League is played in more than 30 countries, though it is most commonly played in the UK (predominantly in northern England), Australia and New Zealand. Of these three, it is in Australia, where it is a winter sport, that Rugby League is most popular, especially in Queensland and NSW.

However, in the UK the game is growing in popularity nationwide, with television figures showing 50 per cent of viewers come from southern England and record participation numbers in the junior game. Nevertheless, the majority of teams still remain in the North.

High-level competitions

The Rugby League International Federation (RLIF) was founded in 1948. The RLIF is the world-governing body for the sport of Rugby League. It is responsible for organising international competitions such as the World Cup and Tri-Nations, as well as fixing the laws of the game and coordinating international development. The RLIF consists of a series of informal meetings between administrators from the leading Rugby League nations.

Super League is a full-time professional Rugby League club competition operating in the northern hemisphere. As a result of current sponsorship from engage Mutual Assurance, the current competition is officially known as the engage Super League.

Super League (Europe) (SLE) began in March 1996 and saw the English season switch from winter to summer for the first time in over 100 years. Most of the teams are based in Great Britain, though initially the league was intended to be European. Following the departure of the only French team, Paris St Germain, in 1997, the league was solely English until Catalans Dragons were admitted for the 2006 season. Since 2009, a Welsh team, the Celtic Crusaders, has taken part in competition.

During the league's regular season, each team plays 27 games over 27 rounds from February to September. At the end of the regular season, the top six teams in Super League take part in the play-offs, which culminate with the Grand Final.

Each year the competition winners play a game against the premiers of the Australasian National Rugby League competition in the World Club Challenge (WCC). Also referred to as the Carnegie World Club Challenge (or CWCC for sponsorship purposes), the WCC is an annual Rugby League match held between the champions of the Australasian National Rugby League and the European Super League competitions to determine the world's best Rugby League club. The first match of its kind was played in 1976, but it did not become a regular part of the World Rugby League calendar until the late 1980s. The WCC's history was also punctuated by the 'Super League War' in the 1990s.

The 'Super League War' was fought in and out of court during the mid-1990s by the News Limited-backed Super League and Kerry Packer-backed Australian Rugby League organisation over control of the top-level professional Rugby League football competition of Australasia.

World Cup

The Rugby League World Cup is the major international competition contested by the men's national Rugby League teams of the member teams of the RLIF. The very first World Cup competition took place 1954 and was contested between the four Test nations: Australia, Great Britain, France and New Zealand. In 2000 a World Cup for the women's national Rugby League teams was inaugurated.

The Bradford Bulls is a professional Rugby League club based in Bradford, a city in northern England. It has been one of the major success stories of the Super League era, with the 2003 season being its best, during which the club won all the major Rugby League honours (Challenge Cup, Super League Championship, World Club Championship, and Minor Premier). The club plays all its home games at Grattan Stadium (formerly called Odsal Stadium), which is located to the south of the city centre. Bradford Bulls is also one of the original 22 rugby clubs that formed the Northern Rugby Football Union in 1895, making Bradford Bulls one of the world's very first Rugby League teams.

Rugby League in Australia

For the development of Rugby League in the United Kingdom, see page 121.

The Australian Rugby League (ARL) is the governing body for the sport of Rugby League in Australia. The ARL is made up of state bodies, including the New South Wales Rugby League (NSWRL) and the Queensland Rugby League (QRL). The ARL Board comprises three members from the NSWRL, three members from the QRL, and a chairman who holds the casting vote.

Since its inception, the ARL has administered the Australian national team and represented Australia in international Rugby League matters. During the 'Super League War' of the mid-1990s (see page 119), the ARL also administered Australia's club premiership until the National Rugby League was formed.

The premier first grade Rugby League competition in Australia had been run by the New South Wales Rugby League from its first season in 1908 until the end of 1994. With further expansion of the competition nationwide implemented for the 1995 season, the NSWRL passed to the ARL control of the Winfield Cup competition, following the inclusion of teams from Perth, Townsville and Auckland.

Following Kerry Packer's announcement that he owned both free-to-air and pay television broadcasting rights for the sport in Australia, News Limited undertook a bold bid to create a rival competition, Super League (Australia). Super League successfully attracted eight of the ARL clubs.

In the State of Origin series of 1995, ARL forbade players of those eight breakaway clubs from participating in the inter-state competition. However, the same eight clubs were allowed to participate in the premiership seasons of 1995 and 1996, while the ARL fought a legal battle to stop the Super League competition from operating.

In 1997, Super League conducted a rival competition in 1997, running parallel to the ARL competition. At the close of the 1997 season, ARL decided that it was not in the best interests of the sport to run two such competitions and approached News Limited and invited the traditional clubs back into the main competition. As a consequence of the negotiations that followed, the National Rugby League (NRL) was formed before the 1998 season from the ARL and Super League competitions.

The NRL has now become Australian Rugby League's major elite competition in Australia, and is conducted as a partnership with News Limited and ARL.

Inclusive game

ARL Development is a not-for-profit company formed by ARL and NRL to develop the sport from grassroots level up to the age of 18 years. Working within the pre-existing development framework established by clubs and state leagues, ARL Development seeks to augment existing programmes and establish new development initiatives. By restricting some rules, youngsters can take part with confidence and learn more about the sport. As the youngsters' interest and skill increase, these same rules can be gradually re-introduced at the more appropriate higher levels of the game.

The two introductory modified codes currently in use in Australia are **mini footy** and **mod league**. On completion of mod league, players make a move to full international Rugby League laws.

Mini footy (also known as **mini league** in England) is a form of Rugby League developed by the Australian Rugby League specifically to introduce children to Rugby League.

These modifications are aimed at providing a child with a safe environment, a firm knowledge of the rules of the sport and time to practise the skills such as tackling, passing, and common defensive and attacking tactics.

Mod league follows on from mini footy. Mod league introduces laws more common to the full international laws of Rugby League, while keeping the core theme of being sport played at an introductory level. Mod league is seen as a necessary bridge between mini footy and the full rigours of international Rugby League.

Table 8.1 Australian Rugby League premiers

Season	Grand Final Information			Minor Premiers
	Premiers	*Score*	*Runners-Up*	Premiers
1995	Sydney Bulldogs	17–4	Manly-Warringah	Manly-Warringah
1996	Manly-Warringah	20–8	St. George	Manly-Warringah
1997	Newcastle Knights	22–16	Manly-Warringah	Manly-Warringah

Indigenous Development Program

The community aspect of the sport is taking steps to include the multi-cultural and indigenous peoples to the game. There are development officers who aim to raise the profile of the sport among ethnic minorities and indigenous peoples of Australia.

IN CONTEXT

As a preliminary to the opening ceremony of the 2008 Rugby League World Cup in Sydney, the New Zealand Maori side played Australia's team, Indigenous Dreamtime, captained by Australian Preston Campbell. When appointed as captain, Campbell described this as the equal of any of his many achievements in the game.

'Winning a premiership is every player's dream, but to represent your people is an honour that all the boys are proud of,' the Gold Coast Titans' Player of the Year said. 'To be named as captain is something I will cherish for the rest of my life.'

Rugby League Tri-Nations

The Gilette Tri-Nations Series Rugby League competition features Australia, New Zealand and Great Britain. In 2001 the first 'Ashes' series was played since Great Britain won in 1994. However, since 2003, the dominance of the Australian team over the last generation has begun to slip.

In 2003 and 2005 New Zealand won the Bill Kelly Memorial Trophy from Australia. In 1999 and 2004 Australia won the first two Rugby League Tri-Nations competitions before being defeated by New Zealand in the final of the 2005 competition. Prior to that defeat Australia had not lost a series since December 1978 (when Australia was defeated by France). In November 2006 Australia lost to Great Britain. This was a huge upset, and the first time since 1988 that the Kangaroos had been beaten by Great Britain in Sydney. The match was Australia's third match of the 2006 Tri-Nations series, Australia having already secured a place in the final with a pair of wins against New Zealand earlier in the tournament. The Australian side managed to re-claim the title of Tri-Nations Champions later in November 2006 with a victory over the New Zealand side in the final. As Australia hosted the competition in 2008, its team automatically qualified.

Rugby Football Union (RFU)

The development of the sport

Rugby Football became popular in the English middle and upper class public schools during the nineteenth century, primarily as recreation for the boys when not studying. Each school played using its own rules, developed by the pupils themselves. For example, the boys at Rugby School, which is situated in central England, played their 'football' on grass using a pig's bladder encased in leather for a ball.

The rules at Rugby School initially forbade handling the ball on the field of play unless the ball was airborne, in which case it could be caught. This situation prevailed up until the mid-1820s when boys started to catch the ball and, instead of standing still, run with the ball in their arms towards the opponent's goal-line. By the 1840s this practice had become the norm.

When the boys of Rugby School left for university or to take up commissions in the armed services, they took the game with them. As a result, clubs sprang up all over England and throughout the British Empire, where the boys now worked either as service personnel or administrators. By 1870 it became clear that the game was being played to a variety of rules, and was in need of some codification.

The birth of the first Rugby Union

On 26th January 1871 a meeting held in London was attended by over 30 people from 22 clubs and schools. As a result of this meeting, the Rugby Football Union (RFU) was founded. A committee was formed and three ex-Rugby School pupils were invited to write a set of laws. The writers were all lawyers and the task was completed and approved by June of that year.

At the same time, the Scottish members of the new Union challenged the English members to a match, and the first international match between Scotland and England was played at Raeburn Place, Edinburgh on 27 March 1871 (Scotland won by 1 goal, 1 try to 1 goal). The Scots formed their own Rugby Union in 1873; the Irish Rugby Football Union was formed in 1879 and the Welsh Rugby Union in 1880.

The 'Great Schism' – professional or amateur?

In 1893 the Committee of the RFU began to hear reports that some players in the north of England were being paid for playing, contrary to the strict amateur code. These payments, commonly known as 'broken time payments', were made to compensate working-class players who would not otherwise have been able to afford to play the game.

There then followed two large general meetings at which efforts were made by the northern clubs to carry a resolution that men should be paid for 'broken time', i.e. when playing football instead of working. The motion was defeated.

As a result, in August 1895 twenty-two clubs seceded from the Rugby Football Union and formed the Northern Union (which in the 1920s became the 'Rugby League'). The loss of these northern clubs (and the many others that followed them) to the Northern Union had a serious impact on the English international side, and it was several years before the loss could be made up.

In 1995 the International Rugby Board announced that the game would become 'open', i.e. players could be paid for playing. So, 100 years after the Northern Union broke away, the ethos of the game had completely changed.

Why did the bastion of amateur sport turn professional in 1995? There were a number of factors:

- player-drain to Rugby League where players could earn a living
- modern sport needs vast financial support – this tends to be attracted by professional sports
- professional sport tends to see a rise in standards, increasing its attractiveness for spectators.

Table 8.2 Advantages and disadvantages of Rugby Union turning professional

Advantages	Disadvantages
Players are full-time and, therefore, playing standards rise as training is more regular, mostly every day.	Over-training can lead to player burnout.
	Physical nature of the game has increased.
Access to best sports science and medicine.	Pressure for results could lead to deviancy such as doping.
Recovery time is effective.	
	Club vs country debate.
Extra income has led to better facilities and pitches which helps increase the standard of play.	More competitions for commercial reasons; don't put players first.

Impact of the World Cup

Success in the Rugby World Cup has led to:

- increasing popularity of the game, both in terms of participation and as a spectator sport
- a growth in clubs, coaches and officials
- a huge injection of money that has improved facilities, training and coaching
- increased media interest
- players became household names and attracted personal sponsorship deals.

Rugby Union in Australia

For the history of Rugby Union in the UK, see Chapter 3.

Rugby Union is a popular team sport played in Australia, with a history dating back to 1864. In Australia, Rugby Union is mainly played at a professional and recreational level. The principal competition in the Australian Rugby Union is the Super 14, which is a multi-regional competition across the southern hemisphere. Within this competition there are four regional franchises from Australia: the Reds (Queensland), the Waratahs (NSW), the Brumbies (Australian Capital Territory), and the Force (Western Australia).

In 2007 the Australian Rugby Championship was introduced as the level below the Super 14. But owing to a lack of interest, this competition ended the same year. Currently, the highest level of domestic competition is made up of the traditional capital city competitions, such as the Shute Shield of Sydney and the Queensland Premier Rugby of Brisbane.

The national Rugby Union team is known as the Wallabies, who have won the Rugby World Cup twice (1991 and 1999). The Wallabies are considered one of the top rugby teams in the world, due to their success at the World Cup and their consistently high world-ranking.

After more than a century of a strictly-enforced amateur code, Rugby Union became an openly professional sport in 1995, with major changes seen in both the club and international game. The Super 12 Rugby competition was born that year. This tournament involved 12 provincial sides from three counties. The year also saw the Tri-Nations Series, between the three Super 12 countries.

In 1999, the Bledisloe Cup match between Australia (the Wallabies) and New Zealand (All Blacks) was staged at the Homebush Olympic Stadium, now known as Telstra Stadium. The game attracted a crowd of 107,042, then a world record for a Rugby Union match. In 2000, this attendance was bettered when a crowd of 109,874 witnessed the 'Greatest Ever Rugby Match', during which a try by Jonah Lomu sealed an All Blacks win over the Wallabies.

The Wallabies were champions of the 1999 Rugby World Cup, held in Wales, claiming their second Webb Ellis Cup trophy. In doing this, Australia became the first multiple winners of the tournament.

In 2003 the fifth Rugby World Cup was staged in Australia. Prior to the tournament, three high profile Kangaroo Rugby League players switched codes. Matches were played all across the country. The tournament was hailed as a huge success. With an estimated 40,000 international spectators travelling to Australia for the event, some estimates claimed that A$100 million may have been injected into the Australian economy. According to the Australian Rugby Union, revenues had exceeded all expectations, with the tournament surplus estimated to be at A$44.5 million. The hosting of the World Cup in Australia also saw an increase in Super 12 crowds and junior participation. In 2005, to celebrate a decade of professional Rugby Union in Australia, the Wallaby Team of the Decade was announced.

Organisation

Rugby Union in Australia is governed by the Australian Rugby Union (ARU), which is a member of the International Rugby Board (IRB). There are constituent state unions, with the New South Wales Rugby Union and Queensland Rugby Union traditionally being the dominant members, reflecting the game's higher status within these states. However, every state and territory in Australia is represented by their respective union and, in recent years, the ACT and Southern NSW Rugby Unions have elevated themselves to equality with NSW and Queensland.

Participation

In 2000, there were just over 42,100 adult Rugby Union players in Australia, of which New South Wales (NSW) and

Queensland account for 82.3 per cent of all senior players. The highest participation rate in the Australian Capital Territory is 0.8 per cent. In NSW major support comes from the many private schools that still maintain Rugby Union over Rugby League.

Exam-style Questions

Australia is a country with a tradition of sporting excellence which began during the colonial period.

Explain the political and cultural factors that extend the tradition of sporting excellence into the twenty-first century.

[5 marks]

American Football

American Football, it has been claimed, sums up the character of the USA: technological, territorial, physically violent and intimidating, a team effort and the epitome of specialisation. It originated from the game of rugby in England, but developed along different lines within its new culture in America. Its development reflected America's attempts to create a new identity, one that was separate from Europe, and the game was influenced by many other different cultures. It was not constrained by the amateur traditions, and its 'win' ethic emerged alongside professionalism.

Today American Football is played by school, college and professional teams and is one of the most popular American sports, attracting thousands of participants and millions of spectators annually. American Football was made popular by teams representing colleges and universities, and therefore had its roots among the white, middle classes of society.

A single game each year between the champions of the leagues has become one of the most popular events in the United States. Because many collegiate football championships were known as 'bowls' because of the bowl-shaped stadiums that hosted them, one AFL owner referred to the new game as a 'super' bowl. The name proved popular with the public and has been used ever since.

The Super Bowl is the final contest of the National Football League (NFL) season. Each year, on a Sunday at the end of January or at the start of February, tens of millions of Americans declare their own unofficial holiday. Americans increasingly have gathered in private Super Bowl parties, where they enjoy food, drink and televised football. An estimated 130 million to 140 million viewers – almost half of the US population – will tune in to some part of the game. Four of the ten most watched television programmes in US history have been Super Bowls.

CHALLENGE YOURSELF

In the USA the development of 'new games' was influenced by the culture of this country.

Describe how Ivy League colleges such as Harvard and Yale helped to develop American Grid Iron Football and explain why American Grid Iron Football is a popular sport in the USA.

[8 marks]

How did this compare to the development of Rugby Football in the UK?

[20 marks]

Baseball

So many people in the USA play the game as children that it has become known as 'the national pastime.'

The exact origins of baseball are unknown, but most historians agree that it is based on the English game of rounders. It became quite popular in the early nineteenth century. In 1845, Alexander Cartwright formalised a list of rules by which all teams could play. Rules, scoring and record-keeping gave baseball gravity. As one sport historian noted, 'Baseball without records is inconceivable.' For example, most devotees in America know that Roger Maris' 61 home runs (balls that cannot be played because they have been hit out of the field) in 1961 broke Babe Ruth's record of 60 in 1927.

Key term

Home run A ball that cannot be played because it has been hit out of the field.

The first professional baseball league was established in America in 1871. By the start of the twentieth-century, most large cities in the eastern United States had a professional baseball team, but baseball only truly came of age in the 1920s, when Babe Ruth (1895-1948) playing for the New York Yankees became a national hero for his playing achievements.

Over the decades, every team has had its great players, such as Jackie Robinson (1919-1972), who played for the Brooklyn Dodgers and was the first black player in the major leagues in 1947. (Prior to Robinson, black players had been restricted to the Negro League.)

Starting in the 1950s, baseball expanded its geographical range. Western cities lured teams to move from eastern cities or formed so-called 'expansion teams' with players made available by established teams. From the start, major league baseball has been divided into the National League and the American League.

The major league baseball season lasts from April to October and includes the regular season, the play-offs, and the World Series. The most victorious team in each league is said to have won the 'pennant'. The two pennant winners meet after the end of the regular season and a series of play-offs within league sub-divisions in the World Series. The winner of this series becomes the major league World Series champion.

Until the 1970s, because of the strict terms of their player-contracts, owners of baseball teams had a great deal of control over the players in their team. Since then, the laws have changed so that players are free (within certain limits) to sell their services to any team. This has resulted in several bidding wars with star players being paid millions of dollars a year. Disputes between the players' union and team-owners have occasionally halted baseball for months at a time. Baseball is both a sport and a business. Many disgruntled fans sometimes view the business side as the dominant one.

Major league baseball (MLB) is the highest level of professional baseball competition in North America, and includes teams from Canada as well as the United States. At the other end of the scale, there are many amateur teams that play in Little League, high school, university, and various community leagues.

Over the course of the twentieth century, baseball spread to many nations and became a demonstration sport at the 1912, 1936, 1956, 1964, 1984 and 1988 Olympic Games. However, in 2005, the International Olympic Committee voted to eliminate baseball from the Olympics after 2008.

At present, baseball does not have an Olympic future.

Ice hockey

Ice hockey is one of the most violent team games – fighting is an intrinsic part of the action, and is expected. The physical speed of the game and the type of implements used (hockey stick, skates, puck) make this game fast, brutal and thrilling to watch. Players are dressed for protection, but carry injury with pride and are willing to play on when injured. Team members play in a confined area with close and vocal supporters to whom winning has an intense emphasis. In contrast to basketball, ice hockey is a sport played and watched by more white people, which is probably due to its origins in sub-arctic Canada. Ice hockey tends to:

- create entertainment through the media and sponsors
- attract families rather than have single sex traditions
- offer extensive facilities that are of a high standard, both in terms of players and spectators
- operate as a business controlled by individual team-owners, with teams heavily marketed with accompanying merchandise
- carry racial identity and preferences
- be very competitive (unlike cricket, draws are not a feature).

The professional ethos of the Lombardian ethic with material rewards for success reflects the capitalist culture of America. Because of the size of the USA, there is not the tradition of 'home' and 'away' fans that is found in Britain. Therefore, crowds are less partisan.

Exam-style Questions

Explain how cultural factors have influenced the development of professional sport in America.

[5 marks]

Basketball

Basketball originated in 1891, when James Naismith, a young physical education teacher in Springfield, Massachusetts, invented a new game that could be played indoors during the cold winter months and that would keep his students occupied and out of trouble. Naismith had the idea of nailing up raised boxes into which players would attempt to throw a ball. Naismith had two bushel baskets nailed to the balcony at opposite ends of the school's gymnasium. He set up two teams (each of nine men), gave them a soccer ball, and told them that the aim of the game was to toss the ball into the basket defended by the opposing team. Most of the rules Naismith drew up still apply in some form today. He called the game 'Basket Ball', the modern version of which is played by over 250 million people worldwide in an organised fashion, as well as by countless others in 'pick-up' games.

Every year, in the second week of February, the National Basketball Association (NBA) interrupts its season to celebrate the annual All-Star game, featuring the game's best players as selected by fans throughout the United States and Canada. At the end of the season, the champions from the Eastern and Western conferences meet in a 'best-of-seven' series to determine the NBA champion.

Superstar players like Michael 'Air' Jordan have increased the popularity of basketball internationally. In 1992, a so-called 'Dream Team', made up of the top American professional basketball players, represented the United States in the Olympic Games for the first time. Many teams in the NBA now have foreign players, who return home to represent their native countries during international competitions, such as the Olympic Games. Dirk Nowitzki who plays for the Dallas Mavericks is Germany's most popular sports export to the USA. FIBA, the Federation of International Basketball, is an independent organisation that governs international basketball and has over 200 organisations affiliated.

Basketball has a unique appeal. As one sport journalist explained, 'The deep appeal of basketball lies in the fact that the poorest of kids can make it rich, and that there is a mystery in how he does it. Neither baseball nor football creates the special, jazzed-up excitement of this game in which the human body can be made to do unearthly things, to defy gravity gracefully. A trust in mystery is part of the foolishly beautiful side of the American dream, which actually believes that the impossible is possible.'

Basketball has more potential for improvisation than either baseball or American Football due to the fluidity of play. The players are free to execute their own individuality and can perform cunningly deceptive moves. Basketball has become a symbol of black identity and black social power.

Exam-style Questions

Outline the reasons why basketball in the USA has evolved into a game dominated by the African-American minority and identify one example of improved provision which has contributed to this development.

[3 marks]

Australian football

Also known as Aussie Rules football, this game dates back to 1858 when two men, Harrison and Wills, decided to design a purely Australian game. The game that emerged showed signs of influences from cricket (oval pitch), Gaelic football (being played by Irish troops) and the English game of rugby. The cricket pitches were used and were controlled by the cricket clubs such as the Melbourne club, which is the oldest, having been founded in 1858. Thus, Aussie Rules also helped to keep cricketers fit in the winter months.

Even today, the size of the playing area is not a set distance but has minimum and maximum dimensions. This is a significant factor in the game not being successful internationally.

Exam-style Questions

Explain why Aussie Rules football is known as a 'new game' and describe how it has developed into a game of the people.

[3 marks]

With Aussie Rules and Rugby League:

- premier matches form a series
- professionals play for their own state rather than the home state of their club
  - *Advantage*: poorer states can use players who have moved to bigger clubs.
  - *Disadvantage*: calculated at player's residence since the age of 15 rather than at birth.
- Aussie Rules has a draft system similar to the USA.

The draft system

In the AFL Draft, clubs receive picks based on the position in which they finish on the ladder during the season. The draft is held each November, with a pre-season draft the following month. Currently to be eligible for the draft, a player must be at least 17 years of age on or before 30 April in the year in which they are drafted. This has been slowly increased over the past few years owing to concerns about school-age players potentially having to leave home to play football in another state.

Priority draft pick rule

In 2006 several changes were made to the rules, including:

- the Priority round was shifted, so that this was held between the First and Second rounds of the draft
- teams would receive a Priority Selection only if they finished the season with fewer than 16.5 premiership points
- if a team finished with fewer than 16.5 premiership points in two consecutive seasons, then their Priority Selection is taken before the First Round.

The Number 1 draft pick is currently awarded to the bottom-placed team, although in some cases it can be traded.

Sport and people with disabilities

In the past sixty years there has been a sea change in attitudes towards people with disabilities. Although there are many areas of life where more improvements could be made, generally disability is no longer seen as a barrier to participation in society. Nowhere is this more true than in sport, from grassroots level to elite performers such as Tanni Grey-Thompson and Eleanor Simmonds. One catalyst for this change in attitudes is the Paralympic Games.

Paralympic Games

Shortly after the Second World War, Sir Ludwig Guttmann, a neurologist at Stoke Mandeville Hospital in Aylesbury who worked with British war veterans suffering from spinal injuries, began using sport as part of the rehabilitation programmes of his patients.

In 1948 he set up a competition with other hospitals to coincide with the Olympics, which were being held in London that year.

Over the next decade Guttmann's care plan was adopted by other spinal injury units in Britain and competition grew.

In 1960 the Olympics were held in Rome, so Guttmann arranged for 400 wheelchair athletes from over 20 countries, including as far away as Australia, to compete in Rome in a parallel competition. The modern Parallel Olympics (or 'Paralympics') were born. In 2008 the Beijing Paralympics over 4,000 athletes from almost 150 countries worldwide competed for medals. The next Paralympics will be held in London in 2010.

Over the years the range of Paralympic sports also expanded:

- **1976 Toronto**: events for blind or partially sighted athletes and amputee athletes
- **1980 Arnhem**: athletes with Cerebral Palsy participated in the Games
- **1996 Atlanta**: events for athletes with intellectual disabilities were included for the first time.

The International Paralympic Committee (IPC) was founded in 1989, with the mandate to organise, supervise and coordinate the Paralympic Games, and promote sport for athletes with disabilities.

In 1990 the Australian Paralympic Federation was established. Ten years later Australia hosted the Paralympic Games in Sydney. The events covered six categories of disability:

1. Spinal cord injury
2. Amputee
3. Cerebral palsy
4. *Les autres* (a range of locomotor disorders)
5. Vision impaired
6. Intellectual disability.

IN CONTEXT

Originally formed in 1990 by members of the National Sporting Organisations for the Disabled (NSOD) and called the Australian Paralympic Federation, the now re-named Australian Paralympic Committee (APC) is the national body responsible for Australia's elite athletes with a disability.

Its primary goal is to create a unified body to coordinate:

- corporate representation (domestically and internationally)
- Paralympic Games participation (summer and winter)
- marketing (sponsorship and fundraising)
- public awareness.

A support goal is to assist 'members' to develop disability sport in Australia. APC membership presently comprises six NSODs plus seven National Sporting Organisations (NSOs).

Its mission statement is to 'to enable Paralympic athletes to achieve sporting excellence and inspire and excite the world'.

The twelfth Paralympic Summer Games took place in Athens in 2004, with athletes from over 130 nations competing for medals. For 17 of these nations this was their first Paralympic Games. During these Games, the Paralympic Village was home to 3,806 athletes, around 2,200 NPC team officials and 1,000 Games officials. Excellent sporting performances in 19 sports resulted in 304 world records and 448 Paralympic records.

China claimed top spot on the final medal tally with a winning total of 141 medals, many of which were gold. Australia was placed second on total medals, winning 101 (26 of which were gold, 39 were silver, and 36 were bronze). The strict selection criteria set by the APC and sports meant that only athletes with the potential to win a medal were selected for the team. As such, the total Australian team size was much smaller than when at Sydney in 2000, when 252 athletes and officials attended from Australia.

At the Beijing Paralympics in 2008 China once again topped the medals table. However, this time Australia had slipped in the rankings.

Table 8.3 Top 10 countries on the medal tally board (Beijing, 2008)

Rank	NPC	Gold	Silver	Bronze	Total
1	China	63	46	32	141
2	Great Britain	35	30	29	94
3	Canada	28	19	25	72
4	USA	27	22	39	88
5	Australia	26	39	36	101
6	Ukraine	24	12	19	55
7	Spain	20	27	24	71
8	Germany	19	28	31	78
9	France	18	26	30	74
10	Japan	17	15	20	52

Since 1981 Australian athletes with disabilities have been able to use the facilities of the Australian Institute of Sport (AIS) In 1989 the first scholarship was offered to the vision-impaired field athlete Russell Short for a place in the AIS Track & Field programme.

During the 1990s a specific 'AIS athletes with disabilities' programme was directed by head coach Chris Nunn and assisted up to 30 world-ranked athletes across a number of sports.

Following the 2000 Paralympic Games, a decision was taken in conjunction with the Australian Paralympic Committee to move towards integrating AIS programmes for disabled athletes with the respective mainstream programmes.

This process began in January 2001 with the integration of the Track and Field component of the programme with the AIS Track and Field Programme. The AIS contributes funds to a Winter Sport Programme for athletes with a disability and this is coordinated by the APC (e.g. the AIS-APC Alpine Skiing programme).

In 2003 the AIS and the Australian Paralympic Committee launched the AIS/APC Swimming programme. This camp-based initiative has become a finishing school for some of Australia's top Paralympic swimmers.

EXAMINER'S TIP

Always be prepared to show your understanding of major social influences, such as amateurism and professionalism, commercialisation and the media, on the development of different sports.

What you need to know

* There are traditional, cultural links between the UK, USA and Australia. Sport has helped to maintain and, in some cases, reinforce these links in competitions such as the Commonwealth Games and the Ashes.
* The UK was the common factor in the early influences of the way sport developed in the USA and Australia.
* Football in the UK was to influence the beginnings of American Football and Aussie Rules football.
* Cricket as an indigenous game in the UK became popular in the colonial period in Australia and has maintained its popularity. The game did not match the new culture of the USA as the USA had developed a more win-orientated approach towards sport.
* Social class was to be influential in all three countries and would be evident in the origins of particular sports. For example, American Football became middle class due to its origins in the universities such as Yale and Harvard, which was similar to the development of rugby in the English public schools of the nineteenth century. Conversely, Association Football in the UK would be dominated by the working-classes in northern England and by the rise of professionalism.

* The development of sports would be affected by differing philosophies and ideals. For example, the payment of players would lead to splits in the game of football and rugby, leading to amateur and professional sides.
* Sport has been, and still is, viewed as a 'way out' for those in low socio-economic groups and ethnic minorities, for whom the traditional educational route may be less accessible.
* The 'big four' of American Football, baseball, basketball and ice hockey reflect the dominant American values of high-scoring, win-ethic mentality, and material rewards for success.
* There has been a growth in disability sport across all three countries with the introduction of new laws to try to eradicate discrimination. A major catalyst for this change has been the Paralympic Games.
* There has been an increase in female participation across all three countries with the introduction of laws such as the Sex Discrimination Act (1975) in the UK and Title IX (1972) in the USA to try to eradicate discrimination.
* The media with its wealth and ability to reach even the remotest parts of a country has been influential in the way sports have developed, or not!

Review Questions

1 What are the European influences evident in the game of Aussie Rules Football?
2 Why did Rugby Union and American Football originate as middle-class games, whereas baseball and Association Football (or soccer) originated as working-class games?
3 Why did cricket become popular in the UK and Australia?
4 How do the 'big four' sports in the USA reflect the culture of the USA?
5 How has basketball helped the fortunes of the lower socio-economic groups in the USA?
6 What evidence shows the growth in the Paralympic Games?
7 What is meant by the 'Super League War' in Rugby League?
8 What are the names of the male and female national football teams in Australia?
9 Why did Rugby Union turn professional in 1995?
10 What impact can turning professional have on a sport such as Rugby Union?
11 Explain the 'priority draft pick' rule as it was changed in 2006.
12 Which teams feature in the Rugby League Tri-Nations competition?

B1: Sports Psychology

Since the second half of the twentieth century the status of sport and physical education within society has increased tremendously. This has been linked, in the main, to developing media, commercial and political interest and has resulted in increased pressure and demands being placed on sports performers. While in turn this has led to major improvements in both technological and physiological preparation, it has also meant that more recognition has been given to the need to prepare performers psychologically.

It has long been recognised that even if a performer is physically trained to near perfection and supported by the best equipment and technology available, this does not guarantee an excellent performance or victory. Research has been carried out by sports psychologists since the early 1960s in order to help us to:

- **understand**: learning/behaviour/performance and situations in sport
- **explain**: learning/behaviour/performance or factors that influence performance/events in a systematic manner
- **predict**: potential learning/behaviour/events or outcomes/performance
- **influence/control**: potential learning/behaviour/performance or events.

When observing sport, commentators and the media often use simplistic terms to explain why certain things happen. Phrases like 'there has been a psychological shift in the game', a performer is 'coping with pressure', a performer has been 'psyched out of the game', a performer has the 'wrong temperament', are all used, along with many others, to explain variations in performance.

Although such phrases are used often without a real understanding of what they mean, they do at least indicate the importance and influence of psychological factors within the context of sport and physical education. As you read through the next two chapters you will gain a greater insight into the underlying theories and concepts which underpin the behaviour of both individuals and groups at all levels of sport. You will also gain a clearer understanding of the various strategies that sports psychologists have used to help develop and prepare performers individually or in groups (teams) to cope with the increased pressures of modern sport. It is generally recognised that the traditional approach to sport psychology (the pre-competition 'rousing pep-talk', the 'up and at them' approach) is of very little 'real' long-term value and in some cases could even be considered 'counter-productive', perhaps leading to poor performance in the short term.

In the same way that an athlete's physical and skills preparation cannot be developed overnight, psychological preparation needs to be developed over a prolonged period of time in order to be effective and retain long-term value. Developing your knowledge of sports psychology should give you a better understanding of the 'causes' and 'effects' of various psychological phenomena which underpin learning and performance in sport.

After reading this whole section on sport psychology you will gain a better understanding of:

- individuals' differences and the resulting influence on sports performance
- social influences and their specific and general effect on both individual, group performers and participants
- management of psychological effects in order to optimise performance.

CHAPTER 9

Individual aspects of performance that influence young people's participation and aspirations

Learning outcomes

By the end of this chapter you should be able to:

- demonstrate knowledge and understanding of the theories of personality, including trait theory, social learning perspectives and the interactionist approach
- explain the effects of personality profiling on the adoption of balanced, active and healthy lifestyles, and evaluate critically personality profiling in sport
- describe and explain the nature of attitudes, the origins of attitudes, and their influence on performance and lifestyles (including the effects of socialisation)
- describe the components of attitudes (cognitive, affective, behavioural)
- evaluate critically attitudes (and behaviour) in sport and lifestyle choice
- describe methods of changing attitudes from negative to positive to promote participation in physical activity and a balanced, active and healthy lifestyle (including the concept of cognitive dissonance)
- outline Atkinson and McClelland's theory of achievement motivation (the need to achieve and the need to avoid failure) and sport-specific achievement motivation (for example competitiveness)
- discuss reasons for success and failure in physical activity with the use of Weiner's Model of Attribution (locus of causality and stability dimensions)
- justify the use of attributional retraining
- demonstrate knowledge and understanding of strategies for the promotion of mastery-orientation and the avoidance of learned helplessness; to raise self-esteem and to develop positive behaviours towards lifetime involvement in physical activity
- evaluate critically the effects of attribution theory on performance and on sustaining a balanced, active and healthy lifestyle
- describe the nature of aggression and assertion, and define channelled aggression
- explain the causes of aggressive behaviour and evaluate critically theories of aggression such as instinct theories, frustration-aggression hypothesis, aggressive-cue hypothesis (Berkowitz) and social learning theories
- describe methods of eliminating aggressive tendencies of performers and explain the effects of these methods on the adoption of active and healthy lifestyles.

CHAPTER INTRODUCTION

Similarities and differences between individuals involved in sport are often obvious, for example, size, shape and gender to mention but a few. Similarities and differences in terms of a performer's physiological behaviour can also be easy to recognise, but the reason why a person *behaves* in a certain way is often not so easy to define.

The search for the 'perfect' profile of a medal-winning performer has been researched for many years. While the use of highly structured talent identification programmes, which search for the correct somatotype (body shape) to match the specific sporting requirements, has been refined to match the physiological characteristics of a champion to potential athletes, the search for the psychological qualities has been more difficult to define.

Many of the great Olympians and World Champions display exceptionally high levels of motivation, commitment and self-sacrifice, but often appear to have very different personalities and methods of dealing with pressurised situations. Research into the personal and individual factors that can influence sporting behaviour has been widespread. Trying to gain a better understanding of the psychological make-up of performers in a sporting setting – that is, 'what makes them tick?' – is now a vital aspect of an athlete's preparation. All too often in the modern sporting arena the margins between victory and also-ran are so marginal that the need to control arousal levels and remain focused will often determine the final outcome, rather than just the physiological and skill factors. The aim of the sports psychologist is to identify the patterns of behaviour of an individual, understand the factors that cause them to react in a certain manner and eliminate any negative behaviour patterns, allowing them to perform at their optimum level.

Personality

There is a vast amount of research in this area that supports the view held by many that personality is a major factor in creating sporting behaviour. The research has traditionally been directed towards the relationship between individual performance and personality variables. Among the questions raised are the following:

- Do the personalities of top-class performers, moderate performers and non-participants differ?
- Can sporting success be predicted as a result of a performer's personality type?
- Are the personalities of performers in various sports different or similar?

At the 2008 Beijing Olympics two of the most successful performers were US swimmer Michael Phelps and British cyclist Chris Hoy. Are their personalities the same or different? Psychologists would like to find similar characteristics they both possess, which could be then combined with the physiological requirements for each sport. However, it is likely that while both men may share similar mental toughness and determination, their own personalities may be very different.

(a)

(b)

Fig 9.1 Do all elite performers have the same personalities?

The early research of the 1960s and 1970s failed to produce many useful conclusions with regard to the relationship between personality and performance in sport. This was mainly as a result of problems with validity and research methodology.

However, the fact that people began to predict how their captain, team-mate, friend or even opponent was going to behave on the basis of what they believed them to be like (that is, stereotyping), means that personality is a concept that has real meaning in the context of sporting interpersonal behaviour. In presenting this 'credulous' approach (Morgan, 1980) where personality is seen as a significant causal factor of behaviour, we must be aware that it is questioned by the 'sceptical' approach, which argues that sporting success is not related to personality. What we must therefore do is take an overview and accept that we need to be aware of all the major theories of personality and how they relate to performance in sport.

Key terms

Credulous approach Approach to the study of personality that supports links between successful sports performance and a particular personality type.
Sceptical approach Approach to the study of personality that questions the link between personality and sports performance.

'Personality' is a term that everybody uses to describe different things. However, a psychologist would not suggest that someone has 'lots of personality' that will help them play sport. Instead, the psychologist would suggest that personality in the context of sport is not something that someone has or does not have, but is more to do with how a person relates to another while taking part in physical activity and how that person deals with the demands of a situation.

For example, think about the behaviour of people you know well, such as the captain of your sports team or a close friend. It would appear that, in the main, their behaviour is hardly ever random or unpredictable. Usually they are consistent in the way they react or approach certain situations – for example, always aggressive and argumentative or stable and reliable. In addition, there are also consistent differences between people we know. Some people are outgoing and easy going, while others are quiet, withdrawn and lack confidence. It is these factors that contribute to both the **behavioural differences** between people and the **behavioural consistency** within people that are referred to as their personality.

Some of the theories you will study suggest that the behaviour of individuals will be the same in every situation and therefore we can identify the specific characteristics that will be required to perform at an elite level. Other theories suggest that individuals will react differently depending on the situation and their behaviour can be modified, which means that a specific personality type may not be required to reach elite levels, only certain aspects of personality such as the ability to cope in highly competitive situations.

Activity 1

Consider your own behaviour characteristics. Write down six characteristics that you think describe your personality (try to be honest!).

With a partner, construct your own definition of personality and then compare it with others in the group and the ones outlined below.

Definitions of personality
Nature or nurture?

Owing to the many different approaches and theories with regard to personality it is almost impossible to present one definition acceptable to all. However, in 1992 Richard Gross put forward a definition that helps us to understand the basic concept being discussed:

'Those relatively stable and enduring aspects of individuals which distinguish them from other people, making them unique but at the same time permit a comparison between individuals.'

Hollander (1971) suggested that:

'Personality is the sum of an individual's characteristics which make him unique.'

Lazarus and Mowat (1979) gave an earlier definition:

'Personality is the underlying relatively stable psychological structures and processes that organise human experience and shape a person's actions and reactions to the environment.'

All the definitions highlight certain questions central to the study of personality and sport.

1 Is personality made up of certain permanent or enduring characteristics?
2 Do these enduring characteristics affect how a person perceives a situation and, therefore, how that person behaves towards it?
3 If these characteristics are enduring, can they be identified?
4 Can these characteristics be measured?
5 Are these characteristics innate (nature)?
6 Can these characteristics be influenced or changed (nurture)?

EXAMINER'S TIP

You may be asked to outline and evaluate each of the theories of personality and its relationship to sports performance. Make sure you include both strengths and weaknesses.

Key terms

Nature Individuals are a product of the genes of their parents. A genetically inherited disposition.
Nurture A learned pattern of behaviour acquired through reinforcement, imitation of the behaviour of others and general environmental influences.

Personality structure

Many people view our personality as a series of complex layers that interact with each other depending on our inherited traits and the situation. Hollander (1967) suggests our behaviour and personality is dependent on three layers, as shown in Figure 9.2.

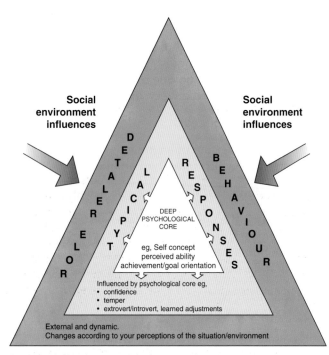

Fig 9.2 Hollander's model of personality

1 **Psychological core**: the most basic level of a performer's personality, it includes your attitudes and values (*see* Attitudes, page 138), motives and perceptions/beliefs about your*self*. These deep-seated components represent the 'real you' and are the most stable and constant.
2 **Typical response**: the ways in which we learn to adjust and adapt to what is happening in the world around us. Usually typical responses lie somewhere between the core and role-related behaviour due to the interaction of the two.
3 **Role-related behaviour**: based upon how we perceive our social situation, this is the most changeable and easily influenced aspect of our behaviour in day-to-day life. This continually changing/dynamic part of our personality allows us to experience and learn, which in turn influences our typical responses over time. Roles can change throughout time. Within one day a performer may experience training for oneself, being focused, etc. They may later be coaching a youth team or performers, that is, acting as a leader, and then going home to be a son/daughter or themselves be parents.

If this suggestion is correct it means that as an individual, even though we may have general behaviour patterns, we can adjust these to suit the situation. For example, if a performer possesses the physiological abilities to excel in a sport, but becomes anxious when placed in competitive situations, using certain stress management techniques he or she can be taught how to control their worries. This may lead to developing the confidence and ability to become a champion.

Activity 2

Consider some of the more well-known sports performers who are currently or have recently been involved in sport such as Wayne Rooney, Roger Federer, Lewis Hamilton and Kelly Holmes. Write down any words that you associate with these performers.

Feedback your answers to the rest of the class and discuss the characteristics identified in terms of any similarities or differences.

The trait approach (nature)

The trait or dispositional approach dominated the early study of personality but has been criticised for not taking into account how a particular situation might also influence an individual's behaviour in different environments. Thus, this approach emphasises the person as opposed to the situation. Traits can be seen as being **relatively stable** and **enduring** characteristics that predispose a performer to act in a certain way, regardless of the situation or circumstance. These stable and enduring predispositions could be used to predict an individual's likely behaviour in a variety of situations. Therefore, in our quest to find the ideal performer, this theory would help us. If an athlete possesses the necessary traits of a champion they should (according to this theory) be able to perform well in highly pressurised competitive situations.

Trait theorists believed that these personal characteristics or traits could be identified, were consistent, and could be generalised across the population as a whole. In other words, an extreme trait approach would suggest that if a person was assessed as being aggressive and competitive, then these characteristics would be displayed in all aspects of the person's behaviour (stable) at all times (enduring). Therefore, it would be possible to predict this particular individual's behaviour in all future situations.

Key terms

Trait Innate, enduring characteristics possessed by an individual that can be used to explain and predict behaviour in different situations.
Trait theory Suggestion that people are born with specific characteristics or traits that determine behaviour.

Two of the better-documented trait/type theories have been associated with Eysenck and Cattell. Although both theories have distinct similarities in that they both propose neurological models, their structures of personality were derived quite differently.

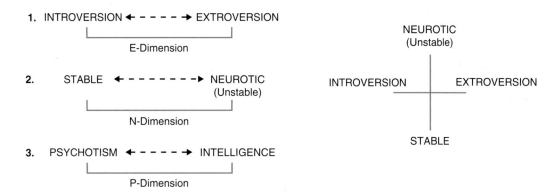

1. INTROVERSION ◄ − − − − ► EXTROVERSION
   E-Dimension

2. STABLE ◄ − − − − − − ► NEUROTIC
   (Unstable)
   N-Dimension

3. PSYCHOTISM ◄ − − − − ► INTELLIGENCE
   P-Dimension

NEUROTIC
(Unstable)

INTROVERSION | EXTROVERSION

STABLE

A third dimension of psychotism intelligence relating to how far a person was prepared to conform to society's rules and conventions was added later, in 1976

Fig 9.3 Major personality dimensions viewed as a continuum

Eysenck's type theory (nature)

Eysenck regarded personality as largely resulting from inherited (innate) tendencies. He attempted to measure these inherited characteristics through a Personality Inventory (EPI, 1964) and Personality Questionnaire (1975). Those tested were expected to give a 'yes' or 'no' answer to a variety of test questions. Using a statistical technique known as factor analysis to identify general trends in his research evidence, Eysenck identified two major personality dimensions, which can be viewed more readily as a continuum (see Figure 9.3).

The better-known extroversion/introversion dimension (E) linked to a person's Reticular Activating System (RAS) is related to how social or unsocial people appeared to be. The stable-neurotic dimension linked to a person's autonomic nervous system refers to the levels of nervousness and anxiety that a person was susceptible to.

The RAS, which Eysenck argued affected the levels of introversion/extroversion, is part of the central cortex of the brain. It acts to either inhibit or excite brain activity in order to maintain optimum levels of alertness or arousal. He suggested that extroverts had an RAS that was biased towards inhibiting or reducing the affects of incoming sensory information, therefore creating a severe state of under-arousal. According to Eysenck, as a result of this, extroverts need increased levels of stimulation to maintain optimum levels of attention and brain functioning. They could become bored very easily and would tend to seek out and be happier in new and challenging situations, particularly those involving other people, thus creating higher levels of stimulation to balance their naturally low levels of arousal. Extroverts, for example, were said to achieve optimum performance at higher levels of arousal, preferably in team-orientated activities or those involving gross motor skills. Activities of a more continuous nature (cross-country and marathon running) could be demotivating to such personalities, as they would not acquire the level of stimulation required.

Introverts on the other hand have high levels of excitation naturally occurring within them (highly over-aroused). They therefore tended not to need external or additional stimulation or excitement in order to function at an optimum level. Introverts, for example, were said to achieve optimum performance at lower levels of arousal, preferably in individual activities requiring more precision (shooting, archery, etc.). The characteristics of extroverts and introverts can be seen in Figure 9.4.

Many claims have been made with regard to extroverts and introverts, and tenuous links have been made with sporting performance (see the Evaluation of Trait Theory, page 135). It was claimed that extroverts were more likely to take part in sport and be more successful, that they prefer team games and that they:

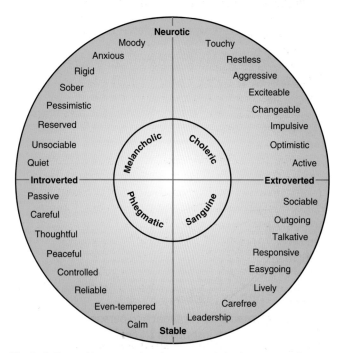

Fig 9.4 Eysenck's personality dimensions linked to personality characteristics (traits) generally displayed

- cope better in competitive and highly charged stressful situations
- cope better in the presence of distracting stimuli (for example audience/noise)
- can cope with pain more easily than introverts.

However, when investigating elite-level performers these claims have regularly proved to be false, with many a variety of personality types succeeding in all sports.

> **Key terms**
>
> **Extrovert** Sociable, outgoing, talkative, active and optimistic.
> **Introvert** Quiet, passive, unsociable, reserved and careful.

The second stable/neurotic dimension (N) is related to emotionality and is based on the autonomic nervous system (ANS). The ANS enables us to react to stressful situations or experiences. A person who tended to display more stable characteristics would have an ANS that was fairly slow to respond to stressful situations. The ANS of a neurotic person would respond more rapidly and strongly to being in a stressful environment, predisposing them to becoming restless, excitable and anxious, none of which would bode well for an elite performer.

Both of these dimensions are independent of each other, therefore performers could be stable extroverts or stable introverts. Most people would score in the middle of the E and N rather than the extreme ends of the continuum.

> **Key terms**
>
> **Stable** Calm, even-tempered, reliable, controlled and logical.
> **Neurotic/unstable** Moody, anxious, touchy, restless and aggressive.

Activity 3

Copy Figure 9.3 and place a cross in the area that you think best describes your personality based on the characteristics listed in Figure 9.4. Compare your assessment with a partner and discuss your findings.

Do you think there is any link between your personality and the type of sports in which you participate?

Cattell's theory (1965)

Cattell also adopted a trait approach to personality, but argued that more than just two or three dimensions were needed in order to create a full picture of a person's personality. He proposed that personality could be reduced to and measured in terms of 16 personality factors, hence his '16 PF Questionnaire'. He argued that measuring these factors via his test would give an appropriate personality profile. In identifying certain common traits (possessed by all) and unique traits (possessed by some) he recognised that personality was more dynamic than Eysenck suggested and could fluctuate according to the situation.

By defining a wider personality profile Cattell's model was seen as providing a more accurate description of personality than Eysenck's. He did not claim that individuals would show similar scores each time they completed his questionnaire, thus enabling deviations from the norm to be more easily observed and assessed. He acknowledged that influences such as mood, motivation and situational factors would affect a person's responses and thus their overall profile.

Type A and Type B personalities

In looking at very specific areas of personality and its effect on coping with stress, a 'narrow-band theory' of personality associated with how people deal with stress was developed by Friedman and Rosenman (1959).

In reviewing the effects of taking part in sport and fitness programmes on personality, researchers have considered two personality dispositions: Type A and Type B personality (Girdano D.A. et al., 1990).

Type A personalities tend to:

- have a very strong competitive drive/need to succeed
- exhibit high levels of agitation/alertness and a tendency to be easily aroused
- generally work at a fast pace, are hasty or have strong sense of urgency
- find it hard to delegate, are intolerant or easily become hostile/angry
- need to be in control of the situation
- experience high levels of stress.

Type B personalities tend to:

- be more relaxed
- delegate easily
- be less competitive
- be less concerned about getting everything done immediately
- be tolerant and methodical, and calm in dealing with problems
- experience low levels of stress.

Although both types were seen as being equally productive, their differences were defined as to do with cognitive emotional aspects linked to the concept of self. The tendency (disposition) towards anger/hostility is thought to increase the likelihood of stress-related disease. The development of these specific tendencies has been related not to specific recent situations (now) but to earlier socio-cultural effects, usually in terms of high expectations of performance due to early pressures. Fitness and exercise programmes have been shown to have a positive effect on the reduction of Type A behaviour patterns, which could lead to reducing the risk of cardiovascular disease.

EXAMINER'S TIP

Make sure you are able to explain the different theories of personality and evaluate their strengths and weaknesses.

Evaluation of trait theory

These two traditional theories received wide criticism and, as a result of further research, both Eysenck and Cattell continued to update their questionnaires. There has been much discussion as to the validity of the trait approach, but it certainly provided a framework from which future personality research could develop. The trait approach:

- was seen as a rather simplistic or limited view of personality
- failed, according to cognitive theorists, to recognise that individuals are actively involved in subjectively constructing their own personalities
- failed, according to situational theorists, to recognise the specific effects of different environmental situations
- failed to recognise that individuals do change.

Traits are seen as poor predictors of behaviour or, at best, predict a limited proportion of behaviour. The view of personality traits as rigid and enduring characteristics is questioned in terms of the validity and long-term reliability of the scales used. It is argued that although people may have certain core tendencies or may be disposed to act in certain ways, these behaviours are not general but are specific to certain situations. Simply knowing a performer's personality traits does not always help us to predict how they will behave in specific circumstances. For example, certain footballers, such as Lee Bowyer, appear to get angry easily during highly competitive situations whereas others, such as Michael Owen, seldom appear angry. However, this does not necessarily mean that Bowyer will be angry in all situations. The predisposition towards anger does not tell us what specific situations will provoke outbursts of unacceptable forms of behaviour. Thus a more interactionist perspective is suggested. The generalisation of specific traits across the population as a whole in order to predict behaviour is also questioned.

Researchers such as Mischel (1973) and Gould (1995) suggest that there is no ideal athletic profile and personality type is not an effective predictive measure of excellence or participation in physical activity.

Further problems associated with assessment and research into personality

The psychologists involved in your studies so far used self-report questionnaires to collect evidence from athletes in order to assess their personality. We should also therefore evaluate the accuracy of this method of data collection.

As we have already seen, early research such as Eysenck's EPQ and EPI, and Cattell's 16 PF, have been criticised for their lack of sophistication and have problems of validity, methodology and interpretation of statistical data. Much of the more up-to-date research has been dogged by similar problems. The ethics of using personality tests have also been raised. Criticism of such tests as the Athletic Motivation Inventory (AMI) devised by Ogilvie and Tutko (1966) seemed to heighten sensitivity over the use and application of such research.

Most sports psychologists, however, still rely heavily on such sport-specific objective inventory tests because of their ease of application and analysis. The Sport Competition Anxiety Test (SCAT; Martens, 1990) is a popular example. Guidelines for the use of such tests have been drawn up to ensure both the validity and the ethical nature of testing (see Figure 9.5).

The advantages of questionnaires such as the EPI, Cattell's 16 PF and Ogilvie and Tutko's AMI include:

- ease of administration
- large numbers can be tested at one time
- questions can be controlled and standardised
- data collection and analysis is straightforward
- time efficient.

However, the use of self-report tests themselves have been widely criticised in terms of:

- accuracy
- a participant's honesty
- a participant's desire to create a favourable impression

---

1) Participants should know the purpose and use of the test.
2) Tests should only be carried out and interpreted by qualified/experienced people.
3) Personality test results should not be used in isolation to predict behaviour.
4) Other information taken should include a person's life history, interview, observations, performance assessments.
5) Sport specific tests should be used.
6) Both trait and state measures should be used.
7) Feedback should be given to participants.
8) Personality tests should not be used for selection purposes and/or to discriminate for places on teams.

Fig 9.5 Guidelines for personality testing – as suggested by the American Psychological Association 1974 in order to ensure tests used are appropriate and ethical

- a participant's possible lack of objectivity
- the fact that neurotics were seen as possibly over-emphasising certain traits
- inappropriate or ambiguous questions.

Answers could also be influenced by:

- the personality of the tester
- time of day
- a participant's previous experience of tests
- a participant's mood swings.

Finally, the concept of personality is seen as far too complex to be measured by a mere 'yes' or 'no' answer.

In more recent research psychologists have developed more sport-specific questionnaires, such as the Sport Competition Anxiety Test (SCAT) and the Competitive State Anxiety Inventory (CSAI-2). These will be discussed in more detail in Chapter 11. Other methods that can be used to assess personality in specific situations include observation and interviews, both of which have their advantages and disadvantages.

Activity 4

In pairs discuss the advantages and disadvantages of using observation and interviews as methods of assessing the personality of an athlete compared to the use of a self-report questionnaire.
Discuss your findings with others in the group.

EXAMINER'S TIP

Ensure that you can name, describe and evaluate different methods of testing related to personality.

Social learning theory of personality (nurture)

The situational perspective is based around theories of social learning. Social learning theory proposes that behaviour is determined more by the individual's situation than by 'unconscious drives' or 'biological predispositions'. Behaviour and personality are said to develop through a process of observational learning (modelling) and social reinforcement (refer back to your notes on Bandura's Social Learning Theory from *OCR PE for AS*, pages 196–7). The situational approach suggests that personality is constructed and shaped as a result of strong environmental influences and indirect reinforcement factors that can override the individual's personality traits. This proposal directly contradicts trait theory.

It can be represented by the following formula:

Behaviour = Function of Environment (B = F(E))

For example, if a high-profile England rugby player is punched, trait theorists would argue a person with high levels of trait aggression would always punch back. Social learning/situational theorists would argue that the response would depend on the situation they were in, i.e.:

- how hard they were hit
- by whom
- in what context of the game (winning or losing)
- previous linked situations
- choices they had in terms of what they had to lose, that is, being sent off, fined, dropped, coach's attitude, their previous record, etc.

Key term

Social learning theory All behaviour is learned from interaction and experiences with the environment.

A person learns to behave in specific situations because of what has been observed and reinforced socially. A performer may appear confident in a specific situation – for example, on the pitch or within the context of a game where assertive behaviour is demanded by the coach and the situation. Outside or away from the same situation, the same assertive performer may behave in a very quiet, unassuming manner. Thus, personality is seen as being relatively enduring, but only in learned specific situations.

While many, such as Mischel (1968), supported this perspective, many psychologists have viewed the approach with a degree of scepticism. It has been felt that in trying to solve the limitations associated with the trait approach, the situational perspective had taken up too extreme a stance as no account was made for any genetic factors. It was seen as being insufficient to predict behaviour accurately.

In our search for potential elite performers this may be a useful approach. The suggestion that behaviour can be modified and learned means that individual deficiencies that may surface in the competitive environment can be altered and we do not have to worry too much about finding an ideal personality profile to excel in sport.

Interactionist approach to personality (nature and nurture)

In deciding between the relative strengths of the person versus situation debate, many psychologists recognise that each, although being limited, represents a degree of 'truth' in explaining the nature of personality. Performers are seen as having certain core elements of personality that predispose them to behave in certain ways, but at the same time are capable of being strongly influenced by changing environmental considerations (think back to the structure of personality as proposed by Hollander). This compromise position is one taken at present by the great majority of sports psychologists: behaviour is explained as the result of a reciprocal interaction between both the individual's consistent psychological traits (core) and the situational factors present.

This is of particular interest to sports psychologists due to the extreme situations in which sports performers can find themselves. They may, for instance, experience very high levels of stress in competitive situations, boredom in training, disappointments from losing or dependence on others in team games. When situational factors are strong, they are more likely to affect behaviour than personality factors. However, when situational factors are not strong then personality is more likely to affect behaviour.

This interactionist approach suggests, therefore, that if we wish to try to understand and predict an individual performer's behaviour we need to consider in depth both the individual person and the specific situation. In doing so, a much more complete picture and explanation of a person's behaviour can be developed.

Key term

Interactionist theory Behaviour is a combination of inherited traits and learned experiences.

An early equation formula suggested by Lewin (1935) represents this relationship as:

$$B = f(PE)$$

where:

B = behaviour (personality)

f = function

P = personality traits

E = environment (e.g., situation or context of game)

This is seen as a much more individualistic approach as it recognises that performers in similar sports do not necessarily exhibit the same behaviour. Just because some top-class marathon runners appear more introverted in their behaviour does not mean that you have to be the same to get to the top. All rugby players are not extroverts all of the time: it is not a prerequisite for success.

Coaches have to develop an in-depth knowledge of each 'unique' performer. Therefore, this becomes a much more dynamic approach. In addition to being aware of a performer's physical, physiological, intellectual and learning capabilities, a coach needs to know about their arousal and anxiety levels, confidence, levels of attention, attributions, achievement motivation, attitudes, etc. All these need to be considered in relation to the specific situations performers find themselves in. In addition, what has been shown to influence behaviour further is the performer's perception (interpretation) of the situation. This has led to increased research to provide coaches with more information on such areas.

In trying to increase our understanding, modern sport psychologists such as Martens (1975), R.S. Weinberg (1995) and Hollander's (1967), *see* Model of Personality, have provided a more systematic and comprehensive framework for understanding the concept of personality.

This approach can be used by the coach to assess common patterns of behaviour and identify the situations in which an athlete may become anxious or aggressive.

IN CONTEXT

As a young international player, David Beckham became, on occasions, over-aroused and displayed signs of frustration and aggression towards opposing players. One notable incident, which resulted in a red card, occurred in the match against Argentina during the 1998 World Cup. England went on to lose the match and was eliminated from the tournament. However, Beckham learned from this experience and, with the help of his coaches, developed strategies to channel his frustrations in a positive manner. He was successful in his efforts and later became an effective captain who would lead by example, rarely displaying aggressive acts but being proactive in calming other players if he felt they were becoming over-aroused.

Personality, sporting performance and a balanced and healthy lifestyle

If we try to summarise our discussions and define an ideal personality for sport we find that research attempting to clarify this issue has been found to be very contradictory. However, the general findings of more up-to-date research indicate that:

1. No obvious sporting personality type differentiates those involved in sport and non-participants.
2. No obvious consistent personality characteristics have been found to distinguish between different types of sports performers (for instance, performers participating in both team or individual sports are not disposed to certain specific types of personality behaviour).
3. Few personality differences have been found between male and female sports performers, particularly at the elite level. There is some evidence to suggest that there is a more marked difference between successful and unsuccessful female performers than male. However, it has been suggested that this is linked more to socio-cultural factors.
4. To be successful in sport a person needs to demonstrate: positive mental health (iceberg profile, see Figure 9.6), positive self-perceptions (self-confidence), and positive/productive cognitive strategies. The iceberg profile (Morgan, 1978) has been related to characteristics associated with elite sports performers; they tend to be more vigorous and have low levels of tension, depression, anger, confusion and fatigue.

5. Sport and Exercise Science research using mood states as a measure was originally carried out to examine people's attitudes towards exercise, related to their positive mental health. It recognised that people's attitudes – and thus behaviour (*see* Components of attitudes, page 139) – often changed according to their 'mood state'. **Mood states** are seen as being temporary, as opposed to personality traits, which are seen as being relatively permanent. Morgan's (1975) work compared successful and unsuccessful athletes. Mood states have been found to differ in successful and less successful performers, with successful performers generally displaying more positive mood profiles. Whether this more positive profile of mood state (POMS) helps to create better performance or whether it is itself caused by the success in sport is inconclusive. Gill argues that less than desirable mood profiles are negatively associated with success in most achievement situations.

6. Successful performers have been found to be able to internalise, that is, use cognitive (mental) strategies such as mental rehearsal, imagery or positive self-talk for coping with anxiety more effectively than unsuccessful performers (*see* Anxiety management techniques, page 200). However, these cognitive strategies have not been found to change personality traits.

7. The claim that sport can influence or develop certain positive or socially desirable characteristics or attributes has not been supported by research evidence. Philosophical statements (often made by physical educationalists and activity centres) that certain sports can develop character and socially desirable types of behaviour are considerably undermined, therefore. There is even some evidence to suggest that taking part in competitive sport can actually have a detrimental effect on social life, by increasing anti-social behaviour and rivalry.

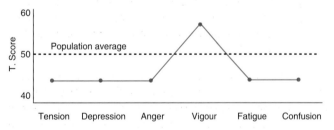

On Profile of Mood States (POMS) scores successful athletes were above the **waterline** (population norm) on vigour, but below the surface on the more negative moods, thus creating the profile of an iceberg.

Fig 9.6 The iceberg profile
Source: Morgan, W.P. et al., 1987, 'Psychological monitoring of overtraining and staleness', *British Journal of Sports Medicine*

EXAMINER'S TIP

Practice drawing and labelling the Profile of Mood State (iceberg profile).

8. The effect of taking part in sport and fitness work has been shown to have an immediate effect on mood states in the specific situation, and also help with a performer's concept of 'self'. The long-term or global influence on our individual personality traits is seen to be of little effect, however.

Key term

Iceberg profile The Profiles of Mood State (POMS) of successful athletes were above the waterline (population norm) on vigour, but below the surface on the more negative moods, creating the 'iceberg' profile.

Attitudes

The development of a positive attitude is vital if a performer is to achieve success at the highest level. It is also important if an individual wishes to maintain a healthy and balanced lifestyle. As you will find later, merely knowing and thinking an 'active lifestyle' is good for your health is not enough to actually make sure you pursue such a lifestyle.

A great deal of research has been undertaken into people's attitudes. However, much of this research has been of a descriptive nature and is, therefore, open to similar criticisms to those levelled at personality research. Within the field of physical/health education and sport, one of the often-stated philosophical objectives is to promote positive attitudes and values, not only in competitive sports performers but also in the population as a whole (for example, the adoption of a healthy lifestyle). In the current climate of rising obesity and increasing numbers adopting a more sedentary lifestyle, it could be inferred that more individuals have a negative attitude towards healthy eating and exercise. As a result, over the past few years there have been many high-profile campaigns to inform the general public, including those still in school, about both the benefits of an active lifestyle and the dangers associated with an inactive lifestyle and poor diet.

Therefore, it is important to know how to promote and maintain positive attitudes towards sport, exercise and health in general. Attitudes are very often linked to the concept of motivation. A performer who is highly motivated usually has a desire to achieve (*see* Achievement motivation, page 145) and thus a positive attitude. They do not look to blame others for any problems associated with performance (*see* Attribution theory, page 148). Later in this chapter we will look in detail at how a negative attitude may be altered.

The term 'attitude' can be viewed in a similar manner to personality in that, although both are seen as relatively stable dispositions, they cannot be measured directly, only inferred from behaviour that can be observed and tested, usually via questionnaires.

Although there has been much debate concerning the definition of attitudes, one of the most frequently used is that by Triandis (1971):

'ideas charged with emotion (positive or negative) which pre-disposes a class of actions to a particular social situation.'

An alternative definition is suggested by Aronson (1994):

'an enduring evaluation – positive or negative – of people, objects and ideas.'

While an early definition by Allport (1935) proposes that it is:

'a mental and neural state of readiness, organised through experience, exerting a directive or dynamic influence upon the individual's response to all objects and situations with which it is related.'

Therefore, we can say that the common components of an attitude include the following qualities.

- Are beliefs that are subjective and evaluative
- Can be positive or negative
- Are relatively stable and enduring
- Develop through experiences
- Are linked to a particular situation or item (commonly known as the 'attitude object').

Activity 5

In small groups construct a list of publicity campaigns and initiatives that have attempted to raise awareness of an 'active lifestyle'. These may include television programmes, national or local campaigns, and the use of high-profile sports stars and celebrities.

Discuss the main messages that each initiative has attempted to promote and evaluate, in your opinion, their effectiveness in making people aware of the benefits of an 'active lifestyle'.

Key terms

Beliefs The knowledge or information we have about the world.
Values Deep-seated feelings or thoughts (emotions) that form the basis for evaluating if something is worthwhile. They are thought to be culturally determined.
Attitudes A blend of beliefs and values. They are learned via our interaction with the social environment (experience) and provide us with a means to express our values in either a positive or negative way.

Attitudes and behaviour

As attitudes are one of the key determinants of our behaviour they can heavily influence the way in which we behave towards different types of '**attitude objects**':

- People
- Objects

- Events
- Ideas.

In her book *Psychological Dynamics of Sport* Diane Gill argues that our attitudes towards these attitude objects are not necessarily all embracing (global): just because a person has a negative attitude towards rugby it does not necessarily mean they have a negative attitude towards all sport, or just because they 'love' netball it does not always mean that they will turn up and train hard at each session. When trying to measure attitudes it is therefore important to be specific.

Key term

Attitude object The focus of an individual's attitude. The object may be training, people, events, places, ideas or specific objects.

Components of attitudes

Attitudes form our beliefs and values, which can influence our behaviour, but not always! To understand the concept of an attitude in more detail Triandis proposed that our attitude is made up of three components that interact. This is known as the 'Triadic model'.

1. **Cognitive component**: what a person believes about the attitude object, for example: 'I believe that jogging is good for me and helps me to keep fit.'
2. **Affective component**: what a person feels about the attitude object. This is usually linked to some form of evaluation related to a performer's values and past experience, for example: 'I enjoy keeping fit and healthy; it is important to maintain my lifestyle.'
3. **Behavioural component**: reflects how a person actually responds or intends to act towards the attitude object as a result of the previous components, for example: 'I go jogging four times a week and encourage others to go jogging. I watch athletics on TV and purchase fitness and health magazines to supplement my knowledge of jogging and fitness.'

This is a simplistic analysis of attitudes, yet it provides a basis from which attitudes can be studied and provides us with a clear indication that, while some components can be positive, it does not necessarily mean that behaviour can be predicted as a result. For example, how many of you think exercise or training is beneficial but don't always exert yourself fully!

EXAMINER'S TIP

Make sure you can explain how an attitude is formed, outline the components of an attitude and evaluate methods of measuring an attitude.

Although most social psychologists would adhere to the three-component analysis of attitudes, they would suggest that a flexible approach must be maintained with regard to its application. There is evidence that it is not always possible to accurately predict a person's behaviour so simply. This is due to the fact that a performer's behaviour does not always reflect the inferred correlation to beliefs (cognitive) and feelings (affective). The classic study by La Piere (1934), although criticised by some, is traditionally used to illustrate the inconsistency between stated or observed attitudes and actual behaviour.

In travelling over 10,000 miles around the USA with a Chinese couple he visited 251 hotels and restaurants. This period in American history was characterised by racial prejudice and stereotyping, however they only experienced one example of discrimination. When he wrote to the various establishments six months later, enquiring as to whether they would indeed accept Chinese people as guests, 92% of the returns stated no, they would not serve Chinese. Further research in this area to support our earlier view from D. Gill begins to suggest that attitudes can only be used to predict behaviour when we measure and assess attitudes to *specific* aspects of our lives and whether or not there is a *stated intention* of behaving in a particular way. A child or performer is more likely to take part in a specific activity, for example swimming, if they have stated a 'behavioural intention' to do so: 'I will take part in the swimming gala.'

General or apparent positive attitudes towards sport will not be a true determinant of actual sporting behaviour. For example, just because a student appears to enjoy swimming and is reasonably good at it does not guarantee that they can be counted on to take part in the gala if they have not specifically said they would.

Research by Fishbein and Ajzen (1975) supports this view that a high degree of specificity between attitudes and behaviour is the key to predicting accurately. Fishbein's model proposes:

1   Specific attitudes towards the sporting act must be considered in order to predict behaviour.
2   Attitudes towards the sporting behaviour along with accepted beliefs (normative) help to predict behavioural intentions more accurately.
3   Behavioural intentions related to sporting activity predict actual behaviour quite well.

The correlation between behavioural intention and actual behaviour is very high. Therefore in order to ensure people adopt and follow an active and healthy lifestyle we need to ensure that performers, beginners or experienced participants:

●   see the relevance of specific fitness and practice programmes to specific activities
●   gain direct experience of the fitness/practice programme, thus providing more information about the attitude object
●   that negative attitudes are dealt with immediately.

Inconsistencies and prejudice in sporting situations

Prejudice is an extreme or strongly held attitude (resistant to change) held prior to direct experience. Situations or people are prejudged. In prejudging a situation or a person we are expecting to see or experience certain types of behaviour in certain situations. Although, as already stated, we cannot accurately predict behaviour as a result of attitudes, they can certainly have a considerable influence on it. Here is an analysis of prejudice via the Triadic model:

●   **Cognitive component** of prejudice = stereotyping
●   **Affective component** is the strong feelings of hostility or liking towards the attitude object
●   **Behavioural component** can be split into five stages according to Allport.

The behavioural component of prejudice can manifest itself in various ways:

●   **Anti-location** – hostile talk, insults, racial jokes, etc.
●   **Avoidance** – keeping a distance
●   **Discrimination** – exclusion from civil rights/team, etc.
●   **Physical attack** – violence against person/property
●   **Extermination** – indiscriminate violence against a certain group.

In relation to people, prejudice (extreme attitudes) serves to develop a certain expectancy of behaviour leading to stereotyping.

Activity 6

Discuss the reasons why it has taken so long for black Americans to enter golfing society.

Why do you think Tiger Woods has been allowed into such a white-dominated sport?

Key terms

Prejudice 'An antipathy either felt or expressed based on faulty or inflexible generalisations directed towards a certain group or an individual who is part of a group.' G.W. Allport (1954)

Stereotyping This term, first suggested by Lippman (1922), relates to a person having a mental picture (cognitive schema) associating certain behaviour traits with a particular group or type of individual.

Research has tended to focus on the negative aspects of stereotyping in relation to issues such as gender and race. Those who hold extreme attitudes (prejudice) can cause people to expect certain types of behaviour resulting in stereotyping. This can then affect our behaviour towards certain individuals or groups of people. For example, if a teacher or coach, as a result of stereotyping, sees boys as having more potential in some sports than girls, this could lead them to have certain expectations of boys and girls. These expectations can influence their behaviour towards both groups. They may be more demanding of the boys, perhaps spending more time with them. The boys' skills will probably improve considerably more than those of the girls as a result of this more positive attitude and behaviour, thus supporting the teacher's or coach's earlier expectations (a self-fulfilling prophecy).

Although stereotypes are rarely accurate they are generally extremely resistant to change. Many are derived from indirect contact. The influence of the media has been responsible for portraying many poor images of certain groups of people. Preconceived views can lead to commonly held stereotypical views. For example:

- Girls are better than boys at aesthetic-type activities
- Boys are more competitive than girls
- People with disabilities cannot play sport
- People with disabilities do not enjoy competitive sport
- Black people are not very good at swimming
- Certain sports are better suited to black people than white.

It has been shown that a person's perceptions of self can be affected by exposure to continuous stereotypical attitudes and certain types of behaviour expectancies. This can influence and lead to differences in sporting achievement.

Activity 7

Discuss the suggestion that stereotyping of behaviour expectancy can have a positive benefit. Illustrate your answer with sporting examples.

IN CONTEXT

During recent years there have been many attempts to break down stereotypical views with the aim of encouraging more people to participate in sporting activities. Within schools and the community the range of sports has increased and participation has become more common and accepted. For example, the number of women's football and rugby teams has grown considerably and is gradually becoming more mainstream as the media increases its coverage of major events. Similarly as the National Governing Bodies of many sports devote more resources to attracting non-traditional performers, the popularity grows. Attitudes towards athletes with disabilities have changed considerably over the past few years due to their success at international level and the emergence of highly recognisable role models such as Tanni Grey-Thompson and Danny Crates.

Key term

Stereotyping 'The general inclination to place a person in categories according to some easily and quickly identifiable characteristics such as age, gender, ethnic group, nationality or occupation and then to attribute certain qualities believed to be typical to members of that category.' R. Tagiuri (1969)

Social and cultural norms in relation to PE and sport have changed considerably over the last 20 years. In order that they continue to change for the potential good of all in society it is important that teachers and coaches in influential positions (significant others) are very careful not to perpetuate unacceptable/negative stereotypes, particularly at the very early stages of development. They must be prepared to challenge any areas of existing or future prejudice in relation to gender, racial or socio-cultural issues.

(a)

(b)

Fig 9.7 Successful performers such as (a) Tanni Grey-Thompson and (b) Arsenal Ladies FC help to break down stereotypical views

Attitude formation

In considering the earlier definition of attitudes you have become aware that attitudes are largely developed through experiences. Therefore it is obvious that positive experiences early in a person's development can have long-lasting effects, just as negative experiences can seriously influence behaviour and possible participation in sporting activities. Attitudes are developed by a combination of the following factors (there may be others):

Activity 8

In pairs discuss the following questions:

● Why did you become involved in your major sport?
● Which activities do you dislike and why?

Compare your answers with other groups.

Activity 9

List the reasons that may contribute to the formation of a negative attitude towards physical activity.

Learning

Attitudes are almost entirely learned, although there is evidence to suggest certain aspects may possibly be genetically instinctive or inherently determined.

Familiarity/availability

If a pupil encounters certain activities or sports on a regular basis they will generally develop a positive attitude towards that activity, especially if they have ease of access. Think of the child who is regularly taken by their parents to watch and play a particular sport at a local club. A positive attitude will probably develop and, if the child is encouraged to use the facilities, they will probably end up (certainly during their early years) playing for the same team or club.

Classical conditioning

Through the association of a certain activity or sport (conditioned stimulus) with a pleasant or unpleasant feeling (unconditioned response) a certain attitude may be formed.

Operant conditioning

Positive reinforcement and rewards have been shown to help positive attitudes, or at least strengthen already-formed attitudes, for example enjoyment of PE lessons, achieving personal goals/success, appreciating the need for a healthy lifestyle.

Socialisation

This is seen as a major influencing factor in the formation of attitudes. Attitudes are learned from significant others, either explicitly through instruction from teachers, parents or coaches, or they may develop through social learning via observation, imitation and modelling. We cannot therefore underestimate the power of the media and high-profile sports stars, particularly in influencing the attitudes of young people. Stereotyping is a major problem created through socialisation, particularly attitudes to issues of gender and different ethnic cultures.

Peer groups and social groupings

Peer groups have also been found to exert a strong influence on people's attitudes. Inter-group attitudes are often formed as a way of defining, maintaining and possibly protecting the group. If there are suitable opportunities for people of similar ages and interests to meet and participate in sport, positive attitudes are more likely to be created.

Compare your ideas to the rest of the group and Table 9.1.

Table 9.1 Factors that contribute to a negative attitude to sport

Disapproval of peers/family
Socialisation against the activity, e.g., rugby league not for females
Race/age/gender constraints
Negative role models
Low status/unpopularity of the activity
High motives to avoid failure
Previous criticism of ability
Use of attribution theory – previous failure attributed to internal stable attributions
Performance goals rather than learning goals
Negative self-concept
Perceived low ability
Fear of failure
Personality of the performer
Previous poor performance – learned helplessness
Perceived high task difficulty
Fear of the danger of the activity
Previous unenjoyable experiences of the activity
Personal constraints – age/gender/race/size

During recent times many high-profile sports stars have been involved in media campaigns and initiatives to promote and involve young people in physical activity. For example, Dame Kelly Holmes is a Sporting Ambassador visiting many schools and clubs, actively trying to encourage girls to remain in sport after leaving school. Similarly the effect of success at the 2008 Beijing Olympics and Paralympics cannot be ignored, with many sports gaining high-profile coverage, creating role models for young, aspiring athletes to emulate, as well as raising the awareness of the general public to new sports and competing groups.

EXAMINER'S TIP

Be ready for the question 'do attitudes predict behaviour?'

Changing attitudes

Up until now we have mainly concentrated on positive attitudes. What happens, however, if a person has a poor or very negative attitude? How easy or difficult is it to change a sportsperson's attitude? Attitude change has been the subject of much research. As we have already explained, the relationship between attitudes and general behaviour does not always appear very strong. Therefore, attempting to change attitudes can be problematic. However, as stated, if the attitude is very specific to an attitude object, it is possible.

Although attitudes are thought to be 'deep seated' and therefore resistant to change, it is felt that attitudes can be influenced or gradually changed through learning, formal or informal social influences, or persuasion.

In a sporting context the conversion to a positive attitude is highly desirable, as the performer may become more motivated, show greater task persistence and work more effectively within a group situation. In other words, the behavioural component of the attitude becomes easier to predict and the individual will participate more regularly.

Psychologists suggest that the two main ways that attitudes may be changed are:

- persuasive communication
- cognitive dissonance theory

Note: In order to assess any attitude change, a person's or group's attitudes need to be measured prior to the attempt to change them and then again afterwards.

Persuasive communication

In their research into how easy it was to persuade a person to adopt a different attitude, Hovland, Janis and Kelly (1953) identified four basic factors (variables) that can affect all persuasion situations:

- **The recipient of the message** and their resistance to change. The individual's past experience and current strength of opinion must be considered
- **The quality of the message.** If the message is presented in a logical format that is clear, precise and informative, the recipient is more likely to pay attention and consider this new point of view
- **The status of the person** delivering the message. If they are a significant other, the message is more likely to be favourably received
- **The context or situation** in which the message is being delivered. The message is more likely to be effective if delivered when there is time to assimilate the information, with adequate resources, and the approach used is not seen as confrontational, with possible support from others.

If we are trying to persuade specific groups of the population that participation in sport is good for them, consider the factors affecting the level of success of such a campaign:

- Is the fitness/health argument used?
- Is the social argument used?
- Is a trend/role model argument used?
- Is the lifestyle argument used?
- Who is going to front the campaign?
- What are the counter-arguments?
- Who is the target group?

In a sporting context, if we are trying to persuade individuals or groups to change their attitudes towards a particular activity, etc. (attitude object), it is important that the person, teacher or coach presenting the persuasion is an expert and thus perceived as having high status or credibility.

Olympic or professional performers are often used to focus attention on campaigns to promote sport. The high profile and clean image of sporting role models such as Gary Lineker, Sir Steven Redgrave, Colin Jackson and Sharron Davis mean they are much in demand; all are now respected media personalities.

During recent years the Sport Relief Mile has been used not only to raise money for charity but to increase the number of people actively involved in some form of exercise. The message is clear: everyone can either run or walk at least a mile and participate in some form of exercise. To support this claim, a host of celebrities and sports stars participate, explaining the reasons for their involvement. This campaign, which is similar to Cancer Research UK's Race for Life, is aimed at fun runners and people who are not likely to run, for example, the London Marathon. The consequences of such events have been to not only raise the awareness of the charities but also to promote the benefits of health and show how easy and enjoyable it can be to participate in some form of exercise.

Teachers and coaches have a vital role to play, using their expertise, likeability and trustworthiness to provide leadership in order to communicate positive attitudes to young people.

You should note that it is important that the person whose attitudes are being influenced does not feel threatened or they may become more defensive (resistant to change).

EXAMINER'S TIP

A common question asks how you can change an attitude. Use at least one of the theories with the correct terminology, and support your answer with practical examples. Don't simply give examples – you need the theory as well.

Cognitive dissonance theory (Festinger, 1957)

According to Festinger an individual knows certain things (cognitions) about their own attitudes, beliefs and thoughts in relation to their own behaviour and surroundings. These cognitions that people know or think about themselves can either be consistent with each other, creating a good feeling (feeling of consonance), or they can be inconsistent, creating a state of dissonance.

Festinger suggests that if a person experiences feelings of **dissonance** then they are generally motivated to change their beliefs, attitudes or thoughts in order to return to a feeling of consonance (psychological harmony). Therefore, the aim is to create a conflict of information that the individual has to consider, assess and form a new judgement. Their opinion may be the same as before but it may also change.

How often have you started a fitness programme, knowing that it is important to keep fit and that at least three sessions per week is desirable, only to lapse after a few sessions or weeks. Not being able to maintain a commitment known to be valuable can create a feeling of 'psychological discomfort', or 'dissonance'. Because of the human need for consonance, you are generally motivated to erase this feeling of dissonance (tension) that is, do something to reduce the imbalance between what we believe and how we are behaving.

In order to rationalise our knowledge, beliefs or thoughts, we can reduce dissonance in various ways:

- make the cognition less important
- change one of the cognitions
- replace one of the cognitions.

One or more of the components of the Triadic model can be targeted to change. For example, if a performer is anxious about participating in gymnastics because they are worried about hurting themselves:

- **Cognitive component** – provide new information that conflicts with existing thoughts, such as outlining the safety measures that are adopted in terms of supporting the performer, explaining the progressive stages that will be used to build up confidence and skill level, as well as observing a demonstration by someone of similar ability
- **Affective component** – ensure the performer enjoys the session and feels safe at all times. The skills are taught progressively in order to develop self-confidence and trust in the coach
- **Behavioural component** – ensure the individual experiences success and such behaviour is reinforced with praise, encouragement and constructive feedback.

Key terms

Consonance Where the cognitions held have a high level of correlation: 'I am being assessed in gymnastics for my A-level assessment. I need to train/practise to develop my skills and therefore I train twice a week outside the class.'

Dissonance A 'negative-drive state' where the cognitions are at odds or in direct conflict with each other, creating a feeling of psychological discomfort or tension: 'I am being assessed in gymnastics for my A-level assessment. I need to train/practise to develop my skills. I don't train/practise outside class at all.'

In applying this theory within a sporting context it is suggested that teachers and coaches can try to change beginners' or elite performers' attitudes by highlighting certain cognitions that may create states of dissonance within the performer's mind. Convincing people to change their attitude is not a simple, short-term process, however, as individuals/teams are generally resistant to change. They tend to distort the truth or evidence that may prove their thoughts and beliefs wrong in order to maintain their perceptions of the status quo. Think of football supporters who regularly see their team lose. In order to justify their commitment to the team, comments may be made, such as 'well, our team always try to play football', 'we don't try to kick our way out of a game', and so on.

Activity 10

Using the theories outlined above discuss how you would alter the negative attitudes in the following scenarios. Use practical examples to support your answers.

- A group of teenage girls think exercise is too hard and boring

- A group of teenage boys only want to play matches when they attend training sessions rather than work on developing their skills
- A group of middle-aged office workers don't take part in exercise because they claim they don't have the time, money or opportunities to participate in the local area.

Discuss your suggestions with the rest of the group.

Strategies to improve a performer's attitude

Compare your answers to the previous activity to the list below:

- Reward the success elements of performance
- Reward the success elements of squad involvement
- Agree targets/goals with the performer
- Give the performer an appropriate role/responsibility
- Use positive role models (significant others, for example parents/coach) to demonstrate positive attitude
- Give positive reinforcement of correct behaviour/attitude
- Coach/teacher/significant others/media/government body give negative feedback/criticism/punishment of unacceptable behaviour/attitudes
- Pressure to conform applied by peer group/team
- Attribute earlier failure to unstable/changeable factors
- Stress benefits, i.e., health, financial, success
- Ensure training/practice is variable/enjoyable to maintain motivation/interest
- Stress performance/process goals rather than just outcome goals

Achievement motivation

Achievement motivation is related to the often-asked questions:

- Why is it that some learners/performers achieve and some do not?
- Why is it that certain performers are driven to be more competitive than others?

'The need to achieve is a relatively stable disposition to strive for success.' (AAHPHERD, 1981)

The term 'achievement motivation' was first put forward by Murray (1938) who, in describing 20 different human motives or needs, identified a human being's need for achievement as being linked to the personality of the performer. Competition is described as an 'achievement situation' whereby performance is compared to a relative or absolute standard. Achievement can, however, take place in non-competitive situations. Whether it is in competition or not, the fact that certain types of people are prepared (more motivated) to place themselves regularly in situations where their achievement is being compared or evaluated in some way generally labels them as being more competitive or 'achievement orientated' than others. Gill (1986) gives the following definition:

'A person who has high levels of achievement motivation would have a tendency to strive for success, persist in the face of failure and experience pride in accomplishments.' (D. Gill)

The level of a person's need to achieve (drive for success) is seen as a relatively stable disposition. A person who has a high need to achieve has a tendency to display a positive approach in relation to their achievement orientation as well as a positive success tendency. They will strive to achieve a high level of performance (mastery accomplishment). Thus, having high levels of achievement motivation can make all the difference to how successful a performer is in both learning and high-level performance situations.

Most of the research associated with achievement motivation in sport has revolved around the early classical theories put forward by Atkinson (1964 and 1974) and McCelland (1961). Although current research has moved on in terms of its interpretations of the cognitive processes affecting achievement motivation, the performance and preference predictions it enables us to make with regard to high and low achievers are still generally accepted.

In trying to explain how a person's need to achieve developed, thus enabling predictions of their future behaviour to be made, Atkinson took an interactionist stance, proposing that both **personality** factors and **situational** factors have to be considered. He recognised that knowledge of a performer's personality traits alone was not enough to give a clear indication of a person's future behaviour.

Atkinson's personality components of achievement motivation

Atkinson suggested that a performer's behaviour is greatly affected (example, achievement motivation, competitiveness) by their ability to balance two underlying motives that we all possess within ourselves:

- **The need to achieve success (n. Ach)** – a person is motivated to achieve success for the feelings of pride and satisfaction they will experience
- **The need to avoid failure (n. Af)** – a person is motivated to avoid failure in order not to experience the feelings of shame or humiliation that will result if failure occurs.

You can probably appreciate from your own experience that sporting situations provide us with regular opportunities to experience success or failure. All sports performers are motivated by a combination of both: a need to be successful and the good positive feelings that are associated with winning, together with a wish to avoid the feelings of shame, embarrassment and possible humiliation associated with losing. Table 9.2 highlights some of the common characteristics of each type of performer. Consider each type of performer and evaluate which behaviours you generally tend to adopt.

Atkinson's research suggested that high achievers in sport tended to have high levels of n. Ach and low levels of n. Af, whereas low achievers in sport tended to have low n. Ach levels and high n. Af levels. Low achievers do not fear failure but they fear the negative evaluation associated with failure.

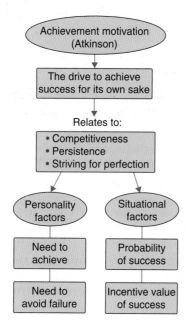

Fig 9.8 Atkinson's component of achievement motivation

Activity 11

Performers have a 'need to achieve' or a 'need to avoid failure' personality. Place the characteristics of each in the appropriate column.

- approach behaviour
- avoidance behaviour
- like being in a challenging situation
- wish to protect their self-esteem
- may opt for the easy option
- view criticism in a positive manner
- see their efforts as a learning experience willing to take risks or attempt new tasks
- concerned about being evaluated
- Does not like feedback or taking responsibility for own actions

Need to achieve	Need to avoid failure

Table 9.2 Comparison of n. Ach and n. Af performer characteristics

Characteristics of a performer motivated to achieve (n. Ach)	Characteristics of a person motivated to avoid failure (n. Af)
Looks for challenges – seeks extremely hard task	Avoids challenging tasks – seeks easy option
Standards are important	Dislikes 50-50 situations
Persists for longer	Gives up easily
Values feedback	Does not like feedback
Enjoys evaluation situation	Dislikes evaluation situations (possible shame)
Not afraid of failure	Performs worse in evaluation situations
Takes responsibility for own actions	Avoids personal responsibility
Attributes performance to internal factors/ controllable factors, e.g., success = effort, failure = lack of concentration	Attributes failure to external factors, e.g., factors out of their control
Optimistic	Pessimistic
Confident (high self-efficacy)	Low in confidence
Looks to complete the task quickly and effectively	Takes a long time over the task
Task goal-orientated	Outcome goal-orientated

The situational component of achievement motivation

Atkinson supports his predictions of behaviour and performance by cross referencing a performer's personality factors with situational factors. He claims that a performer will assess the situation they are faced with and evaluate:

- The probability of success and
- The incentive value of that success.

The probability of success will obviously depend on whom you are competing against and/or the difficulty of the task. Thus, if you are an average club golfer playing against a top professional, the probability of success is not very high. Your chances would be higher against a complete novice. The incentive value, however, of playing against a top professional and the satisfaction gained if you beat him/her, would be far greater. The satisfaction gained from beating the novice would not be as high as you would have expected to win (high probability).

Thus, Atkinson's view of what factors contribute to levels of achievement motivation in people can be expressed by the following equation:

$$\text{Tendency of a person's achievement motivation or competitiveness} = (Ms - Maf) \times (Ps \times \{I - Ps\})$$

Where:

- Ms = motive to succeed
- Maf = motive to avoid failure
- Ps = probability of success
- I = incentive value.

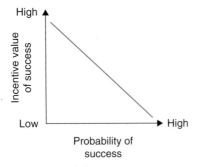

Fig 9.9 Atkinson's suggested relationship between the probability of success and the incentive value

Performers that display a higher motive to achieve (n.Ach) will tend to have approach behaviour, where they will like being in a challenging situation, rise to the challenge in order to gain feelings of satisfaction, even if it is difficult and they may not succeed. They will see their efforts as a learning experience in order to improve their performance in the future and view criticism in a positive manner. However, those performers who are concerned about being evaluated and wish to protect their self-esteem often display avoidance behaviour. In such cases the individual may opt for the easy option or possibly not even attempt the task. It is important that the coach or teacher encourages approach behaviour to ensure future participation and develop a culture of support so that performers are willing to take risks or attempt new tasks without fear of being ridiculed or heavily criticised for their efforts.

> **EXAMINER'S TIP**
>
> Learn the equation related to achievement motivation – it will help you to give full answers.

> **IN CONTEXT**
>
> Elite performers are often faced with situations that require evaluation from the crowd. The nature of sport always creates heroes and villains. Consider a penalty shoot-out at the end of a football match. The coach or manager often asks for volunteers to take the penalty rather than imposing the task on players. Those with a high need to achieve, displaying approach behaviour, will be the ones to take the first set of penalties, knowing they may be the one to miss.

Fig 9.10 Individuals with a high need to achieve will regularly place themselves in highly competitive situations

> **Key terms**
>
> **Approach behaviour** The performer is motivated to attempt a challenging situation even if they may fail.
> **Avoidance behaviour** The performer is motivated to protect their self-esteem and will avoid situations where they may be evaluated.

Activity 12

Using the words listed below complete the following paragraph.

approach	avoidance	easier choice
risks	satisfaction	self-esteem

Performer's who have a higher motive to achieve will tend to display _____ behaviour patterns. They will be prepared to take _____ and rise to the challenge, allowing them to experience feelings of _____ from the task even if they do not succeed. Those who have a higher motive to avoid failure will usually choose display _____ behaviour or not even attempt the task. This is due to them wishing to protect their _____.

Developing achievement motivation and competitiveness

It is not easy in today's society to downplay or easily avoid outcome goals. It is important therefore that teachers and coaches are careful in the way they emphasise certain kinds of behaviour and goals. They can greatly influence a performer's perceptions of success or failure, and thus future motivation, by attributing certain causes or reasons for success or failure (see Attribution theory, below).

In order to develop approach behaviour and encourage a high need to achieve there are several factors that are thought to influence achievement motivation orientation:

- Positive childhood experiences
- Reduction of punishment and negative feelings
- Social environment (social learning)
- Cultural differences
- Encouragement from significant others
- Emphasis (direct or indirect) on task or outcome goals
- Realistic expectations and goals
- Use of correct attributions – those conveyed by the teacher or coach and those expressed by the performer.

EXAMINER'S TIP

The questions may focus on your applied knowledge. Be prepared to give practical strategies to develop approach behaviour and support your answer with sporting examples.

IN CONTEXT

During a school basketball match the teachers from each team approach the game from different perspectives. One teacher encourages the players to shoot for a basket when they have a suitable opportunity and, if they miss, encourages them by saying 'not to worry, it was a good attempt'. The other teacher shouts criticism at the players if they miss a shot or do not shoot when they have the opportunity.

Consider the differences in approach. The first team know that they have the support of the teacher and are willing to attempt to score even if they miss (encouraging approach behaviour). However, the other team are likely to develop avoidance behaviour, resulting in them only shooting when they have an easy shot or making sure they do not get into positions where shooting is an option. The players are too concerned with the consequences of their actions to play to the best of their ability.

Similar situations can be seen during elite sport when players are inhibited in their performance. For example, comments are often made about international players in sports such as football, rugby and cricket not playing to their potential and showing the same skill or flair compared to their club performances. Could they be concerned about evaluation of their performance because the result is of greater importance?

Attribution theory

Definition of attribution – reasons for success and failure in physical activity

Think about the times you have participated in some form of physical activity, either competitively or just for fun. After the event did you evaluate your performance in some way and give reasons for your success or failure? Possibly without realising it you were involved in the 'attribution process'. Attribution theory has been developed as a way of explaining how individuals and teams evaluate their levels of success and failure in performance situations. In addition, it seeks to show how the reasons given by an individual or team for their success or failure may affect future achievement motivation in similar situations.

Achievement situations are assessed by both individuals and teams, who give reasons for how well they have performed. Inferences and assumptions are often made about other people's levels of behaviour that can directly affect a performer's attitude to and behaviour towards them (see Stereotyping, pages 140–1).

Activity 13

With a partner discuss the last time you personally were successful in a physical activity and compare it to a time when you have been unsuccessful.

What reasons did you give for both performances?

Can you suggest reasons why you may have attributed the reasons you did?

Was it possibly to make you feel better about winning or losing?

Key term

Attribution The perceived reasons for the success or failure following an event.

Attributions are seen as being what an individual or team interprets or perceives as being the causes of their or others' particular behaviour, particular outcomes or events. The reasons/causes or attributions that an individual or team gives for their success or failure can affect:

- Immediate emotional reactions
- Actual behaviour
- Future aspirations
- Expectations, motivation and future participation.

In your discussions you will probably have come to realise that the different 'attributions' a person gives to explain success or failure are important. Attributions can affect the *intensity* and *direction* of our behaviour. If a performer taking part in a new activity is struggling to gain any success, the reasons they perceive as being the cause for their apparent

lack of success can have quite serious consequences for their future behaviour.

IN CONTEXT

During a Physical Education lesson students are introduced to a new activity (for example, trampolining). The class achieve differing levels of success; some appear to master new skills such as 'seat-drops' and 'swivel-hips' with ease while others find the activity more difficult and find they can only complete some basic jumps and twists.

After the lesson the teacher discusses the relative levels of success with the group and praises everyone for their effort, concentration and willingness to attempt new skills. Even though not all the students have achieved the same level, they will all probably have a sense of pride and be motivated to participate fully in the next lesson, as they feel they can improve. However, if the teacher were to only praise the students who completed the more difficult moves and ignore the others, or not suggest reasons for their apparent lack of comparable progress, their attitude and motivation towards future lessons may be more negative and even affect future participation altogether.

Weiner's model of attribution

There have been numerous proposed theories of attribution and although Weiner's model is not sport specific, it serves as a useful starting point in helping us to understand the attribution process and its effects. In his research Weiner suggested that all the many thousands of reasons and explanations we might give for what has caused our success or failure can be grouped into certain common categories. These categories could then be related, compared and

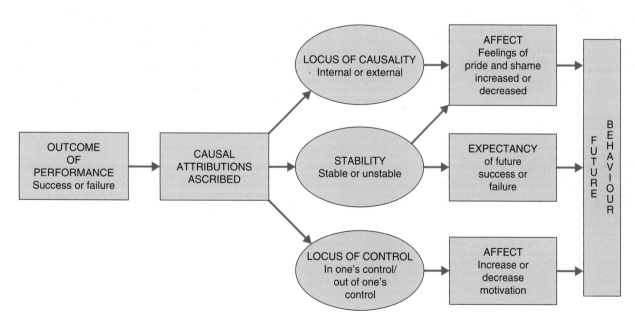

Fig 9.11 The attribution process

initially placed across two dimensions. After further research he later added a third dimension. The two dimensions are:

- **locus of causality** – either internal or external factors
- **locus of stability** – either unstable or stable factors.

The four categories of **causal attributions** given by people for their level of success or failure were:

- ability
- effort
- task difficulty
- luck.

In Figure 9.12(a) you can see how Weiner placed these on his model.

The locus of causality dimension is mainly linked to whether the attributions are:

- **internal factors** – within performers, such as effort and ability
- **external factors** – outside the performer's control (for example, environmental factors such as task difficulty and luck).

The stability dimension refers to whether the reasons/causes are:

- **stable** – being relatively permanent, such as skill level, *ability*, coaching experience and the quality of the opposition or *task difficulty*
- **unstable** – in relation to time: *effort* and *luck* are factors that can change from time to time. For example, the personal level of motivation, arousal levels, quality of the teamwork, tactics, injury, the decisions of the officials and pure luck.

The stability dimension is related to our expectancies of future outcomes; for instance if you attribute success to your ability then, as this is a relatively stable factor (at the time of the activity), you will probably expect to gain success at similar activities or tasks in the future. For example, if we have lost to this team in the past six games it affects expectations about the future: we will probably lose this match too. If we have stable attributions we hold the same expectations. The opposite effect will occur if you attribute failure to the stable factor of ability.

> **EXAMINER'S TIP**
>
> Practise drawing Weiner's model and labelling each box with the correct attributions and suitable practical examples. Draw it in the exam if it helps you to remember the facts.

Following criticisms of his work and further additional research Weiner (1985) reformulated his model, adding a further causal dimension, that of **locus of control**. This helped to explain the effective consequences of attributions that appear to be in or out of a person's control. The **locus of control** dimension has been shown to relate to the intensity of a performer's personal feelings of pride and satisfaction, shame and guilt. This is sub-divided into:

- **personal control** and factors within their control, such as ability (I was better) and effort (I tried hard)
- **external control** and uncontrollable factors, such as I was lucky, and the task was simple.

If internal causes are used then feelings of self-satisfaction and pride will be maximised. As a result motivation will probably continue and possibly increase. The opposite effect will generally occur if failure is also attributed to internal and controllable factors. The emotional effect will be one of increased shame and dissatisfaction leading to possible decreased levels of motivation.

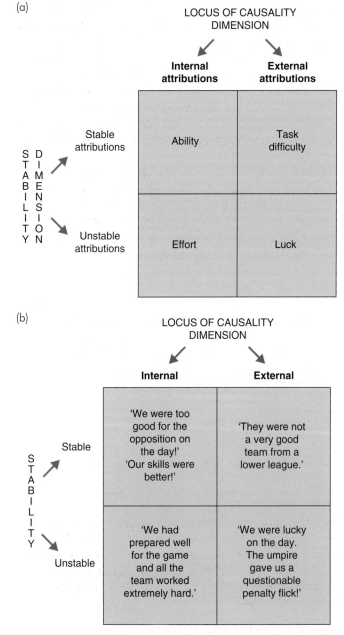

Fig 9.12 (a) Weiner's model (b) Example of Weiners's model – attributions included: reasons why we won the hockey game!

The key points to remember when using attributions are:

- **attribute success to internal factors** – this creates a feeling of pride and satisfaction
- **attribute failure to external or unstable factors** – never to an internal, stable factor such as ability. This may result in low self-confidence and feelings that they can never improve.

EXAMINER'S TIP

Remember you can attribute failure to anything except internal, stable factors, such as ability.

Activity 14

Using Weiner's two-dimensional model of attribution, place the following attributions for success or failure into the model, taking care to consider the various categories:

- 'I'm not very good at badminton'
- 'Our swimming team is the best in the region'
- 'Our team is not really good enough to win the cup'
- 'The referee was biased'
- 'The coach made us play to an unusual pattern'
- 'I couldn't be bothered to try'
- 'The opposition employed better strategies and tactics than us'
- 'They were better organised'
- 'The goalkeeper dropping the ball enabled Gerrard to score'
- 'Everybody tried their best'
- 'The rain caused the match to be abandoned and saved us'

Applying attribution theory in sport and sustaining a balanced, healthy lifestyle

When making attributions performers very often have biases in common, tending to take credit for success and disassociating themselves from failure, blaming external factors. The traditional saying 'a bad workman always blames his tools' reflects this view. Researchers have tried to look at the correlation between the type of attributions given by successful performers and those given by poor performers (that is, winners and losers). The traditional Weinerian view was that winners attribute success to internal factors and losers to external factors in order to reduce feelings of shame and protect their egos.

It has been shown that successful performers do tend to attribute their success to internal factors (ability/effort) to make them feel better about themselves, their group or team (self-esteem is protected or enhanced). This is known as self-serving bias.

Key term

Self-serving bias The tendency of a performer to attribute success to internal factors and failure to external factors to protect their self-esteem.

More up-to-date research, however, has suggested that, contrary to original research and popular belief, unsuccessful performers (losers), particularly individuals, do not try to protect their self-esteem by *always* attributing failure to external factors (task difficulty or luck) in order to reduce feelings of shame. The performer's *perception* of the causes in relation to perceived success/failure is seen as being more important.

This has obvious links back to achievement motivation with regard to outcome goals and task goals. Weiner's original view was that high and low achievers differed in the types of attributions given and that these would affect future behaviour. High achievers were seen as attributing success to internal factors – for example, personal dispositions and high ability, thus they were experiencing more pride. Failure, however, was attributed by high achievers to unstable factors, for example effort. They would therefore be more motivated to seek out, and expect to do well in, achievement situations.

As you can see, the appropriate use of attributions can have a major impact on the attitude and future expectations of an individual. The aim of all those involved with evaluating performance should be to ensure the development of positive self-esteem and the promotion of mastery-orientation.

Activity 15

Watch a post-match interview and compare the reasons the winning and losing teams give for their performance. Place each attribution into Weiner's model. Discuss the findings with your group.

Key term

Mastery-orientation Strong motive to succeed that is found in high achievers. Individuals will expect to be successful at a task but, if not, will still show persistence.

The concept of mastery-orientation involves individuals having the ability to evaluate their actions in a positive manner and attribute success to internal factors and failure to external factors. The characteristics of this type of behaviour are displayed when tasks or situations prove difficult and include the ability to:

- protect 'the self' when failure occurs
- display task persistence

- place an emphasis on achievement
- seize challenges rather than back away from them
- be energised by setbacks.

Alternatively, low achievers tend to attribute success to external factors, for example easy task, luck, generally uncontrollable factors. Failure is attributed to stable factors, for example 'I am too small' or 'I am not good enough', that is, lack of ability. They therefore find achievement situations less satisfying and will be generally less motivated to continue the activity. This has obvious implications when attempting to encourage a healthy lifestyle. If young performers do not have positive experiences during physical activity and develop the opinion that they are unable to improve or gain success, they are less likely to return to the activity in the future.

A performer's attributions will of course be affected by whether they view success or failure in terms of winning or losing (outcome goals) or whether they view it in terms of individual 'task' or 'mastery goals'. If a performer who has lost a tennis match judges their performance against previously set personal performance targets (mastery goals), for example they achieved more first serves and their consistency of ground strokes improved, then their feelings of pride/shame will be different to those of the performer who judges themselves on outcome goals alone (I lost).

Learned helplessness

Dweck categorised performers as 'helpless' or 'mastery-orientated'. Helpless performers attribute failure to themselves and see the task (stable factor) as insurmountable. 'Learned helplessness' is an acquired state or condition related to the performer's perceptions that they do not have any control over the situational demands being placed on them and that failure is, therefore, inevitable (they are 'doomed to failure'). After experiencing initial failure as a result of their perceived lack of ability (internal factor) in relation to the very hard task (stable external factor) they inevitably give up trying.

Characteristics of learned helplessness

- It can be **specific** to one activity or **general** to all sports
- Performer is outcome orientated
- It usually results from previous bad experiences
- Attributions to uncontrollable stable factors (for example, ability)
- Perceptions of low ability (feels incompetent)
- Rarely tries new skills
- Experiencing initial failure in new skills supports perceptions of limited ability
- Feelings of embarrassment
- Future effort is limited (why bother? I'm no good).

Key term

Learned helplessness The feelings experienced by a person when they feel failure is inevitable because of negative past experiences.

IN CONTEXT

Individuals who develop learned helplessness may experience either:

- **General/global learned helplessness** – for example, a young person may have negative experiences when learning to swim and, as a result, feel they will be unable to participate in any water-based activity
- **Specific learned helplessness** – for example a young person may be a strong swimmer and willing to attempt new water-based activities with the exception of those involving any form of canoe or boat as they have experienced capsizing several times and associate those particular activities with negative experience.

Fig 9.13 Learned helplessness can be general or specific

Interestingly it has been noted that often both teacher or coach and performer attribute success or failure to different reasons. Research has shown that when attributing reasons for our own behaviour we tend to relate it to external factors, and when attributing reasons for others' behaviour we tend to relate it to internal factors, such as lack of effort or poor ability. These differences in the application of attributions between an observer and performer are known as fundamental attribution errors. It is important that teachers and coaches are aware that attribution conflict can happen.

The teacher or coach has a very important role to play in preventing the formation of, or changing, inappropriate attributions in order to develop achievement motivation. It is important that when giving feedback to performers the teacher or coach does not negatively influence the performer's interpretation of success or failure by emphasising their lack of ability in relation to the task. If the teacher or coach implies that whatever the performer does they will never achieve the task then this could lead to the performer experiencing even greater levels of 'learned helplessness'.

A performer's lack of success should be attributed to problems with lack of consistency in technique, limited understanding, bad tactical decisions, and lack of experience or insufficient effort. By attributing failure to things that are within their control, that is, things they can do something about, motivation can be maintained through the development and setting of realistic mastery goals in relation to the task. The performer will not become frustrated, behave badly or aggressively and become demotivated.

EXAMINER'S TIP

Learn the definition of learned helplessness and examples of general and specific learned helplessness. Also remember the practical strategies to ensure it does not develop.

Attribution retraining

Getting performers to realise that failure is not inevitable and teaching them how to make appropriate attributions with regard to their performance, especially when they are possibly already experiencing learned helplessness is called 'attribution retraining' and is an important responsibility of the teacher or coach. In her research Dweck reported that attribution retraining was even more effective than initial performance success in ensuring that performers deal more effectively with failure.

Key term

Attribution retraining Process by which individuals are taught to attribute failure to changeable, unstable factors rather than internal, stable factors, such as lack of ability.

The aim of the teacher, coach or significant other should be to alter the person's perception of the reasons they give for their apparent failure. Rather than feeling a lack of success is due to internal factors, such as ability, the reasons should focus on aspects that can be altered and controlled. For example, a change of technique, development of fitness levels, different tactics, the quality of the opposition and so on. This altered perception should in turn alter the emotional feelings linked to the performance; changing from frustration and low self-confidence to optimism and a belief that they can improve in the future.

Strategies to develop mastery-orientation and avoid learned helplessness include:

- Give individual attention
- Emphasise performance goals rather than outcome goals
- Monitor performer's attributions
- Ensure teacher or coach's attributions do not make negative inferences
- Use mental rehearsal
- Avoid social comparisons with other performers
- Ensure early success.

One interesting factor to emerge from Dweck's work is that in heavily influencing the appropriateness of attributions for success or failure in children, teachers and coaches have to be careful not to subconsciously infer gender inequalities; via their expectations of success teachers can considerably influence young children's perceptions of their ability to achieve in and deal with situations.

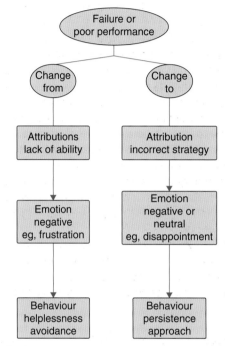

Fig 9.14 Attribution training process

It is also important that teachers and coaches are relatively honest in their approach to performers. There is no point in being unrealistic in the attributions given for success or failure. Young children in particular are relatively astute in perceiving their own levels of competence in relation to what is being asked of them. They need to know that they have the necessary skills to achieve the task even if their initial failure is attributed to a lack of effort. They must be confident in their own ability. If failure is as a result of a performer's limited ability then it is important that the teacher or coach redefines the goals/targets in relation to personal achievement, fitness, and so on, rather than set goals that rely on comparisons (performance goals).

Activity 16

In pairs discuss how you could ensure that learned helplessness does not occur in the following situations:

- Children learning to swim
- School basketball team that has lost its last three games
- Year 8 class learning to throw a javelin
- Adult group being introduced to a fitness gym to improve their health
- Trampolinist entering their first competition.

Aggression and its impact upon performance and behaviour

When we watch modern day sport certain types of behaviour are seen as acceptable and certain types of behaviour are unacceptable. So-called aggressive or unacceptable behaviour is witnessed on a regular basis within many sporting situations. It has been argued that the increase in aggressive and unacceptable behaviour in sport is merely a reflection of general behaviour within society as a whole.

Often commentators and coaches use the term 'aggression' in a context in that sometimes causes confusion. It can be applied in several different ways. Very often coaches demand more aggression from their players to 'win the ball' or 'fight for the ball', and aggressive tactics are often praised, for example serve/volley in tennis, a full court press in basketball, harder tackling in rugby. These examples actually infer that a performer is being energetic or persistent in their actions rather than violent towards another player.

At the same time, however, many actions or types of behaviour are thought of as being unacceptable forms of aggression – for example, a rugby player stamping on a player in a ruck, fights among players on a pitch, verbal abuse of officials, head-butting of opposition players, and so on. None of these can be condoned in any shape or form: the word 'aggression' used in such situations refers to anti-social behaviour intended to harm another.

Opinions of whether an action is acceptable or unacceptable are going to be different for various people, as responses are heavily influenced by subjective judgements. Two people watching a particular hard tackle in rugby or hockey will very often disagree as to its level of acceptability and level of good or bad aggression. It is important, therefore, to note that within sport it is not easy to hang a particular label on actions in order to identify what is meant by aggression.

Activity 17

Discuss the following suggestion: 'Sport is a mirror of society and aggressive acts on the playing field are a reflection of society itself.'

Develop your discussion and consider this second statement: 'Sport is good for society as it allows possible aggressive behaviour to be channelled in a functional way.'

Definitions of aggression

Based on the discussions in Activity 17 you may find that outlining an acceptable definition of aggression is no simple matter. It is important, however, that we do try as problems of misinterpretation by players, administrators and officials could have serious consequences.

Activity 18

Using the definitions outlined below, highlight key terms or phrases that can be used to identify the characteristics of aggression and formulate your own definition. Compare it to the rest of the group's ideas.

- **Maslow (1968)** distinguished between what he called natural/positive aggression (for example self defence) and pathological aggression or violence.
- **Brown (1985)** makes a distinction between aggression that does not always involve injury and violence, which usually does.
- **Moyer (1984)** introduces the idea of aggression being also verbal or symbolic, whereas violence manifests itself in physical damage to person or property.
- **Gross (1991)** defined aggression as the intentional infliction of some form of harm to others. (It is worth noting that anger is not seen as aggression but a state of emotional and physiological arousal – aggression is usually seen as the destructive behavioural expression of anger. The infliction of accidental harm is *not* seen as aggression.)
- **Baron's (1977)** definition of aggression (below) appears to be a compromise/compilation of the various suggestions given above.

'Aggression is any form of behaviour toward the goal of harming or injuring another living being who is motivated to avoid such treatment.' (Baron, 1977)

In relation to sport this definition stresses the idea that aggression is behaviour that is *intentional* and *deliberate* and involves injury to another person. From this, it can be inferred that aggression:

- is a first act of hostility, harm or injury
- involves physical or verbal action/behaviour (thinking is not being aggressive unless it leads to action)
- involves an implied intention (this can be difficult to interpret)
- is ultimately damaging, physically or mentally
- is outside the rules of the game (added later by sports psychologists).

In trying to clarify more clearly what is acceptable and what is not, Buss (1961), Feshback (1964) and Moyer (1976) made the distinction between two types of aggression:

1 Hostile aggression – aimed solely at hurting someone; the primary reinforcement is seeing pain or injury inflicted on another person. Moyer also termed this reactive aggression.
2 Instrumental aggression – a means to an end; aggression to achieve a non-aggressive goal, the primary reinforcement being tangible reward (for example praise, money or victory).

Another term commonly used to describe instrumental aggression is 'channelled aggression'. This form of behaviour appears initially to be more acceptable and covers most examples within sport; both types involve the *intention* to inflict injury or pain and it is debatable whether either should be encouraged in sport as they fall outside the accepted rules of most sporting activities.

During a football match between Arsenal and Birmingham City in 2008, the Arsenal player Eduardo da Silva suffered a broken ankle following a tackle by defender Martin Taylor. The referee decided the tackle had broken the rules, which resulted in a red card and Taylor was sent-off.

However, in a match several seasons earlier the Liverpool striker Milan Baros also suffered a broken ankle following a challenge from Blackburn Rover's Markus Babbel, but no action was taken by the referee. All those concerned were not upset by this incident as shown by the Liverpool manager at the time, Gerard Houllier's reaction after the match: 'The referee did the right thing – it was not even a foul; Markus tackled properly and got the ball and it probably happened when he fell over on the floor.'

As we can see from these two incidents, which both resulted in serious injury to the players involved, it was up to the referee to decide if the cause was aggressive or assertive play.

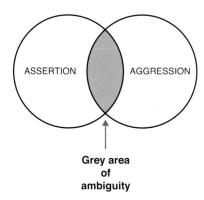

Grey area of ambiguity

Fig 9.15 There is an area of ambiguity between aggression and assertion. It is often left to officials to make the decision which is which

Key terms

Aggression Any form of behaviour intended to harm or injure another living being (Baron, 1977).
Hostile aggression/reactive aggression An emotional response (involving anger) to an individual perceived as an enemy or frustrating rival (Moyer 1984).
Instrumental aggression/channelled aggression Aggression to achieve a non-aggressive goal, the primary reinforcement being tangible reward (for example praise, money or victory).
Assertion Acceptable but forceful behaviour.

Assertive behaviour

In trying to end the confusing use of the word aggression to explain acceptable sporting behaviour the term 'assertive behaviour' was suggested by Husman and Silva (1984).

Assertive behaviour is seen as acceptable but forceful behaviour. The characteristics are:

- goal-directed behaviour
- the use of legitimate verbal or physical force (involving energy and effort that, outside sport, could be interpreted as aggression)
- behaviour that has no *intention* to harm or injure
- behaviour that does not violate the agreed rules/laws/structures of the sport, for example strong tackling in hockey, rugby, football; blocking in basketball; smashing in tennis/badminton, and so on.

While most sports have specific rule structures to control the degree of assertive behaviour allowed, there are still problems associated with subjective interpretations, both general and specific. When, for instance, does a tackle in rugby become high? What in hockey constitutes a deliberate foul in the 'D'? When should a red card be given in football?

Therefore, we can classify behaviour as aggression when the intention is clearly to harm or injure someone *outside* the laws of the game or activity.

Many sports, by their very nature, involve a high degree of physical contact that can lead either to its misuse or to misinterpretation of actions by an official. Officials often take into account the context of the assertive action – for example, what has gone on prior to the action, the stage of the game, where the incident happened on the court or pitch. Thus a member of a team winning 1–0 in an important match, who, as the last defender 'takes out' an attacker in the last few minutes, is generally deemed to have committed a conscious aggressive, not assertive, act (intention to harm or injure). Obviously sports such as rugby, hockey, ice hockey or wrestling have a larger grey area than non-contact sports.

Activity 19

Fill in the gaps using the following words

- Frustration–aggression hypothesis
- Social learning theory
- instinct theories
- Aggressive-cue hypothesis
- assertive

Any behaviour that involves the intention to injure or harm another player and which is outside the laws of the game is known as aggression. However, _____ acts are seen to be acceptable, forceful behaviour even though injury may occur as a result of the action. _____ suggest aggression is innate and a result of evolution, which is needed to provide catharsis. The _____ proposes that frustration always leads to aggression and aggression is always as a result of frustration. The _____ suggests aggressive behaviour is more likely to occur as a result of frustration if social cues are present. Finally, the _____ proposes that aggression is not instinctive but a learned response, acquired by observing others.

> **EXAMINER'S TIP**
>
> Learn the differences between aggression and assertion. Give sporting examples to support your answer.

Theories of aggression

Consider this question: how often have you displayed aggressive behaviour during a sporting contest?

If you have, have you ever actually considered the reasons for your actions and the implications, not only for yourself but the team? In the modern sporting arena, with the increasing pressure from the media, sponsors and supporters, the use of technology and the growing rewards for success, it can be argued that aggressive acts have more consequences than ever before. Performers now have to control their arousal levels because their actions can be far more serious than merely conceding a penalty.

Activity 21

List the possible causes of aggressive behaviour performers may experience and compare your findings with others in the class and the lists below.

Watch a sporting contest that involves some form of physical contact and answer the following questions?

- What are the possible acts of aggression?
- What are the possible causes?
- What the consequences of the aggressive acts?
- What are the acts of assertive behaviour?

Situations that cause aggression

Although activities that have high levels of physical contact are thought to increase the probability of aggression, this only happens if aggression increases the team's chances of winning (performance outcome) or the players interpret the contact as deliberate or intending to inflict harm.

Causes specific to individual aggression are:

- facing defeat (particularly when success has a high intrinsic or extrinsic value)
- officiating is perceived to be unfair
- embarrassment
- physical pain
- playing below expectations.

Activity 20

Tick the appropriate box to show whether you feel the following scenarios are acts of aggression or assertion.

Scenario	Aggression	Assertion
In trying to head a football, a player clashes heads with another player, causing a serious injury to his opponent		
A boxer traps his opponent against the ropes and leads with his head into the chin of the opponent		
A rugby player studs a player at the bottom of a ruck		
Having been tackled hard earlier in the game as the attacking hockey player approaches the 'D', the goalkeeper lifts her stick to catch the defender's hands and head		
Having been forced off the track the rally car driver runs over to the other driver who caused the crash and punches him in the face		
The bowler in cricket beats the batsman with a fast ball and hits him on the thigh		
A basketball player verbally abuses the referee for giving a personal foul against her		
A basketball coach smashes a chair in protest at a referee's decision		
A racing car driver slows down and cuts across the path of a faster driver coming up behind and stops him getting past		
A bowler in cricket bowls a third successive bouncer in one over, hitting the batsman on the head		

General causes of aggression are:

- that the effects or demands of the professional game encourage aggressive behaviour
- competition
- media intervention and comment
- belief that aggression facilitates performance outcome
- belief that it is OK to be more aggressive in sport than in other life contexts
- over-arousal
- over-emphasis on winning or the achievement of goals
- crowd reaction (displaced aggression)
- proximity of the crowd
- home or away venue
- increased rewards
- linked to situational expectations
- coaches and parents
- reinforcement/observation/vicarious processes.

While all of these may be actual causes, we can pose the question 'can the root cause of being aggressive be answered by investigating the nature or nurture debate?' In looking at possible causes of aggression, psychologists have considered the following issues:

- Why are some sports performers more aggressive than others?
- Why do some performers find it hard to control aggression?
- Are aggressive individuals born with certain innate characteristics?
- Are they a product of their learning and environmental influences?

The main theories associated with these questions are:

- Instinct theory
- Frustration–aggression hypothesis
- Aggressive-cue hypothesis
- Social learning theory.

Instinct theory

Instinct theories view aggression as instinctive within human beings that have developed as a result of evolution. In our fight for survival, aggression is seen as inevitable, as with any other species. There are, however, two distinct perspectives on this theory: the psychoanalytical approach and the ethological approach.

Psychoanalytical approach

Freud is the name usually associated with this approach to the instinct theory of aggression; aggression being viewed as a destructive drive. Freudian theory argues that our innate aggressive tendencies are expressed in the self-destructive or **death instinct**. This self-directed, inner drive towards self-aggression is balanced by our **life instincts**. Freud and Lorenze (see Ethological approach below) saw aggression as building up within a person before being directed away from self and into some other form of aggressive behaviour. This could be either acceptable behaviour (sport, expeditions, exploration, and so on) or unacceptable behaviour (crime, brutality or eventually back inside a person's mind, leading ultimately to suicide).

Freud also maintained that when we want to behave in a way that we know is unacceptable, we cope by using 'ego defence' mechanisms, such as **displacement**. For example, if you have had a bad day at the office, rather than hitting your boss when he made you angry you behave aggressively in your match later that evening, which is more acceptable. Thus you redirect your emotional responses from a dangerous target to a more harmless one who will hopefully not retaliate.

Ethological approach

One of the more famous psychologists in this area is Konrad Lorenz who based his views on anthropological studies comparing human behaviour with the 'natural' ritualistic aggressive behaviour of animals. The example of human attempts at territorial control (invasions, etc.) is often cited as justifying the comparison. This perspective sees aggression as building up within humans to create a drive that, if not released in some constructive way achieving catharsis (see below), will inevitably lead to some form of spontaneous destructive or aggressive behaviour. Like Freud, Lorenz argued that in acknowledging our natural aggressive instinct we should be able to control it through socially acceptable competitive sport (for example, invasion games where destructive aggression is controlled by rules and the referee).

Catharsis

For instinct theorists the view that sport and exercise can be used to 'channel' aggressive urges into more socially desirable behaviour (either as a performer or spectator) is very important. This view of purifying the body and reducing drive (catharsis) is not, however, supported by creditable research, particularly in sport. Evidence to show psychological differences before and after aggression has proved equivocal. It has even been suggested that rather than having a cathartic effect (drive reducing), watching aggressive behaviour may be drive enhancing, for example, the spectator who, having seen a particularly vicious boxing match, may be driven to reproduce aggressive behaviour (see Social learning theory of aggression, page 159).

Criticisms of instinct theory

In evaluating instinct theory psychologists feel that the parallels drawn between humans and animals are over simplified. Social learning processes are seen as being much more prevalent in human behaviour and need to be included in any explanation. Other criticisms include:

- No biological innate aggressive drive has ever been identified
- The measuring of any cathartic effect of aggression has proved difficult

- Early human beings were not warriors but 'hunter gatherers', like modern day Inuit
- Cross-cultural studies (Sian, 1985) do not support the view that all human beings are naturally aggressive
- Cultural influences are seen as being more important determinants of human aggression than biological factors
- Human aggression is not seen as being always spontaneous
- Human aggression is seen as reactive and modifiable
- Lorenz does not take into account learning and socialising influences, which are seen as overriding possible innate aggression
- Aggression is seen more as a learned response linked to the human ability to reason.

EXAMINER'S TIP

Make sure you can relate a sporting situation to each of the theories of aggression, and evaluate their respective strengths and weaknesses.

The Frustration–aggression hypothesis

The frustration–aggression hypothesis (Dollard et al., 1939) tried to deal with some of the limitations of instinct theory. Linked to drive theory it proposes that frustration always leads to aggression and aggression is always as a result of frustration.

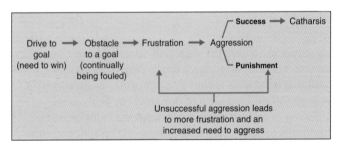

Fig 9.16 The frustration–aggression model is cyclical

Consider how often you have either witnessed aggression as a result of frustration or experienced it yourself. For example, the players in a major final are trying to achieve a good performance (drive) and success (goal-orientated behaviour). If the player is continually tackled and sees the opposition constantly blocking the ball or encroaching (blocking of goal-orientated behaviour) they may become frustrated. They are then driven to do something about it (increase drive), possibly playing or working harder. If the frustration continues, this drive may become an aggressive drive and result in breaking the rules or aggressive behaviour. When held, this player will retaliate with a punch; such aggressive behaviour will reduce frustration, which in turn will have a cathartic effect in the short term. However, in the long term, it may have a negative effect on the game and possibly result in further frustration.

Frustration–aggression hypothesis Suggestion that frustration will lead to aggression, and all aggression is a result of frustration.
Drive Level of motivation or arousal directed towards achieving a specific goal.

Criticism of the frustration–aggression hypothesis

This original model (see Figure 9.16), while initially finding support, has been found to have little credence in sport due, in the main, to its insistence that frustration always leads to aggression. Critics point out that:

- Not all frustration leads to aggression in sport – people have been increasingly shown to be able to deal with frustration in alternative ways, for example learned helplessness
- Aggression can be a learned response and does not always happen as a result of frustration
- Individual and situational differences are not taken into account
- The cathartic effect of aggression in sport is not upheld
- Some aggressive participants have been shown to become more aggressive through participation in sport.

Aggressive-cue hypothesis (cue arousal theory)

As a result of further research several modifications to the original hypothesis have been suggested. Some of Dollard's original theory has been combined with a more social learning approach; Berkowitz (1994) developed the early work and concluded that although frustration may make aggression more likely, other factors also need to be understood and taken into account. Frustration is not seen as being sufficient cause by itself. Berkowitz suggests that frustration creates a 'readiness' for aggression (anger creates psychological or physical pain).

Frustration leads to a predisposition to behave aggressively by increasing anger and arousal. This increased arousal and anger will only lead to aggression if certain socially learned cues or environmental stimuli are present.

For example, a defender in football who is easily beaten by an attacker who could go on to score may lash out or kick the opponent, particularly if the coach or manager has previously accepted such behaviour. Therefore, when encouraging young players in all activities to develop fair play and sportsmanship, the actions of the coach, teacher, parents and team mates are vital to ensure violent play is not encouraged. If aggressive actions by young players are supported and reinforced, they are more likely to occur rather than be controlled in an appropriate manner.

More anger is generated if the frustration is unexpected or seen as unfair. In most cases performers are able to use their developed mental processes of reasoning and thinking, and not always respond to frustration with aggression. Performers may do so, however, if for some reason they cannot think logically at that precise moment.

Evaluation of the aggressive-cue hypothesis

The theory is a more viable explanation of aggression compared to the original versions as it not only accounts for frustration but includes environmental factors, allowing it to view violent behaviour from an interactionist perspective. It also deals with the issue of aggression being an innate response and infers that it can be learnt and reinforced. If this is the case it means that aggression can also be controlled and instances of deviancy can be reduced.

Social learning theory of aggression

Social learning theorists see aggression as being influenced by learning. Bandura (1973) states that aggression is not an instinctive, but a learned, response. In his research Bandura has shown that a performer can learn to be aggressive by either having aggression reinforced (by it being successful or gaining coach approval) or by observation of aggressive behaviour. Bandura's (1965) well-known research demonstrated that children copy adults behaving aggressively in his 'Bobo doll experiment'. Children would often imitate the aggressive behaviour of the adults towards the large inflatable dolls. When the child was rewarded, or witnessed an adult being rewarded for beating the doll, the level of aggression increased.

The application of this theory to sport is obvious. If sports performers, particularly high-status players, are seen to behave aggressively, 'getting away with it' and achieving success, then a young player will be more likely to imitate those actions. This learning through observation of the behaviour of successful 'significant others' is referred to as 'vicarious learning'; this is frequently seen in young players who model their behaviour on the actions of others.

> ### Key term
>
> **Vicarious experience** Performers who watch other achieving the task will often feel they are also capable of being successful.

A young player can receive reinforcement of sporting aggression in many ways. Although teachers, coaches, parents, managers, team mates and professional performers will rarely condone blatant aggression, these significant others may well inadvertently or covertly support or sanction aggressive behaviour. Young players are often encouraged to 'get their retaliation in first', 'make the opposition know you are there'. Gamesmanship and 'psyching out' the opposition are all condoned. Performers very often verbally abuse the opposition (aggression) in order to goad them into retaliation, which may be just enough to put them off their game or sufficient to warrant their being sent off.

Vicarious or observational learning of aggression usually happens very early in a performer's development: a performer will quickly learn what behaviour is acceptable or unacceptable in various specific situations. Through observation and experience a performer will evaluate the consequences of certain aggressive actions, either in terms of punishment or expected reward. When expected rewards (for example prestige, tactical/psychological advantage or victory) are seen to outweigh the value of the punishment (such as a foul given away, booking or possible sin bin) a player will be prepared to transgress the rules.

The situational expectancies of success can be seen as high or low. Social learning theorists believe that reinforcement/punishment values are major factors in influencing sports performers in the selection of aggressive behaviour (Silva, 1979). Thus performers are being socialised towards deviance. However, the social learning perspective also sees the process as having possible positive effects. This more optimistic view suggests that if performers can learn aggressive sporting behaviour then they can also learn to be non-aggressive.

> ### IN CONTEXT
>
> Setting positive examples to younger players has become increasingly important to sporting organisations. The need to maintain a positive image to encourage sponsors, the media, spectators and the next generation of players is vital in the modern sporting world, especially when there are an increasing number of sports to choose from.
>
> Think of your own experiences in sport. Have you watched and copied anyone (either famous or someone such as your coach or teacher)?
>
> Think of the impact senior players in all sports have on young players. All their actions are closely watched and replicated. Consider high-profile footballers such as Wayne Rooney and John Terry; do they portray good sporting behaviour that is then encouraged?

It is vital that positive role models are developed to ensure young people adopt an active and healthy lifestyle for the correct reasons. If an individual sport is seen as particularly violent and aggressive, potential participants may fear for their own safety and develop a negative attitude as a result. It may also result in some individuals becoming involved with the sport purely as a means of committing aggressive acts because they feel it is acceptable to do so within that sporting context. This may lead to further injury to others and a self-perpetuating cycle of violent play and reduction in total number of participants.

Controlling and reducing aggression

Earlier in the chapter we discussed specific situation that may cause aggressive behaviour. It is important to recognise such situations because, if we are aware of what can create or predispose a performer towards aggressive behaviour, we can propose the following strategies for trying to limit or control aggression among sports performers:

1 If a player is observed as displaying signs that may well lead to possible aggressive behaviour, for example continual questioning of official's decisions or committing fouls, then a player should be removed from the game or situation in order to 'cool off' (continuous/rolling substitutions in basketball and hockey allow for this).

2 Stress management techniques (see page 200) can be used to teach sports performers to control their emotions and reactions to frustration. Relaxation prior to the game and mental practice focus efforts more effectively on fulfilling their role in the game.

3 Reduce the emphasis on winning (not so easy in professional sport) – aggression should not be the result of losing. Efforts should be made by the teacher or coach (significant other) to minimise any aggression experienced from losing.

4 Increase rewards for sporting or non-aggressive behaviour, for example fair play awards.

5 Reinforce assertive behaviour not aggressive behaviour.

6 Increase the profile of positive role models and highlight their success because they were not aggressive.

7 Emphasise the result of unacceptable behaviour by role models, for example bad publicity, getting sent off.

8 Ensure that players are aware of the 'wider role' they play in society and the possible damaging effects of their behaviour.

9 Make sure that aggression does not pay dividends – check that rules associated with activities deter acts of aggression (increase numbers of red cards).

10 Increase punishments for aggressive behaviour to reduce legitimacy of the action, for example penalties, sin bins, fines, bans, loss of points, and so on.

11 Players and coaches need to be more sensitive to the differences between assertive and aggressive behaviour in order to reduce the possibilities of retaliation.

12 Educate players and coaches on the appropriateness of certain types of behaviour (ethical/moral development). Emphasise their positive role in the team and discuss how aggressive behaviour may 'let down' their team mates.

13 Contain possible frustration by:
    (a) Increasing performers' levels of fitness in order that they can compete continually throughout a match.
    (b) Ensuring that players have alternative game plans/strategies to deal with situations in which original plans are being frustrated.
    (c) Adapting goals/targets.
    (d) Maintaining performers' attentional control, for example desensitisation to noise/crowd/distractions/intimidation.

EXAMINER'S TIP

Questions will require you to use your knowledge in an applied way, so develop an understanding of how to control aggression if you were in different roles, for example a coach, official or the governing body.

Strategies for controlling spectator aggression

Again, observation of aggressive behaviour has been shown to increase violence off the pitch, but only if certain situational factors are also part of the equation, for example crowd situations and/or large numbers of young males under the influence of alcohol. Controlling strategies include:

- Limiting alcohol or banning it altogether
- Reducing levels of rivalry
- Removing spectators if they display aggressive tendencies
- Increasing effectiveness of game officials, thus reducing aggressive behaviour within the game
- Reducing crowded situations (strict seating control)
- Telling coaches that aggressive behaviour or inciting aggressive behaviour by themselves or their teams will not be tolerated
- Getting the media to support these views by not positively emphasising aggressive behaviour
- Make sporting situations more family orientated
- Increase stewarding.

Methods by which referees/officials can control aggression in sporting competitions

- Officials can only operate within the rules/sanctions allowed within the game
- Apply the rules correctly
- Punish aggressive behaviour immediately (don't allow situations to escalate)
- Officials should be consistent in both judgements, perceptions/interpretation and sanctions awarded
- Officials must apply firmness/consistency/control from the start of the competition.

Activity 22

Observe a live or televised match involving physical contact, such as rugby or football. Identify strategies used by officials, managers, coaches and anyone else involved with the game to limit aggressive behaviour. Evaluate the effectiveness of their actions and suggest alternative strategies that could have been used.

What you need to know

Personality
* Personality is the combination of those characteristics that make a person unique
* Personality refers to those relatively stable and enduring aspects of an individual's behaviour
* The study of personality has tended to consider it as a result of 'nature' or 'nurture'
* Trait theories see personality as being innate and stable predispositions, enabling behaviour patterns to be predicted in all situations
* Social learning theories see personality as being formed as a result of the environment influencing individual learning experiences. Thus it can change in different situations
* Interactionist theories see personality as being a combination of traits and the environment: B = f(PE)
* A variety of methods can be used to test personality, the most common being questionnaires, observation and interviews
* Personality tests should not be used in isolation as there are question marks over their validity
* There are no definite findings suggesting different personalities lead to more successful athletes or specific types of sport
* The closest we can get to predicting the behaviour of an individual is through 'mood states', which link to the suggested 'iceberg' profile
* For success in sport each individual must be viewed differently by the coach according to the three levels of personality: the psychological core, typical response and role-related behaviour.

Attitudes
* Attitudes are specific and related to an attitude object
* Attitudes are formed through experiences
* Attitudes have three components: cognitive, affective and behavioural
* Attitudes can considerably influence behaviour in sport
* Stereotyping is not 'bad' in itself, but it is important for teachers and coaches to be aware of inaccurate stereotypes and challenge them
* Once formed, attitudes are very resistant to change and can lead to prejudice
* Attitudes can be altered by persuasive communication and cognitive dissonance.

Attributions and learned helplessness
* The reasons performers give to explain success or failure (causal attributions) have been found to be very influential on their expectations of future success or failure, level of emotional reactions (feelings of pride or shame) and, thus, future achievement motivation (high or low)

* Weiner's attribution model originally identified two dimensions: locus of causality (internal or external factors) and stability (stable or unstable). A third dimension of locus of control was added later. This related to whether attributions given were under the performer's control or not
* High and low achievers have been found to differ in the attributions they give (self-serving bias)
* A performer who continually focuses on outcome goals and attributes failure to perceived low ability (internal, stable factor), or success to external, unstable factors (luck) – all of which are out of their control – is likely to experience learned helplessness
* Learned helplessness can be general or specific
* Attribution retraining, if used effectively, can help performers reduce feelings of being inevitably 'doomed to failure'.

Aggression
* Aggression is intentional behaviour outside the rules directed towards the goal of harming or injuring another living being, when they are motivated to avoid such treatment
* The main theories associated with the study of aggression are: instinct theory (ethological and psychoanalytical); frustration–aggression hypothesis; aggressive-cue hypothesis and social learning theory
* More up-to-date research has ensured that instinct theory has little support in relation to sport. There is, however, some recognition of limited innate aggressive tendencies
* There is little evidence to support the notion of catharsis
* The revised frustration theory of aggression is seen as having some credibility, particularly when it is linked to social learning theory
* Social learning theory advocates that reinforcement and modelling, either of or by significant others, are the main influential determinants of aggressive behaviour in sport
* Social learning can also be seen as an optimistic approach
* Having an understanding of what can cause aggressive behaviour allows teachers, coaches and performers to be more effective in controlling aggressive behaviour
* Performers can be taught a variety of stress management techniques to control aggressive behaviour
* Coaches, managers and teacher can employ a range to strategies to reduce aggressive acts.

Review Questions

Personality

1 What do we mean by personality?
2 What is the trait perspective view of personality?
3 What are the limitations of the trait perspective?
4 What are the main criticisms of personality tests?
5 What is the social learning theory of personality?
6 How does the interactionist approach differ from the Trait Approach?
7 Explain the equation $B = f(PE)$.
8 What is meant by a personality core? Give an example.
9 What is the iceberg profile? How does it relate to sports performers' 'mood states'?
10 How do type A and type B profiles differ?

Attitudes

1 What is an attitude?
2 Explain the term attitude object.
3 Name and outline the three components of an attitude.
4 Do attitudes really help us to predict behaviour?
5 By giving examples from sport, try to show how attitudes can be formed.
6 Outline the term stereotype.
7 Why are prejudices potentially dangerous?
8 What factors are important when trying to persuade someone to change their attitudes? Illustrate your answer with examples from sport.
9 What is dissonance?
10 Explain how an attitude can be changed using cognitive dissonance.

Attributions and learned helplessness

1 What are Weiner's four types of attribution?
2 What is meant by the term 'causal attributions'?
3 Why do sport psychologists think that attribution theory is important?
4 Explain the locus of control identified in Weiner's model of attributions.

5 Using an example from sport, explain how attributions can affect a performer's future behaviour.
6 What type of attributions might a high achiever give for their success or failure? Give examples.
7 Explain the term 'self-serving bias'.
8 What is meant by 'learned helplessness'? Why is it important?
9 Outline the difference between general and specific learned helplessness.
10 How can teachers or coaches try to alleviate the problem of learned helplessness?

Aggression

1 Give a definition of 'aggression'. How does this differ from assertive behaviour? Give examples.
2 Explain what is meant by:

   (a) Hostile aggression.

   (b) Instrumental aggression.

   (c) Reactive aggression.

3 Why is instinct theory thought to be a too simplistic approach?
4 What is meant by the term 'catharsis'?
5 Using examples from sport, show what you understand by the frustration–aggression hypothesis.
6 Explain how aggression can be socially learned.
7 Why are significant others so important in relation to aggression?
8 How do situational expectancies affect aggressive behaviour?
9 Outline three strategies officials can use to ensure assertive behaviour is encouraged rather than aggressive behaviour.
10 Explain how a coach can reduce the aggressive behaviour of players.

Group dynamics of performance and audience effects that influence people's participation, aspirations and lifestyles

Learning outcomes

By the end of this chapter you should be able to:

- describe the nature of a group/team (mutual awareness, interaction, common goal)
- demonstrate knowledge and understanding of Steiner's model of group performance
- demonstrate knowledge and understanding of motivational factors (social loafing); coordination/cooperation factors (Ringlemann effect) and explain the negative influences that cause dysfunctional behaviour and avoidance of an active and healthy lifestyle
- explain the factors affecting the formation and development of a cohesive group/team
- explain the factors affecting participation in a group/team
- explain group and team effects on behaviour (related to balanced, active and healthy lifestyles)
- demonstrate knowledge and understanding of effective leadership and explain its effects on lifestyle behaviour
- describe the characteristics of leaders (autocratic/task-oriented, democratic/social-oriented, laissez-faire)
- demonstrate knowledge and understanding of emergent and prescribed leaders
- evaluate critically leadership theories (trait, social learning, interactionist theories)
- demonstrate knowledge and understanding of Chelladurai's multi-dimensional model of leadership and explain the effect of leadership expectations on performance and the adoption of a balanced, active and healthy lifestyle
- demonstrate knowledge and understanding of the positive (facilitation) and negative (inhibition) effects of audience and co-actors on performance, participation and lifestyle
- demonstrate knowledge and understanding of links with levels of arousal, and the heightening of the dominant response (Zajonc)
- explain causes and effects of evaluation apprehension
- demonstrate knowledge and understanding of strategies to combat the effects of social inhibition in practical activities (the use of selective attention and mental rehearsal) and in following a balanced, active and healthy lifestyle.

CHAPTER INTRODUCTION

In the previous chapter relating to the psychology of sport we have been concerned mainly with the relationship between the individual performer and various psychological variables, resulting in the creation of certain types of behaviour or 'performance'. We have concluded that a performer's behaviour in relation to certain situations is as a result of many variables.

In accepting this interactionist viewpoint, you should have become aware that a performer's behaviour is rarely a result of individual factors, but usually a result of many interrelated factors.

Every teacher or coach knows that they are not dealing with 'cocooned individuals': most sporting situations

involve some form of social interaction. They have to be aware not only of the previous influences (sporting and non-sporting) of groups and teams on performance, but also that present performance is being either directly or indirectly linked to, or influenced by, the behaviour of others.

This does not mean to say that we ignore all the individual factors discussed earlier in the book; rather, the whole situation becomes more complicated. All the variable factors are impinging on the individual and each individual is affecting the others.

Consider the importance of bringing together a group of highly talented individuals, which will allow them to fulfil their potential and function effectively as a team. In the modern sporting world this process has become

▶

even more complicated by the introduction of the 'support services' required to excel.

Psychologists have carried out a great deal of research into the many different ways in which sports performers interact with one another and how other people's behaviour, or the social situation in which the performance is taking place, can influence performance. This research has then been applied to the competitive environment to ensure preparation, such as 'training camps' and the routines experienced by athletes are well rehearsed in order to maximise their performance.

In this chapter we will explore these direct or indirect effects and you will become aware of what is meant by the following terms and how they can influence sporting performance:

- Group dynamics/cohesion
- Leadership
- Social facilitation.

Group dynamics related to sport performance

Within physical education and sport the study of groups comes under the umbrella of 'social psychology'. Research has generally shown that people tend to behave differently within the context of a group than they do as individuals. As most physical education and sporting situations, including most individual activities, tend to involve the interaction of performers, the study of group dynamics is an important topic.

Research into small group processes in sport has generally revolved around the idea of 'teams' and how teachers and coaches can encourage them to work together to produce an effective performance. It has also been related to such specific areas as group cohesion, leadership, structure, size, motivation, conformity and so on.

This is an important area of study; the importance of developing a cohesive group is vital when you take into account the long-lasting impact of success or failure. Consider the positive impact of the success of the England rugby team at the 2003 World Cup and of Team GB at the 2008 Beijing Olympics. However, also remember how frequently coaches and managers in all sports lose their jobs because of poor results due to below par team performances.

What is a 'group'?

What do we mean by the word 'group'? At first glance it may appear relatively simple: 'several people who come together'? 'A meeting of more than one person'? However, does that include people waiting at a bus stop? Or all the people actually swimming at the local pool?

Activity 1

Think of any successful sporting group or team. List the reasons that identify them as a group and suggest reasons for their success.

The main feature that helps to define a group is that the members of the group must be interacting in some way over a period of time.

This interrelationship within the group will involve mutual interdependence, communication and conformity to the same shared goals, norms and values. The members of the group need to perceive the group's existence, be aware of its effect and that they are all members. They will, therefore, have a group identity that differentiates them from other groups.

'Groups are those social aggregates that involve mutual awareness and potential interaction.'
(MacGrath, 1984)

A group is '… two or more people who are interacting with one another in such a manner that each person influences and is influenced by each other person.'
(Shaw, 1976)

Carron (1982) suggests that groups have some unique characteristics, including:

- Two or more people interacting
- Sharing of a collective identity
- Sharing a common goal
- Structured forms of communication.

Key terms

Group A collection of individuals working together to meet a common goal.
Group dynamics Process by which a group is constantly developing and changing when interaction takes place.

Groups are seen as continually changing and developing units of people – hence the term group dynamics. However, although they are changing dynamically, all groups will exhibit and can be identified by the six Is:

- Interaction (communication over a period of time)
- Interdependence (person and task to achieve common goals)
- Interpersonal relationships (mutual attraction)
- Identical goals/norms/values
- Identity (perception of group's existence)
- Independence.

Establishing effective group performance

In modern day performance-orientated sport it is essential that the teacher or coach can develop the highest standards of performance possible. The process of bringing together talented individuals who interact effectively to produce a successful team is central to the role of a teacher or coach.

Although most sports coaches would support the notion that bringing together the most talented players or performers would increase their chances of team success, they are also aware that this does not necessarily guarantee success. How often have the most talented team lost unexpectedly? Every year there appears to be a major upset in one competition or another, where the favourites have either under-performed or the underdogs raised their game.

Activity 2

We often hear generalised statements from coaches and the media such as:

- 'They are a team of individuals!'
- 'They were all playing for themselves.'
- 'They were the most talented team on paper.'
- 'The best individuals don't always make the best team and win leagues.'

Look at these quotes and discuss what you think they mean. What are the implications for the potential success levels of the teams involved?

Steiner's model of group productivity

The role of the coach, manager or teacher is vital if they are to mould a collection of individuals into a cohesive team. Steiner suggested that a successful team is often more than the sum of its parts (individual talents). Equally so, an unsuccessful team is often less than the sum of its parts. He suggested that group productivity could be measured using the following equation:

$$\text{Actual productivity} = \text{potential productivity} - \text{losses due to faulty group processes}$$

Where:

- **Actual productivity** is their best level of performance
- **Potential productivity** is the quality and quantity of the group's resources relevant to the task
- **Losses due to faulty group processes** include co-ordination losses and motivational losses (see below for further explanation).

The resources relevant to the task include:

- An individual player's motor, physical and perceptual abilities
- An individual player's skills level
- Group skill levels

- Individual/group knowledge/experience
- Individual/group physical/psychological resources (for example size, weight, fitness)
- Individual/group mental (cognitive) resources.

Socially identified resources relevant to the task include:

- Age
- Education
- Religion
- Occupation
- Race
- Gender
- Socialisation.

In assessing a group's potential a coach can either average out or total up the attributes of the individuals concerned. However, the notion that the team possessing 'more' will perform better (while being a 'gut reaction' and one that usually rings true) is not always correct.

According to Steiner's model, individual ability and skill level is probably the major influence on potential success, thus the team with the best individuals has the greater *potential* for success. This very much depends, however, on the type of activity, specific skill and the level of expected play (recreational/fun) or performance. The coach's job is, therefore, to ensure that the talent resources available are used effectively and that potential process losses are minimised. Only when this happens will:

$$\text{Actual productivity} = \text{potential productivity}$$

Activity 3

Observe a sporting contest (it can be a school/college match or one played at elite level). Identify aspects of the performance that could be classed as 'faulty processes' and influenced the actual productivity of the team.

EXAMINER'S TIP

Make sure you understand the faulty processes affecting group productivity and strategies to eliminate them.

Faulty processes within the group process

Very often the underdogs can outshine the top team due to problems with coordination of the relevant resources available (process faults). Process faults can be of two types, either:

1   **Coordination losses:** team work/strategies break down or are not understood or are ineffective. Coaches of very complex team games (for example, basketball or netball) very often blame a team's inability to maintain their 'shape' as a reason for losing a game.

In September 2008 the biannual Ryder Cup golf event was held at the Valhalla Golf Club, Louisville, Kentucky, between Europe and the USA. Europe had held the trophy since 1999 with much of their success based on the well-publicised fact that they were a very cohesive team who played for each other in contrast to the Americans, who appeared to be much more individualistic. The selected European Team were at full strength compared to the USA, who were missing the world's best player, Tiger Woods, and fielding six rookies in the team of 12. However, Paul Azinger, the Captain of the USA selected a team that surprised many and created a climate within the team that allowed them to bond. As a result, they appeared to play with much more commitment and purpose, culminating in victory. After the competition, Phil Mickelson, one of the most experienced players on the American team commented:

'We had six guys who had not experienced losing, who were determined to help turn the United States' performance in the Ryder Cup around, and they did that. Look at their record; it was phenomenal. They brought a game, an attitude, an energy, and it invigorated the US team.'

2   **Motivational losses**: individual or group loss of confidence, incorrect arousal levels, perhaps all team members may not be giving 100 per cent effort or individuals are relying on other 'star' players.

Group coordination and cooperation

When working together as a pair (such as in a tennis doubles) or as a group, research has shown that the most effective teams include not only talented players but players who complement each other. In activities that require complex levels of interaction, such as basketball and rugby, **cooperation** between team members is essential in order that intricate tactical manoeuvres can be carried out effectively. It is also essential that team members can rely on each other to do their own job and not interfere with someone else's efforts. Very often in hockey and soccer, skilful forwards will feel isolated and possibly starved of chances because the midfield are not doing their job in getting the ball 'up front' quickly enough. Therefore, they decide to go back and 'help' to do the job of the midfield players. The midfield players may well now win the ball but are unable to release it forward as there are no forwards in position to give the ball to.

Group size

The size of the group is also thought to be a problem affecting 'productivity' that has to be addressed in terms of both coordination and motivation. In developing a successful team the teacher or coach needs to harness the talents of many individuals, but how many is always a problem. If we follow Steiner's equation, as much of the

supporting research in this area has, we can see that 'more is not always better' and 'too many cooks can spoil the broth', as the traditional sayings go. In other words, there comes a point in a team's development when all the resources for potential success are in place, and adding further so-called talented players may actually be unproductive. Duplication of roles and effort is not necessary as it very often leads to confusion and lack of effort. An interesting aspect of research has shown that group size has a direct correlation with group effectiveness. As group size increases there is a decline in individual effort and eventual productivity. This phenomenon was first noted over 100 years ago by a Frenchman called Ringelmann.

The Ringelmann effect

Research has generally shown that in larger groups each individual does not always give their best effort. In observing a 'tug-of-war' competition during the nineteenth century, Ringelmann noted in various events two, three, and up to eight competitors. As the groups got bigger, the individual effort within the group deteriorated. Instead of the eight-man team pulling eight times as hard as one man, they actually only pulled approximately four times as hard, thus showing a positive decline. Ringelmann showed this decline in productivity as follows:

- One person – 100 per cent
- Two persons – 93 per cent
- Three persons – 85 per cent
- Four persons – 77 per cent
- Five persons – 70 per cent
- Six persons – 65 per cent
- Seven persons – 58 per cent
- Eight persons – 49 per cent.

In other words, he noted that there was an inverse relationship between the number of people performing a task and the amount of effort expended by each of them.

In following up this very early and potentially worrying research, Ingham and colleagues (1974) concluded that this effect, first noted by Ringelmann and originally attributed to poor coordination (such as a lack of simultaneous maximal tension), was actually more related to decreased motivation.

Social loafing

The conclusions of Ingham et al. were that differences or losses in actual group productivity (performance) were more likely as a result of reduced motivation; this has been termed **social loafing**.

Research directed towards explaining social loafing has grown. Latane, Harkins and Williams (1979) proposed that performers demonstrated both **allocation strategies** and **minimising strategies**. This suggests that performers *are* motivated to work hard in groups, but save their best performances for when they are performing alone or under close scrutiny, when it personally benefits them more (allocation strategies). The minimising strategy proposes that performers are motivated to give as much or as little (minimum) effort in order to 'get by' and achieve the task.

Group activities and team games provide plenty of opportunity for performers to 'loaf' and take it easy, as their individual performance is not necessarily being scrutinised or assessed. They may also feel that their performance is not bringing them the recognition it deserves; for example, they feel 'lost' in the crowd or anonymous. Their individual performance/role is not easily identifiable. Performers within a team situation have also been shown to reduce effort as they do not wish to make it easy for less accomplished or less productive individuals to get a 'free ride'. They themselves do not wish to be seen as the 'sucker' doing other people's jobs.

Key terms

Ringelmann effect The performance of an individual may decrease as the group size increases.
Social loafing An individual who attempts to 'hide' when placed in group situations and fails to perform to their potential.

EXAMINER'S TIP

Explain the concepts of the Ringelmann effect and social loafing, as well as strategies to minimise the negative effects on group productivity.

IN CONTEXT

In parts of the UK sport is being used as a vehicle to develop positive attitudes towards group membership and identity, in an effort to reduce levels of dysfunctional behaviour and encourage healthy and active lifestyles.

For example, the Midnight League, a five-a-side football league aimed at tackling crime and social exclusion in Wolverhampton, is a late-night football initiative that operates at the time when most anti-social behaviour occurs in deprived areas of the town (i.e. between 10pm and midnight).

The project is run with the backing of the West Midlands police, and both youth workers and local community groups contribute towards helping the Wolverhampton Wanderers Community Team target and recruit players.

Open to anyone between 16 and 21 who lives in targeted areas of the town, the project aims to provide young people with opportunities to participate in activities that encourage fun, fair play and a sense of responsibility. The benefits include:

- Development of respect for each other, their neighbours and to experience the spirit of teamwork
- Development of socialisation skills and tolerance of others, contributing to the development of community spirit, as well as positive attitudes towards life and learning
- The opportunity to gain qualifications, allowing individuals to extend their involvement to help run the project and gain paid employment
- The chance to visit the local football ground and watch matches
- Regular physical exercise and education about the benefits of an active lifestyle.

The success of the scheme is evident from the comments made by Detective Sergeant Dave Mullett of Wolverhampton Police:

'The first two areas for the Midnight League – Heath Town and Bilston – were both very low in the social exclusion sense with relative high crime levels – mostly based around burglary, vehicle crime and criminal damage. The social make-up of these areas is historically different to other areas in that there was poor or no involvement from important parts of the community, i.e., police/social services and there wasn't a lot for the kids to do.

'This initiative was very much welcomed to ensure these youths are fully utilised in useful skills during their spare time. I don't see this solely as a crime-busting scheme – a lot of it is about teaching the youths life skills, making them aware of the issues surrounding them, teaching them timeliness and how to be part of a team – these are all skills they can take forward into their adult lives.

'There are so many factors that hinder gathering crime stats that we are not able to say the scheme is solely responsible for the reduction in crime, however, in general terms, crime has decreased in these areas and, coincidentally, this has been since the scheme was introduced.'

Strategies for reducing social loafing

As you can see from the example of the Midnight League, the concept of developing teams/groups can extend beyond the initial aim of creating a team and winning in a sporting context. Therefore, it is important to understand how to minimise the impact of social loafing and the Ringelmann effect. Strategies to achieve this include:

1 Identifying situations that allow social loafing to occur and reducing them.
2 Identifying individual contributions and not just group outcomes.
3 Ensuring that individuals understand the importance of their contribution and role within the team.
4 All players' contributions should be identified and evaluated individually, and sometimes publicly (statistics should be kept).
5 Regular feedback on individual's contributions and effort should be given.

6 Although extrinsic rewards/reinforcements can be used to motivate individuals, for example player of the week or tackle of the week, intrinsic motivation should mainly be used.
7 Ensure that players know what others' roles and contributions should be.
8 Games can be videoed to carry out observation checklists.
9 Ensure that fitness is at a high level, thus ensuring that players don't feel the need to take strategic rests (loaf) at crucial times.
10 Develop variety in practice and training to ensure that players stay interested and maintain levels of attention.
11 Develop a good knowledge of each player to ensure that personal or non-game issues are not having a detrimental effect on performance.
12 Develop team cohesion.

Formation and development of a cohesive group/team

A group of individuals is not necessarily a team although all teams, by definition, are groups. In essence, a *team* is any group of people who have in-depth interaction with each other in order to achieve shared objectives.

Although we have stated that groups in sporting terms would generally develop and exhibit the six Is, this process is not a short one. A coach bringing together several individuals would have to work extremely hard over a considerable period of time to develop the six Is in order to maximise performance. Throughout this evolutionary process, teams are constantly developing. A team, therefore, would normally be considered a very *strong* group.

Psychologists have produced several models of group formation. One of the better-known linear models is that developed by Tuckman (1965). In order for groups of individuals to become a 'real team' Tuckman suggested that, although the time scale may differ from situation to situation, they all go through four key progressive stages of development: **forming**, **storming**, **norming** and **performing**.

Stage 1 – Forming

The individuals come together and try to find out about each other (familiarisation). They try to get to know and understand what their and others' roles are within the group (assess strengths and weaknesses – social comparisons). Do they belong? Can they identify with or accept the expected and perceived roles, more formal structures and relationships within the group?

Stage 2 – Storming

In this stage individual members or cliques within the group may begin to question openly certain formal group power structures and, very often, also challenge the status of the leader. Open hostility and stress may result as the members compete for power. The coach/teacher/leader has to work hard to reduce the effects of this situation by communicating with the group openly and objectively.

Stage 3 – Norming

Group instability begins to disappear. The members begin to work together, displaying group cohesion. The members recognise the need for common goals and gain personal satisfaction from achieving tasks collectively and effectively; mutual respect for each member's contribution increases.

Stage 4 – Performing

The members of the group now primarily identify with the team. They all have, and are aware of, their and others' roles within the team structure. All feel that they contribute individually and collectively to the productivity and success of the team. Each individual is said to experience psychological security within the context of the team. Energies are channelled to achieve group success.

Activity 4

Imagine you are a coach of a newly formed team. What strategies might you employ to try to reduce the effects encountered in the storming stage? Discuss with the rest of the group. (You may find it useful to return to this activity after you have read the section on leadership later in this chapter.)

EXAMINER'S TIP

Questions may focus on the stages of group formation and how the process can be made more effective.

Structures and roles within groups and teams

All aspects of group structure are important to the effectiveness of the group or team. The structure will develop as a result of group interaction. During the 'forming stage' the group's structure will begin to develop; because of their perceptions of their own and others' expectations the individuals within the group will begin to adopt certain roles, both formally and informally. A *role* is the specific behaviour expected of a person occupying a certain position in the group's structure.

1 **Formal roles** – teacher, coach, team captain.
2 **Formal task or performance roles** – striker in football/hockey, goalkeeper, penalty taker (hockey/football), goal kicker (rugby), goal shooter (netball).
3 **Informal roles** – team diplomat/social roles, team comedian/joker, team 'hardman' or 'stopper'.

It is important that players within a team or members of a group are aware of their role (role clarity) and are prepared to accept it and function in that role (role acceptability).

The effectiveness of the team can be seriously affected if a player is unaware of, doesn't understand or is unwilling to fulfil the role expected of them by the rest of the team. This area has obvious links to intrinsic motivation and the setting of clear and specific goals by the teacher, coach or leader.

In addition to accepting and taking on certain specific roles within the group/team, members will also adopt certain general and specific patterns of behaviour or beliefs. These are known as the **group norms**. All groups/teams will develop established norms of behaviour and performance—for example, degrees of effort in training, codes of dress, and methods of celebrating or certain aggressive styles of play. Performers and coaches will have different ways of ensuring that team members conform to these norms. These could involve either formal sanctions, such as fines for being late, substitutions or suspensions, or informal sanctions, such as the social pressure of being made fun of. It is very important, therefore, that the teacher or coach establishes clear expectations of behaviour (norms) in order to ensure the highest standards of performance possible within a positive and supportive climate. It is, however, the team members' perceptions of these norms and roles that will be the main influence on whether a positive team climate is established.

Adherence to specific group roles and norms in relation to the task can have a possible negative effect by inhibiting individual flair and development. Groups can also begin to be over comfortable with the situation and limit their effort.

Activity 5

Having looked at how groups are formed, discuss in your groups the types of problems, both positive and negative, that managers or coaches may encounter by bringing into their teams big 'named stars' from different teams.

Cohesion

When considering why some teams are more or less successful than others it is often stated that the successful team was more cohesive and vice versa. Thus the concept of *group cohesion* has become a widely researched area in group dynamics.

There has been much debate about whether group cohesion helps to create a successful team, or whether the fact that a team is initially successful in turn creates cohesion. Certainly there is considerable evidence to support the belief that there is a positive correlation between success and cohesion. Success, particularly early on, leads to greater feelings of self and group satisfaction and, thus, higher cohesion; however, the individual's perceptions of cohesion have also been shown to lead to greater satisfaction with group structure and organisation, although the supporting research is less convincing.

Cohesion is now generally defined as:

'a continuously changing (dynamic) process which is shown by the tendency of a group to stay together in order to achieve certain instrumental objectives, targets or goals or for the satisfaction of its members.' (Carron et al., 1998)

Individuals are seen as being motivated to stay together as a group by either:

1 The attractiveness of the group, that is, the person wants to be involved in the group and values membership; or
2 The benefits they can gain from it (increased recognition).

In this early research the effects of cohesion were also assessed in terms of both interactive and coactive groups. In 'interactive' teams such as basketball, soccer, netball and hockey (where there is a high division of labour and specialised skills are brought together for the good of the whole), perceived cohesion was thought to be important for success. In contrast, team cohesion was seen as less vital for coactive teams such as rowing, swimming and relay, where members rely less on each other and just have to complete their own task successfully.

Key terms

Cohesion The extent to which a group works together to achieve a common goal.
Task cohesion The interaction of the group and how effectively they work together to achieve a common goal.
Social cohesion The interaction of individuals and how well they relate to each other.

Later research developed these two basic assessments of cohesion into two further categories, referred to as **task cohesion** and **social cohesion**.

Task cohesion relates to how well the team works together to achieve common targets or goals, for example win the league. The level of a team's 'desire to win' and be the best is directly linked to their level of group effort and teamwork.

Social cohesion relates to how much the members of the team like each other and integrate socially (interpersonal attractions among members).

Research in this area has raised many questions along the following lines:

● In order to be successful do teams need to have both task *and* social cohesion?
● Is one more effective than the other in developing success?

In order to try to answer these questions Carron (1982) proposed a conceptual model to highlight the many pre-existing variables (antecedents) that could influence the development of group cohesion. Carron's framework identified four major categories of antecedents (factors) that contribute to group cohesion:

- **Situational/environmental elements** (usually consistent): for example, group size, age, contracts, geography, distinctive kit
- **Personal elements** (not always consistent): for example, similar/dissimilar, member satisfaction, gender, motivational reasons(such as task, affiliation, self, attitudes, aspirations, expectations)
- **Team elements**: for example, desire for success, shared team experiences (winning and losing can both create cohesion)
- **Leadership elements**: for example, decision-making style adopted; participative style helps create cohesion, communication, compatibility with performers (see Leadership, page 171).

These four categories of antecedents were seen as affecting both 'task' and 'social' cohesion in relation to either the group or the individual. Thus, while the team's objectives may be the same for all, the individual motives for joining and maintaining the group may well be different.

Fig 10.1 In order to win a team needs all its players working together as a cohesive unit during competitions

> **EXAMINER'S TIP**
>
> Questions may ask you to outline different types of cohesion and the relationship between them.

Taking this view, later research by Carron (1988) and Widmeyer et al. (1985, 1990) began to look in more detail at this apparent circular relationship between success and cohesion, suggesting that both group members' perceptions of the total group (group integration) and the individual's attractions to the group needed to be looked at in detail. Thus both individual and group attributions could be measured and analysed in relation to whether they were either task or socially orientated.

Questionnaires such as the Group Environment Questionnaire (GEQ; Widmeyer, 1985) appear to be the most effective for measuring and evaluating levels of cohesion.

Sociograms have also been used to give an even greater insight into how individuals relate to each other within teams.

In order to understand the levels of interpersonal relationships team members are asked to nominate three people who may relate to specific posed questions, for example:

- Choose three people who you get on best with
- Choose your three best friends
- Choose three people who you would be prepared to room with
- Choose three people who you like best to train with.

Confidentiality is, of course, paramount. From this sociograms can be used to identify:

- Friendship patterns/choices
- Possibility of cliques
- Members' perceptions
- Social isolates
- Level of group attraction.

What this research has shown is that performance success leads to increased cohesion, which in turn leads to increased performance; it also shows that there appears to be a more positive relationship between task cohesion and performance than between social cohesion and performance. Thus, groups performing at the highest professional levels are very often able to put aside their negative personal feelings for one another (poor social cohesion) and work incredibly hard to promote the team effort and performance in order to win (high task cohesion). Questions have been raised, however, as to whether this is because individuals perceive coordination and interdependence on one another as being essential for success and thus work hard to ensure it happens (particularly in interactive team sports rather than coactive sports).

Strategies for developing team cohesion

Carron and Spinks (1997) suggested that both the leader and the individual team members have a part to play. A coach/teacher can employ numerous strategies to encourage both task and social cohesion, which can in turn encourage continued participation. They include:

1 Creating distinctiveness: for example, group name, T-shirts, clothing to form a collective identity.

2 Good coach/team communication.
3 Honest/open discussions.
4 Role clarity (understanding role).
5 Role acceptance (satisfied with and accept role).
6 Team conformity (social and task norms adhered to).
7 Togetherness (team meet regularly or travel together, etc.).
8 Sacrifices (if high-status players make sacrifices for the team).
9 Goals and objectives (clear, challenging group performance goals).
10 Cooperation (ensure group cooperation rather than an individualistic approach).
11 Avoid formation of social cliques.
12 Avoid too many team changes (rapid turnover).
13 Know and understand individuals within and outside the team.
14 Players to give 100 per cent effort at all times (set good example).
15 Social support among team mates (positive reinforcement).

IN CONTEXT

There are numerous examples in sport to highlight how managers and coaches attempt to create a sense of group cohesion. Many are sport related but often social cohesion is developed along with task cohesion. Every four years the British & Irish Lions rugby team is selected from the four home nations of England, Wales, Scotland and Ireland. The managers of the squad have to very quickly create a unity among the players and a sense of identity. They have used various methods including outdoor pursuit and problem solving-type activities, African drum workshops and the creation of the 'Lion's Laws'. The latter is a self-imposed code of conduct, which the players discuss and agree upon, that sets their expectations of behaviour both on and off the field of play. These activities are in addition to the hours spent training and discussing tactics to ensure all players know their personal role within the team structure.

Former player Scott Gibbs commented on the cohesion within the squad:

'There was never anyone who felt alienated in any way. That's a true strength of a squad, that inward support from everybody. That was there in abundance and that was why it was so successful on the field and off the field. We made a lot of friendships and there was never one clique. We had a lot of honesty and I think that was key. There are rules which you all need to adhere to. The fact that this was done in an open forum created a certain list of criteria, which included honesty, desire, ability and conscientiousness, and all those kinds of words that pulled people together and created a strong bond in the team and the squad.'

Fig 10.2 Teamwork among the British and Irish Lions

Leadership and the role of the leader in physical activities

If groups are to be successful and formed into cohesive teams there is no doubt that a leader is required. The study of leaders and leadership has always been based on the assumption that the leadership of a group – the team captain, teacher or coach – is a crucial element affecting overall group performance. Thus, leadership is seen as any behaviour that moves a group closer to attaining its goals.

Leadership is: *'the behavioural process of influencing individuals and groups towards set goals.'* (Barrow, 1977)

Activity 6

Think of two successful sporting leaders; they do not have to be players.

In pairs, discuss what specific and general qualities you think they possess that makes them a good leader?

Compare your list with the rest of your group. Are they similar?

This view probably includes all or most people's ideas of what constitutes the role of leadership in all areas of society, not just sport. We all feel that a leader is good at making decisions and has good interpersonal qualities, such as a high level of communication skills. They can motivate by giving appropriate feedback and are generally tactful and diplomatic. They are confident, show initiative in being able to organise and direct the group, giving good instructions and advice.

The leader must know what the goals and objectives of the group are (have vision) and be able to organise and

Fig 10.3 Influential leaders are vital to team success

structure the situation in order to achieve them. In order to achieve targets a leader should be seen as part of the group. The leader should have all the qualities, skills and beliefs of the group but to a greater degree; they will, therefore, tend to serve as a model for the group in some way. It is important, however, that a leader does not appear too remote or excessively advanced compared to the group, as its other members may feel that they can never achieve the standards being set.

If leaders have the qualities that enable them to inspire and motivate people, they can have a massive impact on the creation of positive attitudes towards participation. PE teachers who deliver high-quality lessons and provide extensive extracurricular activities ensure the benefits of a healthy lifestyle are explained and the values associated with sportsmanship and fair play are upheld. This in turn will not only create enjoyment for individuals but foster a sense of belonging and pride in their actions. Those leaders who are willing to explore and promote new methods of training and other sports, especially those of a life-long nature, will contribute significantly to the long-term well-being of individuals.

> **EXAMINER'S TIP**
>
> Be able to outline the characteristics of a good leader and evaluate the theories of leadership.

Characteristics of leaders

Different styles of leadership were identified as early as 1939 by Lewin et al. In their investigations of adult leadership styles on ten-year-old boys attending after-school clubs Lewin used three basic styles. Different groups of boys experienced different styles of leadership.

Autocratic leaders/task-orientated

This type of leader adopts a very authoritarian style generally based on strong rule structures. They tend to be very inflexible, make all the decisions and rarely get involved on a personal level with the group or team members. They are usually very task orientated. The characteristics of this type of leader include:

- Leader-centred
- Task-orientated, associated with performance of specific tasks/elements of play/meeting specific goals
- Personal authority of leader stressed.

This style of leadership is effective in the following situations:

- More likely to be effective in team sports (with greater number of performers)
- When decisions have to be made quickly
- Better with clear/impersonal goals
- Better in **most** favourable and **least** favourable situations. These include situations where the task is clear, relationships within the group are either very good or need to be established quickly.

Democratic leaders/social-orientated

This type of leader only makes decisions after consulting the group. They are usually more informal, relaxed and active within the group than the autocratic leader. In addition, they show a keen interest in the various people within the group. They are prepared to help, explain and give appropriate feedback and encouragement. The characteristics of this type of leader include:

- Performer-centred
- Cooperative approach that allows performer input into decision making
- Leader set in the context of whole team effort.

This style of leadership is effective in the following situations:

- Individual sports/individual coaching situations
- Better in moderately favourable conditions. These include when there are friendly relationships with the group or when limited facilities are available
- Better when decisions don't have to be made quickly.

Laissez-faire

This type of leader leaves the group to 'get on' by themselves and generally plays a passive role. They do not interfere, either by directing or coordinating. Being generally unsure of the task they tend not to make or give any positive or negative evaluations. The characteristics of this type of leader include:

- Makes no decisions
- Group determines the work to be done and the pace of it
- Acts as a consultant.

The results put forward by Lewin et al. were specifically related to patterns of aggression and cooperation. Those boys in the group with the autocratic leader tended to become aggressive with each other, working independently and in competition with each other. They also worked hard when the leader was present and were generally submissive to the leader.

Those boys with the democratic leader were more consistent in their approach to work – although less work was completed, it was of a similar quality. They related better to one another. They were generally more interested, cheerful and cooperative, altogether more amenable and continued to work when left alone.

The boys in the laissez-faire-led group were also generally aggressive towards each other, being restless and easily discouraged. They also produced very little work.

Lewin et al.'s study indicates that leadership style is a more important factor than personality; that is, that democratic leaders are apparently more effective.

Further research and critics (for example Smith & Peterson, 1988) have argued that the 'effectiveness' of leadership style depends on what the targets or set criteria are. If measured in terms of productivity, then the autocratic leader would have been the more effective as that group produced the most work, but only when directly supervised. The implications of this may be that performers used to an autocratic style of leadership/coaching/teaching do not take responsibility for themselves when the leader is not present. In addition, an authoritarian leadership style may lead to hostility. Alternatively, if the effectiveness of a leadership style was judged on developing good group mood, cooperative behaviour and steady work then the democratic style was best. The fact that the third group did hardly any work at all indicates, however, that leadership of some sort *is* important. This is definitely the case in sport, where the laissez-faire approach is generally not recommended.

Thus, when considering the influence on future participation the effective leader would use a combination of types depending on the situation, but must ensure the individuals are involved so they are motivated to continue when left to make their own choice.

Selection of a leader

Two ways in which leaders develop or are validated have been suggested:

1   **Prescribed leaders** – in a more formal situation the leader is assigned by a higher authority and imposed on a team or a group. The captain of the English cricket team is appointed by the England and Wales Cricket Board, for example.
2   **Emergent leaders** – a leader who achieves their status or authority by having the support of the group usually

emerges from the group as a result of having the appropriate skills, knowledge or expertise that the group members need or value.

Whether a leader **emerges** from the 'pack' or is **prescribed** from above, they will still exert their influence among the team or group by virtue of their personal qualities (which we highlighted earlier). Leadership is generally seen as a very complex social interaction.

Theories related to leadership: nature or nurture?

Three general groups of theories have emerged relating to the effectiveness of a leader: the trait, social learning and interactionist perspectives. As in most of the topics we have discussed, the traditional early research into what makes an effective leader was carried out from either a trait or behaviouristic perspective.

Trait theory

Effective leadership was believed to be as a result of specific innate personality characteristics. Thus, the theory of the 'Great Man' emerged (Carlyle, 1841) that fostered a belief that great leaders, more often than not men, were born not made. These 'great men' were thought to have universal/common traits. Trait theory suggested that certain personality and physical attributes such as height, weight, physical attractiveness, self-confidence, intelligence and sensitivity might be associated with leader success. If this view were true, then we would assume that the same leaders would be effective in all situations. Do you think this is true for all sport?

It may be true that the particular traits identified are all useful or necessary, to some degree, for leadership to be effective. Penman, Hastad and Cords (1974) identified a positive correlation between successful coaches and behaviour tending towards an authoritarian style of leadership. However, a person possessing these particular skills or abilities is not necessarily guaranteed to be a good leader. Research has generally proved inconclusive in identifying consistent personality characteristics, that is, leaders are not consistently found to be particular kinds of people who differ in predictable ways from non-leaders.

Social learning theory

The weakness of the trait approach suggests that leaders cannot develop because they are born to be leaders. By comparison the social learning theory suggests that we learn to become leaders by observing others and copying their actions, especially if they are successful and repeating them when faced with similar situations. In a similar way, aspects of poor leadership are noted and not repeated.

Think back to your studies of Bandura, the stages of learning he suggested and the importance of vicarious experiences. For example, a young player within a team is given the opportunity to be captain for the next game. They will often draw on their own memories and experiences of being captained before deciding how to approach the situation themselves. Those who have only been exposed to

an autocratic leader may well feel this is the only approach to use, and shout and tell the players what to do, rather than build a relationship with them.

However, the critics of this theory argue that leaders are not formed merely through observation of others, and it does not take into account individual personalities and traits as outlined in the previous section.

Interactionist theory

Think back to your studies of personality and recall the interactionist theory. This approach is applied in the same way when discussing leadership. It suggests that the skills of leadership are formed through a combination of inherited personality traits and interaction with the environment. This approach allows for a leader to assess the situation and adjust their style depending on the demands of the task and the people who they are working with.

This theory appears to be a good compromise between the previous suggestions and now holds the most credence.

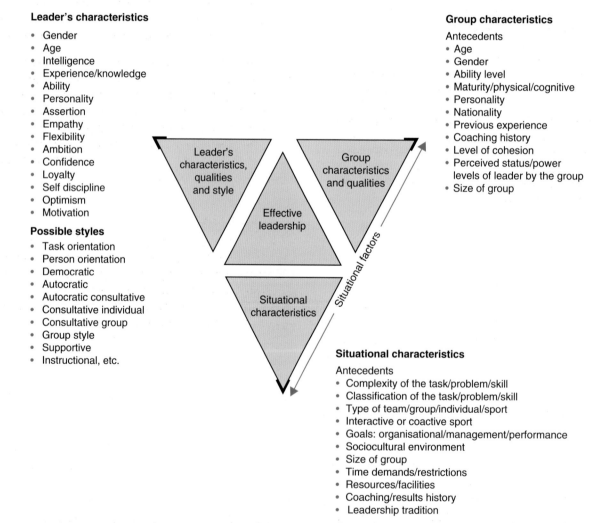

Leader's characteristics

- Gender
- Age
- Intelligence
- Experience/knowledge
- Ability
- Personality
- Assertion
- Empathy
- Flexibility
- Ambition
- Confidence
- Loyalty
- Self discipline
- Optimism
- Motivation

Possible styles

- Task orientation
- Person orientation
- Democratic
- Autocratic
- Autocratic consultative
- Consultative individual
- Consultative group
- Group style
- Supportive
- Instructional, etc.

Group characteristics

Antecedents
- Age
- Gender
- Ability level
- Maturity/physical/cognitive
- Personality
- Nationality
- Previous experience
- Coaching history
- Level of cohesion
- Perceived status/power levels of leader by the group
- Size of group

Situational characteristics

Antecedents
- Complexity of the task/problem/skill
- Classification of the task/problem/skill
- Type of team/group/individual/sport
- Interactive or coactive sport
- Goals: organisational/management/performance
- Sociocultural environment
- Size of group
- Time demands/restrictions
- Resources/facilities
- Coaching/results history
- Leadership tradition

Leader's characteristics, qualities and style

Group characteristics and qualities

Effective leadership

Situational characteristics

Situational factors

Fig 10.4 An interactionist model showing the many components of effective leadership

> **EXAMINER'S TIP**
>
> Questions may require you to outline the theories of leadership and critically evaluate them.

Chelladurai's multidimensional model of leadership related to sport

There has been a great deal of research to try to apply the many non-sporting contingency models and theories to the sporting setting. The so-called 'unique' characteristics of sporting teams/groups, however, together with a lack of specific support and application success, suggested that a more sports-specific model of leadership was required. By bringing together the many positive aspects of different research and contingency models Chelladurai put forward his sport-specific multidimensional model in 1980. Through this model he argued that the style adopted by a leader in sport, and its relative effectiveness, depended not only on the demands and constraints of the situation together with the characteristics of the leader, but also on the characteristics and demands of the *group*. Thus, more detail was added to the effectiveness 'melting pot'.

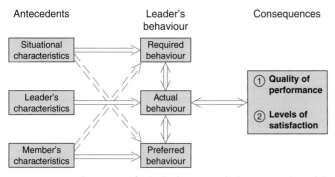

Fig 10.5 An adaptation of Chelladurai's multidimensional model (1980)

His model suggests therefore, that in order to achieve high performance levels and good group team satisfaction (both Chelladurai's measures of effective leadership), a leader has to be even more dynamic and changeable in relation to several antecedents. These include:

1 **Situational characteristics** – factors such as the task difficulty, the size of the group, the time available, the nature of the opposition and the nature of the activity.
2 **Leader characteristics** – personality, skill level, experience and their own preferred leadership style.
3 **Member/group characteristics** – motivation, age, gender, experience and ability.

Three types of interdependent behaviour help to produce the required outcomes.

1 **Required behaviour** – the type of behaviour appropriate to or required by the situation or task, for example teachers are expected to conform to certain norms and express certain accepted values.
2 **Preferred behaviour** – the type of behaviour preferred by the group or performer. Different groups will demand different things from the leader, such as achievement of performance levels (task-orientated) by some, or fun and enjoyment for others – for example, a professional sports team and an over-60s keep fit class.
3 **Actual leader behaviour** – the behaviour shown by the teacher or coach in a specific situation. This is usually as a result of group preferences and situational demands.

The more that the actual behaviour of the teacher or coach matches that of the behaviour preferred by the group, and is demanded by the situation (high congruence), the greater the probability that the desired outcomes will be achieved. That is, the performance will be of a high quality and the group will experience enhanced levels of satisfaction and enjoyment. Thus leadership will have been effective, but only in that specific situation.

> **EXAMINER'S TIP**
>
> Remember that the multidimensional model of leadership relates specifically to sporting situations. Effective leaders adapt their style depending on various factors. Make sure you are able to explain each of the components of the model and support your answer with sporting examples.

IN CONTEXT

A local youth club asks the secondary schools in its area to advertise a new basketball initiative that is aimed at introducing beginners to the game by organising friendly games within the club. The first sessions involve the leaders/coaches developing the basic skills and fundamental knowledge of the game with the focus on fun and enjoyment. As a result many of the children return and tell their friends, who also start attending. However, after several weeks it becomes clear that there are a group of six to eight players who are much better than the rest, having played for various school teams. The leaders of the group start to focus their attention more towards them and games are played specifically to raise their skill levels even further, while the remainder of the group are increasingly left on their own to practise their skills. Several matches are also arranged against other youth clubs instead of the practice sessions. During the next few weeks many of the players in the 'not as good' category fail to turn up to the sessions; they have become demotivated because the leaders have changed the focus and original aim of the basketball initiative. The 'team' players still attend as they are motivated to play and develop their skills.

Activity 8

Consider the situation outlined here and discuss the following points, with reference to Chelladurai's model:

- Were the leaders correct in their actions?
- Explain why some of the players left the group.
- Explain why some of the players remained in the group.
- How could the leaders have approached the situation differently?

The many and various factors (antecedents) that can influence the three dimensions of effective leadership can be seen in Figure 10.4, which highlights the main finding of leadership research, that there is no ideal or perfect type of style that is guaranteed to be effective in all situations. A leader must adopt and adapt the style according to the group and the situation. In this complex and demanding situation, no one can be ignored in order to ensure the smooth interaction between coach, performer and the situation. All may have their own individual, independent and possibly conflicting needs. This should help to ensure that potential develops into successful performance.

Research into performers' preferred styles of leadership have been rather inconclusive and open to cross interpretations and criticism. The research has, however, helped to give the sports profession and sports psychologists in particular certain insights into preferred notional styles.

EXAMINER'S TIP

Remember that optimal performance and group satisfaction occur if the leader's behaviour suits the situation and the preference of the group.

Preferred leadership styles

In any situation, be it competition/training/practice, a coach or leader is continually having to decide what is best for that performers and to balance this against their own ideas and preferences.

In general all performers prefer training, instruction and rewards, thus the coaching/training environment should emphasise:

- Skill development
- Positive feedback
- Concern for self-esteem
- Concern for personal development.

1 **Young players** below mid-teens tend to prefer a relationship-orientated approach with low-level task-orientated behaviours. Positive feedback alongside lots of tactical and technical input was also required.
2 **Slightly older performers** with well-developed (mature) physical skills tend to prefer a more autocratic style of coaching. Equally, as performers get older, they tend to prefer or require a more socially supportive coach.
3 **Elite athletes** tend to prefer a coach to take over control and responsibility for their training. They feel this helps them to achieve their goals more effectively (high task motivation). They have also been shown to prefer high levels of social support in a more democratic atmosphere.
4 **Beginner/novice performers** generally prefer a low level of heavy instruction and training.
5 **Male sports performers** prefer coaches or teachers to demonstrate high levels of autocratic behaviour together with high levels of instructional and training behaviour. They also prefer their coach to be more socially supportive than do female performers.
6 **Female sports performers** tend to prefer teachers or coaches to be more democratic, enabling the performers to participate more in the decision-making process. Male and female athletes tend to be much more alike than different. Their preferences are more dependent upon the nature of the individual performer than gender.
7 **Team sports performers**, particularly those who take part in interactive activities like basketball, football and netball (rather than coactive activities like rowing) prefer a more autocratic style with high levels of demanding training and instruction, but they also require regular rewards and praise.
8 **Coactive sports performers** have been shown to prefer a more democratic style of leadership with higher levels of social support. These findings are similar to those suggested by the path-goal contingency model.

Activity 9

Redraw Chelladurai's model and complete each section based on the following scenarios. How might the leadership style differ for each?

- Leading a group of novice climbers
- Captain of an international team in a major championship.

Social facilitation and inhibition

When involved in sport, at whatever level, be it school, club, national or world level, performers will be observed in some context. The higher the standard usually the greater number of spectators or people connected to the event. The margins between success and failure are small; this makes the influence of those around us even more influential. Usually our presence has an effect on another's sporting performance and the presence of others is seen as having an influence on our own behaviour and performance. Very often we are entirely unaware of these effects – thus the behaviour of a person either taking part in a physical education learning environment or performing at the very highest level is said to be influenced socially either directly or indirectly.

The study of this effect is the study of social facilitation. In a sporting context the presence of others is usually thought of as the 'audience'; however, in social psychology the 'presence of others' takes several different forms. The audience can be primary spectators: those present at the event; or secondary spectators: those watching at home on TV or possibly reading about the event in the media. The audience can be also passive or supportive.

> ### Key terms
>
> **Social facilitation** The influence of the presence of others on performance that has a positive effect.
> **Social inhibition** The influence of the presence of others on performance that has a negative effect.

In addition to those watching, 'others present' can be fellow competitors, both opposition and team mates, teacher and coach. They could also be other people performing the same task or skill but not in direct competition, called 'coactors'. When you practise at a golf driving range, for instance, although you are not in direct competition you are made aware of the presence and calibre of other players by your observation of the direction and length of their shots. This may influence your own efforts as though you were in competition. It has even been suggested that a performer training alone may have thoughts that will be enough to influence behaviour at the present time; for example, spur them on to greater effort as they imagine someone, somewhere, checking training schedules or observing the results of training made evident in a future performance. In other words, they are performing for a hidden audience.

Although the great majority of research in this area relates to work carried out by Zajonc (1965), the earliest recorded research was by Triplett in 1898. He established that the motor performance of cyclists differed according to whether they rode alone, in pairs or groups. To further his understanding of the effect of competition on performance, he supported his earlier findings by conducting laboratory testing of children performing a fishing reel-winding experiment. Triplett originally interpreted his findings in relation to the competitive element involved. The children were seen as unconsciously competing with one another, showing a competitive 'instinct' or 'drive' that served to increase performance speed.

> ### EXAMINER'S TIP
>
> Questions may require you to explain Zajonc's model and the various different types of others. Use practical examples to support your explanations.

However, later research (for example Allport (1924) and Dashiells (1930)), suggested that it was actually the 'mere presence' of others working alongside a person performing (coaction) that was the important factor, not necessarily the competition. Allport suggested that 'coaction' may increase quantity at the expense of quality. Inconsistencies within this early research were evident, with both positive and negative effects being found. The positive effect of others on performance is therefore known as social facilitation, while the negative effects are known as social inhibition.

> ### Key terms
>
> **Coaction** The presence of other people currently performing the same task but not directly in competition.
> **Audience** The other people present but not competing or doing what the performer is doing.

Zajonc and social facilitation

In his later work Zajonc (1965) tried to clear up the inconsistency found in earlier research; as a result, certain patterns of behaviour and specific relationships were recognised.

Zajonc proposed that whether social facilitation occurred, and the level to which it occurred, depended very much on the nature of the activity or task being carried out. His theory was based around the notion of drive theory (refer back to your AS studies, see Arousal on pages 184–185 of OCR PE for AS).

He contended that the presence of an audience in any shape or form raised a performer's level of arousal. This level of arousal would increase a performer's drive. From your understanding of drive theory you will remember that increased drive increased the probability of the dominant response occurring. Thus, the presence of others can serve to enhance the performance of well-learned or simple tasks (for example, sit ups), but have a negative effect on poorly learned skills, or reduce the accuracy when complex skills are involved.

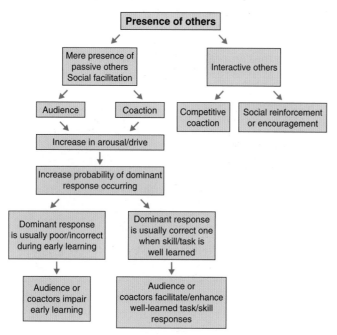

Fig 10.6 Zajonc's view of the relationship between drive theory and social facilitation

A high drive state caused by the presence of an audience is likely to increase the number of mistakes made, particularly by the inexperienced or beginners, thus increasing anxiety and further increasing arousal. This will have a 'snowball' effect, further increasing the chances that irrelevant or incorrect motor performance will be carried out.

EXAMINER'S TIP

Make sure you are able to explain the link between drive theory and social facilitation.

IN CONTEXT

High-profile sporting events such as tennis' Grand Slam events attract large crowds both in the stadium and via various media sources. The crowd at Centre Court at Wimbledon has for many years played an important role in the performance of the players. Extracts from the *Guardian* article by Braney Ronay from the 2008 Championships demonstrates this fact.

This afternoon Andy Murray is due to face the mighty physical specimen that is Rafael Nadal – one of the world's best tennis players. But with the shrieking, flag-ruffling, Chino-wearing Wimbledon crowd behind him, he surely has nothing to fear.

This is what happens at Wimbledon now – at least when a British player is involved. The crowd doesn't simply buy a ticket here. It's one of the competitors – pretty much forehead-to-forehead on court with whatever unfortunate Croat or long-suffering Swede happens to have drawn the short straw.

We got a sense of the crowd's prominence when listening to Murray and his opponent immediately after their match. 'The crowd were awesome,' Murray said. 'The whole tie-break and the fourth and fifth sets, once I got ahead they got behind me more than they ever have before…It almost takes your mind off your physical state when you've got so many people behind you.'

Gasquet had appeared visibly shaken by the brouhaha from the seats. Towards the end, he even took to appealing to the umpire, his only friend out there, for a little peace, some even-handedness, a chorus of the Marseillaise, a hug, anything really.

'The crowd was for him. It was natural. But it helped Andy a lot, for sure,' he said at the end – a remarkably understated comment. 'He played with the crowd…I hope to play against him in Roland Garros. I won't be alone this time.'

As you can see, the crowd had a positive effect on Murray (social facilitation), while it had a negative effect (social inhibition) on his playing partner Gasquet.

Cottrell's evaluation apprehension theory

There are, however, several other views on the origins and effects of social facilitation. Cottrell (1968) argued that it wasn't just the mere presence of others that created higher arousal; there were different types of presence and each could have different effects on arousal (increasing or decreasing). Cottrell went on to suggest that it was more to do with a person's perceptions that they were being 'evaluated' or assessed in some way by the 'others' present that created the higher arousal.

Thus the effects of social facilitation are enhanced by a performer's feelings of evaluation apprehension. The more expert the audience was perceived to be, the more the performance was potentially impaired.

For example, if a group of teenagers are playing a school match, while they may be aroused and aware of spectators, their performance is generally enhanced by their support. If, however, they are aware that a talent-spotting scout from a well-known team is observing them, this may lead to an increase in arousal levels. The effects of being watched are heightened, as the players are concerned that their performance is being evaluated by another, possibly more significant than their coach or teacher.

Key term

Evaluation apprehension Form of anxiety experienced by a performer that is caused by the feeling that they are being judged in some way by the audience.

There are numerous factors that affect the impact of social facilitation and evaluation apprehension. They include:

- Personality of the performer
- Previous experiences
- Levels of trait anxiety
- Age and gender
- Knowledge of the crowd
- Size, proximity and nature of the crowd
- Status of the observers.

Home/away (advantage or disadvantage)

Other psychologists have questioned Zajonc's model (which views the audience in a passive role), arguing that there is no such thing as a passive audience. Research has looked at the effect of 'home' and 'away' venues and supporters on performance. While we may intuitively imagine home advantage as a bonus, it has been shown to have possible negative effects, with players feeling increasingly under pressure due to the greater expectations of the home crowd. The effect has also been shown to vary in relation to different sports.

Home or away (supporting research)

- Most of the research has focused on home advantage
- For major sports, teams tend to win more home matches than away
- Home advantage was mainly due to audience support
- The proximity of crowds to the playing area and resulting noise increase has been seen as a factor
- Home advantage was more noticeable in the early rounds of competitions
- Olympic hosts tend to win more medals than in games before or after
- Home teams tend to play in a more attacking style within the rules (functionally aggressive behaviour)
- Away teams tend to contravene rules more and commit more fouls (dysfunctional aggressive behaviour)
- The more important the game, the greater the negative effect on the home team
- Supportive spectators can create expectations of success
- Potential increases in home players' self-consciousness
- Higher personal expectations cause home players to think too much rather than just playing automatically, causing 'championship choke'
- Coaches are now much more aware of these problems and try not to create too much pressure.

In relating the effects of social facilitation to cognitive factors, Baron (1986; distraction conflict theory) suggested that audience effects occur because the performer is distracted from the task. This distraction creates tension and conflict within their mind, which increases arousal, leading to a greater number of errors.

Due to the inconclusive and equivocal nature of past and current research the main conclusions that can be drawn are that well-learned skills are generally affected in a positive way by the presence of an audience. However, performance can also be inhibited. If we could make more specific predictions then we would be able to explain why even highly experienced and very often 'extrovert' players who are supposed to be able to deal with audience expectations, pressure and evaluation sometimes 'choke' in the final rounds of an important competition.

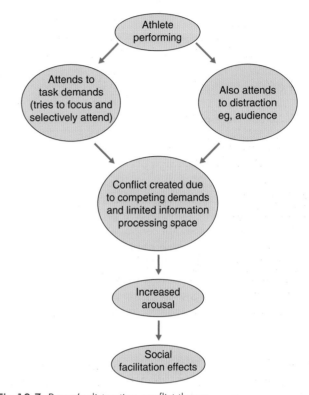

Fig 10.7 Baron's distraction conflict theory

Strategies to combat the effects of social inhibition

It is important to understand that the effects of social inhibition can have a major impact on future participation in physical activities. If the individual always experiences negative emotions when participating they may well look for alternatives activities that create more positive emotions. Practical strategies include:

- Developing the use of mental rehearsal
- Train in front of others and gradually increase the numbers
- Improve selective attention to cut out the effect of the audience
- Reduce the importance of the event
- Avoid social comparison with others
- Encourage team mates to be supportive
- Increase self-efficacy
- Teach/coach in a non-evaluative environment initially
- Use stress management and relaxation techniques
- Use attributions correctly
- Ensure skills are over-learned to encourage the dominant habit to occur as the levels of arousal increase.

What you need to know

Group dynamics and cohesion

* Group dynamics are inter-group processes such as cohesion, communication, power roles, leadership and social facilitation.
* A group in sport has a collective identity and a sense of shared purpose and objectives. It involves interpersonal attraction, person and task interdependence, and very often structured levels and modes of communication.
* Groups are characterised by the six Is.
* Effective groups/teams are formed in four stages: **forming, storming, norming** and **performing**.
* Teachers and coaches are continually striving to enhance the performance of groups/teams by bringing together the best individuals.
* Actual productivity equals potential productivity minus losses due to faulty group processes. Therefore, although the best individuals do usually make good teams, good performance is not always guaranteed.
* The Ringelmann and social loafing effects have been used to explain the effects of an increase of group size and reduced motivation on group effectiveness.
* Social loafing often occurs within a team when a player loses their sense of identity and individuality. Social loafing can be reduced by increasing personal responsibility, identifiability and social incentives.
* Debate over the effects and results of cohesion is still going on but, generally, success is more likely to result in cohesion than derive from it.
* Team cohesion is a dynamic process whereby the members of the team are motivated to stay together as a group.
* Groups are motivated to stay together and work together for either task- and/or social-orientated reasons.
* Cohesion can, therefore, take the form of task cohesion or social cohesion.

Leadership

* Leadership is any behaviour that enables a group to attain its goals.
* Emergent or prescribed leaders possess a variety of characteristics that are both innate and learned, but there are no specific traits that guarantee a good leader.
* Effective leaders learn to be both task-orientated and person-orientated according to their own characteristics/qualities and the demands of the situation, together with the demands and expectations of the group.
* Chelladurai's multidimensional model is specific to sporting situations and states that optimum performance and enhanced satisfaction are more likely to occur when a leader's required, preferred and actual behaviours are consistent.

Social facilitation

* Social facilitation is the arousal effects that the presence of others, either audience or coactors, has on a person's level of performance.
* The presence of others will increase the probability that the dominant response occurs by increasing levels of arousal – this observation is based on drive theory. For beginners or those with poorly learned skills, the dominant response will generally serve to inhibit performance. For experts or those performing well-learned tasks, the effect will generally be to enhance the quality of the performance level.
* Cottrell argued that the effects of social facilitation were enhanced by evaluation apprehension.
* A supportive audience can give home teams an advantage. However, they can also potentially have a negative effect through high expectations.

Review Questions

1 Explain how groups develop through various stages.
2 What factors influence a group's productivity?
3 Why is role clarity and acceptance important?
4 Using a sporting example, explain what is meant by the Ringelmann effect.
5 What is social loafing?
6 Using an example from sport, show how a teacher or coach could try to limit the effects of social loafing.
7 Explain the trait approach to leadership.
8 What advantages does the interactionist approach to leadership have?
9 Within a sporting context, how can a person become a leader? Give examples.
10 Explain the three types of 'leader behaviour' suggested by Chelladurai's model.
11 Using examples from sport, explain the positive and negative effects of an autocratic style of leadership.
12 What is a person-orientated leader?
13 What is the phenomenon known as social facilitation?
14 Explain evaluation apprehension.
15 Outline four strategies a coach could use to limit the effects of social inhibition.

CHAPTER 11

The impact of mental preparation for physical activities on the effectiveness and efficiency of performance

Learning outcomes

By the end of this chapter you should be able to:

- explain the importance and relevance of goal-setting to sport
- explain factors affecting the setting of goals ('smarter' principle)
- evaluate critically the use of short/intermediate/long term goals and process/performance/product goals to improve performance and participation in physical activity
- demonstrate knowledge and understanding of sports confidence (Vealey), and the concepts of trait sports confidence, competitiveness orientation, and state sports confidence
- outline the concept of self-efficacy (Bandura) explaining the influence of performance accomplishments, vicarious experiences, verbal persuasion, and emotional arousal
- explain the effects of self-efficacy on performance and in sustaining a balanced, active and healthy lifestyle
- outline the Cue Utilisation Theory (Easterbrook) and different attentional styles (broad/narrow, internal/external – Nideffer)
- explain the need for differing levels of arousal and their relationship with personality, ability level and complexity of task
- demonstrate knowledge and understanding of peak flow experience and the zone of optimum functioning theory (Hanin)
- describe the nature, and explain the influences of anxiety and state/trait distinction
- demonstrate knowledge and understanding of anxiety management techniques:
  - cognitive techniques such as mental rehearsal/imagery, positive self-talk, thought-stopping and rational/positive thinking
  - somatic techniques such as progressive muscular relaxation and biofeedback relaxation.
- evaluate critically anxiety management techniques in improving performance, participation in physical activity and in sustaining a balanced, active and healthy lifestyle.

CHAPTER INTRODUCTION

Within competitive sport and physical education in general performers are continually in situations that affect their emotional state. Certain emotional states can strengthen a person's motivation and enhance their performance. However, being in an energised state, creating drive and experiencing increased arousal as a result of stress can lead to anxiety, which, in turn, may have a negative effect on performance. Consider how often you have been in a sporting situation where your levels of arousal have altered, possibly linked to your levels of self-confidence. The aim of all performers should be to develop high levels of confidence in their ability to complete the task successfully, which in turn can help to achieve the optimum level of arousal required to excel.

Before you read this chapter it may be beneficial to remind yourself of what is meant by arousal and its associated effects. Originally, drive theory dominated 1960s research as a way of explaining arousal and social facilitation. Arousal was seen to develop as a result of a performer's drives which developed from a performer's basic needs. For example, in competitive sport performers 'need to win' so they train and play hard or may even cheat, if they are frustrated, in order to achieve their objective. The relationship between arousal and performance was seen as a linear one. There is little support for this view in present day sports psychology. For the past 20 years or so the inverted 'U' hypothesis has been found a more convincing explanation for predicting the relationship between arousal and performance. Below par performance is seen as a result of either too high or too low levels of arousal. However, don't forget that not all performers or sports have or need the same levels of optimum arousal.

In your studies last year you also considered some of the newer research in this area — for example, catastrophe theory, which suggests that the relationship between anxiety and performance does not follow the symmetrical, shaped inverted 'U'.

Owing to the multi-dimensional nature of arousal and anxiety many people within sport use the terms 'arousal', 'stress' and 'anxiety' synonymously and continually interchange the terms. It is important, however, that we have clear definitions of each of these three terms in order to appreciate that, although they are very closely related, they are distinct concepts. Within this chapter we will consider the nature of the relationship between stress and arousal and anxiety together with the causes and effects. You will also study the importance of self-confidence and how it can influence performance. In addition, we will consider what effective measures can be taken to control a performer's levels of stress, arousal and anxiety.

Goal-setting

'A goal is what an individual is trying to accomplish. It is the object or aim of an action.'

(Lock, 1981)

Goal-setting is generally seen as an extremely powerful technique for enhancing performance and maintaining motivation to continue participation. However, it must be carried out correctly. When used effectively, goal-setting can help focus a performer's attention, aid self-confidence, enhance both the intensity and persistence dimensions of motivation and, ultimately, have a positive effect on performance. Goal-setting can be used to help performers feel in control of relatively stress-provoking situations and thus help them to cope with their anxieties. However, if you refer back to intrinsic and extrinsic motivation, you will understand that when used improperly the setting of goals (particularly the wrong or unrealistic goals) not only has a negative effect on motivation, but can also be a significant source of stress and anxiety in the immediate performance situation. This can lead to impairment, not enhancement, of performance in the long term. Goal-setting should be used with caution by coaches and teachers. If inappropriate goals are set the individual, rather than be motivated and challenged may be disheartened by their apparent lack of success. This may lead to a reduction in confidence and subsequent participation.

Goals are seen as direct motivational strategies that help when setting standards a performer is psychologically motivated to try to achieve, usually within a specific time. In these discrete terms goal-setting is generally thought to affect performance in the following ways:

- **attention:** goal-setting helps to direct a performer's attention (focus) to the important aspects of the task
- **effort:** goal-setting helps to mobilise or increase the appropriate degree of effort a performer needs to make in relation to specific task
- **persistence:** goal-setting helps a performer maintain their efforts over time
- **new strategies:** goal-setting helps a performer to develop new and various strategies in order to achieve their goals, e.g., learning (problem-solving).

Factors affecting the setting of goals

Most coaches and performers in sport, and people throughout their lives in general, set goals for themselves. The secret for success is to set the *right* goals and use them in the *appropriate* context. Generally, in order to be effective, goals need to provide direction and enhance motivation. Goals are also seen as playing an important role in stress management. They are the standards against which perceived success or failures are measured and thus link to present attributions of success or failure.

If goal-setting is to be effective there are several key principles that should be applied, whatever the situation. The most commonly used principle to set goals can be remembered by the acronym SMARTER. This stands for:

Specific: the goal must be related to the individual, their position and/or event. Any target must not be too vague, for example, 'next time try harder' or 'next time you need to improve your passing'. Instead they may be 'your aim is to have a 75 per cent pass completion rate' or 'aim to transfer your weight when making the pass'. A goal may also be linked to the individual's personality. High achievers (see Achievement motivation) with high n.ach and low n.af motivational levels prefer challenging but realistic goals. In comparison, low achievers (low n.ach/high n.af) avoid challenging goals and usually adopt either very easy or incredibly hard goals. In addition, children in the 'social comparison' stage usually focus on competitive and outcome goals, whilst task orientated performers prefer performance and process goals.

Measureable: the goals should be able to be assessed allowing for direct comparison to ensure progress is being made. It is now a regular occurrence in many sports to complete post-match analysis, which can be highly detailed. Such data have proved invaluable to coaches and performers when identifying areas of strengths and weakness, forming the basis for future training sessions and longer term programmes. However, if evaluation becomes excessive it could possibly lead to an outcome-orientated approach rather than a performance process approach.

Accepted: it is important that the performer is involved in the goal-setting process rather than having them set from some external source. The performer is more able to perceive the targets as fair and achievable and therefore more likely to accept them. They are also far more likely to be prepared to work towards them if they have been responsible for setting the goals in the first place. By understanding the needs and personality of the performer, a coach is more aware of how much time is available for training, etc, and through negotiation can endeavour to foster goal acceptance and commitment.

Realistic: goals must be within the capabilities of the individual or the team. If they are set too high, anxiety may result and individuals may become de-motivated knowing the task is beyond their reach before starting. Therefore, goals do not always have to be based on the end result, especially when competing against higher quality opposition or attempting a difficult task. They may be focused on individual performance and execution of technique.

Time-phased: goals must have specific deadlines, where some form of evaluation and assessment occurs. This is vital, allowing the individual to work towards a set time-frame, knowing their performance will be monitored, rather than their training left to continue with no definite knowledge of when an assessment will occur. The length of time before an evaluation takes place will depend upon the difficulty of the task and the ability of the performer.

Exciting: goals must be seen as challenging to the individual to ensure they are motivated to commit the time and energy to complete the task. It is far better to set goals linked to satisfy intrinsic motivation rather than simply provide extrinsic rewards. Care must be taken to set goals at the correct level. Whilst the goal may be exciting initially, it must be attainable, otherwise there may be a decline in motivation and future participation. It may actually also lead to anxiety and unwanted stress for the performer.

Recorded: finally, any goals set should be recorded, ideally by both the coach and the individual. This action fulfils several functions; it not only provides a record of the goals allowing for feedback, but gives some form of ownership to the individual and creates a sense of responsibility that they must attempt to achieve the target.

> **Key term**
>
> **SMARTER** An acronym for a goal-setting principle that should be followed to ensure effective goals are established.

> **EXAMINER'S TIP**
>
> Learn the SMARTER principle. Be able to explain each component and support your answer with practical examples.

Types of goals

Long, intermediate and short-term goals

Individual research into whether short-, intermediate or long-term goals are best is somewhat equivocal. It has generally supported the view that all need to be set. A performer needs to have an overview of where he or she is heading. At the same time the performer needs to have sub-goals to enhance and reinforce development towards the main long-term goal. Short-term and intermediate goals can be used to give the performer levels of progress and achievement. Interim success can serve to develop confidence, reduce anxiety, and maintain levels of motivation. Developing psychological training goals in order to reduce aspects of anxiety (e.g., learning relaxation techniques) can be seen as short-term goals within the context of overall performance, so remember to set all types of goal.

It may be that, in the light of progress, new short-term goals can be negotiated and set. A performer may be finding the training too easy or may have achieved certain levels of success earlier than expected. New variables not thought of at first may also need to be taken into account. However, goals should not be continually changed as this may lead to a performer's uncertainty. It may also prove difficult to lower goals as performers may perceive this as some form of failure. It is important to emphasise the temporary nature of goals and inform the performer of possible setbacks.

The types of goals a performer either adopts or is set by the coach (goal orientation) can have a significant effect on both the performer and ultimately the performance. In addition to subjective goals, e.g., having fun and enjoyment, and objective goals, e.g., reaching a particular standard, two further goals have been identified: outcome and performance.

Outcome goals

Outcome goals generally focus on the end product. Successful competitive results (for example, winning a match or gaining some tangible reward) are usually the standard or goal set. Performers who continually make social comparisons of themselves against other performers are said to be outcome goal-orientated. Winning and being successful enables this type of performer to maintain a positive self-image as they perceive themselves as having high personal ability (see intrinsic and extrinsic motivation and attribution.) However, a performer may produce the best game or time in their lives and still lose, as their level of achievement depends on the performance of others. They play better; you do not achieve your outcome goal, i.e., failure.

Performance and process goals

These generally focus on a performer's present standard of performance compared with their own previous performance, i.e., they are self-referent. Levels of success are judged in terms of mastering new skills or beating a personal best. Developing a performance goal orientation has been shown to reduce anxiety in competitive situations as the performers are not worrying about social comparisons and demonstrating their competence. They can concentrate on the process of developing their performance further, i.e., process goals. Process goals focus on what can be done in order to achieve the improvement in performance required. For example, keeping your head down and following through more in order to improve your effective strike rate off the tee in golf. Performance-orientated individuals tend to attribute success to internal and controllable factors, e.g., effort, and therefore are able to experience and maintain higher levels of pride and self-satisfaction. A performer adopting performance goals (goal-orientated approach) is able to maintain motivation for longer and more consistently as competition for social comparisons is not the be all and end all of their lives. What matters for them is raising their levels of perceived ability by learning new skills.

Sports psychologists have suggested that performers who adopt different goal-setting styles (outcome or performance) set different types of practice and competitive goals that will affect future cognitions and ultimately performance.

Although it is difficult for performers in modern sport not to consider winning and losing, by continually emphasising and focusing on performance goals the coach should ensure that ultimately outcome goals are achieved. For every outcome goal that is set there should be several performance and process goals.

Key terms

Performance goal Goal that relates to the technique or individual's own standards.
Outcome goal Goal that refers to the end result or finishing position.

Additional factors affecting goals

This point links closely with the fact that a coach must take on the following responsibilities:

1 **Develop goal achievement strategies:** there is no point in goals being set if a performer is not given strategies for reaching those goals. These strategies can be the short-term goals. This is where the teachers or coaches sporting specific knowledge comes into play. Running, training or skills schedules can be put into operation, e.g., a performer may have to cover so many miles per week or train for longer than 20 minutes, three times per week, etc.

2 **Provide goal support:** in order to achieve certain goals the performer will need to make a certain commitment in terms of time and, possibly, even financial. This may need the regular support and understanding of their families. Facilities will be needed along with possible physiotherapy and rehabilitation support. Financial backing, motivation or an occasional shoulder to cry on may be needed.

IN CONTEXT

All performers should set some form of goal, whether they are an elite athlete or a recreational jogger. The 2008 Beijing Olympics proved to be a successful event for two of Britain's young athletes, diver Tom Daley and swimmer Rebecca Adlington. Both went to Beijing with differing goals: Daley, to gain experience in preparation for the 2012 London Olympics, and Adlington, to win a medal and also prepare for the next Olympic Games.

Tom Daley experienced mixed results, finishing seventh in the 10m platform and last in the synchronised event. However, the goals for him were not necessarily to win a medal as his coach Andy Banks pointed out:

'There were three goals when we came out here. Was Tom happy and proud of his performance? Job done! Did he learn as much as possible? He could probably go away and write a book on the subject. And did he have fun? He certainly looked like it!'

Rebecca Adlington went to Beijing with medal hopes and exceeded her expectations by winning not only the 400m freestyle, but also the 800m freestyle in a new World Record time. After the Games, she had to evaluate and modify her future goals, as shown in her comments below;

'I've achieved something that was always my goal, so now I've got to re-set that goal, and aim for something bigger and better. I never thought I would get the world record and two gold medals in Beijing. That was my plan for London. So now that I've achieved it, I've got to go away and get a new ambition.'

Her coach, Bill Furniss, added, 'It's not an unrealistic dream, but it is a difficult dream.'

Even fun runners can benefit from correct goal-setting. Every year thousands of people enter the London Marathon for the first time. Initially, the thought of running over 26 miles can be daunting, but with short-, medium- and long-term goals the task seems more manageable. The process of gradually increasing the mileage covered on a weekly basis, allowing the body to adjust to the new demands, will improve motivation and confidence.

Activity 1

In discussion with your partner, set yourself a performance goal or an outcome goal for your next match or training session. Make sure it is SMARTER. After the event, evaluate the effect the goal had on your motivation and performance.

Investigate how an elite level performer prepares for a major championship and the outline the types of goals they set. How do they follow the SMARTER principle?

Self-confidence

All performers are more likely to produce better performances if they have belief in their own abilities to complete the task. Think about your own experiences; if you have high levels of self-confidence have you achieved a better result? There are numerous examples in sport where victory has gone to the individual or team that possess the most belief in their own abilities. Levels of confidence can change during the course of the event, with dramatic consequences (refer back to your studies of catastrophe theory). How often has one incident during the game changed the motivation and arousal levels of the performers, both positively and negatively?

The role of the coach/teacher should not be just to develop skills, but a self-belief that success is achievable. Many of the aspects of sports psychology you have already studied are focused towards this particular aim. The importance of self-confidence is highlighted by Gould et al:

'the most consistent difference between elite and less successful athletes is that elite athletes possess greater self-confidence.'

Self-efficacy

Bandura (1977) put forward the concept of **self-efficacy**, claiming the concept to be one of the more important explanations of success or failure. In his research he considered how a performer's self-confidence can affect their motivation and ultimate performance. It has formed the theoretical basis adopted for most performance-orientated research in self-confidence and sport. Bandura stated that while self-confidence can be viewed as a global disposition, it is not always general but often specific to certain situations. Self-efficacy is seen as the belief in one's ability in relation to a specific task in a specific situation. In its simplest form:

Self-efficacy = situation specific confidence

Picture the team captain who is very confident during the match, coping with every demand. Yet the same person lacks confidence and feels intimidated when asked to speak to TV reporters after the game or make a speech at the after-match dinner. Generally, in this context 'self-efficacy' relates to the number of similar activities in which the performer feels efficacious.

Imagine again a young swimmer. She may have high levels of self-efficacy when swimming in the shallow end of the pool, when she knows she can touch the bottom if needed. She may not experience high levels of self-efficacy when she first performs in the deep end. It is therefore important that when we try to assess a person's levels of self-efficacy we are aware that, although a performer may feel confident in some aspects of a skill, the same performer may not feel confident in others owing to the variations in perceived demand and perceived ability. A gymnast may feel confident at floor work, but experience low levels of self-efficacy when faced with the vault.

Fig 11.1 (a) Rebecca Adlington, twice-winner of an Olympic Gold medal (b) Tom Daley, Olympic competitor

Bandura suggests that a performer makes judgements with regard to their capabilities to perform a specific task or deal with a certain situation. A performer's perceptions of the situation related to their expected level of self-efficacy will affect their:

- **choice of activity:** high levels ensure continued participation
- **degree of effort:** high levels ensure high levels of motivation and application
- **level of persistence:** high levels ensure good effort and commitment.

In other words, expectations of efficacy explain motivation. Therefore, a performer experiences high or low levels of self-efficacy in a variety of situations. Although Bandura's earlier research provided a clear conceptual model of self-efficacy, claiming it to be the critical variable, later research has shown that high self-efficacy alone is not enough. A performer must also want to succeed and have the capability (i.e., necessary skill levels/techniques) to succeed. In addition, the other cognitive processes underpinning causal attributions will also affect the performer. To account for this additional research, Bandura (1997) re-defined the term self-efficacy, employing the term 'self-regulatory efficacy'.

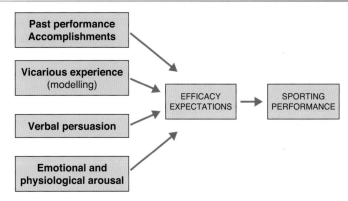

Fig 11.2 Adapted model showing information that affects self-efficacy

Past performance accomplishments

Previous successful experience or mastery of specific or similar skills involved in the particular task faced is seen as the major and most reliable predictor of self-efficacy. If you have regularly practised hockey penalty flicks or basketball free throws and have taken them at critical points in previous matches, then you will feel confident of scoring if a similar situation arises again. The effect would be enhanced further if your previous success was attributed to controllable factors. Practising a specific skill successfully has more effect than being told you will be able to do it by the teacher or coach. This has obvious repercussions for teaching and coaching methodologies where building up a skill and gaining early success, e.g., lowering the net in netball or making games simpler as in short tennis, have a much greater effect on a beginner's future specific confidence and thus effort and participation levels than just telling them they can do it in the main sport. Obviously, previous failure could result in low levels of expected self-efficacy.

Vicarious experience

Sometimes referred to as 'modelling' (refer to observational learning – Bandura), vicarious experiences although less effective than previous success has been found to be a reliable source of self-efficacy. When a performer observes a successful demonstration, particularly by someone of similar ability, they are more likely to feel confident that they too can accomplish the same task. They are less anxious and are encouraged to 'have a go' themselves.

Verbal persuasion

Teachers and coaches often try to persuade performers that they are capable of carrying out certain tasks. Think how often you have heard in gymnastics lessons encouragement being given to students to attempt a certain vault, explaining that it will be perfectly safe, etc, in order to try to boost their confidence. In the majority of situations this type of social persuasion can work, although its effectiveness very much depends on who is doing the persuading.

Occasionally, teachers or coaches may distort results or levels of truth in order to persuade performers that they are better than they are. They must be careful not to undermine their credibility. The learner/performer must have trust in them (significant other) and value their opinion.

Emotional and physiological arousal

Very often performers perceive their 'natural' physiological arousal effects as being something negative. 'Why am I sweating?' 'Why is my heart beating faster?' 'Why am I breathing quickly?' Rather than interpreting these naturally occurring effects as signs of being ready and prepared physiologically for the activity performers often view these as being signs of physiological stress. They think they are not prepared. Bandura saw this as having a negative effect on their self-efficacy. They feel ill-equipped to carry out the activity. Although further studies have questioned this effect, certain research has suggested that very positive psychological preparation via goal-setting, and various relaxation/stress management techniques, can help to change a performer's perceptions of arousal effects, i.e., viewing them as signs that they are ready to compete, and help develop positive self-efficacy. In addition to physiological cues, emotional moods can be influential in developing self-efficacy. Positive emotional states, e.g., happiness, exhilaration, and tranquillity, etc, can help a performer feel energised and therefore experience heightened self-efficacy, whereas negative feelings of anxiety, depression and sadness can have the opposite effect (Maddox and Meier, 1995).

> **EXAMINER'S TIP**
>
> Ensure you are able to outline each of the factors contributing to self-efficacy.

Vealey's sports specific model of sport confidence

Whilst self-efficacy is important and relates to specific situations, Vealey suggested a sports specific model of self-confidence. Her proposal investigates the relationship between levels of competitiveness and self-confidence in sport. Obviously, if we have higher levels of confidence in such situation we are more likely to achieve the correct arousal levels and be motivated to participate. Vealey suggests that sport confidence is:

'the belief or degree of certainty individuals possess about their ability to be successful in sport.'

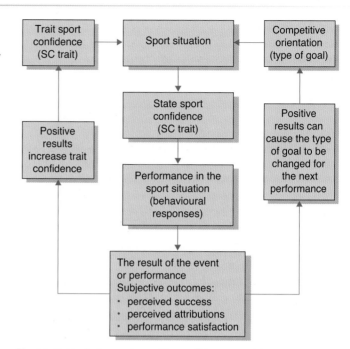

Fig 11.3 Vealey's sport-specific confidence model

The model suggests that each individual will approach the situation from a different perspective due to several factors. Everyone has innate levels of confidence, known as trait sport confidence (SC-trait) which is applied to an **objective sport situation**. The situation may be general or specific, for example playing a game of tennis or serving to save the set.

The level of confidence is also influenced by the player's **competitive orientation**. This refers to how the individual perceives success and the type of goals used to judge their performance. The goals may be performance or outcome-based depending on the nature of the task and consultation with the coach.

When the trait sport confidence and the competitive orientation combine the result is the actual level of confidence or self-efficacy experienced by the performer. This is known as state sport confidence (SC-state). The level of confidence can then influence the behaviour and skill level displayed by the individual. Obviously the more self-confidence the player has the better their performance should be; the reverse is also true. After the match or event the player will judge their performance giving **subjective outcomes**, providing attributions for their success or failure. This is turn will cause emotional responses of either satisfaction or disappointment.

Therefore, it is important to develop self-confidence by setting appropriate goals and using the correct attributions to maintain a high level of state confidence for future events, encouraging approach behaviour. The links to maintaining a healthy lifestyle should be obvious to see; the more positive experiences gained will develop confidence and the desire to continue in the future. It also means that confidence in one sport can be transferred to another sport. Hence, the importance of developing a wide range of skills and experiences, especially at a young age.

EXAMINER'S TIP

You may be required to outline the components of Vealey's model and explain the relationship between each. Ensure that you can also describe how the outcome may affect future participation and levels of self-efficacy.

IN CONTEXT

In the 2004 Athens Olympics, cyclist Victoria Pendleton was overcome by anxiety and effectively froze when competing. She underperformed and left Athens with her confidence crushed. It was a different situation in the 2008 Beijing Olympics. She had to wait until the last day for her event – the sprint – but she won the gold medal comfortably.

With 'compassionate ruthlessness' – mentoring and supporting with total honesty – Pendleton's coaches, Peters and Brailsford, built a team around her to work on all the steps or 'foundation stones' identified that might contribute to gold medal success. In the case of Pendleton, Peters worked hard to remove the fear that can undermine confidence and lead to impulsive decisions. As he says:

'They [performers] learn what part of their brain is giving them completely negative thoughts and they switch over, and that's a skill.'

It took Victoria Pendleton a year to master the skill, to be able to 'switch over' her focus and be able to shut out the negative distractions. Another key phrase that illustrates this is 'logic not emotion'. In the build-up to the 2008 Olympics Pendleton had competed in several major events and performed well, which boosted her self-confidence, resulting in a high level of state sport confidence when she arrived in Beijing on her quest to win that elusive gold medal.

Developing self-efficacy and self-confidence to improve participation

When developing self-efficacy and self-confidence there are several important factors to consider. Remember the aim is to motivate the individual, encouraging them to continue participating, ideally for *intrinsic* reasons rather than extrinsic reward. By creating feelings of satisfaction rather than disappointment this can be achieved relatively easily. Consider your own experiences: when has your own level of confidence increased and why? Success, no matter how small, is a key priority in the development of a performer.

Here is a number of strategies a coach or teacher can employ to help develop positive expectations and build self-confidence:

- experience early success
- observe demonstrations by competent others of similar ability
- set realistic but challenging goals
- set performance goals rather than outcome goals
- offer verbal encouragement and positive feedback
- develop effective stress management techniques
- use mental rehearsal
- avoid social comparison with others and limit the effects of social facilitation
- use attributions correctly by attributing failure to controllable, unstable factors.

EXAMINER'S TIP

Questions may require you to outline strategies to improve levels of self-confidence. Use practical examples to support your answers.

Attentional control

When participating in sporting activity the performer has to be aware of the cues or stimuli around them which affect their decision-making process (refer back to Information-processing in the AS course). There are obvious links to arousal levels and the aim of each individual should be to reach his or her optimum state to maximise chances of success. Factors affecting optimum levels of arousal will be discussed in detail later in this chapter.

It is important for coaches and performers to recognise when they are executing skills correctly and identifying relevant cues as well as those situations when cues are being missed, negatively influencing their performance.

Cue-utilisation theory

The inability of a performer, particularly a beginner, to process the relevant information effectively has been linked to what has been called **perceptual narrowing** and **cue-utilisation theory**. These concepts are closely linked to the Inverted U Theory and help us to understand that as arousal levels increase a performer tries to pay more attention to those stimuli, cues and signals that are more likely and relevant in order to help them carry out the task (cue-utilisation). They focus their attention (perceptual narrowing). However, a performer's ability to focus their attention is severely hampered if arousal levels continue to increase. Perceptual narrowing continues which may cause a performer to miss important cues and signals (ineffective cue-utilisation), and this could have a detrimental effect on performance.

Figure 11.4 illustrates the suggestion that under-aroused performers detect both relevant and irrelevant information. When at optimally aroused, they detect the correct stimuli and when over-aroused, they detect some important cues but miss a number as well.

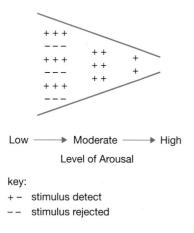

key:
+ – stimulus detect
– – stimulus rejected

Fig 11.4 Adapted model of Cue Utilisation Theory

This effect is even more noticeable if the cues and signals are not what were expected. Extreme levels of arousal can cause such acute levels of perceptual narrowing that a person is not able to concentrate or make decisions effectively, and can even hinder the smooth control of physical movements. This state of 'hyper vigilance' is commonly known as 'blind panic'. Perceptual narrowing is therefore an important aspect of both learning and performance where, in a state of high arousal, reactions to expected stimuli can be enhanced and reactions to inappropriate or unexpected cues and signals can be inhibited.

Attentional styles

Some psychologists have put forward the view that performers need to have the ability to alter their perceptual field and vary the amount and type of information that enters the body depending on the situation and the requirements of the task. For example, during a badminton doubles match, a player will need to focus in a different manner when serving compared to a rally, where more information needs to be assessed. Nideffer's Model of Attentional Focus (1976) proposed that attentional style varies along two dimensions:

1   **Width:** refers to the number of stimuli requiring attention:
    –   **broad:** focuses on a wide range of stimuli e.g. a badminton player needs to detect his own position and that of his opponents on court, as well as the location, flight and speed of the shuttlecock
    –   **narrow:** focuses on a limited range of stimuli, e.g., when serving the player focuses on the place where they wish to hit the shuttlecock
2   **Direction:** refers to the focus of the thought processes of the performer:
    –   **internal:** focuses on their own thoughts and feelings, e.g., the player mentally rehearsing the feelings associated with the correct movement pattern or stress management techniques to control their level of arousal
    –   **external:** focuses on stimuli in the environment, e.g., the location of the players and shuttlecock or the shot being played by the opponent.

IN CONTEXT

Within sport, it is often more common to see evidence of perceptual narrowing during team games involving open skills. For example, during an important game of rugby a player may play well during the opening phases of the game, but become gradually more aroused as the opposition score more points. Later in the game, as the team fall further behind, the player becomes more frustrated and over-aroused. As a result, rather than focus on specific strategies and the correct technical execution of skills, the player tries too hard to change the result and misses vital cues, such as the location of other players who are able to score a try because of an overlap situation. The result is an incorrect decision, such as attempting to score the try themselves. This often results in a breakdown in play or the scoring opportunity being wasted.

Therefore, it would be more appropriate when dealing with inexperienced performers or beginners in a learning situation to ensure that levels of arousal are initially very low. Audiences, evaluation and competitive situations are best avoided.

Based on Figure 11.5 Nideffer identified four attentional styles:

●   **broad/external:** used by players during games to detect fast changing situations and identify the best option
●   **external/narrow:** used by players to concentrate on specific objects or tasks, possibly with limited number of cues

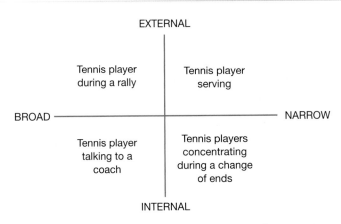

Fig 11.5 Adapted model of attentional focus (Nideffer, 1976)

- **narrow/internal:** used by players to mentally rehearse a skill or task
- **internal/broad:** often used by coaches to analyse performance and plan future strategies and tactics.

The aim of the coach should be to identify the attentional style required in a particular situation. If the performer has a weakness detecting cues during a particular phase of play, this can be highlighted and developed through practice. In many cases, performers will be required to 'switch' between different styles to maximise their performance. Strategies can be developed to encourage this during phases of play. For example, during a badminton match the server may adopt a narrow/internal style to imagine how they are going to play the serve, but then immediately switch to a broad/external style when the rally begins.

Activity 3

Redraw Nideffer's model. Select two sports completely different in nature, e.g. archery and hockey. For each sport identify the appropriate attentional style that would be required at various times throughout the course of the event. Use practical examples to illustrate and justify your answers.
Compare your answers with the rest of the group.

Emotional control

In all forms of sporting participation a certain degree of emotional control is required to perform at your optimum level. There are many cases where a lack of emotional control has caused a major upset in elite sport. Consider how often at major championships during a 4 × 100 metres relay race the baton is dropped by the most experienced of sprinters. In most cases this is not caused by a lack of practice but elevated arousal levels, poor attentional control and anxiety initiated by the situation and the potential reward for winning.

Your previous studies of the inverted U theory (see *OCR PE for AS*, pages 185–188) have given you an insight into the

relationship between arousal and performance. The original theory suggested that optimum arousal levels will vary depending on several factors including the complexity of the task, the personality of the performers and their ability level.

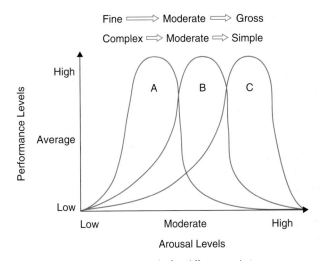

Fig 11.6 The inverted 'U' principle for different tasks: optimum arousal is higher for more simple tasks with more gross-motor control

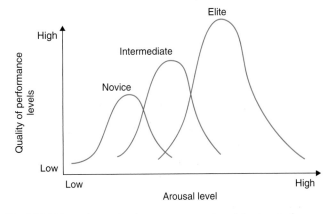

Fig 11.7 The relationship between arousal and the level of expertise or phase of learning

Complexity of the task and arousal

Complex tasks are performed better when one's level of drive (arousal) is low, while simple tasks are performed better when drive/arousal is high. It recognises that there are different degrees of arousal, over or under arousal, and that different people can be affected in different ways depending on the type of tasks they are faced with. Most sports performers and coaches can relate to the principles of the inverted 'U' hypothesis as most of them have experienced performances when both under and over arousal have inhibited their performance. They have also experienced times when their preparation has been exactly right, decisions have been made correctly and effectively and an excellent performance has resulted.

It has been argued that as a general principle, optimum levels of arousal are not the same for all activities or for all performers. The idea that optimum levels of arousal are variable according to the type and complexity of the task in relation to the individual performer has meant that the basic principles can be generalised and used by teachers and coaches to explain and predict behaviour in a whole host of situations. Teachers and coaches began to realise that the usual all-rousing pre-event pep talk was not necessarily the answer for all performers.

It has been found that motor skills generally need an above average level of arousal. If the skills or activity involve mainly gross movements and relatively simple skills using strength, endurance and speed, requiring little decision-making, then higher levels of arousal will be found more effective. Activities involving very fine, accurate muscle actions or complex tasks requiring higher levels of perception, decision-making, concentration and attention will be carried out more effectively if the point of optimum arousal is slightly lower.

It is therefore very important that a teacher or coach assesses the appropriate levels of arousal for each task in order to ensure that the optimum level is achieved. Even within teams the different requirements of each particular role or position may require different levels of arousal at various times. For example, batting and bowling in cricket, where loss of concentration and coordination could be disastrous, require different levels of arousal to those of a general fielder. Adjusting arousal levels to suit both task and situation could involve the coach in trying to increase or decrease a performer's arousal levels. Levels of excitement and anxiety caused by high arousal may need to be controlled by various stress management techniques. As you can appreciate, many sports or tasks involve combinations of both fine and gross skills along with varying levels of information-processing linked to complexity. Even within the context of a game different players will need different levels of arousal and at different times. Past experience, amount of practice and stage of learning will also have an effect on the choice of appropriate level of arousal.

Ability level and arousal

Beginners need different levels of arousal to those of a professional sportsperson. In addition, the level of complexity is relative to the stage of learning and/or experience. What for an experienced performer, i.e. those in the autonomous stage of learning, is a relatively easy task, may be very difficult and involve a great deal of information-processing for a beginner in the cognitive and associate stages of learning. Even at moderate levels of arousal a beginner may 'go to pieces' and be unable to cope with what is required of them; an even lower level of arousal may be more appropriate.

Personality and arousal

Another variable factor that impacts on the optimum level of arousal is the personality of the performer. It is generally agreed that extroverts produce a better performance when the arousal levels are higher. Similarly those who are more introverted in nature would benefit from lower levels of arousal.

This is due to the **reticular activating system** (RAS), which is part of the ascending structure of the spinal cords linked to the fore brain and is responsible for maintaining the general level of arousal or alertness within the body. It plays a part in our selective attention processes and serves either to inhibit or excite incoming sensory information to help our attention processes. The psychologists' interest in arousal has tended to focus on the links between the physiological aroused state and the experience of associated emotions. Just as periods of high intense exercise (e.g., playing football or netball) are associated with all the symptoms of a highly aroused state, e.g., high levels of adrenaline, increased HR, breathing rates, etc, aroused states can be equally associated with the emotional states of fear, anger, apprehension, tension, worry and anxiety. Some evidence suggests that these emotional states are reciprocal with one affecting the other and vice versa.

Therefore, those individuals who are extrovert require higher levels of stimulation and need a higher level of arousal than introverts who have sensitive RAS. If the arousal level increases too much, the result may be anxiety and deterioration in performance.

The various emotional states mentioned above are easily developed and often experienced particularly when exploring the unfamiliar (e.g., meeting something new or being asked to do something important or perform at a new high level of competition) and in the learning or acquiring of motor skills as well as the ultimate performance. Research has shown that levels of arousal can affect levels of perception, attention and movement control, all of which are obviously important in the learning and performance of motor skills. Within a performance situation the player has to be aware of their arousal level and may have to employ strategies to vary this depending upon the specific situation.

Key terms

Arousal is seen as a general internal state of physiological and psychological activity and alertness varying from deep sleep to intense excitement (highly energised), and is linked to the intensity dimension of motivation.

Anxiety is seen as being a negative emotional state usually associated with feelings of apprehension and worry, caused by over arousal due to a person being stressed.

Stress is seen as being the result of the performer perceiving an imbalance between what is being demanded of them (stressors can be physiological or psychological) and whether they think they are capable of meeting that demand, particularly if failure has serious consequences.

Peak flow experience

Sports performers sometimes experience a situation when the timing of movements and actions appears perfect. They seem unable to do wrong. Everything they try works! It's one of those perfect days. They are said to be experiencing the ultimate intrinsic experience. Csikszentmihalyi (1975) describes this as the 'flow experience'. In his research he identified the common characteristics as:

- a feeling that the performer has the necessary skills to meet the challenge
- complete absorption in the activity
- clear goals
- action and awareness are merged
- total concentration on task
- apparent loss of consciousness
- an almost subconscious feeling of self-control
- no extrinsic motivation (goals, rewards, etc.)
- time transformation (appears to speed up)
- effortless movement.

Many researchers in this area have tended to concentrate on analysing the factors which have a negative impact on intrinsic motivation whereas Csikszentmihalyi (1990, 1999) has focused on what makes a task intrinsically motivating. Although it cannot be consciously planned for, the development of 'flow' has been linked to the following factors:

- positive mental attitude (confidence, positive thinking)
- being relaxed, controlling anxiety, and enjoying optimum arousal
- focusing on appropriate specific aspects of the current performance
- physical readiness (training and preparation at the highest level)
- optimum environment and situational conditions (good atmosphere)
- a shared sense of purpose (team games), good interaction.
- balanced emotional state, 'feeling good' and in control of one's body.

It is suggested there is a link between **somatic arousal** (physiological response) and **cognitive arousal** (thought processes). When the performer has reached the correct level of somatic arousal and the cognitive arousal is low, peak flow is more likely to occur. Figure 11.8 illustrates the relationship and emotional states that may occur depending on the different levels of arousal at the time.

By focusing on aspects of their preparation that can help the development of the above factors, elite performers can increase the probability that the 'flow experience' can occur. Psychological preparation is just as important as physiological performance (Jackson et al., 2001).

Obviously, limitations in any of the above factors can result in 'disrupted flow'. For example:

- injury
- fatigue
- crowd hostility
- uncontrollable events
- worrying
- distractions

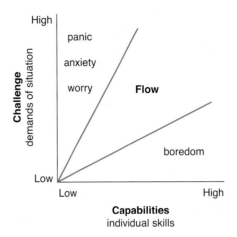

Fig 11.8 Peak flow experience

- lack of challenge
- non optimal arousal
- limited cohesion
- negative self-talk
- poor officials
- poor preparation
- poor performance.

IN CONTEXT

At the 2008 Beijing Olympics, Ben Ainslie became the most successful British sailor by winning his third consecutive gold medal. The following quotations not only shows how he was able to alter his tactics depending on the weather and the requirements of each race, but indicates that he was able to maintain concentration and ignore irrelevant factors that may have hindered his performance. Ainslie's closest rival was the American Zach Riley, and as long as he beat him Riley would win the gold medal.

During the final medal race Ainslie ignored all the other competitors and stayed just ahead of Riley at the back of the field, blocking every attempt he made to pass him.

'I had to string together some top-five finishes and with wins in the second, fourth and fifth races, I was doing well but then I was tenth again. You discount your worst finish, but I had had two bad runs. But in the frustratingly light wind everyone was being erratic. It was really only Zach Riley, the American, who was staying with me. As we got near the end of the regatta, it was all about keeping an eye on him, and hanging on to my lead.'

'We spent a long time hanging around before starting and had raced two legs when the wind just disappeared and the race was abandoned. I had one hand on the gold medal, but had to stay focused.'

However, as the race was abandoned the sailors had to return the following day, but on this occasion a different approach was required.

'... the conditions were completely opposite. It was pouring with rain and we had to come in for a while because visibility was so poor. But when we went back out, the windy conditions allowed me to control the race and finish first.'

Ainslie was able to completely focus on the task and concentrate on his own performance, resulting in a gold medal.

Individual zone of optimum functioning

Closely linked the arousal theories and the peak flow experience is Hanin's concept of the **individual zone of optimal functioning** (IZOF). Hanin studied 46 elite female rowers and measured their levels of state anxiety immediately prior to competition and compared it to the quality of their performance. Based on his research he suggested that each performer has a zone of optimal state anxiety in which their best performance occurs. The feelings associated with being in the zone are similar to those of the 'peak flow experience'. If they are not in this IZOF the performance will decline as shown in Figure 11.9.

> ### Key term
>
> **State anxiety** The level of arousal experienced by a performer at a given time. This can vary from moment to moment depending on the situation at the time.

Hanin's concept, although similar to the inverted U theory, differs in two key aspects:

- the optimum level of arousal does not always occur at the mid-point of the arousal continuum. Variable factors such as the situation and the performer will cause the ZOF to alter.
- the optimum level of arousal does not occur at a specific point but over a 'band width'.

The implications for the coach and performer are that work must be done to allow the individual to recognise when they are both within and outside the IZOF, either needing to relax or become more psyched-up. Also the coach must be aware that within a team there may be performers who have different IZOFs. As a result, simply completing a pre-match psyching-up session that involves everyone may be detrimental to group productivity and the final result.

Stress

As we have already stated, the term 'stress' is very often used in conjunction with or instead of anxiety and vice versa. It is generally seen as a state of psychological tension produced by certain perceived physiological and/or psychological pressures or forces acting on a performer within a certain environment or situation.

Research in this area has suggested that in analysing stress as a sequential process it is important to differentiate between the performer's perceptions of stress and actual potential environmental stressors. The effects of these two aspects have been shown to be different. Additional research (Selye, 1974) has also shown, if the performer's perceptions of the situation are taken into account, that although stress is usually viewed as having a negative or damaging effect on performance and behaviour, it can also have positive effects.

Many top class performers have stated that they need to feel under pressure in order to perform well.

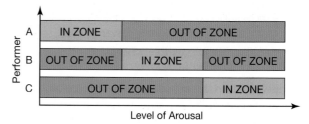

Fig 11.9 Individual zone of optimal functioning (IZOF)

Eustress (good stress)

Many sports performers such as rock climbers and hang-glider pilots, positively seek out so-called stressful situations in order to test their capabilities to the limit. Others claim that being in a relatively stressful situation helps them to focus, pay attention and generally develop skills and enjoyment within the context of sport. The positive benefits in terms of self-satisfaction and enhanced intrinsic motivation gained from having coped with a stressful situation are seen as being greater than the negative effects of the stress. It is, however, the potentially harmful distress or bad stress that has generally generated most of the research. This is more commonly known as anxiety and will be discussed in detail later in this chapter.

> ### Activity 4
>
> Make a list of all the activities in sport that you feel may create eustress.
>
> Compare your list with the rest of the group.
>
> Is your list the same? If not, why not?
>
> Try to explain the sorts of feelings that are developed when taking part in these activities.
>
> Do you think these experiences happen more during or after the activity (retrospectively)? Why?

The stress process

Various sequential models (e.g., McGrath, 1970; Cox, 1975) have been put forward to illustrate the multivariate nature and the stages involved in the stress process. In general *four* basic stages of stress have been identified (see Figure 11.11).

Fig 11.10 Many individuals seek out potentially stressful situations

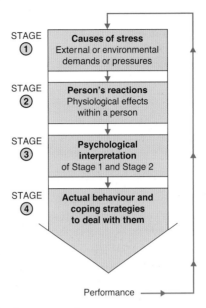

Fig 11.11 The four stages of stress

A performer is said to experience stress when they perceive that they are not capable of carrying out a particular task. Faced with a particular situation, game or task that may have been set by the teacher or coach, a performer will make a quick cognitive evaluation of what is required, comparing this with what they think are their own abilities, skill levels and experience. The demands of the situation/task are then perceived as threatening or not depending on whether an imbalance between task and capabilities is detected.

Key terms

Subjective Personal opinion of the situation not necessarily based on factual evidence.
Objective Factual evidence upon which reliable judgements can be made, not open to dispute or misinterpretation.

Research has shown that problems occur because the performer's subjective perceptions of the situational demands and their own capabilities are used to evaluate the situation, not the objective or actual demands and capabilities. Different performers and athletes will not perceive demands always in the same way and, obviously, they will therefore respond and ultimately perform in different ways. Viewing stress as a sequential process has certain advantages. It has been suggested that it is a cyclic process: the performer's actual behaviour feeds back and affects their future evaluations and perceptions.

Activity 5

In discussion with your group, make a list of all the things that you find stressful. Do you all find the same things stressful or are there differences of opinion? Why do you think this is the case?

Causes of stress

Events, constant irritations or demanding situations that confront us in daily life that lead to stress are called **stressors**. However, people's perceptions of what constitutes a stressor are different. In the final of a tennis competition, a performer who is a finalist for the very first time may perceive the experience as highly stressful. A well-established player may not.

Within life in general there are said to be three basic categories of stressors:

● environmental
● occupational
● life events.

The general stressors a performer may have to face up to in sport are said to fall into two categories: intrinsic within the performer themselves, or those related to the situation. Personal or intrinsic sources of stress are generally related to high trait anxiety, low self-esteem and social physique anxiety. These will have an effect on a performer's interpretation of situational sources of stress in terms of the importance of the event or contest and the uncertainty that surrounds the outcome (Martens 1987). Examples of more sports specific stressors are given below.

Sports specific stressors

Competition

Competitive situations have been shown to be potentially very stressful particularly if the event is important. A cup final or the last game of the season with relegation looming are potentially more stress-producing than a mid-season game. Even within the context of a game there are certain periods more critical than others and thus potentially more stressful (see Anxiety). Uncertainty within players/performers with regard to the outcome or over- evaluation by others has also proved to be a serious source of stress.

Frustration

Frustration occurs when a performer is prevented from reaching their goal and can be a common source of stress (see aggression). It may be that a performer feels generally inadequate or specifically inadequate, for instance, they want to be a good basketball player but are too small or they continually lose to an attacking player on the opposing team. A performer can become frustrated by external factors over which they have no control (see Attributions). Frustration can lead to possible aggression and potentially even more stress.

Conflict

The very nature of physically demanding sport can lead to stress through physical contact. However, conflict in this sense usually refers to a performer experiencing two or more contradictory motives or goals. A player may have to make a decision between playing for their club or a representative team; within the context of a particular game, they may have to decide whether to play it safe or take a chance, and possibly risk losing the game. External influences or domestic difficulties, e.g., family social pressures, may also conflict with a demanding training schedule.

Personal

Many performers will put undue pressure on themselves, thus heightening state anxiety (see later in this chapter) and therefore stress. Performers with high levels of trait anxiety (high A-trait) are predisposed to seeing sporting situations as more threatening than people with a low A-trait. In addition when we discussed personality earlier we described Type A and Type B personalities. People with the Type A personalities who are excessively competitive, tense, constantly work to deadlines, become easily frustrated, hostile and continually need their self-esteem bolstered are susceptible to greater levels of stress. However, many psychologists will argue that Type A behaviour is not really a specific characteristic in itself but a series of sub-characteristics. It does highlight, however, that certain personal characteristics or ways of dealing with life can lead to heightened levels of stress.

Physiological and climatic

Placing the body under severe physical, physiological or climatic strain has also been shown to create stress. Intense or unusual levels of training or playing in very hot, humid conditions can create enormous amounts of physiological stress on a performer. The perceived pressure and necessity to train at extreme levels can also lead to stress. Over-using injuries can develop stress both physically and psychologically.

Audience

While some may find performing in front of an audience an exhilarating experience, others may find it extremely stressful.

Further examples of sporting stressors

These include:

- rewards/incentives/prizes
- prestigious events
- representative honours/games
- social evaluation
- 'win at all costs' attitude
- pre-match pep talks
- parental pressure
- inconsistent coaching/training
- excessive time demands
- repetitive practices
- excessive expectations
- emotional blackmail
- concerns about self-image, e.g., being overweight.

Responding to stress

Having perceived an imbalance between the general or specific demands of the task and their own capabilities, a performer's stress response can either be psychological (cognitive) or physiological (somatic). Their response will vary according to the degree of perceived threat. Anger, apathy and anxiety are the most common psychological (cognitive) responses to stress. When faced with an immediately threatening situation the body reacts in the short term by increasing psychological arousal.

In describing the general adaptation syndrome (GAS) Selye (1956) explained his generally accepted view of how a person's body responds to prolonged stress. Selye identified three stages of the GAS (see Figure 11.12).

Alarm reaction stage

This involves physiological changes associated with the emotions of 'fight or flight' reactions. The sympathetic systems of the ANS (autonomic nervous system) are therefore activated. Levels of adrenaline, blood sugar, heart rate, blood pressure all increase. Sympathetic arousal can continue for some time after the level of stress or perceived threat has reduced or disappeared.

Resistance stage

If the stress continues, the body will try to revert to normal levels of functioning thus coping with the increased adrenaline levels. Usually the level of sympathetic nervous activity decreases.

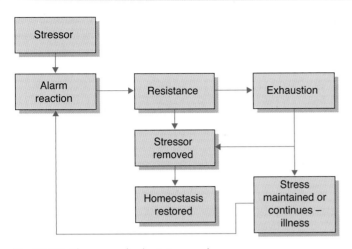

Fig 11.12 The general adaptation syndrome

as the central influence on stress and anxiety. As we have seen when an imbalance between demand and capability is perceived stress occurs and manifests itself in increased arousal which in turn affects both the physiological and psychological balance of the body.

Exhaustion/collapse stage

In trying to deal with the continued stress and coping with the various hormonal changes the body has gradually depleted its own resource. The adrenal cortex fails to function correctly resulting in physiological problems like ulcers, heart disease and high blood pressure. The body is unable to fight infection and in extreme cases death can occur.

Anxiety and performance

Although arousal is a neutral physiological state, the concept of anxiety is linked to the negative emotional feelings a person experiences as a result of the cognitive and physiological effects of arousal and stress. Anxiety is usually associated with feelings such as nervousness, worry and apprehension. These feelings are particularly prevalent in sporting situations when winning or not losing is very important for various reasons. There are several terms associated with anxiety which are discussed in Figure 11.13.

IN CONTEXT

Often stress is inadvertently placed on a performer, particularly young performers. It is most important that teaching and coaching should be appropriate to the individual or team. There are many examples of young sports stars developing 'burnout', due to the high demands placed upon them and the expectations to succeed. At all levels of participation it is therefore vital that the correct goals are set, attributions are used correctly and many of the aspects previously discussed are implemented to reduce the potential negative aspects of stress occurring. It is not only teachers and coaches who have a responsibility in this area, as parents also have a responsibility not to place excessive pressure on their children.

More up-to-date research has tended to focus on controlling levels of arousal which can affect either somatic or cognitive anxiety. Arousal is generally seen

EXAMINER'S TIP

Be able to explain the meaning of each of the types of anxiety and discuss the relationship between them, as well as the impact they may have on performance.

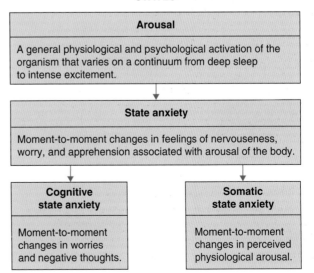

Fig 11.13 Trait anxiety and state anxiety
(*Source:* Weinberg and Gould, 1995)

Trait anxiety

The general acquired behavioural tendency of a person to become worried or anxious, i.e., a stable characteristic, is referred to as '**trait anxiety**'. A person with a high level of trait anxiety is generally predisposed to develop high levels of arousal quickly and easily. They generally react to situations with a very high and often disproportionate level of state anxiety. They have a tendency to over-react in situations that the vast majority of people would view objectively as non-threatening. This has been referred to by some as a possible innate response. More up-to-date research has suggested that it exerts a great deal of influence on a performer's cognitive interpretation of arousal and this can further affect actual physiological arousal.

State anxiety

In certain situations sports performers do not feel anxious at all, whereas in other situations they feel highly anxious. **State anxiety** is a temporary emotional state and refers to subjective but consciously perceived feelings of nervousness and worry as a result of increased arousal when faced with certain situations. A player's levels of state anxiety can vary in intensity from situation to situation and also at various times within the situation. For instance, defending a corner in the last minute of a game you are winning 1–0 will obviously increase your level of state anxiety. State anxiety can be either cognitive or somatic (see below), and research has shown it can even be a learned response, i.e., certain situations create or cause it more than others. More up-to-date research has suggested that:

- somatic state anxiety is related to the performer's *perceptions* of their level of physiological arousal not arousal *per se*
- cognitive state anxiety is related to the mental appraisal of arousal – it can be both negative or positive.

When discussing sports psychology, anxiety is usually seen as having two different components, **cognitive** anxiety and **somatic** anxiety.

Cognitive anxiety

The vague unpleasant thoughts a sportsperson may develop that are usually associated with concerns about under-achieving and negative expectations are said to be the result of cognitive anxiety brought on by stress. A sportsperson experiencing cognitive anxiety would have problems with concentration as levels of attention are interfered with, influenced by images of failure.

Cognitive anxiety is usually experienced earlier than somatic anxiety and will be greatly influenced by the performer's expectations of success.

Somatic anxiety

This type of anxiety is usually as a result of a performer's negative perception of the body's physiological reactions to stress. A performer worries more because they perceive that a queasy stomach, increased sweating, clammy hands and so on – all the body's naturally occurring responses to increased arousal – are going to have a negative effect on performance.

For some performers the prospect of facing an 'extreme' climb, playing in their first big final or facing their first vault in a gymnastic lesson holds no real threat and creates only a slightly increased level of nervousness. They are rarely seriously unnerved by the prospect of new experiences and accept the slight apprehension as natural.

For others, however, the mere thought of being asked to demonstrate in front of a class or audience always triggers extreme arousal and serious levels of anxiety. In their research psychologists have therefore differentiated between anxiety that results from a changing 'mood state' and is usually short-lived and anxiety that is more associated with a person's general characteristics or personality traits.

Anxiety within sport (competitive anxiety)

Performing well in difficult, challenging or highly emotional circumstances, i.e., competitive situations, is a problem to the vast majority of sports performers, in particular those at the most elite of professional levels. Anxiety states can negatively affect a performer's concentration, attention and level of information-processing in competitive situations. It is important that coaches are aware of these effects, can measure and predict them in relation to specific circumstances, and then possibly control them. Important points to note from research into this area are that both elite and average performers experience intense anxiety both prior to, and during, performance; the difference being that elite performers are able to control their anxiety at crucial times within their performance. In addition, the performer's perception of the anxiety is also crucial.

Research in this area has shown that both state and trait anxiety can usually be measured through self-report tests (e.g., Speilberger's STAI). State anxiety can be measured in relation to specific situations and circumstances. The general predisposition of a person to worry more, i.e., trait anxiety, can also be measured. The application of these general research measures to sport has shown that people in sport who are measured as having high levels of trait anxiety (high A-trait) will perceive certain situations, particularly competitive situations, as highly threatening (stressful). Their response will be a disproportionate one, resulting in severe state anxiety (high A-state) together with a possible inhibited performance.

Factors affecting competitive anxiety

Pre-competition a state anxiety can be affected by the performer's perception of:

- fear of failure/making mistakes/performing badly
- fear of evaluation
- fear of competition/importance of event
- fear of injury/danger
- lack of control/good opposition/unfamiliar pitch/biased refereeing.

Factors that can affect anxiety levels during competition include:

- Evaluation of others **during** competition – crowd/opposition/coach/co-actors
- Interaction with others – friendly/aggressive opposition/enjoyment factors/decisions of officials
- Injury during competition/fatigue
- Influence of the environment – weather pitch conditions
- Success/failure **during** competition – time left/ score line
- Type of task – contact or other.

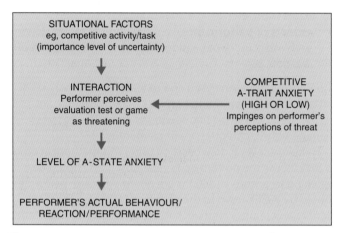

Fig 11.14 Interactionist relationship between a competitive situation and personality factors

Measuring and recognising stress

The measurement of stress levels is an important aspect of a performer's preparation. If individual patterns of behaviour can be identified and linked to specific situations, the coach/teacher can employ various strategies to reduce the performer's anxiety, control arousal levels and allow the athlete to operate in their IZOF.

The following are aids to assessing stress levels in performers.

- Self-report tests, e.g. State Trait Anxiety Inventory (STAI), Sport Competition Anxiety Test (SCAT) and Competitive State Anxiety Inventory (CSAI2)
- Observation
- Biofeedback, e.g., measuring physiological responses.

Self-report questionnaires

These involve performers answering a series of questions concerning their emotions in specific situations. There are numerous advantages to using this method including:

- ease of administration
- large numbers can be assessed quickly
- cheap to administer.

However, there are some drawbacks too:

- misinterpretation or lack of understanding of the questions

- the respondents may not answer honestly as they may wish to appear in a positive light or they may give the answers they think are required or socially desirable
- inappropriate questions may be used, which may lead to biased results
- the actual time of completion may influence the responses
- the available responses may not cater for the exact emotions being experienced.

Martens: sport competition anxiety test (SCAT) & Competitive State Anxiety Inventory (CSAI2): in developing a more specific sports-related test of trait anxiety in sporting situations, Martens (1977) proposed his sport competition anxiety text (SCAT). He felt that although this was seen as a global measure (due to the links between trait and state), this would be a more effective measure of trait, thus a more helpful predictor of possible state anxiety in sport. It is a generally accepted view that competitive situations in sport create anxiety at varying levels in the vast majority of performers. Martens identified that certain performers suffered from this global competitive trait anxiety: a performer's tendency specifically to perceive competitive sporting situations as potentially threatening and to respond to these situations with heightened feelings of apprehension and/or tension. The SCAT test developed over five years was a simple, straightforward 15 item scale self-report test (don't forget that self-report tests in general have been questioned because of bias!). However, generally it proved very reliable in measuring levels of trait anxiety in competitive situations and thus in helping coaches to predict a performer's probable specific anxiety state.

Martens went on to develop his SCAT further in recognition of the more up-to-date multi-dimensional view of the nature of anxiety: The competitive state anxiety inventory (CSAI2) had separate measures for both cognitive and somatic anxiety and has been the most commonly used within sports psychology.

	HARDLY EVER	SOMETIMES	OFTEN
1. Before I compete I worry about not performing well.	a	b	c
2. When I compete I worry about making mistakes.	a	b	c
3. Before I compete I am calm.	a	b	c
4. I get nervous waiting to start a game.	a	b	c

Fig 11.15 Examples of sports competition anxiety test (SCAT) questions – a performer is asked to complete a number of questions of which the following are selected examples; dummy questions are also included to disguise what is being asked (adapted from Martens)

	NOT AT ALL	A LITTLE BIT	MODERATELY SO	VERY HIGHLY SO
1. I am nervous about the competition.	1	2	3	4
2. My body feels tense.	1	2	3	4
3. I feel uncomfortable.	1	2	3	4
4. I don't feel relaxed.	1	2	3	4
5. I am confident.	1	2	3	4
6. I don't think I will perform as well as I can.	1	2	3	4

Fig 11.16 Examples of questions to measure state anxiety (CSAI2) – these are related to feelings expressed by sporting performers prior to a specific competition (up to one hour before); performers are advised that these feelings are natural and to fill in the questions quickly, not worrying over the questions themselves]

The use of such tests as Martens' indicated two general patterns:

- **cognitive anxiety** increases in the days leading up to the competition, remains high, but does not increase just prior to the start of the competition. During the competition it is found to fluctuate normally as a result of the performer's perceptions of success or failure.
- **somatic anxiety** tends to remain low until rising quite dramatically a few hours prior to the event and decreasing during the competition.

Validity of SCAT:

- easy to administrate
- can be used with large groups
- can be open bias/respondents can reply how they think they **should** not how they actually feel
- responses are open to misunderstanding by non-experts
- the questionnaire is not sensitive to small changes in anxiety levels
- the questionnaire system is inconvenient in a real sport situation/can actually interfere with anxiety response
- high scores on the intensity of anxiety do not necessarily mean this state is detrimental.

As research into this area of anxiety developed, the reliability of basic pre-competitive tests as predictors of actual state anxiety and, ultimately, behaviour and performance, is being called into question. Anxiety states, as we have already said, are changing mood states, and these have been shown to alter considerably in relation to arousal once games or competitions have started. Although many performers measure high levels of competitive A-trait this may not directly affect their anxiety state and thus actual performance. They may have learnt through experience to cope with it, or through specific psychological coaching how to reduce their own levels of anxiety.

Observation

Observation of performance, whilst subjective, does allow the performer to be assessed in the actual performance situation. The observer will record two types of data:

- **individual behaviour**, i.e., those behaviours usually associated with nervous actions, such as fidgeting, changes in speech patterns, acts of increased aggression, etc.
- **aspects of performance**, i.e., execution of skilled actions such as accuracy of passing, decision-making, speed of reaction, etc.

The information is analysed and repeated behaviour patterns noted. Detrimental aspects of performance are highlighted during specific situations and relevant stress management techniques are implemented.

There are several drawbacks to using this method. In order to fully assess the performer, several observers should be watching to ensure all actions are noted. Also, the performer should be well-known to the observers, allowing them to identify any unusual and uncharacteristic behaviour patterns.

Biofeedback

Biofeedback involves monitoring the physiological responses of the performer. Data is collected on changes in heart rate, muscle response, respiration rate, sweat production and levels of hormone secretion.

Whilst this provides accurate data there are several drawbacks including the difficulty of recording information during an actual competitive performance (as the athlete has to be 'wired-up' to obtain the results). The potential changes caused as a natural reaction to being evaluated and the replication of the competitive environment is difficult in the laboratory situation.

Anxiety management techniques

In competitive sport the great majority of performers will be under some form or degree of stress. Audiences will always be present. Teams and individuals of equal ability repeatedly compete against each other. Indeed, the whole learning process is one in which the teacher or coach continually sets new and challenging (stressful) tasks for the learner/performer. The skill of the coach/teacher is in knowing and being able to identify, both in the build-up to competition and during, those performers who are feeling just right, those who are too anxious and equally those who may need motivating.

Stress to a certain degree can be good for a performer or even actively sought (eustress). It is important though that the negative aspects of stress and anxiety states, e.g., worrying about not performing to our capabilities, etc., are not allowed to inhibit performance – very often performers get caught up in a downward stress cycle. Therefore, in order to optimise performance they need to be able to manage or cope with stress in order that the optimal combination of arousal related to emotions is achieved.

- As the effects of stress and anxiety are almost unique to each sport performer it is important that the coach has an in-depth knowledge of the performer's psychological and physiological make-up.
- In addition, the coach/performer must be aware of the various effects and responses associated with stress and heightened state anxiety, e.g., both somatic and cognitive anxiety, before they can learn to control them.
- The coach/performer also needs to be aware of the sources of stress.
- Both coaches and performers need to be able to recognise the various signs and realise that some of these are the body's natural ways of preparing. Being aware of these effects can help to reduce cognitive anxiety at experiencing them.

Having got to grips with these points a coach can then ensure that they individualise their coaching programmes in order to boost confidence and ensure optimum performance.

A simplistic way of viewing the management of stress is that teachers and coaches should try to:

- reduce the problem
- reduce the stress
- control arousal.

This can be achieved through either **cognitive** or **somatic techniques**. The techniques can be classed as mainly somatic (relating to physiological aspects, i.e., the body) or cognitive (related to psychological aspects, i.e., thinking). However, as performers can experience both kinds of anxiety at the same time, some of the techniques may also combine elements of each. Top class performers are experts at using either or both in order to maintain psychological control during top level competition.

Control is a key issue here. If a performer feels in control of a situation then stress can be reduced considerably, in particular cognitive anxiety. This will also help to alleviate learned helplessness.

There are numerous stress management techniques which can be used and they fall into two broad categories: cognitive strategies and somatic strategies. Some techniques, however, do combine elements of both.

Cognitive techniques

Imagery

The intervention technique of imagery has become very popular with sports psychologists. However, imagery has been used for many different purposes. As well as the control or regulation of arousal, improving concentration, building confidence and controlling emotional responses, i.e., stress management, it has been used for:

- skill and strategy acquisition (mental rehearsal)
- skill maintenance
- self imagery manipulation
- attention/pain control.

Although imagery and mental rehearsal are often closely associated some psychologists argue that there is a distinction between them.

Imagery is a basic cognitive function and is associated with long-term changes in a performer's behaviour. By recalling appropriate stored information from the memory a player is able to generate images of movement experiences. In many cases this has been shown to be almost as good and effective as actual movement experience.

Imagery can be used to:

- create a mental picture of new experiences in the mind; or
- recreate a mental picture of a previous experience.

Although it is usually associated with visualisation imagery can be:

- **visual** – picture yourself being successful, e.g., hitting a winning smash at Wimbledon
- **auditory** – you hear the sound of the ball hitting the racket
- **kinaesthetic** – tactile, e.g., feel the power and muscular control associated with the smash
- **emotional** – imagine feelings of success, self-satisfaction from the victory, confidence, etc.

Ideally, imagery should involve as many of the senses as possible in order to develop or recreate a more distinct image. Achieving a relaxed state of attention will facilitate the use of all the senses during imagery.

By attaching emotions and feelings to the image performers can help themselves recall situations or behavioural responses more effectively. This can help in the control of current emotions and anxieties and by developing self-confidence in the control of potential emotions and anxieties. Research to support the fact that imagery works

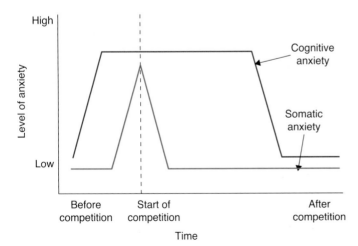

Fig 11.17 Cognitive and somatic anxiety levels may vary before, during and after competitive events

explains that it is only really effective when a performer can link psychological and symbolic coding of movement patterns to psycho/neuro muscular actions.

Factors which a performer should concentrate on to successfully use mental rehearsal:

- the exact details of the movement in question
- the exact details of a successful outcome
- the 'feel' of the movement
- visualising the exact equipment used
- visualising the environment as it would be for physical practice
- recapturing the emotions of being involved in a competitive situation
- mental rehearsal should be practised frequently as it is a skill in its own right
- mental rehearsal should be practised alongside (alternatively with) physical practice
- the use of an appropriate relaxation technique prior to the use of mental rehearsal could help the quality of mental rehearsal e.g., Jacobsen's PMR.

The use of imagery to control arousal

Imagery can be used either to decrease or increase arousal. Research has suggested that imagery can help to:

- improve concentration
- reduce anxiety
- develop confidence
- control emotions.

In order to reduce arousal, images of previous situations when certain responses have had a negative effect on performance are imagined by the performer. They then try to imagine themselves dealing with and controlling the stress in different circumstances. For example, by dealing with a bad call in tennis in a more positive manner, possibly linking an appropriate phrase to remind them to take a deep breath and 'stay cool' in the future. They then imagine themselves carrying out this more positive behaviour. In a more relaxed state they are then able to concentrate more closely on the task and not allow their overall arousal levels to get the better of them in the actual situation when and if it arises. Arousal, and thus state anxiety, can also be reduced by a performer picturing a place where they feel emotionally at ease with themselves and are totally unstressed, perhaps on a beach in the sunshine or by the pool, with 'the sun on your back, the sensation of sand beneath your feet, your body glowing with health and strength'. This process has obvious links with relaxation techniques. The cognitive coping strategy of focusing on emotional images particularly related and relevant to the impending activity has been shown to be very effective in creating positive attitudes, developing confidence and achieving objectives. This has been termed **preparatory arousal**, and is commonly known as 'psyching up'.

There are two basic types of imagery:

- **Internal imagery:** you only see what you would see if you were actually executing the skill yourself. As a hockey player taking a penalty flick you would see the goal, goalkeeper, the ball going in the net and the kinaesthetic feelings associated with your grip on the stick and stance and so on.
- **External imagery:** you see yourself as others would see you, as though you were watching yourself perform on video. Although techniques in relation to others would be seen, as it is external there would be little kinaesthesis attached to the image.

There is evidence to suggest that internal imagery is slightly more effective than external due to the fact that it helps to develop kinaesthetic awareness. The general view, however, is that most performers tend to choose a style which suits them and often continually interchange between both types in order to develop the necessary clear and effective image.

Effective imagery

In order to develop effective imagery a performer and coach should ensure that:

- performers' present image skills levels are evaluated
- imagery is practised regularly and built into the daily routine of the performer
- the performer tries to use as many senses as possible to develop a **vivid** image
- image is **controllable** by the performer
- imagery is carried out in an appropriate setting (initially this may mean no distractions)
- the performer believes it can work
- the performer does not have unrealistic expectations
- the performer builds up the levels and use of imagery over a period of time
- the performer imagines both carrying out the movement and the end result
- images should not be overly long; usually the same length of time as the actual movement
- the performer practises using the image in realistic situations.

After practising and developing imagery skills an experienced performer will be able to use imagery even under potentially distracting circumstances.

Activity 6

Select a sports skill that you have previously completed well in a pressurised situation. Using internal imagery, attempt to recreate the feelings you experienced during the performance. Attempt to remember any visual and auditory cues as well as the kinaesthetic feeling involved. Repeat the action in your mind several times. Before your next event, repeat this process if you feel yourself becoming anxious and practise its use as a stress management control method.

EXAMINER'S TIP

Be able to name and explain different techniques for both cognitive and somatic anxiety. Do not get them confused as they deal with different forms of anxiety.

Self-talk

Self-talk is linked to controlling cognitive anxiety. Interpretations and perceptions of performance during and after an activity can also have a considerable effect on either the present performance or future performance. Different interpretations and reactions can also affect our emotions and feelings. How a performer interprets their actual performance can therefore lead to stress, anxiety, frustration and anger. A performer can interpret both their good and bad performance in either a negative or positive way: this can lead to what is known as **positive** or **negative self-talk**. Comments or thoughts can be directed either against the performance or against their emotions. It is a cognitive modification.

Positive self-talk is used to maintain attention levels and focus positively on the task. Remaining optimistic helps a performer's level of motivation and self-esteem; it can also reduce cognitive state anxiety. Performers are able to focus on the task and what to do better and not on worrying. Positive self-talk is therefore crucial for concentration. A performer should always try to avoid the negatives 'can't', 'never' and 'not'. Mood words are particularly useful: 'stay, tough, fast, hard, I can do it!' etc.

In using **negative self-talk** the performer is usually self-critical and undermines confidence. Negative self-talk serves to increase worry and doubt about future performance, e.g., the next serve. It can lead to frustration, anger and increased muscle tension. For instance, having just double-faulted in tennis the resulting negative self-talk might be:

- 'What a totally stupid shot that was'
- 'What a time to double fault'
- 'I've no chance of getting back into the game now!'

This could result in smashing the racket into the ground. This performer is not concentrating on what can be done or what should be done to improve the situation. In this situation the positive self-talk would be:

- 'I need to watch the ball more when I throw up the ball higher'
- 'This next one goes in'
- 'There's still plenty of time left to turn this match around.'

Thus, while being aware of the difficulties, this positive performer is motivated to carry on and persists. Positive self-talk therefore emphasises the importance of developing and maintaining both a constructive mood and approach. It is important that a performer does not allow negative thoughts to become the focus of attention even though, because of stress, they are usually the ones that come into a player's head or mouth first, because self-fulfilling prophecy may be the result.

Thought-stopping

Thought-stopping involves the individual recognising when they are starting to worry or develop negative thoughts about the performance. Very often experienced performers use cue words to trigger off positive thoughts either to reduce anxiety or increase levels of attention and concentration on specific details. Examples are as follows.

1   A basketball player when learning a new skill such as a set shot may use simple cue words like: 'flex' (knees), 'sight' (basket), 'extend' (knees), 'push' (ball forwards basket), 'flick' (wrist).
2   Tennis players or cricketers who repeatedly fail to watch the ball onto the racket or bat may use self instructional cues of 'watch!' or 'ball' in order to try to break the habit.
3   A skier hitting a mogul may shout 'bend!', 'extend!' or 'down!' and 'up!' in order to remind themselves of the technique.
4   A performer can also motivate themselves, e.g., a 400m runner coming off the last bend can shout to themselves, 'fast! fast! fast!' or 'attack! attack!' in order to help them kick for the line and keep pushing hard!

Rational/positive thinking

As we have discovered stress and anxiety occur as a result of a perceived imbalance between ability and the demands of the task. If the performer can be taught to evaluate the situation and logically plan their course of action, anxiety can be reduced. This may involve the person adjusting their attentional focus and concentrating in the narrow – internal dimension. Any areas of uncertainty can be either discussed with another or internally considered. The aim should be to provide objective evidence to dispel negative thoughts, such as training times achieved, previous success and quality of training undertaken in preparation for the event. This in turn should improve self-efficacy and help to control arousal levels.

Attribution retraining already mentioned can also be helpful in these situations by encouraging a performer to attribute control internally. Being in control of the situation will help a performer develop both general confidence and self-efficacy. By persuading performers to take responsibility for themselves and cope with the situation a teacher/coach can help a performer deal with any problems they may have to face. A performer can be helped to take responsibility by getting them involved in setting their own goals. Realistic short-term and long-term performance goals should be negotiated. Again this should help a performer's self-efficacy together with their ability to cope. Giving a performer as much information as possible about the competitive situation (their progress, goals, etc) can help to reduce a performer's level of uncertainty.

Somatic techniques

Relaxation

Psychologists have suggested and researched many forms of relaxation to reduce stress. Meditation, breathing control, self-hypnosis and biofeedback techniques are all ways that have been used to reduce arousal, and thus reduce stress and anxiety. What has been realised is that just telling someone to relax before or during a game is not enough. The performer needs to know *how* to relax in order that they can have self-control and be able to direct relaxation when and where necessary. Many sports performers actively use and extol the virtues of self-induced relaxation to reduce arousal levels to the optimum. Relaxation helps to inhibit panic and self-doubt enabling the performer to stay calm. By helping people to sleep it also helps reduce the effects of fatigue.

Self-direction relaxation

This purpose of this technique is to reduce specific and general muscle tension in order to relax fully prior to competitive or stressful situations. With help, a performer is able to identify areas of tension and fully relax. Eventually through practice a performer is able to sit quietly and free the tension from muscles in a very short period of time. The progressive technique below is a process for helping performers learn how to relax.

Progressive relaxation technique

This technique has been regularly developed and modified by sports psychologists, although the central theme of it was first developed by Edmund Jacobson in 1938. This is generally a lengthy process whose main purpose is to reduce somatic stress by teaching performers to recognise and feel tension and then to be able to progressively reduce it by 'letting go'. Performers are asked to tense specific muscles. By learning what tension feels like they are then taught to experience relaxing specific muscles. By progressively relaxing and tensing a performer is able to develop an awareness of what tension feels like, as the two feelings are mutually exclusive. Thus, when in a performance situation, they can recognise tension and carry out the relevant relaxation of not only specific muscles but general groups of muscles in order that total relaxation can be experienced. With practice this can be a relatively quick process which can be carried out before, after or during time breaks within games. It is felt that learning to reduce body tension will serve to decrease mental pressure (stress) by allowing the player to worry less. In a relaxed state they can maintain sufficient levels of attention on the necessary techniques of the game and not on muscle tension. Ideally conditions should be appropriate to allowing relaxation to happen, e.g., quiet, subdued surroundings, lying down, loose clothing, etc. More experienced athletes, however, are able to focus and, by using 'trigger' controls, can relax almost at will.

Biofeedback

This technique is again linked to controlling muscular tension and helps a performer deal with long-term stress. Performers are taught to control physiological or autonomic responses, i.e., heart rate, respiration rates and muscle tension, by being attached to a machine which measures and amplifies specific internal muscular nervous action. Through practice the performer learns to relax the specific

muscles that the machine is attached to by using a method that suits them; the performer is able to assess the level of tension in the muscles by the noise levels of the machine and learns to reduce it by relaxing. The machine provides objective biological feedback, either visual or auditory, with regard to their success rate at reducing tension, thus helping motivation. The main point of developing this awareness is so that eventually the performer can transfer this relaxation technique to the competitive or game situation. They no longer have to rely on the machine to inform them of muscle tension, but can recognise the tension via natural physiological changes occurring. Relaxation techniques can then be applied. Biofeedback has also been developed further by some to include the voluntary control of other bodily functions such as heart rate and blood pressure.

Breathing control

There are many general techniques for controlling breathing. Offering a means of controlling breathing has been shown to be an effective method of helping a performer to reduce muscle tension and relax. This again initially reduces the somatic effects of stress and anxiety. However, breathing control can be practised before, after or during the event in order to produce relaxation which can help with imagery, thus helping to enhance technique and performance. Practice is again necessary in order to develop the correct techniques. By consciously controlling the depth and rate of breathing immediately prior, for instance, to an important shot performers can reduce distractions. It will help to maintain their level of control and composure and thus reduce the effects of both somatic and cognitive anxiety.

As you can see a variety of techniques can be employed to improve performance, but must be practised before being successfully transferred to competition.

IN CONTEXT

One of the most recognisable sporting techniques in recent years has been that of England rugby player Jonny Wilkinson preparing to take a penalty kick. This extract from an article by Richard Williams, explains the meaning behind some of his actions and how they help to control his levels of state anxiety.

'The hands, he said, are like a barrier erected against the outside world, helping him to cut out the tens of thousands of opposing fans who are likely to set up a barrage of whistles and jeers in an attempt to disturb his intense concentration. 'As I got more into kicking,' he said, 'I became more involved in looking at other aspects, and one area I looked at was focusing from the inside, slowing down the breathing, relaxation, "centring", which is a way of channelling my power and energy from my core, just behind my navel, down my left leg and into my left foot to get that explosive power. When I was doing this, the position with the hands happened to be the one I adopted. Look at pictures from 1998, and you will see my hands are further apart. Each year they have gradually got closer. For whatever reason, it has become a very strong position for me.'

Wilkinson, together with his permanent technical adviser, Dave Alred, will often practise for hours at a time. They have devised a number of techniques that hone Wilkinson's accuracy, power and consistency.

'In one, in which he tries to land the ball on the crossbar, he pretends that he is a golfer and that his foot is a seven-iron. In another, he imagines a jeering mouth behind the goal and attempts to send the ball down its throat. The funniest technique involves an imaginary woman called Doris, who sits in a particular seat in the stand behind the goal, holding a can of Coke. As Wilkinson prepares to kick, he visualises the flight of the ball ending up in Doris's lap, knocking the drink out of her hands. 'The idea was that, instead of aiming at the posts, you were aiming at something specific 30 yards back,' he said. 'That way we changed the emphasis of where I was aiming and it made me really kick through the ball.'

Kicking through the ball is just one element of a complex technique, which is built up step by step. Another is "hardening" his kicking foot, which Wilkinson does by tapping his left toe on the grass before he kicks, usually in two sets of three taps, thus helping the foot to adopt the shape and the tension he wants when he hits the ball. Other elements are the need to focus on the precise point of the ball he is going to strike, and the importance of allowing the foot to follow through along the line of the ball for as long as possible, like a golfer. Trying to hit it hard, he says, is no good. Hitting it sweetly is the way to project it 40 metres or more, as he routinely does to break his opponents' hearts.'

What you need to know

Goal-setting
* Goals will not be effective unless they are linked to specific and realistic strategies for achieving them.
* The effectiveness of goals is dependent on the interaction between individuals, i.e., coach/performer and the situation.
* Goals can be subjective or objective and can be focused on performance process or outcome.
* Performance goals should adhere to the 'SMARTER' principles.

Self-efficacy
* Self-efficacy theory has provided a model for social psychologists to study the effects of self-confidence on behaviour.
* Self-confidence in specific situations (self-efficacy) has been closely linked to motivation and can affect choice, effort and persistence.
* Self-efficacy is seen as an important factor only when a performer has the necessary skills, abilities and motivation to attempt a task.
* Performance success is seen as the most important factor in developing a performer's expectations of self-efficacy.

Vealey's Sports Confidence
* Performers have Trait Sports Confidence (SC-trait) and a Competitive Orientation, which are linked to the objective sport situation.
* The interactions of these three components creates State Sport Confidence (SC-state)
* High levels of SC-State should improve the performance of the player.

Cue-utilisation theory
* As arousal levels increase a performer tries to pay more attention to those stimuli that are more relevant in order to help them carry out the task (cue-utilisation).
* They focus their attention (perceptual narrowing).
* If arousal levels continue to increase a performer's ability to focus their attention is severely hampered.

Attentional styles
* Attentional style varies along two dimensions: width and direction.
* Width – refers to the number of stimuli requiring attention. It can be **broad**, focusing on a wide range of stimuli or **narrow**, focusing on a limited range of stimuli.
* **Direction** – refers to the focus of the thought processes of the performer. It can be **internal**, focusing on their own thoughts and feelings or **external**, focusing on stimuli in the environment.
* Nideffer identified four attentional styles:
  - **broad/external** – used by players during games to detect fast changing situations and identify the best option
  - **external/narrow** – used by players to concentrate on specific objects or tasks, possibly with limited number of cues
  - **narrow/internal** – used by players to mentally rehearse a skill or task
  - **internal/broad** – often used by coaches to analyse performance and plan future strategies and tactics.

Arousal
* Arousal is a physiological state of alertness and anticipation which prepares the body for action.
* The reticular activating system (RAS) is responsible for maintaining the general level of arousal within the body.
* Levels of optimum arousal will be different according to the complexity and nature of the specific task in relation to the individual's characteristics and the specific situation.
* Over-arousal can create perceptual narrowing.

Peak flow experience

* State that performers sometimes experience during sport when the timing of movements and actions appears perfect.
* This is more likely to occur when the performer has reached the correct level of somatic arousal and the cognitive arousal is low, peak flow.

Individual zone of optimum functioning

* IZOF suggests the individual performer has a zone of optimal state anxiety in which their best performance occurs.
* Variable factors such as the situation and the performer will cause the ZOF to alter.
* The optimum level of arousal does not occur at a specific point but over a 'band width'.

Stress and anxiety

* Stress can be either positive (eustress) or negative.
* The causes of stress are referred to as stressors.
* Stressors can be very specific or general. The level of their effect depends on a person's perceptions of them in relation to their own perceived capabilities (cognitive appraisal).
* Specific examples of sporting stressors are competition, frustration, conflict, environmental factors.
* The general adaptation syndrome has been used as a way of explaining the body's actual stress response.
* The GAS is seen as developing through three stages: alarm/reaction, resistance and **anxiety**.
* Anxiety is a negative emotional state associated with feelings of apprehension and worry caused by over arousal as a result of being stressed.

* There are two distinguishable types of anxiety:
  – Trait anxiety is a predisposition to perceive situations as potentially more threatening than they are.
  – State anxiety is the changing emotional state experienced in specific situations.
* A person with high levels of A-trait anxiety is likely to respond with potentially higher levels of A-state anxiety.
* State anxiety responses can be somatic or cognitive.

Anxiety within sport

* Competitive A-trait has been found to be a general characteristic to perceive competitive situations as highly threatening and to respond disproportionately with higher levels of state anxiety.
* Competitive A-trait can be measured via SCATs.

Managing stress

* Stress management helps reduce both somatic and cognitive anxiety.
* Personal control is seen as a key issue in reducing stressful situations.
* Somatic techniques deal with mainly the physiological aspects of stress and involve various types of 'relaxation' such as progressive relaxation and biofeedback.
* Imagery, goal-setting and cognitive modification techniques can help to improve concentration; improve attention; control emotional states. This is generally known as cognitive stress management.
* All psychological skills training techniques require regular practice and integration into the normal preparation routines of performers.

Review Questions

1 What are the main effects of goal-setting?
2 Explain the difference between outcome goals and performance goals.
3 Explain the SMARTER principle that is taken into account when setting goals
4 Draw Vealey's Model of Sport Confidence and explain the relationship between the different variables.
5 What is self-efficacy and what are the sources contributing to its formation?
6 Outline the Cue-Utilisation theory and its impact on performance.
7 What are the four attentional styles suggested by Nideffer?
8 Explain how personality, ability and complexity of the task affect optimum levels of arousal.
9 What is the peak flow experience?
10 How does the Individual Zone of Optimum Functioning differ from the Inverted U theory of arousal?

11 Using examples from sport explain the difference between trait anxiety and state anxiety.
12 Using examples from sport distinguish between somatic and cognitive anxiety.
13 What do sports psychologists mean by competitive trait anxiety?
14 Explain how psychologists have tried to measure competitive trait anxiety.
15 What are stressors?
16 What are the main ways we can measure and recognise stress?
17 Explain what the technique of imagery involves and how it can help stress management.
18 What is the intervention technique of progressive relaxation?
19 What is the biofeedback technique?
20 Give examples of positive self-talk and explain why it is important.

B2: Biomechanics

Sports Biomechanics is a scientific discipline that examines the different types of motion we see in the sporting arena. Biomechanics is the integration of the laws of physics and physical performance which allows the coach to analyse the forces in action and the motion that results during sporting performance. Whether it is analysing a cricketer's bowling action, or investigating the effect of spin on the flight of a tennis ball, biomechanics can be a useful tool in developing efficient and effective techniques in performers. Biomechanics is also central to the design of sporting products. There is no doubt that the recent successes of the British Track Cycling team is down to the training, commitment and dedication of both performers and coaches. However, the equipment they use has been designed with the use of sophisticated equipment by a team of biomechanical engineers – with the sole aim of adapting the forces in operation during the race to optimal effect.

Furthermore, biomechanics can promote lifelong involvement in a balanced, active and healthy lifestyle since the development of appropriate technique can reduce the possibility of injury and tissue damage.

12 Investigating linear motion in physical activity

Learning outcomes

By the end of this chapter you should be able to:

- apply each of Newton's three laws of motion to a range of practical examples
- explain what is meant by the inertia of a body
- differentiate between vector and scalar quantities of linear motion
- define, calculate and give the correct units of measurements for the following quantities of linear motion:
  - distance
  - displacement
  - speed
  - velocity
  - acceleration
  - mass
  - momentum
- plot and interpret distance-time, speed-time and velocity-time graphs
- calculate the gradient of a graph and use to describe the motion of a performer
- critically evaluate performance with reference to linear motion in the following types of physical activity:
  - running
  - jumping
  - throwing
  - hitting/kicking
  - rotating.

CHAPTER INTRODUCTION

In order to fully understand human motion, a basic understanding of mechanics is required. Biomechanics is a discipline that deals with understanding the internal and external forces that act on the body during sports performance and the effects produced by these forces. An understanding of biomechanics is essential for the coach and athlete in order to analyse performance and develop appropriate technique, and can make the difference between winning and losing. This chapter particularly considers linear motion, which is perhaps the most basic of motions. According to the laws of physics, uninterrupted objects or performers in sport will continue to move in a straight line in a state of uniform motion indefinitely. This chapter helps to explain why this situation is rarely the case in sport, and how forces such as gravity and friction conspire to bring these same objects and performers to rest.

IN CONTEXT

Jonathan Edwards' world record triple jump at the 1995 World Championships still stands today. Few jumpers have come close since this because Edwards was a master technician and had a full understanding of the internal and external forces exerted upon his body during the jump. In 1995, everything from the run up, the hop phase, the step phase, the angle of the jump and the landing were all at an optimal level, resulting in a gold medal and world record jump for Edwards.

Linear motion

You will recall from your study at AS level that linear motion is

movement of a body or object that takes place in a straight line. It occurs when all parts of an object or body move the same distance, in the same direction at the same time.

A good example of a performer undergoing linear motion is a water skier, where all body parts and the skis are moving the same direction, in a straight (or curved) line, covering the same distance at the same speed. Sometimes linear motion can take place along a curved line such as a projectile in flight. This is known as curvilinear motion and an example of this would be a shuttlecock in flight.

Linear motion occurs when a force is applied through the centre of mass (COM) of the body. A force that passes through the centre of mass of a body causing linear motion is called a direct force.

To help us understand and explain linear motion further, we need to revisit Newton's laws of motion.

> **Key terms**
>
> **Linear motion** Movement of a body or object in a straight line, when all parts move the same distance, in the same direction at the same time.
> **Direct force** A force applied through the centre of mass of a body, resulting in linear motion.

Newton's laws of motion

Newton's laws of motion explain the relationship between forces acting on an object or performer and the resulting motion. You will recall from your study of AS that there are three laws of motion.

Newton's first law — the law of inertia

According to Newton's first law of motion:

> *Every body at rest, or moving with constant velocity in a straight line, will continue in that state unless compelled to change by an external force exerted upon it.*

This suggests that a body or an object has a tendency to resist any change in its state of motion — if a body is travelling in a straight line at constant speed, it will continue to do so unless acted upon by a force. Likewise, if an object is at rest, it will not move until a force large enough to overcome its inertia acts upon it. This reluctance of a body to change its state of motion is known as inertia.

> **Key term**
>
> **Inertia** The reluctance of a body to change its state of motion.

At the beginning of a 100m race, an athlete remains stationary in the set position in the blocks. She will remain stationary unless a force is exerted upon the blocks. The force exerted by the leg muscles must be great enough to overcome her inertia and, in doing so, the sprinter will move forward out of the blocks. The inertia of an object is directly proportional to its mass, so a body with a greater mass will need a larger force to overcome its inertia than a body with less mass. A heavier sprinter will therefore need to apply a larger muscular force to drive out of the blocks with the same acceleration.

Fig 12.1 A 100m sprinter in the blocks illustrates Newton's first law of motion

Once out of the blocks, the athlete will quickly accelerate as there has been a change in velocity (which is zero when the sprinter is in the blocks). According to Newton's first law, once in motion the sprinter will move at constant velocity for the remainder of the race. But this is rarely the case, why?

> **Activity 1**
>
> In pairs discuss the reasons why the example of a 100m sprinter may not entirely support Newton's first law of motion.

Newton's second law — the law of acceleration

Newton's second law of motion develops the relationship between force and acceleration.

> *The acceleration of a body is **proportional** to the force causing it, and the acceleration takes place in the **direction** in which that force acts.*

So Newton's second law explains that any change in velocity (acceleration) is dependent upon the force causing it and that this relationship is proportional. It also tells us that in order to generate a greater acceleration, a sports performer must produce a greater muscular force. So the sprinter that applies the greatest force to the starting blocks will be the one who leaves the blocks with the greatest acceleration.

Newton's second law is sometimes expressed as:

$$\mathbf{F} \nabla \mathbf{ma}$$

that is, Force = Mass × Acceleration

Fig 12.2 A sprinter accelerating out of the blocks illustrates Newton's second law of motion

Consider the following situation: a bullet fired from a gun has a large amount of force, as does a train pulling out from a station. The tremendous force of the train results from its large mass, whilst the force of the bullet arises from its great acceleration!

Using the example of a 100m sprinter once again, if the mass and acceleration of the sprinter are known, it is simple to calculate the force required to give that acceleration. For example:

$$\text{mass of athlete} = 74 \text{ kg}$$
$$\text{acceleration} = 4.6 \text{ m/s}^2$$
$$F = ma$$
$$F = 74 \text{ kg} \times 4.6 \text{ m/s}^2$$
$$F = 340 \text{ Newtons}$$

Remember, a Newton is the force that gives a mass of 1 kg an acceleration of 1 m/s^2.

Activity 2

Answer the following questions. Remember to show all your workings.

1 A rugby player successfully kicks a conversion.
   Calculate the force required to give the 400g rugby ball an acceleration of 250 m/s^2.
   Note: remember to convert the mass of the object into kilogrammes first!

2 A 60Kg netball player applies a force of 300N. Calculate her acceleration.

EXAMINER'S TIP

If you are required to perform a calculation in your examination, make sure you show each stage of your workings and ensure you give the correct units of measurement! No units = no marks!

IN CONTEXT

After about five seconds of a 100m sprint we would expect the sprinter to have reached maximum velocity, and (according to Newton's first law) to remain at this constant velocity. So why does the athlete start to slow down? The explanation is relatively simple and arises from both physiological and biochemical effects:

● the muscle stores of ATP and PC which provide the energy for muscular contraction become depleted after 8–10 seconds. This causes the athlete to fatigue somewhat and slow down

● the effects of air resistance (studies have shown that somewhere between 13 per cent and 15 per cent of a sprinter's energy expenditure is used to overcome air resistance).

This slowing down of the athlete represents a change in velocity and therefore is known as deceleration. In fact, most sprinters will start to slow down after 80–90m and the winner will often be the person who takes longer to slow down!

Newton's third law – the law of reaction

Newton's third law of motion states that:

*When one object exerts a force on a second object, there is a force **equal** in magnitude but **opposite** in direction exerted by the second object on the first.*

More simply, to every action there is an equal and opposite reaction.

Our sprinter on the blocks experiences a force propelling her forward. From Newton's third law we can deduce that, as the athlete applies a force backwards and downwards onto the blocks, the blocks apply an equal and opposite force that drives the athlete upwards and forwards out of the blocks.

Reaction forces can easily be seen in all areas of sport:

● A footballer kicking a ball exerts a force upon it in order to set it in motion (N1). According to Newton's third law (N3), the ball will exert an equal and opposite force onto the kicking foot and, of course, it does because we can feel the ball on the foot as we strike it. The ball accelerates away from the player as the mass of the footballer is much greater than the mass of the football.

● In shooting events the performer receives a 'kick back' from the rifle. This recoil of the gun is in fact the reaction force, which is of equal magnitude but in opposite direction to the force causing the acceleration of the rounds.

● The high jumper exerts a force upon the ground in order to gain height. This is because the ground exerts an upward force of equal magnitude upon her. The high jumper accelerates upwards as the mass of the earth is much greater than the mass of the high jumper.

For the high jumper to gain upward acceleration the reaction force must be greater than the weight force of the athlete.

Reaction force ∇ Weight force +
Muscular force applied by the high jumper

Fig 12.3 A sprinter receives an equal and opposite force from the blocks onto their feet propelling them out of the blocks

Scalar quantities are only described in terms of their size or magnitude, usually by a numerical value. For example a long jumper may jump a distance of 5 metres.

Vector quantities are described in terms of both magnitude and direction. Using the example of a long jumper once again, if describing the jump as a vector then we would need to say that the jump of 5 metres was in a south-easterly direction.

It is the direction of a quantity that goes some way in explaining the differences between the terms speed and velocity, distance and displacement and mass and weight, discussed further in the next section.

Key terms

Vector quantity Quantities of linear motion described in terms of size and direction.
Scalar quantity Quantities of linear motion described in terms of size alone.

Activity 3

Use all three of Newton's laws to explain the motion that takes place in each of the following sporting situations:

● High jump
● 100m swim
● Taking a penalty in football
● Serving in tennis.

Describing linear motion
Vector and scalar quantities

The quantities that are used in biomechanics to describe the motion of an object are divided into two groups: **vector** and **scalar**.

Activity 4

1 In small groups determine whether the following quantities of linear motion are vector or scalar quantities:

● Mass
● Speed
● Momentum
● Distance
● Force

● Acceleration
● Displacement
● Velocity
● Weight

2 In small groups determine whether the following units of linear motion are vector or scalar quantities:

● 5 metres
● 30 miles/hour, East
● 65 miles/hour

● 5 metres/second
● 80kg, downwards
● 12km, NNE

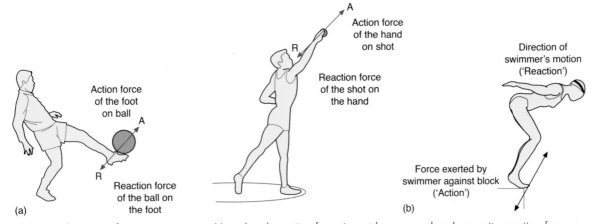

Fig 12.4 Action and reaction forces in operation. Note that the action force is met by an equal and opposite reaction force.

Quantities of linear motion

For your examination you will be required to demonstrate knowledge and understanding of definitions, equations, calculations and units of measurement for the following quantities of linear motion:

- mass
- distance
- displacement
- speed
- velocity
- acceleration
- momentum.

Distance and displacement

Distance is the total length of the path an object covers during its motion from a starting position to the finishing position. It is a scalar quantity and therefore non-directional. A 100m swimmer, for example, covers a distance of 100m during the swim.

Displacement is a vector quantity and considers how far out of place an object is from its starting position. Direction is important here and so the shortest possible route (as the crow flies) from the starting point to the finishing point is used to measure displacement. Taking the example of a 100m swimmer again, displacement will be zero as the swimmer ends up in exactly the same position as the starting point.

Key terms

Distance The total length of the path an object covers during its motion from a starting position to the finishing position; measured in metres (m).
Displacement The shortest distance between the starting and finishing position in a stated direction; measured in metres (m).

Speed and velocity

Just as the terms distance and displacement are different, so to are speed and velocity. Within the sporting arena, we are always concerned with how fast a body or an object is travelling, but should we refer to the speed of an object or its velocity? Speed is a **scalar quantity** and as such no allowances have been made for direction. Information such as a Formula One car travelling at 225 miles/hour refers to speed as no reference to direction is made.

Speed essentially is the rate at which an object covers a specific distance and is calculated using the following equation:

$$\text{Speed} = \frac{\text{distance travelled}}{\text{time taken}}$$

When considering linear motion, biomechanists normally require a direction of travel, indicated by a vector – this is

velocity and it has both size and direction. Velocity therefore is the rate at which a body or object changes its position (the rate of change of displacement). The Formula One car travelling at 225miles/hour in an easterly direction now has velocity as a reference to direction has now been made.

The following equation can be used to calculate velocity:

$$\text{Velocity} = \frac{\text{displacement}}{\text{time taken}}$$

Both speed and velocity quantities are usually measured in metres travelled per second (m/s).

Activity 5

1 Christine Ohuruogu ran 49.61 seconds when she became the World champion for the 400m at the 2007 Osaka World Championships.
   (i) Calculate Christine's average speed during the race
   (ii) Calculate Christine's average velocity during the race.
2 Rebecca Romero was part of the winning Gold medal team for the 3,000m team pursuit at the 2008 World Track Cycling Championships in Manchester. She covered the 3,000m in a time of 3 minutes 25.725 seconds.
   (a) Calculate Rebecca's average speed during the race
   (b) Calculate Rebecca's average velocity during the race.

Activity 6

You will need:

- a compass
- scaled map of your area.

Research the route of a local road race such as a 10k run or a half-marathon in your area. Using a map of the route, show how you could illustrate the displacement that occurs of the runner once he or she completes the run. Describe in terms of magnitude and size the displacement that has taken place. If you are unable to find a route in your local area, then research the route of the London Marathon or the Great North Run.

Key terms

Speed A body's movement per unit of time with no consideration for direction. Measured in metres/second (ms^{-1}).
Velocity The rate of change of displacement. The speed of a body in a given direction. Measured in metres per second (ms^{-1}).

Acceleration and deceleration

In many sporting situations, such as 100m sprint, acceleration should also be considered in order to analyse an athlete's successful performance. Acceleration represents the rate of change of velocity; as such it is a vector quantity, possessing both magnitude and direction.

$$\text{Acceleration (m/s}^2\text{)} = \frac{\text{change in velocity}}{\text{time}}$$

$$\text{or } \frac{v-u}{t}$$

where v = final velocity (m/s)

u = initial velocity (m/s)

t = time (s)

Activity 7

1 A sprinter has an acceleration of 5m/s² during the first 2 seconds of a race. What velocity does she reach?
2 A Formula One car brakes as it approaches a bend in the circuit. Its velocity reduces from 60m/s to 20m/s. What is its acceleration? (Remember that a minus sign denotes negative acceleration; i.e., deceleration.)

Key terms

Acceleration The rate of change (increase) in velocity; measured in metres per second squared (ms⁻²).
Deceleration The rate of change (decrease) in velocity; measured in metres per second squared (ms-²).

Mass and weight

People often confuse the terms **mass** and **weight**. Mass is the amount of matter a body possesses. For example, a basketball is composed of more matter than a tennis ball and, therefore, has a greater mass. Weight is the force a given mass feels due to the gravitational pull of the earth.

On earth the mass of a basketball is approximately 0.6 kg.

The weight of the basketball can be calculated using Newton's second law of motion:

$$F = ma$$

where: F = weight force

m = mass of basketball = 0.6kg

a = the acceleration due to gravity = approximately 10m/s²

weight of basketball = 0.6 kg × 10m/s²

= 6 Newtons

The mass of an object always remains the same no matter where it is placed. However, the weight of that same object can differ depending upon changes in gravity. The basketball mentioned above will have the same mass of 0.6kg on earth and on the moon but its weight will differ as the gravitational pull of the moon is approximately one-sixth that of the earth. The weight of the basketball on the moon will therefore be one-sixth of the weight it is on earth, i.e., 1 Newton (1 N).

Weight is a vector quantity. It has a direction as well as magnitude. In fact, weight always acts downwards from the centre of mass of an object or body. Mass, on the other hand, only has magnitude so is a scalar quantity.

Activity 8

Using bathroom scales, calculate your weight force. Show your workings.

EXAMINER'S TIP

Weight is measured in Newtons. One Newton is the force required to give a 1kg mass an acceleration of 1ms⁻¹.

Key terms

Mass The amount of matter a body possesses; measured in kilogrammes (kg).
Weight The action of gravity on the mass of a body. Weight = Mass × Gravity. Measured in Newtons (N). An athlete with a mass of 70kg will produce a weight force of 700 Newtons (70kg × 10ms⁻²).

Inertia

Inertia is the reluctance of a body to change its state of motion. All objects resist changes in their state of motion. Quite simply, objects will continue to keep on doing what they are doing until some kind of force is applied. The tendency to resist changes in motion varies with an object's mass; the more mass an object has, the greater its inertia. A shot has more mass than a volleyball and is therefore more difficult to change its state of motion — it has a larger quantity of inertia.

Momentum

Momentum is the amount of motion possessed by a moving body. It is the product of mass and velocity:

$$\text{Momentum (kgm/s)} = \text{mass (kg)} \times \text{velocity (m/s)}$$

Thus, a sprinter with a mass of 75 kg and a velocity of 10 m/s has a momentum of 750 kg m/s.

From the above equation it can be seen that a body's momentum can be changed by altering either its mass or velocity. However, in sporting activity the mass of a body or object generally remains constant, so any change in momentum must be due to a change in velocity. (You should recall that a change in velocity is synonymous with the terms acceleration for a positive change or deceleration for a negative one.)

Key term

Momentum The amount of motion a body possesses. It is the product of mass and velocity and measured in $kgms^{-1}$.

Consider the following situation:

As the mass of a long jumper remains constant, any change in their momentum must result from a change in velocity. From Newton's first law of motion, once in the air, the velocity (and mass) of the jumper remains constant; in this instance, momentum is said to be conserved. The long jumper may therefore need to alter their approach run to optimise their velocity and increase their momentum at take off.

This extends Newton's first law of motion and is called the law of conservation of momentum:

In any system of bodies that exert forces on each other, the total momentum in any direction remains constant unless some external force acts on the system in that direction.

EXAMINER'S TIP

The law of conservation of momentum is closely related to Newton's first law of motion.

Fig.12.5 The law of conservation of momentum can be seen in the long jump

Activity 9

1 At what velocity must a 60 kg scrum half run in order to have the same momentum as a 90 kg centre running at 10m/s? Show your workings.

2 A tennis ball has a mass of 67 g and a momentum of 2kgm/s. At what velocity is it travelling? (You will need to convert the mass of the ball into kilogrammes!)

Graphs of linear motion

Graphs of motion can be used to represent the motion of a body which is moving in a straight line.

Table 12.1 A distance-time graph describing the motion of a rugby ball during a penalty kick

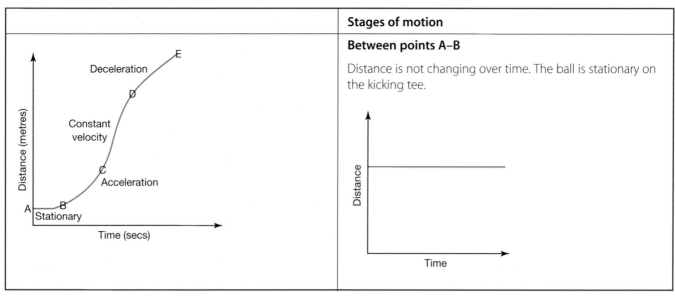

	Stages of motion
	Between points A–B
	Distance is not changing over time. The ball is stationary on the kicking tee.

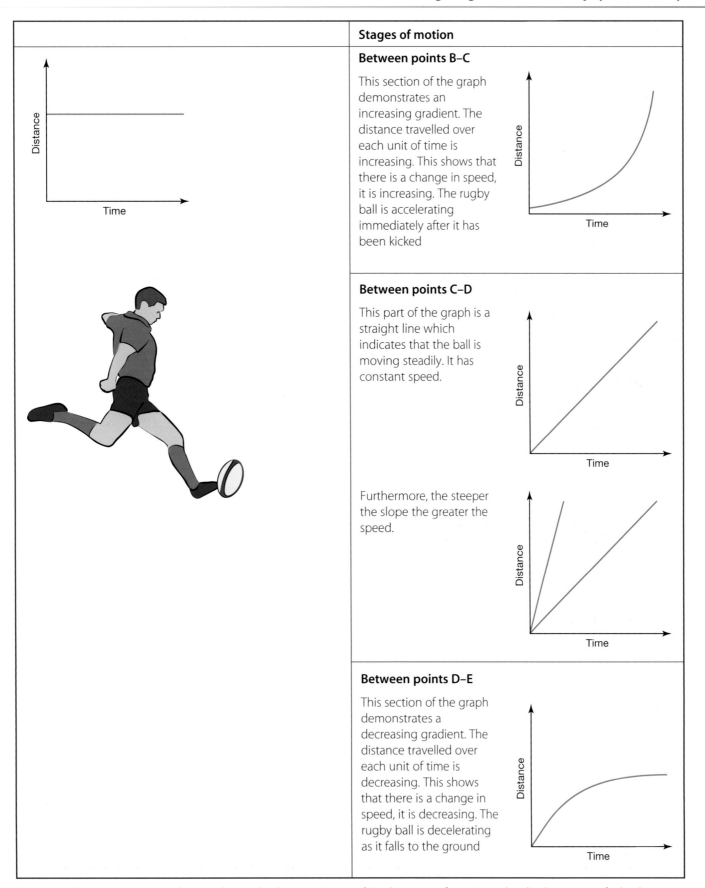

	Stages of motion
	Between points B–C
	This section of the graph demonstrates an increasing gradient. The distance travelled over each unit of time is increasing. This shows that there is a change in speed, it is increasing. The rugby ball is accelerating immediately after it has been kicked
	Between points C–D
	This part of the graph is a straight line which indicates that the ball is moving steadily. It has constant speed.
	Furthermore, the steeper the slope the greater the speed.
	Between points D–E
	This section of the graph demonstrates a decreasing gradient. The distance travelled over each unit of time is decreasing. This shows that there is a change in speed, it is decreasing. The rugby ball is decelerating as it falls to the ground

Note: Displacement-time graphs can show a body's position **and** its direction of motion – the displacement of a body can decrease as well as increase.

Activity 10

A cyclist travels due south when completing the London-Brighton bike ride. The distance he travels is recorded at hourly intervals and shown in Table 12.2.

Table 12.2 Cycling from London to Brighton

Time (hours)		Distance (km)
0	departs London	0
1		22
2		44
3		66
4	arrives Brighton	84

Draw a distance-time graph to represent the cyclist's journey.

1 What is the cyclist's average velocity during the entire journey?
2 From the graph, determine the cyclist's average velocity during the first 3 hours of the journey.
3 From the graph, determine the cyclist's average velocity during the final hour of the journey.
4 What does this tell you about the state of motion of the cyclist in the final hour?

Distance–time graphs

Distance-time graphs illustrate the distance travelled by an object or body over a period of time. It represents the speed of a body at a particular instant. The distance travelled by an object never decreases.

Speed–time graph

Speed-time graphs can be used to show the speed, rate of acceleration and distance travelled by a body. The area under a speed-time graph is equal to the distance travelled by a body.

Table 12.3 Speed-time graphs

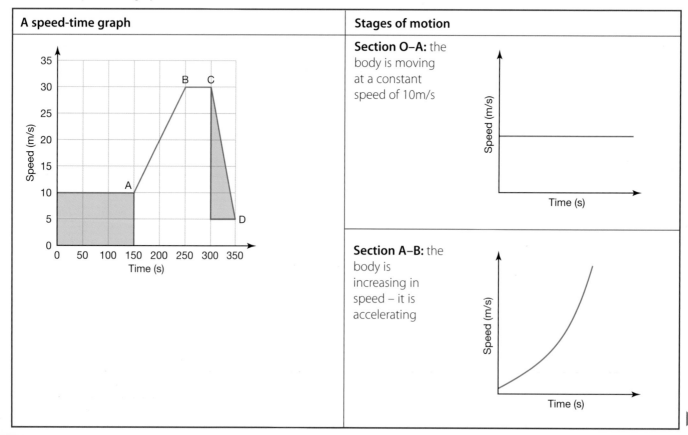

A speed-time graph	Stages of motion
	Section O–A: the body is moving at a constant speed of 10m/s
	Section A–B: the body is increasing in speed – it is accelerating

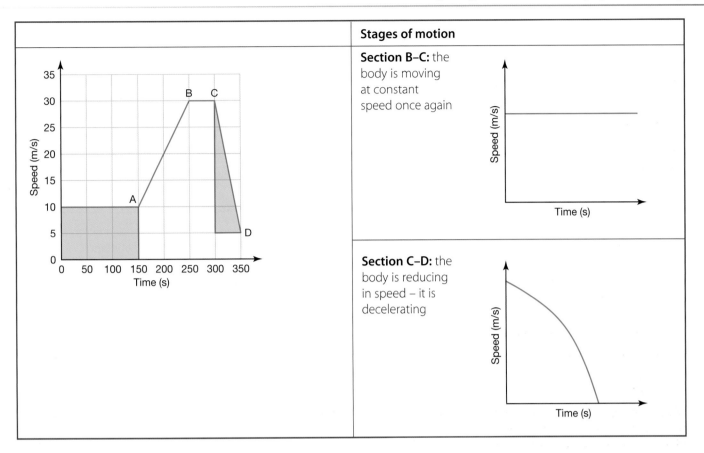

	Stages of motion
	Section B–C: the body is moving at constant speed once again
	Section C–D: the body is reducing in speed – it is decelerating

Velocity–time graphs

The gradient of a velocity-time graph can tell us the rate at which the velocity of an object or body is changing. The gradient can therefore indicate if the body is accelerating, decelerating or indeed moving at constant velocity. Furthermore it is possible to show changes in direction on velocity-time graphs.

Table 12.4 Velocity-time graphs

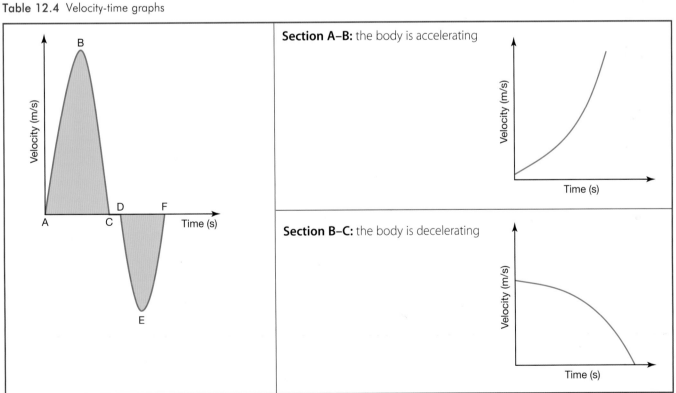

	Section A–B: the body is accelerating
	Section B–C: the body is decelerating

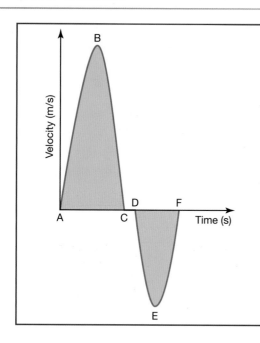

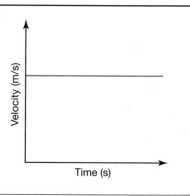

Section C–D: the body is moving at constant velocity

Section D-E: the body has changed direction and accelerated through point E and decelerated until the body comes to rest at point F.

Note: As velocity and acceleration are vector quantities, they are directional. A curve or line below the *x*-axis on a velocity-time graph represents a change in direction.

EXAMINER'S TIPS

The gradient of a straight line can be calculated using the following method:

$$\text{Gradient} = \frac{\text{Change in } y}{\text{Change in } X}$$

Example 1:

$$\frac{\text{Change in } y}{\text{Change in } x} = \frac{3}{3} \qquad \text{Gradient} = 1$$

Example 2:

$$\frac{\text{Change in } y}{\text{Change in } x} = \frac{3}{5} \qquad \text{Gradient} = 0.6$$

Example 3:

$$\frac{\text{Change in } y}{\text{Change in } x} = \frac{-4}{2} \qquad \text{Gradient} = -2$$

The gradient of a distance-time graph gives speed
The gradient of a displacement-time graph gives velocity

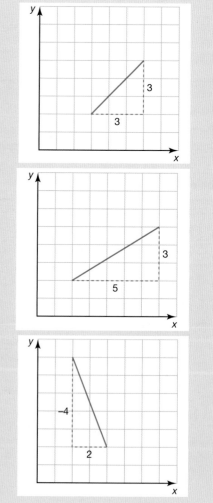

Activity 11

You will need:

- 10 cones (A–J)
- 10 stopwatches
- 10 'stewards'
- 1 runner.

Measure a straight line 100m long, and position each cone along this line at 10m intervals, with the first cone (Cone A) being set 10m from the starting-line. Beside each cone should stand a 'steward' who has his or her own stopwatch.

The runner runs 100m as fast as possible. Watches are stopped as the athlete passes each cone in turn.

Record results in Table 12.5.

Table 12.5 Running 100m

Position	Distance (m)	Time (s)	Time for section (s)	Motion	Average speed (ms^{-1})	Acceleration (ms^{-2})
O	0	0	0	Stationary	0	
A	10					
B	20					
C	30					
D	40					
E	50					
F	60					
G	70					
H	80					
I	90					
J	100					

1 Calculate the time taken for each section and record the results in Table 12.5.
2 Describe the motion of the athlete for each section.
3 Work out the average speed for each section and plot a graph of velocity against time.
   (Velocity = speed; displacement = distance)
4 Using your results for average speed, calculate the acceleration over each 10m section. Remember, if the runner is slowing down you will get a negative value.
5 From the graph, identify the runner's velocity after 2 seconds of the sprint.
6 Use your graph to identify the state of motion throughout the race.
7 Use your graph to calculate the runner's acceleration at 2 seconds.
8 Given that the mass of the runner is (enter the mass of the runner) _____ , calculate the force exerted by the runner during the first 2 seconds of the sprint.
9 Use the data to plot a distance/time graph for the 100m sprint.
   (Distance on the y axis (vertical) and time along the x axis (horizontal).)
10 From the shape of the graph, identify and explain the state of motion during:
   (i) the first 20m section
   (ii) the remainder of the sprint (20-80m).
11 Use the graph to calculate the velocity of the subject at 2 seconds.

Exam-style Questions

1 Table 12.6 shows the speed of a long jumper during his run up before take-off.

Table 12.6 A long jumper during the run up before take-off

Time (secs)	Speed (m/s)
0	0
1	3.0
2	5.5
3	7.5
4	9.0
5	10.0
6	10.0

(i) Plot a graph of speed against time for the long jumper during his run up and calculate the average acceleration of the long jumper during the first 2 seconds of the run. Show all your workings **(4 marks)**

(ii) Sketch a free body diagram showing all the forces acting on the long jumper between 5 and 6 seconds of the run up. Use Newton's Laws of Motion to explain the shape of the curve during this time. **(5 marks)**

CHALLENGE YOURSELF

Draw a velocity-time graph showing the following changes in motion between points:

O–A – the body moves from rest at constant acceleration

B–C – velocity is increasing but acceleration is decreasing

C–D – the body is moving at constant velocity

D–E – the body is decelerating at a constant rate and comes to rest

E–F – the body remains stationary

F–G – the body moves in the opposite direction with constant acceleration

G–H – the body moves at constant velocity

H–I – the body decelerates at a constant rate and eventually comes to rest.

What you need to know

* Inertia is the reluctance of a body to change its state of motion.

* Mass is a measure of an object's inertia. The greater the mass of an object, the more it resists changes in its motion, that is, it has greater inertia.

* The relationship between force, mass and acceleration is expressed as F=ma. This is a form of Newton's second law of motion.

* One Newton (1 N) is the force required to give a 1kg mass an acceleration of 1m/s².

* A scalar quantity has magnitude only; a vector quantity has both magnitude and direction.

* Distance and speed are both scalar quantities; displacement and velocity are vector quantities.

* Displacement is the distance travelled in a particular direction.

* Velocity is the speed in a particular direction.

$$\text{Velocity} = \frac{\text{displacement}}{\text{time}}$$

* Acceleration is the rate of change of velocity; it is a vector quantity.

* The weight of an object is the product of its mass and the pull of gravity on it, i.e.,

Weight = mass × gravity

✱ Momentum is the amount of motion possessed by a moving body.

✱ Momentum = mass (kg) × Velocity (ms^{-1}).

✱ The law of conservation of momentum is related to Newton's first law of motion.

✱ Graphs of motion can be used to represent the motion of a body which is moving in a straight line – particularly distance-time graphs and velocity-time graphs.

✱ The gradient of a graph is measured using the following equation

$$\frac{\triangle y}{\triangle x}$$

Review Questions

1 A weight-lifter exerts an upward force of 2000N on a bar bell of 170 kg. What is the vertical acceleration?

2 Use your understanding of Newton's Laws to explain how a long jumper is able to take off.

3 Explain how distance and displacement differ at the end of a 1500m run.

4 A racing car may have an average speed of 150mph over the course of a lap, but its average velocity over one lap will always be zero. Explain why.

5 What force is required to give a runner with a mass of 50Kg an acceleration of 4m/s²?

6 Define the term momentum and explain why a single sculls boat has a different momentum to that of a double sculls boat travelling at the same velocity.

7 State Newton's second law of motion and explain how its principles affect the outgoing velocity of the tennis ball following a forehand drive.

8 Sketch a distance-time graph to represent the motion of a swimmer sprinting over a distance of 100m.

9 Draw a stick man diagram of a 100m sprinter in the blocks at the moment the gun fires. On your diagram show the action and reaction forces.

CHAPTER 13

Investigating force in sport and physical activity

Learning outcomes

By the end of this chapter you should be able to:

- define and identify the effects of force
- carry out calculations of force using appropriate units of measurement
- explain the concepts of balanced and unbalanced forces giving examples from sport and physical activity
- examine the relationship between force and Newton's laws of motion and the influence of this relationship on the motion of a performer and projectile
- demonstrate your knowledge of vertical forces (weight and reaction) and horizontal forces (friction and air resistance)
- explain the relationship between the relative size of force (both vertical and horizontal) and the magnitude of the resulting motion of a body
- discuss the role of friction in sporting activity with particular reference to footwear and different types of sports surfaces
- draw and interpret free body diagrams; a snap shot showing all vertical and horizontal forces acting on a performer or object during the performance of a skill or action
- define and identify the factors affecting impulse
- explain the relationship between impulse and increasing or decreasing momentum
- sketch and interpret impulse (force-time) graphs during a vertical jump and when sprinting.
- critically evaluate performance with reference to linear motion in the following types of physical activity:
  - running
  - jumping
  - throwing
  - hitting/kicking
  - rotating.

CHAPTER INTRODUCTION

Without force one can argue that there would be no sport. In fact, it is the successful adaptation of force when participating in physical activity that can determine the level of performance. Consider Rebecca Adlington's world record in the 800m freestyle event at the 2008 Beijing Olympic Games. Everything from her dive into the pool, her actual swimming action right through to the specifics of her swimming costume, were all designed to manipulate force to enhance her performance. Central to this successful performance was a complete understanding of all the internal and external forces exerted upon her body.

Forces can either be generated **internally** to the body via muscular contractions or **externally** through the action of gravity, friction and the forces of air and water. Without such forces, movement would not be possible, but optimal performance can only take place when all forces are understood and adapted to the same aim.

Force

Force is the 'push' or 'pull' exerted upon an object or body that can cause the state of motion of a body to change. Within the sporting arena forces can be applied to cause a:

- stationary body to move
- moving body to speed up (accelerate)
- moving body to slow down (decelerate)
- moving body to change direction
- body to change shape.

Activity 1

In pairs, discuss a number of situations from a range of sporting activities where forces can cause a:

- stationary body to move
- moving body to speed up (accelerate)
- moving body to slow down (decelerate)
- moving body to change direction
- body to change shape.

In Chapter 12 you will recall that Newton's second law of motion could be explained using the following equation:

$$\text{Force} = \text{mass} \times \text{acceleration}$$

Therefore, changing the state of motion of an object or body is inextricably linked to force (remember that a change in the velocity of a body constitutes an acceleration or deceleration!)

> ### Key term
>
> **Force** A push or pull exerted on to a body that tends to change its state of motion. Force is measured in Newtons (N).

Balanced and unbalanced forces in determining 'net force'

Force is a **vector quantity** – it has both magnitude and direction. This means that when describing a force that has been applied to a body in sport, an arrow can be used that shows the following information:

- point of application of the force (shown by the origin of the arrow)
- direction of the force (shown by an arrowhead)
- size of the force (shown by the length of the arrow).

Consider Figure 13.1, which depicts the force applied to a hockey ball when performing a push pass.

Fig 13.1 The force that is applied to a hockey ball when performing a push pass can be illustrated by an arrow

We have so far discovered that forces rarely act alone. In fact, when playing sport several forces will act, often in different directions. Where two or more forces act, the resultant force (or 'net force') can be found by adding together all the forces operating. Take a moment to study Figure 13.2.

> ### EXAMINER'S TIP
>
> Forces in the same direction combine by addition whereas forces in the opposite direction combine by subtraction.

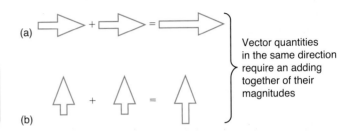

Fig 13.2 Calculating **net force** when two or more forces are acting

> ### Key term
>
> **Net force** Also known as the resultant force, a net force is the final force acting on a body once all the other forces acting have been considered.

Forces typically occur in pairs and can either be balanced or unbalanced.

Balanced forces

As this name suggests balanced forces are equal in size but opposite in direction and therefore do not cause a change in the state of motion.

As the forces are equal but in opposite directions, the two forces cancel each other out and the resulting force or net force is zero. Therefore there is no change in motion. Consider the gymnast performing a handstand in Figure 13.3. Her weight force acting downwards is matched by an upwards reaction force from the floor (from Newton's law of motion). As the length of the arrows are equal there is no change in motion and the gymnast remains balanced.

Other examples where forces cancel each other out to maintain a stationary position might include a tug of war or a rugby scrum, where opposing teams are of equal strength and generate equal force in the opposing directions, resulting in no movement.

This idea of balanced forces does not only affect stationary bodies, however, as zero net force can also act when a body is moving at constant velocity. For example, someone swimming at constant velocity will have zero net force acting as their propulsive force (produced by the muscles) and resistive force (fluid friction or drag of the water) are equal and opposite, cancelling each other out.

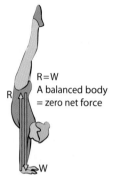

R=W
A balanced body
= zero net force

Fig 13.3 Balanced forces operate when a gymnast performs a handstand resulting in zero net force

Unbalanced forces

Unbalanced forces occur where two or more forces act in opposite directions but they are not equal. In this instance the net force operating is equal to the difference between the two forces and is exerted in the direction of the larger force. Consider the situation of a school rugby team scrummaging against the England team's pack. The force produced by the England pack is likely to be significantly larger than that produced by the pack comprised of schoolboys and therefore a net force is created (equal to that produced by the England team minus that produced by the school teams), causing the school's pack to be driven backwards.

Fig 13.4 A net force might occur in rugby

Parallelogram of forces

Where two forces are acting on a body at the same point but in a different direction, the resultant force can be determined by constructing a **parallelogram** of forces, with the resultant force lying along the diagonal of the parallelogram. Figure 13.5 shows the resultant force of a rugby player travelling at 8 m/s when tackled by an opposition player who imparts a velocity of 6 m/s to the ball carrier. By constructing a parallelogram of forces the resultant velocity can be calculated.

Furthermore, as these two forces are perpendicular to each other a value of the resultant can be calculated using Pythagoras' theorem:

$$\text{Resultant force} = \sqrt{8^2 + 6^2}$$
$$= 10\text{m/s}$$

You will recall from Chapter 12 that all force is measured in **Newtons** where one Newton represents the force required to give a 1 kg mass an acceleration of 1 metre per second squared. However, in Figure 13.5, we have been able to calculate the resultant velocity of the ball carrier following the tackle.

Activity 2

For each of the situations below state whether a balanced or unbalanced force exists:

- a gymnast performing a handstand
- a dancer performing an arabesque
- a high jumper driving upwards over a bar
- a basketball player performing a jump shot
- holding a barbell steady when performing a bicep curl.

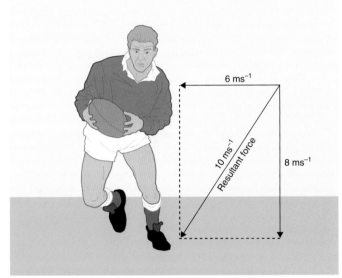

Fig 13.5 The parallelogram of forces. The resultant of two vectors is calculated via the parallelogram of forces

---

EXAMINER'S TIP

Where two forces act at right angles to each other, Pythagoras' theorem can be used to calculate the magnitude of the resultant force.

Types of force

In order to improve performance in sport it may be necessary to develop the technique of the performer. In doing so, the forces acting on and applied by the athlete will alter and, hopefully, enhance the final performance.

For your examination you are required to apply the forces in Table 13.1 to the sporting actions of running, jumping, throwing, hitting, kicking and rotating.

Table 13.1 Forces

VERTICAL FORCES	HORIZONTAL FORCES
• Weight • Normal reaction (buoyancy/up-thrust in water; lift for projectiles)	• Friction (thrust in water) • Air resistance (drag in water)

Most sporting activity will therefore involve a combination of both vertical and horizontal forces.

Vertical forces
Weight force

Weight is a force caused by the gravitational attraction of the earth on the mass of a body or object.

From Newton's second law of motion:

$$\text{Weight force} = \text{Mass of a body} \times \text{Acceleration due to gravity } (10\text{ms}^{-2})$$

As weight is a force, and therefore a vector quantity, it is characterised by a magnitude (proportional to mass), a direction (always downward) and a point of application (always from the centre of mass of an object).

Key term

Weight A vector quantity that is the product of mass and the acceleration of the gravitational pull of the earth. Weight = mass × gravity and is therefore measured in Newtons (N).

Reaction force

Resulting from Newton's third law of motion, reaction or normal reaction forces occur whenever two bodies are in contact with one another. Furthermore, the reaction force acts perpendicular to the surfaces in contact.

According to Newton's third law of motion if weight is the only force acting on an object the normal reaction force will be equal in magnitude but opposite in direction to the weight force, that is:

$$\text{Reaction force} = \text{weight force}$$

Where the reaction force and weight force are equal, there will be no vertical movement of a performer or object up or down.

In many sporting activities, however, the reaction force may be greater than the weight force. This is because of the additional muscular force applied by a performer to a surface, so that:

$$\text{Reaction force} = \text{weight force} + \text{internal muscular force}$$

In this instance, a performer will move vertically upwards (for example, when driving upwards to block in volleyball).

> **Key term**
>
> **Reaction force** A force that acts whenever two bodies come in to contact with one another. It is the equal and opposite force that is exerted by one body on another in response to a force exerted by the first body to the second (from Newton's third law of motion).

Horizontal forces

Frictional force

Friction is a force that acts on the interface of surfaces which are in contact, and acts in the *opposite direction to the direction of motion*. The magnitude or size of the frictional force will determine the relative ease or difficulty of movement for the objects in contact.

The *coefficient of friction* indicates the ease of movement and is determined by the amount of molecular interaction between the two surfaces in contact. For example:

- The coefficient of friction between a rugby boot and grass will be much larger than that between an ice skater's skate and an icy surface and, therefore, provides a better grip.
- In order to increase the coefficient of friction, a rugby player might remove mud and grass from his boots before packing down for a scrum.
- The volleyball court is regularly swept to remove perspiration to enable a firmer grip between shoe and court.

The coefficient may also be increased by maximising the force that presses the surfaces together:

- Mountain-bikers often sit back over the driving wheel when riding up a muddy slope in order to gain a better grip of the tyre on the surface.

Friction forces can further be increased by increasing the surface area in contact with another:

- An athlete wears spikes when running on a tartan track.
- A racket player may wear a glove in order to maintain a firm grip.

> **Key term**
>
> **Friction** A force which opposes the relative motion of two bodies in contact with one another

Air resistance

Air resistance is friction between an object and the air it is moving through. It is a form of fluid friction and opposes the motion of a body.

Air resistance is prevalent in most sporting activity, although its effects on performance can vary greatly and are dependent upon the:

- **speed of the moving body** – the faster a body is moving the greater the air resistance encountered
- **frontal cross-sectional area of the moving body** – the larger the frontal cross-sectional area of the body the greater the air resistance experienced
- **surface characteristics of the moving body** – the rougher the surfaces moving through the air, the greater the air resistance experienced.

> **Key term**
>
> **Air resistance** A form of fluid friction which acts in the opposite direction to the motion of a body travelling through the air.

> ## Activity 3
>
> Consider the examples below. How might air-resistance affect each?
>
> - the long jump
> - projectiles such as balls, shuttlecocks and javelins
> - cyclists
> - sprinters.

> ## IN CONTEXT
>
> The effect of fluid resistance is most clearly illustrated by the forces that act upon the swimmer, illustrated in Figure 13.6.
>
>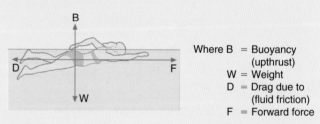
>
> Where B = Buoyancy (upthrust)
> W = Weight
> D = Drag due to (fluid friction)
> F = Forward force
>
> Fig 13.6 The forces acting upon a swimmer who is swimming

The drag force shown in Figure 13.6, is dependent upon four main factors:

1 **The forward cross-section of the swimmer**: to reduce drag, the swimmer should adopt as streamlined a position as possible by maintaining a flat position close to the surface, without dropping the feet.
2 **The surface area in contact with the water.** This concerns the swimmer's body shape – elite swimmers tend to be very lean (verging on ectomorphic), which reduces the friction derived from body contact.
3 **Surface effects.** Swimmers attempt to minimise turbulent flow by wearing shiny swimsuits, wearing swimming hats and 'shaving down' – the practice of removing body hair. These practices allow the water to flow past the body more smoothly and limit the drag force.
4 **Speed of the swimmer.** The relationship between speed and drag is positive – the faster you swim, the greater the drag. As in competitive swimming, the aim is to swim as fast as possible. There is little swimmers can do to prevent drag completely, but adopting an efficient technique that minimise drag while enabling fast swimming should be a priority for all swimmers and coaches.

Free body diagrams

To illustrate the forces acting on a body, a free body diagram can be drawn (see next page). Not only does this illustrate the nature or type of force acting but also the direction (by the arrowhead), the size of the force (by the length of the arrow) and the point at which the force is applied (by the origin of the arrow).

Table 13.2

Force acting	Direction of force
Weight	Always downwards
Normal reaction	Perpendicular to the surface
Friction	In the opposite direction to the direction of motion
Air resistance/drag	In the opposite direction to the direction of motion

EXAMINER'S TIPS

Key points to remember when constructing free-body diagrams:

- Always draw your direction of motion arrow first!
- Make sure your weight arrow originates from the centre of mass of the body

- Make sure your reaction force originates from the point of contact between two surfaces. Note: there may be more than one reaction force acting!
- If there is uniform vertical motion and there is more than one reaction force acting, then the combined length of the reaction force arrows will be equal to the length of the weight arrow
- For upward acceleration, the reaction arrow will be longer than the weight arrow
- For downward acceleration, the reaction arrow will be shorter than the weight arrow
- For forward acceleration, the friction arrow (or thrust) will be longer than the air resistance arrow
- For deceleration, the friction arrow will be shorter than the air resistance arrow.
- Where the friction arrow is equal to the air resistance arrow we can assume zero net force acting and the body is moving at constant velocity.

EXAMINER'S TIPS

There are three key points to remember when describing a force:

1 The point of application (shown by the origin of the arrow)
2 The direction of the force (shown by an arrowhead)
3 The magnitude or size of the force (represented by the length of the arrow).

EXAMINER'S TIP

When drawing your arrows representing force, remember to clearly show the origin of the force, it cannot originate in mid-air; it must be in contact with the object or body to which the force is applied.

Activity 4

Sketch free body diagrams of the sporting situations given below making sure you show all the forces acting on the performer:

- a person standing still
- a runner accelerating
- a high jumper at the point of take off
- a cyclist decelerating.

Table 13.3 Demonstrating how free body diagrams can be used to describe the motion that takes place during the performance of a range of sporting activities

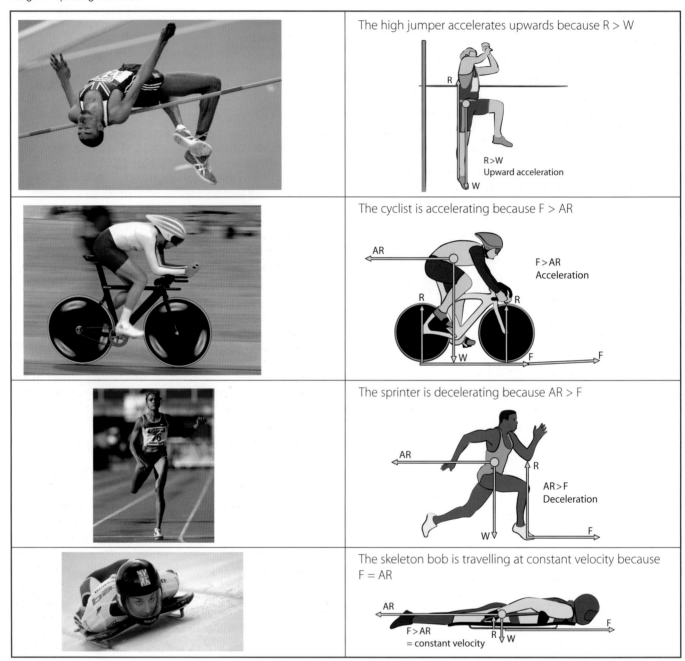

The high jumper accelerates upwards because R > W

R>W
Upward acceleration

The cyclist is accelerating because F > AR

F>AR
Acceleration

The sprinter is decelerating because AR > F

AR>F
Deceleration

The skeleton bob is travelling at constant velocity because F = AR

F>AR
= constant velocity

Key term

Free body diagram A simplified, yet clearly labelled sketch that shows all the forces acting on a body at a particular moment in time.

Exam-style Questions

A rugby player will often change direction and side-step an opponent.

1   Sketch a diagram to show the direction of the force acting upon him which would have this effect. (Draw your force diagram from above and show the direction of the force relative to the direction of travel.)

2   What is the nature of the force created?

3   What factors enable the player to increase the size of this force and side-step more effectively?

Exam-style Questions

A high jumper with a weight of 700N firmly plants his foot on the ground before take off.

1   Sketch a free body diagram showing all the vertical forces acting on the jumper.   **(2 marks)**

2   Explain why it is necessary for the foot contact force to be greater than 700N.   **(2 marks)**

3   Use Newton's laws of motion to explain why it is necessary for the jumper to plant his foot as firmly as possible into the ground just before take off.   **(4 marks)**

Impulse and impact

In Chapter 12 you were introduced to the concept of momentum, which is defined as the amount of motion a body possesses. Momentum becomes more important in sporting situations where collisions or impacts occur. The outcome of the collision depends largely upon the amount of momentum each of the bodies possessed before the collision took place. The body with greater momentum will be more difficult to stop. For example:

●   if a prop forward weighing 90 kg and a scrum half weighing 60 kg were both travelling at the same velocity, the prop forward would have a greater momentum and would need to apply a larger force to stop his path to the try-line.

●   the speed at which the squash ball is struck is determined by the momentum of the racket head at the time of impact.

A change in momentum is synonymous with a change in acceleration and as such relates to Newton's second law of motion (see page 209). This is expressed as:

$$F = ma$$

In order to work out the acceleration (a), the following equations must be used:

$$a = \frac{v - u}{t}$$

thus:

$$F = \frac{m(v - u)}{t}$$

$$a = \frac{mv - mu}{t}$$

$$Ft = mv - mu$$

$$Ft = \text{Change in momentum}$$

Impulse

This final equation suggests that any change in momentum is dependent upon the product of the force and the time that that force is applied to an object, known as **impulse**. It therefore follows that any increase in the force applied or the time over which the force is applied, the outgoing momentum of the object will increase. This has important implications for sporting situations where acceleration of a body or object is essential. For example, a follow-through of a racket or hockey stick will ensure that the time over which the force has been applied is at its maximum; the change in momentum or acceleration of the ball will be greater than if a follow-through had not been performed. This is illustrated in Figure 13.7. The shaded area under the graph represents impulse. A larger impulse results in an increase in the outgoing momentum of a ball.

Application of impulse can also be seen in the shot put. Over time the technique in the shot put has been transformed. Originally a sideways stance was adopted before the put. However, the O'Brien technique (see Figure 13.8) aims to apply a force over a longer period of time by incorporating a 180° turn and increasing the acceleration of the shot. Again by performing a follow-through the athlete can ensure that the time of contact has been maximised. Of course, in addition to developing this technique, the athlete still requires the necessary physical attributes in order to apply a large force to the implement. The O'Brien technique led the way for shot putters. Most rotational throwers now perform a one and three quarter turn before release.

A high jumper will also use their knowledge of impulse to generate maximum upward acceleration. As they plant their foot on take off, they will first land on their heel before rocking onto their toes. This lengthens the time over which they can apply force to the track. Furthermore, they will also lean back slightly at take off, further increasing impulse by increasing the time it takes for their centre of mass (COM) (see Chapter 15) to pass over their take-off foot.

In some instances a small force can be applied over a longer period of time. For example, when playing water polo a player catching the ball with one hand will aim to decrease

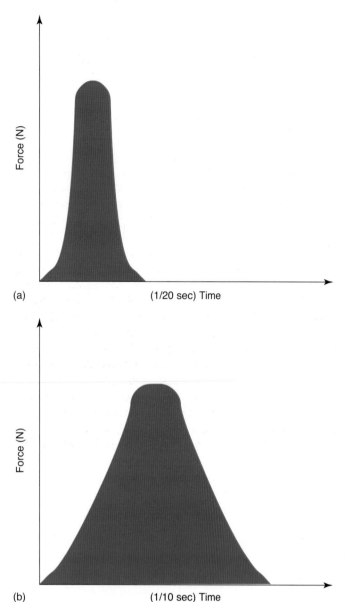

(a)   (1/20 sec) Time

(b)   (1/10 sec) Time

Fig 13.7 The effect of a follow-through on the outgoing momentum of a hockey ball (a) force exerted without a follow-through (b) force exerted with a follow-through

the velocity of the ball over a long period of time and so decrease the force exerted by the ball on the hands. The player does this by meeting the ball early and withdrawing

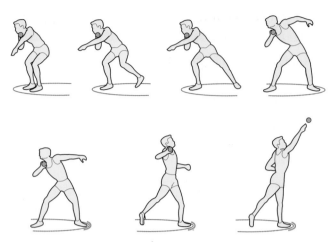

Fig 13.8 The O'Brien technique was developed in the shot put to enable force to be applied to the shot over a longer period of time, increasing the outgoing momentum of the shot

the catching hand in the direction of the ball's motion, thus cushioning the impact; this will prevent the ball hitting the hand and bouncing off uncontrollably (Figure 13.9). Similarly in cricket, when catching a fast-moving cricket ball, the player cradles the ball to reduce the impact on the hands and so prevent injury. Further examples include the use of crash mats in activities such as gymnastics and high jump.

Fig 13.9 A water polo player will decrease the velocity of an incoming ball by meeting the ball early and taking the catching arm back in the direction the ball is travelling in cushioning the impact

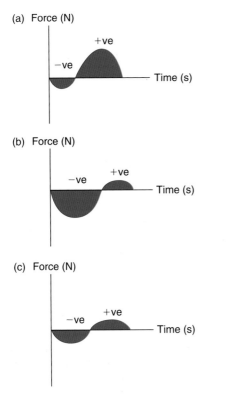

(a) Force (N)

+ve

−ve

Time (s)

(b) Force (N)

−ve   +ve

Time (s)

(c) Force (N)

−ve   +ve

Time (s)

Fig 13.10 Impulse graphs at different stages of a 100m race (a) at the beginning during acceleration (b) at the end of the race when the athlete is decelerating (c) during the middle section of the race when the athlete is running at constant velocity

Activity 5

In small groups, discuss situations from sport where performers will:

● apply a large force over a short period of time
● apply a smaller force over a longer period of time.

Impulse is often illustrated through graphs. We can see from Figure 13.10 that there are two elements to an impulse graph. The first area represents the impulse of a body landing on the ground (this is known as negative impulse), while the second area represents the impulse of the body due to the ground reaction force (positive impulse). In Figure 13.10 (a) there is a small negative impulse but a large positive impulse which indicates a body that is accelerating, its velocity is increasing. A high jumper, for example, imparts a large force over a very short period of time, which causes a large positive impulse that results in vertical acceleration. In Figure 13.10 (b) there is a large negative impulse that is followed by a small positive impulse. This represents a body that is decelerating. For example, a volleyball player upon landing from a block absorbs a large force over a long period of time decreasing his vertical velocity. Figure 13.10 (c) shows a body travelling at constant velocity where positive and negative impulses are equal, and the net impulse is zero, for example, in the middle of a 100 m sprint.

Activity 6

When sprinting after the ball, a games player generates *impulse* at each footfall. Figure 13.11 shows horizontal ground reaction force versus time traces for three students associated with a sprint during a game. Positive forces act on the runner in the direction of the run.

The three situations represented are:

● a point while the player is pushing on the ground at the start of the sprint
● a foot contact just after the player has begun sprinting
● a foot contact in the middle of the sprint.

Consider each of the diagrams X, Y and Z, and match them to the three situations associated with the sprint described above. Explain your answers.

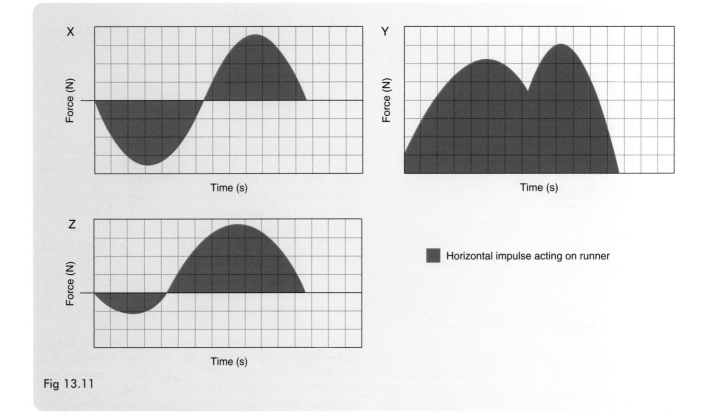

Fig 13.11

Horizontal impulse acting on runner

Exam-style Questions

A hockey player strikes a ball.

1   Sketch a graph of the force applied to the ball against time

2   Explain how using a follow-through would affect the motion of the struck ball.

CHALLENGE YOURSELF

'There can be no sport without force.' Discuss this statement with reference to a range of sporting examples.

(20 marks)

Key term

Impulse The length of time over which a force is applied. It is the product of force and time and is measured in Newton seconds (Ns).

What you need to know

* Force is the push or pull exerted on an object and can be generated internally or externally to the body. Forces can cause a:
  – stationary body to move
  – moving body to speed up (accelerate)
  – moving body to slow down (decelerate)
  – moving body to change direction
  – body to change shape.
* From Newton's second law of motion we can deduce that
  Force = Mass × Acceleration.
* Balanced forces exist where two forces equal in size but opposite in direction operate.

* Unbalanced forces exist where two or more forces operate in opposite directions but are of unequal size.
* A net force is the overall force when all other forces have been considered. This is also known as the resultant force.
* To work out the resultant force a parallelogram of forces can be constructed (which will lie along the diagonal of the two forces acting).
* Forces acting on a body or object are either vertical in nature or horizontal.
* Vertical forces include weight and reaction force.

* Horizontal forces include friction and air resistance.
* The weight of the body is its mass multiplied by the acceleration due to gravity ($10m/s^2$).
* Normal reaction will be equal in size but opposite in direction to the weight force.
* Movement of a body upwards will occur where the reaction force is greater than the weight force.
* Friction is a force which acts on the interface of surfaces which are in contact, and acts in the opposite direction to the direction of motion.
* Some performers will seek to increase friction (for example, by wearing studs in boots), while others will seek to decrease friction for example by waxing skis.

* Air resistance is friction between an object and the air it is moving through. It is a form of fluid friction and opposes the motion of a body.
* Air resistance is dependent upon:
  – the speed of the moving body
  – the frontal cross-sectional area of the moving body
  – the surface characteristics of the moving body.
* Forces acting on a body are illustrated by drawing a free-body diagram.
* Impulse considers the length of time over which a force is applied.
* Increasing impulse can increase the outgoing momentum of an object or body.
* Performing a follow-through can increase the outgoing momentum of an object or body.

Review Questions

1 Give two examples from sport where we might expect to see balanced forces and unbalanced forces at work.
2 Draw free body diagrams of the following, showing all the forces acting upon them:

  (a) A high jumper at take-off

  (b) A gymnast performing a handstand

  (c) A diver at take-off.

3 How do swimmers minimise the size and effects of fluid friction?
4 Give at least three examples from sport where fluid friction (air resistance and drag in water) affects:

  (a) an object

  (b) a sportsperson

  State the effects of this fluid friction in each case.

5 Show all the forces acting on a football as it is kicked. Construct a parallelogram of forces to determine the resultant force acting on a football.

6 Using examples from sport explain how performers manipulate the amount of friction (increasing and decreasing it!) in order to enhance their performance.
7 Sketch a force-time graph to show the effect of a follow-through on a tennis ball and compare it to a ball struck without a follow through.
8 Draw graphs representing the amount of impulse at the following stages of a long jump:

  (a) At the start of the run up

  (b) As the runner reaches a constant velocity

  (c) As the runner takes off

  (d) As the runner lands in the sand pit.

9 How do high jumpers optimise impulse at take off?
10 Use at least three examples from sport to explain when a small force is applied over a (relatively) long period of time.

CHAPTER 14

Understanding fluid mechanics in physical activity

Learning outcomes

By the end of this chapter you should be able to:

- describe and explain the factors affecting air resistance and drag in water (to include velocity, cross-sectional area, mass, streamlining and surface characteristics)
- describe the forces acting on a projectile during flight
- illustrate the resultant force of a projectile using the parallelogram of forces
- explain the relationship between the forces acting on a projectile and the resulting flight path
- explain the Bernoulli principle and show how an upward lift force is produced when throwing the discus and a downward force is created in motor sport, cycling and downhill skiing
- define eccentric force and explain how this creates spin
- describe the types of spin used in sporting activity and explain their impact on flight path and bounce of a ball
- explain how the Magnus effect affects the flight path of projectiles
- critically evaluate performance with reference to linear motion in the following types of physical activity:
  - running
  - jumping
  - throwing
  - hitting/kicking
  - rotating.

CHAPTER INTRODUCTION

In Chapter 13 we discussed the nature of the different forces acting on a performer or object when participating in sporting activity. This chapter specifically investigates the impact of fluid forces such as air resistance and drag in water, and considers how these forces can be manipulated in order to enhance performance. In many ball games spin is an essential element of the performance. This chapter will also explore the factors (such as spin) that affect the flight path of a projectile and how these can be manipulated to once again optimise performance.

Fluid forces in sporting activity

In this chapter we turn our attention to fluid forces that influence sporting activity such as those offered by air and water. When a body or object moves through air or water, it is affected by fluid friction which **acts in the opposite direction to the motion of the moving body.**

Air resistance and drag in water

Air resistance (or drag in water) is prevalent in most sporting activity, although its effects on performance can vary greatly. The amount of air resistance or drag experienced by performers or projectiles in sporting activity depends upon a number of factors, but especially the following:

- **the frontal cross-sectional area of the moving body** – the larger the frontal cross-sectional area, the greater the effects of air resistance
- **the velocity of the moving body** – the faster the body or object is moving, the greater the effects of air resistance
- **the shape and surface characteristics of the moving object or body** – the less the body is streamlined and the rougher the surface of the moving body, the greater the effects of air resistance
- **the mass of the body** – the lighter the body or moving object, the greater the effects of air resistance.

Therefore, in order to optimise performance, performers such as cyclists, swimmers and athletes will attempt to minimise the effects of air resistance and drag by embracing technological and product advancement.

In cycling, for example, the shape of the racing bike has changed dramatically to minimise the area of the cyclist in contact with the air. The racing car manufacturer, Lotus developed the bike on which Chris Boardman won the 1992 Olympic title. This bike possessed an extremely lightweight carbon-fibre frame and disc wheels, both designed to minimise air resistance. Furthermore, the shape of the cycling helmet is tapered and tight-fitting clothing is worn to promote the smooth flow of air past the body and reduce any turbulence. This technology is now available to all and goes some way to explain the recent success of Great Britain's cycling team, in particular Chris Hoy's triple gold medal performance at the Beijing Olympics. There are even reports that suggest that the British Cycling Management are so concerned that other nations will steal their technological ideas from Beijing that all evidence has since been destroyed!

In swimming Speedo™ have recently developed the controversial LZR suit, designed specifically to minimise the effects of drag in the water. This has proved to be a significant advancement in product design since 94 per cent of gold medallists and 23 out of 25 swimmers who broke world records at the 2008 Olympics were wearing these swimming suits, including Michael Phelps.

Fig 14.1 The LZR suit has been developed by Speedo™ to reduce the effects of drag in the water

Key terms

Air resistance The force that acts in the opposite direction to a moving body as it travels through the air.
Drag The force that acts in the opposite direction to a moving body as it travels through a fluid (either water or air).

IN CONTEXT

Swimmer Michael Phelps eclipsed the great achievements of fellow American Mark Spitz by winning eight gold medals at the Beijing Olympics in 2008. Without question, Michael's physical and mental fitness contributed enormously to his success, but attention to the following factors will also have played a part:

- minimising his frontal cross-sectional area by using appropriate technique when swimming
- minimising the surface area in contact with the water, by maintaining a very ecto-/mesomorphic somatotype

- wearing shiny swim suits (i.e. the LZR suit), swimming hats and by 'shaving down' – the practice of removing body hair – in an attempt to minimise turbulent flow.

All of these practices allow the water to flow past the body more smoothly and limit the drag force.

Activity 1

In small groups consider the following sporting examples and discuss the role of air resistance in each case:

- badminton
- track cycling
- sprinting
- the long jump.

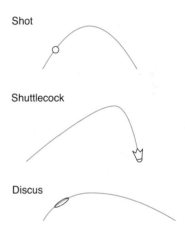

Fig 14.2 The expected flight paths of a shot, badminton shuttlecock and discus

Air resistance and its effect on projectile motion

Air resistance offered to a projectile whilst in flight can have a significant impact upon its final flight path. Some examples of flight paths expected from a variety of projectiles are illustrated in Figure 14.2.

The flight paths of projectiles can be categorised as following one of three shapes:

- parabolic (a uniform symmetrical shape)
- nearly parabolic (a distorted parabola)
- asymmetric.

Once in flight there are **two** key forces acting on a projectile:

- the weight of the projectile
- the air resistance experienced by the projectile during flight.

It is the relative values of weight and air resistance that will ultimately determine the flight path followed by the projectile. Quite simply, when the weight of the projectile is much greater than the air resistance experienced then the flight path is likely to be parabolic (for example, a shot put or a long jumper). Conversely, when air resistance is significantly larger than the weight of the projectile then the flight path will be asymmetric (for example, badminton shuttlecock).

A third force, **lift** may also come into play when analysing a projectile in flight. This acts in the opposite direction to weight and is considered in more depth later in this chapter.

Key terms

Parabola A term used to describe the flight path of a projectile that is a uniform curve and symmetrical about its highest point.
Lift force A force created wherever there is a pressure differential between the airflowing along opposite surfaces of a projectile or object. It is important to note that a lift force can be upwards **or** downwards.

EXAMINER'S TIP

Remember that once a projectile is in flight only two forces act: weight and air resistance. However, a third force of 'lift' may come into play if spin is applied to a projectile or a projectile is released with an appropriate angle of attack.

Not only is flight governed by the ratio of weight to air resistance, it is also dependent upon the size, shape and speed of an object; typically, slower moving or streamlined objects are affected less by air resistance. In fact, the relative contributions of weight and air resistance can actually change during flight. Take the following example of a shuttlecock during badminton.

A badminton shuttlecock struck when performing an overhead clear will initially experience a high level of air resistance since the shuttlecock is travelling very quickly upon leaving the racket. Faster moving objects experience higher degrees of air resistance which causes rapid deceleration of the shuttlecock. This deceleration continues until a point is reached where weight becomes the

determining factor, causing the shuttlecock to drop almost vertically at the back of the badminton court, leading to an asymmetric flight path. The changes in the relative values of weight and air resistance during an overhead clear is illustrated in Figure 14.3.

EXAMINER'S TIP

When drawing a force diagram of a projectile in flight make sure you include the following:
- a direction of motion arrow
- an air resistance arrow
- a weight arrow
- show the relative magnitude of weight and air resistance by the appropriate length of arrow
- show the origin of the arrows from the centre of mass of the projectile.

Resolution of forces acting on a projectile using the parallelogram of forces

The flight path of a projectile can be predicted by considering the resultant force of the two forces acting on the projectile, namely air resistance and weight. The size and direction of the resultant force can be determined by constructing a parallelogram of forces acting on the

EXAMINER'S TIP

To determine the resultant force acting on a projectile, use the weight and air resistance arrows to construct a parallelogram. The resultant force will lie along the diagonal of the parallelogram.

Key term

Resultant force The net force acting on the projectile, having considered all other forces acting; the sum of all the forces acting.

Table 14.1 A comparison of the forces acting on a shot and badminton shuttlecock immediately after release and the resulting flight paths.

	Forces acting	Size of force	Resulting flight path
Shot put	(a)	Weight > Air resistance	Parabolic (symmetric)
Badminton shuttlecock	(b)	Air resistance > Weight	Asymmetric

projectile. Table 14.2 shows how the resultant force is determined through the construction of a parallelogram of the forces acting on a shot and shuttlecock during flight, and how this will ultimately determine the flight path followed.

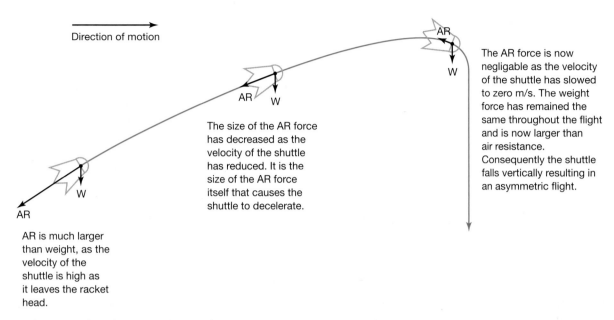

Direction of motion

AR is much larger than weight, as the velocity of the shuttle is high as it leaves the racket head.

The size of the AR force has decreased as the velocity of the shuttle has reduced. It is the size of the AR force itself that causes the shuttle to decelerate.

The AR force is now negligable as the velocity of the shuttle has slowed to zero m/s. The weight force has remained the same throughout the flight and is now larger than air resistance. Consequently the shuttle falls vertically resulting in an asymmetric flight.

Fig 14.3 Changes in the relative contribution of weight and air resistance to the flight path of a shuttlecock during an overhead clear

Table 14.2 Resultant forces acting on projectiles in flight determined by the construction of a parallelogram of forces

Projectile	Forces acting in flight	Explanation	Resultant flight path
Shot put	(a) *diagram: Air resistance, Weight, Resultant force, Direction of motion*	As weight is the dominant force and the effects of air resistance negligible, the size and direction of the resultant force is very similar to the weight force, causing the shot to follow a parabolic flight path	A parabolic flight path
Shuttlecock as it leaves the racket head	(b) *diagram: Air resistance, Weight, Resultant force, Direction of motion*	As air resistance is the dominant force and the effects of weight small, the size and direction of the resultant force is very similar to that of the air resistance force, causing the shuttlecock to follow an asymmetric flight path	An asymmetric flight path

Understanding fluid dynamics in sport

The movement of a projectile through the air is open to manipulation by the sports performer. In the eighteenth century, Daniel Bernoulli conducted a series of experiments that helped to explain the flight paths followed by certain projectiles in the sporting arena and, consequently, contributed to the development of appropriate technique and equipment.

Bernoulli's principle and the creation of lift

The series of experiments conducted by Bernoulli demonstrated that when flow-lines get closer together, velocity increases and there is a resulting drop in pressure. This has had important implications for the design of objects in flight, perhaps the most important being the design of aeroplane wings.

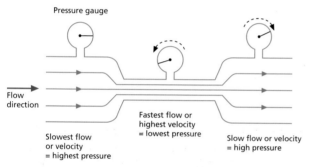

Pressure gauge

Flow direction

Fastest flow or highest velocity = lowest pressure

Slowest flow or velocity = highest pressure

Slow flow or velocity = high pressure

Fig 14.4 Bernoulli's experiments illustrate the inverse relationship between the velocity of airflow and the associated pressure

Figure 14.5 shows that the flow-lines on the upper surface of the wing have to travel further than the flow-lines on the lower surface and must, therefore, increase in velocity in order to reach the back at the same time as those on the bottom. As the velocity increases, pressure decreases. A pressure differential exists between the upper and lower surfaces, and a **lift force** results, keeping the plane in flight.

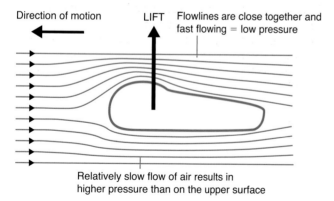

Direction of motion

LIFT Flowlines are close together and fast flowing = low pressure

Relatively slow flow of air results in higher pressure than on the upper surface

Fig 14.5 The Bernoulli principle explains how aeroplanes can stay in flight

Key term

Bernoulli's principle Explains how lift is created as a projectile moves through a fluid (air and water). Bernoulli concluded that the quicker airflows past a projectile, the lower the surrounding pressure. Conversely, slower airflow creates a zone of high pressure. The result of this pressure differential is that the projectile will move from the area of high pressure towards the area of low pressure creating lift.

Activity 2

This activity will show us how the careful design of an aeroplane wing can create lift by lowering the pressure of the air flowing along the upper surface of the wing relative to the pressure flowing along the underside.

You will need:

● half a sheet of A4 paper, cut lengthways
● ruler
● cellotape.

Fold the paper in half along its width, then tape the top edge of the paper so that it is about ½ inch (just over 1 cm) from the bottom edge. This should make the top half of the paper curved like the top of an aeroplane wing. Slide the 'wing' over the ruler so that the curved side is facing up and the folded seam is facing you. Holding the ruler in front of you, with the wing hanging down, blow straight at the folded seam. The wing should lift up from its hanging, resting position.

Now, in groups of two or three, discuss the following:

1 What happens to the distance the air has to travel over the top of the wing compared with the distance it has to travel underneath the wing. Why?
2 Compare the velocity of the air flowing over the top of the wing with that moving underneath it. What happens to the pressure of the airflow above and below the wing? How is the wing lifted?

Activity 3

You will need:

● a funnel
● table tennis ball.

Hold a table tennis ball with a finger at the mouth of the funnel. Take a deep breath and blow as hard and as long as you can down the 'leg' of the funnel.

1 What happens to the table tennis ball
    (i) while blowing into the funnel?
    (ii) when you run out of breath?
2 Explain your answer to the person sitting next to you.

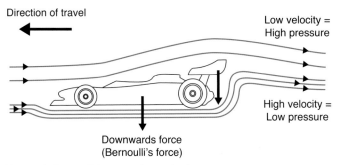

Direction of travel

Low velocity = High pressure

High velocity = Low pressure

Downwards force (Bernoulli's force)

Fig 14.6 Bernoulli's principle applied to motor racing

It is also the Bernoulli principle that governs the technique of the throwing events in athletics, particularly the discus. In order to generate optimum lift, the discus leaves the hand of the thrower at angle. As the discus travels through the air, **the angle of attack** forces the oncoming air to travel further over the top of the discus than the air travelling underneath it. With further to travel the air moves faster over the top of the discus than the air below it, creating an area of lower pressure. This pressure differential creates **a lift force** as the discus moves from the area of relative high pressure (below the discus) to the area of low pressure (above the discus). This lift force allows the discus to stay in the air for longer and greater distance to be achieved by the performer. This application of Bernoulli's principle is illustrated in Figure 14.7.

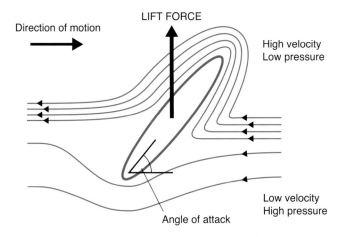

LIFT FORCE

Direction of motion

High velocity Low pressure

Low velocity High pressure

Angle of attack

Fig 14.7 Bernoulli's principle applied to a discus throw. Note how the angle of attack enables a large lift force to be created

This principle has also been applied to Formula One racing cars, but the aerofoil in this case is inverted (called a 'spoiler'), creating a downward force that pushes the car into the track, thus enabling it to hold the bend much better at high speed.

Key term

Angle of attack The most favourable angle of a projectile in flight so that it achieves optimum lift due to Bernoulli's principle.

Activity 4

Using diagrams, show how Bernoulli's principle can be applied to the following performers:

- javelin thrower
- a ski jumper
- track cyclist
- speed skiing.

CHALLENGE YOURSELF

Explain the factors that affect the size of fluid friction acting on a moving body and describe how it can be reduced in order for the body to move faster.

Explain how Bernoulli's principle changes the normal flight path of a projectile in a sport of your choice.

Spinning projectiles and the Magnus effect

Applying spin to a projectile is a feature of many ball games. Whether it is a tennis ball hit with topspin, hook applied to a golf ball or a swerving football, all spin is imparted to a projectile through the application of an eccentric force. You will recall from your AS study that an eccentric force is one which is applied outside the centre of mass of the object and one that causes a projectile to deviate from its expected flight path.

Eccentric force A force applied outside the centre of mass of an object or body that causes a projectile to spin.

The Magnus effect is essentially Bernoulli's principle applied to spinning projectiles, since spin alters the flow of air around the projectile, creating a pressure differential and a lift force.

When an object spins in air (or water), the air molecules in contact with the object *spin* with it, creating a boundary layer (see Figure 14.9).

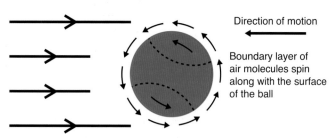

Fig 14.9 The boundary layer – air molecules in contact with a spinning projectile spin along with it

When air molecules spin with the object, they eventually collide head on with the mainstream airflow on one side of the object only. This head-on collision causes a decrease in velocity of the air surrounding airflow resulting in an area of high pressure. This causes a pressure differential with the opposite side of the ball since on this side the boundary layer flows in the same direction as the mainstream airflow. The pressure differential causes a **Magnus force**, directed from the high pressure region to the area of low pressure as illustrated by the tennis ball in Figure 14.10.

Key term

Magnus effect A force created as a projectile spins in the air. A spinning ball creates a pressure differential between the airflow above and below it (or between one side and another). This pressure differential creates a Magnus force and causes the ball to move (swerve) in the direction of the spin.

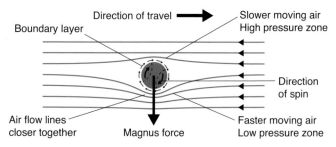

Fig 14.10 The Magnus force created by a tennis ball hit with topspin

Key term

Boundary layer The layer of air (or water) molecules closest to a spinning object that spins along with it which contributes to the creation of a pressure differential resulting in a Magnus force.

IN CONTEXT

Tennis players such as Raphael Nadal are at an advantage when serving with new balls. This is because the Magnus effect is heightened when new balls are used, since the nap or fuzz of the new ball traps a much larger boundary layer resulting in a greater pressure differential.

IN CONTEXT

David Beckham is the master of the free kick. This is because he uses the Magnus force to curve the flight path of the ball to optimum effect. By placing sidespin on the ball, Beckham is able to curve the ball around the wall of defensive players in front of goal; see Figure 14.11.

Table 14.3 The effect of spin on a ball in flight

Type of spin	Diagram	Explanation	Effect on flight path
Topspin	Direction of travel Boundary layer Slower moving air High pressure zone Direction of spin Air flow lines closer together Faster moving air Low pressure zone Magnus force A ball hit with topspin Note: Where velocity of airflow increases, the flow lines get closer together indicating an area of lower pressure	The boundary layer on the **top** surface of the ball travels in the opposite direction to the airflow. This slows the flow of air on the **top** surface and creates a zone of high pressure. The boundary layer on the **bottom** surface travels in the same direction as the oncoming airflow causing the air to travel more quickly than that on the top surface and creates a zone of low pressure.	The pressure differential (high pressure on top of the ball, low pressure below the ball) results in the ball moving towards the low pressure zone causing it to dip and deviate **downwards** from the expected flight path when the ball is struck without spin. Direction of motion Ball dips
Back spin	Magnus force Faster moving air Low pressure zone Air flow lines closer together Boundary layer Direction of spin Slower moving air High pressure zone Direction of travel A ball hit with backspin	The boundary layer on the **bottom** surface of the ball travels in the opposite direction to the airflow. This slows the flow of air on the bottom surface and creates a zone of high pressure. The boundary layer on the top surface travels in the same direction as the on-coming airflow causing the air to travel more quickly than that on the bottom surface and creates a zone of low pressure.	The pressure differential (low pressure on top of the ball, high pressure below the ball) results in the ball moving towards the low pressure zone causing it to float and deviate upwards from the expected flight path when the ball is struck without spin. Direction of motion Ball floats
Sidespin Hook (As viewed from above)	Direction of travel Magnus force Faster moving air = Low pressure zone Slower moving air = High pressure zone A ball hit with sidespin/hook	The boundary layer on the **right-hand** surface of the ball travels in the opposite direction to the airflow. This slows the flow of air on the **right-hand** surface and creates a zone of high pressure. The boundary layer on the **left-hand** surface travels in the same direction as the oncoming airflow causing the air to travel more quickly than that on the right-hand surface and creates a zone of low pressure.	The pressure differential (high pressure on the **right-hand** side of the ball, low pressure on the **left-hand** side of the ball) results in the ball moving towards the low pressure zone, causing it to swerve and deviate **to the left** of its expected flight path when struck without spin. Direction of motion

Type of spin	Diagram	Explanation	Effect on flight path
Sidespin Slice (As viewed from above)	 Direction of travel Magnus force Slower moving air = High pressure zone Faster moving air = Low pressure zone A ball hit with sidespin/slice	The boundary layer on the **left-hand** surface of the ball travels in the opposite direction to the airflow. This slows the flow of air on the **left-hand** surface and creates a zone of high pressure. The boundary layer on the **right-hand** surface travels in the same direction as the oncoming airflow causing the air to travel more quickly than that on the right-hand surface and creates a zone of low pressure.	The pressure differential (high pressure on the **left-hand** side of the ball, low pressure on the right-hand side of the ball) results in the ball moving towards the low pressure zone, causing it to swerve and deviate **to the right** of its expected flight path when struck without spin. Direction of motion

Fig 14.10 A soccer player can use the Magnus effect by placing sidespin on a football to cause the path of the ball to curve

Activity 5

Hook and slice are both forms of sidespin. Draw the expected flight path from above of a golf ball that has been struck with:

● Slice
● Hook.

Activity 6

Taking a situation from football, explain when and how a Magnus force is created.

Exam-style Questions

The graph shows the flight paths of three different types of projectile found in sport.

X represents the flight path of a tennis ball with backspin

Y represents the flight path of a shot in athletics

Z represents the flight path of a badminton shuttlecock.

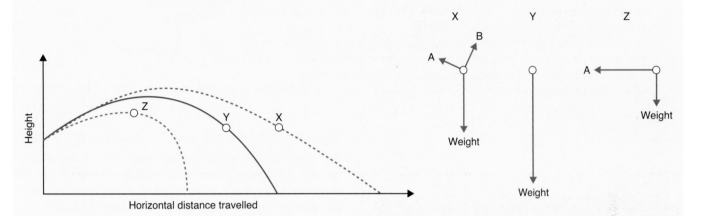

The force diagrams represent the forces acting on the projectiles at the point in the path marked with a large dot in the graph above.

1 Describe the nature of the forces labelled A and B in the diagrams   (2 marks)

2 Explain why each projectile has a very different flight path   (6 marks)

3 What factors affect the horizontal distance travelled by the shot?   (3 marks)

EXAMINER'S TIPS

If asked to draw an airflow diagram in your exam, be sure to include the following points of information:

- identify the direction of motion by drawing on an arrow
- identify the type of spin shown (top, back or side)
- identify whether the projectile is viewed from above or the side
- draw the projectile
- identify the direction of spin inside the projectile

- identify the direction of travel of the boundary layer
- draw on the airflow lines, paying particular attention to the spacing of them on opposite sides of the projectile and the direction of travel (using arrowheads)
- label the area of faster moving air and slow moving airflow
- label the zone of high pressure and low pressure
- draw a Magnus force arrow from the centre of mass (COM) of the projectile
- try to give a brief written explanation, referring to each side of the projectile in turn (for example, 'Above the ball' or 'Below the ball'

Exam-style Questions

Many tennis players use topspin when hitting groundstrokes.

1   With the aid of a diagram, explain how a tennis ball is given topspin. Sketch the contrasting flight paths of a tennis ball hit with topspin and a tennis ball hit without spin.   **(4 marks)**

2   Sketch a vector diagram of all the forces acting on a tennis ball in flight with topspin and include the direction of travel and direction of spin. Show how you could work out the resultant force acting on the ball and explain how it affects the flight path.   **(6 marks)**

Source: OCR, June, 2002.

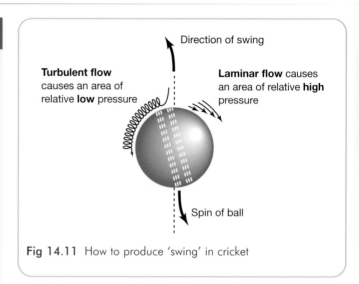

Fig 14.11   How to produce 'swing' in cricket

IN DEPTH

A fast bowler can often cause problems for a batsman by making a cricket ball move whilst in flight, either towards or away from the batsman. But how is this achieved? The answer is in our understanding of fluid dynamics. One side of the ball is polished smooth by fielders constantly rubbing it on their trousers, while the other side of the ball is left to deteriorate through the normal wear and tear of the game resulting in a relatively rough surface. Once in flight, air flows more smoothly over the shiny side of the ball compared to a more turbulent flow of air over the rough surface, causing drag on this side of the ball. The turbulent flow creates a pocket of low pressure in to which the ball 'swings' or moves (remember objects or projectiles will always move from areas of high pressure to areas of low pressure).

Furthermore, swing is increased if the ball is released with the seam at a slight angle. This is because the oncoming airflow is disturbed by the seam creating greater turbulence. To swing the ball away from a right-handed batsman, the rough side of the ball should be on the left with the seam pointing towards second slip. For the in-swinging ball, the opposite is true; the rough side should be on the right with the seam angling towards an imaginary leg slip.

The impact of spin on the bounce of a ball

Spin does not only affect the flight path of a ball, but also its bounce. A ball struck with topspin will accelerate off the surface at a low angle, whilst a ball hit with back spin 'sits up' after the bounce. The answer for this lies in a basic understanding of friction and the application of Newton's third law of motion.

The effect of topspin on the bounce of a ball

A ball hit with topspin rotates in the same direction as the direction of travel; as it lands, the ball applies a backwards force to the surface. Since friction opposes this backwards motion a forward force is created (think of Newton's third law of action/reaction) causing the ball to accelerate quickly from the bounce at a small, shallow angle. The more rapidly the ball spins, the greater the acceleration away from the bounce and the more difficult it is for your opponent to retrieve.

The effect of backspin on the bounce of a ball

A ball hit with back spin rotates in the opposite direction to the direction of travel; as it lands, the ball applies a forward force to the surface. In this instance friction opposes this forward motion creating a backwards force (once again think of Newton's third law of action/reaction) causing the ball to bounce at a much larger angle away from the surface. Furthermore, the more rapidly the ball spins the greater the backwards motion away from the bounce.

For example, in golf an approach shot struck with backspin can land towards the back of the green but the ball can continue moving backwards away from the bounce towards the cup.

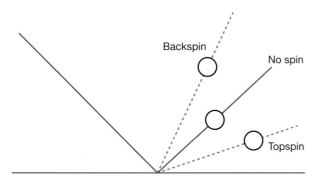

Fig 14.12 The effect of spin on the bounce of a ball

IN CONTEXT

James Willstrop, the British squash player, will use this knowledge of backspin when playing a drop shot. A squash ball struck with backspin will want to accelerate upwards upon striking the front wall. However, the opposing friction will act downwards, causing the ball to drop into the front corner, moving an opponent out of position and making it a difficult shot for them to retrieve.

Exam-style Questions

The flight of a projectile is affected by spin.

(i)   Illustrate the effect of topspin on the flight path of a tennis ball

(ii) Illustrate the effect of backspin on the flight path of a tennis ball

(iii) Illustrate the effect of sidespin on a football, indicating the direction of spin in relation to the resulting swerving effect

(iv) Explain the effect of spin on the bounce of a ball, using appropriate examples from sport.

A ball will react to spin on bouncing. Explain with a diagram what happens when a ball with back spin bounces.

CHALLENGE YOURSELF

Understanding fluid mechanics is essential for effective performance in many sporting activities. Using examples from track cycling and tennis write an extended answer (500 words minimum) expressing how far you agree with this statement.

[20 marks]

Exam-style Questions

Using a diagram to support your answer describe all the forces acting on a shot during flight. Show how the resultant force can be determined and the effect this has on the flight of the shot.

Many performers use spin to control the flight path of a ball. Using an airflow diagram explain the effect of backspin on the flight of a projectile from a sport of your choice.

What you need to know

* Air resistance acts in the opposite direction to the moving body.
* Air resistance and drag in water are both affected by the following four factors:
  - frontal cross-section of the moving body
  - velocity of the moving body
  - shape and surface characteristics of the moving body
  - mass of the body.
* Air resistance together with weight will determine the flight path of a projectile.
* The flight path of a projectile can be classified as either parabolic, nearly parabolic or asymmetrical.

* Where weight is significantly greater than air resistance, a parabolic flight path results.
* Where air resistance is significantly greater than weight, an asymmetric flight path results.
* A parallelogram of forces is used to resolve the forces acting on a projectile determining the resultant force.
* Bernoulli's experiments illustrate the inverse relationship between the velocity of airflow and the associated pressure.
* Where velocity of airflow increases, flow-lines in a fluid get closer together causing a zone of low pressure.

* Where velocity of airflow decreases, flow-lines in a fluid get further apart causing a zone of high pressure.
* Bernoulli's principle can be applied to many sporting situations where there is a pressure differential between two sides of a body or projectile.
* Lift (or a downwards force) is created, since an object, body or projectile will always move from an area of high pressure to area of low pressure.
* Spin is applied by the application of an eccentric force in many sports that involve kicking, throwing or striking a ball.
* The Magnus effect is simply the Bernoulli principle applied to spinning balls.

* Applying topspin to a ball creates a downwards Magnus force, causing it to dip and shorten its flight path.
* Applying backspin to a ball creates an upwards Magnus force, causing the ball to stay in the air for longer, thus extending its flight path.
* A ball struck with hook will cause a ball to deviate left of its expected flight path.
* A ball struck with slice will cause a ball to deviate right of its expected flight path.
* The type of spin applied to a ball will affect the bounce as well as the flight path
* A ball hit with topspin will accelerate away from the surface at a low angle.
* A ball hit with backspin will sit up from the surface at a greater angle.

Review Questions

1 Give three examples, each from a different sporting context, to show how fluid friction affects the sports performer.

2 Taking examples from a sport of your choice, explain three factors that would affect the size of the fluid friction force acting on the moving person or object.

3 Drag in water is a force that acts against a swimmer. How might the swimmer attempt to reduce the size of this force?

4 Air resistance is a force that acts against a moving body. How might a downhill skier try to reduce the size of this force?

5 Sketch a free body diagram showing all the forces acting on a badminton shuttlecock in flight, following an overhead clear at the following stages:

  ● as it leaves the racket head
  ● as it crosses the net
  ● as it drops at the back of the court.

6 Sketch a free body diagram showing all the forces acting on a shot put in flight. Show on your diagram how the resultant force can be determined and briefly explain how the direction of the resultant force helps to explain the path followed by the shot.

7 Explain with the use of a diagram how lift is created on a discus in flight.

8 What do you understand by the term Magnus effect? Explain how a knowledge of Magnus forces can assist a table-tennis player?

9 A basketball player scores a basket from a free throw after striking the backboard. Why would the application of back spin to the ball during the free throw improve the chances of a successful shot?

10 What is the effect of topspin on the bounce of a tennis ball?

Learning outcomes

By the end of this chapter you should be able to:

- define and explain the importance of the centre of mass (COM) to successful sporting performance
- explain how performers can manipulate the position of their centre of mass to enhance performance
- use sporting examples to demonstrate your understanding of how the following factors affect stability:
  - position of the line of gravity
  - height of centre of mass
  - area of the base of support
  - the mass of the body or object
- identify the three classes of lever system in the human body, giving examples from sporting activity when each operates
- explain the relative efficiency of lever systems with reference to mechanical advantage and disadvantage
- define and calculate the torque of simple rotating systems, using the appropriate units of measurement
- describe how rotation is initiated
- using relevant sporting examples, demonstrate knowledge of the types of rotation possible about each of the three axes of rotation (i.e., longitudinal, transverse and frontal)
- define and carry out simple calculations using the appropriate units of measurement for each of the following quantities of angular motion:
  - angular distance
  - angular displacement
  - angular speed
  - angular velocity
  - angular acceleration
- apply each of Newton's three laws to angular motion (analogues of Newton's laws)
- define moment of inertia and explain the factors that determine its value
- explain the relationship between moment of inertia and angular velocity and the resulting effect on the efficiency and ease of movement when somersaulting and spinning
- explain the law of conservation of angular momentum
- using examples from sporting activity, sketch graphical representations of angular velocity, moment of inertia and angular momentum.
- critically evaluate performance with reference to linear motion in the following types of physical activity:
  - running
  - jumping
  - throwing
  - hitting/kicking
  - rotating.

CHAPTER INTRODUCTION

The main focus of this chapter is the investigation into angular motion in sporting activity. Angular motion pervades all sport since it not only occurs when an entire body, object or projectile rotates (for example, when a gymnast performs a somersault or a tennis player applies topspin to a ball), but it also underpins all movement as the levers of the body (bones) rotate about fixed axes of rotation (joints) to enable a performer to move! So, it is impossible to study human movement without exploring angular motion. In fact, an understanding of angular motion is critical in the search for perfection of technique in all sport, whether it is the leg action in sprinting or the body position when somersaulting and twisting in diving.

Before we embark on our exploration of angular motion, we will first review the work studied at AS level on centre of mass and stability.

> **Key term**
>
> **Angular motion** Angular motion, or rotation, occurs when all parts of a body or object move in a circle or part circle about a fixed axis of rotation.

Centre of mass (COM)

The centre of mass is *where the weight of a body tends to be concentrated*. This signifies that point about which the object or body is balanced in all directions. For spherical objects such as a shot the mass is distributed symmetrically around its centre, which therefore indicates its centre of mass. Due to irregular body shapes, however, the centre of mass is not so obvious for humans. For a person standing erect with hands by their sides, the point of centre of mass is approximately at navel height, but this point is constantly changing during movement. For example:

- if a person raises both arms above their head, the centre of mass will move higher up the body
- if the person adducts their arm to the right of the body, the centre of mass will move slightly to the right.

So, depending upon the shape of the body the centre of mass will vary.

Fig 15.1 The Fosbury flop technique in high jump can enable the high jumper's centre of mass to actually travel underneath the bar!

The centre of mass of an object or human body does not have to lie within its actual physical matter. Consider a quoit or rubber ring, for example. The centre of mass of these objects will actually fall at the centre right in the middle of the hole. Similarly, by altering body shape the human performer can manipulate their centre of mass so that it actually lies outside the body.

Athletes and coaches can use their knowledge of this concept in order to improve performance. A perfect

example is the high jump. The Fosbury flop technique was developed so that greater heights could be achieved with similar outlay of effort. By arching the back, the centre of mass will move outside the body, and may pass underneath the bar while the jumper actually travels over the bar! The jumper using the Fosbury flop technique will therefore not need to raise their centre of mass as high as someone performing a western roll or scissor technique when clearing the same height.

> **Key term**
>
> **Centre of mass** The point where the mass of a body tends to be concentrated and is balanced in all directions.

> **Exam-style Questions**
>
> 1   Explain the concept of centre of mass.   **[2 marks]**
>
> 2   Explain how a high jumper changes the position of her centre of mass by changing body shape after take off.   **[3 marks]**
>
> 3   How does the position of the centre of mass change during the performance of a jump shot in basketball?   **[2 marks]**

Stability and balance

Stability is the ability of an object to resist motion and remain at rest. The more stable a body, the greater is its ability to resist motion. In sporting activity stable positions occur when balancing or when defensive positions need to be adopted. More often, however, performers need to become unstable as unstable positions allow performers to change their state of motion and actually move – a central part of most sporting activity!

Fig 15.2 A judo player maximises stability by lowering their centre of mass

Fig 15.3 A gymnast maintains balance in an arabesque by ensuring her centre of mass is over her base of support

Therefore, factors that affect stability include:

- mass of the body or object (the greater the mass, the more stable the body)
- size of the base of support (the larger the base of support, the more stable the body)
- height of the centre of mass (the lower the centre of mass, the more stable the body)
- number of points of contact with the surface (the greater the number of points of contact, the more stable the body)
- proximity of line of gravity to the centre of the base of support (the closer the line of gravity to the centre of the base of support, the more stable the body).

The position of the centre of mass is also important for maintaining balance. An object or person will remain in balance as long as the centre of mass remains directly over its base of support (because the force of mass will always act directly down). As soon as the centre of mass moves away from the base of support, the object will become more unstable. Take the example of a gymnast on a balance beam: as soon as the centre of mass moves outside the beam, the gymnast will become unstable and fall.

If the centre of mass is lowered or the base of support is increased in size, the more stable the object or body. To illustrate this, consider the following examples:

- rugby players forming a platform for a ruck take a large step and lower their hips, which ensures a stable platform, thus enabling them to stay on their feet
- a judo player assumes a wide stance, in order to resist attacks from their opponent.

Key terms

Stability Stability is the ability of an object to resist motion and remain at rest.
Line of gravity An imaginary line which extends from the centre of mass directly down to the ground.

Activity 1

Using examples from a range of different sports, explain occasions when a performer needs to be stable and when they need to be unstable.

Levers, turning effects and angular motion

Levers

Efficient and effective movement is made possible by a system of levers. These are mechanical devices used to produce turning motions about a fixed point (called a fulcrum). In the human body, bones act as levers, joints act as the fulcra and muscle contractions provide the effort to move the lever about the fulcrum.

A basic understanding of lever systems can be used to explain rotational motion, and help athletes develop the most efficient technique for their sport.

There are three types of lever, and each is determined by the relationship of the **fulcrum (F)**, the point of application of force or **effort (E)** and the weight of the lever or **load (L)**.

1 In a first class lever the **fulcrum** lies between the **effort** and the **load.**
2 In a second class lever the **load** lies between the **fulcrum** and the **effort.**
3 In a third class lever the **effort** lies between the **fulcrum** and the **load.**

EXAMINER'S TIPS

A simple way of determining the class or order of the lever system operating during a specified movement is to remember the following rhyme: 'For 1, 2, 3 – think F, L, E' to determine the middle component of the lever system, so that:

- for a first class lever, F is in between L and E
- for a second class lever, L is between F and E
- for a third class lever, E is between F and L.

But beware, as there may be more than one lever system operating at a joint. For example, when flexing the elbow, as in a bicep curl, the effort comes from the point of insertion of the biceps brachii on the radius. This movement involves a third class lever. However, when extending the elbow, as in throwing the javelin, the effort is

▶

generated by the triceps brachii via its point of insertion on the ulna. This movement involves a first class lever.

The majority of movements in the human body are operated as third class levers.

The effort force is applied via the insertion of the agarist muscle.

Table 15.1 The three classes of lever system

Class of lever	Order of components	Examples in the body	Primary function
First class lever EA RA L E F	E, F, L or L, F, E	• Extension of the neck • At the elbow when throwing	Increases the speed at which a given load or object can move
Second class lever RA L E F EA EA > RA = mechanical advantage	F, L, E or E, L, F	• At the ball of the foot where the metatarsals meet the phalanges. Used when standing on tip toe or jumping	Used to overcome heavy loads
Third class lever EA E L F RA RA > EA = mechanical disadvantage	F, E, L or L, E, F	• At the elbow when performing a bicep curl • At the knee when kicking	Increases the speed at which a given load can move

Key terms

Lever Mechanical devices in which an effort force causes the rotation of a rigid bar about a fixed point (fulcrum). In the human body muscles produce the effort force, bones are rigid bars and joints act as the fulcra.

First class lever A lever system in which the fulcrum lies between the effort and the load.

Second class lever A lever system in which the load lies between the effort and the fulcrum.

Third class lever A lever system in which the effort lies between the load and the fulcrum.

Functions of levers

Levers have two main functions:

- to overcome load forces that a given effort can move
- to increase the speed at which a body moves.

First class levers can increase both the effects of the effort and the speed of a body; second class levers tend only to increase the effect of the effort force; whilst third class levers can be used to increase the speed of a body. One example of a third class lever in the body is the action of the hamstrings and quadriceps on the knee joint, which causes flexion and extension of the lower leg. The extent to which this can increase the speed of movement depends upon the relative lengths of the resistance (load) arm and the effort arm.

The resistance arm (RA) or load arm (LA) is the part of the lever between the fulcrum and the resistance. The longer the resistance arm, the quicker the lever system can move. In sport, implements such as bats or rackets are often used to increase the length of the resistance arm, which will increase the outgoing velocity of an object such as a ball. However, the optimal length of an implement should be determined by the strength of the person handling it, which is why, for example, junior tennis rackets have been designed.

The effort arm (EA) is the distance between the fulcrum and the effort; the longer the effort arm, the less effort required to move a given resistance. The effort arm can often be increased to overcome a heavy object.

The relative efficiency of the lever system is expressed as the mechanical advantage (MA), which can be determined as follows:

$$MA = \frac{\text{effort arm (EA)}}{\text{resistance arm (RA)}}$$

Mechanical advantage occurs in a lever system where the effort arm is longer than the resistance arm. This means that the lever system is very effective at overcoming and moving heavy loads.

Mechanical disadvantage occurs in a lever system where the resistance arm is longer than the effort arm. This means that the lever can be put into action very quickly but is not as effective at moving heavy loads or overcoming resistance. The efficiency of levers in the body is illustrated in Table 15.1.

Fig 15.4 The third class lever system operating at the knee joint when kicking a ball

EXAMINER'S TIP

The efficiency of a lever system is determined by the relative lengths of EA and RA. Where EA>RA the system is in mechanical advantage. Where RA>EA the system operates in mechanical disadvantage.

Activity 2

Explain why the third class lever system operating at the elbow is much less efficient at exerting a force on the surroundings than the second class lever system operating at the ankle.

Torques and moments of force

Since levers of the human body are capable of rotational movement only, the majority of movements in sporting activity are of an angular nature about a joint (fulcrum). Consider the movements of the femur about the hip when sprinting or the humerus about the shoulder when bowling a cricket ball: both these examples of skills involve angular motion. The twisting or turning effect of an applied force is known as the moment of force or torque. The moment of force is directly related to the distance between the point of application of the force (muscle insertion) and the fulcrum (joint). This is known as the moment arm (MA) and can be applied either to the effort arm (EA) or the resistance arm (RA).

The largest turning effect or rotation will occur where the moment arm is at its longest or the force applied is at its greatest. For example, when preparing to dive from a platform, the diver will lean out just prior to the dive, causing an increase in the moment arm (resistance arm) and the rotational effect (Figure 15.5). Alternatively, the leg muscles of the diver could produce a much greater effort force.

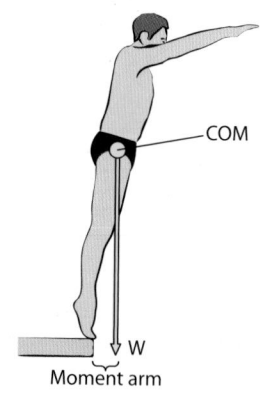

Fig 15.5 The moment of force/torque of a diver is increased by leaning out in preparation for the dive, increasing the moment arm and the overall angular motion

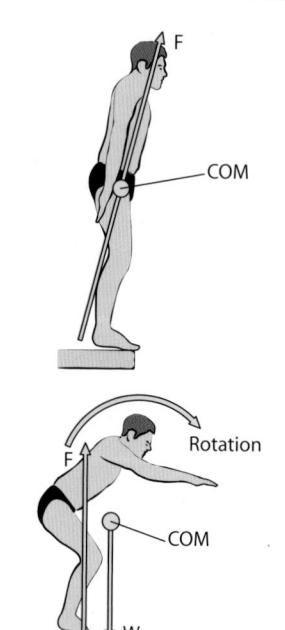

Furthermore, the moment of force or turning effect on the diver is increased when the effort force does not pass through their centre of mass. You will recall that this off-centre force is called an **eccentric force**, and is vital for effective rotation. Look at Figure 15.6. When the force is applied through the centre of mass as in Figure 15.6(a), the resulting motion will be **linear**. But when the force is applied outside the centre of mass as in Figure 15.6 (b), the resulting motion will be **angular**. By moving the centre of mass in front of the effort force, the diver can produce an eccentric force allowing them to maximise their angular motion.

Fig 15.6 Eccentric forces (a) when applying a direct force through the centre of mass, the resulting motion will be linear (b) when applying a force which does not pass through the centre of mass the resulting motion will be angular

So, it can be seen that the turning effect or moment of force of a lever system can be increased by:

- producing a larger effort force
- moving the point of application of the force further away from the fulcrum.

Consider the following example of a bicep curl:

Moment of force	=	size of force (N)	×	the perpendicular distance of force from fulcrum (M)

Moment of force $= 120N \times 0.35M$

$= 42Nm$

> **Key terms**
>
> **Moment of force/torque** The rotational effect of an applied force. It is dependent upon the distance of the point of application of the force from the fulcrum and the magnitude of the force. It is measured in Newton meters (Nm).
>
> **Moment arm** The distance of the point of application of force from the fulcrum and relates to either the effort arm (EA) or resistance arm (RA).

Calculating the moment of force/torque

The moment of a force is equal to the product of the force applied multiplied by the length of the moment arm:

Moment of force	=	size of force (N)	×	the perpendicular distance of force from fulcrum (M)

Units of measurement = Nm

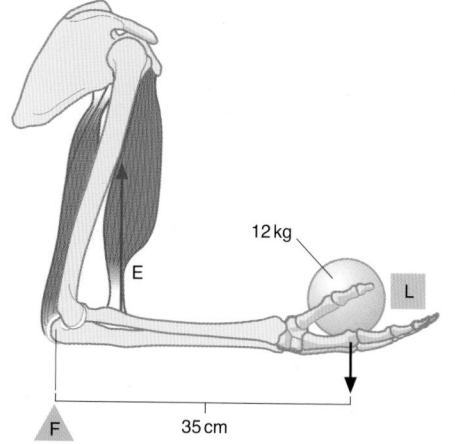

Fig 15.7 The moment of force produced during the performance of a bicep curl

Activity 3

Calculate the moment of force in the first class lever (see Figure 15.8) as an athlete throws a javelin.

Note: remember to show each stage of your calculation, convert given figures into the relevant units (i.e., Newtons and metres) and state the correct units of measurement.

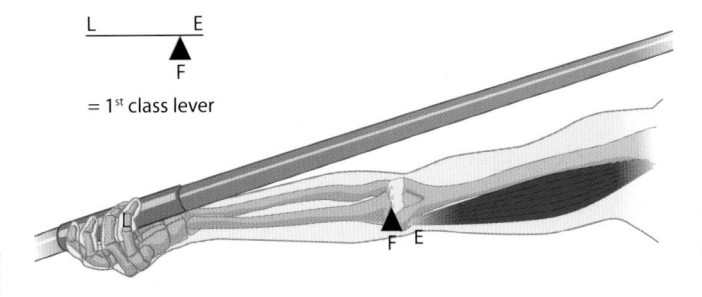

= 1st class lever

Fig 15.8 A lever system operating when throwing the javelin

The principle of moments

In order for a lever system to maintain equilibrium, the moment of force or torque that causes the system to rotate in one direction must be cancelled out by an equal moment of force acting in the opposite direction. This is best explained using the example of a bicep curl. When holding a barbell stationary with the elbows flexed at 90 degrees, as illustrated in Figure 15.9, there is a tendency for this lever to rotate clockwise due to the force of the load. In order for the lever system to remain balanced and the barbell held stationary, the bicep must produce a force equal to the clockwise moment of force.

Total clockwise moment (Lxb)	=	Total anticlockwise moment (E × a)
Clockwise moment	=	load force (N) × distance of load to fulcrum (M)
Anticlockwise moment	=	Effort force (of muscle) × distance of muscle insertion from the joint (M)

This concept is commonly known as the principle of moments, and explains how a system can be balanced about a fulcrum.

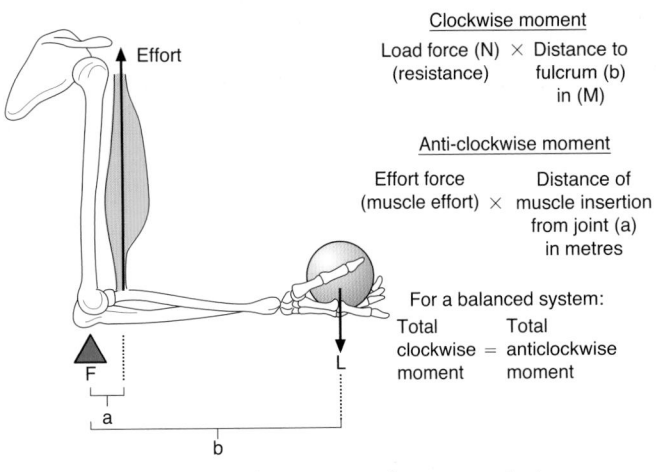

Clockwise moment

Load force (N) × Distance to (resistance)   fulcrum (b) in (M)

Anti-clockwise moment

Effort force × Distance of (muscle effort)   muscle insertion from joint (a) in metres

For a balanced system:

Total clockwise = Total anticlockwise moment   moment

Fig 15.9 The principle of moments is demonstrated when an athlete creates a balanced lever system at the elbow when holding a barbell stationary

Key term

The principle of moments A method of determining the effort force required to maintain a balanced lever system. It is summarised as follows:

Total clockwise moment = Total anti-clockwise moment

EXAMINER'S TIP

To help you determine which is the clockwise moment and which is the anticlockwise moment, draw arrows on your lever system to show the direction of the forces acting. This will help you discover which way the lever system will rotate if it becomes unbalanced.

Activity 4

Use the principle of moments to calculate the effort force produced by the gastrocnemius to hold the body position steady whilst standing on tip toes. Remember to show each stage of your calculation and give the correct units of measurement.

Axes of rotation

Rotation of the body occurs about one (or more) of the three principal axes of the body. Essentially, these axes are imaginary poles that run through the centre of mass of a performer and about which the body can rotate. The longitudinal axis runs through the body from top to bottom, the transverse axis runs from one side of the body to the other and the frontal axis runs front to back. Table 15.2 summarises the sporting and body actions that can occur about each axis.

Table 15.2 Principal axes and their associated movements

Axis	Position in the body	Example from sport where rotation occurs	Angular movements possible at the joints
Longitudinal axis	Runs through the body (or joint) from top to bottom	Spinning ice skater	Pronation, supination, rotation
Transverse axis	Runs through the body (or joint) from side to side	A diver performing a forward or backward somersault	Flexion, extension, dorsiflexion, plantar flexion
Frontal axis	Runs through the body (or joint) from front to back	A gymnast performing a side somersault or cartwheel	Abduction, adduction, lateral flexion

CHALLENGE YOURSELF

The concept of centre of mass (COM) is key to the successful performance of many techniques in sport. Explain how performers manipulate their COM at take off and during flight. Describe the role of the ankle as a lever system at take off. **[15 marks]**

EXAMINER'S TIPS

For your examination you will be required to know the following for each quantity of angular motion:

- a definition
- the relevant equation
- the correct units of measurement.

Quantities of angular motion

Quantities used to explain linear motion also apply to angular motion. For your examination you will be required to define, state the equations for, and use them to calculate, the following quantities of angular motion:

- angular distance
- angular displacement
- angular speed
- angular velocity
- angular acceleration.

Angular distance vs angular displacement

Just as the distance travelled by a body moving linearly can be measured, so can the distance and displacement of a body that is rotating about an axis. Angular distance is the total angle a body has rotated about an axis from start to finish, whereas angular displacement is the shortest change in angular position of a body as it rotates about an axis. It is the smallest angle between the starting and finishing position. Consider the example of a golf swing, illustrated in Figure 15.11. The angular distance is the path followed by the golf club-head, while the angular displacement is shown as the smallest angle between the club head's starting position and finishing position.

You might expect to use degrees as the unit of measurement when analysing the angles through which a body has rotated. However, in our study of angular motion, we will need to use Radians (rads) as the standard unit of measurement. You will need to convert degrees into radians when using angles in any calculations you perform.

1 radian = 57.3 degrees; 1 degree = 0.0175 radians

Key terms

Angular distance The total angle a body turns through when rotating about an axis; measured in radians (rads).
Angular displacement The smallest angle between the starting and finishing position of a body having rotated about an axis; measured in radians (rads).
Radian A measurement of the angle through which a body has rotated where: 1 radian = 57.3 degrees; 1 degree = 0.0175 radians. $360° = 2\pi$ rads.

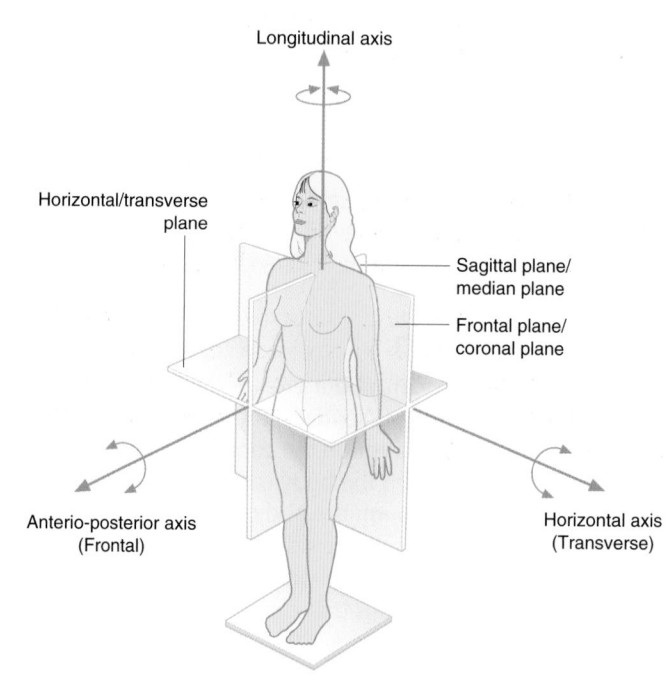

Longitudinal axis

Horizontal/transverse plane

Sagittal plane/median plane

Frontal plane/coronal plane

Anterio-posterior axis (Frontal)

Horizontal axis (Transverse)

Fig 15.10 The principal axes of the body

Angular speed vs angular velocity

Angular speed is the angular distance a body has rotated in a specified time. It is therefore measured in **radians/second** and can be calculated as follows:

$$\text{Angular speed} = \frac{\text{Angular distance (rads)}}{\text{Time taken (secs)}}$$

The angular velocity of a body is the angular displacement resulting from the rotation of a body in a specified time. It is once again measured in **radians/second** and can be calculated as follows:

$$\text{Angular velocity} = \frac{\text{Angular displacement (rads)}}{\text{Time taken (secs)}}$$

Key terms

Angular speed The angular distance a body has rotated in a specified time; measured in rads/sec.
Angular velocity The angular displacement resulting from the rotation of a body in a specified time; measured in rads/sec.

Activity 5

Given that:

$360° = 2\pi$ radians

Calculate the following angular distances in radians an athlete rotates during the following skills from sport:

● a trampolinist performing a half-twist jump
● a high diver performing a triple back somersault
● the rotation of the humerus at the shoulder joint during one complete arm pull in swimming front crawl.

IN CONTEXT

A trampolinist performing a tucked back somersault, turns through 360° in 2 seconds. Their resulting angular speed is therefore 180° per second. However, their angular velocity is zero since the starting and finishing positions of the trampolinist are the same, causing angular displacement to be zero!

Angular acceleration

This is the rate of change of angular velocity, and is measured in radians/sec². It can be calculated using the following equation:

$$\text{Angular acceleration (rads/sec}^2\text{)} = \frac{\text{Change in angular velocity (rads/sec)}}{\text{time taken (secs)}}$$

Key term

Angular acceleration The rate of change of angular velocity. Measured in rads/sec².

Angular analogues of Newton's laws

In attempting to explain angular motion we must once again visit Newton's three laws of motion since the laws that govern linear motion also underpin angular motion. The difference with the angular analogues of Newton's laws lies simply in the language of the law.

Activity 6

Before you read any further, revise Newton's laws of linear motion and see if you can determine the angular analogues of each law.

Newton's first law of angular motion

'A rotating body will continue to turn about its axis of rotation with constant angular momentum unless an external torque or eccentric force is exerted upon it.'

In interpreting this law we can state that a diver performing a somersault will continue to rotate at a constant angular momentum until they enter the water. The water entry creates an external torque causing the angular momentum of the diver to change.

Fig 15.12 The rotation of the trampolinist in a piked position is great as the moment of inertia (it's resistance to angular motion) is law!

This law is also known as the law of conservation of angular momentum. While in flight the only significant force acting on the diver is her weight and as weight cannot alter their angular momentum, it remains unchanged and *is therefore said to be conserved*. This concept will be discussed in more depth later in this chapter.

> **Key term**
>
> **Angular momentum** The quantity of angular motion possessed by a body.

Newton's second law of angular motion

'The angular acceleration (rate of change of angular momentum) of a body is proportional to the size of the torque causing it and takes place in the direction in which the torque acts.'

This law tells us that by increasing the turning effect or torque, a greater angular acceleration can be achieved. An ice skater will increase the torque when performing triple or even quadruple jumps by positioning their arms out to the side and extending one leg behind them just prior to take off, so that the turning moment is as large as possible.

Newton's third law of angular motion

'For every torque that is exerted by one body on another, there is an equal and opposite torque exerted by the second body on the first'

This is the angular form of the action–reaction law and can easily be seen in sporting activity:

- in the long jump, as the legs are brought forward and upward to land, a reaction force causes the arms to be brought forward and downward.
- if a ballet dancer wishes to perform a full twist jump with rotation to the left, they must first create a torque by applying a right-sided force to the floor. This downward and right-sided force (torque) will propel the dancer upwards and to the left.

> **Activity 7**
>
> 1 Apply the analogue of Newton's first law of motion to an ice skater performing a jump with multiple rotations.
> 2 Apply the analogue of Newton's second law of motion to a trampolinist performing a somersault.
> 3 Apply the analogue of Newton's third law of motion to a gymnast performing a pike jump.

Moment of inertia

The moment of inertia of a body is its reluctance to initiate rotation or, if already undergoing angular motion, its *resistance to* change its state of rotation. This can be compared to its linear counterpart.

The moment of inertia of a body is determined by two key factors:

- its **mass**
- the *distribution of its mass around the axis of rotation*.

Mass of the object

The larger the mass of an object, the greater its moment of inertia and vice versa. Consequently, it is more difficult to apply backspin to a shot put than to a basketball as the shot put has a much larger mass and therefore a higher moment of inertia.

The distribution of mass about the axis of rotation

The further the mass of a body is away from the axis of rotation, the greater its moment of inertia and the larger the force required to make it rotate (or stop it spinning if rotation is already occurring). Where the body's mass is concentrated about the axis, the lower the moment of inertia and the faster the rate of rotation.

Moment of inertia The reluctance of a body to change its state of angular motion.

IN DEPTH

The movement of inertia can be calculated as follows:

Moment of inertia = the sum of (mass of body part × distance from the axis of rotation²)

$$MI = \Sigma (m \times r^2)$$

By decreasing the value of r, the moment of inertia is decreased and angular velocity increases.

If r doubles, the moment of inertia increases by $2^2 = 4$.

If r increases four-fold, the moment of inertia increases by $4^2 = 16$.

Applying moment of inertia to sporting activity

The clearest example of the impact of the moment of inertia in a sporting context is seen in trampolining when comparing the rate of spin of a layout somersault and a tucked somersault. In a layout somersault the mass is distributed further away from the axis of rotation, the trampolinist has a large moment of inertia and a comparatively low rate of rotation. In the tucked position the trampolinist's mass is concentrated closer to the axis of rotation, the moment of inertia is lower and the rate of spin higher.

It is possible, of course, to change the moment of inertia once in flight. The trampolinist, for example, performing a tucked back somersault increases her moment of inertia by kicking out of the somersault and extending her body. This slows the rate of rotation and allows the trampolinist to spot her landing.

Similarly, an ice skater can increase his rate of rotation by pulling his arms in tight to his body when performing a spin.

IN CONTEXT

A knowledge of the relationship between moment of inertia and angular velocity is key in developing a successful sprinting leg action. A sprinter such as Usain Bolt will perform leg drills such as high-knee lifts and bottom flicks in their sprint training. These drills allow the lowest possible moment of inertia of their leg during the recovery phase of the sprint action by encouraging maximal flexion at the knee. This enables the flexed leg to rotate about the hip as quickly as possible (high angular velocity) allowing the foot to strike the track for a subsequent drive phase.

IN CONTEXT

A knowledge of the relationship between moment of inertia and angular velocity is key in developing a successful arm action in swimming the front crawl. A swimmer such as Michael Phelps will perform drills that encourage a high elbow, during the recovery phase of the front crawl stroke. The high elbow during recovery encourages flexion at the elbow, which reduces the moment of inertia of the arm. The reduced moment of inertia allows a quicker rotation of the arm at the shoulder joint so that it can enter the water once again for the next propulsive phase of the stroke.

Activity 8

Consider the slalom skier in Figure 15.13. How might a knowledge of moment inertia help when rounding a flag in the quickest time possible?

Fig 15.13 A slalom skier rounding a flag

Angular momentum

Angular momentum is the quantity of angular motion a body possesses and is the product of moment of inertia and angular velocity.

**Angular momentum = moment of inertia ×
angular velocity**

By now, you should have realised that there is an inverse relationship between the moment of inertia of a body and its angular velocity. That is, when moment of inertia is high, angular velocity is low and when moment of inertia is low, angular velocity is high. Furthermore, this inverse relationship is proportional. Consequently, angular momentum of a body in flight remains constant. This concept arises from Newton's first law of angular motion and is referred to as the law of conservation of angular momentum. This law has particular importance when performing those activities requiring rotation of the body such as diving, gymnastics and ice skating.

Applying the law of conservation of angular momentum to sport

As angular momentum cannot be changed once in flight, it is essential that a performer generates as much angular momentum at take off as necessary to allow sufficient rotation for the successful completion of the required skill. A diver will do this when somersaulting about their transverse axis by extending their arms above their heads immediately prior to take off. This increases the moment of inertia and creates a much larger torque (turning moment) maximising their angular momentum at take off. Upon leaving the diving platform the diver will tuck in as tightly as possible so that moment of inertia is reduced and their angular velocity increased. However, due to this inverse relationship, angular momentum remains constant. Immediately prior to entry the diver will once again extend their body, increasing their moment of inertia, thus causing angular velocity to decrease slowing down the rotation of the diver. This should prevent over-rotation and allow a clean entry into the water.

> **Key term**
>
> **Angular momentum** Angular momentum is the quantity of angular motion a body possesses and is the product of moment of inertia and angular velocity.

> **CHALLENGE YOURSELF**
>
> Describe how an ice skater uses the concept of moment of inertia to control her angular velocity at take off, during flight and upon landing. What is the significance of angular momentum to performing a jump with spin?

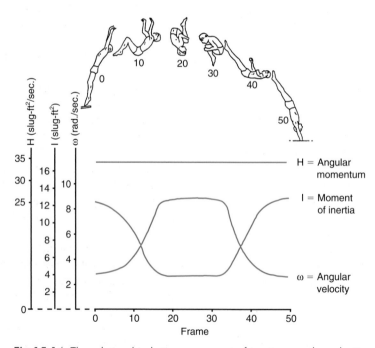

Fig 15.14 The relationship between moment of inertia, angular velocity and angular momentum. Note that angular momentum remains constant throughout the somersault due to inverse proportional relationship between moment of inertia and angular velocity.

What you need to know

* The centre of mass of a body is where the weight tends to be concentrated and the body is balanced in all directions.
* The position of the centre of mass of a body is not fixed; it is dependent upon body shape.
* It is possible for the centre of mass to lie outside the body, such as when performing the Fosbury flop in high jump.
* A body is balanced where the centre of mass lies over the base of support.
* Stability is the ability of an object to resist motion and remain at rest.
* Rotational movement in the body is based around a system of levers.
* Levers in the body have two main functions:
  – to overcome load forces that a given effort can move
  – to increase the rate at which a body moves.
* There are three components to every lever system:
  – an effort force (produced by muscles in the body and applied via the insertion of the agonist muscle)
  – a load force (the weight of a body part and/or implement)
  – a fulcrum (joints in the body).
* There are three classes of lever operating in the body. Which class of lever operates is dependent upon the relative positions of the effort force, load force and fulcrum.
* In a first class lever the fulcrum lies between the effort and load; in a second class lever, the load lies between the effort and the fulcrum; in a third class lever, the effort lies between the load and the fulcrum.
* The efficiency of a lever system is determined by the relative lengths of effort arm (EA) and the resistance arm (RA). Where EA > RA the system is in mechanical advantage. Where RA > EA the system operates in mechanical disadvantage.
* Mechanical advantage in a lever system means that heavy loads can be overcome more easily.
* Mechanical disadvantage in a lever system means that the lever can be put into action very quickly.
* An eccentric force is a force applied outside the centre of mass of a body that causes angular motion to occur.
* Torques or moments of force are the rotational consequences of an applied force.
* Torque = Size of force (N) × Moment arm (m) (perpendicular distance of force from the fulcrum)

* The principle of moments is applied to any balanced lever system; thus;
  Clockwise moment of force (Nm) = Anticlockwise moment of force (Nm)
* There are three principal axes of rotation in the body: the longitudinal axis, the frontal axis and the transverse axis.
* Angular distance is the angle turned about an axis (measured in radians).
* 1 radian = 57.3 degrees; $360° = 2\pi$ rads
* Angular displacement is the smallest angle between starting and finishing positions; measured in radians.
* Angular speed is the angular distance travelled in a specified time (measured in rads/sec).
* Angular velocity is the angular displacement travelled in a specified time (measured in rads/sec).
* Angular acceleration is the rate of change of angular velocity (measured in rads/sec²).
* There are angular analogues to each of Newton's laws of motion.
* The angular analogue of Newton's first law can be stated as 'A rotating body will continue to turn about its axis of rotation with constant angular momentum unless an external torque or eccentric force is exerted upon it.'
* The angular analogue of Newton's second law can be stated as 'The angular acceleration (rate of change of angular momentum) of a body is proportional to the size of the torque causing it and takes place in the direction in which the torque acts.'
* The angular analogue of Newton's third law can be stated as 'For every torque that is exerted by one body on another, there is an equal and opposite torque exerted by the second body on the first.'
* The moment of inertia is the tendency of a body to resist angular motion or if already rotating to resist changes in its state of angular motion.
* The moment of inertia is determined by two key factors:
  – the mass of the body
  – the distribution of the mass of the body from the axis of rotation.
* Moment of inertia (MI) and angular velocity (AV) are inversely proportional so that if MI increases AV decreases proportionally, and vice versa.
* Angular momentum refers to the amount of motion that a rotating body possesses.
* Angular momentum = moment of inertia × angular velocity.

* The law of conservation of momentum results from Newton's first law of motion and explains that the angular momentum of a body cannot be changed once in flight. This is due to the proportionally inverse relationship between moment of inertia and angular velocity.

Review Questions

1 Define centre of mass (COM) and explain its importance when analysing human movement.

2 Name the three principal axes of rotation giving a sporting skill where rotation about each of these axes occurs.

3 Analyse the human lever system during a game of tennis. Give an example when each lever system will be used, sketching diagrams to show each system in action.

4 How can angular momentum be created? Give examples from several different sporting activities.

5 Sketch pin men diagrams of body positions that generate high rates of spin in ice skating and compare these with sketches illustrating body positions that lead to low rates of spin.

6 Use the sport of gymnastics to demonstrate your understanding of the angular analogues of Newton's laws.

7 Using examples from several different sporting activities, demonstrate your understanding of the concept of moment of inertia.

8 How might a sprint coach use his knowledge of the moment of inertia in the coaching of his athletes?

9 Explain why angular momentum is conserved during flight and suggest how an ice skater might maximise their angular momentum at take off.

10 Sketch a graph to show angular velocity against time as a trampolinist travels through a tucked front somersault. Add to your graphs lines representing:

(a) the moment of inertia

(b) angular momentum.

CHAPTER 16

The biomechanical study of performance in selected physical activities

Learning outcomes

By the end of this chapter you should be able to:

- apply your knowledge of biomechanics to a range of physical activities that include:
  - running
  - jumping
  - throwing
  - hitting/kicking
  - rotating.
- critically evaluate performance in terms of quality, effectiveness and efficiency in the following types of activity:
  - running
  - jumping
  - throwing
  - hitting/kicking
  - rotating.

CHAPTER INTRODUCTION

This chapter draws together the biomechanical principles that you have studied and seeks to apply them to a range of practical activities. In your examination you will be required to critically evaluate a performance in terms of its quality, effectiveness and efficiency by the application of biomechanical concepts and principles that you have studied in the preceding chapters. It is hoped that, as you progress through this chapter, you will develop the confidence to draw together your knowledge of biomechanics, thus allowing you to analyse performance and explain the efficiency and effectiveness of technique based on this biomechanical knowledge. Together with a sound knowledge of exercise physiology, it is hoped that this study of biomechanics will help in the enhancement of your own performance and the performance of others.

This chapter illustrates how biomechanical principles can be applied to sporting performance. The application of knowledge to particular sporting activities here is not meant to be definitive or exhaustive. It simply demonstrates the type of information that can be applied to particular sporting activity identified.

Running

Example shown – 100m sprint

Other examples include: sprinting, endurance running, swerving, side-stepping and dodging in team games.

NEWTON'S LAWS

N1 According to Newton's first law of inertia, the sprinter applies a force to the blocks large enough to overcome their inertia. Once in motion the sprinter should move at constant velocity for the remainder of the race, but this is rarely the case owing to external forces that act on the sprinter (e.g. air resistance).

N2 According to Newton's second law of acceleration, the more force the sprinter applies to the track/blocks, the greater their acceleration. Effective application of force is essential so the sprinter will plant their foot actively, thus minimising any braking action on each contact with the track.

N3 Newton's third law of action/reaction in sprinting explains that the sprinter must apply a force downwards and backwards in order to receive an equal and opposite forward and upwards force. A powerful leg extension generates optimal backward force on to the track, which provides an equal and opposite force on to the sprinter.

TYPES OF FORCE

Vertical forces:
1 Weight of sprinter (acts downwards)
2 Reaction force from the track (acts upwards).

Horizontal forces:
1 Air resistance (acts in the opposite direction to the direction of motion)
2 Friction between spikes and track (opposes motion between the foot and track. Therefore, friction acts in the same direction as the direction of motion of the sprinter).

The sprinter seeks to increase friction by wearing running spikes, thus optimising the forward force and maximising acceleration

MOMENT OF INERTIA – THE LEG ACTION

The moment of inertia is the reluctance of a rotating body to change its state of angular motion. This is influenced by the mass of the leg and the distribution of the mass from the axis of rotation. In sprinting the leg rotates about the horizontal axis of the hip joint. During the drive phase the leg is extended where the mass of the leg is a long way from the axis of rotation and, therefore, has a high moment of inertia and a relatively slow angular velocity. Effective sprinting technique requires a fully flexed leg followed by a high knee lift during the recovery phase of the leg action. This brings the mass of the leg closer to axis of rotation, which reduces the moment of inertia and increases the angular velocity. This means that the leg can be brought through quicker, increasing the stride pattern and allowing the leg to land actively, ready to apply force to the track once again.

GRAPH OF MOTION DURING A 100M SPRINT

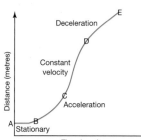

LEVER SYSTEMS

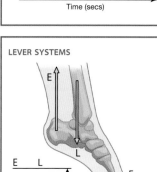

= 2nd class lever

At the ankle:
Second class lever system

Order of components:
F, L, E

EA > RA creating mechanical advantage.

EA = the distance between the effort and the fulcrum

RA = the distance between the load and the fulcrum

This allows the sprinter to shift their body weight more easily. The greater the difference between EA and RA, the more efficient the sprinting technique.

REDUCING AIR RESISTANCE

Minimising air resistance is essential for effective sprinting. To reduce the effects of air resistance and promote laminar flow, sprinters can:

* minimise cross-sectional area by using appropriate sprinting technique
* wear tight-fitting clothes such as Lycra body suits
* wear shiny clothes.

IMPULSE

Impulse considers the length of time a force is applied, i.e:. **Impulse = Force × Time**

In sprinting, a force is applied by the foot striking the track. Efficient and effective sprinting technique requires impulse to be optimised. This can be done by ensuring the leg is fully extended during the drive phase.

From the impulse graph the first section is **negative**, which represents the foot striking the track, which acts opposite to the direction of motion. The second section is **positive**, which represents the foot driving upwards from the track in the same direction as the motion of the sprinter.

At the beginning of the race: The positive section > negative section, which results in acceleration of the sprinter as there is an overall net force acting in a forward direction.

During the middle of the race: The positive section = negative section, which results in constant velocity of the sprinter as there is no net force acting.

Towards the end of the race: The positive section < negative section, which results in deceleration as the net force is backward, causing the sprinter to slow down.

For an example of an **Impulse graph**, see Figure 13.10 on page 231.

NET FORCE

At beginning of the race:
> Friction > Air resistance = Acceleration

There is a forward net force

In the middle of the race:
> Friction = Air resistance = Constant velocity

There is zero net force

At the end of the race:
> Friction < Air resistance = Deceleration

There is a backward net force.

FREE BODY DIAGRAMS

At beginning of the race:
> Friction > Air resistance = Acceleration

In the middle of the race:
> Friction = Air resistance = Constant velocity

At the end of the race:
> Friction < Air resistance = Deceleration

Jumping

Example shown – high jump

Other examples include: long jump, triple jump, jumps in gymnastics and trampolining, ski jumping and some team games.

NEWTON'S LAWS

N1 According to Newton's first law of inertia, the high jumper alters their state of motion by changing from horizontal to upwards acceleration at take-off. The stimulus for this change in the state of motion is the powerful muscular contraction at take-off.

N2 According to Newton's second law of acceleration, the more force the high jumper applies to the track at take-off, the greater their upwards acceleration. Effective application of force is essential so that the high jumper maximises upwards acceleration. The high jumper will achieve this by performing a heel-toe rock in order to generate maximum force.

N3 Newton's third law of action/reaction in high jump explains that the high jumper must apply a very large downwards force at take-off in order to receive an equal and opposite upwards force to propel them upwards and over the bar. When performing the Fosbury flop technique the high jumper must travel over the bar on their back. To ensure they rotate onto their back as they pass over the bar, the high jumper will turn their take-off foot out; thus their take-off foot will face away from the bar.

STABILITY AND CENTRE OF MASS

Stability: The ability of a body to resist motion and to remain at rest. In fact, the high jump requires the performer to become unstable at take-off so that the high jumper can easily change their state of motion. At take-off the base of support is small with only one point of contact (only a one-footed take-off is permitted) and the COM is high. All of these factors facilitate the unstable position required for effective technique. To optimise the efficiency of the Fosbury flop technique, it is essential that the reaction force is very close to, but does not quite pass through, the COM of the high jumper. This allows good upward acceleration, but also allows the high jumper to rotate when travelling over the bar.

Centre of mass (COM): this is where the weight of the body tends to act and signifies the point where the body is balanced in all directions. The Fosbury flop technique causes the high jumper's COM to move outside their body and may actually travel underneath the high jump bar. This means that the high jumper performing the Fosbury flop technique does not need to raise their COM as high as a jumper performing an alternative high jump technique such as the Western roll, making the Fosbury flop the most efficient and effective high jump technique.

TYPES OF FORCE

Vertical forces acting at take-off:
1 Weight of high jumper (acts downwards).
2 Reaction force from the track (acts upwards).
For upward acceleration:
   Reaction > Weight

THE BODY AS A PROJECTILE

Once in flight the high jumper becomes a projectile. Only two forces will act on the high jumper in flight: Weight and Air resistance. As Air resistance is negligible and the high jumper's weight large, Weight becomes the dominant force and the high jumper's flight becomes parabolic.

LEVER SYSTEMS

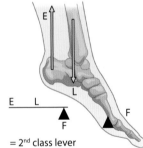

= 2nd class lever

At the ankle:
Second class lever system

Order of components:
F, L, E

EA > RA creating mechanical advantage.

EA = the distance between the effort and the fulcrum

RA = the distance between the load and the fulcrum

This allows the high jumper to overcome their weight more easily. The greater the difference between EA and RA, the more efficient the take-off will be.

IMPULSE

Impulse considers the length of time a force is applied, i.e.:

   Impulse = Force × Time

In the high jump, force is applied by the foot striking the track. Efficient and effective high-jumping technique requires impulse to be optimised at take-off. This can be achieved by performing a 'heel-toe rock' whereby the high jumper plants their heel onto the track and then rocks onto their toes, which allows force to be applied to the track for a longer period of time. At the same time, the high jumper will lean backwards as they plant their take-off foot, thus increasing the time it takes for their body to pass over their take-off foot, further increasing impulse and upward acceleration.

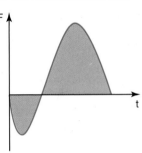

From the impulse graph the first section is negative. This represents the foot striking the track, which acts opposite to the direction of motion.

The second section is positive. This represents the foot driving upwards from the track in the same direction as the motion of the high jumper, thus causing maximum upward acceleration.

NET FORCE

In order for the high jumper to accelerate upwards, the net force must be upwards, i.e.:

   Reaction force > Weight

An upwards net force results from the normal reaction of the track (from Newton's third law equal to the weight of the high jumper) and by the high jumper producing and applying a powerful muscular force to the track so that:

| **Total reaction** | = | **Normal reaction** | + **Internal muscular force** |

FREE BODY DIAGRAMS

There are only vertical forces operating.

At take-off the free body diagram will show reaction force to be significantly larger than weight.

Where R > W the result is upward acceleration.

Throwing

Example shown – javelin

Other examples include shot put, discus, throwing, passing and shooting in team games.

NEWTON'S LAWS

N1 According to Newton's first law of inertia, once the javelin is in flight it will continue to travel at a constant velocity. However, this is rarely the case due to the effects of air resistance that act upon the javelin.

N2 According to Newton's second law of acceleration, the more force the thrower applies to the javelin, the greater its acceleration at the point of release. Effective application of force is essential, so the thrower will seek to maximise the impulse during the execution of the throw by optimising the extension of the shoulder and elbow during the preparation phase.

N3 Newton's third law of action/reaction in javelin-throwing explains that the thrower must apply as large a force as possible backwards onto the track during the execution phase in order to receive an equal and opposite forward force. Some throwers apply such a large force that they are thrown forwards onto the track during the recovery phase of the throw.

TYPES OF FORCE

Vertical forces:
1. Weight of javelin (acts downwards)
2. Lift force (acts upwards)

Horizontal forces:
1. Air resistance (acts in the opposite direction to the direction of motion of the javelin).

The thrower will also seek to maximise friction between the foot and the track by wearing long spikes that are firmly planted into the track and that act as an anchor and axis about which the body rotates during the execution phase of the throw.

LIFT FORCE

The javelin is significantly influenced by aerodynamic forces and a lift force can be created when a javelin is released with an angle of attack. Applying Bernoulli's Principle, air travelling over the upper surface of the javelin has further to travel and must, therefore, travel faster than

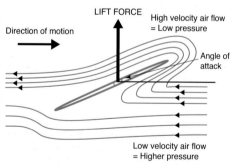

the air travelling along the lower surface. A pressure differential is created between the high pressure created on the bottom of the javelin and the relative low pressure on the upper surface. This difference in pressure creates a lift force from the area of high pressure to the area of low pressure, and the javelin moves upwards, towards the area of low pressure (above the javelin). The lift force allows the javelin to stay in flight for longer than it would if it were released without an angle of attack.

THE FLIGHT OF A JAVELIN

The thrower will apply a large force to the javelin. Once in flight the only forces acting on the javelin will be **weight** and **air resistance**. The thrower will ensure that an additional **lift force** is applied by releasing the javelin with an appropriate angle of attack.

Ultimately, however, air resistance will slow down the javelin so that the weight of the javelin becomes the dominant force.

LEVER SYSTEMS

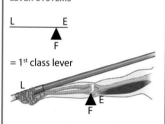

= 1st class lever

At the elbow when throwing:
First class lever system

Order of components:
E, F, L

RA > EA creating mechanical disadvantage

This allows speed to be applied to the javelin so that its acceleration is maximised at the point of release.

TYPES OF FORCE

Forces acting on a javelin:
1. Weight of the javelin (acts downwards).
2. Air resistance force (acts in the opposite direction to the direction of motion).
3. A lift force may also be evident due to Bernoulli's principle (this acts upwards from the COM of the javelin).

IMPULSE

Impulse considers the length of time a force is applied, i.e.:

Impulse = Force × Time

Efficient and effective javelin technique requires impulse to be optimised during the execution and release phases. This is achieved by ensuring that the throwing arm is 'long ' and throws are made from a fully extended position. Additionally, during the execution phase the thrower will rotate the trunk at the hips prior to

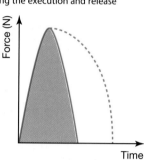

whipping the arm through, which once again extends the time over which muscular force is applied to the javelin, thus maximising outgoing momentum.

The impulse graph illustrates the force applied to the javelin over time. The area represented by the dotted line is where optimum impulse is achieved through maximal extension and follow-through of the throwing arm.

NET (RESULTANT) FORCE ON PROJECTILES

Forces acting on the javelin include Weight, Air resistance (drag) and Lift.

If thrown with an angle of attack, an upwards lift force is created that is greater than the javelin's weight, so the net vertical force is upwards.

The resultant force of the javelin's flight can be illustrated by constructing a parallelogram of forces using the primary forces acting: Lift (which has weight taken into account) and Air resistance.

FREE BODY DIAGRAM OF JAVELIN IN FLIGHT

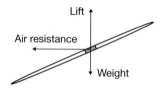

Only forces acting will be Air resistance and Weight.

A lift force may also be seen due to Bernoulli's principle.

The resultant force acting can be calculated by constructing a parallelogram of forces.

Hitting/kicking

Example shown – shots in tennis

Other examples include: shots in badminton, golf, cricket, rounders, free kicks or corner kicks in football, and conversion in rugby.

NEWTON'S LAWS

N1 According to Newton's first law of inertia, the state of motion of a tennis ball is altered every time the player applies a force to it. Once in flight the ball will travel at constant velocity with uniform motion, but this is rarely the case owing to the effects of air resistance, spin, the action of gravity on the ball's mass and the force created as the ball bounces.

N2 According to Newton's second law of acceleration, the more force the tennis player applies to the tennis ball, the greater its acceleration. Effective application of force is dependent upon a number of factors, including appropriate technique and effective timing of the stroke.

N3 Newton's third law of action/reaction in tennis is best seen during the execution of each shot. As the tennis player applies a force to the tennis ball with the racket, the tennis ball applies an equal and opposite force on to the racket. In order to dissipate this reaction force, tennis rackets often have an anti-vibration device built into their shaft.

IMPULSE

Impulse considers the length of time a force is applied, i.e.:

Impulse = Force × Time

Efficient and effective technique in performing tennis strokes requires impulse to be optimised during the execution and recovery (follow through) phases. This is achieved by maximising the time that the racket head is in contact with the tennis ball. Not only does this ensure that the optimal amount of force can be imparted to the tennis ball, increasing outgoing momentum, but it also gives greater control over the direction of travel of the tennis ball.

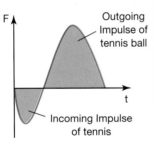

The impulse graph illustrates the force applied to the tennis ball during a forehand drive.

TYPES OF FORCE ON TENNIS BALL

Vertical forces:
1 Weight of tennis ball (acts downwards).
2 Lift force (can act upwards or downwards depending upon the type of spin applied).

Horizontal forces:
1 Air resistance (acts in the opposite direction to the direction of motion of the tennis ball).

The tennis player will also seek to maximise friction between the foot and the court by wearing dimpled tennis shoes which are firmly planted into the court and act as an anchor and axis about which the body rotates during the execution phase of each shot.

THE FLIGHT OF A TENNIS BALL

The flight path of a tennis ball is dependent upon the type of spin imparted onto the ball.

A ball struck with topspin will deviate downwards from its expected flight path, decreasing the distance travelled.

A ball struck with back spin will deviate upwards from its expected flight path, increasing the distance travelled.

Refer to Table 14.3 on page 241.

NET (RESULTANT) FORCE ON PROJECTILES

Forces acting on the tennis ball include Weight, Air resistance (drag) and Lift.

If struck with topspin, a downwards lift (Magnus) force is created which causes the ball to dip.

If struck with backspin an upwards lift (Magnus) force is created that causes the ball to float.

The resultant force of the tennis ball's flight can be illustrated by constructing a parallelogram of forces using the primary forces acting: Weight, Air resistance and any Magnus (lift) force acting.

SPIN AND LIFT/MAGNUS FORCE

When a tennis ball struck with spin travels through the air, the air molecules of the air in contact with the ball spin with it creating a 'boundary layer'. This boundary layer eventually collides head on with the main flow of air on one side of the ball only. This slows down the flow of air on this side of the ball, which increases the pressure on this surface, creating a pressure differential between this surface and the surface on the opposite side of the ball. This pressure differential causes a **Magnus force**, directed from high pressure to low pressure.

When playing topspin: A pressure differential exists between the high pressure along the top surface of the ball and low pressure along the bottom. The Magnus force created pulls down the ball from the area of high pressure to the area of low pressure causing the ball to dip.

When playing backspin: A pressure differential exists between the high pressure along the bottom surface of the ball and low pressure on top. The Magnus force created pulls the ball upwards from the area of high pressure to the area of low pressure causing the ball to float and extend its flight path.

Refer to Table 14.3 on page 241.

LEVER SYSTEMS

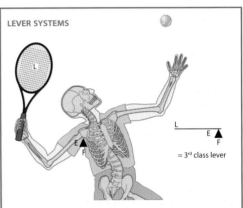

At the shoulder when serving: Third class lever system

Order of components: F, E, L

RA > EA creating mechanical disadvantage. The RA is lengthened with the addition of a racket. The longer the lever, the faster the racket head travels and the greater the outgoing acceleration of the ball.

FREE BODY DIAGRAM OF TENNIS BALL IN FLIGHT

The only forces acting will be Air resistance and Weight.

A lift or Magnus force may also be seen due to the Magnus effect, an extension of Bernoulli's principle when applied to balls struck with spin.

The resultant force acting can be calculated by constructing a parallelogram of forces.

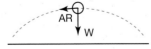

Rotating

Example shown – diving

Other examples include: gymnastics, diving, trampolining, skating and slalom skiing.

EXAMINER'S TIPS

Biomechanical concepts to apply to **rotating** might include: stability, lever systems, rotation, describing angular motion, moment of inertia, angular momentum.

ANGULAR ANALOGUES OF NEWTON'S LAWS

N1 In interpreting Newton's first law of angular motion we see that a diver performing a somersault will continue to rotate at a constant angular momentum until they enter the water. The water entry creates an external torque causing the angular momentum of the diver to change.

N2 This law of angular acceleration tells us that by increasing the turning effect or torque, a greater angular acceleration can be achieved. The diver will increase the torque when performing a double or triple somersault by extending their arms fully above their heads just prior to take-off, so that the turning moment is as large as possible and maximal rotation can occur about the transverse axis.

N3 If a diver wishes to perform a full twisting dive with rotation to the left, they must first create a torque by applying a right-sided force to the diving platform. This downward and right-sided force (torque) will propel the diver upwards and to the left.

AXES OF ROTATION

There are three axes of rotation in the body:

1. When a diver performs a front or backward somersault they will rotate about their transverse axis.
2. When a diver twists they rotate about their longitudinal axis.
3. During a dive the diver may also rotate sideways about their frontal axis.

STABILITY

At take-off, a diver will move from a stable to an unstable position by leaning forward. By leaning forward, the line of gravity is shifted outside the base of support to create instability. This also ensures that the force created by the muscular contractions of the legs at the point of take-off travels outside the COM of the diver, thus producing an eccentric force and initiating rotation of the body.

MOMENT OF INERTIA

The moment of inertia is the reluctance of a rotating body to change its state of angular motion. This is influenced by the mass of the body and the distribution of the mass from the axis of rotation. A diver may rotate about all three axes of the body.

Essentially, the moment of inertia will determine the rate of rotation and, therefore, has important consequences for the effective performance of any particular dive. If during a dive the mass of the body is spread away from the axis of rotation (in a layout position), the rate of spin is low. Conversely, if the mass of the body is close to the axis of rotation (such as in a tucked somersault), the rate of spin is high.

A diver can change their moment of inertia during the dive by altering the shape of their body. For example, by extending the body out of a tucked position, the rate of rotation is slowed, which allows the diver to spot their entry into the water.

ANGULAR MOMENTUM

Angular momentum is the quantity of angular motion a body possesses and is the product of moment of inertia and angular velocity.

Angular = Moment of inertia × Angular velocity
momentum

This relationship is inversely proportional so that when moment of inertia is high, angular velocity is low and when moment of inertia is low angular velocity is high. Consequently, angular momentum of a body in flight remains constant. As angular momentum cannot be changed once in flight, it is essential that a diver generates as much angular momentum at take-off as necessary to allow sufficient rotation for the successful completion of the dive.

A diver will do this when somersaulting about their transverse axis by extending their arms above their heads immediately prior to take-off. This increases the moment of inertia and creates a much larger torque (turning moment), thus maximising their angular momentum at take-off. Upon leaving the diving platform, the diver will tuck in as tightly as possible so that moment of inertia is reduced and their angular velocity increased. However, due to this inverse relationship, angular momentum remains constant.

DESCRIBING ANGULAR MOTION – THE RELATIONSHIP BETWEEN MOMENT OF INERTIA, ANGULAR VELOCITY AND ANGULAR MOMENTUM

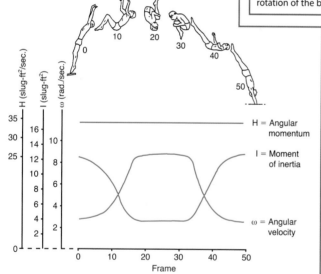

LEVER SYSTEMS

At the ankle:
Second class lever system

Order of components:
F, L, E

EA > RA creating mechanical advantage.

EA = the distance between the effort and the fulcrum

RA = the distance between the load and the fulcrum

This allows the diver to overcome their weight more easily and generate the height at take-off to enable them to perform the required number of rotations to complete the dive competently. The greater the difference between EA and RA, the more efficient the take-off will be and the more power created.

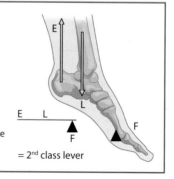

= 2nd class lever

Activity 1

For each of the following types of physical activity mentioned in Table 16.1, apply and explain the biomechanical principles identified in as many sporting examples as possible.

Type of physical activity	Suggested sporting examples	Biomechanical concepts
Running		
Jumping		
Throwing		
Hitting/kicking		
Rotating		

Table 16.1 Biomechanical principles in sport

B3: Exercise Physiology

When examining the performer in action, you need an understanding of physiological concepts within a sporting context. Exercise physiology examines how the body adapts and develops in response to exercise. At the heart of our study is the concept of energy. The body requires energy to perform exercise; it is the aim of the exercise physiologist to seek out ways in which to maximise the amount of energy available to the performer through the implementation of a well-planned training programme. For example, to successfully complete a marathon run, a performer will need to follow a programme comprising continuous methods of training, which will improve the efficiency of the aerobic energy pathway and cause the body to adapt aerobically, facilitating improved performance. Furthermore, the performer will improve energy efficiency by using a number of ergogenic aids, which all aim to enhance performance; for the marathon runner, these aids might take the form of altitude training, glycogen loading or even the use of ice baths.

Therefore, the aim of this section, is for you to develop your knowledge and understanding of the measurement, analysis and improvement of physical fitness and show how the body changes as a result of physical activity. You will be required to use your knowledge gained from this section to explain how physical activity can contribute to a balanced, active and healthy lifestyle.

CHAPTER 17

Energy supply in sport and exercise

Learning outcomes

By the end of this chapter you should be able to:

- define energy, work and power, and identify the units of each
- explain the role of ATP in providing energy in the body
- explain how energy is released from ATP
- describe how ATP is resynthesised via each of the three energy pathways: ATP-PC system, lactic acid system and aerobic system
- identify in each energy system: the type of reaction, the chemical or food fuel used, the site of the reaction, the controlling enzyme, the energy yield (in moles of ATP produced), and any by-products produced
- explain the contribution made by each energy system in relation to the duration and intensity of exercise
- explain how the availability of oxygen and levels of fitness determine which of the energy system operates
- define OBLA and identify the factors that determine when it is reached.

CHAPTER INTRODUCTION

From where do muscles get the energy to provide movement? This chapter aims to answer this and other questions that may arise from our study of physical activity.

Energy is fundamental to the study of sport and, as such, this chapter will examine the sources of energy for muscular contraction and, in particular, the role of adenosine triphosphate (ATP), carbohydrates and fats in the provision of energy.

We will see how the resynthesis of ATP occurs via the ATP-PC (alactic), lactic and aerobic energy systems, and how training can enhance the energy output from the three energy pathways.

Definitions of energy, work and power

Energy is

'the capacity of the body to perform work'

and can exist in many different forms including mechanical, chemical, heat and electrical. Under certain circumstances energy can be transferred from one form to another, and it is this that really interests us here. For example, chemical energy found in food is transformed into mechanical or kinetic energy to enable us to move, or indeed can be transformed into potential energy and stored in the body for use at a later date. The units of energy measurement can be calories (more commonly kilocalories, Kcal) or joules (or kilojoules).

Work done can be defined as

'the product of the force applied to an object and the distance through which the body moves in the direction of the force.'

More simply:

$$\text{work done} = \text{force (N)} \times \text{distance (m)}$$

In order to calculate the work done by a person weighing 80kg walking over 10m we would perform the following calculation:

Work done = force × distance

= (80kg × 10m/s²) × 10m

= 800kgm/s² (N) × 10m

= 8000Nm or joules

Note: in the above calculation we must convert our mass (80kg) into weight. We do this by taking account of acceleration due to gravity (10m/s²), hence our weight force is 80kg × 10m/s².

Power is defined as the amount of work performed per unit of time:

$$power = \frac{work\ done\ (joules)}{time\ (seconds)}$$

Power is therefore measured in joules/sec or Watts. If the person in the above example took 10 seconds to walk the 10m, then the amount of power produced can be calculated as follows:

Power = work done/time

= 8000j/10 s

= 800 Watts

Activity 1

A 65kg woman performs a step test on a 25cm bench for 10 minutes at a rate of 50 steps per minute.

Calculate (a) the work done, and (b) the power output of the woman during the test.

Remember to take account of gravity and to record the distance travelled in metres.

Activity 2

A cyclist wishes to determine his power output when sprinting. A load (resistance) of 80kg is applied to the wheel of the cycle ergometer. The cyclist then sprints over a distance of 200m, which takes him 10 seconds.

Assuming that there are no other forces acting on the cyclist, calculate his power output showing all your workings.

Key terms

Energy The capacity of the body to perform work.
Work The product of force and the distance through which the body/object moves in the direction of the force.
Power The rate at which work is performed or the amount of work performed per unit of time.

The body's energy sources

All movement requires a series of coordinated muscle contractions, which in turn requires a supply of energy. You may think that energy for muscular contraction comes directly from the food we eat, but this food fuel serves only as an indirect source of energy since the body must transfer stored chemical energy from the consumed food into mechanical energy. The chemical energy requirement of a cell is supplied by the breakdown of a high-energy compound called adenosine triphosphate or ATP.

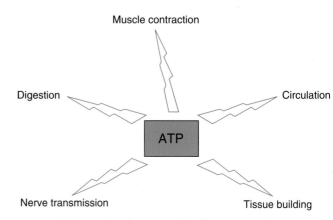

Fig 17.1 ATP supplies the energy for all energy-requiring processes in the body

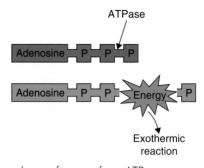

Fig 17.2 The release of energy from ATP

Key terms

Adenosine triphosphate (ATP) The high-energy compound that is the direct source of energy for every energy-requiring process of the body.
Mole A measure of the amount of a substance.

Molecules of ATP consist of atoms held together by a set of bonds that store energy. It is the breaking or splitting of the outermost bond that releases the energy used to fuel all the processes within the body and, in particular, the contraction of skeletal muscle, which facilitates movement. It is the enzyme **ATPase** that helps in the release of energy and, since some of this energy is released in the form of heat, it is known as an exothermic reaction (this is shown in Figure 17.2).

The breakdown of ATP can be summarised as:

$$ATP \rightarrow ADP + Pi + energy$$

EXAMINER'S TIPS

Food is the basic source of energy for cellular activity in the human body. It is ingested, digested, absorbed and stored in the form of various nutrients, which can then be used to resynthesise ATP. The main energy providing nutrients include:

1 Carbohydrates, which are stored in the body as glycogen.
2 Fats, which are stored as triglycerides and are broken down into free fatty acids which provide energy.
3 Proteins or amino acids, which can be utilised for energy once converted to glucose.

Key term

Exothermic reaction A chemical reaction that releases energy (heat).

There is, however, only a limited amount of this high-energy compound in the muscle cell, sufficient only to produce several 'powerful' contractions; or, in a practical context, to run as fast as you can for a few seconds. ATP must therefore be constantly resynthesised in order to provide a continuous supply of energy.

Fig 17.3 The energy to perform a maximum weight lift will be supplied by the splitting of ATP

ATP resynthesis at rest or during prolonged, steady-state exercise occurs via aerobic metabolism – the breakdown of glucose and fat in the presence of oxygen. But, this process is rather slow and cannot meet the demands of high-intensity exercise, such as a 100m sprint, where the body requires energy to recycle ATP very rapidly. The body has therefore adapted several ways in which to resynthesise ATP to ensure a continuous supply of energy.

Fig 17.4 ATP needs to be constantly recycled in order to provide a continuous supply of energy

Exam-style Questions

1 Define the terms energy, work and power, giving the units of measurement for each. **[3 marks]**

2 ATP is a most important compound. Explain why ATP plays such a major role during physical activity. **[3 marks]**

The energy systems

There are three basic pathways or energy systems that govern the replenishment of ATP and, therefore, energy supply. The three energy systems are:

1 The ATP-PC, or alactic system.
2 The lactic acid system.
3 The aerobic system.

Which system operates is largely dependent upon how immediately the energy is required or the duration of the activity, how intense the activity is, and whether or not there is sufficient oxygen available.

Quite simply, the more intense the activity (for example, the faster the athlete runs) the more s/he will rely on anaerobic energy production from the ATP-PC or lactic acid pathways. Conversely, the less intense and the longer the duration of the activity, the more the athlete will rely on the aerobic system of energy production.

EXAMINER'S TIP

It is the intensity and duration of the physical activity that will ultimately determine which method of ATP resynthesis will be in use at any particular time. The higher the intensity, the more we rely on our anaerobic energy systems (ATP-PC and lactic acid systems).

Key terms

Creatine phosphate (phosphocreatine) An energy-rich compound found in the muscle cell that is used to recycle ATP during activities of very high intensity and short duration.
Endothermic reaction A chemical reaction that requires energy (heat).
Sarcoplasm The cytoplasm (fluid-filled watery inner of a cell) of a muscle cell that houses stores of creatine phosphate, glycogen and myoglobin.

The ATP–PC or alactic system

This is the first of the *anaerobic* pathways, which suggests that oxygen is not directly used in the release of energy. This pathway involves the rapid regeneration of ATP through a second energy-rich compound that exists in the muscles called creatine phosphate (also known as phosphocreatine, or PC). Creatine phosphate is broken down in the sarcoplasm of the muscle cell due to the action of the enzyme **creatine kinase**. Creatine kinase is stimulated by the increase in 'free' or inorganic phosphates (Pi) resulting from the breakdown of **ATP into ADP + Pi + energy**. Unlike ATP, the energy derived from the breakdown of phosphocreatine is not directly used for muscle contraction, but instead recycles ATP so that it can once again be broken down to maintain a constant supply of energy. This is an endothermic reaction as energy is consumed in the reaction:

$$Energy + ADP + Pi \rightarrow ATP$$

Once ATP has been broken down to give ADP, a 'free' phosphate and energy, which is used for muscular work, it must be resynthesised for further use.

Since ATP resynthesis requires energy itself, phosphocreatine (PC) is broken down almost simultaneously to provide the energy for ATP resynthesis; it is the energy released from the breakdown of phosphocreatine that is used to rejoin the free phosphate back on to ADP to once again form ATP. This is known as a coupled reaction (see Figure 17.5).

Features of the system

The most important feature of this system is the speed and immediacy with which ATP can be resynthesised through PC since creatine phosphate exists alongside ATP in the sarcoplasm of the muscle cell. This system is therefore used

Table 17.1 Sources of energy to resynthesise ATP in the body

Energy source	Release of energy	Energy provided
ATP	Adenosine triphosphate, existing in muscle tissue is broken down by the enzyme ATPase into adenosine diphosphate (ADP), an inorganic phosphate, and energy	7.6 Kcal/mole
Creatine phosphate	Creatine phosphate existing in muscle tissue is broken down by the enzyme creatine kinase into creatine and free phosphate. The energy released from this reaction is used to resynthesise ATP	7.6 Kcal/mole
Carbohydrate (glycogen)	Carbohydrate is eaten and converted into glycogen where it is stored in the muscles and liver. When needed glycogen is converted to glucose and metabolised via the lactic acid pathway and aerobic system to release energy to resynthesise ATP	4.1 Kcal/g
Fats (fatty acids)	Fats consumed are stored as adipose tissue and triglycerides. When needed, triglyceride is broken down into glycerol and fatty acid molecules. Free fatty acids undergo beta-oxidation and enter the aerobic system, which releases energy to resynthesise ATP	9 Kcal/g
Protein (amino acids)	Nitrogen is removed from the amino acids (deaminated); the remainder is converted into glucose and enters the Krebs cycle	4.1 Kcal/g

Table 17.2 Key features of the ATP-PC system

Site of reaction	Chemical fuel	Controlling enzyme	Energy yield	By-products	Intensity/ duration	Key terms
Sarcoplasm	Creatine phosphate	Creatine kinase	1 mole PC: 1 mole ATP	None	Very high, 3–10 seconds	Coupled reaction

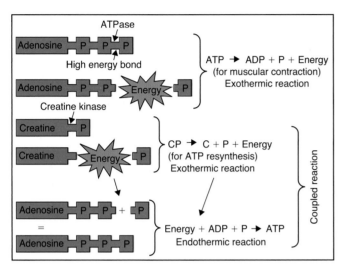

Fig 17.5 ATP resynthesis via the coupled reaction of the ATP-PC system

during the initial stages of very intense muscular activity, such as sprinting, throwing, jumping or, indeed, to provide the energy to start exercising after rest.

The main problem with this system, however, is that like ATP, PC is very limited within the muscle (although there is approximately four times the amount of PC than ATP), and its levels fall as it is used to replenish the depleted ATP. Fatigue occurs when phosphocreatine levels fall significantly and they can no longer sustain ATP resynthesis. This usually occurs after eight to ten seconds of maximum effort, such as that which occurs in a flat out 100m sprint.

> **EXAMINER'S TIP**
>
> The ATP-PC system is used in explosive activities that are of very high intensity but short duration, such as 100m sprinting and many of the athletic field events.

Since the resynthesis of phosphocreatine also requires energy (using energy from ATP again), it can only be replenished when there is sufficient energy available in the body; this is usually through the aerobic pathway when the intensity of exercise is low or during recovery once exercise has stopped.

If exercise continues after the eight to ten second threshold of the ATP-PC system, the muscles must rely on other sources of energy available for ATP resynthesis.

> **Key term**
>
> **Coupled reaction** A reaction in which the product (energy) of one reaction is used by a second reaction.

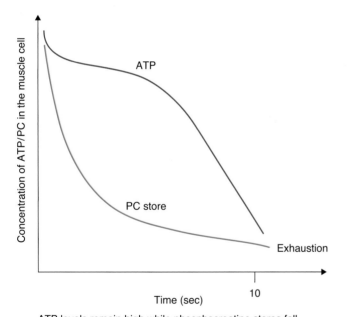

ATP levels remain high while phosphocreatine stores fall rapidly. This is because the energy from phosphocreatine is used to resynthesis ATP, preventing the levels of ATP from falling. After approximately 10 seconds phosphocreatine stores within the muscle are depleted and levels of ATP fall rapidly.

Fig 17.6 The effects of exercise upon muscle phosphogen stores

> **CHALLENGE YOURSELF**
>
> Some performers try to boost their stores of phosphocreatine by taking supplements of creatine monohydrate. The hope is that they can extend the time beyond the typical 10 seconds that they can provide energy from the ATP-PC pathway. Undertake some research on the effects of creatine supplementation.

Table 17.3 An assessment of the value of the ATP-PC system to the sports performer

Advantages	Limitations
• ATP resynthesis is quick • Provides energy for high-intensity activities • PC stores recover quickly • No oxygen is needed • No fatiguing by-products	• Only small stores of PC in muscle cells • Fatigue quickly • Energy provided for only ten seconds • Only 1 mole of ATP from every 1 mole of PC

Exam-style Questions

1   Explain briefly the main process by which ATP is generated during a 60m indoor sprint.   **[4 marks]**

2   A gymnast performing a vault will maintain ATP stores using the ATP-PC system. Using this system as your example, explain the principle of a coupled reaction.   **[4 marks]**

3   Performers may use the ATP-PC system during short, sharp explosive movements. Outline the advantages and disadvantages of this energy system.   **[4 marks]**

IN CONTEXT

A gymnast such as Beth Tweddle will use the ATP-PC system when performing a vault in competition. The vault is a very explosive event that is of very high intensity but of short duration.

The lactic acid pathway

Once stores of phosphocreatine have been depleted within the muscle, ATP must be resynthesised using another energy providing fuel: glycogen. Carbohydrate is eaten in the form of sugar or starch and is stored in the **muscles** and the **liver** as glycogen.

Activity 3

Mark out a 100m track, placing cones at 10m intervals along the 100m distance; a student with a stopwatch is placed on each cone. After a thorough warm up, one student elects to sprint the 100m distance and, on the command 'go', the student starts to sprint and all timers start their stopwatch. As the sprinter passes each 10m interval, the timer should stop their stopwatch, keeping the time on the display until it has been written down and recorded.

Complete the table below:

Section of race (m)	Time at distance	Time for 10m section
0–10		
10–20		
20–30		
30–40		
40–50		
50–60		
60–70		
70–80		
80–90		
90–100		

Explain the process of energy production throughout the run. At what point did the athlete start slowing down? Account for this slowing down.

Key terms

Glycogen The stored form of carbohydrate in the muscles and liver.
Glycolysis The sequence of reactions that converts glucose into pyruvic acid, which releases a small amount (2 moles) of ATP.

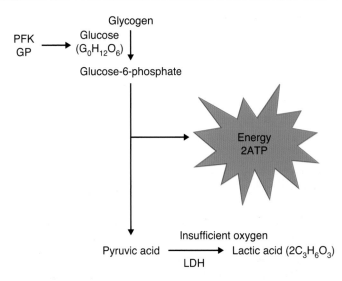

Fig 17.7 A summary of the lactic acid system

Before glycogen can be used to provide energy for ATP resynthesis, it must first be converted into the compound **glucose-6-phosphate**; a process that in itself requires one mole of ATP.

The breaking down of a glucose molecule to liberate energy is known as glycolysis, and since the initial stages of the process are performed in the absence of oxygen, it has become technically known as **anaerobic glycolysis**.

Once glycogen has been converted to glucose-6-phosphate, glycolysis can begin. The glycolytic enzymes **phosphofructokinase (PFK)** and **glycogen phosphorylase (GP)** work on breaking down the glucose molecule in a series of reactions (12 in total) in the sarcoplasm of the cell. Glucose-6-phosphate is broken down into **pyruvic acid (pyruvate)**, which in the absence of oxygen is converted into **lactic acid** by the enzyme **lactate dehydrogenase (LDH)**. This process frees sufficient energy to resynthesise three moles of ATP, but this process uses up energy, so a net gain of 2ATP results:

(a) $C_6H_{12}O_6 \rightarrow 2C_3H_6O_3 + energy$

(b) $energy + 2Pi + 2ADP \rightarrow 2ATP$

Features of the system

The lactic acid system only frees a relatively small amount of energy from the glycogen molecule (approximately 5 per cent) as the lactic acid produced inhibits further glycogen breakdown, which restricts glycolytic enzyme activity. Lactic

acid levels may increase from 1mmol/kg muscle at rest to 25mmol/kg muscle during intense exercise, which causes significant muscle fatigue.

This system does, however, release energy relatively quickly and is therefore responsible for supplying ATP in high-intensity, short-term exercise such as a 400m run or a 100m swim.

Although the lactic acid system is used between 10 seconds and three minutes, it peaks in those events lasting about one minute where the intensity of exercise is high. It also comes into play at the end of aerobic events when the intensity increases, as it does during the sprint finish of a 5000m race.

Table 17.4 Key features of the lactic acid system

Site of reaction	Chemical fuel	Controlling enzyme	Energy yield	By-products	Intensity/ duration	Key terms
Sarcoplasm	Glycogen/ glucose	GP, PFK, LDH	1 mole glycogen: 2 moles ATP	Lactic acid	High intensity, 2–3 minutes	Glycolysis OBLA

Table 17.5 An assessment of the value of the lactic acid system to the sports performer

Advantages	Limitations
• ATP recycled relatively quickly • Can maintain the energy requirements of activities of relatively high intensity • No oxygen is needed • Large stores of glycogen are available	• Lactic acid is produced • Low pH of the muscle cell inhibits enzyme activity • Fatigue relatively quickly • OBLA reached relatively quickly

Key term

Onset of blood lactate accumulation (OBLA) The point at which lactic acid begins to accumulate in the blood. Lactic acid production is greater than lactic acid removal.

EXAMINER'S TIP

The lactic acid system is used during activities that are of high intensity but relatively short in duration (two to three minutes).

IN CONTEXT

A swimmer such as 200m back-stroker Liam Tancock will supply the energy to resynthesise ATP almost entirely from the lactic acid system. Throughout the race lactic acid will be produced and it will start to accumulate once the point where lactic acid production exceeds the rate of lactic acid removal is reached. This signals the onset of blood lactate accumulation, or OBLA, and will cause the muscle 'burn' associated with lactic acid build up.

Activity 4

Run 400 m as fast as you can. At what point did your legs start feeling tired? Account for this onset of fatigue.

Exam-style Questions

1 Some performers will maintain ATP levels in the body almost entirely through the process of glycolysis. Explain what you understand by the term glycolysis and suggest how it might contribute to muscle fatigue. **[4 marks]**

2 This graph shows the levels of lactic acid and glycogen stores in the muscles during a 30-minute interval training session. **[4 marks]**

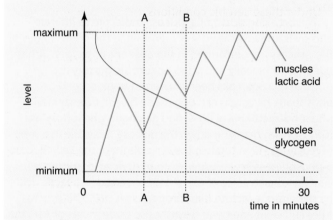

Fig 17.8

3 Use the graph to explain the physiological processes occurring between points A and B. **[4 marks]**

4 Swimmers often rely on the use of the lactic acid system for ATP resynthesis. Describe the lactic acid energy system and discuss the advantages and disadvantages of using this system. **[5 marks]**

The aerobic system

To see how the remaining 95 per cent of energy is released from the glucose molecule, we must look at the aerobic system.

As the name suggests, this energy system differs from the previous two as it requires the presence of oxygen. Although it takes approximately three minutes to extract the remaining 95 per cent of energy from a glucose molecule, the aerobic system has a tremendous energy yield – 18-times greater than anaerobic processes and is therefore worth waiting for!

The initial stages of the aerobic process are similar to those of the lactic acid system, except that the fate of pyruvic acid changes when there is sufficient oxygen available. You will recall that under anaerobic conditions, where there is insufficient oxygen, pyruvic acid is converted to lactic acid, which has a fatiguing effect upon the muscles. In the presence of oxygen, however, during light or low-intensity exercise, pyruvic acid is converted into a compound called **acetyl-coenzyme-A**, which is combined with **oxaloacetic acid** to form **citric acid** before it enters the **Krebs cycle** (see Figure 17.9).

Under these aerobic conditions, the glucose molecule is broken down further in special powerhouses or factories existing in the muscle cell known as mitochondria. These lie adjacent to the myofibrils and exist throughout the sarcoplasm.

> **EXAMINER'S TIP**
>
> Slow-twitch fibres possess a greater number of mitochondria than fast-twitch fibres, which enables them to provide a continuous supply of energy over a long period of time. We would therefore expect marathon runners to have a much higher proportion of slow-twitch muscle fibres than 100m sprinters.

From Figure 17.9, it can be seen that the complete breakdown of one molecule of glycogen can elicit enough energy to resynthesise **38 moles of ATP**:

- 2 during anaerobic glycolysis
- 2 during the Krebs cycle
- 34 during the electron transport system.

Because of the vast energy supply gained through aerobic metabolism, this system is mainly used in the endurance-based activities where energy is required over a long period, as well as supplying the energy required by the body at rest, or while it is recovering from any exercise – aerobic or anaerobic in nature.

> **Key terms**
>
> **Mitochondria** Specialist components of a cell that represent the power plants for ATP resynthesis under aerobic conditions.
>
> **Sarcoplasm** The fluid-filled part of a muscle cell that is the site of energy production for the ATP-PC and lactic acid energy pathways.
>
> **Krebs cycle** A series of chemical reactions of the aerobic system that occur in the matrix of the mitochondria, producing carbon dioxide and water, and yielding sufficient energy to resynthesise 2 moles of ATP.
>
> **Electron transport system** The final stage of the aerobic system that takes place in the cristae of the mitochondria. It involves a series of chemical reactions that yield the majority of energy for ATP resynthesis; 34 moles of ATP can be resynthesised from one mole of glycogen.

> **EXAMINER'S TIP**
>
> The aerobic system is typically used in endurance-based activities that are of low intensity. This system also provides the energy requirements at rest and when recovering from exercise. It can be summarised by the following equation:
>
> $$C_6H_{12}O_6 + 6O_2 \; 6CO_2 + 6H_2O + 38ATP$$
> $$(38ADP + 38Pi \; 38ATP)$$

> **EXAMINER'S TIP**
>
> The mitochondria can be likened to factories. They use the raw materials of glycogen, fatty acids and oxygen to produce a final product – energy. Just like factories, they can also achieve economies of scale. Through training, mitochondria become more efficient through increasing in size *and* number!

Table 17.6 Key features of the aerobic system

Site of reaction	Chemical fuel	Controlling enzyme	Energy yield	By-products	Intensity/ duration	Key terms
Mitochondria	Glycogen/ glucose Fatty acids	GP PFK Lipase	1 mole glycogen: 38 moles ATP	Carbon dioxide Water	Low intensity, >3 minutes	Krebs cycle Electron transport system

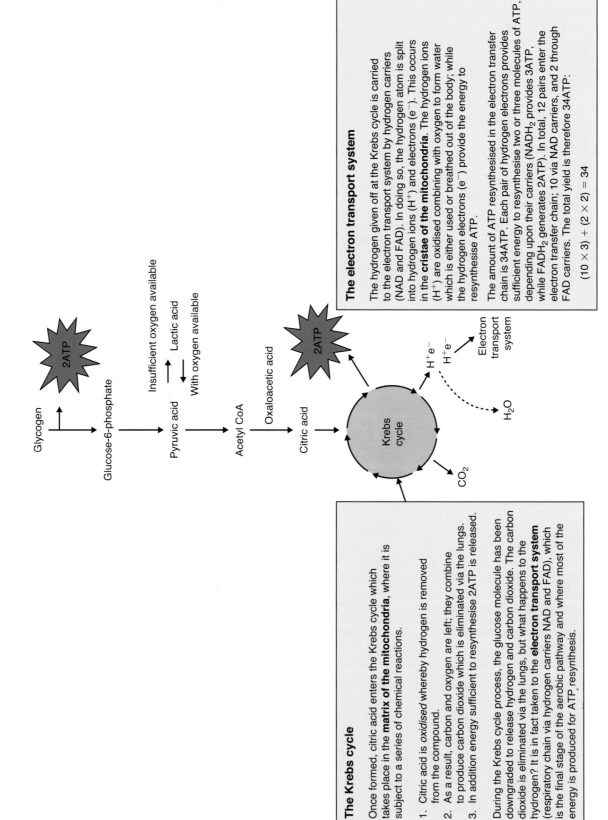

The Krebs cycle

Once formed, citric acid enters the Krebs cycle which takes place in the **matrix of the mitochondria**, where it is subject to a series of chemical reactions.

1. Citric acid is *oxidised* whereby hydrogen is removed from the compound.
2. As a result, carbon and oxygen are left; they combine to produce carbon dioxide which is eliminated via the lungs.
3. In addition energy sufficient to resynthesise 2ATP is released.

During the Krebs cycle process, the glucose molecule has been downgraded to release hydrogen and carbon dioxide. The carbon dioxide is eliminated via the lungs, but what happens to the hydrogen? It is in fact taken to the **electron transport system** (respiratory chain via hydrogen carriers NAD and FAD), which is the final stage of the aerobic pathway and where most of the energy is produced for ATP resynthesis.

The electron transport system

The hydrogen given off at the Krebs cycle is carried to the electron transport system by hydrogen carriers (NAD and FAD). In doing so, the hydrogen atom is split into hydrogen ions (H^+) and electrons (e^-). This occurs in the **cristae of the mitochondria**. The hydrogen ions (H^+) are oxidised combining with oxygen to form water which is either used or breathed out of the body; while the hydrogen electrons (e^-) provide the energy to resynthesise ATP.

The amount of ATP resynthesised in the electron transfer chain is 34ATP. Each pair of hydrogen electrons provides sufficient energy to resynthesise two or three molecules of ATP, depending upon their carriers ($NADH_2$ provides 3ATP, while $FADH_2$ generates 2ATP). In total, 12 pairs enter the electron transfer chain; 10 via NAD carriers, and 2 through FAD carriers. The total yield is therefore 34ATP:

$$(10 \times 3) + (2 \times 2) = 34$$

Fig 17.9 The Krebs cycle and electron transport system – the heart of the aerobic system

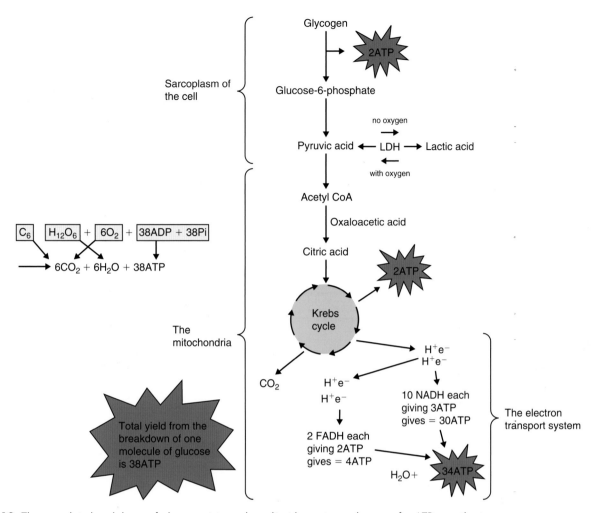

Fig 17.10 The complete breakdown of glycogen into carbon dioxide, water and energy for ATP resynthesis

Activity 5

State the enzymes involved at each stage of energy production:

Stage of energy production	Enzymes responsible
ATP splitting	
Creatine phosphate splitting	
Glycogen pyruvic acid	
Pyruvic acid lactic acid	
The aerobic pathway	

Activity 6

Complete the table below, giving the predominant energy system used for the following activities:

Activity	Energy system used	Fuel	Approximate duration
A gymnastic vault			
100m butterfly swim			
Throwing a cricket ball			
A squash rally			
A steady five-mile run			
Running a marathon			

Table 17.7 An assessment of the value of the aerobic system to the sports performer

Advantages	Limitations
• Large amounts of ATP produced from 1 mole of glycogen or fat • Activity can continue for some hours • Large stores of glycogen and fat • No harmful by-products produced	• Requires oxygen • Relatively slow production of energy • Can only produce energy for activities that are of relatively low intensity

IN CONTEXT

A Tour de France cyclist such as British rider Mark Cavendish will utilise their aerobic system for the majority of each stage. Their bodies have adapted to the demands of the event and, as a result, we would expect the cyclist to have a very high percentage of slow-twitch (Type 1) muscle fibres, which by nature have a much higher density of mitochondria and a higher volume of myoglobin. Together these two components of the muscle cell will ensure that Mark's aerobic system is well developed and functions as effectively as possible.

Activity 7

Place the following terms in the correct order as they appear in the aerobic system:

• Krebs cycle
• Acetyl-coenzyme-A
• Electron transport system
• Citric acid
• CO_2
• 34ATP
• 2ATP

Activity 8

State and explain the process of energy production during a 10,000m run. Give precise details of energy systems used at various stages of the run.
Construct a graph to illustrate the food fuels used against time in this event.

Activity 9

Complete the table below, marking correct statements with a tick in the appropriate box.

Statement	ATP-PC system	Lactic acid system	Aerobic system
Takes place in the presence of oxygen			
Uses glycogen and fatty acids to resynthesise ATP			
Predominates in activities lasting 1–2 minutes			
This system can take place in the absence of oxygen			
This system produces a net gain of two ATP			
Phosphocreatine is the fuel used to resynthesise ATP in this system			
This system is used during sub-maximal exercise			
When I've been using this system it can take me up to 1 hour to recover			
This system relies solely on glycogen			
This system involves a coupled reaction			
This system is my immediate store of energy and is used in activities that are of short duration and high intensity			
This system is sometimes known as anaerobic glycolysis			
This system only takes 2–3 minutes to replenish			
The enzyme known as PFK (phosphofructokinase) is used in this system			
This system predominates in activities lasting over 3 minutes			

Activity 10

Complete the table below with the relevant information.

	ATP splitting	ATP-PC system	Lactic acid system	Aerobic system
Duration	0–3 secs			
Intensity				Low
Site of reaction			Sarcoplasm	
Enzymes	ATPase			
Fuels used		Creatine phosphate		
Equation to summarise				$C_6H_{12}O_6 + 6O_2 + 38ADP + 38Pi \rightarrow 6CO_2 + 6H_2O + 38ATP$

Table 17.8 Major characteristics of each of the three energy systems

	ATP-PC	Lactic acid	Aerobic (carbohydrate)	Aerobic (fat)
Main energy source	ATP, PC	Muscle glycogen	Muscle glycogen	fats, fatty acids
Exercise intensity	Highest	High	Lower	Lowest
Rate of ATP production	Highest	High	Lower	Lowest
Power production	Highest	High	Lower	Lowest
Capacity for total ATP production	Lowest	Low	High	Highest
Endurance capacity	Lowest	Low	High	Highest
Oxygen needed	No	No	Yes	Yes
Anaerobic/aerobic	Anaerobic	Anaerobic	Aerobic	Aerobic
Characteristic track event	100m sprint	800m run	5–42 km run	Marathon
Time factor at maximal use	1–10 seconds	30–120 seconds	More than 3 minutes	20 minutes +

IN CONTEXT

During endurance exercise, such as a wheelchair marathon, the body will have to use a mixture of carbohydrate and fats. At the beginning of the race the athlete will be predominantly using glycogen, but since free fatty acids constitute the preferred fuel under these conditions, the quicker the athlete can introduce fat as a source of fuel, the greater the capacity of the body to conserve glycogen for later in the race when the intensity may increase. The body cannot use fat alone since the solubility of fat in the blood is poor and fatty acids cannot, therefore, be sufficiently transported to the muscle cells to supply the body with all its energy requirements. In this way fat is said to be hydrophobic. The athlete must therefore use glycogen sparingly throughout the race so that s/he avoids 'hitting the wall'. This is the stage where the body has depleted all glycogen reserves, and the body tries to use fat as a sole source of fuel.

1 The body uses oxygen following exercise to enable the body to recover. This results in an elevated rate of aerobic respiration. The first stage of this process involves the breakdown of glycogen to pyruvic acid. Describe the remaining stages that use oxygen to complete the breakdown of glycogen. **[6 marks]**

2 Critically evaluate the relative merits of using fat as a fuel during exercise. **[4 marks]**

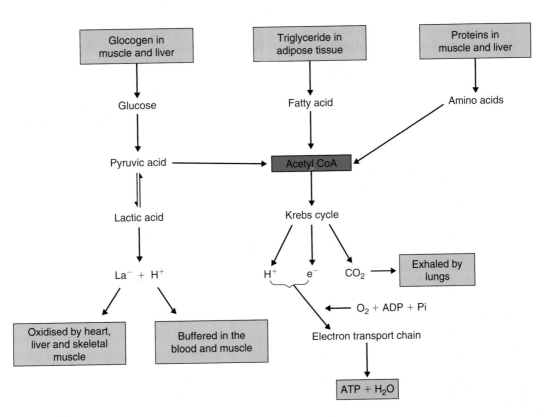

Fig 17.11 Metabolism of food fuels during exercise

The energy continuum

The energy systems do not simply turn themselves on and off when required. In fact all three systems are always in operation during exercise, and even at rest. If I am running a marathon, for example, my body is geared up with full stores of fat and glycogen to be turned on fully and energy to recycle my ATP will be pouring out of them. My stores of phosphocreatine and anaerobic glycolysis, however, will only be dripping and therefore will provide a very tiny percentage of the overall energy requirements of the run.

So it is the relative importance and contribution that each energy system makes to an activity that is important and can change from moment to moment. During a game of football, for example, the ATP-PC system will be predominant during periods of very high intensity such as sprinting for a 50:50 ball. The lactic acid system will operate during sustained periods of high intensity exertion such as when working hard in the midfield. The aerobic system will supply the majority of energy during periods of lower intensity work when the

footballer is jogging back into position for example or when waiting to receive a ball if attacking.

Each activity can be plotted along an energy continuum that shows the relative contribution of each energy pathway. For many activities it is possible to construct an **energy profile**. This is illustrated for a basketball player in Figure 17.14.

> **Key term**
>
> **Energy continuum** The relative importance and contribution that each energy system makes to an activity.

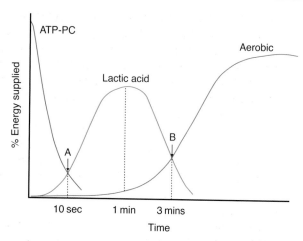

A = ATP-PC LA threshold
The point at which ATP-PC energy system is exhausted and lactic acid system prevails

B = LA O₂ threshold
The point at which lactic acid system is exhausted and the aerobic system takes over

Fig 17.12 Energy supply against time

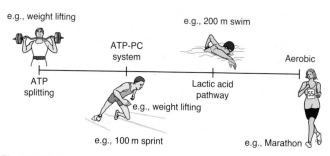

Fig 17.13 An energy continuum

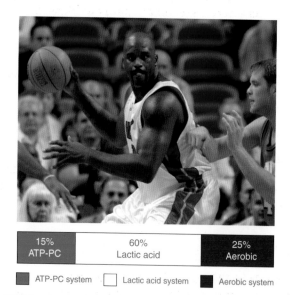

15% ATP-PC	60% Lactic acid	25% Aerobic

■ ATP-PC system □ Lactic acid system ■ Aerobic system

Fig 17.14 An energy profile of a basketball player

Activity 11

On a large sheet of paper, draw an energy continuum that includes ATP splitting at one end and the aerobic system at the other, with the ATP-PC system and the lactic acid system in between.

Now collect a wide range of action photographs covering a variety of sports from magazines or newspapers (if you have access to the internet you could download pictures). Place each photo along the continuum illustrating the predominant energy system in operation during the action taken. Beside each photograph write a short commentary justifying the position you have chosen along the continuum.

Activity 12

Figure 17.14 shows a basketball player and the relative contribution of each energy system in the game. Using the internet or pictures from newspapers and magazines, complete similar energy profiles for a range of sporting activities.

Key term

Threshold The point at which there is a switch from one predominant energy system to another. For example, the ATP-PC/lactic acid threshold is the point where the ATP-PC system exhausts and the lactic acid system takes over. This typically happens after 10 second of intense exercise.

Factors that determine the predominant energy system in use

We have established that the key factors that ultimately determine the energy system in use at any one time is the intensity and duration of the period of exertion. There are a number of other factors to consider, however:

- **Levels of fitness** – a performer with greater levels of aerobic fitness will be able to perform at a higher percentage of their VO₂ max before fatigue sets in. Poor levels of aerobic fitness can cause a person to reach OBLA (onset of blood lactate accumulation) and therefore fatigue prematurely. OBLA essentially relates to the body's ability to remove lactic acid. As long as the removal of lactic acid keeps up with lactic acid production then OBLA can be kept at bay. However, once the production of lactic acid exceeds removal then OBLA will be reached and muscle fatigue quickly ensues. Once the body reaches OBLA the predominant energy system in operation changes from the aerobic system to the lactic acid system. The concept of OBLA will be dealt with in more depth in Chapter 18.

Table 17.9 The energy continuum showing the contribution of aerobic and anaerobic energy supply in various activities

Aerobic (%)	Anaerobic (%)	Activities
0	100	100m sprint Weightlifting
10	90	400m run 100m swim Kilo track cycling
20	80	Squash Volleyball Kayaking
30	70	800m run Tennis Netball Basketball
40	60	200m swim Boxing
50	50	Football Rugby
60	40	Olympic rowing 1500m run
70	30	Cricket Rounders
80	20	1500m swim
90	10	Cross-country running Golf
100	0	Cross-country skiing Marathon running Triathlon

EXAMINER'S TIP

Remember, it is the intensity of the activity at any one time that will determine the predominant energy system in operation.

IN CONTEXT

The energy supply for an Olympic rower is likely to be from approximately 60 per cent aerobic sources and 40 per cent anaerobic.

- **Availability of oxygen** – as soon as sufficient oxygen becomes available to metabolise glycogen and fat stores, the aerobic system becomes the predominant energy pathway. This is because the body always strives to work as efficiently as possible and the aerobic system produces the most energy. A performer with a high VO_2 max will be able sustain aerobic exercise at higher intensities for longer and delay the point at which OBLA occurs. This is because performers with high levels of VO_2 max will typically have well-developed respiratory and cardiovascular systems, meaning they can take in, transport and use a greater amount of oxygen than athletes with a lower VO_2 max.

- **The availability of food fuels** – it takes a short while to begin utilising our glycogen and fat stores, so the body will uses the ATP-PC system in the interim period. Glycogen becomes the major food fuel during the first 20 minutes of exercise with fat assuming the main energy supplier role after this 20 minute threshold. Interestingly, an endurance athlete can only continue exercising for as long as their glycogen stores last (which would be approximately 90 minutes if glycogen was used on its own). This is because the body can only use fat as a fuel when it is used in conjunction with glycogen. This is due to its low solubility in the blood and the additional amount of oxygen required to break it down (about 15 per cent more than that used to break down the equivalent amount of glycogen). As soon as muscle glycogen stores become depleted, the muscles cease to function effectively. In order to maximise their stores of muscle glycogen athletes will often follow a process of glycogen loading.

Exam-style Questions

1   The amount of oxygen available not only has a direct effect on whether energy is released aerobically or anaerobically, but also affects the type of food fuel used. Under what circumstances is carbohydrate used as the predominant food fuel and why?   **[10 marks]**

Key term

Glycogen loading A manipulation of the dietary intake of carbohydrate prior to competition in which athletes try to maximise stores of glycogen.

CHALLENGE YOURSELF

Study Table 17.10, which illustrates how the efficiency and effectiveness of each energy system can be improved with the implementation of a well-considered training programme. Design a training session for a named activity or performer to improve the effectiveness of each energy system.

Table 17.10 Improving the effectiveness of the energy pathways through training

Energy system used	Endurance	Time in use	Examples	Training aimed at	Examples of training
ATP Splitting	Max speed, strength and power	0–3sec	• Max lift • Weight lifting • Tennis serve • Badminton smash	• Increasing stores of ATP • Hypertrophy of fast twitch fibres (Type 2b)	• Max lifts • Sprint starts
ATP-PC	Speed and power	3–10sec	• 100m sprint • Fast sprints • Rallies in racket sports	• Increasing stores of ATP-PC • Increasing size of specific muscles • Hypertrophy of fast twitch fibres (Type 2b)	• Repetition sprints • Acceleration sprints • Short sprint interval training • Run in weighted belts • Running up hills • Running up stairs • High weight/ few reps • Plyometrics
Lactic acid	Local muscular endurance Anaerobic capacity	10sec–3min peaks at 1min	• 400m run • 'Kick' phase in 1,500m • Full court press in basketball • Canoeing	• Overloading the system, causing: large amounts of lactic acid to be produced, increasing lactate tolerance, and increase rate of lactate removal • Hypertrophy of fast twitch fibres (Type 2a)	• Repeated bouts of intense exercise (e.g., run, swim, etc.) • Short recovery • Work relief • Programmes should last several months • Interval training • Circuit training
Aerobic	Aerobic endurance	Excess of 3mins	• Long distance • Running • Team games • 5,000m • Marathon	• Increasing aerobic energy stores of: a) Muscle glycogen b) Triglycerides • Mitochondria • Enzyme capacity • Increasing myoglobin	• Long duration training – up to two hours • Swimming/cycling • Long distance running • Little rest • Continuous training • Aerobic interval training

Exam-style Questions

1   Performers usually rely on all three energy systems for ATP resynthesis. However, at any one time one system may be predominant. Sketch a graph to show how the predominant energy system depends on the duration of exercise.

   [4 marks]

2   During a match a games player will work at different intensities and produce energy from both aerobic and anaerobic pathways. This will affect the energy system and the fuel used. Using examples from a sport of your choice explain when and why a performer uses the ATP-PC, lactic acid and aerobic systems, together with their associated fuels during a competitive match.   **[10 marks]**

3   Compare the relative merits and limitations of the principal energy system used during a triple jump with that used during a 10,000m run.

   [6 marks]

CHALLENGE YOURSELF

During a match, a games player will work at different intensities and produce energy from both aerobic and anaerobic pathways. This will affect the energy system and the fuel used. For example, when a basketball player slam dunks the ball into the basket, they are using the ATP-PC system and the chemical fuel phosphocreatine. Using examples from a sport of your choice, explain when and why a performer uses the lactic acid and the aerobic energy systems and fuels during a competitive match. Discuss the effects of level of aerobic fitness, availability of oxygen and food fuels on the efficiency of the aerobic energy system.   **[20 marks]**

What you need to know

* Energy is the capacity to perform work and is measured in joules or calories.
* Work is the product of force and distance. It is measured in joules.
* Power is the rate at which work is done (or energy created). It is measured in Watts or joules per second.
* All energy required by the body is directly provided by a high-energy compound called adenosine triphosphate (ATP), which is present in all muscle cells.
* The energy required to resynthesise ATP comes from the breakdown of food and other chemical fuels within the body.
* The stores of ATP in the body are limited. There are three main systems responsible for resynthesising ATP in the body: the ATP-PC system, lactic acid system and aerobic system.
* It is the intensity and duration of an activity that determines which energy system operates at any one time.
* The ATP-PC or alactic system is the energy system used for extremely short bursts of high-intensity exercise – up to ten seconds of activity. It is an anaerobic pathway.
* The fuel for ATP resynthesis during the ATP-PC system is phosphocreatine.

* The lactic acid system is a second anaerobic system. This system uses energy from the breakdown of glycogen to resynthesise 2 moles of ATP. This energy system is predominantly used for activities lasting between one and three minutes duration.
* Lactic acid is a by-product of the lactic acid system.
* The aerobic system is the most efficient means of providing energy to resynthesise ATP. With oxygen the glucose molecule can produce a total gain of 38 moles of ATP. The Krebs cycle occurs in the matrix of the mitochondria and removes hydrogen and releases carbon dioxide. Sufficient energy to resynthesise 2 moles of ATP is also released at this stage. Further breakdown of the glucose molecule takes place in the cristae of the mitochondria via the electron transport system, where sufficient energy to resynthesise 34 moles of ATP molecules is released.
* The mitochondrion is the powerhouse of the muscle cell and is where all energy is supplied under aerobic conditions within the body.
* The main energy providing nutrients are glycogen, fats and proteins. For endurance-based events the body relies upon fats and glycogen, while for shorter activities the body will rely solely on glycogen.

* The energy continuum represents the relative importance and contribution that each system makes to an activity.
* It is possible to dip into and out of all three energy system during any specific activity depending upon the intensity of the activity at any particular time.

* The level of a performer's fitness and the availability of oxygen can determine which energy system predominates. With high levels of aerobic fitness, a plentiful supply of oxygen and extensive stores of glycogen and fats, the aerobic system will be the major supplier of energy.

Review Questions

1 Define the terms 'energy', 'work' and 'power'. State the units of measurement for each quantity.
2 Explain the terms endothermic and exothermic in relation to energy supply in the body and give an example of when each takes place during ATP depletion and regeneration.
3 Draw a graph to illustrate how phosphocreatine can maintain levels of ATP within the muscle during a sprint hurdles race.
4 What are the main benefits and limitations of using the lactic acid system to supply energy for ATP resynthesis during physical activity?
5 Explain the role played by the mitochondria in energy provision.
6 What are the major food fuels used to supply energy during a triathlon? Briefly explain how these energy sources are used in the regeneration of ATP.
7 Explain how intensity and duration of exercise play such an important role in the **type of food fuel** we use for energy supply.

8 Construct an energy systems graph that depicts the energy system used against time during a 1,500m run.
9 With reference to the **intensity** of exercise, explain why it is important to view the energy systems as existing as a continuum. Use examples from an activity to support your answer.
10 We only have sufficient glycogen stored in the body to complete around a ten-mile run. Where is glycogen stored in the body, how much can be stored, and explain why endurance athletes can obviously still function for longer than ten miles.
11 Draw an 'energy block profile' for an Olympic rower.
12 Outline some training methods that you would use to develop and improve your ATP-PC system. How do these training methods differ from those used to develop your aerobic system?

CHAPTER 18

Recovery from exercise

Learning outcomes

By the end of this chapter you should be able to:

- define the term 'recovery'
- explain how the body returns to its pre-exercise state
- explain the terms 'oxygen deficit', 'oxygen debt' and 'excess post-exercise oxygen consumption (EPOC)'
- identify the components and duration of the alactacid debt
- identify the components and duration of the lactacid debt
- explain the removal of carbon dioxide and lactic acid
- explain the implications of the recovery process for planning physical activity sessions.

CHAPTER INTRODUCTION

Why is it that a sprinter breathes and pants so deeply after a race, even though they may only have run 100m? Compare this to a 400m runner or even a marathon runner. It is clear that the pattern of recovery for each of these three athletes is different, but why?

Essentially whatever the prior exercise, rapid and deep breathing is commonplace during recovery. It happens because recovery from exercise is dependent upon **oxygen**, and the increased breathing rate helps to increase oxygen consumption. The oxygen utilised during this recovery period is used to rebuild muscular stores of **ATP** and **PC** that may have been depleted, and to **remove any lactic acid** that may have accumulated in the muscle during the preceding exercise. Furthermore, endurance athletes such as a marathon runner will have almost completely depleted their glycogen stores during the run and must eat in order to fully recover. The recovery process is therefore concerned with **returning the body to its pre-exercise state.**

EXAMINER'S TIP

Recovery from exercise requires energy and, since the recovery process itself needs oxygen, the energy to recover is supplied by the aerobic energy system.

Key term

Recovery The return of the body to its pre-exercise state.

Causes of fatigue during exercise

In order to fully understand the process of recovery it is first necessary to consider the causes of fatigue during physical activity. Fatigue is a rather generic term that we use to try to explain feelings of muscular tiredness or perhaps laboured breathing during exercise. However, the causes of fatigue are many, and may differ considerably depending on the activity being undertaken. For example, the experience of fatigue when completing a 400m run to exhaustion will be totally different to that experienced by a runner completing a marathon.

We can summarise the key causes of fatigue as:

- Inability to maintain ATP resynthesis
- Lactic acid accumulation
- Glycogen depletion
- Dehydration and the associated loss of electrolytes
- Reduced availability of calcium

If we are to return to our pre-exercise state and recover fully we must therefore address these causes of fatigue.

IN CONTEXT

Recent research on experienced cyclists has found that after a period of extended high-intensity exercise, small channels in the muscle cell begin to leak calcium. Calcium is an essential element in the process of muscle contraction, and the calcium leaks lead to weakened muscle contractions. It was found that these leaks were repaired within a few days. This helps explain the need to include recovery days in any training programme.

Activity 1

In this activity you will identify the causes of fatigue in a maximal press-up test. You will need a gym mat and stopwatch. On the command 'go' perform as many press-ups as you can. (If you cannot perform full press-ups, box press-ups will suffice.) Your partner will count the number of press-ups and time the duration of the test. It is important to perform press-ups to exhaustion – until you can do no more.

Record your results, including the number of press-ups completed and the time to exhaustion. Now answer the following questions:

1 Did you pace yourself throughout the task or did you start off very fast and slow down towards the end of the task?

2 Which muscle groups felt most fatigue?

3 What 'sensations' or 'feelings' caused you to stop?

4 Based on the intensity and duration of the task discuss the pattern of phosphocreatine and glycogen depletion.

5 Discuss the role that the accumulation of hydrogen ions and lactic acid may have had on your performance.

Excess post–exercise oxygen consumption (EPOC)

Excess post-exercise oxygen consumption represents the total volume of oxygen that is consumed following exercise that enables the body to fully recover and return it to its pre-exercise state. Traditionally the term 'oxygen debt' has been

used to explain the restoration of muscle phosphagens (ATP and PC) and the removal of lactic acid. However, this does not take into account the extra oxygen that is required during the recovery process to keep respiratory rates and heart rates elevated or the repayment of oxygen effectively 'borrowed' from the myoglobin oxygen store. In this way EPOC is now the favoured term, and the oxygen debt is viewed as forming a part of this process.

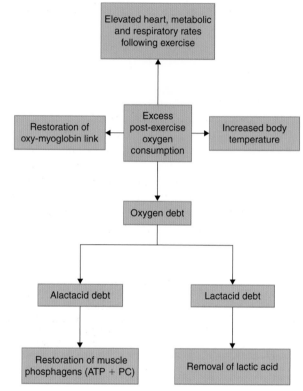

Fig 18.1 The components of excess post-exercise oxygen consumption (EPOC)

Oxygen debt

An oxygen debt will accrue when the body has undertaken some form of exercise anaerobically. This will occur at quite intense levels of exercise, lasting up to three minutes, or when the anaerobic threshold has been exceeded. The debt can be measured by analysing oxygen consumption pre- and post-exercise, or more simply by examining heart rate scores before and after exercise, since the heart rate pattern directly reflects oxygen delivery and usage.

Oxygen deficit

The oxygen debt is used to compensate for the oxygen deficit. This deficit is the amount of extra oxygen required to complete the exercise if all the energy could have been supplied aerobically. As oxygen is not available for approximately the first three minutes of exercise, a deficit will always accrue.

It does not necessarily follow that oxygen debt always equals oxygen deficit because during recovery the oxygen debt must also:

- Supply oxygen to provide energy and resaturate myoglobin with oxygen (the oxy-myoglobin link)
- Supply energy for the **increased cardiac and respiratory rates** that remain elevated during the recovery phase.

Consequently, the amount of oxygen consumed during the oxygen debt is greater than that which might have been consumed during the oxygen deficit.

This is illustrated in Figure 18.2 where you should be able to see that the shaded area of EPOC is larger than the shaded area of oxygen deficit.

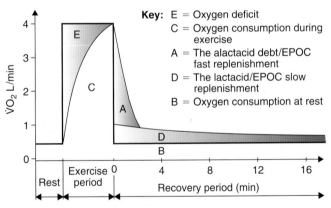

Key: E = Oxygen deficit
C = Oxygen consumption during exercise
A = The alactacid debt/EPOC fast replenishment
D = The lactacid/EPOC slow replenishment
B = Oxygen consumption at rest

Fig 18.2 Oxygen consumption during exercise and recovery

Typically the oxygen debt consists of two components:

1 The alactacid debt or **fast replenishment** of EPOC represented by area A in Figure 18.2.
2 The **lactacid** debt or **slow replenishment** of EPOC represented by area D in Figure 18.2.

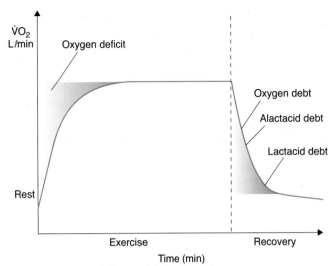

Fig 18.3 Oxygen deficit and debt during low-intensity (sub-maximal) exercise. Note how oxygen consumption plateaus and reaches a period of steady state where oxygen demand is met by oxygen supply

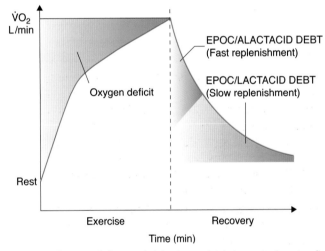

Fig 18.4 Oxygen deficit and debt during high-intensity (maximal) exercise. Note how oxygen consumption continues to increase throughout the duration of the exercise

Alactacid debt (fast replenishment of EPOC)

The alactacid debt is the first component of the oxygen debt that is replenished and aids the recovery process in two ways, as described below.

Replenishment of ATP and PC

As the name of the alactacid debt suggests, it is the volume of oxygen required to restore phosphagens used in the alactic or ATP-PC energy system. It takes a fairly short period of time to resynthesise ATP and PC – approximately two to three minutes – in which time two to three litres of oxygen can be consumed, over and above that which is normally consumed at rest, and used to provide the energy for this resynthesis.

This assumes that following a bout of intense work, such as a 100m sprint, where the predominant energy system used is

ATP-PC, the body should be recovered sufficiently after three minutes of rest to repeat the exercise.

Resaturation of myoglobin with oxygen

Within the fast component of EPOC, the very first amount of oxygen consumed is used to resaturate myoglobin with oxygen.

It was previously mentioned that some oxygen consumed during the oxygen debt may not be attributed to the oxygen deficit that has accrued during exercise. One such factor is the restoration of the **oxy-myoglobin link**, which is the saturation of myoglobin with oxygen, so that oxygen can once again be transported to the mitochondria to release energy from our food fuels.

Through exercise, oxygen is dissociated from myoglobin to enable aerobic glycolysis and, therefore, aerobic energy supply. During recovery the oxygen must be re-associated with myoglobin. To ensure a continuous supply of energy this replenishment occurs very rapidly, and is accomplished within the first minute of recovery; it therefore forms part of the alactacid debt or fast component of EPOC.

Within the fast component of EPOC, the very first amount of oxygen consumed is used to resaturate myoglobin with oxygen.

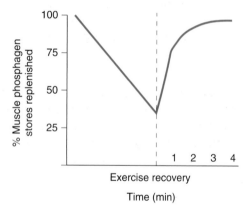

Fig 18.5 Muscle phosphagen replenishment following exercise. Note that 50% of PC stores are replenished after 30 seconds of recovery and full recovery after approximately 3 minutes

Key term

Alactacid debt The initial fast stage of the recovery process, where oxygen consumed in the first two to three minutes following exercise is used to replenish ATP and PC stores and resaturate myoglobin with oxygen.

Activity 2

1 Figure 18.6 shows the depletion of muscle phosphagen stores during a 100m sprint. Copy it onto graph paper and complete the recovery curve using information from Table 18.1.

   If the performer were required to complete another 100m sprint after 120 seconds, what implications will this have for the performer? Draw this pattern of phosphagen depletion and a subsequent 60 seconds recovery on your graph.

   Interval training (bouts of work followed by periods of rest) is central to sprint training. Draw a graph to show the pattern of phosphagen depletion and recovery during one set of 6 × 50m sprints with a 60-second recovery between each work interval.

2 What tactics might a basketball coach employ, having this knowledge of the recovery process?

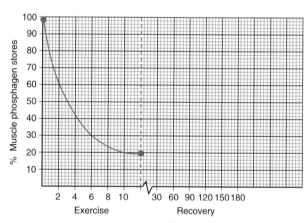

Fig 18.6 The repayment of the lactacid oxygen debt during rest recovery and exercise recivery (active cool-down). NB: repayment of the lactacid debt can be accelerated by following a period of exercise recovery (cool-down) following exercise

Table 18.1 for Activity 2

Time (seconds)	Muscle PC restored (%)
30	50
60	75
90	87
120	93
150	97
180	99

Exam-style Questions

1   Explain the recovery process of an athlete who has just competed in a 100m sprint race.   **[4 marks]**

2   During pre-season a games player participates in an interval training session during which the rate of muscle phosphagen repletion was recorded. The results are shown in the table below:

Recovery time (seconds)	Muscle phosphagen replenished (%)
10	10
30	50
60	75
90	87
120	93
150	97
180	99
210	101
240	102

a)   Using the results shown, plot a graph of percentage of muscle phosphagens restored against recovery time.   **[3 marks]**

b)   From your graph show how you could determine the amount of recovery needed for full replenishment of muscle phosphagen. What resting interval would you recommend?   **[2 marks]**

c)   What would be the effect of commencing the following work period after a resting interval of 30 seconds?   **[2 marks]**

Lactacid debt (slow replenishment of EPOC)

The lactacid debt is the volume of oxygen consumed during recovery used to:

1   Remove lactic acid from the muscles that has accumulated during anaerobic work.
2   Supply the respiratory muscles and heart with energy to remain elevated during the recovery period.

Most of the lactic acid is removed by firstly reconverting it back into pyruvate and then either oxidising it in the mitochondria via the aerobic system to give **carbon dioxide and water** or converting into **muscle and liver glycogen** and **glucose** by the processes of gluconeogenesis and glyconeogenesis. Furthermore, a small amount of lactic acid is converted into protein and removed from the body as sweat and urine. Table 18.2 summarises the key methods by which lactic acid is removed from the muscle cell.

Table 18.2 The removal and ultimate fate of lactic acid

Conversion into	Percentage
Carbon dioxide and water	65
Glycogen	20
Protein including sweat and urine	10
Glucose	5

Key terms

Lactacid debt The slower stage of the recovery process in which oxygen is consumed to remove lactic acid and maintain the heart and respiratory rates.
Gluconeogenesis and glyconeogenesis The formation of glucose and/or glycogen from substrates such as pyruvate or lactic acid.

The process of lactic acid removal takes approximately one hour, but this can be accelerated by undertaking a **cool down** or some form of exercise recovery, which ensures a rapid and continuous supply of oxygen to the muscles, which helps in the dispersion of lactic acid.

IN CONTEXT

A 400m runner such as Nicola Sanders will amass a significant lactacid debt when training. Lactate training involves performing an interval-type training session with incomplete recovery between highly intensive work periods. This allows lactic acid to accumulate more and more with each successive work period in the hope that the performer's body will become more adept at tolerating it. In competition an athlete such as Nicola should therefore be able to work harder for longer (run faster) before the influence of lactic acid takes effect.

Removing lactic acid through buffering

Removal of lactic acid also relies upon the buffering capacity of the body, especially the blood, which weakens and neutralises the effect of lactic acid. The blood is fairly efficient at buffering lactic acid due to the hydrogen carbonate ion (HCO_3^-) produced by the kidneys; this absorbs hydrogen ions from the lactic acid and forms carbonic acid, which is eventually degraded to form carbon dioxide and water, both of which are eliminated via the lungs.

Where
H^+	=	Hydrogen ions from lactic acid
HCO_3^-	=	Bicarbonate ions produced by kidneys
H_2CO_3	=	Carbonic acid
H_2O	=	Water
CO_2	=	Carbon dioxide

$$H^+ + HCO_3^- \rightarrow H_2CO_3 \rightarrow H_2O + CO_2$$

Indeed, some athletes seek to improve their buffering capacity by **soda loading**, which involves drinking sodium bicarbonate several minutes before an event. The idea here is to increase the concentration of the hydrogen carbonate ion in the blood and, therefore, make the 'mopping up' of lactic acid more effective. Although evidence suggests that performance may be improved through this practice, side effects include vomiting and diarrhoea.

Training with small amounts of lactic acid in the system may also improve the resistance and buffering capacity of the body. By improving blood flow to the muscle, the body becomes more efficient at moving lactic acid from the muscle into the blood, which can degrade it and prevent the associated fatiguing effects.

Key terms

Buffering The process by which chemicals can maintain pH values within acceptable limits in the body and neutralise the effects of an acid such as lactic acid.
Soda loading The practice of drinking a solution of bicarbonate of soda an hour or so before an event or training to increase the amount of hydrogen carbonate ions (HCO_3^-) in the blood to facilitate the removal of lactic acid.

The effect of lactic acid accumulation

Even though the blood will always contain a small amount of lactic acid, even at rest (approximately 1–2mmol/litre of blood), during high-intensity work (such as a 400m run) this may increase 15-fold to 30mmol/litre of blood.

During high-intensity exercise, muscle fatigue occurs at a **pH of 6.4** and noticeably affects muscle function. Nobody knows exactly how such acidity causes fatigue, but it is thought that protons dissociate from lactic acid and associate with glycolytic enzymes, thus making them acidic. In this state, the enzymes lose their catalytic ability, become denatured and energy production through glycolysis ceases. Muscle contraction may also be impaired, as high acidity become denatured may inhibit the transmission of neural impulses to the contractile elements of the muscle and obstruct the contraction process. This is particularly true of very high-intensity exercise lasting between 30–120 seconds.

Onset of blood lactate accumulation (OBLA)

OBLA is the point at which lactate begins to **accumulate** in the blood, usually taken as when blood lactate levels reach a figure of 4mmol/litre of blood. It is often used to predict endurance capacities and potential, since the longer an athlete can delay the build-up of blood lactate the longer s/he can continue exercising.

Determining OBLA

OBLA is usually measured by a test of increasing intensity – one that gets progressively more difficult – such as a treadmill test. When a subject takes part in a task of progressively increasing intensity, such as the multistage fitness test, a point is eventually reached where energy can no longer be sustained completely by aerobic means. If intensity increases further, the deficit of energy requirements must be met by anaerobic metabolism. By doing so, blood lactate concentration rises until such a point is reached where lactate concentration is sufficiently high to cause complete muscle fatigue. The point at which lactic acid begins to accumulate in the muscles is the point of OBLA or anaerobic threshold, and is measured as a percentage of VO_2 max reached before this rise in acidity.

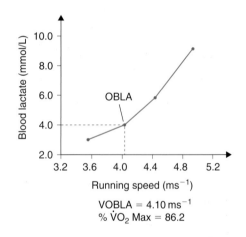

VOBLA = 4.10 ms^{-1}
% $\dot{V}O_2$ Max = 86.2

	Running speed (ms^{-1})			
	3.58	4.02	4.47	4.92
HLa (mmol/L)	2.9	3.7	5.7	9.1
HR (bpm)	166	179	187	197

The test shows that this squash player is using a large percentage of his $\dot{V}O_2$ max, resulting in a more successful endurance performance

Fig 18.7 The OBLA of a national under-19 squash player

Figure 18.7 illustrates the OBLA test results of a national under-19 squash champion working on a treadmill that gets progressively faster. We can see that at low running speeds blood lactate only increases relatively slowly. As running speed increases above 4m/s^2 blood lactate levels increase rapidly and a distinct change in gradient can be seen on the graph. Where the gradient of the graph increases significantly, this reflects the point of OBLA.

Activity 3

Take and record your resting pulse rate. Complete a 400m run at maximum pace, then record your pulse for a 10-second count every minute after the race until your heart rate returns to its original level.

Convert your heart rate values into beats per minute by multiplying your results by six. Plot a graph depicting your results. Describe and explain the pattern of recovery.

Fig 18.8 An 800m runner will accrue a large lactacid debt component

Activity 4

1 Using Figure 18.9, explain what is meant by the oxygen deficit.
2 For what is the oxygen consumed during part 'A' used?
3 Express EPOC using the letters from the key.

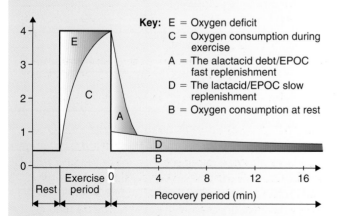

Fig 18.9 Oxygen consumption during exercise and recovery

Exam-style Questions

1 Outline the physiological processes that take place during a ten-minute recovery period following a highly intensive period of anaerobic exercise.   **[6 marks]**

2 A student performs a flat-out 100m freestyle swim. Explain the process of lactate conversion that will take place during the recovery from the swim.   **[4 marks]**

3 During high-intensity exercise such as an 800m run, lactic acid builds up within the working muscles.

  a) How is lactic acid formed in the muscles?
                                         [3 marks]

  b) Identify three possible fates of lactic acid during the recovery process.   **[3 marks]**

Eating for recovery – restoring muscle glycogen stores

One final consideration when discussing the recovery process is the refuelling of the body's energy reserves following the exercise period – namely muscle glycogen stores.

During exercise glycogen may have been depleted in order to provide energy. The repletion of muscle glycogen is a long process and can take up to 48 hours, depending upon the duration and intensity of the preceding exercise.

It is now widely agreed that refuelling with a high-carbohydrate diet within one hour of exercise will speed up the recovery process. This is known as the carbohydrate window. The energy for glycogen replenishment is made available from the aerobic pathway.

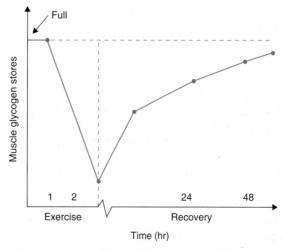

Fig 18.10 Restoration of muscle glycogen stores following a marathon

Delayed onset of muscle soreness

No discussion of fatigue would be complete without mentioning the delayed onset of muscle soreness (DOMS). This is characterised by tender and painful muscles often experienced in the days (usually 48 hours) following heavy or unaccustomed exercise. The explanation of this soreness is relatively simple and results from the damage to muscle fibres and connective tissue surrounding the fibres, and the associated oedema (increased tissue fluid) within the muscle compartment. The soreness is usually temporary and goes within a couple of days as the muscle fibres repair themselves but, in the meantime, it can have a negative effect on the force-generating capacity of the muscles affected. Studies have shown that DOMS is most likely to occur following *eccentric muscle contraction* and can result, therefore, from weight-training, plyometrics or even walking down steep hills.

To reduce the effects of DOMS it is advisable to complete a thorough warm-up prior to exercise and a cool-down following exercise. If possible, in the early stages of a training programme, try to reduce the eccentric aspect of the muscle action. A final factor is to ensure that during the training session you progress from low-intensity work through to higher-intensity bouts of work.

Activity 5

To complete an investigation into muscle soreness you will be required to perform a series of bicep curls in a weight-training or fitness facility.

Perform a warm-up and find your 1 rep-max (1RM) for the bicep curl (that is, a weight with which you can only perform one repetition – this may take several attempts to find: see Chapter 19 for more detail on 1RM).

Now calculate 75 per cent of your 1RM and perform as many repetitions of the bicep curl at 75 per cent 1RM. Repeat three more times, allowing three to four minutes rest between each set.

Answer the following questions:

1 Did you feel any muscle soreness during the activity? If so, can you account for this soreness?
2 Did you feel any muscle soreness 24–48 hours after this exercise? If so, what might have been the causes of this delayed onset?
3 If you felt any delayed onset of muscle soreness, exactly where did you experience it (for example in the centre of the muscle belly, towards the elbow, etc.)?
4 Which part of the action of the bicep curl is most likely to have caused the muscle soreness?

Activity 6

This investigation will determine the energy systems and recovery processes in operation during a simple shuttle run test. Before **Task One**, ensure that you warm-up thoroughly. Following each task, get a partner to record how you are feeling. You may wish to refer to heart rate, respiratory rate, levels of fatigue in the muscles, etc.

Task One: Identify two baselines of a tennis court. Start at one end and, on the command of 'go!', complete a steady 40-length shuttle run (there and back 20 times).

Task Two: Using the same baselines, repeat **Task One**, but this time sprint as fast as you can to the far baseline and back. Get a partner to record your time.

Task Three: Once again repeat **Task One**, but this time sprint to the far end and back five times – a total of 10 shuttles.

Now answer the following questions:

1 Which energy systems are dominant in each run?
2 In which of the three tasks did you recover quickest? Give reasons for this.
3 With reference to **Task Three**, comment on how you felt at various stages of the run. Account for these feelings.
4 For each of the runs, state what fuels are in use and when.
5 How do you think you could improve your times for each of the tasks?
6 Specifically, how will training improve the energy derived from each system?

Activity 7

Copy the following table and complete the recovery time for each factor.

Recovery process	Recovery time
Restoration of oxy-myoglobin link	
Restoration of muscle stores of ATP and PC	
Repayment of fast component of EPOC (alactacid debt)	
Removal of lactic acid with a cool-down	
Removal of lactic acid without a cool-down	
Repayment of slow component of EPOC (Lactacid debt)	
Restoration of muscle glycogen stores	

Exam-style Questions

1. The recovery process is concerned with returning the body to its pre-exercise state. Using relevant sporting examples identify and describe the processes that take place during both the alactacid and lactacid oxygen debt. **[8 marks]**

2. Many games rely on the anaerobic systems to meet their energy requirements. Using a game of your choice show how knowledge of the pattern of recovery can be used to enhance the performance of a games player. **[4 marks]**

3. Why is it important to perform an active cool-down following intense physical activity? **[4 marks]**

4. Following a period of strength training the muscles may become uncomfortable and even painful. What are the reasons for this muscle soreness and what physiological processes may reduce it? **[5 marks]**

5. How could information on oxygen debt recovery be of use to an athlete and coach in the design of training sessions? **[5 marks]**

Planning for physical activity sessions

Knowledge of EPOC and the recovery process can help the coach and athlete to ensure that training and competitive performances are at optimal levels. The coach should make sure that:

- **Athletes warm up thoroughly before training.** This can help 'kick start' the aerobic system and reduce oxygen deficit. It will also help reduce DOMS
- **The athlete is training at the correct intensity.** This is particularly important for endurance-based activities where OBLA should be avoided. In doing so the slow component of EPOC will be reduced
- **When stressing the ATP-PC system** (during sprint interval training, for example) **full recovery is allowed.** This should take a maximum of two to three minutes depending upon duration of the work period. (Remember, 50 per cent of PC stores are recovered within the first 30 seconds!)
- **Athletes undergo active recovery by performing a cool down.** This will speed up lactate removal and reduce the slow component of EPOC. This is particularly essential if athletes are performing in more than one event or training several times a day
- **A meal high in carbohydrates is consumed as soon as possible** (and definitely within 45 minutes to one hour) **following training or competition.** This will speed up the restoration of muscle glycogen stores and help ensure athletes have recovered ahead of subsequent training sessions.

CHALLENGE YOURSELF!

Outline the processes an athlete will go through when recovering from a triathlon event. **[10 marks]**

What you need to know

- ✱ The body requires oxygen to recover from exercise.
- ✱ An oxygen debt will accrue when some form of anaerobic exercise has taken place.
- ✱ Oxygen breathed in and used to facilitate recovery is known as the excess post-exercise oxygen consumption (EPOC).
- ✱ An oxygen debt can be defined as the amount of oxygen consumed during recovery above that which would normally have been consumed at rest during the same period of time.
- ✱ The oxygen deficit is the amount of oxygen that an anaerobic task would require if the task could be undertaken aerobically.
- ✱ An oxygen debt consists of two components: the alactacid debt and the lactacid debt.

- ✱ The alactacid debt is the oxygen consumed to resynthesise ATP and PC and resaturate myoglobin with oxygen. It takes approximately two to three minutes.
- ✱ The lactacid debt is the oxygen consumed to remove lactic acid from the muscles and maintain heart and respiratory rates during the recovery period. It can take up to one hour.
- ✱ Lactic acid can be broken down to form carbon dioxide and water, converted to muscle and liver glycogen, converted into protein, and converted into glucose.
- ✱ Effective removal of lactic acid relies upon the buffering capacity of the muscle and blood.
- ✱ Replenishment of muscle glycogen following exercise may take up to 48 hours.

* The delayed onset of muscle soreness (DOMS) is characterised by the tender and painful muscles experienced in the days following heavy or unaccustomed exercise.

* DOMS is more likely to occur following eccentric muscle contraction.
* To minimise the effect of DOMS it is advisable to perform a thorough warm up just prior to the exercise session.

Review Questions

1 Outline the recovery patterns for:
   (a) A weight lifter who has just completed a maximal lift.
   (b) A 400m hurdler who has just achieved a personal best time.
   (c) A cyclist having completed a 50km training ride.
2 Explain why the oxygen debt is often larger than the oxygen deficit.
3 Immediately following high-intensity exercise what happens to the following:
   (a) Blood and muscle pH.
   (b) Blood lactate levels.
4 What is meant by 'buffering'? How can an understanding of this help the performer and coach?
5 An athlete is to compete in two events at an athletic meeting: an 800m run followed by 1,500m run about one hour later. What advice would you give concerning the recovery process between the two events?

6 What happens to the lactic acid that is removed from the muscle cell during the recovery period?
7 What is meant by OBLA? How does the coach know that an athlete has reached their OBLA?
8 What may be responsible for the decreased effect of lactic acid accumulation that an athlete experiences during exercise following a period of interval training?
9 What do you understand by the term DOMS? What types of activity are most likely to result in a performer experiencing DOMS?
10 Why does a coach often use heart rate as a means to gauge recovery of an athlete during a training session? Use your knowledge of the alactacid (fast) and lactacid (slow) recovery phases to support your answer.

CHAPTER 19

Understanding health–related components of fitness

Learning outcomes

By the end of this chapter you should be able to:

- define aerobic capacity
- explain the concept of VO_2 max and the effect of a performer's physiological make up, level of training, age and sex upon it
- describe and apply methods of evaluating aerobic capacity
- describe and evaluate the different types of training used to develop aerobic capacity
- show your understanding of target heart rates as a measure of the intensity of training
- relate the energy system and food fuels to the performance of aerobic activities
- explain the physiological adaptive responses of the body to aerobic training
- explain and define the different dimensions of strength
- outline the physiological factors that determine the strength of a performer
- describe and apply methods of evaluating each dimension of strength
- describe and evaluate the different methods of training used to develop each dimension of strength
- relate the energy system and food fuels to the performance of strength-based activities
- explain the physiological adaptive responses of the body to strength training
- define flexibility
- outline the factors that contribute to the flexibility of a performer
- describe and apply methods of evaluating flexibility
- describe and evaluate the different methods of training used to develop flexibility
- explain the physiological adaptive responses of the body to flexibility training
- explain the concept of body composition
- describe and apply methods of evaluating body composition
- calculate your own and the body mass index of others
- explain the concept of basal metabolic rate
- critically evaluate your own diet and calorie consumption
- outline the associated health implications of obesity and the role of physical activity in its avoidance.

CHAPTER INTRODUCTION

Exercise physiology is the study of how the body's structures and functions adapt in response to exercise and, in particular, how training can enhance the athlete's performance. Fundamental to sports physiology is a knowledge of health, fitness and training. This chapter explores the dimensions of health-related fitness relevant to a range of sports performers, with a focus on aerobic capacity, strength, flexibility and body composition. Our levels of fitness can affect our health, of course, and we will consider physical activity and fitness in the context of leading a balanced, active and healthy lifestyle.

The components of fitness

You will recall that the components of fitness relate to the requirements of a given sporting activity and can help to explain success or failure in physical activity.

A distinction can be made between components that are generally considered to be health related (health benefits may be gained through improvements in these components) and those that are **skill-related**, although both will affect performance in sport.

Health-related factors are **physiologically based** and determine the ability of an individual to meet the physical demands of the activity; **skill-related-factors** are based on the **neuromuscular system** and determine how successfully a person can perform a specific skill. Both are required in all activities, but the relative importance of each dimension may differ. For example, a person may be physically suited to tennis, possessing the necessary speed, endurance and strength requirements, but may not possess the hand–eye coordination needed to strike the ball successfully. In this instance the individual may be best advised to switch to an activity that requires fewer skill-related components, such as distance running.

Key terms

Fitness The ability to carry out everyday activities without undue fatigue.
Health-related components of fitness Those dimensions of fitness that are physiologically based and determine how well a performer can meet the physical demands of an activity.
Skill-related components of fitness Those elements of fitness that involve the neuromuscular system and determine how successfully a performer can complete a specific task.

Exam-style Questions

1   Explain the division of fitness into health-related and skill-related components.   **[4 marks]**

Health–related components of fitness

Aerobic capacity

Aerobic capacity, or cardio-respiratory endurance, is dependent upon the ability of the cardiovascular system to transport and utilise oxygen during sustained exercise. It can be defined as:

the ability to provide and sustain energy aerobically.

Aerobic capacity is the component of fitness that underpins all endurance-based activities, including long-distance running, cycling or swimming, as well as being a contributory factor to many other sporting situations.

Maximal oxygen uptake (VO₂ max)

A key component of aerobic capacity is the maximal oxygen uptake, or VO_2 max, of a performer, which can be defined as:

the maximal amount of oxygen that can be taken in, transported and consumed by the working muscles per minute.

Key terms

Aerobic capacity The ability to provide and sustain energy aerobically.
Maximum oxygen uptake (VO₂ max) The maximal amount of oxygen that can be taken in, transported and consumed by the working muscles per minute.

Factors affecting aerobic capacity

Physiological factors that determine aerobic performance include the possession of a large proportion of slow-twitch muscle fibres, a proliferation of mitochondria and large myoglobin stores. These help in the production of large amounts of energy via the aerobic pathway.

Perhaps the major influencing factor of cardio-respiratory performance is the maximum volume of oxygen an individual can consume (VO_2 max). This has a very large genetic component and is influenced little by training. Factors affecting aerobic capacity are summarised in Table 19.1.

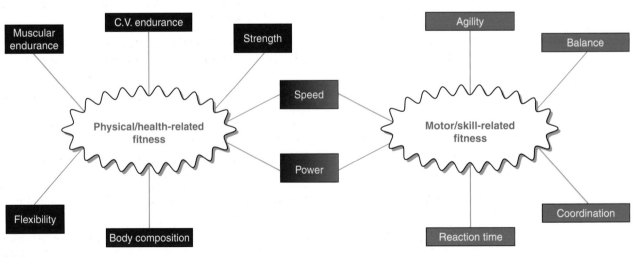

Fig 19.1

Mitochondria The site of energy production under aerobic conditions (when oxygen is present).
Myoglobin A respiratory pigment that acts as a store of oxygen within the muscle cell.
Slow-twitch muscle fibres (Type 1) Muscle fibres designed to produce energy using oxygen over a long period of time.

Activity 1

1 For each of the activities shown, give approximate values of VO$_2$ max for both male and female participants:

- A mid-fielder in hockey
- A 100m sprinter
- A male gymnast
- An Olympic canoeist
- A hammer thrower.

2 Using pictures and photographs from a range of sports, compile a continuum of relative VO$_2$ max.

Exam-style Questions

1 Aerobic capacity is a vital fitness component. Identify the physiological factors that limit aerobic capacity.   **[6 marks]**

Testing aerobic capacity

There are a number of methods of evaluating aerobic capacity, which all focus on determining the VO$_2$ max of a subject. Three tests will be discussed here:

- The multistage fitness test
- PWC170 test
- Direct gas analysis.

The multistage fitness test

The **multistage fitness test** is a progressive shuttle run test (which means that it starts off easily and gets increasingly difficult) that gives a prediction of VO$_2$ max based on the level and shuttle number reached.

Equipment required
- 20m track (or flat non-slippery surface)
- Sports Coach UK CD
- CD player
- Tape measure and marking cones

Follow the instructions given on the CD. Subjects are required to run the 20m distance as many times as possible, keeping in time to the bleeps emitted from the CD. Each shuttle of 20m should be run so that the individual reaches the end line as the bleep is emitted.

The difficulty increases with each level attained, and speed of running will need to be increased accordingly. Continue to run as long as possible until you can no longer keep up with the bleeps. If you fail to complete the 20m shuttle before the bleep is emitted you should withdraw from the test, ensuring that the level and shuttle number attained has been recorded.

Table 19.1 A summary of the factors that determine aerobic capacities

Genetics	Although there is some contention as to exactly how much genetics affect VO$_2$ max, there is no doubt that it is significant. Some studies have suggested as much as 93 per cent.
Physiology	The percentage of slow-twitch muscle fibres, size of heart and lungs, number of red blood cells and density of mitochondria are just a few physiological factors that may contribute to or limit aerobic capacity.
Age	After the age of 25, VO$_2$ max is thought to decrease by about one per cent per year. Regular physical activity, however, can offset some of this decline.
Training	Undertaking the right training can improve VO$_2$ max by 10–20 per cent.
Sex	Women tend to have VO$_2$ max scores that are about 15–30 per cent lower than men of the same group. As a simple rule, subtract 10ml from the equivalent male score.
Body composition	Research suggests that VO$_2$ max decreases as body fat percentage increases. This could contribute to some of the differences in VO$_2$ max between males and females.
Lifestyle	Obviously a lifestyle that involves smoking and a poor diet will have an adverse affect upon VO$_2$ max.
Exercise mode	Care should be taken to select the most appropriate mode of testing VO$_2$ max when testing an athlete. A swimmer should have their VO$_2$ max test conducted while swimming, a runner on a treadmill, and a cyclist on a cycle ergometer. Treadmill tests seem to produce the highest rating.

Table 19.2 Advantages and disadvantages of the multistage fitness test

Advantages	Disadvantages
• Scores can be evaluated by referring to published tables. • Large groups can participate in the test at once. • Little equipment required.	• The test is only a **prediction** and not an absolute measure of VO_2 max. At no point is oxygen consumed actually measured. • The test is maximal and to exhaustion so therefore relies, to a certain extent, on subject's levels of motivation and determination to push themselves to exhaustion. • The test may favour subjects more used to running. Swimmers, for example, may not perform as well as they might in a swimming pool.

Table 19.3 Evaluation of aerobic fitness using multistage fitness test tables

Level	Shuttle	VO_2 max	Level	Shuttle	VO_2 max
6	2	33.6	7	2	37.1
6	4	34.3	7	4	37.8
6	6	35.0	7	6	38.5
6	8	35.7	7	8	39.2
6	10	36.4	7	10	39.9
Level	**Shuttle**	**VO_2 max**	**Level**	**Shuttle**	**VO_2 max**
8	2	40.5	9	2	43.9
8	4	41.1	9	4	44.5
8	6	41.8	9	6	45.2
8	8	42.4	9	8	45.8
8	11	43.3	9	11	46.8
Level	**Shuttle**	**VO_2 max**	**Level**	**Shuttle**	**VO_2 max**
10	2	47.4	11	2	50.8
10	4	48.0	11	4	51.4
10	6	48.7	11	6	51.9
10	8	49.3	11	8	52.5
10	11	50.2	11	10	53.1
			11	12	53.7
Level	**Shuttle**	**VO_2 max**	**Level**	**Shuttle**	**VO_2 max**
12	2	54.3	13	2	57.6
12	4	54.8	13	4	58.2
12	6	55.4	13	6	58.7
12	8	56.0	13	8	59.3
12	10	56.5	13	10	59.8
12	12	57.1	13	13	60.6

Level	Shuttle	VO$_2$ max	Level	Shuttle	VO$_2$ max
14	2	61.1	15	2	64.6
14	4	61.7	15	4	65.1
14	6	62.2	15	6	65.6
14	8	62.7	15	8	66.2
14	10	63.2	15	10	66.7
14	13	64.0	15	13	67.5
Level	Shuttle	VO$_2$ max	Level	Shuttle	VO$_2$ max
16	2	68.0	17	2	71.4
16	4	68.5	17	4	71.9
16	6	69.0	17	6	72.4
16	8	69.5	17	8	72.9
16	10	69.9	17	10	73.4
16	12	70.5	17	12	73.9
16	14	70.9	17	14	74.4
Level	Shuttle	VO$_2$ max	Level	Shuttle	VO$_2$ max
18	2	74.8	19	2	78.3
18	4	75.3	19	4	78.8
18	6	75.8	19	6	79.2
18	8	76.2	19	8	79.7
18	10	76.7	19	10	80.2
18	12	77.2	19	12	80.6
18	15	77.9	19	15	81.3
Level	Shuttle	VO$_2$ max	Level	Shuttle	VO$_2$ max
20	2	81.8	21	2	85.2
20	4	82.2	21	4	85.6
20	6	82.6	21	6	86.1
20	8	83.0	21	8	86.5
20	10	83.5	21	10	86.9
20	12	83.9	21	12	87.4
20	14	84.3	21	14	87.8
20	16	84.8	21	16	88.2

The PWC170 test

Another test of aerobic capacity is the **PWC170 test**. PWC stands for **physical work capacity** and this is a sub-maximal test. Subjects are required to perform three consecutive workloads on a cycle ergometer while their heart rate is monitored. Initially a workload is set that increases the subject's heart rate to between 100 and 115 beats per minute (bpm). The heart rate is measured each minute until the subject reaches steady state. The test is repeated for a second and third workload that increases the heart rate to between 115 and 130, and 130 and 145 bpm, respectively. Each steady state heart rate and respective workload is graphed and used to predict a workload that would elicit a heart rate response of 170 bpm. The score can then be compared to standard tables and a prediction of VO$_2$ max given.

Direct gas analysis

Direct gas analysis is by far the most accurate measure of VO_2 max as it gives the only truly objective measure of oxygen consumption. Subjects are measured at progressively increasing intensities until exhaustion on a laboratory ergometer (treadmills, cycles, rowing machines or swimming benches tend to be the most popular). A computer analyses the relative concentrations of oxygen inspired and expired when the subject performs the test to exhaustion. By performing a simple calculation the VO_2 max consumed by the muscles can be determined.

> **EXAMINER'S TIP**
>
> The units of measurement for VO_2 max are ml/Kg/min for weight-bearing activities such as running, and L/min for non- or partial weight-bearing activities such as cycling.

Fig 19.2 Measuring VO_2 max through direct gas analysis

Activity 2

Outline the benefits of direct gas analysis as a measure of aerobic capacity over the multistage fitness test.

> **Key term**
>
> **Direct gas analysis** The most valid test of aerobic capacity; it analyses actual oxygen consumption during a test of progressive intensity.

Exam-style Questions

1   Describe and critically evaluate two tests of aerobic capacity.   **[6 marks]**

Training aerobic capacity

Continuous methods

Continuous methods of training work on developing endurance and therefore stress the **aerobic energy system**. Central to this method of training is the performance of rhythmic exercise at a steady rate or **low intensity** that uses the large muscle groups of the body over a long period of

Table 19.4 Advantages and disadvantages of the PWC170 test

Advantages	Disadvantages
• This is a sub-maximal test. • Cycle ergometers often contain a pulse monitor, and therefore the heart rate is easily monitored. • Studies have shown this to be a valid test when compared to laboratory tests. • This test has satisfactory levels of validity and reliability.	• As the test is performed on a bicycle it may favour cyclists. • The test relies on the linear relationship between heart rate and workload. • This is only a prediction of VO_2 max based on heart rate scores. At no point is oxygen consumption actually measured.

Table 19.5 Advantages and disadvantages of direct gas analysis

Advantages	Disadvantages
• The only test that actually measures the volume of oxygen consumed. • Different modes of exercise can be used (running, cycling, rowing, swimming). • This test has high validity and reliability.	• This is a maximal test (to exhaustion). • Requires access to a laboratory and sophisticated testing equipment.

Table 19.6 Classification of aerobic fitness (VO_2 max in ml/kg/min)

Age (yrs)	Low	Fair	Average	Good	High
Women:					
20–29	<24	24–30	31–37	38–48	49+
30–39	<20	20–27	28–33	34–44	45+
40–49	<17	17–23	24–30	31–41	42+
50–59	<15	15–20	21–27	28–37	38+
60–69	<13	13–17	18–23	24–34	35+
Men:					
20–29	<25	25–33	34–42	43–52	53+
30–39	<23	23–30	31–38	39–48	49+
40–49	<20	20–26	27–35	36–44	45+
50–59	<18	18–24	25–33	34–42	43+
60–69	<16	16–22	23–30	31–40	41+

Source: American Heart Association, 1972

time (between 30 minutes and two hours). Good examples of such activities include jogging, swimming, cycling or aerobic dance. The intensity of such exercise should be approximately 60 to 80 per cent of HR max, as outlined in the **Karvonen Principle** (see page 306), so the body is not experiencing too much discomfort while exercising.

The great advantage of this type of training, however, is that great distances can be covered without the lactate build-up associated with anaerobic training methods. Distance runners, for example, may total up to 140 miles per week, a distance equivalent of London to Lincoln.

With such high mileage comes the danger of injury, particularly to the muscles and joints, so any programme should be thoroughly scrutinised. Other disadvantages of this type of training are that it can be quite monotonous, and although good in developing an aerobic base for all activities, it is not necessarily sport specific when it comes to team games. The health-related benefits of continuous training have been well documented; jogging and aerobics are very popular, and as long as individuals are made aware of the injury risk factors, there is no reason why the majority cannot participate safely.

Fartlek or speedplay

This is a slightly different method of continuous training. It is a form of endurance conditioning where the **aerobic energy system** is stressed due to the continuous nature of the exercise. The only difference, however, is that throughout the duration of the exercise, the speed or intensity of the activity is varied, so that both the **aerobic and anaerobic systems can be stressed**. Fartlek sessions are usually performed for a minimum of 45 minutes, with the intensity of the session varying from low-intensity walking to high-intensity sprinting. Traditionally, Fartlek training has taken place in the countryside where there is varied terrain, but this alternating pace method could occur anywhere and you could use your local environment to help you, for example:

- 15-minute run at 60 per cent of maximum heart rate
- Sprint for one lamp post then easy jog for three lamp posts (repeat ten times)
- Walk for 90 seconds
- Five-minute run at 75 per cent of maximum heart rate
- Easy jog to finish.

Devised by a Swede, Gösta Holmér, many physiologists have adapted this method of training to suit particular performers. Other examples include the Gerschler and Saltin methods.

Activity 3

Design and participate in a Fartlek session (you may wish to design the session so that it can be completed around your school or college, on a treadmill, bicycle, rowing ergometer or even in a swimming pool!). If available, wear a heart rate monitor during the session. On completion draw a graph to represent your heart rate throughout the duration of the session.

Interval training

This is probably the most popular type of training used in sport for training the elite athlete. It is very versatile and can be used in almost any activity, although it is most widely used in swimming, athletics and cycling. Interval training can improve both aerobic and anaerobic capacities.

In order for the correct capacity to be stressed, several variables can be manipulated which include:

1 Distance of the work interval (duration).
2 Intensity of the work interval (speed).
3 The number of repetitions within a set.
4 The number of sets within a session.
5 Duration of the rest interval.
6 Activity during the rest interval.

In order to train the relevant energy system, the coach must ensure that the variables have been adjusted appropriately.

To train the aerobic system the work interval should be much longer, perhaps up to seven or eight minutes in duration. The intensity should again be moderate (and certainly faster than any pace undertaken during continuous training) and measured as a percentage of personal best times for the distance or using target heart rates. The longer exercise periods mean that fewer repetitions are needed, maybe only three or four in one session, which can be performed in one set. In order to put extra stress on the aerobic system the recovery time is usually much shorter in comparison to the work period. A work:relief (W:R) ratio of $1:\frac{1}{2}$ may be used, where the athlete rests for half the time it took to complete the work period.

The requirements of an interval training session can be expressed as the **interval training prescription**. For example, a swimmer may have the following session prescribed:

$$2 \times 4 \times 200m, W:R = 1:\frac{1}{2}$$

Where:

- 2 = number of sets
- 4 = number of repetitions
- 200m = training distance
- $1:\frac{1}{2}$ = work to relief ratio

For aerobic development:

$$4 \times 5 \text{ minute runs}, W:R = 1:1$$

Where:

- 4 = number of repetitions
- 5 minutes = duration of work period
- 1:1 = 5 minute recovery period

Activity 4

Plan and participate in an interval training session designed to improve aerobic capacity. Be sure to address each of the following variables:

- distance of the work interval (duration)
- intensity of the work interval (speed)
- the number of repetitions within each set
- the number of sets within a session
- duration of the rest interval
- activity during the rest interval.

Key term

Interval training A method of training that involves alternating periods of high-intensity exercise and rest.

Identifying the appropriate intensity of aerobic training

Identifying the appropriate intensity of training is essential for the performer if aerobic development is to occur. Some ways of gauging the intensity of exercise are outlined below:

- Calculating target heart rates, or the **training zone**
- Calculating the performer's VO_2 max and working at a percentage of it
- Calculating the **respiratory exchange ratio**.

For aerobic work, exercise intensity can be measured by calculating an individual's 'training zone'; this is represented by the training heart rate and so involves observing heart rate values. This has become much easier with the increased availability of reliable heart rate monitors.

The most established method of calculating the training zone is known as the **Karvonen Principle**. Karvonen developed a formula to identify correct training intensities as a percentage of the sum of the maximum heart rate reserve and resting heart rate. Maximum heart rate reserve can be calculated by subtracting resting heart rate (HR rest) from an individual's maximum heart rate (HR max):

$$\text{Maximal heart rate reserve} = \text{HR max} - \text{HR rest}$$

An individual's maximal heart rate can be calculated by subtracting their age from 220:

$$\text{Maximum heart rate} = 220 - \text{age}$$

Karvonen suggests a training intensity of between 60 and 75 per cent of maximal heart rate reserve for the average athlete, although this can obviously be adapted to account for individual differences: more experienced performers may work at higher levels, say between 70 and 85 per cent of maximal heart rate reserve.

Consider the following example to illustrate the value of this measure of intensity.

A 20-year-old rower, with a resting heart rate of 65 bpm is aiming to build up his endurance capacities for a forthcoming event. He is advised to train at between 60 and 75 per cent of his training heart rate reserve in the weeks prior to the event. To calculate his training zone, the rower used the Karvonen formula as follows:

$$\text{Training heart rate } 60\% = 0.60 \text{ (HR max − HR rest)} + \text{HR rest}$$

$$= 0.60 \, (200 - 65) + 65$$

$$= 81 + 65$$

$$= \textbf{146 bpm}$$

$$\text{Training heart rate } 75\% = 0.75 \text{ (HR max − HR rest)} + \text{HR rest}$$

$$= 0.75 \, (200 - 65) + 65$$

$$= 101 + 65$$

$$= \textbf{166 bpm}$$

Thus, the rower now has some precise figures to use to ensure that he is training at the correct intensity. In order for some kind of aerobic adaptation to occur, the rower must be exercising within his **target zone**, between 146 and 166 bpm.

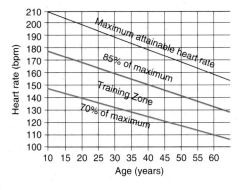

Fig 19.3

Another method of monitoring the intensity of training is through working the athlete at a **percentage of VO$_2$ max**. For the elite endurance athlete, this should be no less than 70 per cent of VO$_2$ max, while those exercising for health-related

reasons will see benefits from training at just 50 per cent of their VO$_2$ max. Figure 19.9 shows the linear relationship between heart rate and oxygen consumption (VO$_2$). If the athlete's HR max is known, then it is possible for the coach to extrapolate the VO$_2$ max from the graph in Figure 19.4.

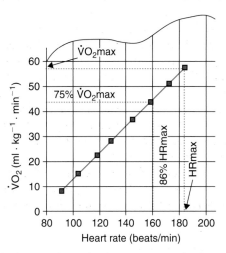

Fig 19.4 The linear relationship between HR and VO$_2$

Activity 5

Use the table in this activity as a calculator to work out your target training zone at various intensities. All scores reflect your heart rate for a 10-second count (don't forget to start counting from zero!). If you fall between age ranges, take the next group up. For example, if you are an 18-year-old and wish to train at 70 per cent of your maximum heart rate, find the age group 20 along the top of the table and move down until you come to 70 per cent of MHR. Your target 10-second pulse rate should be 23 beats. You may wish to convert this to beats per minute, in which case, multiply the figure in the box by six.

		Age												
		15	20	25	30	35	40	45	50	55	60	65	70	75	80
Percentage of maximum heart rate	55%	19	18	18	17	17	17	16	16	15	15	14	14	13	13
	60%	21	20	19	19	19	18	18	17	17	16	16	15	15	14
	70%	24	23	23	22	22	21	20	20	19	19	18	18	17	16
	80%	27	27	26	25	25	24	23	23	22	21	21	20	19	19
	90%	29	28	28	27	26	26	25	24	23	23	22	21	21	20

Now complete a 15-minute run, ensuring your heart rate lies at 70 per cent of your MHR. Sketch the heart rate curve expected.

Activity 6

Using the Karvonen Principle, calculate your training zone. Record your resting pulse rate then, in groups of three, work on a given method of aerobic exercise (for example, running, step-ups, rowing, cycling). One person should be exercising at a steady pace, the second keeps an eye on heart rate, and the third records the results. Record heart rate at the following times:

1 Immediately prior to exercise.
2 Two minutes after exercise commences.
3 Five minutes after exercise commences (ensure you are in the zone).
4 Seven minutes after exercise commences (still in the zone?).
5 Ten minutes after exercise commences (stop exercise now!).
6 One minute after exercise stops.
7 Three minutes after exercise stops.
8 Five minutes after exercise stops.

Copy out and record your results in the table below.

HR rest	Prior to exercise	2 mins during	5 mins during	7 mins during	10 mins during	1 min after	3 mins after	5 mins after

Draw a graph to illustrate your heart rate before, during and after exercise. Identify your training zone on your graph. Comment upon your success at training in your target zone.

The coach has one further method to ensure training is of appropriate intensity, which is to analyse oxygen consumption and carbon dioxide production to determine the **respiratory exchange ratio (RER)**. The RER, or respiratory quotient, is a method of determining which energy providing nutrient is predominantly in use during exercise. It is represented as follows:

$$\text{respiratory exchange ratio} = \frac{\text{Volume of carbon dioxide expired per minute}}{\text{Volume of oxygen consumed per minute}}$$

The closer the value is to 1.0 the more likely it is the body is using glycogen as a fuel; a value of 0.7 suggests that fat is the predominant fuel in use. Intermediate figures suggest that a mixture of fuels is being utilised, which is the expected norm. Obviously the harder the athlete is working the more he or she relies on using glycogen as a fuel. An endurance performer should be utilising a mixture of glycogen and fats.

Exam-style Questions

1 For an elite performer in a named sport of your choice, describe how you would ensure that aerobic capacity is developed during a training programme. **[10 marks]**

Karvonen formula A method that uses training heart rates to determine the most appropriate intensity of training for a performer.

Physiological adaptive responses of the body to aerobic training

Cardiovascular adaptations to aerobic training

Following endurance training, many cardiovascular adaptations arise:

- Cardiac hypertrophy – following aerobic training, the heart increases in size. This enables the heart to work more efficiently, particularly at rest. The increase in thickness of the myocardium (cardiac tissue) enables the left ventricle to fill more completely with blood during the diastole phase of the cardiac cycle. This allows the heart to pump more blood per beat (stroke volume) since the thicker walls can contract more forcibly, pumping more blood into the systemic system and ultimately reaching the muscles.

- **Increased stroke volume** – following training **stroke volume increases** both at rest and during exercise. With an increase in stroke volume at rest, the heart will no longer need to pump as many times per minute to achieve the same amount of blood flowing to the body's tissues.

- **Reduced resting heart rate** (bradycardia) – since the heart seeks to work as efficiently as possible, the heart responds to the increase in stroke volume by decreasing the heart rate at rest, a condition known as bradycardia. This explains the very low resting heart rates often experienced by top endurance athletes.

- **Increased maximum cardiac output** – since an athlete's stroke volume increases with training, so the maximum cardiac output of the athlete also increases. Cardiac output may increase by up to 30–40 L/min in trained individuals. However, it is important to note that there is little or no change in the values of resting cardiac output, due to the decrease in resting heart rate that accompanies endurance training.

Table 19.7 The energy systems and fuels used in developing aerobic capacity

	Energy system stressed	Fuels used
Aerobic capacity	Aerobic system	Glycogen *and* fatty acids

The adaptations mentioned above have focused on the changes to the structure and function of the heart. Training-induced changes may also occur to the vascular system, some of which are outlined below:

- **Capillarisation** – one reason that accounts for greater performances in aerobic events following training is the increased capillarisation of trained muscles. New capillaries may actually develop that enable more blood to flow to the muscles and more oxygen to reach the tissues. Furthermore, existing capillaries become more efficient and allow greater amounts of blood to reach the muscles, which also become more efficient at extracting the oxygen due to the muscular adaptations mentioned above.
- **Enhanced redistribution of blood** – improvements in the ability of the arteries and arterioles to vasoconstrict and vasodilate improve the redistribution of blood by shunting the supply to the active muscles and tissues, so that there is a greater supply of oxygen for energy production in these working muscles.
- **Decreased resting blood pressure** – increased elasticity of the blood vessels following a period of endurance training results in decreased resting blood pressure. Blood pressure during sub-maximal or maximal exercise, however, remains unchanged.
- **Increased blood volume** – increases in blood volume following training can be attributed to an increase in blood plasma (the water component of the blood). This has the important function of decreasing the blood's viscosity and enabling the blood to flow around the body more easily, thus enhancing oxygen delivery to the muscles and tissues.
- **Increased red blood cell volume and haemoglobin content** – red blood cell volume is also higher in the trained athlete, which further facilitates the transport of oxygen around the body. However, although haemoglobin content increases, the increase in blood plasma is greater and, consequently, the blood haematocrit (the ratio of red blood cell volume to total blood volume) is reduced, which lowers the viscosity of the blood and facilitates its progress around the body.

Muscular adaptations to aerobic training

Depending on the type of the prior training, different adaptations will occur in the muscle. Changes that occur following a period of aerobic training include:

- **Hypertrophy of slow-twitch muscle fibres** – regular stimulation of the muscle through aerobic-based exercise will cause changes to occur within the muscle cell. In particular, the structure of the muscle fibres may alter. Since the performance of endurance exercise stresses the slow-twitch muscle fibres, these respond by enlarging by up to 22 per cent. This gives greater potential for aerobic energy production since larger fibres mean a greater area for mitochondrial activity.
- **Increased size and density of mitochondria** – endurance training leads to an increase in both size and number of mitochondria. Some studies have reported mitochondria size to increase by up to 40 per cent and the number by over 100 per cent. Since the mitochondria are the industry of the muscles that produce our aerobic energy, increases in size and number can be associated with the economies of scale achieved by large factories, and an increase in production of energy will result.
- **Increased activity of oxidative enzymes** – endurance training may also improve the efficiency of enzymes within the muscle cell that work on breaking down our food fuel to release the energy stored within. As a result, there is more scope to use glycogen and fat as a fuel. The oxidation of both these fuels increases, providing greater amounts of energy.
- **Increased stores of glycogen and triglycerides** – with hypertrophy of slow-twitch muscle fibres there is a corresponding increase in the muscular stores of glycogen and triglycerides, which ensures a continuous supply of energy, allowing exercise to be performed for a longer period of time.
- **Increased stores of myoglobin** – studies in untrained and trained athletes have revealed increases of up to 80 per cent in myoglobin content within the muscle cell. Myoglobin is the substance within the muscle that carries oxygen to the mitochondria (it is similar in structure to haemoglobin). With greater amounts of myoglobin, more oxygen can be transported to the mitochondria, which further improves the efficiency of aerobic energy production.
- **Increased VO$_2$ max** – all of the above aerobic adaptations associated with endurance training ensure that a higher percentage of VO$_2$ max (maximum oxygen uptake) can be attained before OBLA is reached, which delays the onset of fatigue. Generally, VO$_2$ max is not a product of training as it is largely genetically determined, but these metabolic adaptations within the muscle that occur as a result of training may slightly increase an individual's VO$_2$ max in the region of 10 to 20 per cent.

Respiratory adaptations to aerobic training

Endurance performance depends on oxygen transportation and utilisation, but no matter how good the functioning of these are, improvements in performance will not happen unless we can get oxygen into the body. The respiratory system is responsible for receiving oxygen into the body and dealing with the waste products associated with muscle metabolism.

- **Small increases in lung volumes** – surprisingly, there are only very small increases in lung volumes following training. Vital capacity (the amount of air that can be forcibly expelled following maximum inspiration) increases slightly, as does tidal volume, during maximal exercise. One factor to account for these increases is the increased strength of the respiratory muscles, which may facilitate lung inflation.
- **Enhanced gaseous exchange at the alveoli and the tissues** – pulmonary diffusion (the exchange of gases at the alveoli) will become more efficient following training, especially when working at near maximal levels. The increased surface area of the alveoli during exercise, together with their increased capillarisation, ensures that there is ample opportunity for gaseous exchange to take place and, thus, guarantees sufficient oxygen is entering the blood.
- **Reduced resting respiratory rate** – following training, there is a reduction in both resting respiratory rate and the breathing rate during sub-maximal exercise. This appears to be a function of the overall efficiency of the respiratory structures induced by training.

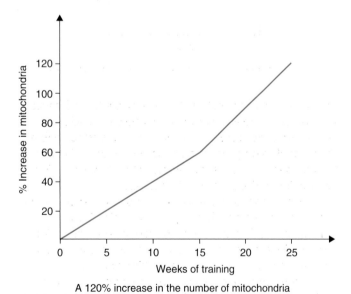

A 120% increase in the number of mitochondria following a 25-week endurance programme. Size of mitochondria may also increase by up to 40%

Fig 19.5 The increase in mitochondrial density following a period of aerobic training

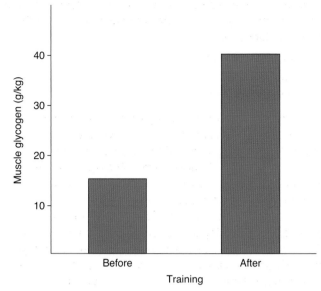

A 20-week, 4 day/week endurance training programme

Fig 19.6 The increase in muscle glycogen stores following a period of aerobic training

Table 19.8 highlights some of the key physiological adaptations that take place following prolonged periods of aerobic training. Essentially, all the structural and physiological changes that occur to the body will contribute to improve the maximal aerobic power, or VO$_2$ max, of the performer.

Activity 7

A student decides to take up distance running and joins a local running club. After following a training programme for three months, a distinct improvement in performance is noted. Account for these changes from a physiological perspective.

Exam-style Questions

1 Identify and explain the physiological adaptations that enable a trained performer to recover faster from physical activity than an untrained individual. **[7 marks]**

Strength

Strength relates to:

the ability of the body to apply a force.

The recognised definition of strength is:

The maximum force that can be developed in a muscle or group of muscles during a single maximal contraction.

However, it is how we apply strength that is important when analysing sporting activity. Three dimensions of strength have been identified:

- Maximum strength
- Elastic strength
- Strength endurance.

An athlete who requires a very large force to overcome a resistance in a single contraction, such as we see in weightlifting, or performing a throw in judo, will require maximum strength. An athlete who needs to overcome a resistance rapidly yet prepare the muscle quickly for a sequential contraction of equal force will require elastic strength. This can be seen in explosive events such as sprinting, triple jumping or in a gymnast performing tumbles in a floor routine. Finally, an athlete who is required to undergo repeated contractions and withstand fatigue, such as a rower or swimmer, will view strength endurance as a vital determining factor to successful performance.

> ### Key terms
>
> **Maximum strength** The maximum force that can be developed in a muscle or group of muscles during a single maximal contraction.
> **Elastic strength** The ability to overcome a resistance rapidly and prepare the muscle quickly for a sequential contraction of equal force.
> **Strength endurance** The ability of a muscle or group of muscles to undergo repeated contractions and withstand fatigue.

Two further dimensions of strength have been identified:

- Static strength
- Dynamic strength.

Static strength

Static strength is a dimension of strength where a force is exerted against a resistance but there is no change in the length of the muscle or movement of the limbs. This is sometimes referred to isometric strength. A gymnast performing a handstand, for example, displays static strength in the muscles of the shoulder and arms.

Dynamic strength

Dynamic strength is a dimension of strength where a force is exerted against a resistance where there is a change in length of the muscle and a change in position of the limbs. This type of strength involves isotonic (concentric and eccentric) muscle contractions. A triple jumper during the hop, step and jump phases of the skill will display dynamic strength in the muscles of the leg.

Factors affecting strength

Cross-sectional area of the muscle

Strength is directly related to the **cross-sectional area of the muscle tissue.** The greater the cross-sectional area of pure muscle tissue, the greater the force produced.

Type of muscle fibre

You will recall from your studies at AS that muscles are composed of different types of muscle fibres (see *OCR PE for AS*, pages 17–20). Fast-twitch (white) muscle fibres, for example, can generate greater forces (and therefore strength) than slow-twitch (red) muscle fibres. However, slow-twitch muscle fibres can continue to contract for much longer periods than fast-twitch fibres, which fatigue rapidly.

> ### Key term
>
> **Fast-twitch muscle fibres (type 2)** Muscle fibres suited to high-intensity anaerobic work. Type 2b fibres are recruited for activities of greatest intensity but fatigue rapidly, while type 2a fibres are engaged in activities that require large forces and yet offer greater resistance to fatigue than type 2b fibres.

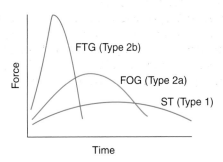

Fig 19.7 Contractional force of different muscle fibre types

Performers that require high levels of strength endurance will possess a larger quantity of slow-twitch muscle fibres. This ensures they receive a rich supply of blood to enable the most efficient production of aerobic energy. This allows the muscles to contract repeatedly without experiencing fatigue due to the build-up of lactic acid.

Activities that require muscular endurance are numerous but can best be highlighted by the example of rowing. Individual muscle groups are required to contract at high intensity for a period of approximately five minutes (or as long as it takes to complete the 2,000m course).

Muscular endurance relies upon the efficiency of the body to produce energy under both anaerobic and aerobic conditions, together with an ability of the body to deal with and 'buffer' the lactic acid.

Table 19.8 Structural and physiological responses of the body to aerobic training

Structural adaptation	Physiological consequence
Increased heart size (cardiac hypertrophy)	The heart adapts by increasing the volume of the ventricular cavities in response to aerobic training (such as continuous training). This enables greater diastolic filling of the heart, which increases stroke volume both at rest and during exercise. Resting heart rate will fall as a consequence (bradycardia). Although resting cardiac output remains the same, it will increase dramatically during exercise
Increased capillary density	With capillarisation comes increased gaseous exchange. More oxygen can reach the exercising tissues and removal of carbon dioxide and lactic acid improves
Enhanced elasticity of blood vessels	Enhanced elasticity enables more effective vasoconstriction and vasodilation, which improves the redistribution of blood via the vascular shunt
Increased blood volume	Increased blood volume facilitates the transport of oxygen and carbon dioxide. An increase in plasma content decreases the viscosity of the blood, speeding up blood flow
Increased red blood cell volume	An increase in red blood cell volume means that there is more haemoglobin available to transport oxygen around to the working muscles
Hypertrophy (and hyperplasia) of slow-twitch muscle fibres	Enlargement of slow-twitch fibres (by up to 22 per cent) and some fibre splitting provide more opportunity for aerobic respiration to take place and provide the energy needed to fuel the muscles during aerobic activity
Increased mitochondrial density	Endurance training signals an increase in the size (by up to 40 per cent) and number (up to 120 per cent) of mitochondria. As these are the factories of aerobic respiration, more and larger factories quite simply mean that more energy is produced for the working muscles
Increased myoglobin volume	An increase (up to 75 per cent) in the myoglobin content of muscle cells means that more oxygen can become available to the mitochondria for the production of aerobic energy
Increased muscle glycogen stores	Increased muscular stores of glycogen provide a larger source of fuel to draw upon during endurance-based exercise
Increased number of oxidative enzymes	This improves the aerobic breakdown of glycogen and fat, which releases more energy to resynthesise ATP. In particular, the increased oxidation of fat, the preferred fuel during endurance activity, leads to the sparing of glycogen and a decrease in the respiratory exchange ratio
Increased maximum pulmonary ventilation	A larger tidal volume and use of available alveoli allows a greater diffusion rate of respiratory gases (O_2 and CO_2)

Key term

Buffering The body's method of maintaining acceptable levels of blood acidity and reduce the effects of lactic acid.

Age

The optimum age to develop strength appears to be in the early to mid-twenties. As the body ages, less protein becomes available in the body for muscle growth, and the stress and anaerobic nature of strength training also makes it an inappropriate method of training during old age.

Table 19.9 A summary of the main factors that determine strength

Type of muscle fibre	Fast twitch fibres can produce high levels of force (maximum and elastic strength) over a short period of time. Slow twitch fibres on the other hand can only produce lower levels of force but over a longer period of time (strength and endurance).
Age	Although strength can be gained at any age, the rate of strength gain appears to be greatest from your teenage years to your early twenties. We are at our strongest at this point.
Gender	Although men's and women's muscle tissue are characteristically the same, men generally have more muscle tissue than women due to the effect of testosterone. So although gender does not affect the quality of the muscle it does the quantity!
Limb and muscle length	The length of limbs determine the body's leverage systems. People with shorter limbs tend to be able to lift heavier weights due to their more advantageous lever systems. In the same way people who have developed longer muscles will have a greater potential for developing size and therefore strength!
Other factors include ...	Point of tendon insertion, lifting technique

Sex

In this age of equality it is highly appropriate to dismiss the notion of a weaker sex. In fact, relative to cross-sectional area of pure muscle tissue, men and women are equal in terms of strength. It is the greater fat content of women and the higher testosterone levels in men that can account for the difference in the cross-sectional area of muscles and, therefore, the increased strength in men.

> **EXAMINER'S TIP**
>
> Make sure you can distinguish between the different types of strength and apply each type to sporting activity.

Evaluating strength

Due to the different types of strength there are a number of tests available for each dimension. Some of the most popular tests are highlighted in Table 19.10.

Tests of maximum strength

The handgrip dynamometer test
Maximum strength can be measured with the use of dynamometers, which give an objective measure of the force generated within various muscles or muscle groups. The easiest strength test to administer is the **handgrip dynamometer**, which measures grip strength generated by the muscles in the forearm.

After adjusting the grip for hand size, squeeze the handle as hard as possible. Record the maximum reading from three attempts for both dominant and non-dominant hands. Table 19.11 evaluates this test of maximum strength.

One repetition maximum test (1 rep max)
Another common test of strength is the **one repetition maximum test** (1RM test). This assesses the maximal weight a subject can lift in one repetition using free weights or other gym equipment.

Table 19.10 Recognised tests for each dimension of strength

Dimension of strength	Recognised test
Maximum strength	Handgrip dynamometer one repetition maximum test
Elastic strength	Wingate cycle test; 25m hop test
Strength endurance	Abdominal conditioning (sit up) test

Table 19.11 Advantages and disadvantages of the handgrip dynamometer test

Advantages	Disadvantages
• A simple and objective measure • Reliability of this test is high.	• The validity of the handgrip test has been questioned, since it only indicates strength of muscles of the forearm.

Table 19.12 Grip strength norms

Classification	Non-dominant (kg)	Dominant (kg)
Women		
Excellent	>37	>41
Good	34–36	38–40
Average	22–33	25–37
Poor	18–21	22–24
Very poor	<18	<22
Men		
Excellent	>68	>70
Good	56–67	62–69
Average	43–55	48–61
Poor	39–42	41–47
Very poor	<39	<41

For persons over 50 yrs of age, reduce scores by 10%.

Source: Data from Cabin, Lindsay and Tolson (1978) Concepts in Physical Education.

> **EXAMINER'S TIP**
>
> Make sure you use the correct units of assessment for each fitness test you perform.

Tests of elastic strength

The Wingate cycle test

This is a 30-second maximum cycle test designed to evaluate anaerobic capacity and elastic strength. The subject pedals against a resistance of 75g per kg of body weight as hard as possible for 30 seconds. The peak power, time to peak power and power decline can all be recorded.

Table 19.13 Advantages and disadvantages of the 1 rep max test

Advantages	Disadvantages
<ul><li>Easy testing procedure</li><li>Most muscle groups can be tested</li><li>Weight training equipment is easily accessible</li><li>Using the following calculation it is possible to convert the weight lifted into a percentage of the performer's body mass: $$\frac{\text{Weight lifted (kg)}}{\text{Body mass (kg)}} \times 100$$</li></ul>	<ul><li>When performing maximal lifts the threat of injury is more apparent and so safety is essential</li><li>It can be difficult to isolate individual muscles</li><li>Trial and error to find the maximum lift may induce fatigue</li></ul>

Table 19.14 Advantages and disadvantages of the Wingate cycle test

Advantages	Disadvantages
<ul><li>Provides objective data</li><li>Many different aspects of elastic strength can be assessed (for example, peak power, time to peak power and power decline)</li><li>This test has high validity and reliability</li></ul>	<ul><li>This is a maximal test that relies on the motivation of the performer to work as hard as possible, often until exhaustion</li><li>Laboratory equipment is required</li><li>As the test involves a cycling action it may favour cyclists</li></ul>

25m hop test

From a flying start the subject hops the 25m distance and the time is recorded. The test is performed firstly with the dominant leg, followed by the non-dominant leg. The average time of the two attempts is calculated and compared to Table 19.15.

Table 19.15 Evaluation of performance on the 25m hop test

Rank (%)	Females (seconds)	Males (seconds)
91–100	3.13–3.75	2.70–3.25
81–90	3.76–4.50	3.36–3.90
71–80	4.51–5.70	3.91–5.00
61–70	5.71–6.90	5.01–6.10
51–60	6.91–8.15	6.11–7.20
41–50	8.16–8.90	7.21–7.90
31–40	8.91–9.45	7.91–8.40
21–30	9.46–10.05	8.41–8.95
11–20	10.06–10.34	8.96–9.25
1–10	10.35–10.70	9.26–9.60

Source: Explosive Power and Strength, Human Kinetics (Chu, 1996)

Tests of strength endurance

A test for muscular endurance should assess the ability of one muscle or a group of muscles to undergo repeated muscular contractions.

Table 19.16 Advantages and disadvantages of the 25m hop test

Advantages	Disadvantages
• Validity in testing the elastic strength of the legs is high • Provides baseline data for self comparison to judge improvement	• Timing is open to human error although this can be rectified through the use of timing gates • Only tests the elastic strength of the legs.

Table 19.17 Advantages and disadvantages of the abdominal conditioning test

Advantages	Disadvantages
• Easy to administer with little equipment required • Large groups can participate at once • The abdominal muscles can be easily isolated • The test is relatively high in validity and reliability	• Correct technique is essential for successful completion of the test, which is difficult to monitor • This is a maximal test and relies to some extent upon the motivation of the performer • It is now recognised that full sit ups should not be completed regularly due to the strain placed on the lower regions of the spine • Only tests the strength endurance and the abdominal muscles

Abdominal conditioning test

A simple test to measure the endurance of the abdominal muscle group is the abdominal conditioning test. The equipment required includes:

- Sports Coach UK CD
- CD player
- Stopwatch
- Gym mat.

Subjects are required to perform as many sit-ups as possible, keeping in time to the bleeps emitted from the CD. Get a partner to count the number of sit-ups completed correctly, and time the duration of the work period. Subjects should withdraw from the test when they can no longer keep in time to the bleeps, or when technique noticeably deteriorates.

Table 19.18 Normative scores for the abdominal conditioning test

Stage	Number of sit-ups	Standard	
	Cumulative	Male	Female
1.	20	Poor	Poor
2.	42	Poor	Fair
3.	64	Fair	Fair
4.	89	Fair	Good
5.	116	Good	Good
6.	146	Good	Very good
7.	180	Excellent	Excellent
8.	217	Excellent	Excellent

Strength training

Strength gains are sought by many athletes and there is no doubt that improvements in strength can enhance performance. There are a number of training methods available to the sports performer; the preferred method, however, will depend on the particular dimension of strength required by the activity.

What is common to all methods of strength training, however, is the use of some form of resistance, whether that be weights, body weight or bungee ropes.

With advances in technology and the improvement in the quality of weight machines, weight training has increased in popularity in both athletic and recreational training regimes. It can be used to develop all aspects of strength: maximum, elastic and strength endurance. Which of these are stressed at a particular time is determined by manipulating the following:

- The weight or resistance
- The number of repetitions
- The number of sets
- The amount of rest or relief.

Central to devising an effective weight training programme is the principle of **one repetition maximum (1RM)**. This is the maximum amount of weight the performer can lift for one repetition. Once this has been found for each exercise, the coach can design a programme adjusting the resistance as a percentage of the athlete's maximum lift.

> **Key terms**
>
> **Repetitions** The number of times the weight is lifted.
> **Sets** A series of repetitions followed by a resting period.

Table 19.19 The development of different dimensions of strength

Objective	Intensity of training load	Repetitions in each set	Number of sets	Recovery between sets	Evaluation procedures	Training of/ value for
Development of maximum strength	85–95%	1–5	Normal 2–4 Advanced 5–8	4–5mins	• Maximum lift • Dynamometer	Weight lifting, shot, discus, hammer, javelin, jumping events, rugby and contact sports, men's gymnastics
Development of elastic strength	75–85%	6–10	(4–6)	3–5mins	• Standing, long and • Vertical jump capability • 25m hop test	All sports requiring 'explosive' strength qualities – sprinting, jumping, throwing, striking
Development of advanced level of strength endurance	50–75% of maximum	15–20	(3–5)	30–45 secs	• Maximum reps possible	Rowing, wrestling, skiing, swimming, 400m, steeplechase etc.
Development of a basic level of strength endurance	25–50% of maximum	15–20	(4–6)	60 secs	• Maximum reps possible	Generally required for all sports suitable for young and novice competitors and fitness participants

EXAMINER'S TIPS

Other considerations when devising a weight-training programme include the type of activity to be undertaken, such as a pyramid system, super sets etc.

Key term

One repetition maximum The amount of weight the performer can lift for one repetition.

Training maximum strength

The most appropriate method of developing maximum strength is through weight training.

Weight training

For activities where maximum strength is required, such as power-lifting or throwing the hammer, training methods that increase muscle strength and size will be required. Essentially, this will involve some form of very high-resistance, low-repetition exercise, for example, performing three sets of two to six repetitions at 80 to 100 per cent of maximum strength, with full recovery between sets, i.e.
3 sets × 6 reps × 80% 1RM (full recovery)

Training elastic strength

Weight training

When weight training to develop elastic strength, the intensity should be of a moderate to high level. The following prescription could be used:

3 sets × 12 repetitions × 75% 1RM ,1–2 minutes between sets

General guidelines for elastic strength development are:

- The movement and contraction period must be explosive to ensure the muscle works rapidly.
- Use very high loads or resistance, which will encourage the muscle to recruit all its motor units.
- Ensure the muscle recovers fully between sets, enabling the relevant energy system to recover.

Plyometrics

Elastic strength or power is the ability to produce maximal muscular forces very rapidly. It is determined by the force exerted by the muscle (strength) and the speed at which the muscle shortens. It therefore follows that by improving either strength or the speed of shortening, elastic strength can be improved. One method of training that can improve the speed at which a muscle shortens is plyometrics.

It has long been established that muscles generate more force in contraction when they have been previously stretched. Think of a rubber band – the greater the band is stretched before firing, the further it will travel. Muscles are the same: by lengthening the muscle, elastic energy can be stored in the muscle fibres and used to produce more powerful contractions. Plyometrics enables this to occur by taking the muscle through an **eccentric (lengthened) phase** whereby elastic energy is stored, before **a powerful concentric (shortening) phase**. This stimulates adaptation within the neuromuscular system whereby the muscle spindles within the muscle cause a **stretch reflex**, which prevents muscle damage and produces a more powerful concentric contraction of the muscle group. This has important consequences for racket sports, sprinting, jumping and throwing events in athletics, as well as in games such as rugby, volleyball and basketball where leg strength is central to performance.

Taking the example of **depth jumping**, here the athlete drops down from a box or platform 50 to 80cm high. On landing, the quadricep muscle group lengthens, pre-stretching the muscle and storing elastic energy. To prevent injury and to stop the muscle from lengthening too much, a stretch reflex is initiated, causing the muscle to give a very forceful concentric contraction and driving the athlete up onto a second platform. Furthermore, the exercise becomes much more effective if the athlete spends as little time as possible in contact with the ground when landing. This particular plyometric activity can also be made sport specific. For example, a basketball player could perform a rebound after dropping down from the box, or a volleyball player perform a block, etc. Due to the high-impact nature of plyometrics individuals would need to be screened for injury and participants would need to undergo a thorough warm-up.

Key points to consider to avoid injury when undertaking a plyometric training session include:

- Warm up thoroughly
- Use a flat, non-slip landing surface that has good shock absorbing properties, such as a grass field
- Make sure any boxes or benches used are sturdy and safe
- Ensure you follow guidelines on technique of the exercises, that is: landing on the ball of your foot, then rocking back onto your heel and then taking off from the ball of the foot again. The sequence should therefore be 'ball-heel-ball'
- Progression in exercise should be gradual to avoid soreness
- If you experience joint or muscular pain stop immediately.

Exercises that might form part of the plyometrics session include:

- Bounding
- Hopping
- Leaping
- Skipping

- Depth jumps (jumping off and onto boxes)
- Press-ups with claps
- Throwing and catching a medicine ball.

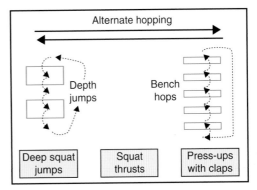

Fig 19.8 A plyometrics circuit

Activity 8

Design a plyometrics session for a sport of your choice. Justify your selection of exercises related to particular skills from your chosen activity.

Key term

Plyometrics A type of training used to develop elastic strength and power in athletes. Activities performed will pre-load a muscle through eccentric muscle contractions before powerful concentric muscle contractions. Activities performed include hopping, bounding, jumping and medicine ball exercises.

Training strength endurance

Weight training

To train for activities that require strength endurance, such as swimming or rowing, a different approach to training will be required. In order to perform more repetitions, a lighter load or resistance is needed and the following programme might be prescribed:

Three sets of 20 repetitions at 50 to 60 per cent of 1RM with partial recovery between sets, i.e.
3 sets × 20 reps × 55% 1RM (partial recovery)

Circuit training

Circuit training involves performing a number of callisthenic exercises in succession, such as press-ups, abdominal curls, step-ups etc. Each exercise is usually performed for a set amount of time or a set number of repetitions, and the circuit can be adapted to meet the specific fitness requirements of a given sport or activity (see Figure 19.9).

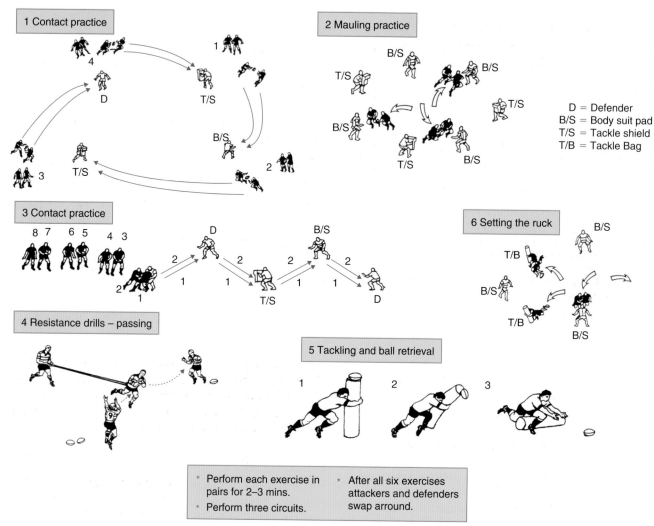

Fig 19.9 A rugby contact circuit

When planning a circuit there are several factors that need consideration. The first of these is the most fundamental: what exactly do you require the circuit for? Once you have answered this you can choose the exercises to include (see some examples of exercises in Table 19.20).

You will also need to consider:

- The number of participants
- Their level of fitness
- The amount of time, space and equipment that is available.

Having considered all these points you can now go ahead and plan the layout of your circuit.

One golden rule when devising the layout of the circuit is that the same body part should not be exercised consecutively. Therefore the sequence of the exercises should be as follows: arms, trunk, cardiovascular, legs, arms, trunk, cardiovascular, etc. The exception is for experienced athletes performing an 'overload' circuit where the endurance of one muscle group is being trained.

The great benefit of circuit training is that it is extremely adaptable, since exercises can be included or omitted to suit almost all activities. It also enables large numbers of participants to train together at their own level. With regular testing, improvements in fitness are easily visible through circuit training as current work can be compared to previous test scores. Figure 19.10 illustrates a 3-in-1 circuit, whereby each participant completes circuits A, B and C. This circuit is particularly good for general conditioning and enables large numbers to participate.

No strength training programme is complete without due consideration of **core stability**. Core stability is the combined strength of all the muscles from your hips to your armpits – and is responsible for many things including posture. An increase in core strength can lead to increases in virtually all other types of strength and dramatically reduces the chance of injury during strength training. The best method of improving core stability is with the use of a Swiss ball. Simply performing abdominal crunches or leg raises on the Swiss ball will strengthen the abdominal and lower back muscles (particularly the multifidus and transverse abdominus), the 'core' of the body's strength.

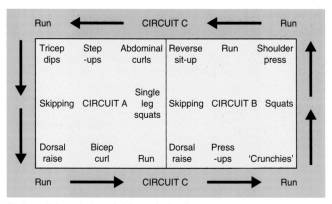

Each participant is to complete each circuit.

Circuit A = 8 exercises × 30 secs = 4 mins
Circuit B = 8 exercises × 30 secs = 4 mins
Circuit C = Run around outside = 4 mins
Repeat 2 or 3 times

Each participant is to complete circuit A, B and C with 60 secs walking recovery between circuit.

Fig 19.10 A general fitness circuit

Activity 9

Design a circuit training session for an activity of your choice. Give reasons for the exercises you have chosen and explain how the principle of progressive overload could be applied. Table 19.20 may help in the selection of some exercises.

Table 19.20 Exercises to include in a circuit

Benefits for	Exercises
Cardiovascular	Running around the gym Skipping Step-ups Cycling on an ergometer Bounding exercises on a mat
Trunk	Abdominal curls Crunches Dorsal rises Trunk twists Medicine ball exercises
Arm	Press-ups/box press Bicep curls Tricep dips Shoulder press Squat thrusts Medicine ball exercises
Leg	Chin-ups to beam Single leg squats Any of the cardiovascular exercises outlined above

Activity 10

Design and carry out a core stability training session using a Swiss ball. Try to include at least eight different exercises.

Table 19.21 The energy systems and fuels used in developing different dimensions of strengtherythropoietin (RhEPO)

Type of strength	Energy system	Fuel used
Maximum strength	ATP splitting/ATP-PC	ATP, PC
Elastic strength	ATP-PC	PC
Strength endurance	Lactic acid	Glycogen

The physiological adaptive responses of the body to strength training

The body adapts to the stress imposed by strength training. The strength gains and muscle hypertrophy associated with the training, however, may only start to become evident after about eight weeks and result largely from the increase in size and volume of the myofibrils.

Muscular adaptations to strength training

- **Hypertrophy of fast-twitch muscle fibres** – following all types of strength training, enlargement of fast-twitch muscle fibres takes place. The growth of type 2a fibres may well follow training designed to improve strength endurance, while type 2b fibres will enlarge following maximum and elastic strength training.
- **Increased stores of ATP and PC** – an increase in the number of muscle cells following strength training will increase the amount of ATP and PC stored within them. This increases the capacity of the ATP-PC energy system, which supplies the energy for all speed and power-based activities.
- **Increased enzyme activity** – the efficiency of the ATP-PC system is further improved through increased activity of the enzymes responsible for breaking down ATP and PC. These include creatine kinase and ATPase.
- **Increased glycolytic capacity** – weight training at high intensities for up to 60 seconds has been shown to increase the glycolytic capacity of the muscle, largely through increasing the activity of glycolytic enzymes. This improves the muscles' ability to break down glycogen in the absence of oxygen and means that the athlete can exercise for longer periods of time before feeling the effects of fatigue.

- **Enhanced buffering capacity** – buffering enables the muscles to tolerate the effects of lactic acid more effectively. When lactic acid accumulates in the muscle, hydrogen ions (H^+) are released, which inhibits glycolytic enzyme activity and interferes with the contractile elements of the muscle, causing muscle fatigue. Bicarbonate ions are the body's natural cleaners; existing in the muscle and the blood they mop up hydrogen ions, reducing acidity and the negative impact of hydrogen ions on muscle contractility. By following a strength training programme, the buffering capacity of the body improves substantially and enables the body to work for longer periods of time and at higher levels of acidity.
- **Delayed OBLA** – the improvements in glycolytic efficiency and buffering capacity contribute to the delay in the onset of blood lactate accumulation or OBLA. OBLA is a product of training, and improvements in this will certainly improve endurance performance, allowing the athlete to work harder for longer.

Flexibility

Flexibility can be defined as:

the range of movement possible at a joint.

Although flexibility is most commonly associated with activities such as trampolining and gymnastics it is, in fact, a requirement in all sports since the development of flexibility

Exam-style Questions

1 Identify the type of strength most relevant to a 100m sprinter and describe a test that can be used to evaluate this type of strength. **[3 marks]**

2 Design a strength training programme that will develop this type of strength, explaining the physiological adaptations that occur as a result of the training programme. **[5 marks]**

can lead to an increase in both the speed and power of muscle contraction.

Two dimensions of flexibility have been identified:

- static flexibility
- dynamic flexibility.

Static flexibility

Static flexibility refers to the range of movement at a joint that occurs without considering the speed of movement. Invariably, it relates to the maximum extent of muscle lengthening, for example when lengthening the hamstrings under control and holding the stretch. Good static flexibility is a necessary prerequisite for good dynamic flexibility; however, having good static flexibility does not in itself ensure good dynamic flexibility.

Table 19.22 A summary of the physiological responses of the body to strength training

Structural adaptation	Physiological consequence
Hypertrophy (and hyperplasia) of fast-twitch muscle fibres	Enlargement of fast-twitch fibres (by up to 22 per cent), due to increased protein synthesis and some fibre splitting (hyperplasia) provide more opportunity for the ATP-PC system and anaerobic glycolysis to take place and provide the energy needed to fuel the muscles during anaerobic activity. This will lead to greater speed, strength and power
Increased recruitment of motor units	The increase in motor unit recruitment is a neural adaptation that, together with enhanced synchronisation, can increase the overall force produced by the muscle when it contracts
Increased levels of ATP and PC within muscle cells	Stores of ATP and PC have been shown to increase by approximately 25 per cent and 40 per cent, respectively. This allows a greater energy yield from the ATP-PC system, which provides more energy more rapidly and delays the point when the lactic acid system 'kicks in'
Increased activity of ATP-PC energy system enzymes	The activity of ATPase and creatine kinase both increase following a period of anaerobic training. This ensures the quick release of energy via the ATP-PC system
Enhanced buffering capacity	Improves the removal of lactic acid from the muscles and can delay the lactate threshold or OBLA. This enables the performer to achieve higher work rates before the arrival of fatigue
Increased number of glycolytic enzymes	The activity of the enzyme PFK can double following a period of anaerobic training. This facilitates the release of energy from glycogen under anaerobic conditions
Increased heart size (cardiac hypertrophy)	The heart adapts by increasing the thickness of the ventricular walls in response to anaerobic training such as weightlifting. This enables a more forceful contraction that increases stroke volume both at rest and during exercise. Resting heart rate will fall as a consequence (bradycardia)

Dynamic flexibility

Dynamic flexibility considers the range of movement at a joint when performing a particular action at speed. A gymnast performing a split leap, for example, must quickly produce a wide range of movement at the hip joint to perform the skill effectively. Similarly, a javelin thrower will have great dynamic flexibility about the shoulder joint in order to launch the javelin by maximising its momentum at release.

> ### Key term
>
> **Momentum** The amount of motion a moving body or object possesses. It is the product of mass and velocity.

Factors affecting flexibility

Flexibility is determined by a number of factors including:

- the elasticity of muscle tissue, ligaments and tendons
- the strength and opposition of surrounding muscles
- the shape of the articulating bones.

Often the degree of movement is determined by the type of joint, since joints are designed either for stability or mobility. The knee joint, for example, is a hinge joint and has been designed with stability in mind. It is only truly capable of movement in one plane of direction, allowing flexion and extension of the lower leg. This is due to the intricate network of ligaments surrounding the joint that restricts movement. The shoulder joint, on the other hand, is a ball and socket joint and allows movement in many planes since relatively few ligaments cross the joint. However, the free movement at the joint comes at a price, as the shoulder joint can easily become dislocated.

Age is another key factor as there is a distinct reduction in mobility from the age of eight years, and following periods of inactivity; older athletes, therefore, need to take flexibility more seriously than their younger counterparts.

Furthermore, flexibility is joint specific so that although a performer may have a wide range of movement at one joint, it does not necessarily follow that they will have a wide range of movement at all joints.

A summary of all the factors affecting flexibility is outlined in Table 19.23 below.

Evaluating flexibility

The most easily accessible test of flexibility is the **sit and reach test**. This test gives an indication of the flexibility of the hamstrings and lower back. The only equipment required is a sit and reach box.

Sit down on the floor with your legs out straight and feet flat against the box. Without bending your knees, bend forwards with arms outstretched and push the cursor as far down as possible and hold for two seconds. Record your score.

Another test of flexibility involves the use of a **goniometer**, a piece of equipment used to measure the range of motion at a joint. The 'head' of the goniometer is placed at the axis of rotation of a joint while the arms are aligned longitudinally with the bone. A measurement in degrees can be taken, giving a very **objective** reading that can be used to assess improvement. One small disadvantage of this piece of equipment is that it is not always easy to identify the axis of rotation of a joint.

Table 19.23 A summary of the factors that contribute to the flexibility of a performer

Internal factors	External factors
• The type of joint – e.g. a ball and socket joint has a greater range of movement than a hinge joint • Bony structures which limit movement e.g. the deep socket of the hip joint restricts some movements • The elasticity of the muscle tissue • The elasticity of the surrounding tendons and ligaments • The temperature of the joint and associated tissues – the warmer the muscle, the less viscous and the greater the ability to lengthen • Strength of the opposing muscle group	• The temperature of the local environment – a warm environment • Age – flexibility tends to decrease with age • Gender – females tend to be more flexible than males due to the hormone oestrogen • Restrictions of clothing • Injury – injury can restrict the flexibility of an individual • Activity level – an active person is likely to have a greater range of movement and therefore a greater degree of flexibility

Table 19.24 Advantages and disadvantages of the sit and reach test

Advantages	Disadvantages
• An easy test to administer • There is plenty of data available for comparison	• The test only measures flexibility in the region of the lower back and hamstrings, so it cannot give an overall score of flexibility • The extent to which a subject has warmed up may well affect results, when comparing to norms

Table 19.25 Normative scores for the sit and reach test

Male (cms)	Female (cms)	Rating (cms)
>35	>39	Excellent
31–34	33–38	Good
27–30	29–32	Fair
<27	<29	Poor

Developing flexibility

Mobility training is the method employed to improve flexibility. It is often a neglected form of training, but should be incorporated into every athlete's training programme as it contributes to a range of different fitness components. Effective flexibility training can improve performance and help prevent the occurrence of injury. Stretching and mobility training should only be performed after a thorough warm-up where an increase in body temperature has occurred. This is easily achieved by performing a period of light cardiovascular exercise, centring upon those muscle groups that are to be stretched. In addition, wear warm clothing while performing the stretches to maintain body temperature; if possible, perform in a warm environment.

The method of stretching used in mobility training should centre on the connective tissue and the muscle tissue acting upon the joint, as these tissues have been shown to elongate following a period of regular and repeated stretching.

Several forms of stretching have been identified and are now outlined below.

Static v dynamic stretching

Static stretching entails lengthening the target muscle and holding the stretch for a period of 15–20 seconds. Dynamic stretching, on the other hand, involves taking the muscle through its full range of motion in a controlled manner, such as when performing lunges. Both static and dynamic forms of stretching should be included in mobility training sessions in order to gain maximum benefit.

Active stretching

Active stretching typically occurs when the athlete performs voluntary muscular lengthening and holds the stretch for a period of 30–60 seconds. No external assistance is required. By consciously relaxing the target muscle at the limit of the range of motion, muscle elongation may occur following regular practice.

Passive stretching

Passive stretching refers to the range of movement that can occur with the aid of an external force. This is generally performed with the help of a partner who can offer some resistance, although body weight and a piece of equipment such as a Dyna band can also be used.

One method of flexibility training that has emerged from passive stretching is **proprioceptive neuromuscular facilitation (PNF)**. This seeks to decrease the reflex shortening of the muscle being stretched (called the stretch reflex), which occurs when a muscle is stretched to its limit.

A simple PNF technique is outlined below:

1 With the assistance of a partner, move the limb or body part to the limit of your range of motion and hold for a few seconds.
2 At the point of discomfort, isometrically contract the target muscle for between six and ten seconds.
3 After the contraction the muscle will release, having stimulated a Golgi tendon organ (GTO) response, which causes further **relaxation** of the target muscle and allows further stretching to take place (with the aid of a partner).

PNF stretching relies on the fact that when a stretched muscle contracts isometrically, the stretch reflex mechanism of the muscle spindles is switched off. The GTO causes relaxation of the muscle and, therefore, enables the muscle to stretch further than previously. A second PNF method is known as the CRAC method (Contract–Relax, Antagonist–Contract).

With continued practice of PNF, a new limit of the muscle stretch may occur, but don't forget that pain is the body's signal that damage is occurring, and athletes should not stretch beyond slight discomfort.

Ballistic stretching

Ballistic stretching is an advanced form of stretching that should only be performed under the watchful eye of a coach. It is not recommended for all performers as it uses the momentum of the body to force or bounce the body beyond its normal range of movement.

The physiological adaptive responses of the body to flexibility training

- Enhanced extensibility and elasticity of muscle tissue
- Increased resting length of connective tissues (tendons and ligaments)
- Increased range of movement.

Although these adaptive responses seem limited at first glance, the fact is that flexibility has a significant impact on the development of other components of fitness such as elastic strength, speed and power.

Body composition

Body composition is concerned with the physiological make-up of the body with regard to the relative amounts and distribution of muscle and fat. Although there are several definitions of body composition, it is most commonly defined as

the component parts of the body in terms of the relative amounts of body fat compared to lean body mass.

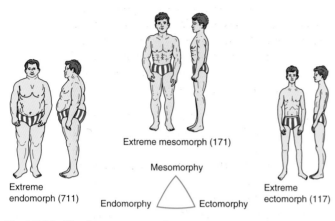

Extreme mesomorph (171)

Mesomorphy

Endomorphy △ Ectomorphy

Extreme endomorph (711)

Extreme ectomorph (117)

Fig 19.11 The three extremes of somatotype

2 **Mesomorphy** – the muscularity of the body.
3 **Ectomorphy** – the linearity or leanness of the body.

The characteristics of a performer's body can be categorised according to these somatotypes and plotted on the delta-shaped graph.

It is very rare that an individual would be classed as an extreme endo, meso or ectomorph at the apex of the delta. More realistically they would possess characteristics of all three, but the relative contributions of each somatotype would differ depending upon the activity. For example, rowers tend to be very lean yet very muscular with little body fat, and are placed accordingly (see Figure 19.14).

Not only does body composition play an important role in the training of elite athletes, more generally it contributes to health and general well-being. Excessive body fat can lead to obesity and the associated complications such as cardiovascular diseases. For the athlete high body fat can result in a reduction in muscle efficiency and contributes to greater energy expenditure, since more weight requires more energy to move around and a consequent increase in oxygen consumption. Body composition requirements vary with different sports but, generally, the less body fat the better. Muscle mass is desirable for those activities or sports that require muscular strength, power and endurance.

Factors affecting body composition

There are many factors that can impact upon an individual's body composition, including:

- Genetics
- Level of fitness and quantity of exercise undertaken
- Age
- Diet
- Sex.

Genetics

Your body composition and body size is, to a certain extent, pre-determined by your genes. The relative shape of the body, or **somatotype**, can also be mentioned at this point. Somatotyping is a method used to measure body shape. Three extremes exist:

1 **Endomorphy** – the relative fatness or pear-shapeness of the body.

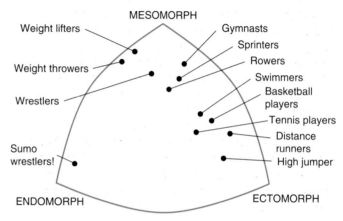

Fig 19.12 Somatotyping relates body composition to sporting activity

Some studies have shown, however, that the body's fat cells are only produced between 0–2 yrs and during puberty. Once we reach full maturation, the number of fat cells remains constant. However, these cells can inflate substantially if a poor diet and inactive lifestyle ensues. It is therefore essential that the diet of children is scrutinised as over-eating during childhood can cause a prolifeation of fat cells leading to a potentially 'fat' adulthood!

Level of fitness and quantity of exercise undertaken

It is generally the case that exercise can cause changes in the body composition of a performer. An aerobic performer will have a high energy expenditure and will utilise fat as well as glycogen as a metabolic fuel, resulting in lean body

Table 19.26 Advantages and disadvantages of hydrostatic weighing

Advantages	Disadvantages
• Validity and reliability are both high, giving accurate predictions of body fat percentage	• Requires a large hydrostatic weighing tank • Some subjects may suffer anxiety from being immersed in the water • The subject's residual volume is needed for the calculation

mass. Similarly, weight training will increase the quantity of muscle mass, which can increase an individual's metabolic rate and also promote lean body mass.

Age

Generally the younger you are, the greater the amount of lean body mass and the lower the quantity of fat mass.

As we age, activity levels tend to fall which can lead to an increase in total body fat.

Diet

A diet high in sugar and saturated fat will lead to an increase in the quantity of fat mass relative to the level of lean body mass.

Sex

Typically men have lower levels of body fat than women. Healthy values for an 18-year-old male range from 14 to 17 per cent body fat; the equivalent for 18-year-old females is 24 to 29 per cent.

Evaluating body composition

Body composition can be measured in a variety of ways.

Hydrostatic weighing

Hydrostatic weighing considers the displacement of water when the body is submerged in a tank. By dividing the body mass of the subject by the volume of water displaced when immersed, body density can be calculated:

$$\text{Body density} = \frac{\text{Body mass}}{\text{Volume of water displaced}}$$

Body density can then be used to predict the percentage of body fat of the individual. The body weighs less in water than out of water because fat floats. A large fat mass will make the body lighter in water. The greater the difference between weight in the water and weight out of the water, the higher the percentage of body fat.

Bioelectrical impedance

Bioelectrical impedance is another popular objective measure whereby a small electrical current is passed through the body from wrist to ankle. As fat restricts the flow of the current, the stronger the current needed, the greater the percentage of body fat. Although this test requires specialist equipment, it is becoming more accessible with the introduction of simple scales or hand-held devices that transmit an electrical current.

Fig 19.13 Body composition assessment through hydrostatic weighing

Body mass index

The most common and simplest measure of body composition is made through the body mass index (BMI). Through calculation of an individual's BMI, body fat can be predicted. BMI is calculated by measuring the body mass of the subject (weight in kg) divided by the height of the individual (in metres squared).

$$\text{BMI} = \frac{\text{Weight in kg}}{\text{Height in m}^2}$$

The higher the score, the greater the levels of body fat:

- Healthy – BMI of 20–24.9
- Overweight – BMI of 25–29.9
- Obese – BMI of 30

Although this test is very quick and a prediction can be made instantaneously, it can obviously be inaccurate since it does not differentiate between fat mass and muscle mass. So large, lean muscular athletes may well fall into the wrong category!

Skin-fold measures

This test requires the measurement of subcutaneous fat on the left side of the body using skin-fold callipers. For men measurements are taken from the chest, abdomen and thigh; for women the triceps, thigh and suprailiac are measured.

Table 19.27 Advantages and disadvantages of skin-fold measures

Advantages	Disadvantages
<ul><li>A simple test that is widely used</li><li>Scores can be used to identify changes in body fat over time</li></ul>	<ul><li>The testing procedure can vary between tester. For example, was the measurement taken in exactly the correct place?</li></ul>

Using the scale via Student Online, locate the sum of the three skin-fold measurements in millimetres, then locate your age on the left-hand scale and connect the two points with a ruler. Read off the percentage body fat from where the line crosses the centre scale.

At this stage, you may wish to make some other anthropometrical measures such as length of bones and overall height, muscle girths or circumferences, and condyle measures at the joints.

Basal metabolic rate (BMR)

The basal metabolic rate (BMR) is the minimum amount of energy that the body requires to sustain life in a resting individual. Quite simply, it is the amount of energy your body would expend during a 24-hour period of sleep. The main determinant of BMR is body weight and body composition.

For the most part, the BMR represents up to 75 per cent of an individual's energy requirements. The remaining energy expenditure depends on the activity levels of the individual.

Measuring your BMR

An individual's BMR is typically measured under standardised conditions in a laboratory after a full night's sleep where the subject is rested and relaxed, and ideally having fasted for the previous 12 hours. However, this is not the most practical method so the following calculations can be used to estimate a subject's BMR.

The Harris–Benedict equation

In order to calculate an individual's approximate basal metabolic rate, the following information is needed:

- Sex of the subject
- Weight (kg)
- Height (cm)
- Age of the subject.

For men:

$$BMR = 66 + (13.7 \times \text{weight in kg}) + (5 \times \text{height in cm}) - (6.8 \times \text{age in years})$$

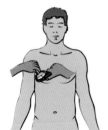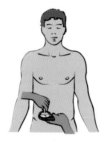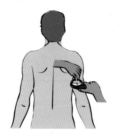

Fig 19.14 Body fat measurements

Table 19.28 The range of factors that affect BMR

Factor	Explanation
Body composition	The greater the lean tissue or muscle mass, the higher the BMR. The higher the percentage of body fat, the lower the BMR
Age	Infants and young children have a high BMR relative to their size due to their rapid growth and development. Younger adults will have a higher BMR than their older counterparts as muscle mass tends to decrease with age
Sex	Men have a higher BMR than women due to their greater muscle mass
Height	Tall, lean people tend to have a higher BMR
Stress	Stress hormones such as adrenaline can raise the BMR
Environmental temperature	Both extreme heat and cold can raise BMR

For women:

$$BMR = 655 + (9.6 \times \text{weight in kg}) + (1.7 \times \text{height in cm}) - (4.7 \times \text{age in years})$$

Activity 11

Calculate your BMR using the Harris-Benedict equation. How does your result compare to the rest of your class? Rank your group BMR results from highest to lowest. What is it that accounts for those students with the highest and lowest BMR scores?

Simple equation

A simpler approach to calculate BMR is:

$$BMR = \text{weight in kg} \times 22 \text{ kcal/kg}$$

Remember, these calculations only give an estimate of the calories required for the body to perform the most basic of functions.

Physical activity and energy expenditure

The rate of energy expenditure of an individual is largely dependent upon the level of physical activity undertaken. On average physical activity accounts for up to 30 per cent of the total daily energy expenditure, but this can be greater in very active people. Table 19.29 indicates the amount of energy (in both calories and joules) required to perform a range of activities.

MET values

A further way to measure energy expenditure is using MET values. MET stands for 'metabolic equivalent' and considers an individual's body weight when calculating energy expenditure. The body typically burns 1 kcal per kilogram of body weight per hour (expressed as 1 kcal/kg/hr) **at rest**, which represents one MET. Sitting quietly at rest, therefore, has a MET value of 1 where the body burns 1 kcal/kg/hr. A game of squash, however, has a MET value of 12, meaning the body burns 12 kcal/kg/hr.

A MET can also be defined as oxygen uptake in ml/kg/min, with one MET equal to the oxygen cost of sitting quietly, equivalent to 3.5 ml/kg/min.

Activity 12

Using Tables 19.29 and 19.30, calculate your energy expenditure in a 24-hour period. You will need to record all forms of activity undertaken during this period, so make sure you write down how much time you spent sitting, studying, sleeping, walking, exercising, etc.

Add together the energy requirements for each activity and you should arrive at your total energy expenditure for that 24-hour period.

What does this tell you about the number of calories you need to consume each day?

Table 19.29 Energy requirements of a variety of daily activities

Activity	KJ/min	Kcal/min
Sleeping	4.6	1.1
Sitting	6	1.4
Studying	7.1	1.7
Standing	7.1	1.7
Washing/dressing	15	3.6
Walking slowly	13	3.1
Walking moderately quickly	21	5.0
Walking up and down stairs	38	9.1
Work and recreation		
Light (domestic work, carpentry, golf, etc.)	20	4.8
Moderate (gardening, dancing, jogging, cycling, tennis)	21–30	5.0–7.2
Strenuous (cross-country running, football, swimming front crawl)	>30	>7.2

Source: Ministry of Agriculture, fisheries and food. *Manual of Nutrition*, London HMSO, 1992

Table 19.30 A comparison of the energy expenditure in different sports

Sport	Duration	Energy expenditure
Swimming	60 mins	5–25 kcal/min
Jogging	30 mins	7–9 kcal/min
Soccer	90 mins	9 kcal/min
Rugby	80 mins	6–9 kcal/min
Tennis	60 mins	6–9 kcal/min
Sprinting	15 secs	90 kcal/min

Key term

MET value (metabolic equivalent) The ratio of the work metabolic rate to the resting metabolic rate.

Activity 13

Use the Compendium of Physical Activities Tracking Guide to calculate your energy expenditure for a 24-hour period using MET values:

http://prevention.sph.sc.edu/tools/docs/documents_compendium.pdf

Activity 14

1 Make a list of everything you eat during one day. Using information on food packaging and/or online calorie counters, calculate the number of calories consumed in the day. Compare this to your answer in Activity 12.

2 What is the impact of this on your weight in the long term (i.e., will it increase, decrease or remain the same)?

3 Work out the relative percentages of carbohydrate, fat and protein you consume. How does this compare with the expected values for an athlete?

4 Critically evaluate your diet and calorie consumption and the long-term effect this may have on your health.

Obesity and weight control

Obesity is a condition that results from a diet high in saturated fats and refined sugar accompanied by an inactive lifestyle. In essence, it is an increase in the body's total quantity of fat.

Obesity can lead to an increased risk of cardiovascular disease, such as atherosclerosis, hypertension, heart disease and strokes, as well as other complications such as diabetes and gall bladder disease. As well as physical symptoms, an obese individual may suffer from a range of psychological problems including dealing with the social stigma of an unacceptable body shape and size, which in turn can lead to a poor self-image and depression.

One method frequently used to estimate the extent of obesity is the BMI (see page 324). It is assumed that the higher the BMI, the greater the level of 'adiposity' or fat. A score of $30kg/m^2$ defines obesity. We do, however, need to be a little careful when using BMI as a measure of obesity as it does not distinguish between fat-mass and fat-free mass (muscle and bones). Consequently, a very muscular rugby player may be classed as obese even if he has very low body fat!

In order to reverse the effects of obesity it is necessary to restrict calorie intake and increase energy expenditure. This creates a deficit in energy provision and the body will be required to draw upon its fat stores to make up the shortfall. Increasing energy expenditure is best done through the implementation of an exercise programme. The best type of exercise to perform for weight loss is aerobic activity, which uses large muscle groups and continues for a minimum of 30 minutes. It is also a good idea to participate in activities that are non- or partial weight bearing such as swimming, cycling or rowing as this will prevent undue stress being placed on the joints of the individual.

Other benefits of performing exercise as part of a weight-control programme include the suppression of appetite, and an increase in the resting metabolic rate, which means that more calories will be burned in the body even if exercise is not taking place.

Key term

Obesity A condition that accompanies over-consumption and an inactive lifestyle. An imbalance between energy intake and expenditure exists, which results in an excessive increase in the body's total quantity of fat. A person is classed as obese when the BMI exceeds $30kg/m^2$.

Exam-style Questions

1 What are the principles behind weight control? What types of exercise would promote fat metabolism and therefore be useful in a weight-control programme? **[5 marks]**

Activity 15

Study Table 19.31, which shows a comparison of the rates of obesity worldwide. Using examples from the table, suggest reasons why the incidence of obesity varies so much from one country to another.

Designing a weight-control exercise programme

Before prescribing an exercise programme, participants should be screened. This is usually accomplished by the participant completing a Physical Activity Readiness Questionnaire (PAR-Q), an example of which is shown in Figure 19.15. If there are any doubts concerning the individual's ability to participate then they should preferably have a medical examination by their doctor.

The intensity of exercise should be light at first, with a very gradual increase in intensity. Ideally, all fitness elements should be included in the exercise programme, although it is advised to keep high-intensity work to a minimum; anaerobic work should never be advised for those with cardiovascular defects since this puts tremendous strain on the heart. Consequently, the aerobic system should be predominantly stressed, using the large muscle group rhythmically at fairly low intensity. Try to avoid high-impact activities, as undue stress on the bones and joints could cause skeletal complications. Swimming and cycling are good forms of exercise for this, since they are non- or partial weight-bearing activities, which obviously reduces the stresses and strains on the body. The American College of Sports Medicine gives the following recommendations for health-related exercise programmes:

● The activity should use large muscle groups that can maintain exercise for a prolonged period of time
● The intensity should be 40 to 85 percent of VO_2 max, or 55 to 90 per cent of age-predicted HR max
● Duration of 15–60 minutes of continuous or interval training
● A frequency of three to five times per week
● Include moderate-intensity strength training of major muscle groups twice per week.

It will be necessary to monitor everyone for signs of distress during the exercise. Care should also be taken to ensure the environment is conducive to such exercise. Older individuals can overheat and dehydrate quickly in hot conditions, and a cold temperature can deprive the heart of oxygen since respiratory and vascular vessels may constrict.

Activity 16

You are asked to prescribe a 10-week, weight-control exercise programme for a group of overweight individuals who have been inactive for some years. What factors will you need to consider when preparing the programme? Justify the types of activity you include. **[10 marks]**

Table 19.31 Percentage of people classified as obese

Percentage classified as obese		Female	Male
USA	1999–2000	34	27.7
Argentina	1997	25.4	28.4
Mexico		25.1	14.9
Russia		25	10
England	2001	23.5	21.0
Germany	1991	19.3	17.2
Finland		19	20
Spain	1997	15.2	11.5
Italy	1999	9.9	9.5
France	1995–1996	7.0	8.0

Source: Food standards agency.
Note: data is not necessarily directly comparable due to different years of survey and varying age ranges.

PAR-Q & YOU

(Physical Activity Readiness Questionnaire)
(for people aged 15 to 69)

Regular physical activity is fun and healthy. Though being more active is very safe for most people, the questions below are designed to assist individuals aged 15 to 69 in determining whether they should see their doctor before increasing physical activity or exercise. Individuals over 69 years of age who are not used to being active should check with their doctor.

Common sense is your best guide when you answer these questions. Read the questions carefully and answer each one honestly

YES	NO	
		Has your doctor ever said that you have a heart condition and that you should only do physical activity recommended by a doctor?
		Do you feel pain in your chest when you do physical activity?
		In the past month, have you had chest pain when you are not doing physical activity?
		Do you lose your balance because of dizziness or do you ever lose consciousness?
		Do you have a bone or joint problem that could be made worse by a change in your physical activity?
		Is your doctor prescribing drugs for a heart condition or drugs that affect your blood pressure?
		Do you know of any other reason why you should not increase your physical activity?

IF YOU ANSWERED: **YES TO ONE OR MORE QUESTIONS**	Talk with your doctor by phone or in person BEFORE you start becoming more physically active or BEFORE you have a fitness appraisal. Tell your doctor about the PAR-Q and which questions you answered yes. You may be able to do any activity you want as long as you start slowly and build up gradually or you may need to restrict your activities to those which are safe for you. Talk with your doctor about the kinds of activities you wish to participate in.
NO TO ALL QUESTIONS	If you answered NO honestly to all PAR-Q questions, you can be reasonably sure that you can start becoming much more physically active - begin slowly and build up gradually, this is the safest and easiest way to go. Take part in a fitness evaluation – this is an excellent way to determine your fitness level.
DELAY BECOMING MUCH MORE ACTIVE:	If you are not feeling well because of temporary illness such as a cold or a fever, wait until you feel better; or If you are or may be pregnant, talk to your doctor before you start becoming more active.

I have read, understood and completed this questionnaire. Any questions I had were answered to my full satisfaction.

Name: _____   DATE: _____

SIGNATURE: _____   WITNESS: _____

SIGNATURE OF PARENT
or GUARDIAN: (for participants under the age of 18)
Adapted from PAR-Q, Canadian Society for Exercise Physiology

Fig 19.15 A Physical Activity Readiness Questionnaire

What you need to know

* Fitness is the ability to carry out everyday activities without undue fatigue.
* Fitness requirements differ tremendously between athletes and activities.
* There are two divisions of fitness: health-related and skill-related.
* Health-related components of fitness are largely physiologically based and include aerobic capacity, strength, flexibility, body composition, speed and power.
* Skill-related components of fitness include agility, balance, co-ordination and reaction time, and are dependent upon the interaction of the nervous system with the muscular system.
* The best measure of aerobic capacity is the maximal oxygen uptake, or VO_2 max. This is the maximum volume of oxygen that can be taken in, transported and consumed by the working muscles per minute. It is the best predictor of aerobic capacity and can only increase through training by 10 to 20 per cent since it has a 93 per cent genetic component.
* Appropriate tests of aerobic capacity include direct gas analysis, the multistage fitness test and the PWC170 test.
* Aerobic capacity can be improved by following a training programme that includes continuous training, fartlek and aerobic interval training.
* Training induces a number of cardiovascular physiological adaptations including cardiac hypertrophy, increased red blood cell volume and hypertrophy of slow-twitch muscle fibres.
* There are three dimensions of strength: maximum strength, elastic strength and strength endurance.
* Appropriate tests of maximum strength include the 1 repetition maximum test and the handgrip dynamometer.
* Weight training is the best method of improving maximum strength.
* Appropriate tests of elastic strength include the Wingate cycle test and the 25m hop test.
* Weight training and plyometrics are the best methods of training to improve elastic strength.
* An appropriate test of strength endurance is the abdominal conditioning test.
* Weight training and circuit training are suitable methods of training to improve strength endurance.

* Training induces a number of structural and functional physiological responses to the muscular system, including the hypertrophy of fast-twitch muscle fibres, increased ATP and PC stores, and increased recruitment of motor units.
* Flexibility is the range of motion possible at a joint.
* Suitable tests of flexibility include the sit and reach test and the use of a goniometer.
* Static and dynamic are two types of flexibility that have been identified.
* Types of stretching practices include static, dynamic, active, passive and ballistic.
* Proprioceptive neuromuscular facilitation (PNF) is the best method of mobility training to increase flexibility.
* Physiological adaptive responses of the body to flexibility training include enhanced extensibility and elasticity of muscle tissue, increased resting length of connective tissues (tendons and ligaments) and an increase in the overall range of movement.
* Body composition can be defined as the component parts of the body in terms of the relative amounts of body fat compared to lean body mass.
* There are many tests of body composition including hydrostatic weighing, bioelectrical impedance, body mass index (BMI) and skin-fold measurements.
* Basal metabolic rate (BMR) is the minimum amount of energy that the body requires to sustain life in a resting individual.
* A MET value is the ratio of the work metabolic rate to the resting metabolic rate; 1 MET is equivalent to 1kcal/kg/hr.
* Obesity is an excessive increase in the body's total quantity of fat:
  - A person is classed as obese when BMI exceeds 30kg/m².
  - Obesity can lead to an increased incidence of cardiovascular disease and diabetes.
* There are many factors that contribute to obesity, but the key factor is the imbalance between calorie intake and calorie expenditure.
* Exercise should form the basis of any weight-control programme as it increases energy expenditure.

Review Questions

1 What physiological factors contribute to the aerobic capacity of an individual?

2 Outline and justify the methods of training you would use to improve the aerobic capacity of a performer.

3 What physiological adaptive responses account for the aerobic improvement of a performer following a period of continuous training?

4 Outline and justify the methods of training you would use to improve the elastic strength of a performer.

5 What weight-training exercises would you include in a strength training programme to improve the strength endurance of the shoulders and upper back muscles? Name each exercise and state the intensity, number of repetitions and sets you would advise.

6 What physiological adaptive responses account for the improvement in maximum strength of a performer following a period of weight training?

7 Outline the factors that contribute to and determine the flexibility of an individual.

8 Outline and justify the methods of training you would use to improve the flexibility of a performer.

9 What physiological adaptive responses account for the increased range of movement of a performer following a period of PNF training?

10 Evaluate the body mass index as an assessment of body composition.

11 Identify two tests to assess each of the following components of fitness:

(a) Aerobic capacity.

(b) Flexibility.

(c) Elastic strength.

(d) Body composition.

12 Outline some of the factors that may result in a person becoming obese.

13 What factors should be taken into account when designing an exercise programme for a person classed as obese?

CHAPTER 20

Applying the principles of training to the design of training programmes

Learning outcomes

By the end of this chapter you should be able to:

- apply each of the following principles of training in the design of a personal health and fitness programme: specificity, progression, overload, reversibility, moderation and frequency
- plan a programme of aerobic training based on your own assessment of aerobic capacity from Chapter 19 and the requirements of your chosen activity
- plan a programme of strength training based on your own assessment of strength from Chapter 19 and the strength requirements of your chosen activity
- plan a programme of flexibility training based on your own assessment of flexibility from Chapter 19 and the flexibility requirements of your chosen activity
- explain what you understand by the principle of periodisation
- define and explain what is meant by the terms macro-cycle, meso-cycle, micro-cycle and training unit in relation to the design of training programmes.

CHAPTER INTRODUCTION

The planning of training programmes is not a hit or miss affair, it is a science! Olympic champions do not happen upon gold medals. Gold medals are the result of a tremendous amount of dedication, hard work and exceptional planning on the part of both coach and athlete. This chapter draws upon knowledge gained from Chapter 19 and considers how planning appropriate training can make the difference between success or failure for a coach and athlete.

The principles of training

The principles of training are essentially the rules or laws that underpin a training programme. If these rules are not followed then any training undertaken will become obsolete and worthless. There are many principles of training that the coach and athlete must bear in mind in the design of an effective training regime. The principles below are the essential ones that you are required to know and apply for your OCR exam.

Specificity

The law of specificity suggests that any training undertaken should be relevant and appropriate to the sport for which the individual is training. For example, it would be highly inappropriate for a swimmer to carry out the majority of his/her training on the land. Although there are certainly benefits gained from land-based training, the majority of the training programme should involve pool-based work.

The specificity rule does not govern just the muscles, fibre type and actions used but also the energy systems that are predominantly stressed. The **energy system** used in training should replicate that predominantly used in the event. The energy systems should also be stressed in isolation of each other so that high-intensity work (stressing the anaerobic systems) should be done in one session, whereas more aerobic and endurance-based work should be completed in a separate session.

When designing a weight-training programme for a shot putter, for example, the coach will ensure specificity by using weights or exercises (such as an inclined bench press) that replicate the action of shot putting. He will ensure that the exercises use the same **muscle groups** and **muscle fibres** that the athlete recruits during the event, and that the repetitions are undertaken explosively, using the alactic (ATP-PC system) energy pathway, which of course is the predominant energy system used during the shot putt.

Key term

Specificity A principle of training which suggests that any training undertaken should be relevant and appropriate to the sport for which the individual is training.

Progression

If exercise takes place on a regular basis the body's systems will adapt and start to cope with the stresses that have been imposed upon it. In order for further improvement to occur, the intensity of training will need to be gradually increased – this process is referred to as progression and can be done by running faster, lifting heavier weights, training for longer or increasing the frequency of training.

Key term

Progression A principle of training which requires a gradual increase in the intensity of training over time to ensure improved levels of performance.

Overload

This rule considers the intensity of the training session. For improvement and adaptation to occur, the training should be at an intensity where the individual feels some kind of stress and discomfort – this signifies overload and suggests that the old adage 'no pain, no gain' has some truth in it, especially for the elite athlete. Overload for the shot putter may therefore involve lifting very heavy weights, or indeed using a shot that is heavier than that used in competition.

Key term

Overload A principle of training that suggests for improved performance the training must put the body under some form of stress.

Reversibility

The principle of reversibility explains why performance deteriorates when training ceases or the intensity of training decreases for extended periods of time. Quite simply, if you don't use it, you lose it! There are several reasons why an athlete may experience reversibility, including injury and rest or transition following a hard season.

Just seven weeks of inactivity can decrease VO$_2$ max by up to 27 per cent, which reflects a fall in the efficiency of the cardiovascular and aerobic systems. During exercise the athlete may experience increases in both blood lactate and heart rate for standard intensities of exercise. Muscle mass and, therefore, strength will also deteriorate, but this happens at a less rapid rate.

The principle of reversibility therefore explains why pre-season training feels so tough even after just six to eight weeks of inactivity.

Key term

Reversibility The principle of training which explains the deterioration in performance following the reduction in training intensity or the halting of a training programme altogether.

Variance (tedium)

Variety is the spice of life! So in order to prevent boredom, staleness and injury through training it is necessary to ensure that the training programme employs a range of training methods and loads so as not to impose too much psychological or physiological stress on the performer. A swimmer, for example, will follow a varied programme of training that includes pool-based work, land training and weight training. In addition, many pools now have the facility to play music underwater, which may allow the swimmer to enjoy their training more!

Key term

Variance A principle of training that requires a training programme to involve a variety of different methods and intensities to prevent boredom and staleness in a performer.

Overtraining/moderation

Overtraining is a common problem to elite athletes as they strive for greater improvement. It is caused by an imbalance between training and recovery that usually occurs when insufficient time has been left for the body to regenerate and cause adaptation before embarking upon the next training session. In their search for the best possible performance in competition, elite athletes are often tempted to increase training loads and frequency of training above optimal levels, which can lead to symptoms of overtraining. These symptoms include enduring fatigue, loss of appetite, muscle tenderness, sleep disturbances and head colds. The coach can identify overtraining syndrome by physiological testing, which may show the athlete having an increased oxygen consumption, heart rate and blood lactate levels at fixed workloads. In order to combat overtraining the coach should advise prolonged rest, and a reduction in training workloads for a period of weeks or even months. This should restore both performance and competitive desire.

Furthermore, by ensuring adequate rest days and following the **3:1 hard:easy ratio**, the coach and athlete should avoid falling into the overtraining trap.

To prevent overtraining it is essential that the training programme is planned sufficiently well to include a variation in training intensities and to include regular rest days. By simply following a ratio of three hard sessions to one easy session, overtraining should be avoided.

> **Key term**
>
> **Moderation** A principle of training that requires the training to be organised in such a way as to prevent overtraining. This is usually based on a 3:1 hard:easy ratio.

The FITT regime

The coach may also wish to consider the FITT regime when designing the training programme. These letters stand for:

- F – frequency of training
  - will depend on the level of ability and fitness of the athlete (e.g. an elite athlete may train every day whereas a lower-level club player may train only once a week)
  - type of training undertaken also dictates frequency (e.g. aerobic training can be followed 5 or 6 times a week, whereas strength training may only be undertaken 3 or 4 times a week
- I – intensity of exercise
  - must take into account the individual differences of the athlete
  - must take into account the type of training being undertaken
- T – time or duration of exercise
  - to be effective, the duration of the training must take into account the intensity of training
- T – type of training
  - influenced by the athlete's needs (e.g. a triathlete will train in all areas of fitness, but will pay especial attention to aerobic and muscular endurance).

> **Key term**
>
> **FITT Regime** The FITT regime is a simplified principle of training that considers the frequency, intensity, time and type of training.

Activity 1

For one of your assessment activities, plan a programme of aerobic training based on your own assessment of aerobic capacity from Chapter 19 and the aerobic requirements of your chosen activity.

Activity 2

For one of your assessment activities, plan a programme of strength training based on your own assessment of strength from Chapter 19 and the strength requirements of your chosen activity.

Activity 3

For one of your assessment activities, plan a programme of flexibility training based on your own assessment of flexibility from Chapter 19 and the flexibility requirements of your chosen activity.

Periodisation of training

It is important to structure the training programme so that the athlete can achieve the best possible improvements in performance, to reduce the likelihood of overtraining and ensure that peak performance occurs at the climax of the competitive season. To achieve this, the training programme should be viewed as a year-long process divided into specific periods designed to prepare the athlete for optimal performances. This is known as periodisation.

The long-term training plan that is usually one year in length but can be longer, (perhaps for an athlete preparing for the Olympic Games or a football player preparing for a World Cup competition) is known as a macro-cycle. This macro-cycle is subdivided into periods of two to eight weeks that concentrate training on particular areas – these phases are known as meso-cycles. Meso-cycles are further divided into weekly training sessions known as micro-cycles, which again have specific aims and objectives. Finally, each training session is called a training unit.

It is essential that the athlete incorporates sufficient rest within each micro- and meso-cycle in order to prevent overtraining. This sometimes happens in a **3:1 ratio** whereby in a micro-cycle (one week's worth of training) the performer may have three 'hard' sessions and one 'easy' session; or in a meso-cycle the athlete may undertake three 'hard' weeks of training and one 'easy' week.

Key terms

Periodisation The organisation of training in to blocks or periods of time, each with a particular focus.
Macro-cycle This is the long-term training or performance goal. Typically, a macro-cycle lasts one year but can last up to four years.
Meso-cycle A block of training of between two and eight weeks' duration. A number of meso-cycles form a macro-cycle.
Micro-cycle A group of training sessions. Usually a week's worth of training.
Training unit The main focus of a particular training session.

The periodised year

There are three main periods of the periodised year:

- The preparation period
- The competition period
- The transition period.

The preparation period (phases 1 and 2)

The preparation period includes the off-season and pre-season aspects of the periodised year.

During the off-season stage, general conditioning is required through a well-rounded programme of aerobic endurance training, mobility training and training to maintain strength to provide a base upon which to build.

Applying the preparation period to a 400m runner – although success in the 400m is largely down to anaerobic fitness, aerobic conditioning is essential. A good aerobic base will help boost anaerobic performance and enable higher intensity and volume of anaerobic training to be undertaken.

During the pre-season stage there is a significant increase in the intensity of training. This is the time when much of the strength work should be undertaken, through lifting heavier weights or working against greater resistances, and working at higher speeds. Towards the end of this period the coach should employ some competition-specific training, for example working on sprint starts for the sprinter.

The competition period (phases 3, 4 and 5)

Training during the competition period should be aimed at maintaining levels of conditioning achieved during the pre-season phase. Maximum strength training is reduced and much of the training should be centred on competition-specific aspects. For the endurance athlete, however, training at high intensity is still important in preparation for competition. In order to ensure that the athlete is perfectly prepared and can **peak** for competition, a process known as **tapering** may be undertaken. Tapering involves manipulating the volume and intensity of training two to three weeks prior to competition to ensure that the athlete is fully recovered from any hard training undertaken, and that muscle glycogen stores can be fully replenished, without the effects of de-training occurring. The two key factors to successful tapering are to:

- Maintain intensity of training
- Decrease the volume of training by approximately one-third. For example, if I normally train at 80 per cent HR max for 45 minutes, when tapering I should maintain the intensity (i.e., continue to train 80 per cent HR max) but reduce the volume of training to 30 minutes. This should hopefully lead to optimal performance during competition.

A 100m sprinter will taper by reducing the total number of repetitions performed in training by 30 to 50 per cent but still working at maximum effort.

The transition period (phase 6)

Following a hard season of competition the body needs to recuperate. The transition period bridges the gap between the season passed and the next training year. Essentially, the transition period should be a period of **active rest** with some low-intensity aerobic work such as swimming or cycling. The transition period is vital and should not be omitted; as well as giving the body a break from all the hard work in physiological terms, it can enhance motivation for training during the following periodised year.

Table 20.1 Activities performed during each phase of the periodised year

Period	Phase	Activities
Preparation	Phase 1	Development of endurance base, general conditioning
	Phase 2	Higher-intensity training, anaerobic work, skills and technique, competition-specific training
Competition	Phase 3	Maintenance of fitness, fine tuning, tactical development
	Phase 4	Tapering
	Phase 5	Season's peak performance
Transition	Phase 6	Recovery/active rest

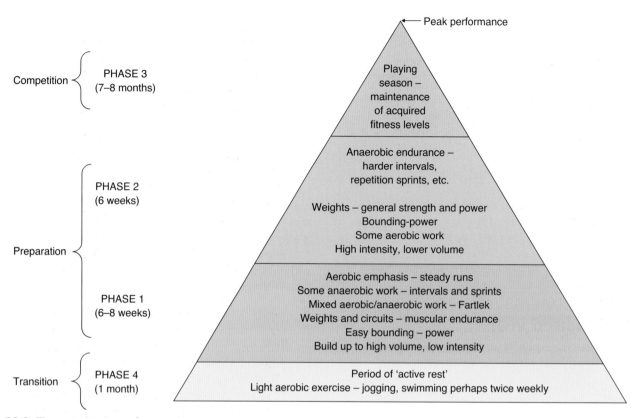

Fig 20.2 The periodised year for a rugby player

Activity 4

The table below shows the periodised year of an international rugby player in a month-by-month format. Study the periodisation and answer the following questions:

Peak months	July	Aug	Sept	Oct	Nov	Dec	Jan	Feb	Mar	Apr	May	June
Heavy weights	✓	✓				✓	✓					
Speed endurance	✓	✓	✓			✓	✓					
Technique and match sharpness			✓	✓	✓			✓	✓	✓	✓	

1 Why are heavy weights performed during the months specified?
2 Explain the timings of the technique and match sharpness sessions.
3 When is the transition period?
4 Why are Oct/Nov, Feb/March and April the 'peak months'?
5 Using the four phases of periodisation (preparation 1, preparation 2, competition and transition) complete the periodised year for a 100m sprinter on the calendar below:

Oct	Nov	Dec	Jan	Feb	Mar	Apr	May	June	July	Aug	Sept

6 Some sportspeople require a double-periodised year. Explain this term and show how this might occur on the calendar below:

Oct	Nov	Dec	Jan	Feb	Mar	Apr	May	June	July	Aug	Sept

What you need to know

* The principles of training are the laws that ensure adaptation from effective training.
* Specificity suggests that any training undertaken should be relevant and appropriate to the sport for which the individual is training.
* Specificity relates to muscle fibres, energy systems, muscle groups and movement actions.
* The principle of progression requires a gradual increase in the intensity of training over time to ensure improved levels of performance.
* The principle of overload suggests that, for improved performance, the training must put the body under some form of stress.
* The principle of reversibility explains the deterioration in performance following the reduction in training intensity or the halting of a training programme altogether.
* The principle of variance requires a training programme to involve a variety of different training methods and intensities to prevent boredom and staleness in a performer.
* The FITT regime is a simplified principle of training that considers the frequency, intensity, time and type of training.
* Periodisation of training is the organisation of training into blocks or periods, each with a particular focus.
* A periodised year is subdivided into macro-cycles, meso-cycles, micro-cycles and training units.

* A macro-cycle is the long-term training or performance goal. Typically, a macro-cycle lasts one year but can last up to four years.
* A meso-cycle is a block of training of between two and eight weeks' duration. It comprises of a number of micro-cycles.
* A micro-cycle is a group of training sessions that usually forms a week's worth of training.
* A training unit is the main focus of a particular training session.
* There are three distinct periods that make up a periodised year: the preparation period, the competition period and the transition period.
* The preparation period consists of two phases (phases 1 and 2) and is the period that focuses mainly on the development of fitness and technique.
* The competition period consists of three phases (phases 3, 4 and 5) and seeks to maintain fitness levels acquired during the preparation phase, allow the performer to taper their training and ensure the athlete peaks for major competitions.
* The transition period consists of one phase (phase 6) and is a period of active rest that allows the performer to recover from the endeavours of the previous season's competition and training before the new season commences.

Review Questions

1 Explain how the principle of specificity can be applied to the design of a training programme for a squash player.
2 Explain how you would apply the principles of training to a performer training for a half-marathon.
3 What do you understand by the following terms?
   (a) Macro-cycle
   (b) Meso-cycle
   (c) Micro-cycle
   (d) Training unit
4 How can a coach prevent their performer from overtraining?

5 Tapering is a feature of the competition phase of the periodised year. What are the two key considerations for successful tapering?
6 Identify the following:
   (a) The three periods of a periodised year
   (b) The six phases of the periodised year
7 What activities would you include during the preparation period (phases 1 and 2) for a 100m sprinter?
8 How can a coach ensure that an athlete performs at their peak during a major competition?

CHAPTER 21

Enhancing performance through ergogenic aids

CHAPTER INTRODUCTION

Sports culture is filled with pills, potions, powders, new training equipment and psychological techniques that all claim to give athletes the 'winning edge' and to increase the adaptive responses outlined previously.

An ergogenic aid can be defined as:

any substance, object or method used by an athlete with the sole aim of improving or enhancing performance.

Ergogenic aids are not a new phenomenon. Indeed, in ancient Greece athletes are reported to have eaten magic mushrooms to improve their chances of winning the laurel wreath, while the Aztecs reportedly ate human hearts to gain advantage over their rivals.

EXAMINER'S TIP

In your exam you will be required to critically evaluate the use of ergogenic aids by performers. This essentially requires you to discuss the perceived benefits and consider any disadvantages such as associated health risks.

Key term

Ergogenic aid Any substance, object or method used by an athlete with the sole aim of improving or enhancing performance.

Classifying ergogenic aids

Ergogenic aids are classified according to the nature of the physiological and psychological benefits or outcomes. What follows is a brief discussion outlining the different categories of ergogenic aid together with a number of examples of each. The range of ergogenic aids open to a sports performer is very extensive and it would be impossible to deal with each in detail here. Consequently, this chapter covers those aids specifically required for your exam. This is not meant to be a prohibitive list, however, and you should consider the complete array of ergogenic aids available to the performer. Indeed, some of the activities in this chapter will require you to investigate a number of ergogenic aids not specifically mentioned in the specification.

Five classes of ergogenic aid have been identified:

- Physiological
- Hormonal or pharmacological
- Nutritional
- Mechanical

- Psychological (note that psychological aids are not required for your exam but will be discussed briefly to deepen your level of understanding).

Physiological aids

These aids are ones that seek to boost the physiological adaptive responses of the body, such as improved oxygen transport. Some of these aids are perfectly legal – such as altitude training – but others such as **blood doping** and **recombinant erythropoietin (RhEPO)** are illegal.

Blood doping (illegal)

Blood doping is a practice where between 450ml and 1800ml of blood is removed from an athlete several weeks before a key competition and then kept chilled or frozen. The body adapts and compensates by producing more blood. The blood is then re-infused into the athlete several hours ahead of competition resulting in an increase in total blood volume and enhanced oxygen transport. Because of the negative impact the removal of blood has on an athlete's training regime some performers will omit the removal stage and directly infuse the blood of a second person of the same blood group immediately prior to competition. Due to the improved oxygen transport, blood doping is mainly associated with endurance-based activities such as cycling and cross-country skiing. Table 21.1 evaluates the use of blood doping as an ergogenic aid.

IN CONTEXT

The practice of drinking turtle blood has been widespread among some groups of Chinese athletes, along with the ingestion of many other traditional medicines. The haemoglobin and myoglobin of turtles is much more effective at transporting, storing and releasing oxygen to the muscles than that of humans. This is why turtles can remain underwater for long periods of time. With this knowledge the temptation could be to inject turtle blood rather than the athlete's own blood when blood doping!

Indeed, scientists from Cambridge University have already produced a haemoglobin hybrid that is part human and part crocodile, designed to help patients with circulatory problems. The potential advantage to sports performers is clear – quite simply the athlete will be able to perform at higher intensities for longer.

Activity 1

Place each of the following ergogenic aids under the appropriate heading:

Physiological	Hormonal/pharmacological	Nutritional	Mechanical	Psychological

- altitude training
- amphetamines
- anabolic steroids
- beta blockers
- blood doping
- bungee ropes
- colostrum
- cooling aids
- creatine supplements
- drag shorts
- gene doping
- glycogen loading

- goal-setting
- human growth hormone
- imagery
- isotonic sports drinks
- lycra body suits
- medicine balls
- mental rehearsal
- nasal strips
- parachutes
- protein shakes
- RhEPO
- soda loading

Table 21.1 Advantages and disadvantages of blood doping

Advantages (perceived benefits)	Disadvantages (associated health risks)
• Increase in red blood cell count and haemoglobin levels by up to 20% • Improved oxygen transport and uptake • It is difficult to determine if blood doping has taken place when the athlete's own blood has been used – however, there is now a test to determine the presence of somebody else's blood	• An increase in blood viscosity decreases cardiac output and blood flow velocity • Increased risk of blood clotting leading to possible heart failure • Possible transfusion reactions and viral infections (such as hepatitis and HIV) can occur when blood other than the athlete's is used

Table 21.2 Advantages and disadvantages of recombinant erythropoietin (RhEPO)

Advantages (perceived benefits)	Disadvantages (associated health risks)
• Increase in red blood cell count and haemoglobin levels • Improved oxygen transport and uptake (VO$_2$ max)	• An increase in blood viscosity decreases cardiac output and blood flow velocity • Increased risk of blood clotting leading to possible heart failure • The production of the body's natural form of EPO is affected • A urine test now exists that can detect the difference between synthetic and naturally occurring EPO

Recombinant erythropoietin (RhEPO) (illegal)

A synthetic product that mimics the body's naturally occurring hormone EPO, which is produced by the kidneys and stimulates the body to manufacture more red blood cells in the bone marrow. With an increase in red blood cells oxygen transport should be improved. By injecting RhEPO the athlete's aim is to increase the concentration of red blood cells in the blood and, consequently, their aerobic capacity. For this reason RhEPO abuse is most commonly found in endurance-based activities such as distance running and tour cycling. Table 21.2 evaluates the use of RhEPO as an ergogenic aid.

IN CONTEXT

The stories of **Johan Sermon, Fabrice Salanson and Marco Pantani** highlight the dangers of RhEPO. All were young, fit cyclists. All died in their sleep from fatal heart attacks. All had exceptionally high haematocrit, pointing to the use of RhEPO. This drug's most serious effect is hyper-viscosity, which can ultimately lead to a heart attack, as the sludge-like blood travels too slowly around the body leading to blood clots and vascular blockages.

Key terms

Haematocrit The proportion of red blood cells in a given volume of blood. Normal haematocrit for males occurs in the region of 42 to 45 per cent, and females 36 to 38 per cent. Foul play is assumed if an athlete has a haematocrit reading of 50 per cent or more.
Hyper-viscosity Excessive resistance to the flow of blood. Essentially the blood becomes excessively thick.

Gene doping

Gene doping is considered to be the next big thing to challenge the integrity of sport. Gene doping involves the illegal use of gene therapy to enhance performance. Gene therapy is typically used in medicine to alter a person's DNA so that they can combat disease more effectively. Indeed, it is used to encourage the production of blood cells and boost muscle growth. With these physiological outcomes it is clear, therefore, why some performers may be tempted by gene doping. Although as yet there is no hard evidence of performers doing it, the threat is certainly there. Table 21.3 evaluates the use of gene doping as an ergogenic aid.

Table 21.3 Advantages and disadvantages of gene doping

Advantages (perceived benefits)	Disadvantages (associated health risks)
• Engineering of hormones to increase muscle mass • Engineering of hormones to increase the production of red blood cells • Testing may be unable to distinguish between naturally produced red blood cells or testosterone and that which the body has been genetically engineered to produce naturally	• This practice is still in an experimental stage; there could be significant health risks attached • There is a moral and ethical issue with altering the very fabric of a person

IN CONTEXT

It has been suggested that blood and even tissue samples from all medal winners from major competitions will be kept for a period of eight years, which will allow anti-doping laboratories to establish detection techniques. Indeed in October 2008 following the Olympic Games the samples of all athletes were re-tested for a new advanced form of RhEPO.

Cooling aids (legal)

Exercising in warm environments can cause the body to overheat, leading to performance impairment. Blood flow to the exercising muscle may be reduced because there is greater blood flow to the surface of the skin in an attempt to cool the body down. Athletes have also been known to suffer from a phenomenon called cardiovascular drift where the heart rate increases despite a constant work rate. Indeed, it is suggested that for every 1° increase in body temperature the heart rate increases by approximately 10 bpm. Cooling aids generally consist of clothing adapted to maintain the core temperature of the body. Clothing is usually manufactured using material designed to absorb water or indeed to have a liquid coolant integrated into it. Simple examples of cooling aids include bandanas, headbands and vests. Table 21.4 evaluates the use of cooling aid as ergogenic aids.

Key term

Cardiovascular drift Cardiovascular drift is the phenomenon whereby heart rate 'drifts' upwards over time despite the performer working at a constant rate. It typically occurs in warmer environments and is associated with increased sweating and dehydration.

Soda loading (legal)

A solution of bicarbonate of soda is consumed an hour or so before an event or training to increase the amount of bicarbonate ions (HCO_3^-) in the blood. You will recall from Chapter 18 that bicarbonate ions act as buffers to maintain the pH of the blood by attracting hydrogen ions from lactic acid, therefore neutralising it. In this way soda loading helps to improve the athlete's tolerance to lactic acid, thereby delaying OBLA and enabling the performer to work harder for longer. Soda loading appears to be of benefit, particularly for those activities that operate at near-maximum intensities of between one and seven minutes, including 400m runners, 1km track cyclists and rowers. Table 21.5 evaluates the use of bicarbonate of soda as a cooling aid.

IN CONTEXT

One study by the Australian Institute of Sport found that elite male rowers rowing for six minutes at maximal effort on an ergometer, increased the distance rowed from an average of 1813m to 1861m following a dose of 300mg of bicarbonate of soda per Kg of body mass.

Activity 2

Some endurance performers will undertake a period of altitude training prior to competition. Research this legal physiological ergogenic aid and address the following points:

● Which performers are most likely to benefit?
● Outline the advantages and disadvantages of this practice.
● What is the current thinking on altitude training?

Table 21.4 Advantages and disadvantages of cooling aids

Advantages (perceived benefits)	Disadvantages (associated health risks)
• Maintains core body temperature • May prevent dehydration arising from excessive sweating	• Increased energy expenditure due to heavier clothing

Table 21.5 Advantages and disadvantages of soda loading

Advantages (perceived benefits)	Disadvantages (associated health risks)
• Increased buffering capacity • Increased removal and tolerance to lactic acid • Athletes can perform at higher intensities for longer • No significant health risks	• Possible stomach cramping and diarrhoea • Can cause vomiting due to the unpleasant taste

Exam-style Questions

1   In order to optimise performance, some sports performers may be tempted to take illegal ergogenic aids such as recombinant erythropoietin (RhEPO) and anabolic steroids. Discuss the perceived benefits and harmful side effects to an athlete in taking both these performance-enhancing drugs.   **[8 marks]**

CHALLENGE YOURSELF

For some endurance athletes, the pressure to perform at the highest level means that the temptation to gain unfair aerobic training benefits from ergogenic aids, despite the dangers, becomes too great. Identify a physiological aid that would benefit such an athlete and briefly outline what it is and how it enhances performance. Discuss health risks that are associated with its use and explain the advantages it has over altitude training.   **[10 marks]**

Hormonal/pharmacological aids

The majority of pharmacological aids are illegal. They seek to enhance athletic performance by boosting the levels of hormones and neural transmitters that are naturally released by the body. Examples of illegal pharmacological aids include **anabolic steroids**, **amphetamines** and **human growth hormone (HGH)**.

Anabolic steroids (illegal)

Anabolic steroids are a group of synthetic hormones related to the male hormone testosterone. Taken orally or injected, they promote the storage of protein and the growth of tissue. Anabolic steroids may be used by athletes to train harder through increases in muscle size and strength. Examples of anabolic steroids known to have been taken by sports performers include tetrahydrogestrinone (THG) and nandrolone. Anabolic steroids are the drug of choice for performers who work at the highest intensities such as sprinters and field event athletes. Table 21.6 evaluates the use of anabolic steroids as an ergogenic aid.

Human growth hormone (illegal)

Human growth hormone (HGH) is a synthetic product that mimics the body's natural growth hormone, which is produced in the pituitary gland in the brain and is responsible for the growth of muscle tissue, cartilage and bone. When synthetic HGH is injected it can stimulate protein synthesis, increasing muscle mass and promoting bone growth. Its use is most commonly seen in those activities requiring power and short bursts of explosive strength, such as weightlifters, or indeed to speed up the rehabilitation of an injured athlete. Table 21.7 evaluates the use of human growth hormone as an ergogenic aid.

IN CONTEXT

One anecdote tells of a French cyclist who had to change his shoes because his shoe size increased significantly half-way through the season as a consequence of his human growth hormone habit!

Table 21.6 Advantages and disadvantages of anabolic steroids

Advantages (perceived benefits)	Disadvantages (associated health risks)
• Increased muscle mass leads to increased strength • Enables athletes to train harder at higher intensities • Increased anabolic hormones in the blood leads to faster recovery times • New 'designer' steroids are being produced by pharmaceutical companies all the time in an attempt to remain one step ahead of the testers	• Liver damage • Heart failure • Increased aggression and mood swings – 'roid rage' • Development of masculine effects in females such as deepening of the voice and growth of facial hair • Testicular atrophy, reduced sperm count, baldness and breast development in males • In adolescents growth can be halted through the premature maturation of the skeleton • Fortunately there are now many tests available to detect the use of a wide range of different anabolic steroids

Table 21.7 Advantages and disadvantages of human growth hormone (HGH)

Advantages (perceived benefits)	Disadvantages (associated health risks)
• Increased muscle mass leads to increased strength • Enables athletes to train harder at higher intensities • Facilitates the recovery from training • Decreases percentage of body fat by increases in metabolic activity • Increases bone density • As HGH occurs naturally in the body it can be difficult to test	• Abnormal development of bone and muscle tissue • Excessive enlargement of vital organs such as the heart can lead to heart failure • Broadening of the hands, face and feet can occur (known as acromegaly) • Increased risk of some cancers

Exam-style Questions

1   A weightlifter may be tempted to illegally dope through the use of steroids and human growth hormone in order to improve their maximum strength. Critically evaluate the use of both these ergogenic aids in the pursuit of maximising strength.   **[10 marks]**

Activity 3

Research the use of diuretics as an ergogenic aid. Use your research to determine which type of performer is most likely to use them and why. Make sure you comment upon the perceived benefits and the associated health risks.

Nutritional aids (generally legal)

Nutritional aids largely include dietary supplements such as **vitamins**, **creatine** and **glutamine** and, by and large, are legal. However, it should be observed that excessive doses of these supplements can be illegal. For example, the International Olympic Committee (IOC) has banned caffeine above a urine level of 12 micrograms/ml. Other legal forms of nutritional aid include the consideration of **pre- and post-competition meals** and **glycogen loading**.

Glycogen loading (legal)

Glycogen loading involves manipulating the consumption of carbohydrates in the week prior to a competition in order increase muscle glycogen storage capacity. Essentially, the process involves the depletion of existing stores of glycogen

seven days prior to a competition by undertaking some form of endurance-based activity followed by the restriction of carbohydrate for the following three days. In the final three days leading up to the competition the athlete will consume carbohydrate-rich meals (500 to 600g of carbohydrate) while reducing training volume or even resting.

Some performers following a glycogen-loading regime such as the one displayed in Table 21.8 have experienced a doubling of their muscle glycogen stores since the depletion phase appears to trigger a mechanism in the body to store as much carbohydrate as possible once it becomes available. Because of the availability of greater stores of energy, this method of dietary manipulation has been widely practised by endurance performers such as marathon runners and triathletes. Table 21.9 evaluates the use of glycogen loading as an ergogenic aid.

Table 21.8 A suggested glycogen loading regime

Day 1	Moderately long exercise bout (should not be exhaustive)
Day 2	Mixed diet; moderate carbohydrate intake; tapering exercise
Day 3	Mixed diet; moderate carbohydrate intake; tapering exercise
Day 4	Mixed diet; moderate carbohydrate intake; tapering exercise
Day 5	High-carbohydrate diet; tapering exercise
Day 6	High-carbohydrate diet; tapering exercise or rest
Day 7	High-carbohydrate diet; tapering exercise or rest
Day 8	Competition

Table 21.9 Advantages and disadvantages of glycogen loading

Advantages (perceived benefits)	Disadvantages (associated health risks)
• Increased glycogen synthesis • Increased muscle glycogen stores • Increased endurance capacity • Delays fatigue and can prevent endurance performers 'hitting the wall'	• Water retention and bloating • Weight increase that can lead to greater energy expenditure • Muscle stiffness and fatigue during the depletion stage • Irritability and feelings of weakness during the depletion stage

Pre- and post-competition meals

Pre- and post-competition meals are the dietary considerations of a performer on the day of a competition.

Pre-competition meals should be eaten at least two hours prior to the event and should consist mainly of carbohydrates that are easily digestible such as cereals, toast and juices in order to top-up muscle glycogen and maintain blood glucose levels. For endurance-based activities such as a 10Km road run the performer may wish to consider carbohydrates that release their energy more slowly (foods with a low glycaemic index), such as porridge oats or granary bread, so that blood glucose levels are maintained throughout the duration of the event. Sugary foods that have a high glycaemic index should be avoided, however, as although they may give an immediate boost of energy, this can be counterproductive as greater levels of insulin will be released, ultimately leading to a dip in blood sugar levels.

Following exercise performers will need to eat in order to promote recovery. You will recall from Chapter 18 that the replenishment of muscle glycogen stores can take up to 48 hours following endurance activities such as triathlons or marathons; most activities, however, will not require anywhere near this length of time.

The synthesis of glycogen is at its most efficient within the first two hours of the end of the exercise period and so an athlete should be encouraged to consume a carbohydrate-rich meal within the first 45 minutes to an hour of finishing a competition. This period of time after exercise, when the muscles are most receptive to refuelling with glycogen, is known as the **carbohydrate window**. The main problem with hitting the carbohydrate window, however, is that exercise is in fact an appetite suppressant and performers rarely feel like eating so soon after the competition.

Fluid intake (legal)

The consumption of water and of sports drinks is chiefly designed to replace fluids and electrolytes lost by sweating and boost blood glucose levels. Ahead of competition performers will need to consider their fluid intake in order to prevent dehydration. Losing the equivalent of two per cent of your body weight as sweat can impair performance by up to 10 to 20 per cent. If you do not replace the lost water then core body temperature will rise, bringing with it a number of performance inhibitors. The blood becomes 'thicker' or more viscous, which slows down the flow to the working muscles. To try and compensate, the heart beats faster, putting the body under greater stress. The loss of electrolytes through sweating can cause fatigue and cramps,

Fig 21.1 A carbohydrate-rich meal is needed pre- and post-competition

Table 21.10 Advantages and disadvantages of fluid intake

Advantages (perceived benefits)	Disadvantages (associated health risks)
• Fluid replacement prevents dehydration • Isotonic sports drinks maintain levels of electrolytes in the body, which allows the muscle cells to function properly • Hypotonic and hypertonic sports drinks can help to maintain blood glucose levels during endurance activity	• Drinking too much fluid can dilute the levels of blood sodium levels and induce fatigue (a condition known as hyponatremia)

Activity 4

Record your fluid intake over the course of a day. Comment upon the amount of fluid consumed together with the carbohydrate, electrolyte and caffeine content of the fluid consumed (you may need to refer to the nutrition labels of products that you buy). Are you consuming sufficient fluid for your daily needs? Research the range of sports drinks available on the market. What differences are there in the nutritional content of each?

IN CONTEXT

The glycaemic index (GI) is a measure of the effect different foods have on your blood glucose levels. Foods with a high GI provide a rapid surge in blood glucose levels, while those with a low GI release their energy more slowly. We might expect increases in blood glucose that accompany consumption of high GI foodstuffs to be useful in providing energy – but in fact it will only give us a relatively fleeting high and, in the long run, will be detrimental to performance. This is because in order to maintain blood glucose levels within a 'healthy' range the pancreas releases insulin, which carries the glucose out of the blood and into the cells. Excessive consumption of high GI foodstuffs results in an increased release of insulin, which in fact causes blood glucose levels to fall rapidly.

so it is essential that performers remain hydrated. As a general rule it is recommended that approximately 15 minutes before training or competition performers should drink between 400 and 500ml of fluid, whilst during exercise 150 to 200ml should be drunk every 15 to 20 minutes.

Isotonic sports drinks are designed to replace electrolytes lost through sweating. The main electrolytes include sodium, potassium and chlorine, which help to maintain the correct rate of exchange of nutrients and waste products into and out of the muscle cell so that effective muscle contraction can take place. Hypertonic and hypotonic sports drinks, on the other hand, can provide a well needed boost to blood glucose levels for the performer exercising over an hour or so. Table 21.10 evaluates the use of fluid intake as an ergogenic aid.

Creatine supplementation (legal)

Creatine supplementation is the consumption of creatine monohydrate in powder, capsule or liquid form, which can increase the levels of phosphocreatine stored in the muscle cell by up to 50 per cent. As it delays the alactic/lactic threshold, using supplements of creatine is common among performers such as sprinters and weightlifters where short bursts of energy and explosive strength are required. Table 21.11 evaluates the use of creative supplementation as an ergogenic aid.

Caffeine (legal)

Caffeine is a mild stimulant that occurs naturally and is predominantly found in coffee, tea and colas. It is probably the most widely available and accessible pharmacological aid. Until 2004, caffeine was listed as a banned substance by

Table 21.11 Advantages and disadvantages of creatine supplementation

Advantages (perceived benefits)	Disadvantages (associated health risks)
• Increased PC stores (between 20 and 50%) • Increased maximum and elastic strength (power) • Allows performers to train at higher intensities • Delays the point at which the ATP-PC system exhausts • A naturally occurring 'muscle builder', creatine supplementation is legal	• Increased weight gain (often mistaken for muscle mass!) • Increased water retention • Muscle cramps • Stomach cramps and diarrhoea • Studies have yet to be conducted on the effect of long-term usage on health

Table 21.12 Advantages and disadvantages of caffeine

Advantages (perceived benefits)	Disadvantages (associated health risks)
• Enhanced nervous stimulation • Increased levels of concentration • Increases endurance capacity by promoting the release of adrenaline, which increases the strength of muscular contraction and dilates respiratory structures • Promotes glycogen sparing by metabolising more fatty acids	• Caffeine is a diuretic and therefore can promote dehydration • Possible sleep deprivation • Muscle and abdominal cramping

the World Anti-doping Agency (WADA) as its consumption was deemed to give performers an unfair advantage. Some studies cite that caffeine reduces the athlete's perception of muscle fatigue and results in an increased ability of the muscle to mobilise and utilise fat as a fuel. Consequently, caffeine is deemed to be of particular benefit to endurance performers such as runners and cyclists. Table 21.12 evaluates the use of caffeine as an ergogenic aid.

Alcohol (legality is at the discretion of individual sports governing bodies)

The relationship between sport and alcohol in a historical context is well documented; in fact, drunkenness was a pre-requisite to the playing of mob football in the eighteenth century. The effect of alcohol is largely dependent upon the quantities consumed. While a little may give some psychological ergogenic effects, such as increased self-confidence, too much can cause total physiological and psychological breakdown!

The legality of alcohol in a competitive setting is quite difficult to determine. The IOC has left the banning of alcohol to the discretion of individual sports governing bodies. At the 2004 Athens Olympics, for example, certain Olympic sports prohibited the use of alcohol for the duration of the games or in-competition testing period. These sports included archery, gymnastics, modern pentathlon, triathlon and wrestling. Table 21.13 evaluates the use of alcohol as an ergogenic aid.

IN CONTEXT

Alcohol played a significant part in the death of one of Britain's finest touring cyclists, Tommy Simpson. He collapsed and died of heat stroke on Mont Ventoux, a mountain on the Tour de France. His post-mortem showed that he had taken a cocktail of brandy and amphetamines that allowed him to push himself far beyond his natural limits.

Exam-style Questions

1 An ergogenic aid is any substance that enhances performance. Discuss the following as aids to enhancing performance:
   (a) The use of dietary manipulation.
   (b) Pre-competition meals.
   (c) Post-competition meals.   [10 marks]
2 Creatine supplementation is a nutritional ergogenic aid. Discuss the use of this aid in terms of:
   (a) The type of performer benefiting.
   (b) The performance-enhancing qualities.
   (c) The associated side effects.   [6 marks]

Mechanical aids (legal)

Mechanical ergogenic aids are specialised equipment or devices that enhance performance. Examples include equipment used to increase resistance, such as **parachutes and pulleys**, **aerodynamic helmets in cycling** and low-drag **Lycra body suits** for sports such as speed skating and swimming. Mechanical aids by and large are legal, although there may be some restrictions on equipment in competition.

Resistance equipment (legal)

The vast array of resistance equipment available to the sports performer is largely designed to enable the body to work harder against a resistance yet maintain the technique used in the event. Examples include the use of bungee ropes, pulleys, parachutes, and medicine balls.

Aerodynamic equipment and streamlined clothing (legal)

There is now a whole industry based around the development of ergogenic equipment and clothing, which largely seeks to improve streamlining and reduce the effect

Table 21.13 Advantages and disadvantages of alcohol

Advantages (perceived benefits)	Disadvantages (associated health risks)
• Enhances self-confidence • Reduces anxiety associated with competition • Can reduce the sensation of pain, which allows athletes to push themselves to the limit • Reduces muscle tremor and, therefore, can benefit sports such as archery or shooting.	• Impairs perceptual motor abilities such as reaction time • Can cause dehydration • Decreases the availability of glucose causing blood glucose levels to fall, leading to hypoglycaemia • Can cause hypothermia when exercising in cold environments • Long-term consumption can lead to liver damage

of air resistance and drag in water. Speedo, for example, have recently released their range of LZR suits that claim to be the most drag efficient yet; with many world records already broken by those wearing these mega low-drag suits, their claims appear to be substantiated. The world of cycling has for some years now relied on Formula 1 technology when designing drag efficient bikes. Even sprinters can benefit as some studies have shown that as much as 20 per cent of total energy expenditure is reportedly used simply to overcome air resistance during the sprint – it is no wonder they kit themselves out in Lycra! Table 21.14 evaluates the use of aerodynamic tight fitting equipment and clothing as ergogenic aids.

IN CONTEXT

In the pool at the 2008 Beijing Olympics, 23 out of 25 world records (92 per cent), 94 per cent of gold medals and 89 per cent of all medals were achieved by swimmers wearing Speedo's LZR suits. Perhaps Speedo's greatest advertisement is Michael Phelps, who won eight gold medals in eight days, seven of them in world-record time, all while wearing a LZR suit.

Activity 5

A swimmer will use a range of different mechanical ergogenic aids when training and competing. These include the use of equipment such as floats, hand paddles, bungee cords, fins and clothing such as drag shorts, shark-skin suits and the latest LZR suits designed by Speedo.

For a named activity investigate the range of mechanical aids available to performers and explain the reasons behind their use. [8 marks]

Exam-style Questions

1   Name two ergogenic aids that might affect performance in explosive activities. Describe the physiological benefits of each aid. [6 marks]

Psychological aids (not examined)

This form of performance enhancement revolves mainly around mental training and conditioning techniques that are used to boost concentration levels and to combat the stress and anxiety associated with competition. Examples include **self-hypnosis**, **visualisation**, **cue utilisation** and **goal setting**, all of which are perfectly legal.

Imagery

This is a cognitive technique used to alleviate anxiety whereby performers remove themselves from a stressful situation by thinking about pleasurable experiences, such as lying on a beach.

Mental rehearsal

A cognitive technique used to alleviate anxiety. A performer will create a mental picture or video of themselves performing a skill or action successfully.

CHALLENGE YOURSELF

Research and critically evaluate the use of a range of other ergogenic aids in sport. Your research might include examining the use of:

- Colostrum
- Amphetamines
- Beta blockers
- Altitude training.

CHALLENGE YOURSELF

Discuss the following statement: 'Sports performers should be allowed to use performance-enhancing drugs like any other training aid.' [20 marks]

Table 21.14 Advantages and disadvantages of aerodynamic equipment and streamlined clothing

Advantages (perceived benefits)	Disadvantages (associated health risks)
• Shiny material promotes the smooth flow of air past the performer's body • Reduced drag • More efficient use of performer's energy	• Equipment and clothing can be expensive • May erode the value of true athletic ability • A situation might occur where winners are determined by their wealth and not their ability • Some performers may be sponsor-tied and cannot benefit from newly developed equipment

What you need to know

* An ergogenic aid is any substance, object or method used by an athlete with the sole aim of improving or enhancing performance.
* Ergogenic aids can be divided into five different categories: physiological, hormonal/pharmacological, nutritional, mechanical, psychological.
* The legality of an ergogenic aid usually depends on the associated health risks. An ergogenic aid is likely to be illegal if the health risks associated with it are deemed to be severe.
* Physiological aids generally seek to boost the transport of respiratory gases such as oxygen. Examples include recombinant erythropoietin (RhEPO) and blood doping.
* Hormonal/pharmacological aids are man-made drugs that mimic the body's naturally produced hormones. Examples include anabolic steroids and human growth hormone (HGH).

* Nutritional aids include dietary supplements and manipulation. Examples of supplements include creatine monohydrate and protein shakes, while forms of dietary manipulation include glycogen loading and pre- and post-event meals.
* Mechanical aids include the plethora of training aids and equipment that enable the body to work harder. Examples include the use of pulleys or parachutes. Mechanical aids also include competitive equipment or clothing that seeks to maximise energy efficiency in the body. Examples include streamlined clothing such as Lycra body suits or shark-skin suits used in swimming.
* Psychological aids seek to boost concentration and reduce levels of anxiety and stress. Examples include mental rehearsal and imagery.

Review Questions

1 Name the five categories of ergogenic aid.
2 Blood doping is a practice sometimes undertaken by endurance athletes such as cyclists. Briefly outline this method and critically evaluate the value of blood doping as an ergogenic aid.
3 What is soda loading and why do some sports performers follow this practice?
4 Marathon runners will often seek to boost their muscle glycogen stores prior to competition through glycogen loading. What advice would you give to a marathon runner who wishes to glycogen load but is unsure about how to go about it?
5 On the morning of a half-marathon Sarah eats a full English breakfast together with a large glass of water. Comment upon Sarah's pre-competition meal.
6 Critically evaluate the use of sports drinks (as opposed to water) as mechanisms of fluid replacement.

7 What are the issues that surround the use of gene doping as an ergogenic aid?
8 What nutritional advice concerning pre- and post-competition meals would you give to a rugby player involved in a two-day long rugby sevens tournament?
9 How might caffeine improve athletic performance?
10 What are the risks involved with using anabolic steroids and human growth hormone?
11 How does the consumption of moderate amounts of alcohol affect athletic performance?
12 What mechanical aids might a 100m sprinter use to enhance their performance?
13 List some examples of cooling aids and evaluate their use as an ergogenic aid.

UNIT 2

The improvement of effective performance and the critical evaluation of practical activities in physical education (Unit G454)

The following chapter (Chapter 22) will help you to acquire knowledge and demonstrate your understanding necessary to be successful in your coursework. Through participation in the roles of performer, coach or official, you will learn of the different pathways to success. These include:

● outwitting opponents
● accurate replication
● exploring and communicating ideas, concepts and emotions
● performing at maximum levels
● identifying and solving problems
● exercising safely and effectively.

The concept of success underpins this unit of study.

Chapter 22 will also help you to prepare for your oral response on the evaluation, appreciation and the improvement of performance section of the coursework unit. This component requires you to demonstrate your knowledge of the relationship between skill, tactics and fitness, and explain how each can contribute to successful performance.

Finally, Chapter 22 will help you to acquire knowledge and demonstrate your understanding of the short- and long-term health and fitness benefits of participation in physical activity as well as the opportunities for participation and progression in your chosen activity, both locally and nationally.

CHAPTER 22

How to be successful in your coursework

Learning outcomes

By the end of this chapter you should be able to:

- understand the requirements of the coursework unit
- understand the assessment criteria for each area of the coursework
- develop a plan to improve your ability in the role of performer, coach or official
- appreciate and evaluate the performance of others
- develop an action plan to improve the performance of others
- justify your evaluative comments by applying relevant knowledge and concepts from the physiological, psychological and socio-cultural areas you have studied.

CHAPTER INTRODUCTION

This chapter seeks to help you get to grips with the coursework section of your A2 physical education course. One of the underlying themes of this A2 course is for candidates to show their ability to apply skills, knowledge and understanding through physical activity. This specification enables you to achieve this by having the opportunity to participate in physical activity either as a performer, an official or a coach. The main difference between practical assessment at AS and A2 is that, at A2, candidates are required to perform in a more open competitive environment.

This unit is synoptic, which means that it requires candidates to demonstrate their ability to apply theory work studied in the classroom to their own practical performance and the performance of others. It will therefore be necessary for you to apply relevant knowledge from physiological, psychological and socio-cultural areas you have studied during both your AS and A2 course.

The coursework unit contributes 15 per cent to your overall A Level mark (30 per cent of your A2 mark).

> **Key term**
>
> **Synoptic** The drawing together of knowledge and concepts studied at both AS and A2 level.

What are the coursework requirements?

You have the choice of several different pathways to successfully complete your coursework at A2. Which pathway you choose will depend on your own individual strengths and the advice given to you by your teacher. There are two components to this unit, both of which need to be completed. The choice of route through this unit is illustrated in Table 22.1.

You must choose a performance, coaching/leading or officiating activity that you were assessed in at AS.

Your ability to apply skills and demonstrate your knowledge and understanding from Unit G451 and G453 will therefore be assessed through:

- Participation in one practical activity as a performer and/or a coach and/or official, together with
- An oral assessment based on your observations of another performer.

There are 60 marks in total available for this unit: 40 marks for your participative role and 20 marks for the oral assessment.

Table 22.1 Pathways through your coursework assessment

Unit G454	Component 1	and	Component 2
Pathway 1	Assessment in one practical performance	and	Oral assessment in the evaluation, appreciation and the improvement of performance
Or			
Pathway 2	Assessment in coaching/leading one activity	and	Oral assessment in the evaluation, appreciation and the improvement of performance
Or			
Pathway 3	Assessment in officiating one activity	and	Oral assessment in the evaluation, appreciation and the improvement of performance
Marks available	40 marks		20 marks

What activities can I be assessed in?

Remember, at A2 you are required to choose one of the activities in which you were assessed at AS. Activities at A2 are the same as those available at AS level. You may recall that activities are grouped together into 'activity areas'. Table 22.2 outlines the different activity areas and some examples of activities that fall into that group. If you cannot see a particular activity in the table that you wish to be assessed in, ask your teacher if it is possible or check at www.ocr.org.uk.

How will I be assessed?

You will be assessed in the first instance by your teacher. They will keep an ongoing record of assessment in your role as performer, coach or official throughout the year and must submit your marks to the exam board by the end of March. They will also keep a video log of your performance to justify the marks that have been awarded to you. This video will also help you to identify your strengths and weaknesses and determine what you need to do to improve your performance. For activities that are not offered in your school or college it may be possible to be assessed by an external coach under the guidance of your PE teacher.

At some point in May a number of candidates from each centre will be subject to external moderation. This is led by a practical moderator from the exam board and the process guarantees the standardisation of marks across the country so that all teachers are marking to the same level.

Table 22.2 Examples of coursework activity areas

Activity area	Activity examples
Athletic activities	Track and field athletics, Olympic weightlifting, track cycling
Combat activities	Judo, boxing, fencing
Dance activities	Contemporary dance, Irish dance
Invasion games	Association football, basketball, field hockey, netball, rugby league, rugby union
Net/wall games	Badminton, squash, tennis, volleyball
Striking/fielding games	Cricket, rounders
Target games	Golf, archery
Gymnastic activities	Gymnastics, trampolining
Outdoor and adventurous activities	Mountain walking, sailing, skiing
Swimming activities	Competitive swimming
Safe and effective exercise activities	Circuit training

Table 22.3 General assessment criteria for each of the roles: performer, coach and official

Performer	Coach/leader	Official
Candidates will be assessed on their: • Level of acquired and developed skills and standard of accuracy, control and fluency under pressure • Selection and application of advanced techniques and standard of accuracy, control and fluency under pressure • Use of appropriate strategies demonstrating an understanding of perceptual requirements. And will need to: • Demonstrate a range of basic and advanced skills • Demonstrate appropriate selection and application of tactics and strategies • Demonstrate physical endeavour, creativity and sportsmanship • Demonstrate an understanding and application of rules, regulations and codes of practice. **Note**: the skills are required to be performed in an open competitive environment in which the activity is normally performed.	Candidates will be assessed on their: • Level of basic and advanced coaching/leadership skills • Use of appropriate strategies demonstrating understanding of perceptual aspects • Level of awareness of health and safety. And will need to: • Coach/lead sessions • Demonstrate competence in organisational skills related to the planning and delivery of sessions • Demonstrate appropriate communication skills • Demonstrate an understanding of health and safety procedures • Implement risk assessment procedures • Demonstrate an awareness of the health and fitness benefits of the activity • Demonstrate an awareness of child protection issues • Operate the principle of inclusion in their sessions • Evaluate sessions delivered and plan for improvement. **Note**: the Sports Leaders UK Level 2 or Level 3 in Sports Leadership or a Governing Body Level 3 coaching qualification gives you some idea of the level required. It may be a good idea to gain either of these during your course. However, you must still fulfil all the assessment criteria.	Candidates will be assessed on their: • Level of basic and advanced officiating skills • Use of appropriate strategies demonstrating an understanding of perceptual aspects • Level of awareness of health and safety. And will need to: • Officiate sessions • Demonstrate competence in decision-making skills related to the application of the rules/regulations and conventions of the activity • Demonstrate appropriate communication skills • Demonstrate an understanding of health and safety procedures • Implement risk assessment procedures • Demonstrate an awareness of the health and fitness benefits of the activity • Demonstrate an awareness of child protection issues • Evaluate sessions officiated and plan for improvement. **Note**: a governing body level 3 officiating award gives you some idea of the level required. It may be a good idea to gain this during the course. However, you must still fulfil all the assessment criteria.

Key term

Moderation The standardisation of coursework assessment. A moderator from the examination board will observe a sample of candidates' performance from your centre across several activities to ensure assessment has been completed at the appropriate level.

Part 1: Performance assessment

What are the assessment criteria for performance, coaching and officiating?

The assessment criteria will vary depending on whether you are being assessed as a performer, coach or official. Table 22.3 highlights the general themes of assessment for each role; these general themes can then be applied to each activity. The activity-specific assessment criteria can be viewed on the OCR website at www.ocr.org.uk.

If you are choosing to be assessed as a coach/leader or official, remember that, in addition to your performance, you are required to keep a log of your coaching/leading or officiating experiences over a six-month period. Table 22.4 outlines the information required in your log.

Activity 1

Access the OCR website (www.ocr.org.uk). Find the A2 Physical Education pages and print off the relevant assessment criteria for your chosen activity.

Activity 2

Find out about clubs in your school, college or local area for your chosen activity. If you are hoping to be assessed in the role of official or coach, contact the NGB or development officer for your chosen activity and discover what opportunities there are for level 3 qualifications in your local area.

How can I improve my level of performance, coaching and officiating?

It is essential that you dedicate some time to improve your skills as a performer, coach and/or official. Joining clubs whether in school or outside will give you the opportunity to perfect your skills through performing, coaching or officiating.

The performer

As a performer you will need to work on:

- Quality and range of skills
- Fitness
- Tactics and strategies
- Knowledge, understanding and application of rules.

It is a good idea to get yourself videoed while performing so that you can identify your own strengths and weakness and see for yourself what you need to improve on. Table 22.5 highlights the key areas a performer should focus on in order to improve the quality of their performance.

Activity 3

Research a range of coaching points and coaching activities that can be used to improve the performance of a number of basic and advanced skills for your chosen performance.

Table 22.4 Information required in the coach's/leader's and official's log of experiences

Information required in the coach's/leader's log	Information required in the official's log
• A record of your coaching/leading experiences • A personal video diary that provides at least 40 minutes of coaching/leading footage • A scheme of work that allows participants to demonstrate progression including at least ten hours of session plans • Evaluations of each session led • A record of risk assessments carried out • Evidence of a first aid qualification • Details of the health and safety issues relevant to the activity • Details of the child protection issues related to the activity • Your view on the health and fitness benefits of the activity/coaching the activity • Any other relevant information such as additional coaching/leading qualifications	• A record of your officiating experiences • A personal video diary that provides at least 40 minutes of officiating footage • At least four assessor evaluations of the sessions that you have officiated • A record of risk assessments carried out • Details of the health and safety issues relevant to the activity • Details of the child protection issues related to the activity • Your view on the health and fitness benefits of the activity/officiating the activity • Any other relevant information such as additional officiating qualifications

Table 22.5 Areas on which a performer should focus in order to improve the quality of their performance

Performer focus	Factors to consider
Preparation	**Improving the quality and range of skills** – as you will be assessed on the application of skills in an authentic competitive setting (e.g., full game situation for games), it is essential that you practise and perfect the quality and range of your technical skills. This will involve you attending practice sessions and accessing good-quality coaching. Once you have perfected your skills in training it will be easier to replicate them in the full authentic competitive setting and, therefore, enhance your performance. **Improving fitness** – consider the key components of fitness that are central to successful performance and devise an appropriate training programme to improve these fitness elements. **Accessibility to facilities and coaching** – to improve the range and quality of your skills it will be necessary to ensure that you have access to good-quality facilities and coaching. If your school or college does not offer the activity in which you wish to be assessed, then it is essential that you join a local club to receive the coaching necessary to improve your performance. **Kit and equipment** – make sure you have the appropriate kit and equipment for your chosen activity.
Performance	Your overall performance is based on a number of factors. You should be able to: • Replicate skills in an authentic competitive situation • Demonstrate appropriate levels of fitness for your chosen activity • Select appropriate skills, tactics and strategies for a given situation • Display appropriate physical endeavour, creativity and sportsmanship • Demonstrate understanding of rules, regulations and codes of practice. To improve your overall level of performance it will therefore be necessary to incorporate them into and reflect upon them following each performance.
Evaluation and reflection	Ask a friend or colleague to video your performances. You can then study these with your coach and/or teacher to identify your strengths and weaknesses. This will help you prioritise areas of improvement. Make sure you consider your strengths and weaknesses in relation to technical ability (skills), fitness and tactics/strategies. You will also need to evaluate and reflect upon physical endeavour, creativity and sportsmanship.
Technical knowledge	**Rules and regulations** – it is essential that you keep up to date with, and show an understanding of, the rules and regulations of the activity. In some activities rules change fairly regularly so make sure you have access to the most recent rule book. **Technical models, practices, tactics and strategies** – to help hone the quality of your skills, make certain that you are aware of the correct technical models for a wide range of skills, along with related coaching points and progressive practices. Together with an understanding of the most appropriate tactics and strategies, this will help improve and enhance your performance.

The coach or leader

As a coach you will need to work on:

- Control and organisation of individuals and groups
- Choice and delivery of appropriate drills and progressive practices
- Choice of appropriate fitness sessions
- Awareness of health and safety and child protection issues.

It is again a good idea to get yourself videoed while coaching so that you can identify your strengths and weaknesses and see for yourself what you need to improve on.

Table 22.6 highlights the key areas a coach or leader should focus on in order to improve the quality of their performance.

Fig 22.1 Performers will need to conduct themselves appropriately on the field of play

The official

As an official you will need to work on:

- The rules and regulations of the activity
- Decision making related to the rules and regulations of the activity
- Fitness
- Awareness of health and safety and child protection issues.

Again, it is a good idea to get yourself videoed while officiating so that you can identify your strengths and weaknesses and see for yourself what you need to improve on. Table 22.7 highlights the key areas an official should focus on in order to improve the quality of their performance.

Table 22.6 Areas on which a **coach/leader** should focus in order to improve the quality of their performance

Coach/leader focus	Factors to consider
Planning and organisation	**Scheme of work** – produce a scheme of work that includes an overview of your coaching plan that outlines the aims, content and outcomes of each session **Facilities and equipment** – consider the availability, costs and accessibility of facilities and equipment **Group information** – age, sex, numbers, ability etc **Health and safety issues** – carry out appropriate risk assessments; make yourself aware of the emergency procedures; have a first aid kit available; conduct an appropriate warm up and cool down etc **Child protection issues** – what are they? How will you put them into operation? **Time keeping** – make sure you are on time for sessions, allowing plenty of time at the beginning and end to organise equipment; manage your time effectively during the session.
Delivery	**Appearance** – make sure you are neat and tidy and dressed appropriately for the activity **Communication** – positioning so that everybody can see/hear, varied voice tone, clear instructions and use of accurate demonstrations **Presence and personality** – control the group perhaps by sitting them down when giving instructions or using a whistle; be enthusiastic and give praise and feedback when appropriate **Relationships** – foster positive relationships with the group, treat members of the group equally and ensure that everybody is included in all activities.
Evaluation and reflection	You will need to evaluate both your performance and the performance of others. Coaching/leading for example, requires you to observe members of the group, assess their performance and give suggestions for improvement. You will also need to evaluate your own performance, both during and following a session. If an activity is not working during a session, then change the activity; do not continue with it just because it's on your scheme of work. Following your session make an honest written appraisal of how the session went. What went well? What might need to be changed next time you lead that session?
Technical knowledge	**Technical models, practices, tactics and strategies** – in order to ensure that you are giving appropriate and accurate information to your group members/participants, it is essential that you keep up to date with coaching ideas. Coaching manuals and videos will provide the correct technical models along with related coaching points and progressive practices, together with the most appropriate tactics and strategies to improve and enhance the performance of your group members/participants.

Activity 4

Make a video of yourself as a performer, coach and/or official. Analyse your performance with your teacher or coach and develop an action plan for improvement.

Activity 5

Assess the fitness requirements of your chosen activity. Design a training programme to improve the fitness components that you have established are essential to effective performance.

Activity 6

Contact the NGB for the activities in which you will be assessed and request the latest rules and regulations handbook.

Table 22.7 Areas on which an **official** should focus in order to improve the quality of their performance

Officiating focus	Factors to consider
Planning and organisation	**Awareness of the participants** – you must make sure that you are aware of the age, sex and ability level of the participants that you will be officiating **Awareness of the competition** – make sure you know the regulations of the competition you will be officiating. For example, if it is a cup competition do you know what happens if the score is equal at full time? **Knowledge of the venue** – do you have directions to the venue? **Preparation of equipment** – ensure you have checked that all your equipment is in order: that your stopwatch and whistle work, that you have scorecards and disciplinary cards if required **Health and safety issues** – leave yourself sufficient time to carry out the necessary risk assessment on the facility and the equipment to be used **Fitness** – you must ensure that your fitness is at a level to meet the demands of the competition you will be officiating.
Officiating	**Appearance** – make sure you are neat and tidy and dressed appropriately for the activity to be officiated **Communication** – clear verbal and non-verbal communication of decisions that should be understood by all is required. You must also get yourself into good positions so that appropriate decisions can be made **Decision-making** – you must be clear, confident and firm in the decisions you make **Interaction with participants** – you must be impartial and treat all players fairly. Be firm and fair! Humour can be displayed when appropriate **Interaction with other officials** – It may be necessary to work with other officials; if this is the case, make sure communication between all the officials is effective. Decisions should be made based on the views and opinions of all officials.
Evaluation and reflection	You will need to evaluate your performance following each session that you officiate. Following each session make an honest written appraisal of how your officiating went. Were you confident in the decisions you made? Did you communicate your decisions effectively? What can you improve on before you officiate your next session? It will also be necessary to have an assessed observation by an experienced official to help identify any areas that require improvement. Your evaluations should address your planning and organisation (including levels of fitness), your level of officiating, and your knowledge of the rules and regulations.
Technical knowledge	**Rules and regulation**s – in order to ensure that you are making appropriate and accurate decisions, it is essential that you keep up to date with the rules and regulations of the activity. In some activities rules change fairly regularly so make sure you have access to the most recent rule book.

Activity 7

If you are to be assessed as a coach or official you will need to demonstrate an understanding and appreciation of the health and safety and child protection issues relevant to your activity.

Conduct a risk assessment for either a coaching session or competitive fixture.

Contact the NGB for your activity and identify the issues surrounding child protection.

Part 2: Evaluation, appreciation and the improvement of performance

In addition to the assessment of you in the role of performer, coach or official, you are required to observe a live performance of a fellow candidate in your assessed activity and carry out an oral response based on what you have observed. This aspect of the coursework follows on from the evaluation and planning for improvement of performance section that you undertook as part of your AS coursework. Your oral response should evaluate the performance and provide ideas on how the performance can be improved, justifying your action plan with relevant knowledge from the physiological, psychological and socio-cultural areas that you have studied. Your response should therefore focus on:

- Identifying the strengths of the performance in relation to skills, tactics and fitness
- Identifying the weaknesses of the performance in relation to skills, tactics and fitness
- Prioritising elements of the performance requiring improvement
- Formulating a realistic action plan that can be implemented to improve the weaknesses identified. This should include coaching points, progressive practices and fitness sessions, as well as giving some idea of timescale
- Applying physiological, psychological and socio-cultural knowledge to justify the evaluative comments that you make and the action plan you suggest.

EXAMINER'S TIP

The fewer prompts needed the better – so try and do most of the talking and limit the number of supplementary questions your teacher/moderator asks.

What questions can I expect in the evaluation and planning for improvement section?

The questions posed by your teacher and/or the moderator will be very open ended questions that will allow you to show and apply your knowledge. You will be directed to the performer or aspect of performance you are to be focused on:

'I would like you to observe the performance of ……………… I would like you to comment on:

- *The strengths of the performance observed in relation to skills, tactics and fitness*
- *The weaknesses of the performance observed in relation to skills, tactics and fitness*
- *Justify your evaluative comments by applying relevant physiological, psychological and socio-cultural knowledge*
- *The areas of the performance you would prioritise for improvement*
- *Create a viable action plan to improve those areas of performance, including detailed coaching points and progressive practices*
- *Justify your action plan by applying relevant physiological, psychological and socio-cultural knowledge*
- *The opportunities locally and nationally for performers to participate and improve in the activity*
- *The health and fitness benefits of the activity observed.'*

How should I structure my oral response?

It is best to break down the response into a number of logical steps, otherwise you can end up confused, losing your train of thought and becoming tongue tied. The following passage provides a suggested route through your oral response.

Step 1: Observe the performance

Observing a performer is more difficult than it may first appear. In order to gather all the required information it may be necessary for you to observe from a number of different vantage points. For example, when observing individual skills it may require you to view from the side, front and from behind. Observing tactical appreciation may require you to get a much broader picture and observe from further away, however.

When observing the live performance it is a good idea to make a few notes to help prompt you when outlining the performer's strengths and weaknesses. You will not be allowed to use pre-prepared notes in your assessment, however.

Step 2: Identify the movement or analytical phases of your activity

These phases help you to focus on particular aspects of performance, such as the arm action in swimming or the preparation phase when performing an overhead clear in badminton.

Identifying the phases of movement should feature early in your response. You may start by saying something like:

The phase of movement for throwing the javelin are:

- *Initial stance, grip and preparation*
- *Travel and trunk position*
- *Throwing action*
- *Release*
- *Overall efficiency.*

I will now comment on the strengths and weaknesses of the throw related to each of these phases…'

Some examples of the analytical phases of movement are highlighted in Table 22.8.

Step 3: Identify the strengths and weaknesses of the performance

You should focus on the strengths and weaknesses of the following three areas of the performance:

Activity 8

Find out from the OCR website (www.ocr.org.uk) the phases of movement related to your activity.

Skills when performed in an authentic competitive situation

You are required to be aware of the relevant 'technical models' of the particular skills you are observing. These technical models refer to the performance of 'text book' skills considered to be of a very high standard. You can find technical model resources in coaching manuals, instructional videos, photographs and other live events. Knowing how a skill should be performed will help you to justify your evaluations (strengths or weaknesses). When performing under pressure the competitor may perform some skills poorly (compared to the technical model) or inconsistently, make the wrong choice of shot or even choose not to perform the skill at all. These would all constitute weakness in skill reproduction.

Try to refrain from saying that the arm action in swimming is simply good or bad without offering any justification. You should phrase your response something like this:

'The pull phase of the arm action is strong. It pulls down the mid-line of the body, which ensures the swimmer maximises her forward movement in the water. This results from Newton's third law of motion – 'for every action there is an equal and opposite reaction' – as the force applied to the water by the swimmer is met by an equal and opposite force from the water onto the swimmer, propelling her forward. However, the straight arm recovery (extension at the elbow)

Table 22.8 Analytical phases for particular activity groups

Activity	Analytical phases
Competitive swimming, e.g., butterfly	• Arm action • Leg action • Body position • Breathing • Overall efficiency
Track and field athletics – track events	• Posture • Arm action • Leg action • Head carriage • Overall efficiency
Invasion games, e.g., Association football, rugby, netball, hockey	• Preparation • Execution • Recovery • Result • Overall efficiency

is a weakness as it slows the arm pull down. The swimmer can only move if a force is applied to the water, so it is important for the recovery aspect of the stroke to be as quick as possible, so that the arm can enter the water and once again apply another force. A bent arm recovery with a high elbow is, therefore, favoured as this is more efficient, wasting less energy and ensuring a quicker recovery phase of the stroke. From my study of biomechanics I know that if a swimmer reduces the length of the arm by flexing at the elbow during the recovery phase, the moment of inertia is reduced and angular velocity increased, allowing quicker arm entry into the water…'

Activity 9

Using a variety of coaching media such as coaching manuals, internet sites (such as www.bbc.co.uk/sportacademy) or software (such as Dartfish or Quintec) begin compiling your own coaching handbook based on the technical models for a range of skills for your activity. Your manual should include:

- Images or photos of correct technique
- Video footage of correct technique
- Coaching points for each skill
- A list of common faults for each skill.

Tactics and strategies

You will need to have a good level of understanding of the main tactics and strategies that are appropriate in the activity you are observing and then comment upon the performer's application of these. Tactics and strategies will vary greatly from activity to activity. Some activities, for example, may require you to comment on the effective use of team play. As well as teamwork, other comments you make may refer to an individual's decision-making ability or their selection of the most appropriate skill. It really does depend upon the activity though.

'The squash player demonstrated some really good attacking strategies. They seem fully aware of their opponent's position on the court and select the most appropriate shot. For example, I noticed that when their opponent has been taken to the back of the court they usually follow up by playing a drop shot to one of the front corners, making retrieval by their opponent more difficult. The player must be aware not to perform the same shot too regularly, however, as their opponent may start to anticipate this shot. One weakness I've noticed is that the player is playing a left-handed player yet continues to start serving from the right- hand side of the court. It is usual to start serving from the left hand side as then the serve will be to the opponent's backhand, usually a weaker stroke…'

Activity 10

Using a variety of coaching media, such as coaching manuals and internet sites, research a number of tactics and strategies appropriate for your activity.

Fitness

You will need to determine the required components of fitness used in the observed activity and compare the performer's demonstrated level with the required or expected level of these components. For the purpose of A2 study, the following components should be used:

- stamina
- strength
- speed
- suppleness.

However, if you have studied exercise physiology, you should discuss the following components:

- aerobic capacity
- strength
- speed
- flexibility
- body composition.

You may, for example, comment that suppleness at the hip joint is fundamental to an effective split leap in dance and gymnastics but the lack of flexibility about the hip of the observed performer has resulted in a poorly executed leap. However, the dancer has demonstrated some high levels of leg strength, confirmed by the height of the leap; this is to be expected of the dancer as it allows more time for movement into and out of the splits position.

'From the rugby performance I have just observed it is clear that the major fitness strengths of the player observed is their strength and speed. They have made several breaks and they appear to be able to accelerate rapidly over the first five metres. They obviously have good leg strength too, as they have also broken several tackles and remained on their feet well when tackled. From the period of play observed I would suggest that their main weakness in fitness is their stamina as they find it increasingly difficult to get into the correct position the longer the play continues. So much so that by the fourth or fifth phase of play they are rarely involved. I can only assume that this is due to poor cardiovascular fitness…'

Step 4: Formulate an action plan to improve performance

Once you have observed and identified the strengths and weaknesses of the performance you will need to arrive at an 'action plan' that addresses the weaknesses recognised. Your action-plan should include the following information:

Activity 11

Use the 'fitness wheel' to identify the fitness requirements of an activity. Observe a friend or classmate in this same activity and compare their level of fitness to the required fitness.

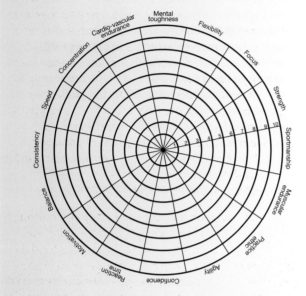

Fig 22.5 The fitness wheel

- **Clear, realistic goals** – select a major weakness in skill, fitness and tactics. If it is relevant you may make the following sort of comment:

  'I want to increase the percentage of first serves the performer makes into the box from 53 per cent to 65 per cent,' or 'the performer must increase their shoulder flexion from 18cm to 25cm.'

- **Timescale** – how often will training take place and how many weeks will your action plan take in total? If it is relevant you may make the following sort of comment:

  'The performer will follow a strength training programme that requires them to attend the gym three times a week for one hour over a period of 12 weeks.'

- **Method of achieving your goals** – what coaching points, drills, practices or fitness training methods will you use to improve performance? If it is relevant you may make the following sort of comment:

  'In order to promote the bent arm recovery in front crawl I will demonstrate the correct action to the swimmer. I will have them place a pull buoy (float) between their legs so that the swimmer is concentrating solely on the arm action and get them to perform the following exercises:

  1   *4 × 50m 'catch up', which encourages a high elbow recovery.*

  2   *4 × 50m drawing the thumb up the side of the body from waist to armpit, which encourages a high elbow recovery.*

  3   *4 × 50m arms only, concentrating on the relevant teaching points: high elbow, entry point in line with shoulder etc.'*

Activity 12

Using a variety of coaching media, such as coaching manuals and internet sites (e.g., www.brianmac.demon.co.uk), research a range of coaching sessions aimed at improving each of the following:

- Stamina
- Suppleness
- Speed
- Strength.

Be sure to include information on the FITT principle:

- Frequency – how often you should train
- Intensity – how hard you should train
- Time – how long should each session last
- Type – what method of training should be used.

- **Method of evaluating the goals you have set** – how will you know if your action plan has been successful? If it is relevant you may make the following sort of comment:

  'The number of assists made (in basketball) will be monitored, recorded and assessed prior to and following the action plan. If the action plan has been successful then the number of assists will have increased significantly.'

Activity 13

Observe a number of different performers and answer the following questions:

- What are the major weaknesses identified in the performance?
- Outline a corrective practice or drill to improve the performance.

Step 5: Justification of evaluative comments and their action plan, through the application of physiological, psychological and socio-cultural knowledge

You must validate the strengths and weaknesses you identify in the observed performer's skills, fitness and tactics by applying knowledge from your study of the theoretical units of AS and A2 PE. You might, for example, account for the performer's strengths in accurately selecting appropriate shots in tennis by explaining that:

'The performer I am currently observing is in the autonomous stage of learning and, therefore, performance is almost automatic as skills are performed effectively without too much conscious control. Also, the performer is able to process information easily, concentrating only on the relevant cues, which is known as selective attention. This speeds up their decision-making process…'

Similarly, you must justify your prescribed action plan. For example, you may have identified a weakness in a performer's speed and suggested a training programme of sprint interval training. As well as prescribing the training programme, you will need to explain why the training will improve the performer's speed. Your answer may include some of the following:

'Sprint interval training stresses the ATP-PC energy system, which responds by increasing the stores of ATP and PC in the muscle cells. This increase occurs as hypertrophy (enlargement) of fast twitch (type 2b) muscle fibres occurs, which contract rapidly contributing to an increase in speed. Furthermore, some of these muscle fibres split, which is called hyperplasia, again increasing the amount of muscle cells and therefore the level of ATP and PC and their associated enzymes…'

EXAMINER'S TIP

It is important to draw upon all three theoretical areas equally in your justification if you want to access the higher assessment bands.

Step 6: Discuss the role of the activity in promoting healthy lifestyles and the opportunities for increased participation

You should conclude your oral response by making some comment on:

● **The health and fitness benefits of the activity** – for this section you need to consider the long-term adaptive responses of the body to training and the impact this has on the health and fitness of the individual. You should try to **critically evaluate** and perhaps acknowledge any negative impact that exercise might also have on health.

'The health and fitness benefits of participation in an athletic event such as the 1500m are great. The performer may notice many physiological adaptations such as an enlarged heart, known as cardiac hypertrophy, which may lead to an increased stroke volume and a reduced resting heart rate (bradycardia). This places less stress on the cardiovascular system and can keep blood pressure within a healthy range. By performing aerobic-type exercise bone density may also increase and so prevent skeletal disease such as osteoporosis. However, the performer must be careful not to over-train as she may become susceptible to overuse injuries such as stress fractures or even osteoarthritis. Generally, however, participating in any physical activity is going to help reduce stress and promote the feel-good factor. I believe that more GPs should prescribe exercise as a remedy to certain physical and mental health conditions. Providing gym memberships, for example, might go some way in preventing obesity and even treating some forms of depression…'

● **The range of opportunities both locally and nationally for progression in the activity** – for this section you need to consider factors that may have influenced the opportunity for development and improvement within the activity. It is important that you consider issues such as physical education experiences, provision of facilities, effectiveness of national and local organisations, government initiatives, funding and the influence of role models.

'In my local area there are a number of hockey clubs, however, there are only two or three AstroTurf pitches. Demand for these pitches is high and they are always booked, particularly, at the evenings and weekends. I have to rely on my college to play hockey but regionally it seems that fewer and fewer schools and colleges are putting out teams so we mainly train; therefore, I only play a dozen or so matches in the season. I am keen to improve but the lack of facilities and coaches in the immediate area would mean I would need to travel, which will be expensive and, therefore, prohibitive. I believe that England Hockey should provide more AstroTurf pitches and develop more grass roots schemes to provide greater opportunity for participation.'

EXAMINER'S TIP

Evaluation, appreciation and the improvement of performance requires regular practice and a good knowledge of the observed activity.

Activity 14

Select an activity to observe and use the template below to help prepare for your evaluation, appreciation and the improvement of performance oral response.

Activity 15

1 In the space below identify the phases of movement for your activity:

-
-
-
-
-
-

2 Now observe a performer demonstrating one skill/event/stroke from your activity. Use your knowledge of coaching points to comment on the strengths and weaknesses of the performance in terms of **skill**, related to each of the phases listed above.

Phase	Phase description	Strengths	Weaknesses
1			
2			
3			
4			
5			
6			

3 Now comment on the strengths and weaknesses of the performer in terms of tactics and strategies:

Tactic/strategy	Strengths	Weaknesses

4 Now comment on the strengths and weaknesses of the performer in terms of fitness:

Fitness component	Strengths	Weaknesses

5 Select one major weakness identified for a skill component and one for a fitness component and create an action plan to improve them:

   a) Major skill weakness:

_____

_____

_____

      Action plan:

      Clear, realistic goals:

      Timescale:

      Method for achieving goals, e.g., progressive practices, training:

      Method for evaluating achievement of goals:

   b) Major fitness weakness:

_____

_____

_____

      Action plan:

      Clear, realistic goals:

      Timescale:

      Method for achieving goals, e.g., progressive practices, training:

      Method for evaluating achievement of goals:

▶

6 Now make a list of points that you wish to make to demonstrate your application of knowledge from theory areas you have studied. These points should help to justify the comments and action plan that you have formulated.

Points I wish to raise:

- Physiological (anatomy and physiology, exercise physiology, biomechanics):

  Health benefits of participation:

- Psychological (acquiring movement skills, sports psychology):

- Socio-cultural: (socio-cultural studies, historical, comparative):

  Opportunities for participation (local and national):

What you need to know

* You are required to be assessed in one activity at A2 – either as a performer, coach or official.
* You will be assessed according to the relevant assessment criteria for your activity.
* If you wish to be assessed as a coach or an official you will be required to keep a detailed log of your experiences.
* Assessment criteria for performance considers your level of overall performance, level of physical and mental fitness, and your level of understanding of the activity rules and regulations in an authentic competitive situation.

* Assessment criteria for coaching considers your overall level of coaching or leading, level of organisational skills, knowledge of rules and regulations, awareness of child protection and health and safety issues.
* Assessment criteria for officiating considers your overall level of officiating, level of organisational skills, application of rules and regulations, awareness of child protection and health and safety issues.

* You are also required to observe the live performance of another candidate, evaluate it and plan an appropriate strategy for improvement, justifying your evaluative comments through the application of physiological, psychological and socio-cultural knowledge. This will take the form of an oral response.
* Assessment of your evaluation and plan for improvement will focus on:
  - Your description of strengths and weaknesses of the observed performance
  - Your priority of performance improvement
  - Your creation of a viable action plan
  - Your justification of the evaluative comments you make through the application of physiological, psychological and socio-cultural knowledge
  - Your appreciation of the health and fitness benefits of the activity
  - Your appreciation of the range of opportunities both locally and nationally.

Review Questions

1 Outline the assessment criteria for your chosen activity – what will you be required to do?
2 What factors require consideration when seeking to improve performance in your chosen activity?
3 Identify the fitness requirements for your chosen activity. For each component give an example of a training session designed to improve it.
4 Identify three skills integral to successful performance in your chosen activity. Write down the key coaching points for each skill.
5 For each of the skills given above (in question 4) describe a number of progressive practices that can be used to help improve your performance.
6 Outline the six steps to a successful evaluation, appreciation and improvement of performance.
7 State the analytical phases of your chosen activity.
8 Selecting specific situations from your chosen activity, explain the tactics and strategies you would use and why.
9 Outline the health benefits of participating in your chosen activity.
10 Investigate the opportunity to participate in your chosen activity in:
   (a) Your local area.
   (b) In the wider region.
   (c) Nationally.

Index